About the Cover

TV Rules, Social Media Gains

The prior edition of this book featured public relations queen Lady Gaga on its cover. Since then, celebrities—and everyone else, for that matter – have gotten more prickly, more risk-averse, more protective about their images; and thus today's communications queen, Taylor Swift, after ruminating for months, respectfully turned down your author's request for cover treatment.

But to the rescue rode NBC television personality Raina Seitel (Don't ask!), who thankfully agreed to grace the cover. (Eat your heart out Taylor Swift!) And how appropriate that she did. TV, you see, is the place where more than half of all Americans still turn for their news and current events, but Facebook, Twitter, YouTube, and other online sites are coming on strong as sources of news and information, particularly for millennials.

Public relations professionals must understand all of them—traditional print and broadcast media as well as social media upstarts, alike. Dealing strategically with all these 21st century information channels and all the new ones to come is the front—line responsibility of *The Practice of Public Relations*.

Fraser P. Seitel

The Practice of
PUBLIC RELATIONS

THIRTEENTH EDITION

Fraser P. Seitel

Managing Partner, Emerald Partners

Adjunct Professor, New York University

PEARSON

Boston   Columbus   Indianapolis   New York   San Francisco   Amsterdam
Cape Town   Dubai   London   Madrid   Milan   Munich   Paris   Montréal   Toronto
Delhi   Mexico City   São Paulo   Sydney   Hong Kong   Seoul   Singapore   Taipei   Tokyo

Vice President, Business Publishing: Donna Battista
Editor-in-Chief: Stephanie Wall
Editor-in-Chief: Ashley Dodge
Senior Sponsoring Editor: Neeraj Bhalla
Editorial Assistant: Eric Santucci
Vice President, Product Marketing: Maggie Moylan
Director of Marketing, Digital Services and Products: Jeanette Koskinas
Field Marketing Manager: Lenny Ann Raper
Product Marketing Assistant: Jessica Quazza
Team Lead, Program Management: Ashley Santora
Team Lead, Project Management: Jeff Holcomb
Project Manager: Becca Groves
Operations Specialist: Carol Melville
Creative Director: Blair Brown
Art Director: Janet Slowik
Vice President, Director of Digital Strategy and Assessment: Paul Gentile
Manager of Learning Applications: Paul DeLuca
Full-Service Project Management, Composition and Design: Integra
Printer/Binder: LSC Communications
Cover Printer: LSC Communications

Library of Congress Cataloging-in-Publication Data

Seitel, Fraser P., author.
  The practice of public relations/Fraser P. Seitel.—Thirteenth edition.
    pages cm
  ISBN 978-0-13-417011-4—ISBN 0-13-417011-3   1. Public relations—United States.   I. Title.
  HM1221.S45 2016
  659.20973—dc23
                                                                    2015032218

2 16

ISBN 10:   0-13-417011-3
ISBN 13: 978-0-13-417011-4

Dedicated to

The world's greatest kiddies—**David, Hunter, Raina**, and **Theo**.

Brief Contents

Contents

Chapter 16   Integrated Marketing Communications   334

Chapter 17   Crisis Management   355

Foreword

David Rockefeller *(Photo courtesy of Virginia Sherwood)*

Opaque, confused, and inadequate communications by business and financial leaders characterized both the response to the 2008 financial crisis and the dizzying descent into global economic recession, as well as the subsequent effort to recover and rebuild. Unfortunately, their political brethren did not do a much better job then and sowed confusion rather than enlightenment in the years since. As a result, all institutions are under unprecedented stress and scrutiny, and the level of public dissatisfaction with both the private sector and government is at very high levels.

As Fraser P. Seitel shows in the 13th edition of his text, good public relations will not solve these problems, but the dissemination of principled policies by seasoned professionals will allow the rest of us to understand the basic issues and lead to the formulation of more appropriate and effective policies.

Regaining and maintaining public confidence is essential as we move forward. But saying it and doing it are two different things. For students, and even for professionals who have worked in the field for some time, *The Practice of Public Relations* is an excellent place to start. Seitel bridges the gap between theory and practice in a compelling and vivid way. His use of case studies, interviews, news photos, and other techniques, as well as his humorous and lucid text, brings the process brilliantly to life.

Leaders in the public, private, and not-for-profit sectors have learned from painful experience that they should rely on their public relations counselors for cogent advice on strategy and policy as well as communications. I learned to trust Mr. Seitel's instincts and abilities long ago when I was the chair and chief executive officer of The Chase Manhattan Bank. I continue to rely on his advice to this day.

For those who are working to restore and enhance the capacity of our institutions and their leaders to deal honestly and effectively with the public, this book will provide useful and essential guidance.

—*David Rockefeller*

David Rockefeller, who celebrated his 100th birthday in June 2015, is one of the most influential figures in the history of U.S. business, finance, and philanthropy. He is considered by many to be "America's last great business statesman." Over four decades, Mr. Rockefeller served as an executive with The Chase Manhattan Bank, joining as assistant manager in the foreign department in 1946 and retiring in 1981, after 11 years as chair and CEO. During the 100 years of his life, Mr. Rockefeller has met hundreds of world leaders and traveled around the globe many times. Since his retirement, Mr. Rockefeller has continued to stay active, with wide-ranging interests and involvement in the fields of international relations and civic affairs. He is the last remaining child of John D. Rockefeller Jr., who hired Ivy Lee in 1914 as the first modern-day public relations counselor.

Preface

First, thank you for buying my book. I appreciate it.

This book has been around for a good while, as have I.

Public relations continues to be a practice that is "contemporary" in every respect: new research findings, new communication methods, new social media communication techniques, and constantly changing case studies. Stated another way, a text like this one can't afford to rest on its laurels. It has to keep up to remain current.

In that context, your author is fortunate to continue to spend each day engaged in the practice of public relations, as a teacher and working consultant, with real clients, who demand real publicity and occasionally find themselves in real crises.

This helps keep the text fresh and up-to-date and practically grounded, so that events and innovations can be approached in proper public relations context. For example, social media, which has become so important in the field, is approached here in a realistic, practical application sense as an important public relations "tool," but a tool nonetheless.

The point is that the approach of this book, unlike other basic texts, is intensely practical—long on reasoning and justification and applications that work and short on ethereal philosophy, dubious theory, or new wave communication panaceas. This 13th edition of *The Practice of Public Relations* will prepare you for real-world public relations work in the second decade of the 21st century.

What's New in the 13th Edition of *The Practice of Public Relations*?

- Twelve new, full cases featuring the most current and relevant topics in the industry, including:
  - General Motors recall
  - National Football League's domestic abuse scandal
  - Uber's global problems
  - Sony's e-mail embarrassment
  - Chris Christie's "Bridgegate"
  - China's "Under the Dome" scandal
  - Walmart's Tracy Morgan crash
  - Starbuck's gun policy
  - Alex Rodriguez's comeback
  - Bill Cosby's meltdown
  - The ALS Ice Bucket Challenge
- Refortified emphasis on ethics with 17 brand-new ethics mini-cases, including:
  - Vladimir Putin's public relations counsel
  - Alec Baldwin's meltdown
  - Brian Williams' fall from grace
  - Product claims of Dr. Oz

- New England Patriots' Deflategate
- Edward Snowden: Criminal or hero?
- Diet Soda is good for you study
- Violating Wikipedia's rules
- Dolce Gabbana's same sex marriage battle
- Subway Jared's child pornography scandal
- The death of Cecil the lion

- **Five new "From the Top" interviews with today's top authorities in the worlds of management, media, and academia, including:**
  - Obama Presidential Press Secretary Josh Earnest
  - Noted public relations professors Denise Hill and Jay Rayburn
  - Reputation management leader Sandra Macleod
  - Writing specialist Hoa Loranger

- **New, expanded social media content in Chapter 10, "Public Relations and Social Media,"** encompassing the most up-to-date (at least as we write this) analysis of social media applications to public relations practice. In addition, comprehensive coverage of the role of social media in Public Relations is discussed throughout the text.

- **Updated "Public Relations Bookshelf"** features the most current public relations literature—primarily post-2005—as well as one new contemporary "Pick of the Literature" per chapter.

- **Every chapter begins with a contemporary issue relating to the chapter content**—from ISIS terrorists' use of public relations for diabolical ends to Kim Kardashian's tweeting controversy to her stepfather Caitlyn Jenner's coming-out communications.

Social media applications run throughout the chapters and, as noted, the chapter devoted to "Public Relations and Social Media" offers a comprehensive, updated discussion of social media vehicles and how they relate to public relations practice.

As important as social media has become to public relations work, the field still depends on technical skill, experience, and judgment, all grounded in solid relationships with colleagues, constituents, and media.

Above all, public relations responses and relationships must be based on the single concept of *doing the right thing*. Indeed, acting *ethically* lies at the heart of the solutions for the more than three dozen case studies that this edition presents.

With economic and political uncertainty around the world, the practice of public relations has never been a more potent force in society or a more valuable factor in an organization's reputation. In the second decade of the 21st century, public relations crises and opportunities are front-page news on a daily basis.

The field remains, at heart, a personal, relationship-oriented practice, demanding experienced judgment, and finely-honed interpersonal communications skills. And so, this 13th edition of *The Practice of Public Relations* places its emphasis on the principles, processes, and practices that lead to building positive relationships in a 24/7 communications environment.

This contemporary, real-life approach is intended to increase your enthusiasm for public relations study and practice.

Among the highlights of the 13th edition:

Comprehensive Social Media Content

As in so many other lines of work, mastering social media has become a key tool for public relations practitioners to engage in "direct conversations" with public relations publics. Public relations professionals must understand the communications opportunities and limitations of mobile and tablets; Facebook, Twitter, SnapChat, and YouTube; blogs, podcasts, and Pinterest; and all the rest.

No public relations textbook offers a more comprehensive discussion of social media than the 13th edition of *The Practice of Public Relations*.

Refortified Emphasis on Ethics

Proper public relations practice must be underpinned by a strong sense of ethics. The principle of *doing the right thing* is what should distinguish the practice of public relations.

This edition of *The Practice of Public Relations* focuses on the ethical base that provides the theoretical foundation of effective communications and public relations.

The book's introductory chapters place significant attention on how an understanding of and facility with communications research, theory, and public opinion can be applied to strategic public relations planning and creation of believable and persuasive messages.

Also included is a mini-case "A Question of Ethics" in each chapter. These cases bring to life the daily ethical dilemmas that confront professional public relations practitioners.

New Contemporary Cases

Public relations practice confronts an ever-changing landscape of problems and opportunities. It is imperative, therefore, that a textbook in the field keep current with the most contemporary examples of the good, the bad, and the ugly in public relations work.

This 13th edition does so by chronicling the most important contemporary public relations cases—from GM's troubling cover up and then recall of unfit automobiles to Taylor Swift's use of public relations to rise to the top of the world popularity, from Sony's mishandling of hacked e-mails to Alex Rodriguez's astonishing reputational comeback from baseball purgatory.

Every case is designed to test your application of the theories discussed in solving real-world challenges.

Additional New Elements

The strength of this book continues to reside in its application of theory to real-life practice.

In addition to the new, contemporary cases and the expanded Social Media discussion, unique elements in the 13th edition include:

- **NEW! From the Top** interviews with distinguished communicators including President Obama's press secretary. These complement interviews with legendary public relations counselors Harold Burson, Howard Rubenstein, and Richard Edelman; former Johnson and Johnson communications director Ray Jordan; and three late icons, management guru Peter Drucker, USA Today founder Al Neuharth, and Edward Bernays, one of the "fathers" of public relations.

- **NEW! PR A Question of Ethics mini-cases**, which highlight the ethical challenges that public relations professionals face on a daily basis—from the harsh employee communications of Cosi's CEO to the forced resignation of a star-crazed congressman to Target's savvy handling of a plus-sized controversy.

- **NEW! FYI** features that expose off-line curiosities that make the practice of public relations such a fascinating art form.

- **NEW! Public Relations Bookshelf and Pick of the Literature** features, encompassing the most comprehensive, post-2005 bibliography in public relations literature.

- **NEW! Newscom photos**, taken straight from the news wire, add a real-life feel to this edition that isn't found in any other textbook.

All of these elements add to the excitement of this book. So, too, does the full-color format that underscores the liveliness, vitality, and relevance of the field.

Unique Perspective

Clearly, *The Practice of Public Relations*, 13th Edition, isn't your grandma's PR textbook.

This book is a lot different from other introductory texts in the field. Its premise is that public relations is a brutally practical field, whose emphasis is on doing the work—counseling, writing, promoting, and dealing with constantly changing circumstances. The extensive explanation of Social Media and its application to public relations practice is unique in public relations textbooks.

Although other texts may steer clear of the contemporary major cases, perplexing ethical mini-cases, thought leader interviews, "how to" counsel, and the public relations conundrums that force you to think, this book confronts them all.

It is, if you'll forgive the vernacular, an *in-your-face* textbook for an *in-your-face* profession.

Most important, *The Practice of Public Relations*, 13th Edition, is built around the technical knowledge of theory, history, process and practice, judgmental skills and personal relationships that underlie public relations practice and will be so essential in building the trust and respect of diverse communities in the second decade of the 21st century.

Happy reading, and thanks again for buying the book.

Acknowledgments

The author and the publisher would like to thank the following reviewers for providing feedback for this revision.

Joseph Basso, Rowan University
Richard T. Cole, Michigan State University, East Lansing
Suzanne Fitzgerald, Rowan University
Dr. Andrew Lingwall, Clarion University
Jack Mandel, Nassau Community College
Michael Smilowitz, James Madison University

About the Author

Fraser P. Seitel is a veteran of five decades in the practice of public relations, beginning, he claims, "as a child." In 2000, *PR Week* magazine named Mr. Seitel one of the *100 Most Distinguished Public Relations Professionals of the 20th Century.*

In 1992, after serving for a decade as senior vice president and director of public affairs for The Chase Manhattan Bank, Mr. Seitel formed Emerald Partners, a management and communications consultancy, and also became senior counselor at the world's largest public affairs firm, Burson-Marsteller.

Mr. Seitel has been a regular guest on television and radio, appearing on a variety of programs on the Fox News Network and CNN, ABC's *Good Morning America*, CNBC's *Power Lunch*, as well as on MSNBC, Fox Business Network, the Fox Radio Network, and National Public Radio.

Mr. Seitel has counseled hundreds of corporations, hospitals, nonprofits, associations, and individuals in the areas for which he had responsibility at Chase—media relations, speech writing, consumer relations, employee communications, financial communications, philanthropic activities, and strategic management consulting.

Mr. Seitel is an Internet columnist at Forbes.com and odwyerpr.com and a frequent lecturer and seminar leader on communications topics. Over the course of his career, Mr. Seitel has taught thousands of public relations professionals and students. For the past decade, Mr. Seitel has been an adjunct professor in public relations at New York University.

After studying and examining many texts in public relations, he concluded that none of them "was exactly right." Therefore, in 1980, he wrote the first edition of *The Practice of Public Relations* "to give students a feel for how exciting this field really is." In four decades of use at hundreds of colleges and universities, Mr. Seitel's book has introduced generations of students to the excitement, challenge, and uniqueness of the practice of public relations.

The Practice of
PUBLIC RELATIONS

Chapter 1

Defining
Public Relations

Chapter Objectives

1. To define the practice of public relations and underscore its importance as a valuable and powerful societal force in the 21st century.

2. To explore the various publics of public relations, as well as the field's most prominent functions.

3. To underscore the ethical nature of the field and to reject the notion that public relations practitioners are employed in the practice of "spin."

4. To examine the requisites—both technical and attitudinal—that constitute an effective public relations professional.

FIGURE 1-1 **Public relations terrorists.**
The brutal Islamic State used macabre public relations techniques, such as videos and social media, to shock the world with its brutality.
Photo: Ropi/ZUMA Press/Newscom

The practice of public relations—barely into its second century—has never been more powerful or more valuable. Indeed, in the latter half of the second decade of the 21st century, most accepted that the practice of public relations had become one of society's most potent forces.

Everyone from the Pope to the Queen of England, from the President of the United States to the President of Russia, from Apple to Walmart, from George Clooney to Ariana Grande practices public relations on a daily basis.

Perhaps the greatest testimony to that reality came from one of the most evil enemies the civilized world has ever known, the terrorist group that labeled itself, "Islamic State," also known as Daesh or ISIS or ISIL. Even though IS began as a ragtag group of anti-social fanatics, lacked the weapons of an established military and had no air power whatsoever, its terrorist stature grew as it used public relations techniques to shock the world (Figure 1-1). Among the techniques, ISIS:

- Used an aggressive social media campaign to release statements of its conquests and major battles,

- Staged elaborate events, particularly parades, to showcase the weapons it captured, and

- Posted chilling high-quality videos of torture and beheadings of prisoners, including American journalists, to underscore the group's brutality (Figure 1-1).

As IS used its public relations power in seizing parts of Iraq and Syria, it replaced the equally demonic Al Qaeda as terrorist enemy number one.[1]

In the 21st century, few societal forces are more powerful than the practice of public relations, especially when combined with social media—the agglomeration of Facebook and Twitter, Instagram and Snapchat, instant messages, e-mail, cell phone photos, blogs, wikis, Web casting, RSS feeds, and all the other emerging technologies of the World Wide Web.

Together, the combination of the two—social media and public relations—has revolutionized the way organizations and individuals communicate to their key constituent publics around the world.

What exactly is the practice of public relations?

That's a question that still perplexes many, including those in the field, who can never seem to agree on precisely what it is they do.

In fact in 2012, when the Public Relations Society of America (PRSA) tried to reach a common definition of the practice by asking the 200,000-plus people in the United States and the thousands of others overseas who practice public relations, the effort was greeted, as *The New York Times* put it, with *"widespread interest, along with not a small amount of sniping, snide commentary and second-guessing."*[2] The PRSA received 927 suggested definitions from public relations professionals, academics, students, and the general public, finally selecting the winning definition:

> *Public relations is a strategic communication process that builds mutually beneficial relationships between organizations and their publics.*

Not bad, although practitioners still grumbled and even the CEO of PRSA admitted, "Like beauty, the definition of 'public relations' is in the eye of the beholder."[3]

In a society overwhelmed by communications—from traditional and increasingly threatened newspapers and magazines, to 24/7 talk radio and broadcast and cable television, to nontraditional social media—the public is bombarded with nonstop messages of every variety. The challenge for a communicator is to cut through this clutter to deliver an argument that is persuasive, believable, and actionable.

The answer, more often than not today, lies in public relations. Stated another way, in the 21st century, the power, value, and influence of the practice of public relations have never been more profound.

1 Prominence of Public Relations

In the 21st century, public relations as a field has grown immeasurably both in numbers and in respect. Today, the practice of public relations is clearly a growth industry.

- In the United States alone, public relations is a multibillion-dollar business practiced by 208,000 professionals, according to the U.S. Bureau of Labor Statistics. Furthermore, the Bureau projects public relations specialist employment will grow 12% between 2012 and 2022. During that time period, an additional 27,400 jobs will need to be filled.[4]

■ Around the world, the practice of public relations has grown enormously. The International Public Relations Association, founded in 1948, boasts a strong membership in more than 80 countries.

■ The field's primary U.S. trade associations have strong membership, with the PRSA encompassing nearly 22,000 members and 11,000 college students in 330 chapters and the International Association of Business Communicators including 12,000 members in 80 countries.

■ Approximately 250 colleges and universities in the United States and many more overseas offer a public relations sequence or degree program. Many more offer public relations courses. Undergraduate enrollments in public relations programs at U.S. four-year colleges and universities are conservatively estimated to be well in excess of 20,000 majors. Graduate education in public relations is also growing, with one study reporting the number of graduate public relations programs increasing from 26 to 75 since the start of the new century.[5] Moreover, in the vast majority of college journalism programs, public relations sequences ranked first or second in enrollment.[6] One reason for this trend was that the income gap between public relations specialists and journalists was growing, with the annual median income of public relations people standing at $54,940 while the equivalent for a journalist was $35,600.[7]

■ The U.S. government has thousands of communications professionals—although none, as we will learn, are labeled *public relations specialists*—who keep the public informed about the activities of government agencies and officials. The Department of Defense alone has 7,000 professional communicators spread out among the Army, Navy, and Air Force.

■ The world's largest public relations firms are all owned by media conglomerates—among them Omnicom, The Interpublic Group, and WPP Group—which refuse to divulge public relations revenues. The field is dominated by smaller, privately held firms, many of them entrepreneurial operations. A typical public relations agency has annual revenue of less than $1 million with fewer than 10 employees. Nonetheless, the top 10 independent public relations agencies in the United States record annual revenues in excess of a billion dollars, with the top independent firm, Edelman Public Relations, with 5,308 employees, earning more than $797 million in annual revenues.[8]

In the 21st century, as all elements of society—companies, nonprofits, governments, religious institutions, sports teams and leagues, arts organizations, and all others—wrestle with constant shifts in economic conditions and competition, security concerns and shifting public opinion, the public relations profession is expected to thrive as increasing numbers of organizations are interested in communicating their stories.

Indeed, public relations people have already attained positions of prominence in every aspect of society. The U.S. President's press secretary is quoted daily from his televised White House press briefings. Former Press Secretary Robert Gibbs remains a close adviser to President Barack Obama. Karen Hughes, a public relations advisor to George W. Bush for many years, moved from a Special Assistant to the President position in the White House to become Undersecretary of State for Public Diplomacy responsible primarily for changing attitudes internationally about the United States. Corporate professionals, at the top of the wage scale, earn seven figure salaries. Where once public relations was a profession populated by anonymous practitioners, today's public relations executives write books, appear on television, and are widely quoted. When United Parcel Service (UPS) appointed communications professional Christine Owens to its top internal body in 2005, CEO Mike Eskew said, "Communications is just too important not to be represented on the management committee of this company."[9]

Perhaps the most flattering aspect of the field's heightened stature is that competition from other fields has become more intense. Today the profession finds itself vulnerable to encroachment by people with non–public relations backgrounds, such as lawyers, marketers, and general managers of every type, all eager to gain the management access and persuasive clout of the public relations professional.

The field's strength stems from its roots: "A democratic society where people have freedom to debate and to make decisions—in the community, the marketplace, the home, the workplace, and the voting booth. Private and public organizations depend on good relations with groups and individuals whose opinions, decisions, and actions affect their vitality and survival."[10]

As people around the world continue to strive to secure their own freedoms, the power of communications—of public relations—will continue to ascend.

What Is Public Relations?

The PRSA's 2012 definition—"*Public relations is a strategic communication process that builds mutually beneficial relationships between organizations and their publics*"—is really pretty good.

Public relations is, indeed, a "strategic" process, which focuses on helping achieve an organization's goals. Its fundamental mandate is "communications," and its focus is "building relationships."

Another approach to a definition is, *"Public relations is a planned process to influence public opinion, through sound character and proper performance, based on mutually satisfactory two-way communication."*

At least that's what your author believes it is.

This definition adds the elements of "planning," so imperative in sound public relations practice, the aspect of "listening" through "two-way communications," as well as the elements of "character" or "ethics" and "performance." Public relations is most effective when it is based on ethical principles and proper action. Without these two essential requisites—character and performance—achieving sustained influence might be either transitory or impossible; in other words, you can fool some of the people some of the time but not all of the people all of the time; in other words, *"You can't pour perfume on a skunk!"*

The fact is that there are many different definitions of public relations. American historian Robert Heilbroner once described the field as *"a brotherhood of some 100,000, whose common bond is its profession and whose common woe is that no two of them can ever quite agree on what that profession is."*[11]

In 1923, the late Edward Bernays described the function of his fledgling public relations counseling business as one of providing

> *Information given to the public, persuasion directed at the public to modify attitudes and actions, and efforts to integrate attitudes and actions of an institution with its publics and of publics with those of that institution.*[12]

And way back in 1975, when people didn't have a clue what "public relations" was, one of the most ambitious searches for a universal definition was commissioned by the Foundation for Public Relations Research and Education. Sixty-five public relations leaders participated in the study, which analyzed 472 different definitions and offered the following 88-word sentence:

> *Public relations is a distinctive management function which helps establish and maintain mutual lines of communications, understanding, acceptance, and cooperation between an organization and its publics; involves the management of problems or issues; helps management to keep informed on and responsive to public opinion; defines and emphasizes the responsibility of management to serve the public interest; helps management keep abreast of and effectively utilize change, serving as an early warning system to help anticipate trends; and uses research and sound and ethical communication techniques as its principal tools.*[13]

In adopting its 2012 definition, the PRSA noted that its definition implied the functions of research, planning, communications dialogue, and evaluation, all essential in the practice of public relations.

No matter which formal definition one settles on to describe the practice, to be successful, public relations professionals must always engage in a planned and ethical process to influence the attitudes and actions of their target audiences.

Influencing Public Opinion

What is the process through which public relations might influence public opinion? Communications professor John Marston suggested a four-step model based on specific functions: (1) research, (2) action, (3) communication, and (4) evaluation.[14] Whenever a public relations professional is faced with an assignment—whether promoting a client's product or defending a client's reputation—he or she should apply Marston's R-A-C-E approach:

1. **Research.** Research attitudes about the issue at hand.
2. **Action.** Identify action of the client in the public interest.
3. **Communication.** Communicate that action to gain understanding, acceptance, and support.
4. **Evaluation.** Evaluate the communication to see if opinion has been influenced.

The key to the process is the second step—action. You can't have effective communication or positive publicity without proper action. Stated another way, performance must precede publicity. Act first and communicate later. Indeed, some might say that public relations—PR—really should stand for *performance recognition*. In other words, positive action communicated straightforwardly will yield positive results.

This is the essence of the R-A-C-E process of public relations.

Public relations professor Sheila Clough Crifasi has proposed extending the R-A-C-E formula into the five-part R-O-S-I-E to encompass a more managerial approach to the field. R-O-S-I-E prescribes sandwiching the functions of objectives, strategies, and implementation between research and evaluation. Indeed, setting clear objectives, working from set strategies, and implementing a predetermined plan are keys to sound public relations practice.

Still others suggest a process called R-P-I-E for research, planning, implementation, and evaluation, which emphasizes the element of planning as a necessary step preceding the activation of a communications initiative.

All three approaches, R-A-C-E, R-O-S-I-E, and R-P-I-E, echo one of the most widely repeated definitions of public relations, developed by the late Denny Griswold, who founded a public relations newsletter.

Public relations is the management function which evaluates public attitudes, identifies the policies and procedures of an individual or an organization with the public interest, and plans and executes a program of action to earn public understanding and acceptance.[15]

The key words in this definition are *management* and *action*. Public relations, if it is to serve the organization properly, must report to top management. Public relations must serve as an honest broker to management, unimpeded by any other group. For public relations to work, its advice to management must be unfiltered, uncensored, and unexpurgated. This is often easier said than done because many public relations departments report through marketing, advertising, or even legal departments.

Nor can public relations take place without appropriate action. As noted, no amount of communications—regardless of its persuasive content—can save an organization whose performance is substandard. In other words, if the action is flawed or the performance rotten, no amount of communicating or backtracking or post facto posturing will change the reality.

The process of public relations, then, as Professor Melvin Sharpe put it, "harmonizes long-term relationships among individuals and organizations in society."[16] To "harmonize," Professor Sharpe applied five principles to the public relations process:

- Honest communication for credibility
- Openness and consistency of actions for confidence
- Fairness of actions for reciprocity and goodwill
- Continuous two-way communication to prevent alienation and to build relationships
- Environmental research and evaluation to determine the actions or adjustments needed for social harmony

And if that doesn't yet give you a feel for what precisely the practice of public relations is, then consider public relations Professor Janice Sherline Jenny's description as *"the management of communications between an organization and all entities that have a direct or indirect relationship with the organization, i.e., its publics."*

No matter what definition one may choose to explain the practice, few would argue that the goal of effective public relations is to harmonize internal and external relationships so that an organization can enjoy not only the goodwill of all of its publics but also stability and long life.

A Question of Ethics

Repping the Russian Lion

Ever since the first time he became president of Russia in 2000, Vladimir Putin (Figure 1-2)—"the lion of Russia"—has been a constant thorn in the side of the United States.

Putin's periodic criticisms of U.S. imperialism, even while Russia pushed the boundaries of its power, and his almost impish provocations of U.S. presidents hearkened back to an earlier era of "cold war" between the United States and the old Union of Soviet Socialist Republics (USSR). Putin seemed eager to keep the flame of conflict burning.

FIGURE 1-2   **Strongman rides.**
Ketchum Public Relations received beaucoup criticism for its representation of Russian president
and constant U.S. thorn Vladimir Putin.
Photo: Alexey Druzhinyn/ZUMAPRESS/Newscom

That's why in 2006 when one of the world's most respected public relations agencies, Ketchum, agreed to represent Russia and its president to influence public opinion, many wondered if the agency had done the right thing.

The Ketchum relationship started innocently enough, with the firm representing Russia's interests in hosting the Group of 8 meeting in St. Petersburg. Ketchum then helped Putin be selected as Time magazine's "Person of the Year" in 2007. But soon thereafter, things started going downhill for Ketchum and its client.

Critics of the Russian government began turning up dead. In 2008, Russia fueled a war with the Republic of Georgia, a former USSR state. In 2013, Putin published an Op-Ed column in *The New York Times* that criticized the whole notion of American "exceptionalism." In 2014, Russian-backed troops began a civil war in another former USSR entity, Ukraine. The United States immediately responded with economic sanctions against Russia and its leaders. And the U.S. ambassador to the United Nations called Russia's actions in Ukraine a "threat to all of our peace and security."

Ketchum, which from 2006 to 2012 was reportedly paid almost $23 million in fees and expenses on its Russia account, began to feel the heat. The firm cut back its staff assigned to the Russian account and generally kept a low profile.

Ketchum, it must be said, wasn't the only public relations firm representing questionable foreign governments and leaders. Over the years, public relations firms have represented a host of U.S. antagonists from Libya's Muammar Gaddafi to Syrian President Bashar al-Assad.

Indeed, some public relations professionals argue that representing a controversial nation and its president is akin to representing a company that sells arms or cigarettes.

For its part, Ketchum defended the Russian relationship. Said its senior manager on the Russian account, "Where we can help facilitate communication, at the end of the day that can only help."

One former Ketchum executive, Angus Roxburgh, who left the agency and wrote a book in 2011, said that in signing up for lucrative fees from Russia and working for Kremlin leaders, it meant "helping them disguise all the issues that make it unattractive: human rights, invasions of neighboring countries, etc."

Questions

1. Do you think a public relations agency should represent a nation that holds views contrary to the United States? Why or why not?

2. Should Ketchum have resigned the Russian account after the 2014 invasion of Ukraine? Why or why not?

3. Where should a public relations agency draw the line in representing controversial clients?

Note: For further information, see Brett Logiurato, "Meet the PR Firm That Helped Vladimir Putin Troll the Entire Country," *Business Insider*, September 12, 2013; Ravi Somaiya, "PR Firm for Putin's Russia Now Walking a Fine Line," *The New York Times*, August 31, 2014; and Joe Weisenthal, "Vladimir Putin Calls Out U.S. Exceptionalism in Intense NYT Op-Ed," *Business Insider*, September 11, 2013.

Management Interpreter

The late Leon Hess, who ran one of the nation's largest oil companies and the New York Jets football team, used to pride himself on *not* having a public relations department. Mr. Hess, a very private individual, abhorred the limelight for himself and for his company.

But times have changed.

Today, the CEO who thunders "I don't need public relations!" is a fool. He or she doesn't have a choice. Every organization *has* public relations whether it wants it or not. The trick is to establish *good* public relations. That's what this book is all about—professional public relations, the kind you must work at.

Public relations affects almost everyone who has contact with other human beings. All of us, in one way or another, practice public relations daily. For an organization, every phone call, every letter, every face-to-face encounter is a public relations event.

Public relations professionals, then, are really the organization's interpreters.

- On the one hand, they must interpret the philosophies, policies, programs, and practices of their management to the public.

- On the other hand, they must convey the attitudes of the public to their management.

Let's consider management first.

Before public relations professionals can gain attention, understanding, acceptance and, ultimately, action from target publics, they have to know what management is thinking.

Good public relations can't be practiced in a vacuum. No matter what the size of the organization, a public relations department is only as good as its access to management. For example, it's useless for a senator's press secretary to explain the reasoning behind an important decision without first knowing what the senator had in mind. So, too, an organization's public relations staff is impotent without firsthand knowledge of the reasons for management's decisions and the rationale for organizational policy.

The public relations department in any organization can counsel management. It can advise management. It can even exhort management to take action. But it is management who must call the shots on organizational policy.

It is the role of the public relations practitioner, once policy is established by management, to communicate these ideas accurately and candidly to the public. Anything less can lead to major problems.

Public Interpreter

Now let's consider the flip side of the coin—the public.

Interpreting the public to management means finding out what the public really thinks about the firm and letting management know. Regrettably, history is filled with examples of powerful institutions—and their public relations departments—failing to anticipate the true sentiments of the public.

- In the 1960s, General Motors (GM) paid little attention to an unknown consumer activist named Ralph Nader, who spread the message that GM's Corvair was "unsafe at any speed." When Nader's assault began to be believed, the automaker assigned professional detectives to trail him. In short order, GM was forced to acknowledge its act of paranoia, and the Corvair was eventually sacked at great expense to the company.

- In the 1970s, as both gasoline prices and oil company profits rose rapidly, the oil companies were besieged by an irate gas-consuming public. When, at the height of the criticism, Mobil Oil spent millions in excess cash to purchase the parent of the Montgomery Ward department store chain, the company was publicly battered for failing to cut its prices.

- In the 1980s, President Ronald Reagan rode to power on the strength of his ability to interpret what was on the minds of the electorate. But his successor in the early 1990s, George H. W. Bush, a lesser communicator than Reagan, failed to "read" the nation's economic concerns. After leading America to a victory over Iraq in the Gulf War, President Bush failed to heed the admonition, "It's the economy, stupid," and lost the election to upstart Arkansas Governor Bill Clinton.

- As the 20th century ended, President Clinton forgot the candid communication skills that earned him the White House and lied to the American public about his affair with an intern. The subsequent scandal, ending in impeachment hearings before the U.S. Congress, tarnished Clinton's administration and ruined his legacy.

- At the start of the 21st century, Clinton's successor, George W. Bush, earned great credit for strong actions and communications following the September 11, 2001, attacks on the nation. The Bush administration's public relations then suffered when the ostensible reason for attacking Iraq—weapons of mass destruction—failed to materialize. Bush's failure to act promptly and communicate frankly in subsequent crises, such as Hurricane Katrina, hurt his personal credibility and irreparably tarnished his administration.

- Bush's successor, Barack Obama, was hailed for his messianic communications skills as he stormed into the White House with a message of "hope and change" in 2008. But by the end of his first term in 2012, with the economy flagging from an unprecedented financial meltdown, Obama struggled to regain his "communications mojo."

In the midst of the second decade of the 21st century, individuals and institutions continued to struggle, on a daily basis, to "interpret" their actions to the public. Whether in the midst of natural disasters, like the 2015 killing earthquakes that rocked Nepal or the devastating incidents of police shootings of unarmed young black men in the United States, the importance of rapid communication to explain action remained critical.

The point remains that the savviest individuals and institutions—be they government, corporate or nonprofit—understand the importance of effectively interpreting their philosophies, policies and practices to the public and, even more important, interpreting back to management how the public views them and their organization.

2 Public Relations Publics

The term *public relations* is really a misnomer. *Publics* relations, or relations with the publics, would be more to the point. Practitioners must communicate with many different publics—not just the general public—each having its own special needs and requiring different types of communication. Often the lines that divide these publics are thin, and the potential overlap is significant. Therefore, priorities, according to organizational needs, must always be reconciled (Figure 1-3).

Technological change—particularly social media, mobile devices, blogs, satellite links for television, and the wired world in general—has brought greater interdependence to people and organizations, and there is growing concern in organizations today about managing extensive webs of interrelationships. Indeed, managers have become interrelationship conscious.

Internally, managers must deal directly with various levels of subordinates as well as with cross-relationships that arise when subordinates interact with one another.

Externally, managers must deal with a system that includes nongovernmental organizations (NGOs), government regulatory agencies, labor unions, subcontractors, consumer groups, and many other independent—but often related—organizations. The public relations challenge in all of this is to manage effectively the communications between managers and the various publics, which often pull organizations in different directions. Stated another way, public relations professionals are mediators between client (management) and public (all those key constituent groups on whom an organization depends).

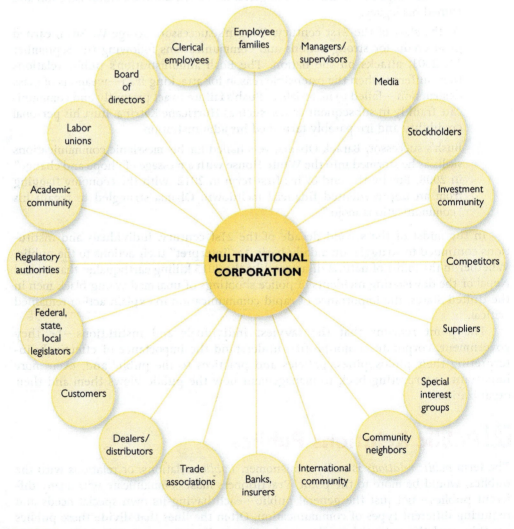

FIGURE 1-3   Key publics.
Twenty of the most important publics of a typical multinational corporation.

Interpreting a Sensitive, Sexual Issue

Approximately 17 million viewers in May 2015 tuned in to see a most bizarre ABC TV interview.

Bruce Jenner, a former U.S. Olympic decathlon gold medalist, told "20/20" interviewer Diane Sawyer and a worldwide audience about his journey to become a woman. Jenner, father of six who was formerly married three times—the last to reality star and Kardashian clan matriarch, Kris—announced to one and all that he considered himself a transgender woman (Figure 1-4).

Jenner's announcement, which had been the subject of media speculation for months, drew one of the biggest audiences in "20/20" history and drew 972,000 tweets on social media. While some criticized the Olympic hero for maximizing the publicity of what should have been a private decision—Jenner also agreed to be the subject of a reality show following his transition—others commended him for bringing national attention to the transgender issue.

Adding to the intrigue was that Jenner also acknowledged that his political views tended to the conservative, unlike most others in Hollywood. The leader of the Log Cabin Republicans, a gay and lesbian conservative Republican group congratulated Jenner "*in the tremendous courage he demonstrated*" and for "*being true to himself both in terms of his personal identity as well as his political identity.*"

Jenner, himself, vehemently protested that his interview with Sawyer "*was not a publicity stunt.*" Indeed, Jenner's candor and straightforwardness in the two-hour interview with Sawyer qualified as the first "*interpretation*" of the transgender world to many of the millions viewing.

Questions

1. Do you think it was a wise idea for Bruce Jenner to choose ABC-TV for his announcement?

2. What other options might you have suggested in announcing that he was transgender?

FIGURE 1-4 **Coming out party.**
It was big news in the spring of 2015 when Bruce Jenner told ABC's Diane Sawyer that he intended to live the rest of his life as a transgender woman.
Photo: Christopher Sadowski/Splash News/Newscom

Note: For further information, see Jacob Bernstein, "The Bruce Jenner Story Goes from Gossip to News," *The New York Times*, February 4, 2015; and Sean Dooley et al., "Bruce Jenner: 'I'm a Woman,'" *ABC News*, April 24, 2015.

Definitions differ on precisely what constitutes a public. One time-honored definition states that a public arises when a group of people (1) faces a similar indeterminate situation, (2) recognizes what is indeterminate and problematic in that situation, and (3) organizes to do something about the problem.[17] In public relations, more specifically, a public is a group of people with a stake in an issue, organization, or idea.

Publics can also be classified into several overlapping categories:

- **Internal and external.** Internal publics are inside the organization: supervisors, clerks, managers, stockholders, and the board of directors. External publics are those not directly connected with the organization: the press, government, educators, customers, suppliers, and the community.

- **Primary, secondary, and marginal.** Primary publics can most help—or hinder—the organization's efforts. Secondary publics are less important, and marginal publics are the least important of all. For example, members of the Federal Reserve Board of Governors, who regulate banks, would be the primary public for a bank awaiting a regulatory ruling, whereas legislators and the general public would be secondary. On the other hand, to the investing public, interest rate pronouncements of the same Federal Reserve Board are of primary importance.

- **Traditional and future.** Employees and current customers are traditional publics; students and potential customers are future ones. No organization can afford to become complacent in dealing with its changing publics. Today, a firm's publics range from women to minorities to senior citizens to homosexuals. Each might be important to the future success of the organization.

- **Proponents, opponents, and the uncommitted.** An institution must deal differently with those who support it and those who oppose it. For supporters, communications that reinforce beliefs may be in order. But changing the opinions of skeptics calls for strong, persuasive communications. Often, particularly in politics, the uncommitted public is crucial. Many a campaign has been decided because the swing vote was won over by one of the candidates.

It's true that management must always speak with one voice, but its communication inflection, delivery, and emphasis should be sensitive to all constituent publics.

Public Relations Functions

There is a fundamental difference between the functions of public relations and the functions of marketing and advertising. Marketing and advertising promote a product or a service. Public relations promotes an entire organization.

Modern public relations is all about managing relationships, crafting strategic stories, conveying expertise and solving organizational problems through strategic communications.

The functions associated with modern public relations work are numerous. Among them are the following:

- **Writing**—the fundamental public relations skill, with written vehicles from news releases to speeches and from brochures to advertisements falling within the field's purview.

- **Media relations**—dealing with the press is another frontline public relations function.

- ■ **Social media interface**—creating what often is the organization's principle interface with the public: its Web site, as well as creating links with social media options, such as Facebook, Twitter, YouTube, Instagram, Snapchat and all the rest. Also important is monitoring the World Wide Web and responding, when appropriate, to organizational challenge.

- ■ **Planning**—of public relations programs, special events, media events, management functions, and the like.

- ■ **Counseling**—in dealing with management and its interactions with key publics.

- ■ **Researching**—of attitudes and opinions that influence behavior and beliefs.

- ■ **Publicity**—the marketing-related function, most commonly misunderstood as the "only" function of public relations, generating positive publicity for a client or employer.

- ■ **Marketing communications**—other marketing-related functions, such as promoting products, creating collateral marketing material, sales literature, meeting displays, and promotions.

- ■ **Community relations**—positively putting forth the organization's messages and image within the community.

- ■ **Consumer relations**—interfacing with consumers through written and verbal communications.

- ■ **Employee relations**—communicating with the all-important internal publics of the organization, those managers and employees who work for the firm.

- ■ **Government affairs**—dealing with legislators, regulators, and local, state, and federal officials—all of those who have governmental interface with the organization.

- ■ **Investor relations**—for public companies, communicating with stockholders and those who advise them.

- ■ **Special publics relations**—dealing with those publics uniquely critical to particular organizations, from African Americans to women to Asians to senior citizens.

- ■ **Public affairs and issues**—dealing with public policy and its impact on the organization, as well as identifying and addressing issues of consequence that affect the firm.

- ■ **Crisis communications**—dealing with key constituent publics when the organization is under siege for any number of urgent situations that threaten credibility.

This is but a partial list of what public relations practitioners do. In sum, the public relations practitioner is manager/orchestrator/producer/director/writer/arranger and all-around general communications counsel to management. It is for this reason, then, that the process works best when the public relations director reports directly to the CEO.

3 The Sin of "Spin"

So pervasive has the influence of public relations become in our society that some even fear it as a pernicious force; they worry about the power of public relations to exercise a kind of thought control over the American public.

Which brings us to *spin*.

In its most benign form, spin signifies the distinctive interpretation of an issue or action to sway public opinion, as in putting a positive slant on a negative story. In its most virulent form, spin means confusing an issue or distorting or obfuscating it or even lying.

The propensity in recent years for presumably respected public figures to lie in an attempt to deceive the public has led to the notion that "spinning the facts" is synonymous with public relations practice.

It isn't.

Spinning an answer to hide what really happened—that is, lying, confusing, distorting, obfuscating, whatever you call it—is antithetical to the proper practice of public relations. In public relations, if you lie once, you will never be trusted again—particularly by the media.

Nonetheless, public relations spin has come to mean the twisting of messages and statements of half-truths to create the appearance of performance, which may or may not be true.

This association with spin has hurt the field. *The New York Times* headlined a critical article on public relations practice, "Spinning Frenzy: P.R.'s Bad Press."[18] Other critics admonish the field as "a huge, powerful, hidden medium available only to wealthy individuals, big corporations, governments, and government agencies because of its high cost."[19]

The term *spin* was coined in the Clinton administration, when a bevy of eager communications counselors, such as James Carville, Paul Begala, and Lanny Davis, eagerly spun the tale that intern Monica Lewinsky was, in effect, delusional about an Oval Office affair with the president. (*She wasn't!*)[20] In the Bush administration, high-level advisors Karl Rove and Lewis Libby were implicated in a spinning campaign against former Ambassador Joseph Wilson, who questioned the motives of the war in Iraq. In 2005, Libby, Vice President Dick Cheney's top aide, was convicted for "obstruction of justice, false statement, and perjury" in the Wilson case.[21] In 2013, President Barack Obama, in the midst of fighting for his contentious and groundbreaking healthcare plan, mistakenly used the campaign line, "If you like your healthcare, you can keep it."[22] After the plan's passage, this turned out not necessarily to be the case, and Obama was criticized for "spinning" to grease the skids for the bill's passage.

Sadly, the practice of public relations is often blamed for the existence of "spin." Faced with this era of spin and continued public uncertainty about the ethics of public relations, practitioners must always be sensitive to and considerate of how their actions and their words will influence the public.

Above all—in defiance of charges of spinning—public relations practitioners must consider their cardinal rule: *to never, ever lie.*

4 What Manner of Man or Woman?

What kind of individual does it take to become a competent public relations professional?

A 2004 study of agency, corporate, and nonprofit public relations leaders, sponsored by search firm Heyman Associates, reported seven areas in particular that characterize a successful public relations career:

1. Diversity of experience

2. Performance

3. Communications skills

4. Relationship building

5. Proactivity and passion

6. Teamliness

7. Intangibles, such as personality, likeability, and chemistry[23]

Beyond these success-building areas, in order to make it, a public relations professional ought to possess a set of specific technical skills as well as an appreciation of the proper attitudinal approach to the job. On the technical side, the following six skills are important:

1. **Knowledge of the field.** The underpinnings of public relations—what it is, what it does, and what it ought to stand for.

2. **Communications knowledge.** The media and the ways in which they work; communications research; and, most important, how to write.

3. **Technological knowledge.** Familiarity with computers and associated technologies, as well as with the World Wide Web, are imperative.

4. **Current events knowledge.** Knowledge of what's going on around you—daily factors that influence society: history, literature, language, politics, economics, and all the rest—from Kim Jong Un to Kim Kardashian; from Dr. Phil to Dr. Dre; from Three Penny Opera to 50 Cent; from Ice T to Ice Cube to Vanilla Ice to ISIS. A public relations professional must be, in the truest sense, a Renaissance man or woman.

5. **Business knowledge.** How business works, a bottom-line orientation, and a knowledge of your company and industry.

6. **Management knowledge.** How senior managers make decisions, how public policy is shaped, and what pressures and responsibilities fall on managers.

In terms of the "attitude" that effective public relations practitioners must possess, the following six requisites are imperative:

1. **Pro communications.** A bias toward disclosing rather than withholding information. Public relations professionals should want to communicate with the public, not shy away from communicating. They should practice the belief that the public has a right to know.

2. **Advocacy.** Public relations people must *believe in* their employers. They must be advocates for their employers. They must stand up for what their employers represent. Although they should never ever lie (Never, ever!) or distort or hide facts, occasionally it may be in an organization's best interest to avoid comment on certain issues. If practitioners don't believe in the integrity and credibility of their employers, their most honorable course is to go to "Plan B"—find work elsewhere.

3. **Counseling orientation.** A compelling desire to advise senior managers. Top executives are used to dealing in tangibles, such as balance sheets, costs per thousand, and cash flows. Public relations practitioners deal in intangibles, such as public opinion, media influence, and communications messages. Practitioners must be willing to support their beliefs—often in opposition to lawyers or human resources executives. They must even be willing to disagree with management at times. Far from being compliant, public relations practitioners must have the gumption to say *no*.

4. **Ethics.** The counsel that public relations professionals deliver must always be ethical. The mantra of the public relations practitioner must be to *do the right thing*.

5. **Willingness to take risks.** Most of the people you work for in public relations have no idea what you do. Sad, but true. Consequently, it's easy to be overlooked as a public relations staff member. You therefore must be willing to stick your neck out...stand up for what you believe in...take risks. Public relations professionals must have the courage of their convictions and the personal confidence to proudly represent their curious, yet critical, role in any organization.

6. **Positive outlook.** Public relations work occasionally is frustrating work. Management doesn't always listen to your good counsel, preferring instead to follow attorneys and others into safer positions. No matter. A public relations professional, if he or she is to perform at optimum effectiveness, must be positive. You can't afford to be a "sad sack." You win some. You lose some. But in public relations, at least, the most important thing is to keep on swinging and smiling.

Last Word

Spin, cover-up, distortion, and subterfuge are the antitheses of good public relations.

Ethics, truth, credibility—these values are what good public relations is all about.

To be sure, public relations is not yet a profession like law, accounting, or medicine, in which all practitioners are trained, licensed, and supervised. Nothing prevents someone with little or no formal training from hanging out a shingle as a public relations specialist. Such frauds embarrass professionals in the field and, thankfully, are becoming harder to find.

Indeed, both the PRSA (**Appendix A**) and the International Association of Business Communicators (**Appendix B**) have strong codes of ethics that serve as the basis of their membership philosophies.

Meanwhile, the importance of the practice of public relations in a less certain, more chaotic, overcommunicated, and social media–dominated world cannot be denied.

Despite its lingering problems—in attaining leadership status, finding its proper role in society, disavowing spin, and earning enduring respect—the practice of public relations has never been more valuable or more prominent. In its first 100 years as a formal, integrated, strategic-thinking process, public relations has become part of the fabric of modern society.

Here's why.

As much as they need customers for their products, managers today also desperately need constituents for their beliefs and values. In the 21st century, the role of public relations is vital in helping guide management in framing its ideas and making its commitments. The counsel that management needs must come from advisors who understand public attitudes, moods, needs, and aspirations.

Contrary to what misinformed critics may charge, "More often than not, public relations strategies and tactics are the most effective and valuable arrows in the quiver of the disaffected and the powerless."[24] Civil rights leaders, labor leaders, public advocates, and grassroots movements of every stripe have been boosted by proven communications techniques to win attention and build support and goodwill.

Winning this elusive goodwill takes time and effort. Credibility can't be won overnight, nor can it be bought. If management policies aren't in the public's best interest, no amount of public relations effort can obscure that reality. Public relations is not effective as a temporary defensive measure to compensate for management misjudgment. If management errs seriously, the best—and only—public relations advice must be to get the truthful story out immediately. Indeed, working properly, the public relations department of an organization often serves as the firm's "conscience."

This is why the relationship between public relations and other parts of the organization—legal, human resources, and advertising and marketing, for example—is occasionally a strained one. The function of the public relations department is distinctive from that of any other internal area. Few others share the access to management that public relations enjoys. Few others share the potential for power that public relations may exercise.

No less an authority than Abraham Lincoln once said: "Public sentiment is everything ... with public sentiment, nothing can fail. Without it, nothing can succeed. He who molds public sentiment goes deeper than he who executes statutes or pronounces decisions. He makes statutes or decisions possible or impossible to execute."[25]

Stated another way, no matter how you define it, the practice of public relations has become an essential element in the conduct of relationships for a vast variety of organizations in the 21st century.

Discussion Starters

1. How prominent is the practice of public relations around the world in the 21st century?
2. What is the PRSA's definition of public relations? How would you define the practice of public relations?
3. Why is the practice of public relations generally misunderstood by the public?
4. How would you describe the significance of the planning aspect in public relations?
5. Within the R-A-C-E process of public relations, what would you say is the most critical element?
6. In what ways does public relations differ from advertising or marketing?
7. If you were the public relations director of the local United Way, whom would you consider your most important "publics" to be?
8. What are the seven functions of public relations practice?
9. How do professional public relations people regard the aspect of "spin" as part of what they do?
10. What are the technical and attitudinal requisites most important for public relations success?

Pick of the Literature

Rethinking Reputation: How PR Trumps Advertising and Marketing in the New Media World

Fraser P. Seitel and John Doorley. New York: Palgrave Macmillan, 2012

One outstanding educator and another person critique how a social media-dominated society with declining journalistic societal standards impacts the quest for credibility.

The authors demonstrate how public relations can help build successful enterprises, even with a minimum of advertising support. The book focuses on real-life cases, including student designers of a successful footwear company who market themselves through networking, Facebook, and Twitter; Merck CEO Roy Vagelos, who developed a cure for river blindness and ensured the drug was made available where needed for free; and Exxon-Mobil, which resurrected its reputation through on-the-ground meetings with critics and a more accessible public relations posture.

The book also reviews the new 21st-century public relations realities, in which even "taking the low road" can lead to success, as in the cases of Donald Trump, Al Sharpton, Nancy Grace, and Dominic Strauss-Kahn. They forcefully argue, though, that "taking the high road," a la Paul Volcker and T. Boone Pickens, is eminently preferable. Worth buying, if for no other reason than one of the authors needs the money!

Case Study The New CEO's Trial by "Switchgate" Fire

At the start of 2014, Mary Barra made history as the first woman in the 106-year history of the General Motors Corporation to be named chief executive officer.

Barra's CEO honeymoon as the most powerful woman in the history of the auto industry lasted exactly two months.

In March, the new CEO found herself confronting the most damaging safety/cover-up scandal in General Motors' history—even more hurtful than GM's battle with consumer activist Ralph Nader 50 years earlier.

The company was charged with no less than a dozen charges of GM car drivers dying as the result of faulty ignition switches. Even worse, reports indicated that GM management had known about the ignition switch problem for a decade but never corrected it nor divulged the problem publicly.

"Switchgate" would dominate the headlines and consume the new CEO for the next year. How Mary Barra handled her moment in the crucible would largely define her reputation as chief of America's largest car company.

Here's how CEO Barra responded to her first critical public relations challenge.

Fix the Problem

The most important part of crisis management is *"fixing the problem."*

Most people don't understand that effective "public relations" must start with performance, not cosmetics. It's axiomatic that *"you can't pour perfume on a skunk."* Positive public relations demands taking action first to fix the problem and then communicating. In public relations, as in much of life, it is axiomatic, as the saying goes, *"you never get a second chance to make a first impression."*

In Barra's case, she moved decisively to recall the affected vehicles, reassure car owners, and remedy the ignition switch problem. In the first months after the problem surfaced, GM recalled and vowed to quickly fix 1.6 million-affected vehicles—all older models and two of which, Pontiac and Saturn, that no longer were in production. The CEO also named a 40-year GM veteran as the company's new vice president of global safety and appointed a high level internal task force to take control of the recall.

On the public side, she apologized profusely to the victims of the defective switches, called the incident a *"terrible, tragic problem"* and told a room full of reporters, at an unprecedented—especially for General Motors in the midst of a recall—press conference, *"Our goal is to make sure that something like this never happens again."*

So in terms of "first impressions," Barra appeared to be taking proper action to fix the problem.

Get the Bad News Out

A second principle in such a public relations dilemma where the reputation of the company is on the line is to get out all of the bad news as quickly as possible, in order to put it behind you and move on.

Accordingly, GM followed the Switchgate recall with another recall of 1.7 million newer vehicles, whose airbags were faulty. At the same time, the company announced that it would take a $300 million first quarter charge for its recall repairs; this, again, was unprecedented for a company as tradition-bound as General Motors, which historically took a much more deliberative approach to paying for mistakes.

In lumping in all this bad news right at the front of the crisis, Barra properly sought to immediately absorb a big hit so the negative impact of the devastating knock on GM's reputation might begin to diminish.

Find Out Why What Happened, Happened

CEOs are judged by how "seriously" they attack the issues that led to the problem, i.e. are they *really* interested in stopping bad behavior or are they just giving lip service?

The awful reality of Switchgate was that General Motors executives knew for years that its ignition switches were potentially harmful; yet they refused to recall them. Why? And who at GM was responsible for the decision? Barra, herself, was GM's global product development chief at the time. Yet she steadfastly testified that she wasn't involved with the ignition switches. But if she wasn't involved, which executives were responsible?

To her credit and to answer that question, Barra launched an internal investigation to find out who knew what, when, and why no action was taken. That was the good news. The less good news was that she placed at the helm of the investigation, a representative of King and Spaulding, GM's outside legal firm which presided over ignition switch settlement cases.

Appointing the same firm that pleaded GM's case in court hinted to critics the notion of a lack of objectivity in the investigation, even a potential *"conflict."* Barra dismissed the concern and stuck with the outside law firm.

Bridle the Lawyers

In a major crisis like GM's, lawyers properly tell you what you *"must"* do to defend yourself in a court of law. Public relations advisors, by contrast, tell you what you *"should"* do to defend yourself in the court of public opinion.

There's a big difference.

In GM's case, people wondered how the company would ultimately settle with the families of those killed or injured by the faulty ignition switches. This was a complicated matter For one thing, the liability for the defects, technically, belonged to the predecessor company "Old GM"—a company that declared bankruptcy—rather than the "New GM" that Ms. Barra now headed.

So technically, lawyers could have argued that the new company owed victims nothing, since the liability pre-dated the new company. For another thing, some victims already settled with GM, unaware of the company's apparent cover up over 10 years. In such an unclear legal environment, it would be understandable if GM had listened to hard-nosed lawyers and held the line on payouts.

FIGURE 1-5 On the hot seat.
General Motors CEO Mary Barra prepares to face the finger pointers in the U.S. House of Representatives in June 2014.
Photo: MICHAEL REYNOLDS/EPA/Newscom

But Barra chose to go outside the company for an impartial arbiter to decide what damages to pay claimants. She brought in Kenneth Feinberg, the lawyer who presided over the claims settlements both in the 9/11 World Trade Center tragedy and the BP Gulf of Mexico oil spill. Feinberg's hiring reassured victims and the public that the GM claims would be adjudicated fairly.

Sure enough, he announced that GM would "rip up" all prior settlements and provide compensation ranging from $20,000 to several million dollars to anyone injured in accidents involving 2.6 million GM cars.

Be Visible and Human

Finally, when faced with such an epochal public relations event, a good CEO must be visible and exhibit "humanity," even in the face of strong criticism.

That means talking to the staff, to the press, to the Congress and becoming the *"face"* of the company's response. Several years prior to the GM crisis, car rival Toyota learned—to its billion dollar detriment—that trying to stay in the background off the radar screen when faced with such a public crisis is a sure-fire recipe for disaster. Toyota was excoriated, in particular, by the U.S. Congress.

So the GM CEO learned from Toyota's mistakes and agreed to make the trek to Capitol Hill and appear before U.S. senators and representatives. As a lifetime auto executive, she was clearly

uneasy in commanding the spotlight and untrained in being glib or charismatic. And it was also quite true that GM's tragedy wasn't her doing. But she agreed nonetheless and faced withering questions; many from self-promoting politicians.

Throughout her Congressional testimony and, more important, with the survivors of accidents and the families of those who didn't survive, CEO Barra was quick to apologize on behalf of her company. *"I'm truly sorry for your loss,"* she repeated over and over as she met with victims at a two-hour meeting at GM's Washington, D.C. office.

By the summer of 2015, General Motors and its new CEO were ready to get back to producing quality American cars, as "Switchgate" faded in the rear view mirror.

Questions

1. How would you assess the way CEO Barra handled the "Switchgate" crisis?

2. Do you agree with her decision to allow GM's outside lawyers to lead the internal investigation?

3. What was the public relations benefit of hiring Kenneth Feinberg to supervise the claims process?

4. What recommendations would you make for GM's public relations process going forward?

Note: For further information, see Jeff Bennett, "GM Recall Compensation Plan Sees Payouts from $20,000 to Millions," *The Wall Street Journal*, June 30, 2014; Ben Geier, "GM's Mary Barra: Crisis Manager of the Year," December 28, 2014; Fraser P. Seitel, "GM's Recall Scandal: A Scorecard on CEO Mary Barra," *Fortune.com*, March 21, 2014; and Bill Vlasic, "General Motors Chief Pledges to Move Beyond Recalls," *The New York Times*, January 8, 2015.

From the Top

An Interview with Harold Burson

Harold Burson is the world's most influential and gentlemanly public relations practitioner. He has spent more than a half century serving as counselor to and confidante of corporate CEOs, government leaders, and heads of public sector institutions. As founder and chairperson of Burson-Marsteller, he was the architect of the largest public relations agency in the world. Mr. Burson, widely cited as the standard bearer of public relations ethics, has received virtually every major honor awarded by the profession, including the Harold Burson Chair in Public Relations at Boston University's College of Communication, established in 2003.

How would you define public relations?

One of the shortest—and most precise—definitions of public relations I know is "doing good and getting credit for it." I like this definition because it makes clear that public relations embodies two principal elements. One is behavior, which includes policy and attitude; the other is communications—the dissemination of information. The first tends to be strategic, the second tactical—although strategy plays a major role in many, if not most, media relations programs.

How has the business of public relations changed over time?

Public relations has, over time, become more relevant as a management function for all manner of institutions—public and private sector, profit and not-for-profit. CEOs increasingly recognize the need to communicate to achieve their organizational objectives. Similarly, they have come to recognize public relations as a necessary component in the decision-making process. This has enhanced the role of public relations both internally and for independent consultants.

How do ethics apply to the public relations function?

In a single word, pervasively. Ethical behavior is at the root of what we do as public relations professionals. We approach our calling with a commitment to serve the public interest, knowing full well that the public interest lacks a universal definition and knowing that one person's view of the public interest differs markedly from that of another. We must therefore be consistent in our personal definition of the public interest and be prepared to speak up for those actions we take.

At the same time, we must recognize our roles as advocates for our clients or employers. It is our job to reconcile client and employer objectives with the public interest. And we must remember that while clients and employers are entitled to have access to professional public relations counsel, you and I individually are in no way obligated to provide such counsel when we feel that doing so would compromise us in any way.

What are the qualities that make up the ideal public relations man or woman?

It is difficult to establish a set of specifications for all the kinds of people wearing the public relations mantle. Generally, I feel five primary characteristics apply to just about every successful public relations person I know.

- They're smart—bright, intelligent people; quick studies. They ask the right questions. They have that unique ability to establish credibility almost on sight.

- They know how to get along with people. They work well with their bosses, their peers, their subordinates. They work well with their clients and with third parties like the press and suppliers.

- They are emotionally stable—even (especially) under pressure. They use the pronoun "we" more than "I."

- They are motivated, and part of that motivation involves an ability to develop creative solutions. No one needs to tell them what to do next; instinctively, they know.

- They don't fear starting with a blank sheet of paper. To them, the blank sheet of paper equates with challenge and opportunity. They can write; they can articulate their thoughts in a persuasive manner.

What is the future of public relations?

More so than ever before, those responsible for large institutions whose existence depends on public acceptance and support recognize the need for sound public relations input. At all levels of society, public opinion has been brought to bear in the conduct of affairs both in the public and private sectors. Numerous CEOs of major corporations have been deposed following initiatives undertaken by the media, by public interest groups, by institutional stockholders—all representing failures that stemmed from a lack of sensitivity to public opinion. Accordingly, my view is that public relations is playing and will continue to play a more pivotal role in the decision-making process than ever before. The sources of public relations counsel may well become less structured and more diverse, simply because of the growing pervasive understanding that public tolerance has become so important in the achievement of any goals that have a recognizable impact on society.

Public Relations Bookshelf

Broom, Glen M. *Cutlip and Center's Effective Public Relations* (11th ed.). Upper Saddle River, NJ: Prentice Hall, 2012. The granddaddy of comprehensive textbooks in the field.

Center, Allen H., Patrick Jackson, and Stacey Smith. *Public Relations Practices* (8th ed.). Upper Saddle River, NJ: Pearson, 2012.

Dillenschneider, Robert L. *The AMA Handbook of Public Relations.* New York: American Management Association, 2010. A legendary practitioner offers his prescription for communicating in the 21st century.

Dinan, William, and David Miller. *A Century of Spin: How Public Relations Became the Cutting Edge of Corporate Power.* Ann Arbor, MI: Pluto Press, 2008. A review of corporate public relations with a decidedly Scottish twist.

Doorley, John, and Helio Fred Garcia. *Reputation Management: The Key to Successful Public Relations and Corporate Communication* (3rd ed.). New York: Routledge, 2015. The two smartest professors in the field discuss what really counts in terms of public relations effectiveness.

Ewen, Stuart. *PR! A Social History of Spin.* New York: Basic Books, 1996. A not-nice-at-all analysis of the growth of public relations in society, written by a sociologist who doesn't seem to have much regard for the burgeoning profession.

Gehrt, Jennifer, and Colleen Moffitt. *Strategic Public Relations: 10 Principles to Harness the Power of PR.* Xlibris Corporation, 2009. Two veteran public relations counselors use lessons from others to respond to the new 21st-century communication landscape.

Guth, David W., and Charles Marsh. *Public Relations: A Values-Driven Approach* (5th ed.). Upper Saddle River, NJ: Pearson Education, 2012. Two distinguished professors offer a look at today's public relations, including such unique theoretical aspects as contingency theory of accommodation, reflective paradigm, and heuristic versus theoretical approaches.

Heath, Robert L. *The Sage Handbook of Public Relations.* Thousand Oaks, CA: Sage Publications, 2010. A comprehensive overview of the field, including sections on investor relations, sports public relations, and the role of public relations in promoting healthy communities.

Lattimore, Dan, Otis Baskin, and Suzette Heiman. *Public Relations: The Profession and The Practice* (Kindle ed.). New York: McGraw-Hill College, 2011. Worthwhile contributions from a variety of scholars and professionals in the field.

Newsom, Doug, Judy Vanslyke Turk, and Dean Kruckeberg. *This Is PR: The Realities of Public Relations* (11th ed.). Boston, MA: Wadsworth Publishing Company, 2013. Well regarded text authored by top-line academic practitioners.

Pohl, Gayle M. *No Mulligans Allowed: Strategically Plotting Your Public Relations Course.* Dubuque, IA: Kendall Hunt Publishers, 2005. A fresh, creative, and useful perspective on charting a public relations career, authored by one of the nation's foremost public relations educators.

Rampton, Sheldon, and John Stauber. *Trust Us, We're Experts: How Industry Manipulates Science and Gambles with Your Future.* New York: J.P. Tarcher/Putnam, 2002. A super-cynical look at what public relations people do for a living, authored by two of the industry's most ardent—yet lovable—critics.

Ries, Al, and Laura Ries. *The Fall of Advertising and the Rise of PR.* New York: Harperbusiness, 2004. An old ad hand and his daughter blow the lid off the advertising profession.

Slater, Robert. *No Such Thing as Over-Exposure: Inside the Life and Celebrity of Donald Trump.* Upper Saddle River, NJ: Financial Times/Prentice Hall, 2005. The story, if you can bear it, of Donald Trump, in which the promotion-craving megalomaniac sat for 100 hours of private conversations. (Not for the faint of heart!)

Smith, Ron. *Public Relations: The Basics.* New York, NY: Routledge, 2014. Excellent introduction to the field and its functions.

Solis, Brian, and Deidre Breakenridge. *Putting the Public Back in Public Relations.* Upper Saddle River, NJ: Pearson Education, 2009. Two experts on public relations for the Social Media Age present new concepts to engage old and new publics.

Swann, Patricia. *Cases in Public Relations Management.* New York, NY: Routledge, 2010. Contemporary cases in public relations.

Wilcox, Dennis, Glen T. Cameron, and Brian H. Reber. *Public Relations: Strategies and Tactics* (11th ed.). Boston: Allyn & Bacon, 2014. Fine, long-standing text; good introduction.

Yaverbaum, Eric. *Public Relations Kit for Dummies* (2nd ed.). Foster City, CA: IDG Books Worldwide, 2006. A tongue-in-cheek, but useful, primer.

Endnotes

1. Zeina Karam and Vivian Salama, "Has The World Been Bamboozled by the ISIS PR Machine?" *Associated Press* (September 10, 2014).
2. Stuart Elliott, "Public Relations Defined, After an Energetic Public Discussion," *The New York Times* (March 1, 2014).
3. Ibid.
4. U.S. Bureau of Labor Statistics, U.S. Department of Labor, Occupational Outlook Handbook 2012–13 Edition, Public Relations Managers and Specialists, www.bls.gov/ooh/Management/Public-relations-managers-and-specialists.htm, March 25, 2015.
5. Gail E. Rymer, "The Number of Public Relations Graduate Programs Increasing—But Inconsistent Curricula Create Confusion," *Commission on Public Relations Education*, October 17, 2011.
6. Kirk Hallahan, "Challenges Confronting PR Education," *Public Relations Society of America* Web site, www.prsa.org, November 2005.
7. "PR-Journalism Pay Gap Presents Challenges for the Public Relations Industry," *Pew Research Center* (August 13, 2014).
8. O'Dwyer's, "Worldwide Fees of Top Independent PR Firms with Major U.S. Operations," www.odwyerpr.com/pr_firm_-rankings/independents.htm, March 2015.
9. Company Expands Its Management Committee to Include Communicator," *Ragan Report* (September 19, 2005): 2.
10. "The Design for Undergraduate Public Relations Education," a study cosponsored by the public relations division of the Association for Education and Journalism and Mass Communication, the Public Relations Society of America, and the educators' section of PRSA, 1987, 1.
11. Cited in Glen M. Broom, *Cutlip and Center's Effective Public Relations*, 10th ed. (Upper Saddle River, NJ: Prentice Hall, 2008).
12. Edward L. Bernays, *Crystallizing Public Opinion* (New York: Liveright, 1961).
13. Rex F. Harlow, "Building a Public Relations Definition," *Public Relations Review 2*, no. 4 (Winter 1976): 36.
14. Ibid.
15. John E. Marston, *The Nature of Public Relations* (New York: McGraw-Hill, 1963): 161.
16. Dr. Melvin I. Sharpe, professor and coordinator of the Public Relations Sequence, Department of Journalism, Ball State University, Muncie, IN, 2001.
17. John Dewey, *The Public and Its Problems* (Chicago: Swallow Press, 1927).

18. Timothy L. O'Brien, "Spinning Frenzy: P.R.'s Bad Press," *The New York Times* (February 13, 2005): B1.

19. Derrick Jensen, "The War on Truth: The Secret Battle for the American Mind," interview with John Stauber, www.mediachannel.org (June 7, 2000).

20. Fraser P. Seitel and John Doorley, *Rethinking Reputation* (New York: Palgrave Macmillan, 2012): 187–189.

21. "White House Official I. Lewis Libby Indicted on Obstruction of Justice, False Statement and Perjury Charges Relating to Leak of Classified Information Revealing CIA Officer's Identity," news release of Office of Special Counsel (October 28, 2005), www.usdoj.gov/usao/iln/osc.

22. Louis Jacobson, "Barack Obama Says That What He Said Was You Could Keep Your Plan If It Hasn't Changed Since the Law Passed," *Tampa Bay Times* (November 6, 2013).

23. "Heyman Associates Study Finds Critical Patterns for Public Relations Success," news release of Heyman Associates (June 28, 2004), www.heymanassociates.com.

24. Fraser P. Seitel, "Relax Mr. Stauber, Public Relations Ain't That Dangerous," www.mediachannel.org (June 7, 2000).

25. Abraham Lincoln, Lincoln–Douglas Debates, Ottawa, IL, August 21, 1858.

Chapter **2**

The History and Growth
of Public Relations

Chapter Objectives

1. To track the development of the practice of public relations from ancient times to the present.
2. To underscore the contribution to the field of two pioneers, in particular, Ivy Lee and Edward Bernays, whose philosophies and policies set the tone for modern-day public relations.
3. To chart the growth of public relations and its emergence as a major societal force in the 21st century.
4. To examine the factors, like social media, that have propelled the practice of public relations as a powerful and valuable force in this new century.

FIGURE 2-1 *The Man in the Gray Flannel Suit.* Gregory Peck's 1956 portrayal of a harassed and tortured public relations man didn't do much for the field's reputation. But at least he bathed regularly.
Photo: akg-images/Newscom

In its first 100 years, the practice of public relations has come a long way baby—from the days of *The Man in the Gray Flannel Suit*. The 1956 film starred the immortal Gregory Peck (Figure 2-1), who returns from the war and interviews for a position in public relations.

"But I know nothing about public relations," says an embarrassed Peck to his television network interviewer.

"Nonsense," retorts the personnel man, *"You've got a freshly-pressed suit and you apparently bathe regularly. What more is there to know?"*

Not a particularly auspicious beginning for a field that today is responsible for billions of dollars in revenue.

Nearly three decades later, the practice of public relations came of age.

On Sept. 30, 1982, the Johnson & Johnson (J&J) Company of New Brunswick, New Jersey, confronted the most diabolical crisis in the field's young history—the sabotaging of company products resulting in the murder of company customers. The respectful and public way that J&J handled "The Tylenol Murders" is the subject of the case at the end of Chapter 4 and a large reason why the field enjoys such prominence today.

Johnson & Johnson's "Credo" of corporate values that it considers sacrosanct is a model for companies around the world.

But public relations is a continually evolving social science. And none other than the legendary Johnson & Johnson company learned that lesson in the fall of 2010, when it was forced to recall a series of products, from its children's liquid Tylenol to tens of thousands of artificial hips to millions of contact lenses, all produced by J&J units. The spate of highly publicized product problems cast a pall over the commodity that Johnson & Johnson had fought so valiantly to uphold in the face of the Tylenol murders 30 years earlier—its integrity.[1]

Such is the fragility of a public relations reputation.

Unlike accounting, economics, medicine, and law, the modern practice of public relations is still a young field, a little more than 100 years old.

Modern-day public relations is clearly a 20th-century phenomenon. The impetus for its growth might, in fact, be traced back to one man.

John D. Rockefeller Jr. (Figure 2-2) was widely attacked in 1914 when the coal company he owned in Ludlow, Colorado, was the scene of a bloody massacre staged by Colorado militiamen and company guards against evicted miners and their families. When a dozen women and small children were killed at the Ludlow massacre, Rockefeller called in journalist Ivy Ledbetter Lee to help him deal with the crisis.

Lee, whom we discuss later in this chapter, would go on to become "the father of public relations." His employer, John D. Rockefeller Jr., whose legendary father had

FIGURE 2-2 **Pondering a crisis.**
John D. Rockefeller, Jr. (center) needed public relations help in 1914, when the Colorado coal company he owned was the scene of a massacre of women and children.
Photo: Rockefeller Archive Center

always adhered to a strict policy of silence in public affairs, would bear responsibility for the birth of a profession built on open communications.

Building a Strong Profession

The relative youthfulness of the practice of public relations means that the field is still evolving. It is also getting *stronger* and gaining more *respect* every day. The professionals entering the practice today are by and large superior in intellect, training, and even experience to their counterparts of decades ago (when few studied "public relations").

The strength of the practice of public relations today is based on the enduring commitment of the public to participate in a free and open democratic society. Several society trends have influenced the evolution of public relations theory and practice:

1. **Growth of big institutions.** The days of small government, local media, mom-and-pop grocery stores, tiny community colleges, and small local banks have largely disappeared. In their place have emerged massive political organizations, worldwide media and social networks, Walmarts, Home Depots, Googles, Apples, statewide community college systems and nationwide banking networks. The public relations profession has evolved to interpret these large institutions to the publics they serve.

2. **Heightened public awareness and media sophistication.** First came the invention of the printing press. Then came mass communications: print media, radio, and television. Later it was the development of cable, satellite, videotape, videodisks, video typewriters, portable cameras, word processors, fax machines, and cell phones. Then came the Internet, blogs, podcasts, wikis, and, most prominently, social media that have helped fragment audiences. Fifty years ago, McGill University Professor Marshall McLuhan predicted the world would become a "global village," where people everywhere could witness events—no matter where they occurred—in real-time. In the 21st century, McLuhan's prophecy has become a reality.

3. **Increasing incidence of societal change, conflict, and confrontation.** Minority rights, women's rights, senior citizens' rights, gay rights, animal rights, consumerism, environmental awareness, downsizings, layoffs, and resultant unhappiness with large institutions all have become part of day-to-day society. With the growth of social media, activists throughout the world have become increasingly more daring, visible and effective. Today, anyone who owns a computer can be a publisher, a broadcaster, a motivator of others.

4. **Globalization and the growing power of global media, public opinion, and democratic capitalism.** While institutions have grown in size and clout in the 21st century, at the same time the world has gotten increasingly smaller and more interrelated. Today, news of a cyclone that ravages Myanmar or an earthquake that imperils Nepal is broadcast within moments to every corner of the globe. The outbreak of democracy and capitalism in China, Latin America, Eastern Europe, the former Soviet Union, South Africa, and even, in recent years, in Middle East nations from Afghanistan and Iraq to Libya and Egypt (although not without pain and suffering) has heightened the power of public opinion in the world. The process has been energized by media that span the globe, especially social media that instantaneously connect like-minded individuals. In China alone, the most popular microblogging service, Sina Weibo,

has more than 500 million registered members and 54 million daily users, who even criticize the government—often at great risk.[2]

5. **Dominance of the Internet and growth of social media.** Today, more than three billion people use the Internet, many of them through social media.[3] The extraordinary growth of the Internet and social media have made billions of people around the world not only "instant consumers" of communication but also, especially with the advent of social media, "instant generators" of communication as well. The profound change this continues to bring to society—and the importance it places on communications—is monumental.

1 Ancient Beginnings

Although modern public relations is a 20th-century phenomenon, its roots are ancient. Leaders in virtually every great society throughout history understood the importance of influencing public opinion through persuasion. For example, archeologists have found bulletins in Iraq dating from as early as 1800 B.C. that told farmers of the latest techniques of harvesting, sowing, and irrigating.[4] The more food the farmers grew, the better the citizenry ate and the wealthier the country became—a good example of planned persuasion to reach a specific public for a particular purpose—in other words, public relations.

The ancient Greeks also put a high premium on communication skills. The best speakers, in fact, were generally elected to leadership positions. Occasionally, aspiring Greek politicians enlisted the aid of sophists (individuals renowned for both their reasoning and their rhetoric) to help fight verbal battles. Sophists gathered in the amphitheaters of the day to extol the virtues of particular political candidates. Thus, the sophists set the stage for today's lobbyists, who attempt to influence legislation through effective communications techniques. From the time of these early sophist lobbyists, the practice of public relations has been a battleground for questions of ethics. Should a sophist or a lobbyist—or a public relations professional, for that matter—"sell" his or her talents to the highest bidder, regardless of personal beliefs, values, and ideologies? When modern-day public relations professionals agree to represent repressive governments, such as Iran or Zimbabwe or North Korea or even Russia, or to defend the questionable actions of troubled celebrities, from Lindsay Lohan and Floyd Mayweather to Chris Brown and Justin Bieber, these ethical questions remain a focus of modern public relations.

The Romans, particularly Julius Caesar, were also masters of persuasive techniques. When faced with an upcoming battle, Caesar would rally public support through published pamphlets and staged events. Similarly, during World War I, a special U.S. public information committee, the Creel Committee, was formed to channel the patriotic sentiments of Americans in support of the U.S. role in the war. Stealing a page from Caesar, the committee's massive verbal and written communications effort was successful in marshaling national pride behind the war effort. According to a young member of the Creel Committee, Edward L. Bernays (later considered by many to be another "father of public relations" and the subject of the interview at the end of this chapter), "This was the first time in U.S. history that information was used as a weapon of war."[5]

Even the Catholic Church had a hand in the creation of public relations. In the 1600s, under the leadership of Pope Gregory XV, the church established a College of Propaganda to "help propagate the faith." In those days, the term *propaganda* did not have a negative connotation; the church simply wanted to inform the public about

FIGURE 2-3   Public relations Pope.
Pope Francis, who assumed the Papacy in March 2013, has forged a positive public relations image around the world, even including outstripping Kanye West in terms of Twitter followers.
Photo: ANGELO CARCONI/EPA/Newscom

the advantages of Catholicism. Today, the pope and other religious leaders maintain communications staffs to assist in relations with the public. Indeed, the chief communications official in the Vatican maintains the rank of Archbishop of the Church. It was largely his role to deal with perhaps the most horrific scandal ever to face the Catholic Church—the priest pedophile issue at the start of the 21st century. In the aftermath of that scandal, the Vatican has become super sensitive to public relations, with Pope Francis—the "People's Pope"—becoming a public relations star with 10 million Twitter followers—right behind Kanye West![6] (Figure 2-3).

Early American Experience

The American public relations experience dates back to the founding of the republic. Influencing public opinion, managing communications, and persuading individuals at the highest levels were at the core of the American Revolution. The colonists tried to persuade King George III that they should be accorded the same rights as English men and women. "Taxation without representation is tyranny" became their public relations slogan to galvanize fellow countrymen and countrywomen.

When King George refused to accede to the colonists' demands, they combined the weaponry of sword and pen. Samuel Adams, for one, organized Committees of Correspondence as a kind of revolutionary Facebook to disseminate anti-British information throughout the colonies. He also staged events to build up revolutionary fervor, such as the Boston Tea Party, in which colonists, masquerading as American Indians, boarded British ships in Boston Harbor and pitched chests of imported tea overboard—as impressive a media event as has ever been recorded sans television.

Thomas Paine, another early practitioner of public relations, wrote periodic pamphlets and essays that urged the colonists to band together. Paine's first pamphlet was called "Common Sense," a paean to human liberty, published in January 1776. In a nation of fewer than three million people, it sold a half-million copies.[7] In one essay contained in his *Crisis* papers, Paine wrote poetically: "These are the times that try men's souls. The summer soldier and the sunshine patriot will, in this crisis, shrink from the service of their country." The people listened, were persuaded, and took action—testifying to the power of early American communicators.

Later American Experience

The creation of the most important document in America's history, the Constitution, also owed much to public relations. Federalists, who supported the Constitution, fought tooth and nail with anti-Federalists, who opposed it. Their battle was waged in newspaper articles, pamphlets, and other organs of persuasion in an attempt to influence public opinion. To advocate ratification of the Constitution, political leaders such as Alexander Hamilton, James Madison and John Jay banded together, under the pseudonym Publius, to write letters to leading newspapers. Today those letters are bound in a document called *The Federalist Papers* and are still used in the interpretation of the Constitution.

After its ratification, the constitutional debate continued, particularly over the document's apparent failure to protect individual liberties against government encroachment. Hailed as the father of the Constitution, Madison framed the Bill of Rights in 1791, which ultimately became the first 10 amendments to the Constitution. Fittingly, the first of those amendments safeguarded, among other things, the practice of public relations:

Congress shall make no law respecting an establishment of religion, or prohibiting the free exercise thereof; or abridging the freedom of speech, or of the press, or the rights of the people peaceably to assemble, and to petition the government for a redress of grievances.

In other words, people were given the right to speak up for what they believed in and the freedom to try to influence the opinions of others. Thus was the practice of public relations ratified.

Into the 1800s

The practice of public relations continued to percolate in the 19th century. Among the more prominent, yet negative, antecedents of modern public relations that took hold in the 1800s was press agentry. Two of the better-known—some would say notorious—practitioners of this art were Amos Kendall and Phineas T. Barnum.

In 1829, President Andrew Jackson selected Kendall, a Kentucky writer and editor, to serve in his administration. Within weeks, Kendall became a member of Old Hickory's "kitchen cabinet" and eventually became one of Jackson's most influential assistants.

Kendall performed just about every White House public relations task. He wrote speeches, state papers, and messages, and he turned out press releases. He even conducted basic opinion polls and is considered one of the earliest users of the "news leak." Although Kendall is generally credited with being the first authentic presidential press secretary, his functions and role went far beyond that position.

Among Kendall's most successful ventures in Jackson's behalf was the development of the administration's own newspaper, the *Globe*. Although it was not uncommon for the governing administration to publish its own national house organ, Kendall's deft editorial touch refined the process to increase its effectiveness. Kendall would pen a Jackson news release, distribute it for publication to a local newspaper, and then reprint the press clipping in the *Globe* to underscore Jackson's nationwide popularity. Indeed, that popularity continued unabated throughout Jackson's years in office, with much of the credit going to the president's public relations advisor.*

Most public relations professionals would rather not talk about P. T. Barnum as an industry pioneer. Barnum, some say, was a huckster whose motto might well have been "The public be fooled." Barnum's defenders suggest that although the impresario may have had his faults, he nonetheless was respected in his time as a user of written and verbal public relations techniques to further his museum and circus.

Like him or not, Barnum was a master publicist. In the 1800s, as owner of a major circus, Barnum generated article after article for his traveling show. He purposely gave his star performers short names—for instance, Tom Thumb, the midget, and Jenny Lind, the singer—so that they could easily fit into the headlines of narrow newspaper columns. Barnum also staged bizarre events, such as the legal marriage of the fat lady to the thin man, to drum up free newspaper exposure. And although today's practitioners scoff at Barnum's methods, in this day of Paris Hilton, Lindsay Lohan and presidential candidates (groan) Donald Trump and Al Sharpton, not to mention the Kardashians, there are still many press agents practicing the ringmaster's techniques. Indeed, when today's public relations professionals bemoan the specter of shysters and hucksters that still overhangs their field, they inevitably place the blame squarely on the fertile mind and silver tongue of P. T. Barnum.

Emergence of the Robber Barons

The American Industrial Revolution ushered in many things at the turn of the century, not the least of which was the growth of public relations. The 20th century began with small mills and shops, which served as the hub of the frontier economy, eventually giving way to massive factories. Country hamlets, which had been the centers of commerce and trade, were replaced by sprawling cities. Limited transportation and communications facilities became nationwide railroad lines and communications wires. Big business took over, and the businessman was king.

The men who ran America's industries seemed more concerned with making a profit than with improving the lot of their fellow citizens. Railroad owners led by William Vanderbilt, bankers led by J. P. Morgan, oil magnates led by John D. Rockefeller, and steel impresarios led by Henry Clay Frick ruled the fortunes of thousands of others. Typical of the reputation acquired by this group of industrialists was the famous—and perhaps apocryphal—response of Vanderbilt when questioned about the public's reaction to his closing of the New York Central Railroad: "The public be damned!"

Little wonder that Americans cursed Vanderbilt and his ilk as "robber barons" who cared little for the rest of society. Although most who depended on these industrialists for their livelihood felt powerless to rebel, the seeds of discontent were being sown liberally throughout society.

---

*Kendall was decidedly not cut from the same cloth as today's neat, trim, buttoned-down press secretaries. On the contrary, Jackson's man was described as "a puny, sickly looking man with a weak voice, a wheezing cough, narrow and stooping shoulders, a sallow complexion, silvery hair a seedy appearance." (Fred F. Endres, "Public Relations in the Jackson White House," *Public Relations Review 2*, no. 3 [Fall 1976]: 5–12.)

FYI

P. T. Barnum Redux

Kourtney, Kim, Khloé, and Kris and the Never-Ending Quest for Publicity

Self-respecting public relations professionals despise the legacy of P. T. Barnum, who created publicity through questionable methods. They lament, as noted in Chapter 1, that public relations communication should always reflect "performance" and "truth."

Ah, were it so.

Alas, Barnum's publicity-seeking methods are just as effective with 21st-century media as they were with 19th-century media.

Doubt it?

Then consider the Kardashians, those walking/talking/publicity-generating masters of media, who have parlayed their peculiar personal predicaments into reality-TV fame, public relations renown, and oodles of nonstop cash. P. T. Barnum never met publicity he didn't like, and neither have the Kardashians.

The Kardashian girls—Kourtney, Kim, Khloé, mother Kris Jenner (former wife of Los Angeles attorney Robert Kardashian and remarried to U.S. Olympic gold medalist-turned-transsexual Bruce Jenner), and younger sisters Kendall and Kylie—are celebutantes, famous for, well, being "famous."

The Kardashian girls parlayed their fame into a reality-TV series, *Keeping Up with the Kardashians*, which spawned the reality show *Khloé and Lamar* about Khloé and troubled basketball-playing husband Lamar Odom. The Kardashians also cashed in on clothing lines, perfume franchises, a retail store in Las Vegas, and Kim's 72-day wedding to professional basketball player Kris Humphries.

While cynics doubted the staying power of the Kardashians, the media continued to report their every movement. Somewhere, P. T. Barnum is smiling (Figure 2-4).

FIGURE 2-4   **Here come the Kardashians.**
Forget the Obamas. America's first publicity family is the extended Kardashian klan, featuring Kris, Khloe, Kendall, Kim, Kanye, Baby North West and assorted others on their way to church on Easter Sunday 2015, as the paparazzi dutifully followed.
Photo: WP#EAG/ZOJ/WENN/Newscom

Enter the Muckrakers

When the axe fell on the robber barons, it came in the form of criticism from a feisty group of journalists dubbed *muckrakers*. The "muck" that these reporters and editors "raked" was dredged from the supposedly scandalous operations of America's business enterprises. Upton Sinclair's novel *The Jungle* attacked the deplorable conditions of the meatpacking industry. Ida Tarbell's *History of the Standard Oil Company* stripped away the public façade of the nation's leading petroleum firm. Her accusations against Standard Oil Chair Rockefeller, many of which were unproven, nonetheless stirred up public attention.

Magazines such as *McClure's* struck out systematically at one industry after another. The captains of industry, used to getting their own way and having to answer to no one, were wrenched from their peaceful passivity and rolled out on the public carpet to answer for their sins. Journalistic shock stories soon led to a wave of sentiment for legislative reform.

As journalists and the public became more anxious, the government got more involved. Congress began passing laws telling business leaders what they could and couldn't do. Trust-busting became the order of the day. Conflicts between employers and employees began to break out, and newly organized labor unions came to the fore. The Socialist and Communist movements began to take off. Ironically, it was "a period when free enterprise reached a peak in American history, and yet at that very climax, the tide of public opinion was swelling up against business freedom, primarily because of the breakdown in communications between the businessman and the public."[8]

For a time, these men of inordinate wealth and power found themselves limited in their ability to defend themselves and their activities against the tidal wave of public condemnation. They simply did not know how to get through to the public. To tell their side of the story, the business barons first tried using the lure of advertising to silence journalistic critics; they tried to buy off critics by paying for ads in their papers. It didn't work. Next, they paid publicity people, or press agents, to present their companies' positions. Often these hired guns painted over the real problems of their client companies. The public saw through this approach.

Clearly, another method had to be discovered to get the public to at least consider the business point of view. Business leaders were discovering that a corporation might have capital, labor, and natural resources, yet be doomed to fail if it couldn't influence public opinion. The best way to influence public opinion, as it turned out, was through honesty and candor. This simple truth—the truth that lies at the heart of modern-day, effective public relations practice—was the key to the accomplishments of American history's first great public relations counselor.

2 Ivy Lee: The Father of Public Relations

Ivy Ledbetter Lee was a former Wall Street reporter, the son of a Methodist minister, who plunged into publicity work in 1903 (Figure 2-5). Lee believed neither in Barnum's public-be-fooled approach nor Vanderbilt's public-be-damned philosophy. For Lee, the key to business acceptance and understanding was that the public be informed.

Lee disdained the press agents of the time, who used any influence or trick to get a story on their clients printed, regardless of the truth or merits. By contrast, Lee firmly believed that the only way business could answer its critics convincingly was to present its side honestly, accurately, and forcefully. Instead of merely appeasing the public, Lee thought a company should strive to earn public confidence and goodwill.

FIGURE 2-5 **Father of public relations.**
Ivy Lee.
Photo: Courtesy of Seely G. Mudd Manuscript Library, Princeton University Library, Ivy Lee Papers, Public Policy Papers, Department of Rare Books and Special Collections

In 1914, John D. Rockefeller Jr., son of one of the nation's most maligned and mis-understood men, hired Lee to assist with the fallout from the Ludlow massacre, which was affecting his Colorado Fuel and Iron Company. Lee's advice to Rockefeller was simple:

> *Tell the truth, because sooner or later the public will find it out anyway. And if the public doesn't like what you are doing, change your policies and bring them into line with what the people want.*[9]

Despite the tragedy of Ludlow, Lee encouraged Rockefeller to create a joint labor–management board to mediate all workers' grievances on wages, hours, and working conditions. It was a great success. The mine workers—and the public—began to see John D. Rockefeller Jr. in a different light. Most important, he began to see them in a new light as well. As Rockefeller's youngest son, David, recalled nearly a century later, "My father was changed profoundly by his meetings with the workers. It was a lesson that stayed with him throughout the rest of his life and one of the most important things that ever happened to our family."[10]

In working for the Rockefellers, Lee tried to "humanize" them, to feature them in real-life situations such as playing golf, attending church, and celebrating birthdays. Simply, Lee's goal was to present the Rockefellers in terms that every individual could understand and appreciate.

Ironically, even Ivy Lee could not escape the glare of public criticism. In the late 1920s, Lee was asked to serve as advisor to the parent company of the German Dye

Trust, which, as it turned out, was an agent for the policies of Adolf Hitler. For his involvement with the Dye Trust, Lee was branded a traitor and dubbed "Poison Ivy" by members of Congress investigating un-American activities. Ironically, the smears against him in the press rivaled the most vicious ones against any of the robber barons.[11]

Ivy Lee's critics cite his unfortunate involvement with the Dye Trust and even his association as spokesperson for John D. Rockefeller Jr. as proof that his contributions weren't particularly profound. They argue that Lee "was not someone who was particularly effective at getting business to change its behavior."[12]

Ivy Lee's proponents, on the other hand (and your author is one of them), argue that Lee was among the first to counsel his clients that "positive public relations starts with action, with performance" and that positive publicity must follow positive performance.[13] This is why Ivy Lee is recognized as the individual who began to distinguish "publicity" and "press agentry" from "public relations" based on honesty and candor. For his seminal contributions to the field, Ivy Lee deserves recognition as the *real* father of public relations.

③ The Growth of Modern Public Relations

Ivy Lee helped to open the gates for modern public relations. After he helped establish the idea that high-powered companies and individuals have a responsibility to inform their publics, the practice began to grow in every sector of American society.

Government

During World War I, President Woodrow Wilson established the Creel Committee under the leadership of journalist George Creel. Creel's group, composed of the nation's leading journalists, scholars, and public relations leaders, mounted an impressive effort to mobilize public opinion in support of the war effort and to stimulate the sale of war bonds through Liberty Loan publicity drives. Not only did the war effort get a boost, but so did the field of public relations. The nation was mightily impressed with the potential power of publicity as a weapon to encourage national sentiment and support.

During World War II, the public relations field received an even bigger boost. The Office of War Information (OWI) was established to convey the message of the United States at home and abroad. Under the directorship of Elmer Davis, a veteran journalist, the OWI laid the foundations for the U.S. Information Agency as America's voice around the world.

World War II also saw a flurry of activity to sell war bonds, boost the morale of those at home, spur production in the nation's factories and offices, and, in general, support America's war effort as intensively as possible. By virtually every measure, this full-court public relations offensive was an unquestioned success.

The proliferation of public relations officers in World War II led to a growth in the number of practitioners during the peace that followed. One reason companies saw the need to have public relations professionals to "speak up" for them was the more combative attitude of President Harry Truman toward many of the country's largest institutions. For example, Truman's seizure of the steel mills touched off a massive public relations campaign, the likes of which had rarely been seen outside the government.

Later in the century, the communications problems of President Richard Nixon, surrounding the "cover-up" of the Watergate political scandal, brought new criticism of public relations. It didn't matter that Nixon was surrounded by alumni of the advertising industry, rather than public relations professionals. The damage to the field's reputation was done. But the administration of the "great communicator" Ronald Reagan reaffirmed the value of public relations. And later, the communications skills of President Bill Clinton—before a nasty scandal in the Oval Office submerged him in controversy—added to the importance of the practice in government. In the 21st century, the communications ability of President Barack Obama reinforced the power of communication in the White House, especially early in his first term and later in his second term.

Counseling

The nation's first public relations firm, the Publicity Bureau, was founded in Boston in 1900 and specialized in general press agentry. The first Washington, D.C. agency was begun in 1902 by William Wolff Smith, a former correspondent for the *New York Sun* and the *Cincinnati Enquirer*. Two years later, Ivy Lee joined with a partner to begin his own counseling firm.

The most significant counselor this side of Ivy Lee was Edward L. Bernays, who began as a publicist in 1913 and was instrumental in the war bonds effort. He was the nephew of Sigmund Freud and author of the landmark book *Crystallizing Public Opinion* (see interview at the end of this chapter).

Bernays was a giant in the public relations field for nearly the entire century. In addition to contributing as much to the field as any other professional in its history, Bernays was a true public relations scholar. He taught the first course in public relations in 1923 and was also responsible for "recruiting" the field's first distinguished female practitioner, his wife Doris E. Fleischman.

Fleischman, former editor of the *New York Tribune*, was a skilled writer, and her husband was a skilled strategist and promoter. Together they built Edward L. Bernays, Counsel on Public Relations into a top agency. In many ways, Fleischman was the "mother" of public relations, paving the way for a field that is today dominated by talented women (Figure 2-6).

FIGURE 2-6 **Dynamic duo.**
Edward L. Bernays and his wife, Doris Fleischman, formed the 20th century's greatest public relations tandem.
Photo: Courtesy of the Museum of Public Relations, www.prmuseum.com

Bernays's seminal writings in the field underscored the importance of strategic communications advice for clients. For example, Bernays wrote:

> At first we called our activity "publicity direction." We intended to give advice to clients on how to direct their actions to get public visibility for them. But within a year we changed the service and its name to "counsel on public relations." We recognized that all actions of a client that impinged on the public needed counsel. Public visibility of a client for one action might be vitiated by another action not in the public interest.[14]

Due to his background, Bernays was fascinated by a wide range of psychological theories and practices beginning to emerge in society. One of his major contributions to the practice of public relations was transforming the practice from a purely journalistic-based approach to one underpinned by psychology, sociology, and social-psychology to reach individuals in terms of their unconscious desires, fears, and needs.[15]

After Bernays's pioneering counseling efforts, a number of public relations firms, most headquartered in New York, began to take root, most notably among them Hill & Knowlton, Carl Byoir & Associates, Newsom & Company, and Burson-Marsteller. One of the earliest African American counselors was D. Parke Gibson, who authored two books on African American consumerism and advised companies on multicultural relations.

For many years, Hill & Knowlton and Burson-Marsteller jockeyed for leadership in the counseling industry. One early counselor, Harold Burson (see From the Top in Chapter 1), emphasized marketing-oriented public relations "to help clients sell their goods and services, maintain a favorable market for their stock, and foster harmonious relations with employees." In 2000, Burson was named the most influential PR person of the 20th century.[16]

In the 1990s, the counseling business saw the emergence of international super agencies, many of which were merged into advertising agencies. Indeed, both Hill & Knowlton and Burson-Marsteller were eventually merged under one corporation, WPP, which also included the J. Walter Thompson and Young & Rubicam advertising agencies. Another mega-communications firm, Omnicom Group, owned seven major public relations firms, including Fleishman-Hillard, Porter Novelli, and Ketchum. In the 21st century, with the growth of such large agencies, occasional lapses in ethical standards confronted the profession (see A Question of Ethics in this chapter). Despite these communications conglomerates, most public relations agencies still operate as independent entities. The largest of these, Edelman Public Relations, founded by another legendary public relations pioneer, Daniel Edelman in 1952, collects nearly $800 million in annual fees.[17] Nonetheless, local agencies, staffed by one or several practitioners, still dominate the industry.

In the 21st century, then, the public relations counseling business boasts a diverse mix of huge national agencies, medium-sized regional firms, and one-person local operations. Public relations agencies may be general in nature or specialists in everything from consumer products to entertainment to health care to social media and technology.

Corporations

After World War II, as the 20th century rolled on, the perceptual problems of corporations and their leaders diminished. Opinion polls ranked business as high in public esteem. People were back at work, and business was back in style.

Smart companies—General Electric, General Motors (GM), and American Telephone & Telegraph (AT&T), for example—worked hard to preserve their good names through both

A Question of Ethics

Burson Fumbles Facebook Flap

As noted, there is no more respected individual in the practice of public relations than Harold Burson. The agency he founded, Burson-Marsteller, has a long and proud tradition of ethical practice. (Your author, himself, is a proud alumnus of the firm.)

But in the spring of 2011, Burson-Marsteller was caught red-handed in an embarrassing scheme to make a client's competitor look bad. The fact that the client was Facebook and the competitor was Google—two of the most powerful names in the social media world—only added to Burson's dilemma (Figure 2-7).

It all started when two Burson staff members—both former journalists—approached daily newspapers and Internet bloggers about authoring articles critical of a feature on Google's Gmail service called "Social Circle." The social media feature, said the Burson representatives, was guilty of trampling the privacy of millions of users and violating federal fair trade rules.

When the bloggers pressed Burson to reveal its client, Burson refused. One blogger was so enraged with the Burson whispering campaign that he posted Burson's entire pitch online. The blogger reported that Burson offered to ghost write an op-ed column, let the blogger sign his name to it, and then help get it published in the *Washington Post, Politico, The Hill, Roll Call,* and *The Huffington Post.*

This led to a chain reaction in the media. *USA Today* ran a Money section front-page story, "PR Firm's Google Attack Fails," exposing the two former journalists, one former CNBC news anchor Jim Goldman and the other, former *National Journal* political columnist John Mercurio, as the surreptitious leakers.

Meanwhile, Google began fielding media calls about the little-known service and issued its own statement: "We have seen this e-mail reportedly sent by a representative of the PR firm Burson-Marsteller. We're not going to comment further. Our focus is on delighting people with great products."

Facebook quickly came out to separate itself from its public relations agency. Said a Facebook spokesperson, "No 'smear' campaign was authorized or intended," adding that it hired Burson to "focus attention on this issue, using publicly available information that could be independently verified by any media organization or analyst."

A chastened Burson said Facebook asked to be anonymous but acknowledged that the misguided effort was "not at all standard operating procedure and is against our policies."

The public relations industry was quick to denounce the clumsy "fake news" efforts of Burson and the two reporters-turned–public relations professionals. Said the chair of the Public Relations Society of America (PRSA), "This reflects poorly upon the global public relations profession. Burson took the road of misleading and not disclosing who they were representing. In the essence of the public relations code of ethics 101, that's a no-no."[*]

No-no.

Questions

1. How should Burson have handled its Facebook assignment?

2. Should a public relations client always be identified?

FIGURE 2-7 **Thumbs down.** The world's leading social media company was caught with egg on its face(book) as a result of the sneaky campaign of its public relations agency to plant incriminating stories about its competitor, Google.
Photo: PETER DaSILVA/EPA/ Newscom

*For further information, see Bryon Acohido and Jon Swartz, "PR Firm's Google Attack Fails," *USA Today,* May 10, 2011, pp. B-1, 2; and Greg Hazley, "Burson Becomes Target in Facebook Flap," O'Dwyer's, June 2011, p. 10.

words and actions. Arthur W. Page became AT&T's first public relations vice president in 1927. Page was a legendary public relations figure—memorialized in today's Arthur Page Society of leading corporate and agency public relations executives—helping to maintain AT&T's reputation as a prudent and proper corporate citizen. Page also was one of the few public relations executives to serve on prestigious corporate boards of directors, including Chase Manhattan Bank, Kennecott Copper, Prudential Insurance, and Westinghouse Electric.[18]

Page's five principles of successful corporate public relations are as relevant now as they were in the 1930s:

1. To make sure management thoughtfully analyzes its overall relation to the public
2. To create a system for informing all employees about the firm's general policies and practices
3. To create a system giving contact employees (those having direct dealings with the public) the knowledge needed to be reasonable and polite to the public
4. To create a system drawing employee and public questions and criticism back up through the organization to management
5. To ensure frankness in telling the public about the company's actions[19]

Another early corporate public relations luminary was Paul Garrett. A former news reporter, he became the first director of public relations for mighty GM in 1931, working directly for GM's legendary CEO Alfred Sloan. Garrett once reportedly explained that the essence of his job was to convince the public that the powerful auto company deserved trust, that is, "to make a billion-dollar company seem small." Ironically, as good as Garrett was, according to the late maestro of management Peter Drucker (see From the Top in Chapter 5), he nevertheless reflected the universal public relations complaint, still common today, of "never feeling like an insider" within his organization. Drucker, who counseled CEO Sloan, said that because Garrett was a "communications professional" and not a "car man," GM executives often treated him with wariness.[20]

One would think that companies today all recognize the importance of proper public relations in the conduct of their business. Most do. But, as the corporate financial scandals of the first decade of the 21st century—that torpedoed entrenched firms such as Lehman Brothers, Bear Stearns, Countrywide, and Washington Mutual and laid low the respected names of Goldman Sachs, Morgan Stanley, Merrill Lynch, Bank of America, and Citigroup—show, CEOs don't know everything. The point is that in a day dominated by social media and cable TV, smart corporate leaders more than ever need to seek out the counsel of trained public relations professionals in dealing with their key constituent publics.

4 Public Relations Comes of Age

As noted, public relations came of age largely as a result of the confluence of five general factors in our society:

Growth of Large Institutions

Ironically, the public relations profession received perhaps its most important thrust when business confidence suffered its most severe setback. The economic and social upheaval caused by the Great Depression of the 1930s provided the impetus for corporations to seek public support by telling their stories. Public relations departments sprang up in scores of major companies, among them Bendix, Borden, Eastman Kodak, Eli Lilly, Ford, GM, Standard Oil, and U.S. Steel. The role that public relations played in regaining post-Depression public trust in big business helped project the field into the relatively strong position it has enjoyed since World War II.

Today, businesses of every size recognize that aggressively communicating corporate products and positions can help win public receptivity and support and ward off government intrusion. The best companies in the 21st century are those that have learned, as Ivy Lee preached, that proper action results in the best public relations.

Heightened Public/Media Awareness

In the 1970s and 1980s, companies were obligated to consider minority rights, consumer rights, environmental implications, and myriad other social issues. Business began to contribute to charities. Managers began to consider community relations a first-line responsibility. The general policy of corporations confronting their adversaries was abandoned. In its place, most large companies adopted a policy of conciliation and compromise.

This new policy of corporate social responsibility (CSR) continued into the 1990s. Corporations came to realize that their reputations are a valuable asset to be protected, conserved, defended, nurtured, and enhanced at all times. In truth, institutions in the 1990s had little choice but to get along with their publics. The general prosperity of the 1990s, fueled by enormous stock market gains, helped convey goodwill between organizations and their publics.

By 2012, 98% of American homes had television, more than 50% of Americans subscribed to basic cable, and 273 million North Americans used the Internet.[21] Ironically, where once three television networks—ABC, CBS, and NBC—dominated America's communication nexus, now a plethora of channels and cable networks, talk radio stations, as well as millions of blogs, Web sites, and social media outlets cater to every persuasion, enabling media consumers to choose what they want to view.

As a result of all this communication, publics have become much more fragmented, specialized, and sophisticated.

Societal Change, Conflict, and Confrontation

Disenchantment with big institutions peaked in the 1960s, coincident with an unpopular Vietnam War.

The social and political upheavals of the 1960s dramatically affected many areas, including the practice of public relations. The Vietnam War fractured society. Movements were formed by various interest groups. An obscure consumer advocate named Ralph Nader began to look pointedly at the inadequacies of the automobile industry. Women, long denied equal rights in the workplace and elsewhere, began to mobilize into activist groups such as the National Organization for Women (NOW). Environmentalists, worried about threats to the land and water by business expansion, began to support groups such as the Sierra Club. Minorities, particularly African Americans and Hispanics, began to petition and protest for their rights. Gays, lesbians and transgender people, AIDS activists, senior citizens, birth control advocates, and social activists of every kind began to challenge the legitimacy of large institutions. Not since the days of the robber barons had large institutions so desperately needed professional communications help.

By the 21st century, such movements had morphed into established, well-organized and powerful interest groups. Nongovernmental organizations (NGOs), united by the Internet, proliferated around the globe. By the presidential election of 2008, public disapproval of the Iraq War, concerns about energy supplies and prices, climate change and global warming, and a host of other issues, as well as renewed disenchantment with those in charge of government and business, generated a new round of activism. Women rallied around the candidacy of Senator Hillary Clinton. The enthusiasm, among young people, generated by Senator Barack Obama and his call for "hope and change" was illustrative of the mood. When Senator Obama was elected the nation's first African American president and Senator Clinton was named his secretary of state in 2009—and presumed Democratic candidate for President in 2016—it was clear that traditional times in America had, indeed, "changed".

Spread of Democracy and Capitalism

In the 21st century, democracy and capitalism, as someone once said, have "broken out everywhere."

In recent years, significant events to spur democracy—all conveyed in real-time by pervasive global media—have been breathtaking.

- In 2005, after the defeat of Saddam Hussein signaled the potential for a democratic Iraq, an astounding 10 million citizens—70% of eligible voters—went to the polls to elect new leaders.

- In 2008, Kosovo declared its independence from Serbia in a stunning signal of freedom. Also, democratic revolutions in Georgia and Ukraine challenged Russian dominance.

- In 2011, the political uprising that swept through the Middle East represented the most significant challenge to authoritarian rule since the collapse of Soviet communism. Champions of democracy demanded that tyrants cede power as the "Arab Awakening" extended into totalitarian nations such as Syria well into the winter of 2013.

The setbacks in 2015 that these brave attempts suffered—from continuing repression, terrorism and war in the Middle East to Russia's attempts to turn back democratic ideals among its neighbors, like Ukraine—haven't silenced democratic longings.

While the world remains a troubled place, the growth of democracy remains an inexorable force that can't be denied. Even in nations that aren't democracies, like China, the spirit of capitalism, of individuals free to earn a living based on their own industriousness and entrepreneurship, pervades. Moreover, with the world near-completely "wired," the power of communication and public relations to bring down tyrants and build up democracy is profound.

Growth of Social Media

In the 21st century, true two-way communication has arrived largely as a result of the growth of online access. Social media, cable, satellite, mobile, instant messaging, pagers, bar code scanners, voice mail systems, videodisk technologies, and a multitude of other developments revolutionized the information transmission and receiving process. The emergence of the Internet and the World Wide Web radically intensified the spread of communications even further.

The Internet began during the cold war in 1969 as a U.S. Department of Defense system. In 2000, 22% of Americans had bought a product online. The rate grew to 49% in 2007. Revenues from Internet purchases grew from $7.4 billion in the third quarter of 2000 to an estimated $34.7 billion in the third quarter of 2007. And today, with close to 87% of adults online and most connected to social media platforms, sales via e-commerce surpassed $300 billion for the first time in 2014.[22]

The impact of the Web and social media on public relations practice has been phenomenal. E-mail dominates internal communications. Journalists, like many other Americans, regard the Internet as their primary choice of most organizational communications. In the 21st century, knowledge of and facility with the Internet—from Facebook to Twitter, from Instagram to Pinterest to mobile apps of every variety—has become a front-burner necessity for public relations practitioners.

Public Relations Education

As the practice of public relations has developed, so too has the growth of public relations education. In 1951, 12 schools offered major programs in public relations. Today, well in excess of 200 journalism or communication programs offer concentrated study in public relations, with nearly 300 others offering at least one course dealing with the profession.

The last major study of public relations education was done more than a decade ago by the Commission on Public Relations Education, chartered by the PRSA. This commission recommended a public relations curriculum imparting knowledge in such nontraditional but pivotal areas as relationship building, societal trends, and multicultural and global issues.[23]

While public relations education isn't generally incorporated into most business schools, it should be. As noted, the practice has become an integral part in the daily workings and ongoing relationships of most organizations—from companies to churches, from governments to schools. Therefore, business students should be exposed to the discipline's underpinnings and practical aspects before they enter the corporate world.

Likewise, in journalism, with more than 70% of U.S. daily newspaper copy—and 80% of UK newspaper copy—estimated to emanate from public relations–generated releases, journalists, too, should know what public relations is all about before they graduate.[24]

Last Word

From humble beginnings 100 years ago, the practice of public relations today is big business around the world.

- The U.S. Bureau of Labor Statistics reports that close to 229,000 individuals practice public relations across the country, with an annual increase of 12% anticipated between now and 2022.[25]

- The PRSA, organized in 1947, boasts a growing membership of 22,000 in 100 chapters nationwide.

- The PRSA, formed in 1968 to facilitate communications between students interested in the field and public relations professionals, has more than 10,000 student members at close to 300 college chapters in the United States and one in Argentina.

- The International Association of Business Communicators boasts 12,000 members in more than 80 countries.

- More than 5,000 U.S. companies, 2,100 trade associations, 189 foreign embassies, and 350 federal government departments, bureaus, agencies, and commissions have public relations departments.[26]

- More than 1,400 independent public relations agencies exist in the United States, with more than 700 public relations firms residing in 80 foreign countries.[27]

- Top communications executives at major companies and agencies draw six-figure salaries, and more than a few make in excess of a million dollars a year.

The scope of modern public relations practice is vast. Media relations, government relations, Web relations, employee communications, public relations counseling and research, local community relations, audiovisual communications, contributions, interactive public relations, and numerous other diverse activities fall under the public relations umbrella. This may be one reason public relations is variously labeled *external affairs, corporate communications,* *public affairs, corporate relations*, and a variety of other confusing euphemisms.

Just as the name of the field generates confusion, so too does its purpose. Specifically, public relations professionals lament that the practice is still often accused of being a haven for snake oil salespeople peddling cosmetics, subterfuge, and spin. What many fail to understand is that proper public relations—the kind that builds credibility—must begin and end with one important commodity: *truth.*

Indeed, there is no more important characteristic for public relations people to emulate than the candor that comes from high ethical character. The field's finest ethical moment, in fact, occurred when the Johnson & Johnson (J&J) Company, in the wake of unspeakable tragedy brought about by its lead product Tylenol, didn't hesitate to choose the ethical course. As the case study at the conclusion of Chapter Four suggests, the handling of the Tylenol tragedy was public relations' most shining hour. (And as the J&J example at this chapter's commencement indicates, positive public relations must be refortified all the time.)

Despite the stereotypes that still overhang the field, with hundreds of thousands of men and women in its practice in the United States and thousands more overseas, public relations has become solidly entrenched as an important, influential, and professional component of 21st-century society.

Discussion Starters

1. What societal factors have influenced the spread of public relations?
2. Why do public relations professionals think of P. T. Barnum as a mixed blessing?
3. What is the significance to the practice of public relations of American revolutionary hero Samuel Adams?
4. What did the robber barons and muckrakers have to do with the development of public relations?
5. Why are Ivy Lee and Edward Bernays considered two of the fathers of public relations?
6. What impact did the Creel Committee and the Office of War Information have on the development of public relations?
7. What was the significance of Arthur Page to the development of corporate public relations?
8. Where should the practice of public relations be situated in a university?
9. What are some of the yardsticks that indicated that public relations had "arrived" in the latter part of the 20th century?
10. What are some of the issues that confront public relations in the 21st century?

Pick of the Literature

A Century of Spin: How Public Relations Became the Cutting Edge of Corporate Power (paperback)

David Miller and William Dinan, London, England: Pluto Press, 2008

Two British sociology professors present a not-so-flattering view of how public relations developed and became the powerful societal force it is today.

The authors' bias is that public relations was hatched by covertly political types, interested in "spinning" propaganda to forward their purposes. It traces these roots to modern-day British politicians, right up to British Prime Minister David Cameron.

The book begins by calling public relations one of the world's most powerful forces, conceived by corporations to impose business interests on public policy. The notion of "public relations ethics" is an oxymoron, according to these professors.

Worth reviewing, at least to see how the naysayers think.

Case Study   Welcome to the NFL

In 2015, the annual compensation of the commissioner of the National Football League (NFL), Roger Goodell, was $44 million. And why not?

The NFL's annual revenues exceeded $9.5 billion, the highest for any world professional sports league. The NFL's 32 teams collect more than $1 billion yearly in sponsorship revenues. The league has a $400 million contract with Microsoft for exclusive technologies on the sidelines and a $4 billion partnership with DirectTV to broadcast every football game. The 2015 NFL Super Bowl drew an average audience of 114 million TV viewers, the most watched broadcast in U.S. television history.

So you would think that Commissioner Goodell and the NFL would be enjoying the moment. Well, you'd be wrong.

In the second decade of the 21st century, the league was rocked by a series of scandals, the most damaging of which stemmed from society's growing concern over domestic violence, particularly the abuse of women and children.

Fight in an Elevator

The NFL's problems began in February 2014 when star Baltimore Ravens running back Ray Rice and his then fiancée, Janay Palmer, were involved in an early-morning fight in an Atlantic City hotel elevator. Both were charged with simple assault and released by the Atlantic City Police Department.

A day later, TMZ.com released a video showing Rice dragging Palmer out of the elevator. Ravens Coach Jim Harbaugh responded to the video by alluding to his conversation with Rice about what happened and the fact that the couple would attend a seminar to deal with the incident. Meanwhile, the NFL said nothing, allowing the team to deal with what appeared to be a minor problem.

A month later, after an Atlantic City grand jury charged Rice with third-degree aggravated assault, the Ravens issued a statement: *"This is part of the due process for Ray. We know there is more to Ray Rice than this one incident."*

Rice and Palmer then got married, and Rice acknowledged his actions were "inexcusable." In July, the NFL issued the star

FIGURE 2-8   Abused and abuser.
Former NFL star Ray Rice and his wife, Janay Palmer, attend arbitration hearing with NFL Commissioner Roger Goodell in November 2014.
Photo: ANDREW GOMBERT/EPA/Newscom

player a two-game suspension, after meeting personally with the couple. By August, Goodell was being roundly criticized for the lightness of Rice's punishment, and on August 28, the league reacted by adopting a stricter domestic violence policy. Announced a chagrined Goodell:

> *My disciplinary decision led the public to question our sincerity, our commitment, and whether we understood the toll that domestic violence inflicts on so many families. I take responsibility both for the decision and for ensuring that our actions in the future properly reflect our values. I didn't get it right. Simply put, we have to do better. And we will.*

The new goodwill lasted a week.

Video Knockout

On September 8, TMZ.com released new surveillance video from inside the elevator, showing Rice punching Palmer and knocking her senseless.

The outrage from the public was immediate and uncompromising. Celebrities and other NFL players immediately condemned Rice's behavior. Nike dropped its sponsorship of him. EA Sports announced it would delete the running back from its popular video games. The Ravens offered to exchange Rice jerseys for those of other players, and the team terminated his contract. The NFL then suspended Rice indefinitely—all as a result of the TMZ video.

The league and the team both claimed they had never before seen the video that TMZ published. Rice's now wife issued a statement on Instagram talking about the *"horrible nightmare"* her family was now living through. She begged forgiveness for her husband and pleaded that he be allowed to go back to his work to support the family. Rice, himself, texted the media, expressing fear that he wouldn't be allowed to play again. *"I'm just holding strong for my wife and kid that's all I can do right now,"* he wrote.

Inevitably, demands grew for Rice's permanent suspension from football and Goodell's firing. Commissioner Goodell, in full damage control mode, went on national television and announced the recruitment of domestic abuse specialists and plans to lead a campaign against national domestic violence. He also said he couldn't rule out that Ray Rice would never again play in the NFL.

Learning the Hard Way

In the wake of the Ray Rice disaster, the NFL and its commissioner had learned their lesson.

A week after the Rice video, another NFL star running back, Adrian Peterson of the Minnesota Vikings, was indicted in a child abuse case in which he used a wooden switch to discipline his four-year-old son. In this case, however, NFL justice was swift and severe.

Goodell immediately announced that Peterson would be suspended without pay for the remainder of the league season. Declared the commissioner in invoking the punishment:

> *The difference in size and strength between you and the child is significant, and your actions clearly caused physical injury to the child. While an adult may have a number of options when confronted with abuse—to flee, to fight back, or to seek help from law enforcement—none of those options is realistically available to a four-year-old child. Further, the injury inflicted on your son includes the emotional and psychological trauma to a young child who suffers criminal physical abuse at the hands of his father.*

As for Ray Rice, he ultimately appealed his NFL suspension in federal court and won the right to become a free agent, eligible to be picked up by a team for the 2015 season. However, two weeks before the season started, Rice still hadn't been signed by a new team.

Unfortunately for the player and his family—but certainly understandable in light of the domestic abuse baggage he carried—no team was willing to take a chance on the one-time star who had become a public relations pariah.

Questions

1. Had you been public relations advisor to the NFL commissioner, what advice would you have given him after the Ray Rice incident was first reported?

2. What is your view on the fairness of the Rice suspension after the second TMZ video was exposed?

3. Should the NFL allow players like Rice and Peterson and future domestic abusers to remain in the league?

4. What public relations initiatives would you recommend the NFL take relative to domestic and child abuse?

Note: For further information, see Madeline Boardman, "Adrian Peterson: Minnesota Vikings Player Indicted in Child Abuse Case," *US Weekly* (September 13, 2014); Ike Ejiochi, "How the NFL Makes the Most Money of Any Sport," *CNBC.com* (September 4, 2014); Ryan Gorman, "Baltimore Ravens Announce Ray Rice Jersey Exchange as Nike Drops Endorsement," *US Weekly* (September 9, 2014); "Key Events in the Ray Rice Timeline," CNN (September 11, 2014); Esther Lee, "Adrian Peterson Suspended by NFL for Rest of 2014 Season After Child Abuse Scandal," *US Weekly* (November 18, 2014); Kate McDonough, "Ray Rice Video's Second Horror: Why It Never Should Have Been Published in the First Place," *Salon* (September 8, 2014).

From the Top

An Interview with Edward L. Bernays

Photo courtesy of Barry Spector

Edward L. Bernays, who died in 1995 at the age of 103, was a public relations patriarch. A nephew of Sigmund Freud, Bernays pioneered the application of the social sciences to public relations. In partnership with his late wife, he advised presidents of the United States, industrial leaders, and legendary figures from Enrico Caruso to Eleanor Roosevelt. This interview was conducted with the legendary counselor in his 98th year.

When you taught the first public relations class, did you ever envision the field growing to its present stature?
I gave the first course in public relations after Crystallizing Public Opinion was published in 1923. I decided that one way to give the term "counsel on public relations" status was to lecture at a university on the principles, practices, and ethics of the new vocation. New York University was willing to accept my offer to do so. But I never envisioned at that time that the vocation would spread throughout the United States and then throughout the free world.

What were the objectives of that first public relations course?
The objectives were to give status to the new vocation. Many people still believed the term "counsel on public relations" was a euphemism for publicity man, press agent, or flack. Even H. L. Mencken, in his book on the *American language*, ranked it as such. But in his *Supplement to the American Language*, published some years later, he changed his viewpoint and used my definition of the term.

What are the most significant factors that have led to the rise in public relations practice?
The most significant factor is the rise in people power and its recognition by leaders. Theodore Roosevelt helped bring this about with his Square Deal. Woodrow Wilson helped with his New Freedom, and so did Franklin Delano Roosevelt with his New Deal. And this tradition was continued as time went on.

Do you have any gripes with the way public relations is practiced today?
I certainly do. The meanings of words in the United States have the stability of soap bubbles. Unless words are defined as to their meaning by law, as in the case of professions—for instance, law, medicine, architecture—they are in the public domain. Anyone can use them. Today, any plumber or car salesman or unethical character can call himself or herself a public relations practitioner. Many who call themselves public relations practitioners have no education, training, or knowledge of what the field is. And the public equally has little understanding of the meaning of the two words. Until licensing and registration are introduced, this will continue to be the situation.

What pleases you most about current public relations practice?
What pleases me most is that there are, indeed, practitioners who regard their activity as a profession, an art applied to a science, in which the public interest, and not pecuniary motivation, is the primary consideration; and also that outstanding leaders in society are grasping the meaning and significance of the activity.

How would you compare the caliber of today's public relations practitioner with that of the practitioner of the past?
The practitioner today has more education in his subject. But, unfortunately, education for public relations varies with the institution where it is being conducted. This is due to the lack of a standard definition. Public relations activity is applied social science to the social attitudes or actions of employers or clients.

Where do you think public relations will be 20 years from now?
It is difficult to appraise where public relations will be 20 years from now. I don't like the tendency of advertising agencies gobbling up large public relations organizations. That is like surgical instrument manufacturers gobbling up surgical medical colleges or law book publishers gobbling up law colleges. However, if licensing and registration take place, then the vocation is assured a long lifetime, as long as democracy's.

Public Relations Bookshelf

Bernays, Edward L. *Crystallizing Public Opinion.* New York: Liveright, 1961. The original 1923 version was the first significant book in the field. It deserves to be read for its historical value as well as for the amazingly progressive ideas that its author forwarded about the modern practice for which he was so responsible.

Bernays, Edward L. *Public Relations.* Norman: University of Oklahoma Press, 1963. This book offers an informative history of public relations, from Ancient Sumeria through the 1940s, and includes Bernays's view of what public relations ought to stand for.

Bernays, Edward L. *The Later Years: Public Relations Insights, 1956–1986.* Rhinebeck, NY: H & M, 1987. Essentially, this is a series of columns that Edward Bernays authored for the late *Public Relations Quarterly.*

Boorstin, Daniel J. *The Image: A Guide to Pseudo Events in America.* New York: Harper & Row, 1964. A not-very-flattering account of America's emphasis on image over reality, written 40 years ago by one of the nation's most eminent 20th-century thinkers.

Burson, Harold. "A Decent Respect to the Opinion of Mankind." Speech delivered at the Raymond Simon Institute for Public Relations (Burson-Marsteller, 866 Third Avenue, New York, NY 10022), March 5, 1987. This speech highlights public relations activities that have influenced the United States from colonial times to the present day.

Burson, Harold. *E Pluribus Unum: The Making of Burson-Marsteller.* New York: Burson-Marsteller, 2004. This 166-page memoir traces the life of one of the patriarchs of public relations, Harold Burson, from newspaperman in Memphis through war correspondent to founding his legendary public relations firm.

Chomsky, Noam. *Necessary Illusions: Thought Control in Democratic Societies.* Boston: South End Press, 1989. A contrary view to Bernays's concept of public relations, this book, written by a well-known social critic, expresses all "that is wrong" about the media and attempts to persuade the public.

Cutlip, Scott M. *Public Relations History from the 17th to the 20th Century.* Hillsdale, NJ: Lawrence Erlbaum Associates, 1995. A one-of-a-kind historical reference.

Cutlip, Scott M. *The Unseen Power—Public Relations, A History.* Hillsdale, NJ: Lawrence Erlbaum Associates, 1994. This 800-page book is perhaps the definitive history of public relations in the 20th century. And it's not always "positive," either.

Ewen, Stuart. *PR! A Social History of Spin.* New York, NY: Basic Books, 1996. And oldie, but baddy, at least in terms of its view of public relations. This Hunter College history professor is no fan of public relations, and the book is worth reading for that reason alone.

Olasky, Marvin N. "Roots of Modern Public Relations: The Bernays Doctrine." *Public Relations Quarterly,* Winter 1984. Olasky wages a spirited defense of Bernays as a more pragmatic and effective public relations representative than Ivy Lee.

Slater, Robert. *No Such Thing as Over-Exposure: Inside the Life and Celebrity of Donald Trump.* Upper Saddle River, NJ: Prentice Hall, 2005. If you've ever wondered about the phrase "a legend in his own mind," read this book and find out what it means.

Tedlow, Richard S. *Keeping the Corporate Image: Public Relations and Business, 1900–1950.* Greenwich, CT: JAI Press, 1979. An analytical and comprehensive history of corporate public relations in the first half of the 20th century.

Tye, Larry. *The Father of Spin: Edward L. Bernays and the Birth of Public Relations.* New York: Henry Holt, 1998. The author's background as a *Boston Globe* journalist, not a public relations practitioner or professor, both limits the depth of this biography and offers the refreshing viewpoint of an "outsider."

Endnotes

1. Natasha Singer and Reed Abelson, "After Recalls of Drugs, a Congressional Spotlight on J&J's Chief," The *New York Times* (September 28, 2010).
2. Xuecum, Murong, "Busting China's Bloggers," *The New York Times* (October 15, 2013).
3. World Internet Users June 2014, Internet World Stats: Usage and Population Statistics, www.internetworldstats.com, Miniwatts Marketing Group, 2014.
4. Scott M. Cutlip, Allen H. Center, and Glen M. Broom, *Effective Public Relations,* 8th ed. (Upper Saddle River, NJ: Prentice Hall, 2000): 102.
5. Fraser P. Seitel, "The Company You Keep," www.odwyerpr.com (July 22, 2002).
6. Katie Engelhart, "The PR Guru Behind the Pope Who Is Charming the World," *Vice* (November 21, 2013).
7. Alexander Green, "The Propagandist Who Changed the World," *Spiritual Wealth* (March 14, 2014).
8. Ray Eldon Hiebert, *Courtier to the Crowd: The Story of Ivy L. Lee and the Development of Public Relations* (Ames: Iowa State University Press, 1966).
9. John E. Harr and Peter J. Johnson, *The Rockefeller Century: Three Generations of America's Greatest Family* (New York: Simon & Schuster, 1988): 130.
10. Interview with David Rockefeller, New York, NY, November 30, 2005.
11. Cited in Alvin Moscow, *The Rockefeller Inheritance* (Garden City, NY: Doubleday, 1977): 23.
12. Interview with Stuart Ewen, "Spin Cycles: A Century of Spin," *CBC Radio* (January 19, 2007).
13. Interview with Fraser Seitel, "Spin Cycles: A Century of Spin," *CBC Radio* (January 19, 2007).
14. Edward L. Bernays, "Bernays: 62 Years in Public Relations," *Public Relations Quarterly* (Fall 1981): 8.
15. Interview with Stuart Ewen, op. cit.
16. "Burson Hailed as PR's No. 1 Influential Figure," *PR Week* (October 18, 1999): 1.
17. "O'Dwyer's Ranking of PR Firms with Major U.S. Operations," *O'Dwyer's Newsletter* (March 9, 2015).
18. Cited in Noel L. Griese, "The Employee Communications Philosophy of Arthur W. Page," *Public Relations Quarterly* (Winter 1977): 8–12.
19. Noel L. Griese, *Arthur W. Page: Publisher, Public Relations Pioneer, Patriot* (Tucker, GA: Anvil Publishers, 2001).
20. Fraser P. Seitel, "An Afternoon with Peter Drucker," *The Public Relations Strategist* (Fall 1998): 10.
21. "Internet Users in the Americas December 31, 2011," World Stats—Web Site Directory, Miniwatts Marketing Group, 2012.
22. Allison Enright, "U.S. Annual E-Retail Sales Surpass $300 Billion for the First Time," *Internet Retailer* (February 17, 2015).
23. John L. Paluszek, "Public Relations Students: Today Good, Tomorrow Better," *The Public Relations Strategist* (Winter 2000): 27.
24. "'Churnalism' Study Claims News Mainly PR and Wire Copy," www.pressgazette.co.uk/story.asp?storycode=40123, February 1, 2008.
25. Bureau of Labor Statistics, U.S. Department of Labor, Occupational Outlook Handbook, 2014–15 Edition, Public Relations Specialists, www.bls.gov/oco/ocos086.htm, January 8, 2014.
26. Jack O'Dwyer (Ed.), *O'Dwyer's Directory of Corporate Communications* (New York: J. R. O'Dwyer Co., 2005).
27. Jack O'Dwyer (Ed.), *O'Dwyer's Directory of Public Relations Firms* (New York: J. R. O'Dwyer Co., 2013).

Chapter **3**

Communication

Chapter Objectives

1. To discuss the goals and theories of modern communication as they relate to the practice of public relations.

2. To explore the importance and proper use of words and semantics to deliver ideas and persuade others toward one's point of view.

3. To discuss the various elements that effect communication, including the media, the bias of receivers, and the individuals or entities delivering messages.

4. To examine the necessity of feedback in evaluating communication and formulating continued communication.

FIGURE 3-1   Call me Caitlyn.
In June 2015, the former Olympic gold medalist Bruce Jenner shocked the world by reintroducing himself on the cover of *Vanity Fair* magazine as Caitlyn Jenner. *Photo: Newscom*

Remember Olympic gold medalist Bruce Jenner from Chapter 1? Well forget him. He is now a *she,* specifically Caitlyn Jenner, transgender woman, who chose to announce her new identity and assets with a *Vanity Fair* cover story one June day in 2015 that drew more than 1.1 million followers hours after it went online (Figure 3-1). By day's end, six million people had viewed the *Vanity Fair* story, and a new Caitlyn Jenner Twitter account had attracted one million followers in four hours and three minutes; shattering the old record (held by Barack Obama) for fastest person on Twitter to reach the one-million follower milestone.[1] The Jenner coming-out cover soon became the lead story on national broadcasts, in newspapers and online.

The *Vanity Fair* article and Twitter account was just another step in the new Ms. Jenner's carefully orchestrated public relations campaign that commenced with the TV interview cited in Chapter 1. All of this publicity led to a new reality show on the E! network and a new public identity for the former decathlete and Kardashian father.

When asked about the perception from journalistic purists that the *Vanity Fair* article was simply part of a promotional campaign to further Ms. Jenner's career in the limelight, editor Graydon Carter sniffed, *"All stories are part of some coordinated rollout, all stories everywhere."*[2]

And he had a point.

Communication in the 21st century—with the Net and social media tying people around the world together as never before—has become very much a public relations phenomenon, where everything from movie releases to presidential campaigns are meticulously calibrated to achieve maximum impact.

For organizations and individuals, especially those in the public eye, the days of "quiet communications" are over.

In the 21st century world of pervasive social media, nearly the whole world is truly "wired." The power of communication, through the oral and written word and the images that flash around the world to millions of people in real-time, is more awesome than any individual, group, or even nation.

What happens at a market in Kirkuk is witnessed in a matter of seconds in Berlin, Bangkok, and Boise. The world has truly become a "global village."

As a consequence, *communication* has never been a more potent tool, and *communications* must be handled with great care.

Which brings us back to public relations.

First and foremost, the public relations practitioner is a professional communicator. More than anyone else in an organization, the practitioner must know how to communicate.

Fundamentally, communication is a process of exchanging information, imparting ideas and making oneself understood by others. It also includes understanding others in return. Indeed, *understanding* is critical to the communications process. If one person sends a message to another, who disregards or misunderstands it, then communication hasn't taken place. But if the idea received is the one intended, then communication has occurred. Thus, a boss who sends subordinates dozens of e-mails isn't necessarily communicating with them. If the idea received is not the one intended, then the sender has done little more than convert personal thoughts to words—and there they lie.

Although all of us are endowed with some capacity for communicating, the public relations practitioner must be better at it than most. Before public relations practitioners can earn the respect of management and become trusted advisors, they must demonstrate a mastery of many communications skills—writing, speaking, listening, promoting, and counseling. Just as the comptroller is expected to be an adept accountant, and the legal counsel is expected to be an accomplished lawyer, the public relations professional must be the best communicator in the organization.

1 Goals of Communication

When communication is planned, as it should be in public relations, every communication must have a goal, an objective, and a purpose. If not, why communicate in the first place?

What are typical communications goals?

1. **To inform.** Often the communications goal of an organization is to inform or educate a particular public. For example, before holidays, the Automobile Association of America (AAA) will release information providing advice on

safe driving habits for long trips. In so doing, AAA is performing a valuable information service to the public.

2. **To persuade.** A regular goal of public relations communicators is to persuade people to take certain actions. Such persuasion needn't be overly aggressive; it can be subtle. For example, a mutual fund annual report that talks about the fund's long history of financial strength and security may provide a subtle persuasive appeal for potential investors.

3. **To motivate.** Motivation of employees to "pull for the team" is a regular organizational communications goal. For example, the hospital CEO who outlines in an Intranet memo to employees, the institution's overriding objectives in the year ahead is communicating to motivate the staff to action.

4. **To build mutual understanding.** Often communicators have as their goal the mere attainment of understanding of a group in opposition. For example, a community group that meets with a local plant manager to express its concern about potential pollution of the neighborhood is seeking understanding of the group's rationale and concern.

The point is that whether written release, online memo, speech, or meeting, all are valid public relations communications vehicles designed to achieve communications goals with key constituent publics. Again, the best way to achieve one's goals is through an integrated and strategically planned approach.

Traditional Theories of Communication

Books have been written on the subject of communications theory. This book is *not* one of them. Consequently, we won't attempt to provide an all-encompassing discussion on how people ensure that their messages get through to others. But in its most basic sense, communication commences with a source who sends a message through a medium to reach a receiver, who, we hope, responds in the manner we intended. Books have been written on the subject of communications theory.

Many theories exist—from the traditional to the contemporary—about the most effective ways for a source to send a message through a medium to elicit a positive response. Here are but a few.

- One early theory of communication, the *two-step flow theory*, stated that an organization would beam a message first to the mass media, which would then deliver that message to the great mass of readers, listeners, and viewers for their response. This theory may have less relevance today when media is less "mass" than it is "targeted"—through social media, Web sites, blogs, cable TV, talk radio, etc.—people today are influenced by a great many factors, of which the mass media may be one but is not necessarily the dominant one.

- Another theory, the *concentric-circle theory*, developed by pollster Elmo Roper, assumed that ideas evolve gradually to the public at large, moving in concentric circles from great thinkers to great disciples to great disseminators to lesser disseminators to the politically active to the politically inert. This theory suggests that people pick up and accept ideas from leaders, whose impact on public opinion may be greater than that of the mass media. The overall study of how communication is used for direction and control is called *cybernetics*.

■ The communications theories of the late Pat Jackson have earned considerable respect in the public relations field. Jackson's public relations communications models, too, emphasized "systematic investigation—setting clear strategic goals and identifying key stakeholders."[3] One communications approach to stimulate behavioral change encompassed a five-step process:

1. **Building awareness.** Build awareness through all the standard communications mechanisms that we discuss in this book, from publicity to advertising to public speaking to social media to word of mouth.

2. **Developing a latent readiness.** This is the stage at which people begin to form an opinion based on such factors as knowledge, emotion, intuition, memory, and relationships.

3. **Triggering event.** A triggering event is something—either natural or planned—that makes you want to change your behavior. Slimming down in time for beach season is an example of a natural triggering event. Staged functions, rallies, campaigns, and appearances are examples of planned triggering events.

4. **Intermediate behavior.** This is what Jackson called the "investigative" period, when an individual is determining how best to apply a desired behavior. In this stage, information about process and substance is sought.

5. **Behavioral change.** The final step is the adoption of new behavior.

■ Another traditional public relations theory of communications is the basic *S-E-M-D-R communications process.* This model suggests that the communication process begins with the source (S), who issues a message (M) to a receiver (R), who then decides what action to take, if any, relative to the communication. Two additional steps, an encoding stage (E), in which the source's original message is translated and conveyed to the receiver, and a decoding stage (D), in which the receiver interprets the encoded message and takes action, complete the model. It is in these latter two stages, encoding and decoding, that the public relations function most comes into play.

■ Confirmation bias suggests that people seek out messages that agree with or "confirm" their own attitudes; they avoid messages that disagree or are "dissonant" to their own attitudes. So the fact that liberals watch *MSNBC* and conservatives watch *Fox News* is an example of such "confirmation bias."[4]

■ There are even those who focus on the growing import of the "silent" theories of communication. The most well known of these, Elisabeth Noelle-Neumann's *spiral of silence*, suggests that communications that work well depend on the silence and nonparticipation of a huge majority. This so-called silent majority fears becoming isolated from and therefore ostracized by most of their colleagues. Thus, they invariably choose to "vote with the majority."[5]

All of these theories and many others have great bearing on how public relations professionals perform their key role as organizational communicators.

Contemporary Theories of Communication

Many other communications theories abound today as social media and Internet communication changes the ways and speed at which many of us receive our messages. Professor Everett Rogers talks about the unprecedented "diffusion" of the Internet as a communications vehicle that spans cultures and geographies. Others point to the new reality of "convergence" of video, data and voice, mobile and fixed, traditional and new age communications mechanisms with which public relations professionals must be familiar.

The complexity of communications in contemporary society—particularly in terms of understanding one's audience—has led scholars to author additional "audience centric" theories of how best to communicate.

- *Constructivism* suggests that knowledge is *constructed* not transmitted. Constructivism, therefore, is concerned with the cognitive process that precedes the actual communication within a given situation rather than with the communication itself.

   This theory suggests that in communicating, it is important to have some knowledge of the receiver and his or her beliefs, predilections and background. Simply dispensing information and expecting receivers to believe in or act on it, according to this theory, is a fool's errand. The task of the communicator, rather, is to understand and identify how receivers think about the issues in question and then work to challenge these preconceived notions and, hopefully, convert audience members into altering their views.[6]

- *Coordinated management of meaning* is a theory of communications based on social interaction. Basically, this theory posits that when we communicate—primarily through conversation—we construct our own social realities of what is going on and what kind of action is appropriate. We each have our own "stories" of life experience, which we share with others in conversation. When we interact, say the creators of this theory, we attempt to "coordinate" our own beliefs, morals, and ideas of "good" and "bad" with those of others so that a mutual outcome might occur.

   The point, again, is that communication, rather than being the simple "transmission" of ideas, is a complex, interconnected series of events, with each participant affected by the other.[7]

- Other widely discussed theoretical models of public relations communications are the *Grunig-Hunt public relations models*, formulated by Professors James E. Grunig and Todd Hunt. Grunig and Hunt proposed four models that define public relations communications.

1. **Press agentry/publicity.** This early form of communication, say the authors, is essentially one-way communication that beams messages from a source to a receiver with the express intention of winning favorable media attention.

2. **Public information.** This is another early form of one-way communication designed not necessarily to persuade but rather to inform. Both this and the press agentry model have been linked to the common notion of "public relations as propaganda."

3. **Two-way asymmetric.** This is a more sophisticated two-way communication approach that allows an organization to put out its information and to receive feedback from its publics about that information. Under this model, an organization wouldn't necessarily change decisions as a result of feedback but rather would alter its responses to more effectively persuade publics to accept its position.

4. **Two-way symmetric.** This preferred way of communicating advocates free and equal information flow between an organization and its publics, based on mutual understanding. This approach is more "balanced"—*symmetrical*—with the public relations communicator serving as a mediator between the organization and the publics.[8]

A Question of Ethics

Irate Actor Takes to the Air

Alec Baldwin is an Academy Award-nominated actor, heralded for the breadth of his acting talent, from comic turns in network sitcoms to dramatic performances in feature films. He is truly a gifted communicator.

But the actor's real-life performance as a put-upon American Airlines passenger, left most observers scratching their heads.

The whole thing started when Baldwin refused to stop playing the popular mobile phone game, "Words With Friends," while the plane waited to taxi to the runway. According to airline officials, he was rude and foul-mouthed. And so he was booted from the flight.

And that's when the communications fun started.

Incensed, Baldwin immediately tweeted, "Flight attendant on American reamed me out 4 playing WORDS W FRIENDS while we sat at the gate, not moving. #nowonderamericanairisbankrupt"

The actor's tweet reached five million people.

Now many large companies, worried about making the situation worse, would have left the incident right there. But American would have none of it. If the outraged actor would use social media to lash out at the airline, American would fight fire with fire.

The morning after Baldwin's tweet went viral, American posted this statement on its Facebook page:

> Since an extremely vocal customer has publicly identified himself as being removed from an American Airlines flight, we have elected to provide the actual facts of the matter as well as the FAA regulations which American, and all airlines, must enforce.
>
> Cell phones and electronic devices are allowed to be used while the aircraft is at the gate and the door is open for boarding. When the door is closed for departure and the seat belt light is turned on, all cell phones and electronic devices must be turned off for taxi-out and take-off. This passenger declined to turn off his cell phone when asked to do so at the appropriate time. The passenger ultimately stood up (with the seat belt light still on for departure) and took his phone into the plane's lavatory. He slammed the lavatory door so hard, the cockpit crew heard it and became alarmed, even with the cockpit door closed and locked. They immediately contacted the cabin crew to check on the situation.
>
> The passenger was extremely rude to the crew, calling them inappropriate names and using offensive language. Given the facts above, the passenger was remqved from the flight and denied boarding.

FIGURE 3-2 **Fallen star.**
A disgruntled Alec Baldwin lands in New York, after being thrown off his initial flight for refusing to heed flight attendant requests to turn off his phone.
Photo: PacificCoastNews/Newscom

The American Airlines Facebook post reached more than 75,000 people, was rebroadcast around the country and put the enraged actor squarely on the defensive; a not-so-sympathetic victim in the last act (Figure 3-2).*

Questions

1. How would you assess the "fairness" of Baldwin's response to American's action, and the airline's response to Baldwin's tweet?

2. Did American Airlines do the right thing? What other options did the airline have?

Sources: For further information, see Erin Calabrese, "Alec Baldwin Thrown Off AA Flight at LAX for 'Playing Game' on Phone," *New York Post* (December 6, 2011); Sheila Marikar, "American Airlines Fights Back After Alec Baldwin's Rant," *ABC News* (December 7, 2011); and Matt Wilson, "American Airlines Calmly Handles Celebrity Blow-up," *Ragan PR Daily* (October 21, 2013).

These are but a few of the prominent theories of communications—all revolving around "feedback"—of which public relations practitioners must be aware. In Chapter 4, we review relevant theories in forming public opinion.

2 The Word

Communication begins with words. Words are among our most personal and potent weapons. Words can soothe us, bother us, or infuriate us. They can bring us together or drive us apart. They can even cause us to kill or be killed. Words mean different things to different people, depending on their backgrounds, occupations, education and geographic locations. As anyone who has ever walked into a Starbucks and ordered a "small" caramel mocha macchiato only to be handed a "tall" caramel mocha macchiato knows, what one word means to you might be dramatically different from what that same word means to someone else. For example, when former First Lady and presidential candidate Hillary Clinton was pressed by an interviewer to justify her $5 million in speaking fees, she replied, "You have no reason to remember, but we came out of the White House not only dead broke, but in debt." Her words came back to haunt her, as Republicans in the 2016 race for the White House continually reprised them as a sign of Mrs. Clinton's insensitivity to the problems of real Americans.[9] The study of what words really mean is called *semantics*, and the science of semantics is a peculiar one indeed.

Words are perpetually changing in our language. Every day, especially with the Internet, words are added to the lexicon. In 2012, when Marc Zuckerberg's Facebook stock floundered in its initial public offering, those who bought the stock were said to have been *Facebooked* or, worse, *Zucked*. Indeed, *Zuck* became an instant, new four-letter word.[10] What a word denotes according to the dictionary may be thoroughly dissimilar to what it connotes in its more emotional or visceral sense. Even the simplest words—*liberal, conservative, profits, consumer activists*—can spark semantic skyrockets. For example, in 2007, McDonald's launched a petition to get the Oxford English Dictionary to alter its definition of *McJob* as "an unstimulating low-paid job with few prospects."[11]

Particularly sensitive today is so-called discriminatory language—words that connote offensive meanings—in areas such as gender, race, ethnicity, and physical impairment. Words such as *firemen, manpower, housewife, cripple, midget*, and *Negro* may be considered offensive. While "political correctness" can go too far, it is nonetheless incumbent on public relations communicators to carefully assess words before using them.

Many times, without knowledge of the territory, the semantics of words may make no sense. Take the word *fat*. In U.S. culture and vernacular, a person who is fat is generally not associated with the apex of attractiveness. A person who is thin, on the other hand, may indeed be considered highly attractive. But along came 50 Cent and Kanye West and Jay-Z and hip-hop, and pretty soon *phat*—albeit with a new spelling—became the baddest of the bad, the coolest of the cool, the height of fetching pulchritudinousness (if you smell what I'm cookin').

Words have a significant influence on the message conveyed to the ultimate receiver. Thus the responsibility of a public relations professional, entrusted with *encoding* a client's message, is significant. Public relations encoders must understand, for example, that in today's technologically changing world, words and phrases change meaning and drop out of favor with blinding speed (see FYI in this chapter). During the past century, the English language has added an average of 900 new words every year.[12]

For an intended message to get through, then, a public relations "interpreter" must accurately understand and effectively translate the true meaning—with all its semantic complications—to the receiver.

The Message

The real importance of words, in a public relations sense, is using them to build the messages that move publics to action. Framing "key messages" lies at the top of every public relations to-do list. This is where "the rubber meets the road" in public relations. Leaders have plenty of ideas, but framing these ideas in messages that motivate and inspire is a special and important task.

Messages may be transmitted in myriad communications media: social media, speeches, newspapers, radio, television, news releases, press conferences, broadcast reports, and face-to-face meetings. Communications theorists differ on what exactly constitutes the message, but here are three of the more popular explanations.

1. **The content is the message.** According to this theory, which is far and away the most popular, the content of a communication—what it says—constitutes its message. According to this view, the real importance of a communication—the message—lies in the meaning of an article or in the intent of a speech. Neither the medium through which the message is being communicated nor the individual doing the communicating is as important as the content. This is why professional public relations people insist on accurate and truthful content in the messages they prepare.

2. **The medium is the message.** Other communications theorists argue that the content of a communication may be less important than the medium in which the message is carried. This theory was originally proffered by the late Canadian communications professor Marshall McLuhan. This theory is relevant in today's hyper-media society, where the reputation and integrity of a particular media source may vary wildly. For example, a story carried on an Internet blog would generally carry considerably less weight than one reported in *The New York Times*. That is not to say that for some receivers, a particular blog's credibility might surpass that of the *Times*. Personal bias, as we will discuss, is always brought to bear in assessing the power and believability of communications messages. That's why conservatives see *Fox News* as the "fair-and-balanced last word" in credibility, while liberals turn to *MSNBC*.

3. **The man—or, to avoid political incorrectness, the person—is the message.** Still other theorists argue that it is neither the content nor the medium that is the message, but rather the speaker. For example, Führer Adolf Hitler was a despicable man, but a master of persuasion. His minister of propaganda, Josef Goebbels, used to say, "Any man who thinks he can persuade, can persuade." Hitler practiced this self-fulfilling communications prophecy to the hilt. Feeding on the perceived desires of the German people, Hitler was concerned much less with the content of his remarks than with their delivery. His maniacal rantings and frantic gestures seized public sentiment and sent friendly crowds into frenzy. In every way, Hitler himself was the primary message of his communications.

   Today, in a similar vein, we often refer to a leader's charisma. Frequently, the charismatic appeal of a political leader may be more important than what that individual says. Such was the historic appeal of Fidel Castro in Cuba or

Muammar Gaddafi in Libya, for example. Political orators in particular, such as former Presidents Bill Clinton and Ronald Reagan, could move an audience by the very inflection of their words. The smooth and confident speaking style of Barack Obama was a major plus in his winning the presidency in 2008. Indeed, motivational speakers in every field, from sports to politics to business can rally listeners with their personal charismatic demeanor.

FYI

Profizzle of Lexicizzle

The 21st-century lexicon of current words and phrases is ever-changing. What's *in* today is *out* tomorrow.

Doubt it?

Then see if you can be *on fleek*—or, if you prefer, on point—with respect to the following phrases that your parents considered colloquial.

- *I'll be a monkey's uncle*
- *This is a fine kettle of fish*
- *Knee high to a grasshopper*
- *Going like 60*
- *Iron Curtain*
- *The rubber meets the road (sound familiar?)*

Or explain what they meant by the following items.

- *Boob tube*
- *L.D.*
- *Segregation*
- *Mailman*
- *Stewardess*

Or reconcile what you mean with what they mean by the following terms.

- *Gay*
- *Menu*
- *Virus*
- *Crack, smack, snow,* and *blow*

Words change so quickly these days that we even have new instant languages being created before our eyes. Among them, the *gangsta* lexicon of one, Snoop Dogg (Figure 3-3), affectionately known as *izzle speak*, is designed primarily to confuse anyone who isn't an urban Black rapper. To wit:

- *Valentizzle*
- *Tonizzle*
- *Televizzle*
- *Barack Obizzle*
- *Kim Kardashizzle*

All of which means that for public relations professionals in the 21st century, properly interpreting messages to key publics has become a complicated proposition.

Fo shizzle.

FIGURE 3-3   Profizzle of Lexicizzle.
Rapper Snoop Dogg.
Photo: RUNE HELLESTAD/UPI/Newscom

The point is that a speaker's words, face, body, eyes, attitude, timing, wit, presence—all form a composite that, as a whole, influences the listener. In such cases—even though theoretical purists may avert their eyes when it's stated—the source of the communication may well become every bit as important as the message itself.

3 Receiver's Bias

Communicating a message is futile unless it helps achieve the desired goal of the communicator. As the bulk of the communications theories cited in this chapter suggest, the element of feedback is critical. This is why Web 2.0 technology—social media, instant messaging, blogs, and the like—is important and pervasive. Key to feedback is understanding the precognitions and predilections that receivers bring to a particular message.

Stated another way, how a receiver decodes a message depends greatly on that person's perception. How an individual comprehends a message is a key to effective communications. Everyone is biased; no two people perceive a message identically. Personal biases are nurtured by many factors, including stereotypes, symbols, semantics, peer group pressures and—especially in today's culture—the media.

Stereotypes

Everyone lives in a world of stereotypical figures. Gen Xers, policy wonks, feminists, bankers, blue-collar workers, bluebloods, PR types and thousands of other characterizations cause people to think of specific images. Public figures, for example, are typecast regularly. The dumb blond, the bigoted right-winger, the bleeding-heart liberal, the computer geek, and the snake oil used car salesperson are the kinds of stereotypes perpetuated by our society.

Like it or not, most of us are victims of such stereotypes. For example, research indicates that a lecture delivered by a person wearing glasses will be perceived as significantly more believable than the same lecture delivered before the same audience by the same lecturer without glasses. The stereotyped impression of people with glasses is that they are more trustworthy and more believable. (Or at least that's the way it was before Lasik surgery!)

Also, like it or not, such stereotypes influence communication.

Symbols

The clenched-fist salute, the swastika, and the thumbs-up sign all leave distinct impressions on most people. Marshaled properly, symbols can be used as effective persuasive elements. The Statue of Liberty, the Red Cross, the Star of David, and many other symbols have been used traditionally for positive persuasion. On the other hand, the symbols chosen by the terrorists of September 11, 2001—the World Trade Center, the Pentagon, and most likely the U.S. Capitol and the White House—were clearly chosen because of their symbolic value as American icons (Figure 3-4).

Semantics

Public relations professionals make their living largely by knowing how to use words effectively to communicate desired meanings. Occasionally, this is tricky because the same words may hold contrasting meanings for different people. Today's contentious debate about abortion is a case in point, with the debate buttressed by confusing

FIGURE 3-4

Freedom symbol.
Fanatical terrorists chose to attack New York's World Trade Center on September 11, 2001, because it stood as a global beacon of freedom and democracy.
Photo: REX/Newscom

semantic terms—*pro-life* to signify those against abortion and *pro-choice* to signify those in favor of allowing abortions. By the same token, Republican semanticist Frank Luntz warns his party to talk about the *death tax*, rather than the "estate tax," and *economic freedom*, rather than "capitalism."[13]

Controversy also surrounds the semantics associated with certain forms of rap and hip-hop music. To critics, some artists preach a philosophy that promotes gun violence and hate and prejudice against women. But misogynist gangsta rappers, from the self-promoting Kanye West to the downright filthy Lil John, claim that they are merely "telling it like it is" or "reporting what we see in the streets." When reporters and record company executives give credence, that is, "street cred," to such misguided rhetoric, they become just as responsible as the artists for the often-unfortunate outcomes that result—for example, the child pornography charges against and subsequent 2008 trial of singer R. Kelly.

Because language and the meanings of words change constantly, semantics must be handled with extreme care. Good communicators always consider the consequences of the words they plan to use before using them.

Peer Groups

In one famous study, students were asked to point out, in progression, the shortest of the following three lines.

A _____

B _____

C _____

Although line B is obviously the shortest, each student in the class except one was told in advance to answer that line C was the shortest. The object of the test was to see whether the one student would agree with his peers. Results generally indicated that, to a statistically significant degree, all students, including the uncoached one, chose C.

Such an experiment is an example of how peer pressure prevails in terms of influencing personal bias. Public relations professionals, intent on framing persuasive communications messages, must understand the importance of peer group influences on attitudes and actions.

Media

The power of the media—particularly as an agenda setter—is substantial. Agenda-setting is the creation of public awareness by the media—the ability to tell us what issues are important.

Today, with social media and the Internet so pervasive, cable news and talk radio so popular, and newspaper readership down, some argue that traditional media have lost some clout as agenda-setters. Perhaps. But it is still the case that most national agendas are set by the most powerful national media, such as *The New York Times, The Washington Post,* and *USA Today.* For example, in June 2013 when former U.S. National Security Agency contractor Edward Snowden chose to expose to the world thousands of pages of classified documents, he did so by leaking them to the *Times, Post,* and several other major world newspapers.

By the same token, in interesting the media to pursue client-oriented stories, public relations professionals also have a direct role in setting the agenda for others. The point is that people base perceptions on what they read or hear, often without bothering to dig further to elicit the facts. This is a two-edged sword: Although appearances are sometimes revealing, they are also often deceiving.

4 Feedback

A communicator must get feedback from a receiver to know what messages are or are not getting through and how to structure future communications.

You really aren't communicating unless someone is at the other end to hear and understand what you're saying and then react to it. This situation is analogous to the old mystery of the falling tree in the forest: Does it make a noise when it hits the ground if there's no one there to hear it? Regardless of the answer, effective communication doesn't take place if a message doesn't reach the intended receivers and exert the desired effect on those receivers.

Even if a communication is understood clearly, there is no guarantee that the motivated action will be the desired one. In fact, a message may trigger several different effects.

1. **It may change attitudes.** This result, however, is difficult to achieve and rarely happens.

2. **It may crystallize attitudes.** This outcome is much more common. Often a message will influence receivers to take actions they might already have been thinking about taking but needed an extra push to accomplish.

3. **It may create a wedge of doubt.** Communication can sometimes force receivers to modify their points of view. A persuasive message on cable TV can cause viewers to question their original thinking on an issue.

4. **It may do nothing.** At times, the best laid communication plans result in no action at all.

Whether the objectives of a communication have been met can often be assessed by such things as the amount of sales, number of followers, viewers, or votes obtained.

If individuals take no action after receiving a communication, feedback must still be sought. In certain cases, although receivers have taken no discernible action, they may have understood and even passed on the message to other individuals.

Last Word

Knowledge of how and when and to whom to communicate is the primary skill of the public relations practitioner. Above all else, public relations professionals are professional communicators. That means they must not only be knowledgeable about the various Web-based techniques and tactics available to communicators in the 21st century but also understand the theoretical underpinnings of what constitutes a credible message and how to deliver it.

The early years of the 21st century indicate that effective communication has never been more important. With the emergence of worldwide terrorism; the deepening cultural chasm between West and East, rich and poor, and haves and have-nots; along with social and economic challenges from the cost of climate change to the threat of global recession, to the emergence of China and India as economic super powers—the need for honest, straightforward, and credible communication is critical.

There is no trick to effective communication. In addition to mastery of techniques, it is knowledge, experience, hard work, and common sense that are the basic guiding principles. Naturally, communication must follow action; organizations must back up what they say with what they do. Omnipresent advertising, a winning Web site and social media presence, slick brochures, engaging speeches, intelligent articles, and good press may help capture the public's attention, but in the final analysis the only way to obtain continued public support is through proper performance.

Discussion Starters

1. Why is it important that public relations professionals understand communication?
2. What are some principal goals of communication, and what are some contemporary examples?
3. Why do words such as *liberal, conservative, profits*, and *consumer activist* spark semantic skyrockets?
4. What is the role of a public relations professional in the S-E-M-D-R communications process?
5. What is the difference between the symmetric and asymmetric models of communication?
6. What is meant by constructivism and coordinated management of meaning?
7. What is meant by the media as *agenda setter*?
8. Why is feedback critical to the communications process?
9. What common mistakes do people make when they communicate?
10. What are some contemporary examples of the changing meanings of words over time?

Pick of the Literature

The Power of Communication
Helio Fred Garcia, Upper Saddle River, NJ: Pearson Education, 2012

One of the brightest lights in the communication profession, Professor Garcia draws on first-hand experience to detail how communication is as powerful as any factor in the 21st century.

The book draws heavily on current examples to link leadership and communication. From Bill Gates to John McCain, David Letterman to Steve Jobs to the CEOs of Hewlett-Packard and Netflix, Garcia applies sensible lessons to contemporary cases.

Through his experience as a teacher and practitioner and especially as counselor to leaders in the military, Garcia offers a valuable text for any public relations practitioner. As the author puts it, "Words matter. Words shape world views." And as one contributor adds, "If you can't communicate, you can't lead."

Case Study | Race Relations with That Soy Latte?

In the old days, before CEOs made 330 times more than the average worker, the men (and they were all mostly "men") who ran America's biggest corporations were eager to communicate to the public, by standing up for what they stood for. CEOs like Chase's David Rockefeller, General Electric's Jack Welch, Citicorp's Walter Wriston, and Dupont's Irving Shapiro would regularly give speeches, testify before Congress, and meet with the media to forward their own and their corporations' viewpoints.

Not so much anymore.

Today's CEOs, with precious few exceptions, are timid, more inclined to be not seen and not heard, while they rake in their excessive bounty. One glowing exception, however, is Howard Schultz, CEO of Starbucks.

Mr. Schultz is a concerned, fearless, plain-speaking Brooklyn native, who cares about his country and isn't afraid to use his corporate muscle to communicate his views. Sometimes, it gets him and his company into the kind of hot water that isn't compatible with brewing.

Drop Your Weapons

In 2013, with America reeling in the wake of horrific gun violence in movie theaters, ship yards and elementary schools, Howard Schultz wrote an "*Open Letter*" to gun owners and placed it in *The New York Times, Washington Post, Wall Street Journal*, and other major newspapers. It said in part:

Dear Fellow Americans,

Few topics in America generate a more polarized and emotional debate than guns. In recent months, Starbucks stores and our partners (employees) who work in our stores have been thrust unwillingly into the middle of this debate. That's why I am writing today with a respectful request that customers no longer bring firearms into our stores or outdoor seating areas.

From the beginning, our vision at Starbucks has been to create a "third place" between home and work where people can come together to enjoy the peace and pleasure of coffee and community. Our values have always centered on building community rather than dividing people, and our stores exist to give every customer a safe and comfortable respite from the concerns of daily life.

The CEO explained that while in the past, Starbucks allowed patrons to pack heat in "open carry" states that allowed firearms to be concealed, the company was henceforth changing its policy. Wrote CEO Schultz:

We are respectfully requesting that customers no longer bring firearms into our stores or outdoor seating areas—even in states where "open carry" is permitted—unless they are authorized law enforcement personnel.

Predictably, Starbucks was immediately excoriated by gun enthusiasts, as the company's Facebook page lit up with sentiments like "*You are weak*" and "*I won't shop in your stores now*" and "*My ability to protect myself is more important than my caffeine intake.*"

Schultz, himself, became a target of pro-gun advocates, who considered Starbucks a symbol of liberal, left-leaning Seattle. Despite the criticism, the Starbucks CEO stuck to his, well, guns.

Tell Me about Your Race

Two years later, the outspoken Starbucks CEO was at it again, this time joining the nation's ongoing discussion of race relations.

In the spring of 2015, after racially charged skirmishes with police erupted in several American cities, CEO Schultz decided that Starbucks should again take the public opinion lead. So the company announced its "*Race Together*" program, wherein 50,000 busy Starbucks baristas in its 20,000 stores would initiate discussions about race with customers, as they sipped on their caffe macchiatos (Figure 3-5).

Almost immediately, the public pushback against the well-meaning program made the earlier no-gun initiative look like a walk in the park. Critics questioned how coffee servers would be willing, able and competent enough to engage customers in conversation about race, and if customers would tolerate such an intrusion into their simple daily act of buying coffee. Journalists flocked to Starbucks locations to talk to baristas about race, while patrons in line fumed. Twitter, for one social medium, erupted accordingly:

- Really mad at this Starbucks employee who wrote #RaceTogether on my croissant.
- Starbucks #RaceTogether is actually useful—as a demonstration of what's wrong with the way US employers treat their workers.
- #RaceTogether is trending nationwide on Twitter tonight, not really for the reasons @Starbucks wanted.

Things got so bad that a few days into the campaign, Starbucks global communications director announced he was deleting his Twitter account because, "*I felt personally attacked in a cascade of negativity.*" Oofa!

And so, a week after Starbucks had announced its campaign to confront the race issue, a sadder-but-wiser CEO Schultz announced that the initiative would be ending. As the CEO put it in a staff memo:

"*While there has been criticism of the initiative—and I know this hasn't been easy for any of you—let me assure you that we didn't expect universal praise.*"

What Starbucks and its determined CEO got, instead, was a reminder that influencing public opinion is no easy task.*

FIGURE 3-5 **Wrong race?**
Starbucks CEO Howard
Schultz had high hopes
for the company's ill-fated
"Race Together" campaign
in 2015.
*Photo: DAVID RYDER/REUTERS/
Newscom*

Questions

1. What would you have counseled CEO Schultz on his idea to keep Starbucks locations free of guns?

2. What about your counsel relative to his idea to start conversations among baristas and patrons on the subject of race?

3. Is it a good idea for companies to communicate publicly about their viewpoints? If so, should there be any public relations restrictions on the issues companies take on?

4. What other public relations options did Schultz have in his quest to bring Starbucks into the race issue?

*For further information, see Rachel Alexander, "Starbucks Should Stick to Coffee and Leave Guns Alone," *The Guardian* (September 19, 2013); "An Open Letter from Howard Schultz, CEO of Starbucks Coffee Company," *The New York Times* (September 17, 2013); Jessica Contrera, "Starbucks Will Stop Writing 'Race Together' on Your Cups Now," *Washington Post* (March 22, 2015); Fraser Seitel, "Howie Schultz Goes over the Cliff," *odwyerpr.com* (March 28, 2015); and Matt Wilson, "Starbucks CEO: Don't Bring Guns into Our Stores," *Ragan PR Daily* (September 19, 2013).

From the Top

An Interview with Denise Hill

Denise Hill is a distinguished faculty member in the School of Communications at Elon University, where she teaches strategic communications courses. She has more than 30 years of agency and corporate communications experience, including positions in which she served in the senior communications role and as a member of the executive leadership team. Most recently, she spent four years as vice president, corporate communications and public relations for Delhaize America, the U.S. operation of global Fortune 500 grocery retailer Delhaize Group. Previously, she was senior vice president of communications at a business unit of Wyndham Worldwide Corporation and held vice president of communications roles at CIGNA, Novartis Pharmaceuticals Corporation, and Quest Diagnostics. Ms. Hill has also taught communications courses at New York University and the University of North Carolina at Chapel Hill.

How essential is "communications" in public relations?
Absolutely essential. Communication is the essence of what we do in public relations, whether it is through writing, speaking, and/or using visuals. In fact, without communication, there is no public relations. Communication involves ensuring that clear messages are delivered via channels that resonate with audiences and that those messages are not just received, but understood by recipients. As part of the communication process, public

relations professionals help facilitate two-way communication between organizations and their publics. George Bernard Shaw said, "The single biggest problem in communication is the illusion it has taken place." A public relations professional helps ensure that communication has actually taken place.

What are the communications skills that a successful public relations professional must have?

He or she must be able to effectively use the written and spoken word. Public relations professionals must be able to create clear written messages, and they must have strong verbal communication skills. In addition, good listening and non-verbal communication skills are key, as is the ability to assess the internal and external environment in which communications will be delivered and know when and how to adapt accordingly; also, strong influence, persuasion, and counseling skills.

What elements of theory must a public relations communicator possess?

There are a number of communication models and theories that are applied in the practice of public relations. Two that come to mind are the two-step flow theory and agenda setting: 1) The two-step flow theory highlights the importance of opinion leaders in audiences' decision making. Public relations professionals often identify opinion leaders as an important audience and frequently rely on them to help reach other audiences.

2) Agenda setting proposes that the media influence and determine the importance of topics on the public agenda. This theory can be summarized with the statement:

The media don't tell the public what to think, rather they tell the public what to think about. It's important that public relations professionals have an understanding of this theory, especially when posing an additional question: If the media tell the public what to think about, who tells the media what to think about? In some instances, the answer to that question is: the public relations professional.

Must a public relations professional be a writer?

Yes; a resounding yes. Given that so much of communication involves the written word, the public relations professional must not only be a writer, but a good writer.

What are the attitudinal attributes that a professional communicator must possess?

A professional communicator must be able to work well under pressure and be adaptable to changing circumstances. He or she must be intellectually curious and creative, with the ability to work well individually and as a team member. Additionally, a professional communicator must be focused, diligent, and able to work effectively at the macro and micro levels, often simultaneously. The term "juggling multiple priorities" is frequently used when describing the work of a professional communicator. The ability to be empathic is also important. Given that public relations professionals usually communicate to a broad range of audiences, it's important they know and understand their audiences. In addition, a professional communicator must have a strong moral compass and must be committed to practicing ethically.

Public Relations Bookshelf

Brown, Paul B., and Alison Davis. *Your Attention, Please: How to Appeal to Today's Distracted, Disinterested, Disengaged, Disenchanted, and Busy Audiences*. Avon, MA: Adams Media, 2006. Excellent treatise on how to deal with the information overload with which all of us are afflicted. The trick to getting through, according to the authors: Be fast and write punchy.

Caywood, Clarke L. (Ed.). *Strategic Public Relations and Integrated Marketing Communications*. New York, NY: McGraw-Hill Companies, 2012. A distinguished Northwestern University public relations professor makes use of the knowledge of leading academics to present a thorough communications public relations communications primer.

COMM.PR.biz, commpro_daily_headlines@commpro.biz, 362 Atlantic Avenue, Brooklyn, NY 11217. Guest columnists discuss the pertinent public relations news of the day. And it's free!

Cone, Steve. *PowerLines: Words that Sell Brands, Grip Fans, and Sometimes Change History*. New York: Bloomberg Press, 2008. A fascinating synopsis of the memorable words and phrases indelibly etched in the public cranium, from "Bond, James Bond" to "Virginia Is for Lovers" to "Live Free or Die."

Diggs-Brown, Barbara, *The PR Style Guide: Formats for Public Relations Practice*. 3rd ed. Boston, MA: Wadsworth, 2013. A compendium of public relations vehicles, from annual reports to audio news releases, brochures to direct mail campaigns, media tours to new media.

D'Vario, Marisa. *Building Buzz: How to Reach and Impress Your Target Audience*. Franklin Lakes, NJ: Career Press, 2006. This is a combination pop psychology/communication primer on how to get you and your company and its products noticed.

Hackman, Michael Z., and Craig E. Johnson. *Leadership: A Communication Perspective*. 5th ed. Long Grove, IL: Waveland Press, Inc., 2009. Examples, case studies, and explanation on the intersection between leadership and effective communication.

Krishnamurthy, Sriramesh, Ansgar Zerfass, and Kim Jeong-Nam (Eds.). *Public Relations and Communication Management*. New York, NY: Routledge, 2013. Scholarly compilation of public relations communication theories.

McPhail, Thomas L. *Global Communications: Theories, Stakeholders, and Trends*. 2nd ed. Malden, MA: Blackwell Publishing, 2006. Contemporary view of global communications innovations and challenges.

Pacelli, Lonnie. *The Truth about Getting Your Point Across...and Nothing But the Truth*. Upper Saddle River, NJ: Prentice Hall, 2006. This book is a terrific primer on how to get your message across convincingly whether writing or speaking, texting or tweeting.

PR Daily News Feed, webmgr@ragan.com, *Ragan.com*, Lawrence Ragan Communications, 111 East Wacker Drive, Chicago, IL 60601. Pointed online commentary on current communications issues. And it's also free!

Shepherd, G. J., Jeffrey St. John, and Ted Striphas (Eds.). *Communications as...Perspectives on Theory*. Thousand Oaks, CA: Sage Publications, 2006. Communications, the authors say, is a "process of relating," and this book explains how relationships are built.

Endnotes

1. Hannah J. Parkinson, "Caitlyn Jenner Smashes Twitter World Record, Reaching a Million Followers," *The Guardian* (June 1, 2015).

2. Ravi Somaiya, "Caitlyn Jenner, Formerly Bruce, Introduces Herself," *The New York Times* (June 2, 2015): B1.

3. Patrick Jackson, "The Unforgiving Era," *Currents* (October 1998).

4. Thomas H. Bivins, *Public Relations Writing,* 7th ed. (New York: McGraw-Hill, 2010): 31–32.

5. Serge Moscovici, "Silent Majorities and Loud Minorities," *Communication Yearbook 14* (1991): 298–308.

6. J. Delia, B. O'Keefe, and D. O'Keefe, "The Constructivist Approach to Communication," *Human Communication Theory* (New York: Harper and Row, 1982): 147–191; Also see E. Griffin, *A First Look at Communication Theory,* 4th ed. (New York: McGraw-Hill, 2000): 110–120; and Julia. T. Wood, *Communication Theories in Action: An Introduction* (Belmont, CA: Wadsworth, 1997): 182–184.

7. W. Barnett Pearce and Vernon E. Cronen, *Communication, Action and Meaning: The Creation of Social Realities* (New York: Praeger, 1980); Also see G. Philipsen, "The Coordinated Management of Meaning: Theory of Pearce, Cronen, and Associates," *Watershed Research Traditions in Human Communication Theory,* Donald Cust and Branislave Kovocic, Eds. (Albany, NY: State University of New York Press, 1995): 13–43.

8. James E. Grunig and Todd Hunt, *Managing Public Relations* (New York: Holt, Rinehart and Winston, 1984): 21–27; See also Anne Lane, "Working at the Interface: The Descriptive Relevance of Grunig and Hunt's Theories to Public Relations Practices in South East Queensland Schools," http://praxis.massey.ac.nz/working_interface.html, 2003.

9. Emily Thomas, "Hillary Clinton: We Were 'Dead Broke' Upon Leaving White House," *Huffington Post* (June 9, 2014).

10. "DealBook Online," *The New York Times* (May 25, 2012): B4.

11. "McDonald's Launches Face-Saving Petition," *Bulldog Reporter's Daily Dog* (May 25, 2007).

12. Richard Lederer, "The Way We Word," *AARP Magazine* (March/April 2005): 86–93.

13. Justin Elliott, "GOP Message Man 'Frightened to Death' of Occupy," *Salon.com* (December 1, 2011).

Chapter 4

Public Opinion

FIGURE 4-1 **Punch in the gut.**
Civil rights activist Al Sharpton stands next to Michael
Brown, Sr., whose son was shot by a white police officer
in Ferguson, Mo., triggering the beginning of a slide in
public confidence in U.S. police officers.
Photo: BILL GREENBLATT/UPI/Newscom

Chapter Objectives

1. To discuss the phenomenon of public opinion, contemporary examples of it, the areas that impact it, and how it is formed.
2. To explore the issue of attitudes, how they are influenced, motivated, and changed.
3. To discuss the area of persuasion, its various theories, and how individuals are persuaded.
4. To examine reputation, particularly corporate image, and how companies might enhance their reputation.

Public opinion is an elusive and fragile commodity. It can take an organization or individual many years to build the credibility and nurture the trust that goes into winning favorable public opinion. But it can take only a matter of minutes to destroy all that has been developed.

Consider police officers across America.

From an early age, children are taught to respect law enforcement, to listen to what police officers say, and to obey their commands. But in the summer of 2014, that time-honored maxim was challenged as public opinion about police officers and their motives was questioned by several high profile incidents involving the police and African Americans.

The first incident that attracted national attention occurred in Ferguson, Mo., where an 18-year-old black man, Michael Brown, was shot and killed by a white police officer, reportedly after raising his arms in the air and pleading, "*Hands up, don't shoot.*" The shooting sparked outrage and riots in Ferguson, and outside activists, from ubiquitous protestor Al Sharpton to rapper Nelly flocked to Ferguson to demand justice. It seemed to matter little that young Brown was being followed because he stole several packages of cigarillos from a nearby convenience store, nor was there proof that he had, in fact, cooperated with the arresting officer and raised his hands. Nonetheless, Ferguson became the symbol of police brutality and racism, and the public opinion of police across the nation took a major hit[1] **(Figure 4-1).**

Suffering a loss in public opinion isn't a trivial matter. Individuals and companies in the public eye can't afford to tarnish their reputations. Often, this translates into a loss of prestige and business. And that's why most public relations agencies bill themselves as experts in the field of "reputation management."

Society is littered with the reputational carcasses of once respected organizations and individuals who tested the goodwill of the public once too often. For example:

- In 2008, the nation witnessed a parade of several of its richest financial leaders, from Citigroup CEO Chuck Prince to Merrill Lynch CEO Stanley O'Neal to Bear Stearns CEO Alan Schwartz to Lehman Brothers CEO Richard Fuld, being pilloried by media and Congress for squandering shareholder trust and resources in the disastrous subprime mortgage lending fiasco.

- In 2012, the vaunted U.S. Secret Service was rocked by scandal when it was reported in April that 11 agents, including supervisors, had engaged prostitutes prior to President Obama's trip to Colombia. Most of those involved left the agency or were demoted.[2] Then, two years later, the Secret Service was mortified again when uninvited guests showed up at White House state dinners and fence jumpers scaled the White House fence. It was also reported that employees of another government agency, the General Services Administration, responsible for monitoring the federal budget, had spent $820,000 of taxpayer money to fly 300 bureaucrats to Las Vegas for a "congratulatory conference" at a lavish spa and casino.[3]

- In 2015, the most powerful governing body in all of sports, the Federation Internationale of Football Association (FIFA) was rocked by scandal, with 14 people, including nine current or former FIFA officials, charged with racketeering by the U.S. Dept. of Justice. The scandal reaches to FIFA's autocratic president, Sepp Blatter, who resigned in disgrace.[4]

The point is that these individuals and the organizations they represented, like many others in all areas of society, suffered serious setbacks in terms of their standing with the public as a result of their actions.

The related point is, as we put it in Chapter 1, *You can't pour perfume on a skunk.*

The best public relations campaign in the world can't build trust when reality is destroying it. If your product doesn't work, if your service stinks, if you are a liar, then no amount of "public relations" will change that. You must change the "action" before credibility or trust can be built.

Such are the vulnerabilities of public opinion in a culture driven by media, fueled by the Internet, and dominated by celebrity. Public opinion in the 21st century is a combustible and changing commodity.

As a general rule, it's difficult to move people toward a strong opinion on anything. It's even harder to move them away from an opinion once they reach it. Nonetheless, the heart of public relations work lies in attempting to affect the public opinion process.

Public relations professionals therefore must understand what public opinion is, how it is formed, how it evolves from people's attitudes, and how it is influenced by communication. This chapter discusses attitude formation and change and public opinion creation and persuasion.

1 What Is Public Opinion?

Public opinion, like public relations, is not easily explained. Newspaper columnist Joseph Kraft called public opinion "the unknown god to which moderns burn incense." Edward Bernays called it "a term describing an ill-defined, mercurial, and changeable group of individual judgments."[5]

Princeton Professor Harwood Childs, after coming up with no fewer than 40 different yet viable definitions, concluded with a definition by Herman C. Boyle: "Public opinion is not the name of something, but the classification of a number of something."[6]

Splitting public opinion into its two components, *public* and *opinion*, is perhaps the best way to understand the concept. Simply defined, *public* signifies a group of people who share a common interest in a specific subject—stockholders, for example, or employees or community residents. Each group is concerned with a common issue: the price of the stock, the wages of the company, or the building of a new plant.

An *opinion* is the expression of an attitude on a particular topic. When attitudes become strong enough, they surface in the form of opinions. When opinions become strong enough, they lead to verbal or behavioral actions.

Attitudes
   └─→ *Opinions*
          └─→ *Actions*

A forest products company executive and an environmentalist from the Sierra Club might differ dramatically in their attitudes toward the relative importance of global warming and continued industrial production. Their respective opinions on a piece of environmental legislation might also differ radically. In turn, how their organizations respond to that legislation—by picketing, petitioning, or lobbying—might also differ.

Public opinion, then, is the aggregate of many individual opinions on a particular issue that affects a group of people. Stated another way, public opinion represents a consensus. That consensus, deriving as it does from many individual opinions, begins with people's attitudes toward the issue in question. Trying to influence an individual's attitude—how he or she thinks on a given topic—is a primary focus of the practice of public relations.

2 What Are Attitudes?

If an opinion is an expression of an attitude on a particular topic, what then is an *attitude*?

Unfortunately, that also is not an easy question to answer. It was once generally assumed that attitudes are predispositions to think in a certain way about a certain topic. But research indicates that attitudes may more likely be evaluations people make about specific problems or issues. These conclusions are not necessarily connected to any broad attitude. For example, an individual might favor a company's response to one issue but disagree vehemently with its response to another. Thus, that individual's attitude may differ from issue to issue.

Attitudes are based on a number of characteristics.

1. **Personal**—the physical and emotional ingredients of an individual, including size, age, and social status.

2. **Cultural**—the environment and lifestyle of a particular country or geographic area. The cultures of the United States and off again/on again ally Pakistan,

for example, differ greatly; on a less global scale, cultural differences between rural and urban America are vast.

3. **Educational**—the level and quality of a person's education. To appeal to the increased number of college graduates in the United States today, public communication has become more sophisticated.

4. **Familial**—people's roots. Children acquire their parents' tastes, biases, political partisanships, and a host of other characteristics.

5. **Religious**—a system of beliefs about God or a higher power. After a period of people turning away from religion, in the 21st century, even after several evangelical scandals, religious fervor has reemerged.

6. **Social class**—position within society. As people's social status changes, so do their attitudes. For example, college students, unconcerned with making a living, may dramatically change their attitudes about such concepts as big government, big business, wealth, prosperity, and politics after entering the job market.

7. **Race**—ethnic origin, which today increasingly helps shape people's attitudes. Minorities in our society, as a group, continue to improve their standard of living and their relative position. African Americans head major corporations, hold cabinet positions, sit on the Supreme Court, and even become two-term presidents of the United States. Latinos and Asian Americans have become coveted interest groups. And women, in many sectors—among them, college students and public relations professionals—are no longer considered a minority.

Research indicates that attitudes and behaviors are situational—influenced by specific issues in specific situations. Nonetheless, when others with similar attitudes reach similar opinions, a consensus, or public opinion, is born.

How Are Attitudes Influenced?

Strictly speaking, attitudes are positive, negative, or nonexistent. A person is for something, against it, or neutral. Studies show that for any one issue, most people don't care much one way or the other. A small percentage expresses strong support, and another small percentage expresses strong opposition. The vast majority is smack in the so-called muddled middle—passive, neutral, indifferent. Many years ago, former U.S. vice president Spiro T. Agnew called this group "the silent majority."

It's hard to change the mind of a person who is staunchly opposed to a particular issue or individual. Likewise, it's easy to reinforce the support of a person who is wholeheartedly in favor of an issue or individual.

Social scientist Leon Festinger discussed this concept when he talked about the *theory of cognitive dissonance*. He believed that individuals tend to avoid information that is dissonant or opposed to their own points of view and tend to seek out information that is consonant with, or in support of, their own attitudes.[7]

Similarly, *social judgment theory* suggests that people may have a range of opinions on a certain subject, anchored by a clear attitude.[8] Again, while it is seldom possible to change this anchor position, communicators can work within this range, called a person's "latitude of acceptance," to modify a person's opinion.

For example, while most people might not discriminate against eating Canadian seafood products, they might object to the clubbing of baby seals. Therefore, in trying to pressure Canada to stop the seal hunt, the Humane Society of the United States attempts

FIGURE 4-2
Save the seals.
The Humane Society's campaign to stop Canada's commercial seal hunt used graphic mailings, Web video, and photos to influence public opinion.
Photo: Courtesy of the Humane Society of the United States

to link the hunt with Canada's seafood industry. In so doing, it attempts to sway the undecided to take action and also to influence others within an acceptable range **(Figure 4-2)**.

Understanding the potential for influencing the silent majority is extremely important for the public relations practitioner, whose objective is to win support through clear, thoughtful, and persuasive communication. Moving a person from a latent state of attitude formation to a more aware state and finally to an active one becomes a matter of motivation.

Motivating Attitude Change

People are motivated by different factors, and no two people respond in exactly the same way to the same set of circumstances. Each of us is motivated by different drives and needs.

The most famous delineator of what motivates people was Abraham Maslow. Maslow's *hierarchy of needs theory* helps define the origins of motivation, which in turn helps explain attitude change. Maslow postulated a five-level hierarchy:

1. The lowest order is physiological needs: a person's biological demands—food and water, sleep, health, bodily needs, exercise and rest, and sex.

2. The second level is safety needs: security, protection, comfort and peace, and orderly surroundings.

3. The third level is love needs: acceptance, belonging, love and affection, and membership in a group.

4. The fourth level is esteem: recognition and prestige, confidence and leadership opportunities, competence and strength, intelligence and success.

5. The highest order is self-actualization, or simply becoming what one is capable of becoming; self-actualization involves self-fulfillment and achieving a goal for the purposes of challenge and accomplishment.[9]

According to Maslow, the needs of all five levels compose the fundamental motivating factors for any individual or public.

Another popular approach to motivating attitude change is the *elaboration likelihood model*, which posits that there are essentially two ways that people are persuaded:

1. When we are interested and focused enough on a message to take a direct "central route" to decision making, and

2. When we are not particularly engaged on a message and need to take a more "peripheral" route.

Translating this theory into action means that the best way to motivate interested people is with arguments that are strong, logical, and personally relevant. On the other hand, the way to motivate people who are less interested might be through putting them in a better mood—with a joke, for example, or demonstrating, through speech or clothes or mannerism, that you are very much "like" them. Such techniques, according to this theory, might help encourage listeners to accept your arguments.[10]

3 Power of Persuasion

Perhaps the most essential element in influencing public opinion is the principle of persuasion. Persuading is the goal of the vast majority of public relations programs.

Persuasion theory has myriad explanations and interpretations. Basically, persuasion means getting another person to do something through advice, reasoning, or just plain arm-twisting. Books have been written on the enormous power of advertising and public relations as persuasive tools.

According to classic persuasion theory, people may be of two minds in order to be persuaded to believe in a particular position or take a specific action.

■ First is the "systematic" mode, referring to a person who has carefully considered an argument—actively, creatively, and alertly.

■ Second is the "heuristic" mode, referring to a person who is skimming the surface and not really focusing on the intricacies of a particular position to catch flaws, inconsistencies, or errors.[11]

That is not to say that all systematic thinkers or all heuristic thinkers think alike. They don't. Things are more complicated than that. Let's say your little brother wants a pair of basketball shoes and your dad accompanies him to the store to buy them. Both are systematic thinkers. But they have different questions.

Your dad asks:

1. How much do they cost?

2. How long will they last?

3. Is the store nearby so I can get back to watch the ball game?

4. Will they take a personal check?

Your brother asks:

1. Does LeBron James endorse them?

2. Do all my homeboys wear them?

3. Will Wanda Sue go out with me if I buy them?

The point is that all of us are persuaded by different things, which makes the challenge of public relations persuading much more a complex art form than a science. No matter how one characterizes persuasion, the goal of most communications programs is, in fact, to influence a receiver to take a desired action.

What kinds of "evidence" will persuade?

1. **Facts.** Facts are indisputable. Although it is true, as they say, that "liars figure and figures lie," empirical data are a persuasive device in hammering home a point of view.

2. **Emotions.** Maslow was right. People do respond to emotional appeals—love, peace, family, patriotism. Arguably, the most riveting moment in George W. Bush's presidency came in the Oval Office on September 13, 2001, two days after the most horrific event in U.S. history, when a reporter asked about Bush's personal concerns.

   The President: *Well, I don't think about myself right now. I think about the families, the children. I am a loving guy, and I am also someone, however, who has got a job to do—and I intend to do it. And this is a terrible moment. But this country will not relent until we have saved ourselves and others from the terrible tragedy that came upon America.*[12]

   In less than 50 words, a visibly shaken Bush had made an emotional connection with the American public that proved elusive through much of his presidency.

3. **Personalizing.** People respond to personal experience.

   - When poet Maya Angelou talks about poverty, people listen and respect a woman who emerged from the dirt-poor environs of the South in a day of segregation.

   - When *America's Most Wanted* TV host John Walsh crusades against criminals who prey on children, people understand that his son was abducted and killed by a crazed individual.

   - When former baseball pitcher Jim Abbott talks about dealing with adversity, people marvel at a star athlete born with only one arm.

   Again, few can refute knowledge gained from personal experience.

4. **Appealing to "you."** The one word that people never tire of hearing is *you. What is in this for me?* is the question that everyone asks. One secret to persuading, therefore, is to constantly think in terms of what will appeal most to the audience.

As simple as these four precepts are, they are often difficult for some to grasp. Emotion, for example, is a particular challenge for business leaders, who presume, incorrectly, that showing it is a sign of weakness. This, of course, is wrong. The power to persuade—to influence public opinion—is the measure not only of a charismatic but also of an effective leader.[13]

Influencing Public Opinion

Public opinion is a lot easier to measure than it is to influence. However, a thoughtful public relations program can crystallize attitudes, reinforce beliefs, and occasionally change public opinion. First, the opinions to be changed or modified must be identified and understood. Second, target publics must be clear. Third, the public relations professional must have in sharp focus the "laws" that govern public opinion—as amorphous as they may be.

A Question of Ethics

The Doctor Is Piqued

In the 21st century, as Sly and the Family Stone once crooned before you were born, "Everybody is a star." And everybody—from pawn brokers to hip-hop gangstas to couples with 19 children—is a TV star. And that includes medical doctors.

And far and away, the most famous TV medical doctor was one Mehmet Oz, a distinguished heart surgeon-turned television talk show host, who operated out of Columbia University's respected Columbia Presbyterian Hospital in New York City.

Dr. Oz, who owed much of his TV success to appearances on the Oprah Winfrey Show, was a staple of afternoon television and the destination for many famous guests (**Figure 4-3**). Dr. Oz was particularly enthusiastic about lecturing the common people on diet and exercise, vitamins and nutrients. It was in the course of recommending such cures, however, where Dr. Oz ran into trouble.

The first salvo came in an appearance before Congress, when Dr. Oz received a public tongue-lashing by senators for touting a supplement called green coffee bean extract as "a magic weight loss cure for every body type." Social media quickly joined on the anti-Oz bandwagon calling him a "quack," and in the spring of 2015 a group of 10 distinguished

physicians wrote an open letter to Columbia University urging the firing of Dr. Oz for "his disdain for science and evidence-based medicine."

Where others might shrink from such a public reputational attack, the good doctor came out swinging. Not only did the daytime host publicly defend his reputation, he devoted an entire TV episode to paint himself as a victim of powerful interests and explain why he hadn't violated the public trust.

"My job," he explained, *"is to be a cheerleader for my audience. When they think they don't have hope,* I look everywhere for alternative healing traditions that I believe might be supportive for them."

And with that declaration, Dr. Oz kept right on keepin' on, as his critics continued to protest.*

Questions

1. How would you assess the ethics of Dr. Oz's recommendations for miracle cures?

2. What public relations options did Dr. Oz have in response to the criticism of his methods?

3. What do you think of his response to the challenge in terms of public opinion?

FIGURE 4-3
Jumpin' Quack Flash?
The world's most high profile doctor and his First Lady of Fitness TV guest.
Photo: Consolidated News Photos/Newscom

*For further information, see Bill Gifford, "Dr. Oz Is No Wizard, but No Quack Either," *The New York Times* (April 25, 2015); Michael Hiltzik, "Dr. Oz Fires Back at Critics with Misdirection and an Absurd Defense," *Los Angeles Times* (April 24, 2015); and Mary E. Williams, "Dr. Oz Will Not Be Silenced Of Course: The Self-Aggrandizing Showbiz Doc Defends Himself Against Attacks," *Huffington Post* (April 23, 2015).

In that context, the "Laws of Public Opinion," developed many years ago by social psychologist Hadley Cantril, remain pertinent. The events following the September 11 attacks on America are a case in point.[14]

1. **Opinion is highly sensitive to important events.** Events of unusual magnitude are likely to swing public opinion temporarily from one extreme to another. Opinion doesn't become stabilized until the implications of events are seen in some perspective. For example, after despised terrorist Osama bin Laden was killed by U.S. forces in 2011, President Obama's popularity rose.

2. **Opinion is generally determined more by events than by words—unless those words are themselves interpreted as an event.** In a speech to a joint session of Congress nine days after the 9/11 terrorist attacks, the president vowed to "lift the dark threat of violence from our people and our future. We will rally the world to this cause by our efforts, by our courage. We will not tire, we will not falter, and we will not fail." Bush's words became a rallying cry for the nation and, temporarily at least, transformed his presidency.[15]

3. **At critical times, people become more sensitive to the adequacy of their leadership. If they have confidence in it, they are willing to assign more than usual responsibility to it; if they lack confidence in it, they are less tolerant than usual.** Relatively few voices rose in protest when the Bush administration, in the cause of fighting terrorism, imposed sweeping changes in privacy rights regarding such areas as securing court orders before wiretapping suspected American evildoers. Indeed, it took the nation till the summer of 2015 to begin to push back on privacy restrictions as a result of the 9/11 terrorist attacks.[16]

4. **Once self-interest is involved, opinions are slow to change.** Even after the United States invaded Iraq to oust Saddam Hussein in March 2003, American support continued for the war effort. That support began to wane when the 2000th American soldier was killed in October 2005.[17]

5. **People have more opinions and are able to form opinions more easily on goals than on methods to reach those goals.** For example, few questioned the need for a new U.S. Department of Homeland Security to protect the land within our borders from terrorism.

6. **By and large, if people in a democracy are provided with educational opportunities and ready access to information, public opinion reveals a hardheaded common sense.** In the weeks and months following the attacks of September 11, as Americans became more enlightened about the implications and threats of terrorism within the United States, the administration's strategy of continuous communication helped solidify public opinion. But again, as progress in the Middle East waxed and waned and American troops were made to serve extended tours in long, drawn-out conflicts, by 2011—after 4500 American deaths and 30,000 Americans wounded—public opinion clearly agreed when President Obama formally declared the end of the Iraq war.[18]

4 Polishing the Corporate Image

Most organizations today and the people who manage them are extremely sensitive to the way they are perceived by their critical publics. The days of "The public be damned!" are long behind us.

Today, organizations—particularly large ones—have little choice but to go public. CEOs are regular guests on CNBC, Fox Business, and Bloomberg financial television programs. The accounting and corporate scandals of the early years of the 21st century and the credit crisis at the end of the decade that embroiled such now-former companies as Enron, Worldcom, Lehman Brothers, Bear Stearns, Countrywide, and Arthur Andersen threatened the confidence of the American capitalistic system.

In the second decade of the 21st century, with 24/7 communication the rule, companies are constantly reminded about the importance of sustaining a positive public image.

- In 2010 and 2011, Wall Street was rocked by a continuous stream of Ponzi schemes, insider trading scams, and other assorted disasters that threw formerly respected multi-millionaire investors, such as Bernie Madoff, Allen Sanford, and Raj Rajaratnam, and enablers like former McKinsey & Company head Rajat Gupta, right into the slammer.

- In 2012, having learned that such "silence isn't golden," JP Morgan Chase CEO Jamie Dimon didn't shrink from public view when his company reported an embarrassing $2 billion trading loss. Dimon confronted the issue with two congressional appearances, took the heat, and came out relatively unscathed.

- Another Wall Street firm, the once-reviled Goldman Sachs, also got the message. The formerly imperious investment bank began a Twitter account, hired a respected veteran government public relations executive to head its communications, and Goldman CEO Lloyd Blankfein took to YouTube to endorse same-sex marriage.[19]

FYI

Winning Reputation...

How do you measure reputation?

For more than a decade, survey firm Harris Interactive has polled consumers on what companies they feel have the highest reputation.

Harris asks 17,555 respondents to rank organizations on six primary measures of reputation: (1) emotional appeal, (2) financial performance, (3) products and services, (4) vision and leadership, (5) workplace environment, and (6) social responsibility. Other characteristics, such as ethics and sincerity of corporate communications, were also probed.

The 2015 Harris data underscore the ephemeral quality of corporate reputation. Only three of the companies ranked among the Top 10 in 2008 repeated in 2012. At the top of the 2015 list was a newcomer, Wegman's Food Markets, a Rochester, NY regional grocer with 85 stores and a reputation for exceptional customer treatment. Big tech companies dominated the most recent list, with Amazon, Samsung, Apple, and Google all represented. Meanwhile, recalls drove traditional reputation bellwether Johnson & Johnson (See case study at end of this chapter) from second in 2008 to fifth in 2015. And not one financial or oil company made the list.

Here are the top 10 companies for 2015 and 2008.

Top 10—2015

1. Wegman's Food Market
2. Amazon.com
3. Samsung
4. Costco
5. Johnson and Johnson
6. Kraft
7. LL Bean
8. Publix Super Markets
9. Apple
10. Google

Top 10—2008

1. Google
2. Johnson & Johnson
3. Intel Corporation
4. General Mills
5. Kraft Foods Inc.
6. Berkshire Hathaway Inc.
7. 3M Company
8. The Coca-Cola Company
9. Honda Motor Co.
10. Microsoft

For further information, see "The 2015 Harris Poll Annual RQ Public Summary Report," Harris Interactive, February 2015.

FYI

. . . Losing Reputation

And then there were the companies who tied their fortunes to hip-hoppers.

Eager to appear hip to attract a younger market, large companies have learned the hard way in recent years that paying rappers to endorse your products can wind up torching your corporate reputation.

In the stretch of one week in 2013, Reebok dropped its ties to rapper Rick Ross over objectionable lyrics, and PepsiCo's Mountain Dew did the same to Lil Wayne and Tyler the Creator.

Lil Wayne's lyrics outraged the relatives of Emmett Till, the black teenager murdered during the civil right era, whom the rapper had mentioned in a vulgar context. Pepsi dropped Tyler the Creator after black scholars called his soda commercial racist.

Perhaps most objectionable of all was Rick Ross (**Figure 4-4**), whose casual lyrics about rape drew outrage from nearly everybody. In one lyrical burst, Mr. Ross talked about nonconsensual sex, using slang for the drug Ecstasy. *"Put molly all in her champagne, she ain't even know it/I took her home and I enjoyed that/she ain't even know it."*

Red-faced Reebok didn't quite see the artistic merit and, concerned about its reputation, immediately severed promotional ties with the controversial rapper.*

FIGURE 4-4   Bum rap.
Reebok's reputation took a pounding after it momentarily sponsored outrageous rapper Rick Ross, who rhymed about rape.
Photo: JLJ/ZOJ/JLN Photography/WENN/Newscom

*For further information, see Jon Caramanca, "Rap, Both Good and Bad for Business," *The New York Times* (May 7, 2013).

The point is that most organizations and individuals in the spotlight today understand, first, that credibility is a fragile commodity, and second, to maintain and improve public support they must operate with the "implicit trust" of the public. That means that for a corporation in the 21st century, winning favorable public opinion isn't an option—it's a necessity, essential for continued long-term success.

Managing Reputation

For an organization or an individual concerned about public opinion, what it comes down to is managing reputation. Reputation is gained by what one *does,* not by what one *says.* Reputation is present throughout our lives. It's how we choose business partners, which dentist or mechanic to visit, the stores we frequent, the neighborhood we live in, and the friends we keep. In recent years, *reputation management* has become a buzzword in public relations and in the broader society. At the start of the century, the term was little known. Today, a Google search on "reputation management" produces nearly 22 million results.

Many public relations firms have introduced reputation management divisions, and some have even billed themselves as being in the business of "relationship management." Generally defined, relationship management aligns communications with an organization's character and action. It creates recognition, credibility, and trust among key constituents. It stays sensitive to its conduct in public with customers and in private with employees. It understands its responsibilities to the broader society and is empathetic to society's needs. Edelman's highly respected, Trust Barometer annually researches the trust of the public around the world in business and government. (In 2014, the gap between little trust in government and increasing trust in business was the largest since the Barometer's founding in 2001.)

While reputation itself may be difficult to measure, its value to an organization or an individual is indisputable. And it's also indisputable that "managing" reputation is a front-line responsibility of public relations.

Last Word

Influencing public opinion remains at the heart of professional public relations work. Public opinion is a powerful force that can impact the earnings of corporations through such actions as product boycotts, union threats, strikes, and the misdeeds of key executives; influence government legislation through campaign support, product recalls, and letters and e-mails from constituents; and even unify a nation through calls to action by strong and committed leaders.

To influence public opinion, public relations professionals must anticipate trends in our society. At the start of the 21st century, one self-styled prognosticator, John Naisbitt, predicted the new directions that would influence American lives in the near future. Among them were the following:

- Inflation and interest rates will be held in check.
- There will be a shift from welfare to workfare.

- There will be a shift from public housing to home ownership.
- CEOs in a global economy will become more important and better known than political figures.[20]

As we progress through the second decade of the new century, a number of Nesbitt's "megatrends" appear to be coming to pass. Public relations professionals need to take note of these and other trends in gauging how public opinion will impact their organizations. They also should consider what the late public relations counselor Philip Lesly once pointed out: "The real problems faced by business today are in the outside world of intangibles and public attitudes."[21]

To keep ahead of these intangibles, public attitudes, and kernels of future public opinion, managements will turn increasingly for guidance to professional public relations practitioners.

Discussion Starters

1. What is the relationship between public relations and public opinion?
2. What are attitudes, and on what characteristics are they based?
3. How are attitudes influenced?
4. What is Maslow's hierarchy of needs?
5. What is the theory of cognitive dissonance?
6. How difficult is it to change a person's behavior?

7. What are several key public opinion laws, according to Cantril?
8. What kinds of evidence persuade people?
9. What are the elements involved in managing reputation?
10. In assessing the list of best and worst companies in terms of reputation, what specific characteristics influence these rankings?

Pick of the Literature

The New York Times, nytimes.com, and The Wall Street Journal, wsj.com

Public relations can be practiced only by understanding public opinion, and two of the most prominent daily forums in which to study it are *The New York Times* and *The Wall Street Journal* or, as is increasingly the case, their online vehicles, nytimes.com and wsj.com.

Despite the 21st-century problems of newspapers, these two most venerable news organizations reveal the diverse views of pundits, politicians, and plain people. The *Times* is arguably the primary source of printed news in the world. The *Journal,* likewise, is the primary printed source of the world's business and investment news—an area of increasingly dominant importance.

Both papers, through their opinion pages and in-depth stories, express the attitudes of leaders in politics, business, science, education, journalism, and the arts, on topics ranging from abortion rights to genetic engineering to race relations. Occasionally, the *Times* and the *Journal* supplement their usual coverage with public opinion polls to gauge attitudes and beliefs on particularly hot issues. Sure, the news is often infuriating, but it's also a joy to know more about what's going on than virtually anyone else.

The *Times* and the *Journal* are clearly the most important reference works any public relations professional can read (even including this book!).

Case Study   The Tylenol Murders

Arguably, the two most important cases in the history of the practice of public relations occurred within four years of each other to the same product and company.

For close to 100 years, Johnson & Johnson Company of New Brunswick, New Jersey, was the epitome of a well-managed, highly profitable, and tight-lipped consumer products manufacturer.

Round I

That image changed on the morning of September 30, 1982, when Johnson & Johnson faced as devastating a public relations problem as had confronted any company in history.

That morning, Johnson & Johnson's management learned that its premier product, extra-strength Tylenol, had been used as a murder weapon to kill three people. In the days that followed, another three people died from swallowing Tylenol capsules loaded with cyanide. Although all the cyanide deaths occurred in Chicago, reports from other parts of the country also implicated extra-strength Tylenol capsules in illnesses of various sorts. These latter reports were later proved to be unfounded, but Johnson & Johnson and its Tylenol-producing subsidiary, McNeil Consumer Products Company, found themselves at the center of a public relations trauma the likes of which few companies had ever experienced.

Tylenol had been an astoundingly profitable product for Johnson & Johnson. At the time of the Tylenol murders, the product held 35% of the $1 billion analgesic market. Throughout the years, Johnson & Johnson had not been—and hadn't needed to be—a particularly high-profile company. Its chairperson, James E. Burke, with the company for almost 30 years, had never appeared on television and had rarely participated in print interviews.

Caught by Surprise

Johnson & Johnson's management was caught totally by surprise when the news hit. The company recognized that it needed the media to get out as much information to the public as quickly as possible to prevent a panic. Therefore, almost immediately, Johnson & Johnson made a key decision: to open its doors to the media.

On the second day of the crisis, Johnson & Johnson discovered that an earlier statement that no cyanide was used on its premises was wrong. The company didn't hesitate. Its public relations department quickly announced that the earlier information had been false. Even though the reversal embarrassed the company briefly, Johnson & Johnson's openness was hailed and made up for any damage to its credibility.

Early on in the crisis, the company was largely convinced that the poisonings had not occurred at any of its plants. Nonetheless, Johnson & Johnson recalled an entire lot of 93,000 bottles of extra-strength Tylenol associated with the reported Chicago murders. In the process, it telegrammed warnings to doctors, hospitals, and distributors and suspended all Tylenol advertising.

But what about all those millions of dollars worth of Tylenol capsules on the nation's shelves?

The company was convinced such a massive recall wasn't warranted by the facts. It was convinced that the tampering had taken place during the product's Chicago distribution and not in the manufacturing process. Further, the FBI was worried that a precipitous recall would encourage copycat poisoning attempts. Nonetheless, five days later, when a copycat strychnine poisoning occurred in California, Johnson & Johnson did recall all extra-strength Tylenol capsules—31 million bottles—at a cost of more than $100 million.

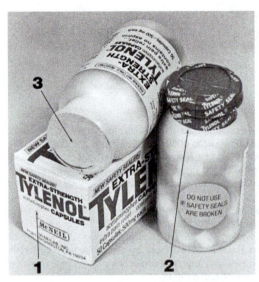

FIGURE 4-5 **New packaging.**
The triple-safety-sealed, tamper-resistant package for Tylenol capsules had (1) glued flaps on the outer box, (2) a tight plastic neck seal, and (3) a strong inner foil seal over the mouth of the bottle. A bright yellow label on the bottle was imprinted with a red warning: "Do not use if safety seals are broken." As it turned out, all these precautions didn't work.
Photo: Courtesy of Johnson & Johnson

Although the company believed it had done nothing wrong, Johnson & Johnson acted to assuage public concerns. It also posted a $100,000 reward for the killer or killers. Through advertisements promising to exchange capsules for tablets, through thousands of letters to the trade, and through statements to the media, the company hoped to put the incident into proper perspective.

Loyal Users but...

At the same time, Johnson & Johnson commissioned a nationwide opinion survey to assess the consumer implications of the Tylenol poisonings. The good news was that 87% of Tylenol users surveyed said they realized that the maker of Tylenol was "not responsible" for the deaths. The bad news was that 61% still said they were "not likely to buy" extra-strength Tylenol capsules in the future. In other words, even though most consumers knew the deaths weren't Tylenol's fault, they still feared using the product.

But Chairperson Burke and Johnson & Johnson weren't about to knuckle under to the deranged saboteur or saboteurs who had poisoned their product. Despite predictions of the imminent demise of extra-strength Tylenol, Johnson & Johnson decided to relaunch the product in a new triple-safety-sealed, tamper-resistant package (**Figure 4-5**). Many on Wall Street and in the marketing community were stunned by Johnson & Johnson's bold decision.

So confident was Johnson & Johnson's management that it launched an all-out media blitz to make sure that people understood its commitment. Chairperson Burke appeared on television shows and in newspaper interviews.

Welcoming *60 Minutes*

The company even invited the investigative news program *60 Minutes*—the scourge of corporate America—to film its executive strategy sessions to prepare for the new launch. When the program was aired, reporter Mike Wallace concluded that although Wall Street had been ready at first to write off the company, it was now "hedging its bets because of Johnson & Johnson's stunning campaign of facts, money, the media, and truth."

Finally, on November 11, 1982, less than two months after the murders, Johnson & Johnson's management held an elaborate video news conference in New York City, beamed to additional locations around the country, to introduce the new extra-strength Tylenol package.

In the months that followed Burke's news conference, it became clear that Tylenol would not become a scapegoat. In fact, by the beginning of 1983, despite its critics, Tylenol had recaptured an astounding 95% of its prior market share. Morale at the company, according to its chairperson, was "higher than in years." It had acted true to the "Credo," which spelled out the company's beliefs (**Figure 4-6**). The euphoria lasted until February 1986 when, unbelievably, tragedy struck again.

Round II

Late in the evening of February 10, 1986, news reports began to circulate that a woman had died in Yonkers, New York, after taking poisoned capsules of extra-strength Tylenol.

Unbelievably, the nightmare for Johnson & Johnson was about to begin again.

And once again, the company sprang into action. Chairperson Burke addressed reporters at a news conference a day after the incident. A phone survey found that the public didn't blame the company. However, with the discovery of other poisoned Tylenol capsules two days later, the nightmare intensified. The company recorded 15,000 toll-free calls at its Tylenol hotline. Once again, production of Tylenol capsules was halted. "I'm heartsick," Burke told the press. "We didn't believe it could happen again, and nobody else did either."

This time, the firm decided once and for all to cease production of its over-the-counter medications in capsule form. It offered to replace all unused Tylenol capsules with new Tylenol caplets, a solid form of medication that was less tamper-prone (**Figure 4-7**). The withdrawal of its capsules cost Johnson & Johnson more than $150 million after taxes.

Once again, in the face of tragedy, the company and its CEO received high marks. As President Reagan said at a White House reception two weeks after the crisis hit, "Jim Burke of Johnson & Johnson, you have our deepest appreciation for living up to the highest ideals of corporate responsibility and grace under pressure."

Today, 30 years after the first customers were murdered after ingesting Tylenol capsules, the Tylenol case study stands as a model in how to conduct positive public relations—honestly, openly, transparently—even in the face of unspeakable tragedy.

OUR CREDO

We believe our first responsibility is to the doctors, nurses and patients,
to mothers and fathers and all others who use our products and services.
In meeting their needs everything we do must be of high quality.
We must constantly strive to reduce our costs
in order to maintain reasonable prices.
Customers' orders must be serviced promptly and accurately.
Our suppliers and distributors must have an opportunity
to make a fair profit.

We are responsible to our employees,
the men and women who work with us throughout the world.
Everyone must be considered as an individual.
We must respect their dignity and recognize their merit.
They must have a sense of security in their jobs.
Compensation must be fair and adequate,
and working conditions clean, orderly and safe.
We must be mindful of ways to help our employees fulfill
their family responsibilities.
Employees must feel free to make suggestions and complaints.
There must be equal opportunity for employment, development
and advancement for those qualified.
We must provide competent management,
and their actions must be just and ethical.

We are responsible to the communities in which we live and work
and to the world community as well.
We must be good citizens — support good works and charities
and bear our fair share of taxes.
We must encourage civic improvements and better health and education.
We must maintain in good order
the property we are privileged to use,
protecting the environment and natural resources.

Our final responsibility is to our stockholders.
Business must make a sound profit.
We must experiment with new ideas.
Research must be carried on, innovative programs developed
and mistakes paid for.
New equipment must be purchased, new facilities provided
and new products launched.
Reserves must be created to provide for adverse times.
When we operate according to these principles,
the stockholders should realize a fair return.

Johnson & Johnson

FIGURE 4-6
**The Johnson &
Johnson credo.**
*Photo: Courtesy of
Johnson & Johnson*

A special message from the makers of TYLENOL® *products.*

If you have TYLENOL capsules, we'll replace them with TYLENOL caplets.

And we'll do it at our expense.

As you know, there has been a tragic event. A small number of Extra-Strength TYLENOL® Capsules in one isolated area in New York have been criminally tampered with.

This was an outrageous act which damages all of us.

Both federal and local authorities have established that it was only capsules that were tampered with.

In order to prevent any further capsule tampering, we have removed all our capsules from your retailers' shelves. This includes Regular and Extra-Strength TYLENOL capsules, CO-TYLENOL® capsules, Maximum-Strength TYLENOL® Sinus Medication capsules, Extra-Strength SINE-AID® capsules, and DIMENSYN® Menstrual Relief capsules.

And Johnson & Johnson's McNeil Consumer Products Company has decided to cease the manufacture, sale, and distribution of **all** capsule forms of over-the-counter medicines.

If you're a regular capsule user, you may be wondering what to use instead. That's why we'd like you to try TYLENOL caplets.

The caplet is a solid form of TYLENOL pain reliever, which research has proven is the form most preferred by consumers. Unlike tablets, it is specially shaped and coated for easy, comfortable swallowing.

And the caplet delivers a full extra-strength dose quickly and effectively.

So, if you have any TYLENOL Capsules in your home, do one of the following:

1. Return the bottles with the unused portion to us, together with your name and address on the form below. And we'll replace your TYLENOL capsules with TYLENOL Caplets (or tablets, if you prefer). We'll also refund your postage. Or...

2. If you prefer, you can receive a cash refund for the unused capsules by sending the bottle to us along with a letter requesting the refund.

We are taking this step because, for the past 25 years, over 100 million Americans have made TYLENOL products a trusted part of their health care.

We're continuing to do everything we can to keep your trust.

Send to:
**TYLENOL® Capsule Exchange
P.O. Box 2000
Maple Plain, MN 55348**
Please send my coupon for free replacement caplets or tablets to:
Please print
Name
Address
City
State _____ Zip _____
Offer expires May 1, 1986

(Courtesy of Johnson & Johnson)

Questions

1. What might have been the consequences if Johnson & Johnson had decided to "tough out" the first reports of Tylenol-related deaths and not recall the product?

2. What other public relations options did Johnson & Johnson have in responding to the first round of Tylenol murders?

3. Do you think the company made a wise decision by reintroducing extra-strength Tylenol?

4. In light of the response of other companies not to move precipitously when faced with a crisis, do you think Johnson & Johnson should have acted so quickly to remove the Tylenol product when the second round of Tylenol murders occurred in 1986?

5. What specific lessons can be derived from the way in which Johnson & Johnson handled the public relations aspects of these tragedies?

6. What was the media environment when the Tylenol crises occurred? How might the results have differed if the crises occurred today?

7. See what information Johnson & Johnson offers for its customers on the Tylenol Web site (www.tylenol.com). Follow the links to the Care Cards, House Calls, and FAQ sections. How do these sections demonstrate Johnson & Johnson's concern for customers? How do you think Johnson & Johnson would use this Web site to communicate with the public if new health scares surfaced?

For further information on the first round of Tylenol murders, see Jerry Knight, "Tylenol's Maker Shows How to Respond to Crisis," *Washington Post* (October 11, 1982): 1; Thomas Moore, "The Fight to Save Tylenol," *Fortune* (November 29, 1982): 48; Michael Waldholz, "Tylenol Regains Most of No. 1 Market Share, Amazing Doomsayers," *The Wall Street Journal* (December 24, 1982): 1, 19; and *60 Minutes,* CBS-TV (December 19, 1982). For further information on the second round of Tylenol murders, see Irvin Molotsky, "Tylenol Maker Hopeful on Solving Poisoning Case," *The New York Times* (February 20, 1986); Steven Prokesch, "A Leader in a Crisis," *The New York Times* (February 19, 1986): B4; Michael Waldholz, "For Tylenol's Manufacturer, the Dilemma Is to Be Aggressive—But Not Appear Pushy," *The Wall Street Journal* (February 20, 1986): 27; and "Tylenol II: How a Company Responds to a Calamity," *U.S. News & World Report* (February 24, 1986): 49. For an overall view of Johnson & Johnson and Tylenol, see Lawrence G. Foster, *Robert Wood Johnson n: The Gentleman Rebel.* State College, PA: Lillian Press, 1999.

From the Top

An Interview with Ray Jordan

Ray Jordan is Senior Vice President of Corporate Affairs at Amgen. For nine years, he was Corporate Vice President, Public Affairs and Corporate Communication for Johnson & Johnson, responsible for public relations and corporate communication for the broadly based, diversified global health care company. He oversaw the public affairs responsibilities and activities of the company's more than 250 operating companies in 57 countries around the world. This interview was conducted during his tenure at J&J, which ended in 2012.

What was your primary mission as Johnson & Johnson's chief communications officer?
Our function had a clear vision and strategy, broad enough to be relevant and applicable to all our businesses, and my principal role was to drive that throughout the organization. Our mission involved three primary components: (1) maintaining and enhancing the reputation of the company and our businesses, (2) ensuring our core values, and (3) improving the environment for growth.

How did you manage the worldwide J&J communications network across international borders?
We managed more than 200 people around the world, including those who reported up through various solid and dotted lines. We didn't have communications people in all of our countries. Our corporate team was about 20 professionals. We operated through a council of senior communications officers, responsible for each of our four primary groups: (1) consumer, (2) pharmaceuticals, (3) surgical care, and (4) comprehensive care.

How did you influence perceptions in different geographies?

At Johnson & Johnson, our *Credo* was the galvanizing element across all geographies and businesses. That was at the core of driving reputation externally and our behavior inside the company.

Has the Tylenol case influenced the way J&J conducts itself around the world?

Yes. It's a powerful story and representation of how J&J thinks as a company. Those stories, like Tylenol, and the people who have lived and carry them are powerful influencers in the J&J culture.

How important is it for communications officers to interact constructively with corporate lawyers?

To be effective in my job, this is essential. Our lawyers are facilitators not roadblocks. One obligation we have as communicators is to help ensure that our company's actions are consistent with who we are. That means we need to reflect on how other constituencies might react to a particular corporate action—before we take it. Lawyers are always engaged around potential actions. So a good relationship with lawyers means they will bring us into an assessment of whether an impending action may have consequences for other stakeholders. We were fortunate that at the corporate level of Johnson & Johnson, the communications group was always invited into discussions of this sort. And I lobbied our communications staff around the world to build strong working relationships with their senior lawyer—and also their senior finance officer. It's curious that many communications people tend to shy away from dealing with legal or finance groups. But they are both critically important for a communicator to get to know and work with.

How do you measure your success in your job?

Measurement in our business has always been a conundrum. My CEO gave me good guidance early on. He suggested focusing on a five-year mission at any given time. You need that much time to make meaningful change in terms of realizing a particular mission. So we managed our group in terms of priorities over the next five years. We assessed progress against these larger objectives clearly embraced by management. We met each fourth quarter with our senior executives to review what, if anything, we needed to change in our framework, what environmental factors weighed on our priorities, and what commitments we planned to make for the year ahead. We used these updates to strike the theme for all subsequent communications—annual report, internal town hall meetings, analyst meetings, etc. In this way, our communications messages were consistent across geographies and businesses. And we could track progress in conveying these messages.

What qualities do you value most in a communications professional?

I look for three things:

1. *Business acumen is vital.* You must be able to relate to business leaders on the basis of what the business is and how to think about it.

2. *Excellent writing or editing capacity.* This is still vitally important in what we do.

3. *Tenacity to help the business operate in "the right way" is third.* You've got to possess a passion for this.

Public Relations Bookshelf

Asher, Herbert. *Polling and the Public*. 7th ed. Washington, DC: CQ Press, 2007. A comprehensive examination of research methods and public opinion surveys.

Berinksky, Adam J. (Ed.). *New Directions in Public Opinion*. New York: Routledge, 2012. A contemporary discussion of what influences public opinion in such controversial topics as same-sex marriage, politics, and trust in public opinion polls.

Bernays, Edward. *Crystallizing Public Opinion*. New York, NY: Open Road Integrated Media, 2015. The grand daddy of public relations public opinion texts, written in the 1920s, is available now on Kindle.

Bloomgarden, Kathy. *Trust: The Secret Weapon of Effective Business Leaders*. New York: St. Martins Press, 2007. Ruder Finn's co-CEO traces a road map for corporations to build support among their most important publics.

Chomsky, Noam and David Barsamian. *Propaganda and the Public Mind*. Chicago, IL: Haymarket Books, 2015. This paperback reprint of a 2001 Chomsky best-seller is a good introduction to the point-of-view of those who have little tolerance for modern day public relations.

Claggett, William J. M. and Byron E. Shafer. *The American Public Mind*. New York: Cambridge University Press, 2010. Worthwhile historical background on the major events that underpin the United States, including the Depression, New Deal, and civil rights.

Friedman, Barry. *The Will of the People*. New York: Farrar, Strauss, and Giroux, 2009. A study of how public opinion has influenced Supreme Court interpretation of the Constitution.

Haggerty, James F. *In the Court of Public Opinion: Strategies for Litigation Communications*. Chicago, IL: American Bar Association, 2009. Interesting review of famous legal cases, from Martha Stewart to HealthSouth, from the perspective of a lawyer.

McCombs, Max, Lance Holbert, Spiro Kiousis, and Wayne Wanta. *The News and Public Opinion*. Cambridge, UK: Polity Press, 2011. A British view on how what's reported influences public opinion.

Murray, Allan. *Revolt in the Boardroom*. New York: HarperCollins, 2007. A *Wall Street Journal* editor traces reasons why the "reputations" of corporations are prone to suffering in a post-Enron world.

Oxley, Zoe M. *Public Opinion: Democratic Ideals, Democratic Practice* (Paperback). Washington, DC: CQ Press, 2008. A scholarly discussion of public opinion research and its relation to social psychology.

Sobel, Richard, Peter Furia, and Bethany Barratt. *Public Opinion and International Intervention*. Dulles, VA: Potomac Press, 2012. Fascinating exposition on the different views of the Iraq war in 12 countries.

Tessler, Mark. *Islam and Politics in the Middle East*. Bloomington, IN: Indiana University Press, 2015. Translating public opinion of citizens in perhaps the world's most challenging hot spot.

Woodly, Deva R. *The Politics of Common Sense*. London, England: Oxford University Press, 2015. A scholarly view of political discourse and its impact on public opinion from a British scholar.

Endnotes

1. Jay Balfour, "Nelly, T.I. React to St. Louis Protests; Nelly Visits Ferguson," *HipHop DX* (August 19, 2014).

2. Michael S. Schmidt and William Neuman, "U.S. Expands Inquiry of Suspected Misconduct by Agents in Colombia," *The New York Times* (April 19, 2012).

3. Sheryl G. Stolberg and Michael S. Schmidt, "Agency Trip to Las Vegas Is the Talk of Washington," *The New York Times* (April 3, 2012).

4. Austin Knoblauch and Barry Stavro, "A Timeline on the FIFA Scandal," *Los Angeles Times* (June 2, 2015).

5. Cited in Edward L. Bernays, *Crystallizing Public Opinion* (New York: Liveright, 1961): 61.

6. Cited in Harwood L. Childs, *Public Opinion: Nature, Formation, and Role* (Princeton, NJ: Van Nostrand, 1965): 15.

7. Leon A. Festinger, *A Theory of Cognitive Dissonance* (New York: Harper & Row, 1957): 163.

8. Richard M. Perloff, *The Dynamics of Persuasion: Communication and Attitudes in the 21st Century*, 2nd ed. (Mahwah, NJ: Lawrence Erlbaum Associates, 2003). Ample discussion of social judgment theory, pioneered by Muzafer and Carolyn Sherif in 1967.

9. Abraham Maslow, *Motivation and Personality* (New York: Harper & Row, 1954).

10. Richard E. Petty and John T. Cacioppo, *The Elaboration Likelihood Model of Persuasion* (New York: Academic Press, 1986).

11. Timothy C. Brock and Sharon Shavitt, *Persuasion: Psychological Insights and Perspectives* (Chicago: Allyn & Bacon, 1999).

12. George W. Bush, Press Conference from the Oval Office, September 13, 2001.

13. Saul D. Alinsky, *Rules for Radicals* (New York: Vintage Books, 1971): 81.

14. Hadley Cantril, *Gauging Public Opinion* (Princeton, NJ: Princeton University Press, 1972): 226–230.

15. Daniel T. Max, "The 2,988 Words That Changed a Presidency: An Etymology," *The New York Times* on the Web (October 7, 2001).

16. Alex Swoyer, "Rand Paul's NSA Protest Makes Him Most Popular GOP Candidate on Social Media," *Breitbart.com* (June 1, 2015).

17. Saad Abedine, "U.S. Death Toll in Iraq Reaches 2000," *CNN.com* (October 26, 2005).

18. Tom V. Brook, "U.S. Formally Declares End of Iraq War," *USA Today* (December 15, 2011).

19. Jason Farago, "Goldman Sach's CEO Shows Gay Marriage Is a No-Risk Trade," *The Guardian* (February 7, 2012)

20. John Naisbitt and Patricia Aburdene, *Megatrends 2000* (New York: Morrow, 1990).

21. Philip Lesly, "How the Future Will Shape Public Relations—and Vice Versa," *Public Relations Quarterly* (Winter 1981–1982): 7.

Chapter 5

Management

Chapter Objectives

1. To discuss public relations as a "management" function that serves the organization best when it reports to the CEO.

2. To explore in detail the elements that constitute a public relations plan.

3. To discuss public relations objectives, campaigns, and budgets.

4. To compare and contrast the internal public relations department and the external public relations agency.

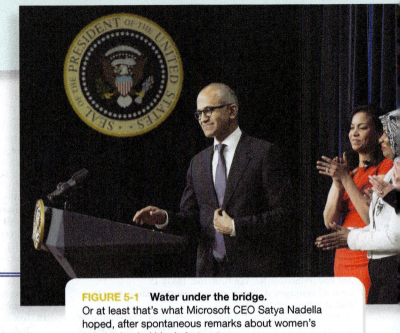

FIGURE 5-1 Water under the bridge.
Or at least that's what Microsoft CEO Satya Nadella hoped, after spontaneous remarks about women's salaries landed him in hot water.
Photo: ROBERT GALBRAITH/REUTERS/Newscom

After too many years of bombastic billionaire Steve Ballmer as CEO, long-suffering Microsoft shareholders were delighted in 2014 when Ballmer left to own a basketball team and computer executive Satya Nadella became the new CEO (**Figure 5-1**).

"Delighted," that is, until the new CEO opened his mouth.

At a seminar on "Women in Computing," CEO Nadella was asked about how women should ask for raises. He replied, *"It's not really about asking for a raise, but knowing and having faith that the system will give you the right raise."* Alas, the "system" that the CEO referenced was one that paid women 78% as much as men. And in the heart of computing territory, Silicon Valley, men with graduate degrees earned 73% more than female counterparts, and men

with bachelor's degrees earned 40% more. After the predictable ensuing commotion, a chagrined Nadella acknowledged, *"I answered that question completely wrong."*[1]

Such are the communications obstacles that confront management.

These days, as *Fortune* magazine put it, "it takes a village to sell a CEO to both Wall Street and Main Street"; meaning that today's boss requires a village of communications advisors, including:

- Executive coach to help polish communications strategies and skills.

- Social media guru to create their tweetings and other postings to employees.

- Speechwriter to hone the words and thoughts of the CEO so they sound profound.

- Media coach to advise on how best to handle those nasty reporter questions that a CEO must answer.

- Positioning coach to counsel on building a CEO's "personal brand as a manager and thought leader."

- Reputation manager to research, evaluate, and advise on helping the CEO build the desired corporate image.

- Personal stylist (although most won't admit it!) to recommend what to wear and how to look in order to make the most managerial impression.[2]

In many ways, then, the primary function of a top manager is to serve as the organization's communicator—or, if you will, public relations person. In fact, it has been said that the only difference between the public relations director and the CEO is that the latter gets paid more.

In many ways, that's quite true. The CEO, after all, is the firm's top manager, responsible for, in addition to setting strategy and framing policy, serving as the organization's chief spokesperson, corporate booster, and reputation defender—not at all unlike the responsibilities assigned to the public relations professional.

Accordingly, to be effective—and respected—in his or her job, the public relations professional in the 21st century must understand management. That means that public relations people must master knowledge of such management functions as planning, budgeting, objective setting, and how top management thinks and operates. That's what this chapter discusses.

It also deals with the differences between working as a staff public relations practitioner inside a corporation, nonprofit, or other organization, where the job is to support management in achieving its objectives, and working as a professional in a public relations agency, where the job is to contribute to the revenue generation of the company. Finally, it provides some feel of what to expect in terms of income in public relations.

1 Public Relations Management Process

Like other management processes, professional public relations work emanates from clear strategies and bottom-line objectives that flow into specific tactics, each with its own budget, timetable, and allocation of resources. Stated another way, public relations today is much more a planned, persuasive social managerial science than a knee-jerk, damage-control reaction to sudden flare-ups.

Don't get me wrong. As we will learn later, the public relations professionals who have the most organizational clout and get paid the most are those who demonstrate the ability to perform in a crisis. Thinking "on your feet" is a coveted ability in the practice of public relations. But so, too, is the ability to think strategically and plan methodically to help change attitudes, crystallize opinions, and accomplish the organization's overall goals.

Managers insist on *results,* so the best public relations programs can be measured in terms of achieving results in building the key relationships on which the organization depends. The relevance of public relations people in the eyes of top management depends largely on the contribution they make to the management process of the organization.

With nearly a century under its belt, the practice of public relations has developed its own theoretical framework as a management system. According to communications professors James Grunig and Todd Hunt, public relations managers perform what organizational theorists call a *boundary* role: They function at the edge of an organization as a liaison between the organization and its external and internal publics. In other words, public relations managers have one foot inside the organization and one outside. Often this unique position is not only lonely but also precarious.

As boundary managers, public relations people support their colleagues by helping them communicate across organizational lines both within and outside the organization. In this way, public relations professionals also become systems managers, knowledgeable about and able to deal with the complex relationships inherent in the organization.[3]

Top managers are forced to think strategically about reaching their goals. So, too, should public relations professionals think in terms of the strategic process element of their own roles.

It is this procedural mindset—directed at communicating key messages to realize desired objectives to priority publics—that makes the public relations professional a key advisor to top management.

Reporting to Top Management

The public relations function, by definition, must report to top management.

If public relations, as noted in Chapter 1, is truly to be the "interpreter" for management philosophy, policy, and programs, then the public relations director should report to the CEO.

In many organizations, this reporting relationship alas, is not the case. Public relations is often subordinated to advertising, marketing, legal, or human resources. Whereas marketing and advertising promote the product, public relations promotes the entire organization. Therefore, if the public relations chief reports to the director of marketing or advertising, the job mistakenly becomes one of promoting specific products rather than one of promoting the entire organization.

For the public relations function to be valuable to management, it must remain independent, credible, and objective. This mandates that public relations professionals have not only communication competence but also an intimate knowledge of the organization's business. Without the latter, according to research, public relations professionals are much less effective as top-management advisors.[4]

Public relations should be the *corporate conscience.* An organization's public relations professionals should enjoy enough autonomy to deal openly and honestly with management. If an idea doesn't make sense, if a product is flawed, if the general institutional wisdom is wrong, it is the duty of the public relations professional to challenge the consensus. As Warren Buffet, the legendary CEO of Berkshire Hathaway, put it, "We can afford to lose money—even a lot of money. But we cannot afford to lose reputation—even a shred of reputation."[5]

This is not to say that advertising, marketing, and all other disciplines shouldn't enjoy a close partnership with public relations. Clearly, they must. All disciplines

A Question of Ethics

Deflated Standards

By the summer of 2015, no professional sports team was more celebrated or more despised than the New England Patriots, Super Bowl champions of the National Football League (NFL).

The ever-winning Patriots team—owned by the eccentric but charitable Robert Kraft, coached by the furtive and anti-social Bill Belichick and quarterbacked by the dashing and "perfect" Tom Brady—was idolized in New England and loathed just about everywhere else. Over the years, the Patriots were subject to a series of embarrassing events (**Figure 5-2**).

- In 2015, New England's high paid, star receiver Aaron Hernandez was convicted of murder.

- In 2007, the team admitted illegally videotaping an opponent's play-call signals.

- In 1982, the team had a snowplow operator clear a space so that its kicker could kick the winning field goal against the Miami Dolphins, coached by the legendary Don Shula, who called the Patriots' conduct, "*the most unfair act in the history of the league.*"

So it came as little surprise to many when, in the days leading up to the 2015 Super Bowl, the Patriots were charged with another violation of league rules; specifically, deflating the pressure of footballs so that quarterback Brady could get a better grip.

"*Deflategate*" became a national obsession. The Patriots, from the owner on down, denied any such malfeasance and publicly predicted that the outside investigator hired by the NFL to investigate would corroborate the team's innocence. When the investigator came back with a conclusion of "*guilty as charged*" and implicated golden boy Brady in the offense, owner Kraft blew up.

> "*To say we are disappointed in its findings, which do not include any incontrovertible or hard evidence of deliberate deflation of footballs at the AFC Championship Game, would be a gross understatement,*" Kraft

FIGURE 5-2   Deflated egos.
Quarterback Tom Brady and New England Patriots owner Robert Kraft before "Deflategate."
Photo: USA Today Sports/Newscom

thundered immediately after the league dropped its Brady bombshell. Nonetheless, the Patriots' owner vowed, *"We will accept the findings of the report and take the appropriate actions based on those findings as well as any discipline levied by the league."*

But when the NFL reacted to the report by fining the team $1 million, taking away two draft picks and suspending Brady for four games—Kraft went ballistic and intimated he had changed his mind. Said the team's statement: *"Despite our conviction that there was no tampering with footballs, it was our intention to accept any discipline levied by the league. Today's punishment, however, far exceeded any reasonable*

expectation. It was based completely on circumstantial rather than hard or conclusive evidence."

But in the end Brady had his suspension overturned in a federal court appeal; the golden boy refused to be "deflated."

Questions

1. How would you assess the management communications performance of Robert Kraft?

2. How would you suggest the Patriots deal with their reputation for failing ethics?

3. How would you have advised the owner of the Patriots when confronted by the "Deflategate" accusations?

*For further information, see Mike Cole, "Report: Robert Kraft's 'Out of His Mind with Anger' over Patriots' Punishments," *NESN* (May 12, 2015); Fraser P. Seitel, "Roger Goodell's Next PR Opportunity," *odwyerpr.com* (May 7, 2015); and Shalise M. Young, "Robert Kraft Unhappy with Harsh Discipline for Patriots," *Boston Globe* (May 12, 2015).

---

must work to maintain their own independence while building long-term, mutually beneficial relationships for the good of the organization. However, public relations should never shirk its overriding responsibility to enhance the organization's credibility by ensuring that corporate actions are in the public interest.

② The Public Relations Plan: Conceptualizing

Strategic planning for public relations is an essential part of management. Planning is critical not only to know where a particular campaign is headed but also to win the support of top management. Indeed, one of the most frequent complaints about public relations is that it is too much a "seat-of-the-pants" activity, impossible to plan and difficult to measure. Management's perspective is, "How do we know the public relations group will deliver and fully leverage the resources they're asking for?" They must see a plan. With proper planning, public relations professionals can indeed defend and account for their actions.

Before organizing for public relations work, practitioners must consider objectives and strategies, planning and budgets, and research and evaluation. The broad environment in which the organization operates must dictate the overall business objectives. These, in turn, dictate specific public relations objectives and strategies. Once these have been defined, the task of organizing for a public relations program should flow naturally.

Environment
    └─➤ *Business objectives*
            └─➤ *Public relations objectives and strategies*
                        └─➤ *Public relations programs*

Setting objectives, formulating strategies, and planning are essential if the public relations function is to be considered equal in stature to other management processes. Traditionally, the public relations management process involves four steps:

1. **Defining the problem or opportunity.** This requires researching current attitudes and opinions about the issue, product, candidate, or company in question and determining the essence of the problem.

2. **Programming.** This is the formal planning stage, which addresses key constituent publics, strategies, tactics, and goals.

3. **Action.** This is the communications phase, when the program is implemented.

4. **Evaluation.** The final step in the process is the assessment of what worked, what didn't, and how to improve in the future.

Each of these four process steps is important. Most essential is starting with a firm base of research and a solid foundation of planning.

The Public Relations Plan: Creating

The public relations plan must be spelled out in writing. Its organization must answer management's concerns and questions about the campaign being recommended. Here's one way it might be organized and what it should answer.

1. **Executive summary**—an overview of the plan.

2. **Communication process**—how it works, for understanding and training purposes.

3. **Background**—mission statement, vision, values, events that led to the need for the plan.

4. **Situation analysis**—major issues and related facts the plan will deal with.

5. **Message statement**—the plan's major ideas and emerging themes, all of which look to the expected outcome.

6. **Audiences**—strategic constituencies related to the issues, listed in order of importance, with whom you wish to develop and maintain relationships.

7. **Key audience messages**—one- or two-sentence messages that you want to be understood by each key audience.

8. **Implementation**—issues, audiences, messages, media, timing, cost, expected outcomes, and method of evaluation—all neatly spelled out.

9. **Budget**—the plan's overall budget presented in the organization's accepted style.

10. **Monitoring and evaluation**—how the plan's results will be measured and evaluated against a previously set benchmark or desired outcome.[6]

The beauty of creating a plan is that it clearly specifies tactics against which objectives can be measured and evaluated. In devising the public relations plan along these lines, an organization is assured that its public relations programs will reinforce and complement its overall business goals.

Activating the Public Relations Campaign

Any public relations campaign puts all of the aspects of public relations planning—objectives, strategies, research, budgeting, tactics, and evaluation—into one cohesive framework. The plan specifies a series of *what's* to be done and *how* to get them done—whatever is necessary to reach the objectives.

Every aspect of the public relations plan should be designed to be meaningful and valuable to the organization. The four-part skeleton of a typical public relations campaign plan resembles the following:

1. **Backgrounding the problem.** This is the so-called situation analysis, background, or case statement that specifies the major aims of the campaign. It can

be a general statement that refers to audiences, known research, the organization's positions, history, and the obstacles faced in reaching the desired goal.

2. **Preparing the proposal.** The second stage of the campaign plan sketches broad approaches to solve the problem at hand. The elements of the public relations proposal may vary, depending on the subject matter, but generally include the following:

- Situational analysis—description of the challenge as it currently exists, including background on how the situation reached its present state.

- Scope of assignment—description of the nature of the assignment: What the public relations program will attempt to do.

- Target audiences—specific targets identified and divided into manageable groups.

- Research methods—specific research approach to be used.

- Key messages—specific selected appeals: What do we want to tell our audiences? How do we want them to feel about us? What do we want them to do?

- Communications vehicles—tactical communications devices to be used.

- Project team—key players who will participate in the program.

- Timing and fees—a timetable with proposed costs identified.

3. **Implementing the plan.** The third stage of a campaign plan details operating tactics. It may also contain a time chart specifying when each action will take place. Specific activities are defined, people are assigned to them, and deadlines are established. This stage forms the guts of the campaign plan.

4. **Evaluating the campaign.** To find out whether the plan worked, evaluation methods should be spelled out here.

- Did we implement the activities we proposed?

- Did we receive appropriate public recognition for our efforts?

- Did attitudes change—among the community, customers, management—as a result of our programs?

The inclusion of a mechanism for evaluation is imperative in terms of verifying results based on shifts in public opinion or actions taken to benefit an organization and its goals.[7]

Finally, although planning the public relations campaign is important, planning must never become an end in itself. The fact is that no matter how important planning may be, public relations is still assessed principally in terms of its action, performance, and practice.

3 Setting Public Relations Objectives

An organization's goals must define what its public relations goals will be, and the only good goals are ones that can be measured. Public relations objectives and the strategies that flow from them must achieve results. As the baseball pitcher Johnny Sain used to say, "Nobody wants to hear about the labor pains, but everyone wants to see the baby."

So, too, must public relations people think strategically. Strategies are the most crucial decisions of a public relations campaign. They answer the general question, *How will we manage our resources to achieve our goals?* The specific answers then become the public relations tactics used to implement the strategies. Ideally, strategies and tactics should profit from pretesting.

FYI

Disappearing Roots

It is axiomatic that public relations planning must precede implementation; which is what actor Ben Affleck found out the hard way in 2015 (**Figure 5-3**).

Affleck agreed to participate in the PBS program, *"Finding Your Roots,"* in which Harvard Professor Henry Louis Gates traces a guest's ancestors. In Affleck's case what Gates uncovered was a distant relative who owned slaves. "Woops," said Affleck, who wrote the host to ask that this slave-owning element in his family's roots not be shared with the public.

And the actor probably would have gotten his way, had the e-mails from Gates to the show's producer, SONY, not been exposed by Wikileaks, when it hacked into SONY executive e-mails. The Gates' e-mails to SONY revealed that the show's host was aghast that the Batman movie star would try to censor the program. Wrote Gates, *"We've never had anyone ever try to censor or edit what we found. What do we do?...To do this would be a violation of PBS rules, actually, even for Batman."*

A week after the disappearing slave-owner controversy reared its ugly head, Affleck took to Facebook to explain himself. Said the star, "I didn't want any television show about my family to include a guy who owned slaves. I was embarrassed. The very thought left a bad taste in my mouth." Affleck, whose mother marched for civil rights in the 1960s, added, *"While I don't like that the guy is an ancestor, I am happy that aspect of our country's history is being talked about."*

No doubt next time, he'll plan ahead.*

FIGURE 5-3   Good roots.
Actor Ben Affleck had no trouble being pictured with his current family, but he wasn't planning on information leaking about a distant slave-owning ancestor.
Photo: BDA/ZOJ/WENN/Newscom

*For further information see Salon staff, "Ben Affleck: I Didn't Want Any Television Show About My Family to Include a Guy Who Owned Slaves: I Was Embarrassed," *Salon* (April 21, 2015); and Mary E. Williams, "Don't Hide from Your Family Slave-Owning Past, Ben Affleck," *Salon* (April 20, 2015).

As for objectives, good ones stand up to the following questions:

- Do they clearly describe the end result expected?
- Are they understandable to everyone in the organization?
- Do they list a firm completion date?
- Are they realistic, attainable, and measurable?
- Are they consistent with management's objectives?

Increasingly, public relations professionals are managing by objectives (MBO) and by results (MBR) to help quantify the value of public relations in an organization. The two questions most frequently asked by general managers of public relations practitioners are, *How can we measure public relations results?* and *How do we know whether the public relations program is making progress?* MBO can provide public relations professionals with a powerful source of feedback. MBO and MBR tie public relations results to management's predetermined objectives in terms of audiences, messages, and media. Even though procedures for implementing MBO programs differ, most programs share four points:

1. Specification of the organization's goals, with objective measures of the organization's performance
2. Conferences between the superior and the subordinate to agree on achievable goals
3. Agreement between the superior and the subordinate on objectives consistent with the organization's goals
4. Periodic reviews by the superior and the subordinate to assess progress toward achieving the goals

Again, the key is to tie public relations goals to the goals of the organization and then to manage progress toward achieving those goals. The goals themselves should be clearly defined and specific, practical and attainable, and measurable.

Public Relations Budgeting

Like any other business activity, public relations programs must be based on sound budgeting. After identifying objectives and strategies, the public relations professional must detail the particular tactics that will help achieve those objectives. No organization can spend indiscriminately. Without a realistic budget, no organization can succeed. Likewise, public relations activities must be disciplined by budgetary realities.

In public relations agencies responsible for producing revenue, *functional budgeting* is the rule; that is, dollars for staff, resources, activities, and so on are linked to specific revenue-generating activities. Employees are required to turn in time sheets detailing hours worked on behalf of specific clients. In organizations where public relations is a "staff" activity and not responsible for revenue generation, *administrative budgeting* is the rule; that is, budget dollars are assigned generally against the department's allocation for staff and expenses.

The key to budgeting may lie in performing two steps: (1) estimating the extent of the resources—both personnel and purchases—needed to accomplish each activity, and (2) estimating the cost and availability of those resources. With this information in hand, the development of a budget and monthly cash flow for a public relations program becomes easier. Such data also provide the milestones necessary to audit program costs on a routine basis and to make adjustments well in advance of budget crises.

Most public relations programs operate on limited budgets. In a growing number of instances, "pay-for-performance" public relations has emerged. The premise of this arrangement is that the buyer pays only for what he or she gets, meaning that fees are based on the depth of coverage and the circulation or audience rating of the venue in which coverage appears. If no coverage is achieved, no fee is paid. Most public relations agencies, however, make "no guarantees" that their efforts will be successful and therefore frown on pay-for-performance contracts.[8]

Most public relations agencies treat client costs in a manner similar to that used by legal, accounting, and management consulting firms: The client pays for services rendered, either on a monthly or yearly retainer basis or on minimum charges based on staff time. Time records are kept by every employee—from chairperson to mail clerk—on a daily basis to be sure that agency clients know exactly what they are paying for. Hourly charges for public relations agency employees can range from double figures per hour upwards to $500–$600 an hour and even as high as $1,000 an hour for a handful of agency superstars.

Agencies generally organize according to industry groupings, with specialization in industry functions—media relations, government relations, social media, investor relations, etc. Larger agencies are divided into such areas as health care, sports, fashion, technology, finance, and so on. Account teams are assigned specific clients. Team members bill clients on an hourly basis, with most firms intending to retain two-thirds of each individual's hourly billing rate as income. In other words, if an account executive bills at a rate of $300 per hour—and many senior counselors do—the firm expects to retain $200 of that rate toward its profit.

Because agency relationships are based on trust, it is important that clients understand the derivation of costs. Out-of-pocket expenses—for meals, hotels, transportation, and the like—are generally charged back to clients at cost. But when an agency pays in advance for larger expense items—printing, photography, graphics, design—it is standard industry practice to mark up such expenses by a factor approximating 17.65%. This figure, which the vast majority of agencies use, was borrowed from the advertising profession and represents the multiplicative inverse of the standard 15% commission that ad agencies collect on advertising placement.

The guiding rule in agency budgeting is to ensure that the client is aware of how charges are being applied so that nasty surprises might be avoided when bills are received.

Public Relations Implementation

The duties and responsibilities of public relations practitioners are as diverse as the publics with whom different institutions deal. Specific public relations tasks are as varied as the organizations served. Here is a partial list of public relations duties:

- **Media relations:** Coordinating relationships with the online, print, and electronic media, which includes arranging and monitoring press interviews, writing news releases and related press materials, organizing press conferences, and answering media inquiries and requests.

- **Social media marketing:** The digital revolution has introduced a whole new component to public relations skills sets. The Web, where everyone is a publisher and conversations are the rule, has transformed the publication of information into a legitimate two-way street. Marketing via social networking sites, from Facebook to Twitter, from Pinterest to Tumblr to all the rest has become a frontline responsibility of public relations professionals.

- **Internal communications:** Informing employees and principals through a variety of means, including intranet, newsletters, television, and meetings. Traditionally, this role has emphasized news-oriented communications rather than benefits-oriented ones, which are usually the province of personnel departments.

- **Government relations and public affairs:** Coordinating activities with legislators on local, state, and federal levels. This includes legislative research activities, lobbying, and public policy formation.

- **Community relations:** Orchestrating interaction with the community, perhaps including open houses, tours, and employee volunteer efforts designed to reflect the supportive nature of the organization to the community.
- **Investor relations:** Managing relations with the investment community, including the firm's present and potential stockholders. This task emphasizes personal contact with securities analysts, institutional investors, and private investors.
- **Consumer relations:** Supporting activities with customers and potential customers, with activities ranging from hard-sell product promotion activities to "soft" consumer advisory services.
- **Public relations research:** Conducting opinion research, which involves assisting in the public policy formation process through the coordination and interpretation of attitudinal studies of key publics.
- **Public relations writing:** Coordinating the institution's printed voice with its publics through reprints of speeches, annual reports, quarterly statements, and product and company brochures.
- **Special interest publics relations:** Coordinating relationships with outside specialty groups, such as nongovernmental organizations, suppliers, educators, students, nonprofit organizations, and competitors.
- **Institutional advertising:** Managing the institutional—or non-product—advertising image as well as being called on increasingly to assist in the management of more traditional product advertising.
- **Graphics:** Coordinating the graphic and photographic services of the organization. To do this task well requires knowledge of desktop publishing, typography, layout, and art.
- **Web site management:** Coordinating the organization's online "face," including Web site design and ongoing counsel, updating, and even management of the site.
- **Philanthropy:** Managing the gift-giving apparatus, which ordinarily consists of screening and evaluating philanthropic proposals and allocating the organization's available resources.
- **Special events:** Coordinating special events, including travel for company management, corporate celebrations and exhibits, dinners, groundbreakings, and grand openings.
- **Management counseling:** Advising managers on alternative options and recommended choices in light of public responsibilities.
- **Crisis management:** Taking charge when crisis strikes is another first-line responsibility of public relations professionals, who are looked to provide guidance to management in confronting the media and the often perilous situation.

Again, this is but a partial list of the tasks ordinarily assigned to public relations professionals.

4 Public Relations Departments

Public relations professionals generally work in one of two organizational structures: (1) as a staff professional in a public relations department of a corporation, university, hospital, sports franchise, political campaign, religious institution, and so on, whose task is to support the primary business of the organization; or (2) as a line professional in a public relations agency, whose primary task is to help the organization earn revenue.

Consider the public relations department. Once an organization has analyzed its environment, established its objectives, set up measurement standards, and thought about appropriate plans, programs, and budgets, it is ready to organize a public relations department. Departments range from one-person operations to far-flung networks of hundreds of people, such as at the U.S. Department of Defense, Johnson & Johnson, or ExxonMobil, with staff around the world, responsible for relations with the press, investors, civic groups, employees, and many different governments.

Today, appropriately, about half of all corporate communications departments report to the chairperson, president, and/or CEO. This is an improvement from the past and indicative of the higher stature that the function enjoys. About one-sixth of public relations departments report to advertising or marketing, and another one-sixth report to a vice president of administration.[9] Clearly, reporting to the CEO is eminently preferable to reporting to a legal, financial, or administrative executive, who may tend to "filter" top-management messages.

In government, public relations professionals (although, as we will see later in this book, they're not called *public relations*) typically report directly to department heads. In universities, the public relations function is frequently coupled with fundraising and development activities. In hospitals, public relations is typically tied to the marketing function.

In terms of structure, corporate public relations departments today are faced with stakeholders who are more "empowered" than ever. The days of "top down" communication, where CEO pronouncements were the only ones that counted, are over. Today, everybody is on the Net and using social media—activists, employees, consumers, bloggers of every stripe and attitude. For the first time in history, corporate communicators and their superiors no longer control the conversation.[10]

This group of diverse influencers means that companies must organize communications departments to reflect a new diverse group of influencers (**Figure 5-4**). This new reality suggests that corporate communications departments must focus more on "engaging" their constituent publics in two-way dialogue, to keep informed about their views and to keep them informed as to the company's motives and actions.

FIGURE 5-4 Organizing for public relations.
These diverse publics are some of those who make up the evolving ecosphere of influencers of MasterCard Worldwide.
Courtesy MasterCard Worldwide

Public Relations Agencies

Now consider the public relations agency. The biggest difference between an external agency and an internal department is perspective. The former is outside looking in; the latter is inside looking out (sometimes literally for itself!). Here's what is meant by "perspective." Sometimes the use of an agency is necessary to escape the tunnel-vision syndrome that afflicts some firms, in which a detached viewpoint is desperately needed. An agency, unfettered by internal corporate politics, might be better trusted to present management with an objective reading of the concerns of its publics.

An agency has the added advantage of not being taken for granted by a firm's management. Unfortunately, management sometimes has a greater regard for an outside specialist than for an inside one. This attitude frequently defies logic but is nonetheless often true. Generally, if management is paying (sometimes quite handsomely) for outside counsel, it tends to listen carefully to the advice.

In recent years, as clients have begun to manage resources more rigorously, agencies have gotten much more systematic in measuring success and in keeping customers from migrating to a competitor. Indeed, the most difficult part of agency work is not *attracting* clients but *retaining* them.

Public relations agencies today, as noted, are huge businesses. And public relations, itself, is a multibillion-dollar industry. In 2013, the global public relations industry recorded fee income of $12.5 billion, employing about 80,000 people, according to the Holmes Report.[11]

Over the past two decades, most of the top public relations firms have been subsumed by communications holding companies, the most prominent of which, along with some of the agencies they own, are the following:

- **Omnicom:** Fleishman-Hillard, Ketchum, Porter-Novelli, Brodeur Worldwide, Clark & Weinstock, Kreab Gavin Anderson & Company, and Cone

- **Interpublic Group:** Axis Agency; Cassidy & Associates; Current; DeVries Public Relations; Film Fashion; Fitzgerald & Co.; Frank About Women; Golin; Inside Edge; KRC Research; McCann Health; McCann World Group; Mullen Lowe Group; PMK BNC; Powell Tate; Promoqube; Rogers & Cowan; Spong; Tierney Public Relations; and Weber-Shandwick Worldwide

- **WPP Group:** Burson-Marsteller; Carl Byoir Associates; Cohn & Wolfe; GCI Group; Glover Park Group; Hill & Knowlton; Grey Global Group; Ogilvy Public Relations Worldwide; Public Strategies Inc.; and numerous others.

- **Havas:** Abernathy MacGregor; Arnold Public Relations; Cake; Euro RSCG; Havas Worldwide; and many others.

- **Publicis:** Kekst and Company; Manning, Selvage & Lee; Publicis Dialog; Rowland Worldwide; and others.

- **Chime Communications PLC:** Bell Pottinger; The Blaze Agency; CSM Worldwide; Good Relations; Corporate Citizenship; and other international agencies.

Public relations purists bemoan the incursion of these mammoth companies because many are dominated by advertising agencies. Defenders point to the potential synergy between the two disciplines. One casualty of the takeover of the world's leading public relations firms by these holding companies is that the largest agencies no longer make public their annual revenues and earnings. Nonetheless, a compilation of the net fees of the largest independent public relations firms still shows robust annual revenues (**Table 5-1**), with the largest, Edelman, employing 5300 employees and earning in excess of $797 million annually. What is indisputable is the tremendous growth of the profession.

TABLE 5-1 O'Dwyer's Rankings: Worldwide Fees of Top Independent PR Firms with Major U.S. Operations—May 2014

Beyond the largest public relations firms, most owned by advertising-oriented multinational holding companies, are thousands of independent public relations firms—many entrepreneurial in nature. Others, like the family-owned Edelman Company—begun by father Dan and now run by son Richard (see From the Top in Chapter 10)—are huge organizations.

Many of these independent shops are thriving. In 2014, many of the top 25 independent public relations firms enjoyed double-digit gains in fee income, testifying to the strength of the public relations counseling business.

Firm	2014 Net Fees	Empl.	% Fee Change from 2013
1. Edelman, New York, NY	$797,328,238	5308	+8.6
2. APCO Worldwide, Washington, DC	118,112,600	635	−1.9
3. Waggener Edstrom Communications, Bellevue, WA	106,676,000	705	−9.3
4. W2O Group, San Francisco, CA	82,625,000	402	+10.1
5. Ruder Finn, New York, NY	73,891,000	522	+16.8
6. Finn Partners, New York, NY	52,796,000	339	+19.0
7. MWWPR, New York, NY	51,775,000	248	+7.8
8. ICR, New York, NY	50,687,714	144	+19.4
9. DKC Public Relations, New York, NY	41,500,000	199	+26.2
10. Zeno Group, New York, NY	39,921,576	276	+11.2
11. Allison+Partners, San Francisco, CA	37,000,000	207	+28.3
12. Global Strategy Group, New York, NY	32,378,000	76	+29.5
13. PadillaCRT, Minneapolis, MN	31,624,111	185	−2.2
14. Racepoint Global, Boston, MA	27,274,597	188	+14.0
15. G&S Business Communications, New York, NY	25,438,112	140	+13.1
16. Coyne PR, Parsippany, NJ	23,010,000	154	+14.8
17. Taylor, New York, NY	21,700,000	108	+2.8
18. Prosek Partners, New York, NY	20,300,000	85	+17.0
19. Hunter PR, New York, NY	20,250,000	101	+10.2
20. 5W Public Relations, New York, NY	18,961,046	112	+18.4
21. French | West | Vaughan, Raleigh, NC	18,753,747	87	even
22. Fahlgren Mortine, Columbus, OH	18,616,471	110	+10.5
23. LEVICK, Washington, DC	17,231,618	61	+40.4
25. Peppercomm, New York, NY	16,294,726	90	+14.4

Courtesy Jack O'Dwyer Company, odwyerpr.com.

Reputation Management

Many public relations agencies in recent years, particularly those purchased by the large advertising agency conglomerates, have declared special emphasis on what they suggest is the more "strategic" *reputation management*.

What is reputation management? Public relations purists argue that this is precisely what they have been doing all along—helping to "manage strategically" an organization's "reputation," that is, its brand, position, goodwill, or image.

Essentially, an organization's reputation is composed of two elements: (1) the more "rational" products and performance, and (2) more "emotional" behavioral factors, such as customer service, CEO performance, personal experience with the company, and the like. Stated another way, reputation is gained by what one *does*, not by what one *says*.[12]

Reputations matter because a company with a good reputation can charge premium prices, have greater access to new markets and products, have greater access to capital, profit from greater word-of-mouth endorsement, and possess an unduplicated identity. Such distinctive organizations as Tiffany, Google, Dreamworks, and the New York Yankees are all examples of entities with unique and positive reputations that translate into hard-nosed advantages. One quantitative study of reputation concluded that more than one-quarter of a company's stock market value was attributable to intangibles such as its reputation.[13]

Reputation management, then, is *the ability to link reputation to business goals to increase support and advocacy and increase organizational success through profits, contributions, attendance, and so on.*

What do reputation managers do? The behaviors they attempt to influence include (1) persuading consumers to recommend and buy their products, (2) persuading investors to invest in their organization, (3) persuading competent job seekers to enlist as employees, (4) persuading other strong organizations to joint venture with them, and (5) persuading people to support the organization when it is attacked.

As the extraordinarily successful former commissioner of the National Basketball Association, David Stern, put it, "I am the protector of the brand and its integrity. That's a job that every CEO has, and I consider it my job to be out there to be protective and to respond so that I can be the spokesperson."[14]

Assisting the CEO in "managing" the reputation of the organization is the public relations professional. Indeed, for the public relations person, reputation management reflects the function's fundamental mandate to promote, maintain, defend, enhance, and sustain the organization's credibility, as the economists put it, "in perpetuity"; in other words, forever.

Where Are the Jobs?

The long-term future of the practice of public relations promises to be steady and strong. Consider the numbers for public relations agencies in 2014:

- More than 70% of public relations firms saw revenue grow.
- Firms grew at an average of 10%, the fifth year in a row the agency experienced such growth.
- Nearly half of public relations firms expected client budgets to increase in 2015.[15]

What kinds of public relations jobs were most in demand?

- First, according to the PR Council, was demand for digital media specialists. Social media outreach has become an integral part of a public relations specialist's responsibilities. Social media is a mechanism through which Millennials, in particular, communicate, and has, therefore, introduced new public relations opportunities for them in particular.
- Media relations specialists ranked next in terms of demand. Despite social media and the rise of going direct to the consumer on the Internet, top managers still value the traditional skill of public relations managers to work with the media to pursue third party endorsement.
- Next came the function of client relationship managers to help manage an organization's reputation. Also, the specific areas of investor relations and crisis management. The increase in demand for specialists in these three high-level areas probably explains why public relations salaries have increased markedly in recent years.[16]

In every realm of society, public relations is growing. Public relations agencies, wiser and more experienced after the boom-bust phenomenon of the early years of the 21st century, will continue to expand. Meanwhile, global corporations, faced with increased scrutiny from the media, government, and the general public to act ethically and behave responsibly, have recognized the need for talented, top communications managers. Once the media never gave public relations news much notice, but in 2015 when McDonald's and Amazon appointed former Obama Press Secretaries Robert Gibbs and Jay Carney, respectively, to top public relations posts, it was major news.[17]

In the nonprofit realm, public relations positions in healthcare are likely to grow as managed care becomes the reality and health care organizations become more competitive in attracting patients and winning community approval. Other nonprofits—charities, schools, museums, associations—all faced with fewer resources and more competition for community funding—will also require increased public relations help to attract development and membership funds.

Finally, one other public relations skill that will be in increased demand, certainly for the remainder of this decade, is employee communications. Employees in the 21st century, empowered by the Internet and burned by layoffs, pension fund losses and restructurings, and failures of management to be credible, must be convinced that their organizations deserve their allegiance. This will be a job largely for public relations practitioners—to win back employee trust.[18]

And if you still aren't convinced that public relations jobs will blossom in the years ahead, consider this. Pope Benedict XVI, in the summer of 2012, hired Vatican Fox News correspondent Greg Burke to assist the church in its sometimes-wanting public relations policy around the globe. By 2015, Burke was being praised for his work, behind the scenes, in catapulting Pope Francis to, well, "saintly status," in terms of his public relations.[19] The point is that in the last half of the second decade of the 21st century, even the Pope needs public relations!

What Does It Pay?

Without question, the communications function has increased in importance and clout in the new century. Top communications professionals in many large corporations today draw compensation packages well into six figures, with a select few earning more than $1 million annually. According to *PR Week,* the media salaries of U.S. public relations practitioners were healthy indeed:

- Median annual corporate public relations salaries in 2015 were $120,000, the same as a year earlier.

- Median annual public relations agency salaries in 2015 were $90,000, up from $85,000 in 2014.

- Median annual nonprofit public relations salaries were $75,000 in 2015, down from $80,000 in 2014.[20]

- In a more general census, the U.S. Bureau of Labor Statistics reported that the annual wage for the nation's 208,000 public relations specialists was $54,170 in May 2012.[21]

According to the PRSA, average salaries for public relations professionals by job title in 2012 ranged thusly:

Executive vice president	$160,600
Senior vice president	$138,300
Vice president	$112,700
Account supervisor	$75,600
Senior account executive	$60,600
Account executive	$37,400

The survey, quoted by the PRSA, found that salaries were higher in New York, Los Angeles, Atlanta, and Chicago and lower in Boston, Dallas, Houston, Washington, and San Francisco.[22] Another survey indicated that public relations agency vice president/group directors earned between $112,000 and $185,000 annually and that corporate public relations vice presidents earned between $113,500 and $182,000 annually.[23]

A 2012 Korn/Ferry study of 148 "chief communications officers (CCO)" polled the senior-most communication executives at Fortune 500 companies. This survey revealed a wide disparity among companies in terms of pay packages for communication officers. Two-thirds of those polled earned $175,000 and $349,000 a year. A handful had salaries in excess of $700,000 a year. And most were entitled to bonuses and equity compensation, with such annual bonuses averaging between $150,000 and $200,000.

The Korn/Ferry study was instructive in that nearly half these high-earning respondents reported to the company CEO and possessed an advanced degree, more than half were in the 46- to 55-year-old category, and most supervised a staff of less than 50 people. The survey concluded that "the CCO function is becoming broader and more vital to companies, especially as they are challenged to manage all of their stakeholder relations and their reputations."[24]

Women and Minorities

Two decades ago, the practice of public relations was overwhelmingly a bastion of white males. Today, it is women who predominate in public relations work. And minorities—African Americans, Asians, and Hispanics—while still small in total numbers in the field, have nonetheless increased their participation in public relations.

Fifty years ago, 27% of public relations practitioners were female; today that figure has grown to nearly 85%. Of the PRSA's 21,000 members, 73% are women.[25] Women have flocked to public relations for many reasons, among them that salaries are higher than equivalent journalism jobs, public relations positions are increasing while journalism opportunities are shrinking, and in public relations, there is ample opportunity for advancement and increased power.[26] Also, there is the "glamour factor," immortalized by the portrayal of public relations diva Samantha Jones in the hit show, *Sex and the City* (**Figure 5-5**).

The issue of increased feminization of public relations—the establishment of a so-called velvet ghetto—is a particularly thorny one for the practice. One area of constant consternation is the traditional discrepancy between men's and women's salaries and upper-management positions—the glass ceiling for women in public relations.

The PRSA's "2010 Work, Life & Gender Survey" indicated that the average annual income for men in public relations was about $120,000; the figure for women was about $72,000. The study's conclusion: While the numbers of women entering public relations is growing, the salary gap between men and women is widening.[27] Many scholars have examined this troubling phenomenon and come up with theories. One researcher noted the fact that many in top management consider women as "natural born communicators," possessing "general feminine values such as cooperation, respect, interconnection, justice, equity, honesty, sensitivity, intuition, fairness, morality, commitment, etc." Such a belief "is a dangerous myth and represents highly questionable gender stereotypes."[28] Another researcher bluntly concluded that the 14% differential in pay between men and women in public relations could only be attributable to one thing: "gender discrimination."[29]

FIGURE 5-5 Glamour job.
Actress Kim Cattrall (left), as public relations firebrand Samantha Jones, and her pals in the blockbuster *Sex and the City* helped boost the glamour quotient of the public relations field.
Photo: Album/Newscom

The fact is that 90% of chief communications officers at Fortune 500 companies are white men, while 2% are African American or black, 2% are Hispanic, and 6% are either Asian/Pacific Islander, multiracial, Native American/Alaska Native, or declined to state.[30]

One brighter ray in this gender picture is that recent experience may suggest that times are changing, albeit more slowly than some would prefer. University public relations programs across the country report a preponderance of female students, outnumbering males by as much as 80%. Moreover, the number of women executives in public relations has also increased in recent years. While the number of male public relations executives still exceeds the number of female public relations executives, the existence of a glass ceiling may be a phenomenon in decline.[31] Also, the field's record on promoting African Americans to leadership positions is also woeful.[32]

So the fact remains as we head toward the end of the second decade of the 21st century that the practice of public relations still has a ways to go in providing women and minorities opportunity for growth, development, and higher pay.

Last Word

In the 21st century, the practice of public relations is firmly accepted as part of the management process of any well-run organization. Indeed, the function of a CCO—chief communication officer—is a growing one throughout industry.

That's the good news. The challenge, however, that accompanies that new-found public relations power is that significant jobs in the field carry significant responsibility and stress. Indeed, *CareerCast's* list of "the most stressful jobs in America" puts public relations executives in the number #6 most stressful job slot, just behind fire fighters and airline pilots.[33]

Public relations objectives and goals, strategies, and tactics must flow directly from the organization's overall goals. Public relations strategies must reflect organizational strategies, and tactics must be designed to realize the organization's business objectives. Stated another way, public relations programs are worth little if they fail to further management's and the organization's goals.

As social media and all manner of wireless communications have proliferated and an organization's reputation has become more essential, the practice of public relations enjoys a significant management role and challenge in this new century. As society gets bigger and more complex and individuals express less "trust" in the large organizations that dominate their lives, management in every sector must depend on the able assistance of proper public relations practice to help reestablish trust in society's major institutions.

That may be one reason why the U.S. Bureau of Labor Statistics projects employment of public relations specialists will grow 12% between 2012 and 2022. During that time period, an additional 27,400 jobs will need to be filled.[34] Or, in the words of one public relations recruiter, "There has never been a better time to be in the business. And that will continue for the next 10 to 20 years."[35]

Discussion Starters

1. What is the management process of public relations?
2. Why is it imperative that public relations report to top management?
3. What are the elements that make up a public relations plan?
4. What questions must be answered in establishing valid public relations objectives?
5. What elements go into framing a public relations budget?
6. What were the "ethical implications" that confronted Fleischman-Hillard with its Canadian client?
7. What are the fundamental differences between working in a corporation and working in an agency as a public relations professional?
8. What are several of the primary tactical tasks assigned to the public relations function?
9. What may be the primary areas of opportunity for public relations professionals in the years ahead?
10. Why has the field of public relations been accused of being a "velvet ghetto"?

Pick of the Literature

Reputation Management: The Key to Successful PR and Corporate Communication, 3rd Edition

John Doorley and Helio Fred Garcia, New York: Routledge, 2015

Two eminent public relations professors (full disclosure: I work with 'em, but they're still "eminent!") prescribe a best-case formula for achieving positive recognition for any organization.

Both authors bring a wealth of corporate and consulting experience to this seminal work that transcends any other in the area of "reputation management." For one thing, the authors contend that reputation management can be measured, and they present methods to help quantify the elusive, but essential, commodity.

The authors dissect the various elements of managing one's reputation, from community relations to crisis. In terms of the latter, they detail, as definitively as anyone ever has, how an organization can respond effectively in the midst of crisis, by assessing specific measures that trigger strategic action. And they also offer five guest chapters, written by experienced practitioners, who have helped build reputations at leading corporations. Clearly, Doorley and Garcia have written the number-one text on "reputation management" in the practice of public relations.

Case Study   Uber Success Brings Uber Public Relations Problems

Behold the phenomenon that is Uber.

The 21st century personal taxi cab service, headquartered in San Francisco, is worth approximately $50 billion and isn't even public. It is a staple in 300 cities in 58 countries, employs 300,000 drivers and generates annual revenues of $10 billion.

Uber Impactful

Uber was founded in 2009 by Travis Kalanick and Garrett Camp as a transportation network company that uses an app to allow consumer to submit a trip request then routed to Uber's nexus of drivers. Uber lore suggests that Kalanick and Camp hatched the idea one snowy night in Paris when they couldn't find a cab.

Almost immediately, the concept disrupted taxi companies and governments around the world.

Meanwhile, private investors piled on to finance the upstart company, assuring it of one of history's most monumental public offerings—if and when it decides to go public.

Uber's impactful growth appeared unstoppable. In the summer of 2015, CEO Kalanick announced plans to invest $1 billion in China, increasing to 65 the number of Chinese cities served by Uber. Despite challenges from entrenched taxi companies and the Chinese government, Kalanick predicted that China might turn out to be a more important market for Uber even than the U.S.

Uber Arrogant

Despite Uber's roaring success, it suffered public relations problems from its start.

One primary reason was its not-yet-40-year-old CEO Kalanick. While any Silicon Valley "disruptor" must be a feisty competitor by nature, the Uber founder found himself in more hot water virtually every time he opened his mouth.

- On the long-standing industry he wished to dethrone, CEO Kalanick immediately enraged taxi drivers and local governments when he declared, *"It's not Pinterest where people are putting up pins. You're changing the way cities work, and that's fundamentally a third rail. We're in a political campaign, and the candidate is Uber and the opponent is an a—hole named Taxi."*

- On the upstart competitor Lyft raising money to challenge Uber, Kalanick made a veiled threat to investors, *"Just so you know, we're going to be fund-raising after this, so before you decide whether you want to invest in them, just make sure you know that we are going to be fund-raising immediately after."*

- When asked by an interviewer about his skyrocketing "desirability" as young CEO of a multi-billion company, he responded, *"Yeah, we call that 'Boob-er.'"* And if that didn't reflect enough public relations tone deafness, Kalanick followed the comment up by blaming the media for reporting a claim by a political organizer that she was choked by an Uber driver; dismissing the accusation that Uber was somehow liable *"for these incidents that aren't even real in the first place."*

Unfortunately for the CEO and his company, Uber's public relations "incidents" kept on coming.

Uber Crises

Kalanick's "take no prisoners" attitude permeated his company and antagonized taxi drivers and governments throughout the world.

In cities from Paris to London, from Shanghai to Mexico City, taxi companies and unions protested against Uber alleging that

FIGURE 5-6
Not so jolly Old London.
London taxi drivers blocked the streets with a go-slow protest outside the Transport for London offices to protest Uber's invasion in the spring of 2015.
Photo: Guy Bell/REX Shutterstock/Newscom

its use of unlicensed drivers was unsafe and illegal **(Figure 5-6)**. Joining the protests were city governments and their taxi commissions that regulated taxis and depended on cab revenues. In New York and other cities, governments proposed regulations that would rein in car-service apps.

Then there were mounting safety issues stemming from allegations against Uber drivers.

- A woman in New Delhi accused an Uber driver of raping her, and in response, the Indian capital banned the taxi-booking service.

- In Chicago and London, female passengers accused Uber drivers of sexually assaulting them.

- In Los Angeles, an Uber driver was arrested and charged with kidnapping a drunk woman and taking her to a hotel to sexually assault her.

Then on top of all the other public relations challenges being thrown at it, an Uber executive acknowledged in the winter of 2014 of telling reporters at what he thought was an off-the-record gathering that he proposed spending $1 million to dig up damaging information that would discredit journalists critical of the company. According to BuzzFeed, he singled out one technology reporter, saying he wanted to prove a "particular and very specific claim" about her personal life. When BuzzFeed exposed the story and the company was engulfed in a social media firestorm, even the pugnacious Kalanick unreservedly apologized for his subordinate's stupefying stupidity.

And even as the revenues rolled in, the public relations problems just kept on coming, from criticisms for aggressively poaching drivers and using dirty tricks to undermine rival services to offering rides to "hot chicks" to promote Uber in France to allegedly pushing subprime auto loans on drivers to not doing enough to address female passengers receiving unwanted sexual attention.

No wonder that in 2015, Kalanick, according to TechCrunch, had embarked on a public relations campaign to convey a "kinder, gentler Uber."

And not a moment too soon.*

Questions

1. Were you Uber's public relations director, what strategy would you recommend the company adopt relative to the taxi industry and competitors?

2. How would you attempt to "clean up" the image of Uber's CEO?

3. What public relations response would you recommend Uber adopt relative to the claims of sexual harassment by drivers?

4. What public relations strategies would you use to prepare the company for going public?

---

*For further information, see Kevin Allen, "The Continuing Saga of Uber PR," *Ragan PR Daily* (December 20, 2014); Johana Bhuivan, "Uber's Travis Kalanick: Takes 'Charm Offensive' to New York City," *BuzzFeed* (November 14, 2014); Jessica Guynn and Elizabeth Weise, "Uber's Plot to Spy on Reporter Is Latest Controversy," *USA Today* (November 18, 2014); Neil Irwin, "Uber Scandals Highlight Silicon Valley's Grown Up Problem," *The New York Times* (November 19, 2014); Mickey Rapkin, "Uber's Cab Confessions," *Gentlemen's Quarterly* (March 2014); Veronica Rocher, "Uber Driver Accused of Kidnapping Clubgoer, Taking Her to Motel," *Los Angeles Times* (June 3, 2014); and Kara Swisher, "Man and Uber Man," *Vanity Fair* (December 2014).

From the Top

An Interview with Peter Drucker

Peter Drucker, who died in 2005 at the age of 95, was called the "greatest thinker management theory has produced" by the *London Economist*. His work influenced Winston Churchill, Bill Gates, Jack Welch, and the Japanese business establishment. His more than three dozen books, written over 66 years and translated into 30 languages, also delivered his philosophy to newly promoted managers just out of the office cubicle. Dr. Drucker counseled presidents, bishops, baseball managers, CEOs, and symphony conductors on the finer points of management success. In his 88th year, Dr. Drucker sat with the author for this interview.

What would you say have been your greatest contributions to business and society?
One, I made management visible. People say I've discovered management—that's nonsense. I made it into a discipline.

Second, I was also the first one who said that people are a resource and not just a cost, and they have to be placed where they can make a contribution. The only ones who took me up on it were the Japanese for a long time.

The third one is knowledge—that knowledge work would be preeminent.

Four, I was the first to say that the purpose of business is to create the customer and to innovate. That I think is a major contribution. That took a long time to sink in—that management

is not this mad dog of internal rules and regulations, that it's a discipline that can be learned and taught and practiced.

I think those four. The rest are secondary.

What is your view of today's public relations practice?
There is no public relations. There's publicity, promotion, advertising; but "relations" by definition is a two-way street. And the more important job and the more difficult is not to bring business and the executives to the outside but to bring the outside to these terribly insulated people. And this will be far more important in the next 20 years, when the outside is going to change beyond all recognition. I'm not only talking business CEOs but also university presidents and even bishops—several of my charity patients are bishops—all need to know what's going on outside.

Can you elaborate?
With an example. Have you ever heard of Paul Garrett?

Paul Garrett came out of journalism. He wanted to build a proper public relations department, to bring to General Motors what the outside was like. He would have been very effective. But GM didn't let him. Alfred Sloan (GM's CEO) brought Garrett in 1930 to keep GM out of *Fortune. Fortune* was founded as a muckraking magazine with investigative journalism.

Why didn't Sloan, supposedly one of the greatest managers of all time, want to listen to Garrett?
Neither Sloan nor anybody else in top management of General Motors wanted to hear what Garrett would have told them. And this was still the case much later.

Paul Garrett was a professional who would have told them things they didn't want to hear and wouldn't believe. Killing the messenger is never the right policy.

And in GM's case, the employee relations people totally failed to warn the company of the horrible sit-down strike they would suffer. And then when investor relations became important, it wasn't assigned to the public relations people.

And to this day, most institutions still look upon public relations as their "trumpet" and not as their "hearing aid." It's got to be both.

What do you see as the future of the practice of public relations?
I think there is a need. It is a very complicated and complex function. The media are no longer homogenous and are much more critical. But there is a need for an intermediary to tell the truth to management. Public relations people today don't do that because they're scared, because the people they work for don't like to hear what they don't want to hear.

Let's face it. There's an old saying, "If I have you for a friend, I don't need an enemy."

Public Relations Library

Austin, Erica W. and Bruce E. Pinkleton. *Strategic Public Relations Management*. 2nd ed. Mahwah, NJ: Lawrence Erlbaum Associates, 2006. Solid emphasis on public relations planning and research theory and technique.

Aylward, Scott and Patty Moore. *Confessions from the Corner Office*. New York: John Wiley & Sons, 2007. Two communications executives, who rose through the ranks, credit their mastery of "the art of survival and behavior."

Bloom, Robert H. and Dave Conti. *The Inside Advantage: The Strategy that Unlocks the Hidden Growth in Your Business*. New York: McGraw-Hill, 2007. Words of wisdom from an experienced business CEO, who suggests that every company has "hidden strengths," which it must find, unleash, and communicate.

Croft, Alvin C. *Managing a PR Firm for Growth and Profit*. New York: Haworth Press, 2006. A public relations agency executive offers advice on attracting, winning, and keeping clients.

Ki, Eyun-Jung, Jeong-Nam Kim, and John A. Ledingham, *Public Relations as Relationship Management*. 2nd ed. New York: Routledge, 2015. Scholarly study of the relationship between an organization and its publics.

Gregory, Anne. *Planning and Managing Public Relations Campaigns*. 3rd ed. London, England: Kogan, 2010. Detailed discussion on how research, planning, and theory contribute to solving public relations problems.

Ihlen, Oyvind, Betteke V. Ruler, and Magnus Fredrikkson (Eds.). *Public Relations and Social Theory*. New York: Routledge, 2009. Confronting public relations as a social phenomenon with a decidedly global perspective.

Lukaszewski, James E. *Why Should the Boss Listen to You? The 7 Disciplines of the Trusted Strategic Advisor*. New York: Jossey Bass/ Wiley, 2008. An experienced management counselor offers advice on landing a seat at the management table, based on trustworthiness, thinking strategically, and developing a management perspective.

Moss, Danny and Barbara DeSanto. *Public Relations: A Managerial Perspective*. Thousand Oaks, CA: Sage, 2011. A number of distinguished professors author chapters on various elements of public relations management.

Rivkin, Steve and Fraser P. Seitel. *Ideawise: How to Transform Today's Ideas into Tomorrow's Innovations*. New York: John Wiley & Sons, 2002. Two communications veterans (one of whom is exceedingly good looking) provide common sense rules on sparking creativity and "finding the muse."

Smith, Ronald D. *Strategic Planning for Public Relations*. New York: Routledge, 2009. Worthwhile explanation of the importance of reasoned and logical planning in solving public relations problems, with a wide array of contemporary cases included.

Swann, Patricia. *Cases in Public Relations Management*. 2nd ed. New York: Routledge, 2014. Good discussion of contemporary cases in media relations, ethical public relations, and other areas.

Theaker, Alison. *The Public Relations Handbook*. 4th ed. New York: Routledge, 2012. Soup-to-nuts glossary of public relations practice, with elements of management.

Toth, Elizabeth (Ed.). *The Future of Excellence in Public Relations and Communication Management*. Mahwah, NJ: Lawrence Erlbaum, 2007. A research-oriented, scholarly discussion, with contributions from leading academics in the field.

Endnotes

1. Robert Williams, "How Investors Respond to CEO Apologies," *Wall Street Daily* (November 24, 2014).
2. Erika Fry, "Packaging The Boss," *Fortune* (October 27, 2014).
3. James E. Grunig and Todd Hunt, *Managing Public Relations* (New York: Holt, Rinehart, & Winston, 1984): 89–91.
4. "Study Results Find Communications Competence Must Be Combined with Knowledge of the Business," study sponsored by Deloitte & Touche and IABC Research Foundation, June 14, 2001.
5. Ibid.
6. Lester R. Potter, "How to Be a Credible Strategic Counselor to Your Organization," Delivered at IABC International Conference, Chicago, June 2002.
7. Stuart Z. Goldstein, "Information Preparedness," *Strategic Communication Management 3*, no. 1 (December/January 1999).
8. Richard Virgilio, "Is the Road to ROI Paved with Pay-for-Placement PR?" *PR News* (August 10, 2005).
9. "O'Dwyer's Director of Corporate Communications 2005" (New York: J. R. O'Dwyer Company, 2005): A5.
10. Remarks by Harvey Greisman, senior vice president/group executive global communications group, MasterCard Worldwide, May 15, 2007, Tarrytown, NY.
11. Aaron Sudhaman, "Global PR Industry Growth Surges to 11% in 2013," *World PR Report* (July 7, 2014).
12. Thomas Murray, "In Retreat from Excellence," *Ragan Report* (June 11, 2007): 1.
13. Pete Engardio and Michael Arndt, "What Price Reputation?" *Business Week* (July 9, 2007): 70.
14. Ken Wheaton, "NBA's Stern Gets It: Brand Image Is Key to Game Plan," *Advertising Age* (June 23, 2008).
15. Kathy Cripps, "PR's Growth Spurt Continues-A Look at the Council's Latest Data," *PR Council* (January 28, 2015).
16. "Salary Survey 2015," *PR Week* (March 2, 2015).
17. Hiroko Tabuchi, "McDonald's Hires Robert Gibbs; Ex-Press Secretary for Obama," *The New York Times* (June 9, 2015).
18. Fraser P. Seitel, "Reputation Management," *odwyerpr.com* (July 9, 2002).
19. Katie Engelhart, "The PR Guru Behind the Pope Who Is Charming the World," *Vice InHuman Kind* (November 21, 2013).
20. "Salary Survey 2015," op. cit.
21. "Public Relations Specialists," *U.S. Bureau of Labor Statistics* (January 8, 2014).
22. "Salaries for PR Professionals," PRSA Job Center, www.prsa.org/jobcenter/career_resources/resource_type/tools_tactics/salary_information/salaries_pr/, adopted from "The Official PR Salary and Bonus Report—2012," Spring Associates, Inc., New York, NY.
23. "2012 Salary Guide," The Creative Group, creativegroup.com, 2012.
24. "The Chief Communications Officer," Korn/Ferry's 2012 Survey of Fortune 500 Companies, Korn/Ferry International, 2012.
25. Russell Working, "Women Dominate the PR Industry: Why?" *Ragan PR Daily* (October 4, 2010).

26. Olga Khazan, "Why Are There So Many Women in Public Relations?" *The Atlantic* (August 8, 2014).

27. Bey-Ling Sha, "PR Women: New Data Show Gender-Based Salary Gap Is Widening," *Ragan PR Daily* (March 8, 2011).

28. Romy Frohlich, "The Friendliness Trap," *Communication Director* (April 2010).

29. David M. Dozier, "No Equal Pay in PR: Today's Gender Pay Gap of 14% Can Be Blamed on Discrimination," *COMMPRO.Biz LLC* (August 4, 2011).

30. "The Chief Communications Officer," op. cit.

31. Richard Bailey, "A Glass Ceiling in PR?" *PR Studies* weblog from Leeds Business School at Leeds Metropolitan University, http://prstudies.typepad.com (April 2, 2005).

32. Mike Paul, "PR Firms Need to Back Diversity Words with Top Hiring Action," *odwyerpr.com* (April 27, 2015).

33. Matt Wilson, "PR Execs Have the 6th Most Stressful Job in America," *Ragan PR Daily* (January 8, 2014).

34. "Public Relations Specialists" (January 8, 2014).

35. "Salary Survey 2005," *PR Week* (February 21, 2005).

Chapter **6**

Ethics

Chapter Objectives

1. To discuss the one aspect that should differentiate public relations from the law and other business pursuits—ethics.

2. To explore ethics—or the lack thereof—in today's business, government, media, and public relations cultures.

3. To discuss the concept of corporate social responsibility.

4. To underscore the bedrock importance of public relations professionals "doing the right thing."

FIGURE 6-1   Liar, liar, pants on fire.
Golden State Warriors Coach Steve Kerr, with a simon-pure reputation for honesty, stunned the sports world in 2015 by lying to give his team an extra edge.
Photo: Bob Donnan/USA Today Sports/Newscom

Say it ain't so, Coach!

That's what Steve Kerr fans said to themselves in the summer of 2015 when the five-time National Basketball Association champion as a player and now the coach of the Golden State Warriors acknowledged he had lied to the press and public before a pivotal playoff game (**Figure 6-1**).

With Kerr's Warriors down two games to one in the championship series against the Lebron James-led Cleveland Cavaliers, Kerr lied about his plans to shake up the starting lineup, so that his opponents would be taken by surprise.

Said the coach, whose record as a player, broadcaster and general manager was impeccable up until his playoff fib, *"I could evade the question, which would start this Twitter phenomenon. Who is going to start for the Warriors? Or I could*

lie. So I lied. Sorry but I don't think they hand you the trophy based on morality. They give it you if you win."[1]

Well said, if not ethically executed.

Is it more important to get an edge in business or to tell the truth? Is winning worth lying?

Those are the kinds of questions public relations practitioners face every day. The answers to practitioners who care about their profession should be simple. The practice of public relations is all about earning *credibility*. Credibility, in turn, begins with telling the truth. Public relations, then, must be based on "doing the right thing"— in other words, acting ethically; in other other words, never lying.

The fact is that ethics should be the "great differentiator" that separates public relations professionals from other professions, like lawyers. The reality is that this is not always the case.

- In 2010, the U.S. Federal Trade Commission settled a complaint against public relations firm Reverb Communications for using employees to pose as ordinary customers to post glowing reviews of client video games on Apple's iTunes store.[2]

- In 2011, former Bill Clinton White House apologist Lanny Davis grudgingly resigned from serving as public relations representative for murderous Ivory Coast leader Laurent Gbagbo. Davis, who wrote a book about the importance of "transparency" in public relations, was the subject of withering criticism for serving as a hired gun for a Gbagbo regime that reportedly committed legendary human rights abuses.[3]

- That same year, the executive of the Los Angeles office of the giant public relations firm Fleishman-Hillard was sent to prison and the company was ordered to pay millions of dollars for overcharging the city's Department of Water and Power about $50,000 a month for three years.[4]

- In 2012, Walmart cut its ties with Mercury Public Relations after a junior staff member at the L.A. public relations firm showed up at an anti-Walmart union news conference, posing as a reporter. The union discovered the ruse and alerted the media.[5]

1 Ethical Issues Abound

In the 21st century, with scandals popping up periodically in every sector of society—from politics to religion, from business to sports—the subject of ethics is a pervasive one.

What precisely are *ethics*?

A sociologist posed that question to business people and got these answers:

- "Ethics has to do with what my feelings tell me is right or wrong."
- "Ethics has to do with my religious beliefs."
- "Being ethical is doing what the law requires."
- "Ethics consists of the standards of behavior our society accepts."
- "I don't know what the word means."

Classical ethics means different things to different people. Ethics theories range from utilitarianism (i.e., the greatest good for the greatest number) to deontology (i.e., do what is right, though the world should perish).

While the meaning of ethics may be hard to pin down, there's no secret to what constitutes unethical behavior. Unfortunately, it's all around us. Consider the following:

- In **government**, ethical lapses know no party affiliation. Washington seems perpetually rocked by ethical scandals. In 2010, longtime New York congressman Charley Rangel was convicted of a variety of ethical offenses, all stemming from his misuse of power.[6]

(The disgraced Rangel, whose career would have been doomed in any other profession, came back to win primary reelection in 2012. But hey, that's politics!) In 2011, Rangel's New York colleague Anthony Weiner resigned from the House after it was revealed he had sent provocative tweets to female followers.[7] On the Republican side, delusional Chicago Congressman Aaron Schock resigned his seat in the spring of 2015, when it was revealed he spent $40,000 to redecorate his office in the style of the popular Public Broadcasting show, "Downton Abbey" and used campaign contributions for private jet flights, concert tickets, and all forms of entertainment.[8] In the summer of 2015, former Republican Speaker of the House Dennis Hastert was accused of illegally structuring bank withdrawals to disguise payoffs to a person with whom he committed underage sexual misconduct[9] (**Figure 6-2**).

- In **business**, insider trading scandals, where Wall Street fat cats bilked unsuspecting investors out of millions, have dominated the news in recent years. Hedge fund titans Bernie Madoff, Allen Stanford, Raj Rajaratnam, and disgraced former McKinsey & Co. CEO Rajat Gupta all faced hard time after their unethical behavior was displayed before the world.

- In **sports**, several of history's most legendary baseball players, from slugging Mark McGwire to fire-balling Roger Clemens to slammin' Sammy Sosa to all-everything Alex "A-Rod" Rodriguez, were all tarnished in the wake of the

FIGURE 6-2 **Silent speaker.**
Former Speaker of the House of Representatives Dennis Hastert leaves Chicago Federal Court after denying that he violated bank regulations to provide hush money to a victim of sexual misconduct.
Photo: BRIAN KERSEY/UPI/Newscom

sport's 21st century steroids scandal. Formerly revered cyclist Lance Armstrong was disgraced when, after lying for years, he admitted that illegal doping gave him an unfair advantage.[10]

■ In **entertainment,** one of America's most cherished television "role models," comedian Bill Cosby, was accused of sexual assault by more than 40 women, who came forward by 2015. Cosby vehemently denied the allegations but lost much of his popularity. (See Case Study at the end of this chapter.)

■ In **education,** the president of Penn State University was drummed out in 2011 in the wake of the pedophilia scandal that also cost football coach Joe Paterno his job—and, some argued, his life. President Graham Spanier, whom all agreed did a superlative job in building Penn State's reputation, nonetheless was found wanting in covering up the awful Jerry Sandusky scandal.[11]

■ Similar charges of sexual abuse embroiled the venerable **Catholic Church** in ethical scandals from the beginning of the decade under Pope John Paul II and later under his successor, Pope Benedict XVI. It was left to Pope Francis to clear the air to rid the Church of the aftertaste of ethical scandal.

■ In the realm of **nonprofit organizations,** supposed to aid those less fortunate, ethical improprieties also weren't uncommon. For example, in 2012, CNN revealed that a charity designed to serve veterans with disabilities had instead squandered millions of dollars on marketing costs that benefited Disabled Veterans National Foundation's organizers.[12]

■ As noted, not even the practice of **public relations** could escape serious ethical lapses, as the Fleishman-Hillard, Walmart, Lanny Davis, and other ethical scandals revealed.

Again, public relations professionals are expected to *do the right thing*. The cardinal rule of public relations is to *never lie*.

Nonetheless, in one startling survey at the turn of the century of 1700 public relations executives, it was revealed that 25% of those interviewed admitted they had "lied on the job," 39% said they had exaggerated the truth, and another 44% said they had felt "uncertain" about the ethics of what they did.[13]

While the industry never repeated that survey (Wonder why?), the PRSA did invest $100,000 in revamping its code of ethics. The code (see Appendix A), underscored by six fundamental values that the PRSA believes vital to the integrity of the profession (**Figure 6-3**), demonstrates the significance of ethics to the practice of public relations.

Doing the Right Thing

What exactly are ethics? The answer isn't an easy one.

The Josephson Institute, which studies ethics, defines ethics as *standards of conduct that indicate how one should behave based on moral duties and virtues.*

In general, ethics are the values that guide a person, organization, or society—concepts such as right and wrong, fairness and unfairness, honesty and dishonesty. An individual's conduct is measured not only against his or her conscience but also against some norm of acceptability that society or an organization has determined.

Roughly translated, an individual's or organization's ethics comes down to the standards that are followed in relationships with others—the real integrity of the individual

PRSA Member Code of Ethics 2000

PRSA Member Statement of Professional Values

This statement presents the core values of PRSA members and, more broadly, of the public relations profession. These values provide the foundation for the Member Code of Ethics and set the industry standard for the professional practice of public relations. These values are the fundamental beliefs that guide our behaviors and decision-making process. We believe our professional values are vital to the integrity of the profession as a whole.

ADVOCACY

We serve the public interest by acting as responsible advocates for those we represent. We provide a voice in the marketplace of ideas, facts, and viewpoints to aid informed public debate.

HONESTY

We adhere to the highest standards of accuracy and truth in advancing the interests of those we represent and in communicating with the public.

EXPERTISE

We acquire and responsibly use specialized knowledge and experience. We advance the profession through continued professional development, research, and education. We build mutual understanding, credibility, and relationships among a wide array of institutions and audiences.

INDEPENDENCE

We provide objective counsel to those we represent. We are accountable for our actions.

LOYALTY

We are faithful to those we represent, while honoring our obligation to serve the public interest.

FAIRNESS

We deal fairly with clients, employers, competitors, peers, vendors, the media, and the general public. We respect all opinions and support the right of free expression.

The Public Relations Society of America, 33 Irving Place, New York, NY 10003-2376

FIGURE 6-3 **PRSA's six values.**
The values of advocacy, honesty, expertise, independence, loyalty, and fairness form the basis of the PRSA ethical code.
Copyright Public Relations Society of America. Reprinted by permission

or organization. Obviously, a person's ethical construct and approach depend on numerous factors—cultural, religious, and educational, among others. Complicating the issue is that what might seem right to one person might not matter to someone else. No issue is solely black or white but is rather a shade of gray—particularly in making public relations decisions.

That is not to say that classical ethical distinctions don't exist. They do. Philosophers throughout the ages have debated the essence of ethics.

- *Utilitarianism* suggests considering the "greater good" rather than what may be best for the individual.
- To Aristotle, the *golden mean of moral virtue* could be found between two extreme points of view.
- Kant's *categorical imperative* recommended acting "on that maxim which you will to become a universal law."
- Mill's *principle of utility* recommended "seeking the greatest happiness for the greatest number."
- The traditional *Judeo-Christian ethic* prescribes "loving your neighbor as yourself." Indeed, this golden rule makes good sense as well in the practice of public relations.

Because the practice of public relations is misunderstood by so many—even including some of those for whom public relations people work—public relations people, in particular, must be ethical. They can't assume that ethics are strictly personal choices without relevance or related methodology for resolving moral quandaries. Public relations people must adhere to a high standard of professional ethics, with truth as the key determinant of their conduct.

Indeed, ethics must be the great differentiator between public relations practice and other functions. Public relations people must always tell the truth. That doesn't mean they divulge "everything" about those for whom they work. But it does mean that they should never, ever lie. All one has in public relations is his or her reputation. When you lie, you lose it. So a high sense of ethical conduct must distinguish those who practice public relations.

Professional ethics, often called *applied ethics,* suggests a commonly accepted sense of professional conduct that is translated into formal codes of ethics.

The essence of the codes of conduct of both the PRSA and the International Association of Business Communicators is that honesty and fairness lie at the heart of public relations practice. Indeed, if the ultimate goal of the public relations professional is to enhance public trust of an organization, then only the highest ethical conduct is acceptable.

Inherent in these standards of the profession is the understanding that ethics have changed and continue to change as society changes. Over time, views have changed on such issues as discrimination, the treatment of women and minorities, pollution of the environment, concern for human rights, acceptable standards of language and dress, and so on. Again, honesty and fairness are two critical components that will continue to determine the ethical behavior of public relations professionals.

Boiled down to its essence, the ethical heart of the practice of public relations lies, again, in posing only one simple question to management: *Are we doing the right thing?* In posing that critical question, the public relations officer becomes the "conscience" of the organization.

Often the public relations professional will be the only member of management with the nerve to pose such a question. Sometimes this means saying no to what the boss wants to do. Public relations professionals must be driven by one purpose—to preserve, defend, sustain, and enhance the health and vitality of the organization. Simply translated, the bottom-line for public relations professionals must always be to counsel and to do what is in the best long-term interests of the organization.

2 Ethics in Business

For many people today, regrettably, the term *business ethics* is an oxymoron. Its mere mention stimulates images of disgraced CEOs being led away in handcuffs after bilking their shareholders and employees out of millions of dollars. In one period alone, the 2012 "summer of shame," a dizzying array of corporate executives was charged with ethical violations.

- The summer began with Irving H. Picard, the trustee overseeing the liquidation of Bernard Madoff's investment advisory firm, receiving permission to "claw back" profits from those Madoff rewarded in his Ponzi scheme that bilked investors out of some $7.3 billion—the most costly swindle in investing history.

- The Madoff number was just slightly more than high-flying Texas financier R. Allan Stanford who was convicted of swindling out of investors over a two-decade scam involving 30,000 investors in 113 countries.

- In June, the conviction of Rajat Gupta was perhaps the most shocking scandal of all. Gupta, former McKinsey CEO and a member of the board of premier investment banker Goldman Sachs, was an eminently respected business leader. But he also turned out to be a common criminal, feeding insider information to convicted hedge fund felon Raj Rajaratnam.

Gupta's conviction culminated a wave of insider trading cases that yielded 66 indictments and 60 convictions over two-and-a-half years. These followed business scandals earlier in the decade that exposed subprime lenders as crooks, banks and other financial institutions as less-than-responsible stewards of public wealth, and CEOs as suspect in terms of ethics and credibility. With venerable companies such as Bear Stearns and Lehman Brothers going out of business and other less venerable ones like Washington Mutual and Countrywide Mortgage meeting the same fate, the early part of the 21st century was not a stellar period for business credibility.

No wonder confidence in business has deteriorated. One survey by the Ethics Resource Center found that although employees seemed more ethical in their own jobs, more employees had negative views of the ethics of their supervisors. Confidence in senior leadership fell to 62% in 2011, matching the historic low of 2000 and down six points from just two years earlier. One-third of U.S. employees said their own managers "didn't exercise ethical behavior."[14]

Indeed, many believed "crooked CEO" was redundant. One book, written by former management consultants, described CEOs thusly:

Among the more than 14,000 publicly registered companies in the U.S. and the even larger number of privately held companies there is a class of people who will lie to the public, the regulators, their employees and anyone else in order to increase personal wealth and power.[15]

A Question of Ethics

Sorry for Your Loss but .... Nice Bag

In the last half of the second decade of the 21st century, celebrity sells.

The more celebrities that can be seen wearing our product, the more our sales will increase. So there's nothing unusual about a high-end fashion company promoting itself with photos of a Hollywood actress wearing its clothes or carrying one of its couture handbags. So why all the fuss in the winter of 2014 when Valentino sent the following e-mail, with photo, to the media:

"We are pleased to announce Amy Adams carrying the Valentino Garavany Rockstud Duble bag from the Spring/Summer 2014 collection on Feb. 6 in New York."

Here's why.

Adams, dressed in black and escorted by her husband, was carrying the Valentino bag to the funeral of Adams's film co-star Philip Seymour Hoffman, Oscar winner and father of three, who died of a drug overdose (**Figure 6-4**).

Almost immediately, Adams's representative quickly distanced the actress from Valentino and said she had no idea the photo would be used that way.

A chagrined Valentino also wasted little time in responding, after Web sites and tabloids pointed out the bad taste photo. Said the company:

"We sincerely regret releasing a photo to the media…of Amy Adams with a Valentino Bag. We were not aware the photograph was taken while she was attending the wake of Philip Seymour Hoffman. It was an innocent mistake and we apologise to Ms Adams who was not aware, or a part of, our PR efforts."

Questions

1. How would you assess Valentino's reaction to the publicity surrounding its promotional e-mail?

2. What might the company do to avoid a similar ethical public relations lapse in the future?

FIGURE 6-4
Bereavement bag.
Actress Amy Adams and her husband arrive at the New York City funeral of Philip Seymour Hoffman, unaware that the Valentino bag the actress carried would be at the heart of a public relations firestorm.
Photo: infusny-69/141/240/ Mauceri/MacFarlane/ INFphoto.com/Newscom

*For further information, see Luke O'Neill, "Fashion Label Uses Philip Seymour Hoffman's Wake as PR Opportunity," *Gawker* (February 9, 2014) and Matt Wilson, "Valentino Apologizes After Promoting Handbag with Photo from Celebrity Wake," *Ragan PR Daily* (February 10, 2014).

To stem the feeling that chief executives and their companies weren't acting ethically, a number of firms increased their efforts to make their activities more transparent to the public. Companies from Coca-Cola to Amazon.com to General Electric announced plans to make accounting procedures more understandable. One CEO, Henry Paulson of investment banking giant Goldman Sachs, called on his fellow CEOs, in a memorable speech, to reform before regulation forced them to do so: "In my lifetime, American business has never been under such scrutiny. To be blunt, much of it is deserved."[16] Paulson's call for business ethics helped secure his selection as Secretary of the Treasury under President George W. Bush; where later he presided over the meltdown and eventual recovery of the U.S. financial system.

Corporate Codes of Conduct

By the second decade of the 21st century, most organizations devoted an increasing amount of time and attention to corporate ethics.

The vast majority of companies conducted periodic risk assessments, with more than half doing so annually. Three-quarters of all companies conducted training in such areas as sexual/workplace harassment, conflicts of interest, and protecting confidential information. Many firms devoted upwards of $500,000 a year, exclusive of personnel costs, for ethics and compliance programs.[17]

Most organizations also adopted formal codes of conduct to guide their activities. A code of conduct is a formal statement of the values and business practices of a corporation. A code may be a short mission statement, or it may be a sophisticated document that requires compliance with articulated standards and that has a complicated enforcement mechanism. Whatever its length and complexity, the corporate code of conduct dictates the behavioral expectations that an organization holds for its employees and agents.

Formal codes of conduct can help accomplish a number of public relations purposes.

- **To increase public confidence.** Scandals, credit crises, product recalls, etc., have all shaken investor confidence and have led to a decline of public trust and confidence in business. Many firms have responded with written codes of ethics.

- **To stem the tide of regulation.** As public confidence has declined, government regulation of business has increased. Some estimated the cost to society of compliance with regulations at $100 billion per year. Corporate codes of conduct, it was hoped, would help serve as a self-regulation mechanism.

- **To improve internal operations.** As companies became larger and more decentralized, management needed consistent standards of conduct to ensure that employees were meeting the business objectives of the company in a legal and ethical manner.

- **To respond to transgressions.** Frequently, when a company itself is caught in the Web of unethical behavior, it responds with its own code of ethics.

Ralph Waldo Emerson once wrote, "An organization is the lengthened shadow of a man." Today, many corporate executives realize that just as an individual has certain responsibilities as a citizen, so, too, does a corporate citizen have responsibilities to the society in which it is privileged to operate.

3️⃣ Corporate Social Responsibility

Closely related to the ethical conduct of an organization is its corporate social responsibility (CSR). Simply stated, CSR is about how companies manage the business processes to produce an overall positive impact on society. This implies that any social institution, from the smallest family unit to the largest corporation, is responsible for the behavior of its members and may be held accountable for their misdeeds.

In the late 1960s, when this idea was just emerging, initial responses were of the knee-jerk variety. A firm that was threatened by increasing legal or activist pressures and harassment would ordinarily change its policies in a hurry. Today, however, organizations and their social responsibility programs are much more sophisticated. Social responsibility is treated just like any other management discipline: Analyze the issues, evaluate performance, set priorities, allocate resources to those priorities, and implement programs that deal with issues within the constraints of the organization's resources. Many companies have created special committees to set the agenda and target the objectives.

Social responsibility touches practically every level of organizational activity, from marketing to hiring, from training to work standards. A partial list of social responsibility categories might include the following:

- **Product lines**—dangerous products, product performance and standards, packaging, and environmental impact
- **Marketing practices**—sales practices, consumer complaint policies, advertising content, and fair pricing
- **Corporate philanthropy**—contribution performance, encouragement of employee participation in social projects, and community development activities
- **Environmental activities**—pollution control and climate change projects, adherence to federal standards, and evaluation procedures for new packages and products
- **External relations**—support of minority enterprises, investment practices, and government relations
- **Employment diversity in retaining and promoting minorities and women**—current hiring policies, advancement policies, specialized career counseling, and opportunities for special minorities such as the physically handicapped
- **Employee safety and health**—work environment policies, accident safeguards, and food and medical facilities

More often than not, organizations have incorporated social responsibility into the mainstream of their practices. Most firms recognize that social responsibility, far from being an add-on program, must be a corporate way of life. They recognize that in a skeptical world, business must be responsible to act ethically and improve the quality of life of their workforce, their families, and the broader society.

Ethics in Government

Politics has never enjoyed an unblemished reputation when it comes to ethics. In the first two decades of the 21st century—with the U.S. political system polarized between hard right and hard left—politicians seemed to be losing more ground in terms of trustworthiness and ethical values.

Both the legislative and executive branches of the federal government took a beating in the public eye. Americans' job approval rating for Congress hovered around 15% in 2014, close to the record-low yearly average of 14% in 2013. The highest yearly average was measured in 2001, at 56%. Yearly averages haven't exceeded 20% during the Obama Administration.[18]

The president generally fared better than Congress, but presidential approval still had trouble consistently piercing the 50% approval barrier.

The advent of 24-hour cable news and the 24/7 Internet blogosphere cast a perpetual 21st century spotlight on the activities of the president and his allies. No administration could escape the harsh glare of prying eyes noting ethical failures. President Bill Clinton suffered the ultimate ethical ignominy: being impeached by the House of Representatives for his inexplicable and shocking behavior with a young intern in the White House. Both President George W. Bush and Vice President Dick Cheney were criticized harshly for everything from the disposition of and reasons for war in Iraq to their past corporate energy affiliations. President Obama also was attacked by critics for everything from politicizing his declaration of a path to citizenship for children of illegal immigrants to his Justice Department's "Fast and Furious" decision to provide guns to Mexican arms traffickers.

The "sleaze factor" in government continued to poison politics.

- In 2010, former Vice President Al Gore made headlines when an Oregon masseuse accused him of assault among other sordid details; meanwhile his wife of 40 years divorced him.

- In 2011, Democrat Congressman Anthony Weiner was drummed out of the House for sexting young women pictures of his...well, never mind.

- In 2012, former Democrat senator and presidential candidate John Edwards was exonerated from charges of using campaign funds to hide a mistress and love-child, although the damage to his career was done.

- In 2013, the mayor of Toronto, Canada, Rob Ford, was reported by Gawker as having been seen on a video smoking crack cocaine. For the next several months, Ford led the media on a cat-and-mouse excursion of continuing allegations and denials, through rehab and back again (**Figure 6-5**).

- In 2014, the administration of New Jersey Gov. Chris Christie was found to have purposely created traffic jams on the George Washington Bridge to get back at a political opponent. Despite his continued claims that he "knew nothing" of the lane closures, Christie stock as a Republican national candidate descended rapidly.

- In 2015, one of New York State's most powerful politicians, Assembly Speaker Sheldon Silver, was charged with taking millions in illegal payoffs over the years. A few months later, Silver's counterpart, New York State Senate Leader Dean Skelos resigned his leadership post after being charged in a corruption scheme to help his son.

Get the picture? Whew!

After all the white-collar crime and political scandals that have marked the first two decades of the 21st century, the public is less willing to tolerate such ethical violations from their elected officials. It is likely that ethics in government will become an even more important issue as voters insist on representatives who are honest, trustworthy, and ethical.

FIGURE 6-5
Laughing stock.
Toronto Mayor Rob Ford lit up two countries with his questionable antics in 2013, as he fought off allegations of smoking crack on video.
Photo: AARON HARRIS/ REUTERS/Newscom

FYI

Test Your Workplace Ethics

So you want to enter the workplace? The question of ethics looms larger today than at any previous time, especially with the advent of technology and the potential abuses it brings.

To test how you might measure up as an ethical worker, answer the following questions. And don't cheat!

Questions

1. Is it wrong to use company e-mail for personal reasons?

2. Is it wrong to use office equipment to help your family and friends with homework?

3. Is it wrong to play computer games on office equipment during the workday?

4. Is it wrong to use office equipment to do Internet shopping?

5. Is it unethical to visit pornographic Web sites using office equipment?

6. What's the value at which a gift from a supplier or client becomes troubling?

7. Is a $50 gift to a boss unacceptable?

8. Is it okay to take a pair of $200 football tickets as a gift from a supplier?

9. Is it okay to take a $120 pair of theater tickets?

10. Is it okay to take a $100 holiday fruit basket?

11. Is it okay to take a $25 gift certificate?

12. Is it okay to accept a $75 prize won at a raffle at a supplier's conference?

Answers

From a cross-section of workers at nationwide companies, the answers to these questions were compiled by the Ethics Officer Association, Belmont, Massachusetts, and the Ethical Leadership Group, Wilmette, Illinois.

1. 34% said personal e-mail on company computers is wrong.

2. 37% said using office equipment for homework is wrong.

3. 49% said playing computer games at work is wrong.

4. 44% said Internet shopping at work is wrong.

5. 87% said it is unethical to visit pornographic sites at work.

6. 33% said $25 is the amount at which a gift from a supplier or client becomes troubling. Another 33% said $50. Another 33% said $100.

7. 35% said a $50 gift to the boss is unacceptable.

8. 70% said it is unacceptable to take $200 football tickets.

9. 70% said it is unacceptable to take $120 theater tickets.

10. 35% said it is unacceptable to take a $100 fruit basket.

11. 45% said it is unacceptable to take a $25 gift certificate.

12. 40% said it is unacceptable to take the $75 raffle prize.

Ethics in Journalism

The Society of Professional Journalists is quite explicit on the subject of ethics (**Figure 6-6**).

Journalists at all times will show respect for the dignity, privacy, rights, and well-being of people encountered in the course of gathering and presenting the news.

1. The news media should not communicate unofficial charges affecting reputation or moral character without giving the accused a chance to reply.

2. The news media must guard against invading a person's right to privacy.

3. The media should not pander to morbid curiosity about details of vice and crime.

And so on.

Unfortunately, what is in the code often doesn't reflect what appears in print or on the air. More often than not, journalistic judgments run smack into ethical principles—especially in a day when every citizen is a publisher on the Internet.

■ Plagiarism scandals at three of the nation's leading newspapers—*The New York Times, Washington Post,* and *Boston Globe*—resulted in the firings of high-profile journalists. The *Times* fell victim to the new century's most embarrassing instance of suspect journalistic ethics. In 2003, the "Great Gray Lady" was stunned when one of its promising young reporters, Jayson Blair, was discovered to have fabricated numerous dispatches for the paper over an extended period. The *Times* found out about Blair's fraud only when a reporter from another paper tipped it off. Blair was immediately fired, and the *Times* took a major reputation hit.

■ In 2005, the *Times* was shocked again after one of its star reporters, Judith Miller, served 85 days in prison for refusing to reveal confidential administration sources related to stories involving the leak of the name of a CIA operative married to a Bush administration critic. On her release, the *Times* criticized her for being too cozy with the White House. Miller hastily resigned after 28 years at the *Times* and was hired by Fox News.

■ In 2010, the *Times, Washington Post, Guardian* of London, and other major newspapers made the decision to publish a cache of a quarter million confidential diplomatic cables, purloined by WikiLeaks, an organization dedicated to revealing secret documents. Some questioned the ethics of putting diplomats and the nations they worked for at risk.[19]

■ In 2015, the anchor of the NBC Nightly News, Brian Williams, became immersed in an ethical scandal that ripped at his credibility and that of the network he represented. Williams admitted to making up facts about being attacked in a helicopter in Iraq during the war; specifically Williams' helicopter wasn't involved in any attack. NBC suspended the veteran anchor

FIGURE 6-6
Journalists' code.
The Society of Professional Journalists has elaborated in some detail on the ethical guidelines that should govern all journalists. *Copyright © 1996–2007. Reprinted by permission of the Society of Professional Journalists, www.spj.org*

Society of Professional Journalists

C⊙DE *of* ETHICS

PREAMBLE

Members of the Society of Professional Journalists believe that public enlightenment is the forerunner of justice and the foundation of democracy. Ethical journalism strives to ensure the free exchange of information that is accurate, fair and thorough. An ethical journalist acts with integrity.

The Society declares these four principles as the foundation of ethical journalism and encourages their use in its practice by all people in all media.

SEEK TRUTH AND REPORT IT

Ethical journalism should be accurate and fair. Journalists should be honest and courageous in gathering, reporting and interpreting information.

Journalists should:

▶ Take responsibility for the accuracy of their work. Verify information before releasing it. Use original sources whenever possible.

▶ Remember that neither speed nor format excuses inaccuracy.

▶ Provide context. Take special care not to misrepresent or oversimplify in promoting, previewing or summarizing a story.

▶ Gather, update and correct information throughout the life of a news story.

▶ Be cautious when making promises, but keep the promises they make.

▶ Identify sources clearly. The public is entitled to as much information as possible to judge the reliability and motivations of sources.

▶ Consider sources' motives before promising anonymity. Reserve anonymity for sources who may face danger, retribution or other harm, and have information that cannot be obtained elsewhere. Explain why anonymity was granted.

▶ Diligently seek subjects of news coverage to allow them to respond to criticism or allegations of wrongdoing.

▶ Avoid undercover or other surreptitious methods of gathering information unless traditional, open methods will not yield information vital to the public.

▶ Be vigilant and courageous about holding those with power accountable. Give voice to the voiceless.

▶ Support the open and civil exchange of views, even views they find repugnant.

▶ Recognize a special obligation to serve as watchdogs over public affairs and government. Seek to ensure that the public's business is conducted in the open, and that public records are open to all.

▶ Provide access to source material when it is relevant and appropriate.

▶ Boldly tell the story of the diversity and magnitude of the human experience. Seek sources whose voices we seldom hear.

▶ Avoid stereotyping. Journalists should examine the ways their values and experiences may shape their reporting.

▶ Label advocacy and commentary.

▶ Never deliberately distort facts or context, including visual information. Clearly label illustrations and re-enactments.

▶ Never plagiarize. Always attribute.

MINIMIZE HARM

Ethical journalism treats sources, subjects, colleagues and members of the public as human beings deserving of respect.

Journalists should:

▶ Balance the public's need for information against potential harm or discomfort. Pursuit of the news is not a license for arrogance or undue intrusiveness.

▶ Show compassion for those who may be affected by news coverage. Use heightened sensitivity when dealing with juveniles, victims of sex crimes, and sources or subjects who are inexperienced or unable to give consent. Consider cultural differences in approach and treatment.

▶ Recognize that legal access to information differs from an ethical justification to publish or broadcast.

▶ Realize that private people have a greater right to control information about themselves than public figures and others who seek power, influence or attention. Weigh the consequences of publishing or broadcasting personal information.

▶ Avoid pandering to lurid curiosity, even if others do.

▶ Balance a suspect's right to a fair trial with the public's right to know. Consider the implications of identifying criminal suspects before they face legal charges.

▶ Consider the long-term implications of the extended reach and permanence of publication. Provide updated and more complete information as appropriate.

ACT INDEPENDENTLY

The highest and primary obligation of ethical journalism is to serve the public.

Journalists should:

▶ Avoid conflicts of interest, real or perceived. Disclose unavoidable conflicts.

▶ Refuse gifts, favors, fees, free travel and special treatment, and avoid political and other outside activities that may compromise integrity or impartiality, or may damage credibility.

▶ Be wary of sources offering information for favors or money; do not pay for access to news. Identify content provided by outside sources, whether paid or not.

▶ Deny favored treatment to advertisers, donors or any other special interests, and resist internal and external pressure to influence coverage.

▶ Distinguish news from advertising and shun hybrids that blur the lines between the two. Prominently label sponsored content.

BE ACCOUNTABLE AND TRANSPARENT

Ethical journalism means taking responsibility for one's work and explaining one's decisions to the public.

Journalists should:

▶ Explain ethical choices and processes to audiences. Encourage a civil dialogue with the public about journalistic practices, coverage and news content.

▶ Respond quickly to questions about accuracy, clarity and fairness.

▶ Acknowledge mistakes and correct them promptly and prominently. Explain corrections and clarifications carefully and clearly.

▶ Expose unethical conduct in journalism, including within their organizations.

▶ Abide by the same high standards they expect of others.

The SPJ Code of Ethics is a statement of abiding principles supported by additional explanations and position papers (at spj.org) that address changing journalistic practices. It is not a set of rules, rather a guide that encourages all who engage in journalism to take responsibility for the information they provide, regardless of medium. The code should be read as a whole; individual principles should not be taken out of context. It is not, nor can it be under the First Amendment, legally enforceable.

after other exaggerated stories came to light, and its nightly news broadcast lost 700,000 viewers in the wake of the scandal.[20]

■ And then, of course, there were the screamers. Cable television news, in particular, was rocked by the phenomenon in the 21st century of "nonstop screaming," where adversaries on either side spent most of their air time declaring a "my way or the highway" point of view. Partisanship was the order of the day. Such popular programs as Fox News Channel's *The O'Reilly Factor with Bill O'Reilly*, MSNBC's *Hardball with Chris Matthews*, and *CNN Headline News' with Nancy Grace*, all distinguished by their voluble hosts, added plenty of heat but little light to the national dialogue. Indeed, by 2012, CNN, the one cable network that tried to remain neutral, had lost so miserably in the ratings wars that it brought in NBC veteran Jeff Zucker to become its new president. Zucker immediately vowed to "broaden the definition of what news is."[21]

A 2014 Gallup poll revealed that while 24% of Americans rated journalists "high or very high" in terms of "Honesty/Ethics," a larger 30% rated them "low or very low," ahead of bankers and lawyers.[22] Such was the challenging state of journalistic ethics in the last half of the first decade of the 21st century.

4 Ethics in Public Relations

Ethics is—or at least, should be—the great differentiator between public relations and other professions. In light of numerous misconceptions about the practice of public relations, it is imperative that practitioners emulate the highest standards of personal and professional ethics (**Figure 6-7**). Within an organization, public relations practitioners must be the standard bearers of corporate ethical initiatives. By the same token,

---

Council of PR Firms Code of Ethics

Members of the Council commit to standards of practice that assure clients, the public and media, employees, and business partners and vendors the highest level of professionalism and ethical conduct in every relationship with a Council member. This commitment is a requirement for application and continued membership in the Council.

Member firms will serve their **clients** by applying their fullest capability to achieve each client's business objectives, and charging a fair price for that service. Members and their employees will be honest and accurate when recording time charges and seeking reimbursement of expenses, and member firms will not solicit or accept kickbacks or under-the-table payments in connection with business development efforts. Members will avoid representing any conflicting client interests without the expressed approval of those concerned. Council firms and their employees will respect client confidences and the privacy of client employees, and will refrain from directly soliciting client employees with whom they are engaged in ongoing projects.

In communicating with the **public** and **media**, member firms will maintain total accuracy and truthfulness. To preserve both the reality and perception of professional integrity, information that is found to be misleading or erroneous will be promptly corrected and the sources of communications and sponsors of activities will not be concealed.

Council members will respect the personal rights of their **employees** and former employees. They will provide employees the necessary tools to serve their clients and opportunities to develop their professional skills. They will safeguard the privacy and handle with respect the professional reputation of current and former employees. Members will adopt policies that assure equal opportunity for all job candidates without regard to race, color, religion, national origin, sex, sexual orientation, age, veteran status, disability or any other basis prohibited by applicable federal, state or local law.

Commercial relationships with business **partners** and **vendors** will be handled in a businesslike manner, and credit will be given for ideas and services provided by others.

FIGURE 6-7 **Doing the right thing.**
The Council of Public Relations Firms board of directors revised its Code of Ethics in 2009 to exhort members to commit to the highest level of ethics.
Courtesy Council of Public Relations Firms

public relations consultants must always counsel their clients in an ethical direction—toward accuracy and candor and away from lying and hiding the truth.

The public relations department should be the seat of corporate ethics. At least four ethical theories are relevant to the practice of public relations.

- The *attorney/adversary model*, developed by Jay Barney and Ralph Black, compares the legal profession to that of public relations in that (1) both are advocates in an adversarial climate and (2) both assume counterbalancing messages will be provided by adversaries. In this model, Barney and Black suggest practitioners have no obligation to consider the public interest or any other outside view beyond that of their client.

- The *two-way communication model*, developed by Jim Grunig, is based on collaboration, working jointly with different people, and allowing for both listening and give-and-take. In this model, Grunig suggests that the practitioner balances his or her role as a client advocate with one as social conscience for the larger public.

- The *enlightened self-interest model*, developed by Sherry Baker, is based on the principle that businesses do well by doing good. In this model, Baker suggests that companies gain a competitive edge and are more respected in the marketplace if they behave ethically.

- The *responsible advocacy model*, developed by Kathy Fitzpatrick and Candace Gauthier, is based on the ideal of professional responsibility. It postulates that practitioners' first loyalty is to their clients, but they also have a responsibility to voice the opinions of organizational stakeholders. In this model, Fitzpatrick and Gauthier suggest that the practitioner's greatest need for ethical guidance is in the reconciliation of being both a professional advocate and a social conscience.

The PRSA has been a leader in the effort to foster a strong sense of professionalism among its membership, particularly in its new code of ethics. Its six core values underpin the desired behavior of any public relations professional.

- **Advocacy.** The PRSA Code (see Appendix A) endorses the Fitzpatrick and Gauthier model in stating: "We serve the public interest by acting as responsible advocates for those we represent." For example, public relations professionals must never reveal confidential or private client information, even if a journalist demands it. The only way such information might be revealed is after a thorough discussion with the client.

- **Honesty.** For example, a client asking a public relations representative to "embellish" the performance the company expects to achieve should be told diplomatically, but firmly, no. Public relations people don't lie.

- **Expertise.** For example, a client in need of guidance as to whether to accept a sensitive interview invitation for a cable TV talk show must be carefully guided through the pros and cons by a skilled public relations practitioner.

- **Independence.** For example, when everyone in the room—lawyer, human resources, treasurer, and president—agree with the CEO's rock-headed scheme to disguise bad news, it is the public relations professional's duty to strike an independent tone.

- **Loyalty.** For example, if a competing client offers a practitioner more money to abandon his or her original employer, the public relations professional should understand that his or her loyalties must remain constant.

■ **Fairness.** For example, when a rude and obnoxious journalist demands information, a practitioner's responsibility is to treat even the most obnoxious reporter with fairness.

What these tenets indicate is that proper public relations practice is just the opposite of what many accuse public relations people of being—deceivers, obfuscators, con artists, spinners, or even liars. Rather, public relations people and practice ought to be "transparent."[23]

Sadly, the practice hasn't always lived up to these ethical principles. As a consequence, the field, even more sadly, regularly ranks toward the bottom on credibility surveys. One 2014 Texas Tech study found that while 91% of those surveyed considered public relations professionals to be "smart and informed," only 11% considered them to possess positive ethical traits.[24] Changing this view to one of a more ethical and honest practice is a great challenge for public relations leaders in the 21st century.

Last Word

The scandals in government and business and journalism in the first two decades of the 21st century have placed a premium in every sector of society on acting ethically. More than half of the 3000 workers who took part in a National Business Ethics Survey said they witnessed at least one type of ethical misconduct on their job.[25] That's disgraceful. As the CEO of Eaton Corporation, the manufacturing giant, put it, "There is no truer window into a corporation's soul than its approach to ethics."[26]

The same can be said for the practice of public relations.

The success of public relations in the 21st century will depend largely on how the field responds

to the issue of ethical conduct. Public relations professionals must have credibility in order to practice. They must be respected by the various publics with which they interact. This is as true overseas as it is in the United States. To be credible and to achieve respect, public relations professionals must be ethical. It is that simple.

Stated another way, for public relations practice in general and individual public relations professionals in particular, credibility in the next few years will depend on how scrupulously they observe and apply the principles and practice of ethics in everything they do.

Discussion Starters

1. How would you define ethics?
2. How would you describe the state of ethics in business, government, and journalism?
3. How important is the ethical component of the practice of public relations?
4. Why have corporations adopted corporate codes of conduct?
5. What is corporate social responsibility?
6. What were the ethical implications of Scott McClellan's memoirs?
7. What are the pros and cons of the attorney/adversary public relations model compared to the enlightened self-interest model?
8. Is the public more tolerant or less tolerant of ethical violators today? Why?
9. What is the significance of the six ethical values that underscore the PRSA Code of Ethics?
10. What are the ethical responsibilities of a public relations professional?

Pick of the Literature

Ethics in Public Relations, 2nd Edition

Patricia J. Parsons, Philadelphia, PA: Kogan Page Ltd., 2008

Excellent overview of the various aspects of ethics in the practice of public relations, authored by a distinguished professor at Mount St. Vincent University in Halifax, Nova Scotia, Canada.

The bias of this book is that most public relations professionals conduct themselves with honesty and integrity, and that "spin" is the enemy (She's right!).

She writes that "recognizing, facing, and dealing with ethical dilemmas in everyday practice are the three most important aspects of ethics." (Again, she's right!) The book proposes an ethical framework for practitioners, beginning with history and definitions and evolving into moral relativism and situational ethics. In the process, she examines such germane aspects as ethics in media relations, whistle-blowing, ethics and client relations, ethics in decision-making, and a host of other issues.

This is truly an exhaustive summary of an imperative topic in the practice of public relations.

Case Study | Ethical Hammer Falls on Daddy Huxtable

For decades, there was no more beloved television figure than Bill Cosby.

As the star of TV's number one rated *The Cosby Show* in the 1980s, the comedian played patriarch Cliff Huxtable of an upper middle-class African American family in Brooklyn Heights. Daddy Cliff regularly counseled his five children with wise and ethical advice. And the comedian, himself, who had risen from the projects of Philadelphia to become one of the brightest entertainment stars of his era, enjoyed a reputation for ethics and honesty around the world.

And then, 30 years after his meteoric rise to stardom, Bill Cosby's ethical reputation absorbed a hammer blow that would ultimately prove fatal to his career.

Initial Disturbing Rumblings

In 2005, with Cosby continuing to enjoy popularity as a standup comedian and a prominent voice among African Americans, two women raised allegations that began to shake the Cosby empire (**Figure 6-8**).

The first came from a Temple University graduate who claimed that Cosby, whom she considered a mentor, had touched her inappropriately on several occasions. After ABC News picked up the story, Cosby said nothing but his lawyer came out swinging, dismissing the woman's accusations as "utterly preposterous" and "plainly bizarre." Eventually, Cosby reached an out-of-court settlement with his accuser.

On the heels of this controversy, another woman appeared on the NBC Today Show and claimed that Cosby had drugged and sexually assaulted her in the 1970s. Once again, the comedian's lawyer was quick to condemn the accuser, claiming the comedian didn't even know the woman.

In 2006, *People Magazine* reported that several other women, including actresses who had worked with him, had accused Bill Cosby of inappropriate sexual relationships, and that the comedian agreed to pay some of them.

Despite the mounting allegations against him, Bill Cosby continued to be an outspoken voice in the first decade of the 21st century for the need for African American parents, particularly fathers, to inculcate in their children higher standards of morality. Other African American leaders, including Barack Obama, hewed to the Cosby line of advice.

A Drip Becomes a Flood

By 2014, Bill Cosby—actor, author, philanthropist, spokesman for Jell-Oo and other wholesome products—now approaching 80 years old was in discussions with Netflix for a brand new comedy special.

And then Bill Cosby's world imploded.

In February, *Newsweek* interviewed two of the women who had charged Cosby years earlier with sexual misconduct; both described the beloved comedian as a calculating and manipulative predator. Once again, Cosby said nothing, but his publicist responded that the claim was "*a 10-year-old discredited accusation that proved to be nothing at the time and is still nothing.*"

Other media picked up the Cosby story, and more than a dozen other women came forward with tales about Cosby's alleged improprieties. Both Netflix and NBC, which had contemplated a Cosby sitcom return, announced they were shelving plans for the comedian's comeback.

FIGURE 6-8   The accused.
After decades of revered status as an ethical and honorable leader, comedian Bill Cosby saw it all come tumbling down in 2014.
Photo: BARRY GUTIERREZ/REUTERS/Newscom

For the first time, other African American comedians began to attack the legendary comic, accusing him of rape. In response, Cosby's public relations team invited social media followers to "Go Ahead. Meme Me," with a meme to a link generator on the Cosby Web site. Although the memes had to be submitted for approval, few followed the guidelines and instead posted screen shots of the comic, tweeted under the hashtag #CosbyMeme, with captions like:

■ "My two favorite things—Jell-O Pudding and Rape."

■ "More than a dozen women have accused me of rape."

■ "Had a drugged up sista about a week ago."

As the allegations continued and the parade of accusers got longer, the comedian agreed to be interviewed with his wife by Scott Simon, the gentle but savvy host of National Public Radio's (NPR) "Weekend Edition." Ostensible subject of the interview was to discuss the Cosbys' loan of African art for a Washington, D.C. exhibition. After several minutes of niceties about the art, Simon asked about the allegations of sexual misconduct. No response. After Simon asked again and received the same silent treatment from Cosby, the interviewer concluded the interview. After the broadcast Cosby's lawyer explained that his client "won't dignify these allegations with any response."

End of an Icon

After the NPR radio silence, Bill Cosby found himself hopelessly inundated by bad publicity.

Over the next several months, numerous additional accusers—upwards of 30—emerged with similar stories of how Cosby had drugged them to commit acts of sexual misconduct in the 1960s, 1970s, and 1980s. A Cosby Show employee acknowledged that he was in charge of "delivering payoffs" to keep women quiet. And Cosby's biographer took to Twitter to apologize for not including the accusations in his book. Throughout the ordeal, Cosby's lawyer condemned the "media-driven feeding frenzy" over old accusations. And few of Cosby's fellow entertainers came to his aid.

The bad news for the fallen icon continued through 2015. Gloria Allred, notorious pit bull attorney for women claiming to be victims of assault, announced she was representing a number of the accusers. A New York theater canceled two upcoming Cosby performances; the U.S. Navy stripped Cosby of his honorary chief petty officer designation; and an unknown vandal scrawled "rapist" on Cosby's star on the Hollywood Walk of Fame (**Figure 6-9**).

Through it all, Bill Cosby himself refused to address the mounting allegations. Indeed, in February 2015 when it was reported that Eddie Murphy refused to play Cosby in a sketch for the 40th anniversary of Saturday Night Live, Cosby responded simply, "I am very appreciative of Eddie, and I applaud his actions." And three months later, when Cosby sat down for an interview on ABC's Good Morning America, he once again refused to confront directly the growing list of abuse charges that had scuttled his once-impeccable reputation.*

Questions

1. How would you assess the Cosby public relations strategy of allowing lawyers and others to answer charges?

2. What would you have advised the comedian upon receiving the invitation to appear on NPR?

3. What public relations advice would you have given Bill Cosby do deal with the allegations?

FIGURE 6-9   The accusers.
Pit bull attorney Gloria Allred holds press conference court in 2015, introducing two more accusers that claimed Bill Cosby sexually assaulted them.
Photo: DARREN ORNITZ/ REUTERS/Newscom

*For further information, see Matt Giles and Nate Jones, "A Timeline of the Abuse Charges Against Bill Cosby," *Vulture* (March 3, 2015); Jessica Goodman, "Bill Cosby Responds to Rape Allegations in GMA Interview with Near Gibberish," *Huffington Post* (May 15, 2015); and Scott Neuman, "In NPR Interview, Bill Cosby Declines to Discuss Assault Allegations," *NPR The Two-Way* (November 15, 2014).

From the Top

An Interview with Howard J. Rubenstein

Howard J. Rubenstein, president of Rubenstein Associates since founding the firm in 1954, is one of the world's most well-known and respected public relations counselors, advising some of the world's most influential corporations, organizations, and opinion leaders. In addition to managing the day-to-day activities of his firm, Rubenstein is involved in numerous civic and philanthropic organizations. A Phi Beta Kappa graduate of the University of Pennsylvania, he finished first in his class in the night school division of St. John's University School of Law, which subsequently awarded him an honorary Doctor of Law degree. As an attorney, he served as assistant counsel to the House of Representatives Judiciary Committee.

How would you define the practice of public relations?
Public relations is the art of conveying an idea or message to a wide variety of publics utilizing multiple forms of communications. It can be broadly applied and used to advance the interests of businesses, governments, and society in general. It can achieve objectives as narrow as promoting a product or as broad as creating a movement. The communications themselves can be targeted to the general public or to very select groups of individuals, conveyed via media or person to person. The tools employed encompass a wide array, from press releases, news conferences, special events, speaking engagements, webinars, blogs, and grassroots organizations down to a single conversation with one influential person.

How important is communications for organizations in today's society?
Communications in its many forms creates and projects messages with the power to affect great change and achieve tremendous success, while a breakdown in communications can lead to dismal failure. Clearly, communications is critical

for organizations as they seek public acceptance, support, and understanding of their activities. Communication today is a major focus for presidents, prime ministers, and legislators, as well as religious leaders, as they try to shape the directions of entire societies and world events.

What are the key attributes that distinguish the best public relations professionals?

Ethics, intelligence, and willingness to put in the time and hard work are core characteristics. Good PR professionals should have the ability to write well and speak effectively. The final attribute is creativity and imagination, combined with an understanding of reality and practicality. Professionals in the field should be able to stretch the envelope as far as technique and methodology go, without forgetting what they are trying to achieve.

What is the key to interesting a journalist in a client's story?

There are many keys to piquing media interest. First, however, you must know the media outlet and understand what a news story is and what a reporter wants to see as the components of a story. You must target and reach out selectively, rather than just send out releases. Then, once you know where to go, find the human-interest angle, keep the pitch succinct, and offer what the reporter needs to cover the story. Forget the term *spinmeister.* Offer a story that is accurate, do it in an honorable and forthright way, and help the reporter do his or her job well. Above all, don't waste reporter's time with something that isn't right for the publication or the beat the reporter covers. And don't be nasty if your idea is rejected. You'll likely want to approach that reporter again some day. Instead take that rejection as a sign that you need to refine the pitch or find a better fit for it.

What inspired you, personally, to go into public relations?

I was inspired to enter public relations by my father, who was a crime reporter with the *New York Herald Tribune.* From his perspective as a journalist, he believed that PR had the untapped potential to be a great career. Not only did he get me my first account, he explained to me the importance of ethics, honesty, and integrity in dealing with the press, conducting business, and communicating with the public. He taught me the importance of good writing, finding the news value in a story, and working hard to achieve coverage in the media. He was very supportive when I began my company with that single account at my new office, which was also known as *my mother's kitchen table!* He encouraged me and always believed that public relations had a bright future. I remember him saying that public relations as a field was malleable, like clay, and could be formed to fit any idea that I had. As a result, I started out believing that if I was honest, thoughtful, and hard working, I could be successful, earn a living, and establish a good reputation in what was then a barely recognized field. That's what happened, so I guess my father was right.

What are the greatest challenges facing the practice of public relations?

In every aspect of society, leaders seek public relations counsel. Because media scrutiny is so intense today, it takes a professional to understand and advise society's leaders as to how best to respond and engage. As a result, PR people today are professionals with as much credibility and weight as lawyers, accountants, bankers, architects, or engineers. We alone offer the ability to design communications programs, judge their potential, and execute them to achieve results. That guarantees for PR professionals tremendous opportunity and a seat at the table at the highest levels.

Yet for all that progress in the evolution of the profession, there are still too many people, especially in the general public, who hold public relations in low esteem. PR professionals are still viewed in many quarters as snake-oil salesmen, ready to stoop to conquer or employ deceptive tactics. The great challenge today is changing that perception and winning for the profession the respect that it deserves. The way to meet that challenge as an industry is through superb professional performance and continued adherence to the highest ethical and business standards.

Public Relations Bookshelf

Black, Jay and Chris Roberts. *Doing Ethics in Media.* New York: Routledge, 2011. A discussion of the ethics that people in communication—journalism, public relations, advertising, marketing—ought to emulate.

Fitzpatrick, Kathy and Carolyn Bronstein (Eds.). *Ethics in Public Relations: Responsible Advocacy.* Thousand Oaks, CA: Sage Publications, Inc., 2006. A book all about "responsible advocacy," representing clients and organizations.

Frederickson, George H. and Richard K. Ghere (Eds.). *Ethics in Public Management.* New York, NY: Routledge, 2013. Interesting perspective on managing the public trust.

Lipschultz, Jeremy H. *Social Media Communication.* New York, NY: Routledge, 2015. Excellent section on the ethics of social media, including theories, trust and transparency.

McClellan, Scott. *What Happened.* New York: Public Affairs, 2008. The prodigal son of the George W. Bush White House gives his side of the events that led him to turn on his former employer with this tell-all memoir.

O'Leary, Rosemary. *The Ethics of Dissent.* Washington, DC: CQ Press, 2006. A lively treatise, focusing on ethical issues, problems, and downright abominations in government.

Stauber, John and Sheldon Rampton. *Trust Us, We're Experts.* New York: Penguin Putnam, 2001. An oldie but a goodie. The anti–public relations authors of *Toxic Sludge Is Good for You* are at it again. This time they explain—from their unique perspective—how "corporations and public relations firms have seized upon remarkable new ways of exploiting your trust to get you to buy what they have to sell." Strap yourself in.

Endnotes

1. Steve Popper, "Truth Be Told, Not by Kerr," *The Record* (June 14, 2015).
2. Grant Gross, "FTC Settles Complaint About Fake Video Game Testimonials," *IDG News Service* (August 26, 2010).
3. Justin Elliott, "The Lobbyist and the Despot," *Salon* (December 22, 2010).
4. Kevin Roderick, "Former LA PR Exec Dowie Must Begin Prison Term," *Associated Press* (January 7, 2011).
5. Alice Hines, "Stephanie Hartnett, Member of PR Team Hired by Walmart, Fired for Posing as Reporter," *The Huffington Post* (June 14, 2012).
6. Andy Newman, "Rangel's Ethics Violations," *The New York Times* (November 16, 2010).
7. Raymond Hernandez, "Weiner Resigns in Chaotic Final Scene," *The New York Times* (June 16, 2011).
8. Dana Bash, Jeff Zeleny, and Alexandra Jaffe, "Aaron Schock Resigns Amid Scandal," *CNN Politics* (March 18, 2015).
9. Monica Davey, Julie Bosman, and Mitch Smith, "Denis Hastert Pleads Not Guilty in Federal Case Targeting Bank Withdrawals," *The New York Times* (June 9, 2015).
10. Jim Vertuno, "Lance Armstrong Doping Charges: USADA Makes New Allegations," *The Huffington Post* (June 13, 2012).
11. Andrew McGill, "Penn State President Graham Spanier Resigns in Wake of Scandal," *The Morning Call* (November 10, 2011).
12. "Charity Fraud: Disabled Veterans National Foundation Squanders Millions on Marketing Services," *The Huffington Post* (May 8, 2012).
13. "In Public Relations, 25% Admit Lying," *The New York Times* (May 8, 2000): C20.
14. "2011 National Business Ethics Survey," Ethics Resource Center, 2011.
15. A. Larry Elliott and Richard J. Schroth, *How Companies Lie: Why Enron Is Just the Tip of the Iceberg* (New York: Crown Publishers, 2002).
16. Henry M. Paulson, Address to the National Press Club, Washington, DC (June 5, 2002).
17. CSR, "Ethics and the Board of Directors," *Ethisphere* Q3 (2007): 8.
18. Rebecca Riffkin, "2014 U.S. Approval of Congress Remains Near All-Time Low," *Gallup* (December 15, 2014).
19. Scott Shane and Andrew W. Lehren, "Leaked Cables Offer Raw Look at U.S. Diplomacy," *The New York Times* (November 28, 2010).
20. Michael Storr, "'NBC Nightly News' Loses 700K Viewers After Brian Williams Scandal," *The New York Post* (February 18, 2015).
21. Dylan Byers and Mackenzie Weinger, "Jeff Zucker's CNN: Fast Changes and New Hires," *Politico* (January 29, 2013).
22. "Honesty/Ethics in Professions," *Gallup Poll* (December 2014).
23. Fraser Seitel, "Public Relations Ethics," *O'Dwyer's PR Report* (April 2007): 36.
24. "Texas Tech Professors Tackle Public Relations Perception Through Study," *Texas Tech University* (October 27, 2014).
25. Teresa M. McAleavy, "Survey: Ethics Abuses on Rise," *The Record* (October 13, 2005): B1.
26. James P. Thompson, "Enforcing the Code of Conduct," *NYSE Magazine* (January 2006): 23.

Chapter 7

The Law

FIGURE 7-1   Not so fast, General.
The smiles on the faces of General Mills' top executives turned to frowns in 2014, when an overzealous privacy policy landed the Cheerios maker in hot milk, uh, water.
Photo: NYSE EURONEXT/PR NEWSWIRE/Newscom

Chapter Objectives

1. To discuss the relationship between public relations professionals and lawyers and the importance to public relations practitioners of understanding the law.

2. To explore, in particular, the First Amendment, from which free speech emerges.

3. To discuss the various areas of the law relevant to public relations professionals, including defamation, disclosure, insider trading, copyright, and Internet law.

4. To underscore the new importance in the 21st century of litigation public relations.

Food giant General Mills, famous for Cheerios, Trix, and assorted other delicacies, was sent scrambling in the spring of 2014 when its updated "customer privacy policy" was reported in *The New York Times* (**Figure 7-1**).

As the *Times* told it, the new policy would prohibit consumers who engaged with the brand in any way—downloading coupons, linking to or "liking" any General Mills product, entering company-sponsored contests, etc.—from suing the company. The *Times* reported that the company's legal terms "require all disputes related to the purchase or use of any General Mills product or service to be resolved through binding arbitration."

Predictably, the company's attempt to avoid lawsuits drew immediate pushback on social media, where it was branded "overly legalistic and insensitive." A red-faced General Mills quickly pushed back against the pushback by clarifying, *"No one is precluded from suing us merely by purchasing our products at the store or liking one of our brand Facebook pages."*[1]

The General Mills dust storm illustrated the ever-contentious relationship that exists between the dueling disciplines of law and public relations.

Indeed, there has always been a natural tension between public relations practitioners and lawyers. Ideally, public relations counselors and lawyers should work together to achieve a client's desired outcomes. And this is often the case. But there is also a fundamental difference in legal versus public relations advice.

- Lawyers correctly advise clients on what they *must* do, within the letter of legal requirements, to defend themselves in a court of law.

- Public relations advisors counsel clients on not what they *must* do but what they *should* do to defend themselves in a different court—the court of public opinion.

There is a vast difference between the two.

In recent years, however, lawyers have moved increasingly to pursue the publicity turf traditionally manned by public relations professionals. Some lawyers have become ubiquitous—on radio and television and in the middle of press conferences—in using public relations techniques to further their clients' and their own ends.

In many ways, it makes sense that lawyers and public relations people should work in concert. Public relations and the law both begin with the First Amendment to the Constitution that guarantees freedom of speech in our society.

But in the 21st century, ensuring freedom of speech is not as easy as it sounds. One question, that was underscored by the leaked classified documents of U.S. security consultant Edward Snowden in 2013 (see this chapter's A Question of Ethics), is, *Where does one's freedom start and another's end?* Another question is, *How much freedom of speech is appropriate—or advisable—in any given situation?* And yet another question is, *How does the freedom of the Internet impact on communications rights and responsibilities?*

Such are the dilemmas in the relationship between public relations principles and legal advice.

1 An Uneasy Alliance

While public relations professionals and lawyers have worked more closely in recent years, the legal and public relations professions have historically shared an uneasy alliance. Public relations practitioners must always understand the legal implications of any issue with which they become involved, and a firm's legal position must always be the first consideration.

From a legal point of view, normally the less an organization says prior to its day in court, the better. That way, the opposition can't gain any new ammunition that will become part of the public record. A lawyer, the saying goes, tells you to say two things: *"Say nothing, and say it slowly!"*

From a public relations standpoint, though, it may make sense to go public early on, especially if the organization's integrity or credibility is being called into public question. In the summer of 2003, for example, when NBA star Kobe Bryant was accused of raping a woman at a Colorado hotel, on the advice of his lawyers and public relations counsel Bryant immediately held a press conference, with his wife at his side, to acknowledge he had erred but denied the charges. A year later, the sexual assault charge was dismissed, and, Kobe Bryant, his credibility restored, returned to the NBA to lead his Los Angeles Lakers to the NBA championship in 2009 and to continue playing through the 2015 season. By contrast, domestic icon Martha Stewart listened to her lawyers' exhortation to remain silent when charged with lying to federal prosecutors in 2004, and she wound up in the slammer.

The point is that legal advice and public relations advice may indeed be different. In an organization, a smart manager will carefully weigh both legal and public relations counsel before making a decision.

It also should be noted that law and ethics are interrelated. The Public Relations Society of America's Code of Professional Standards (see Appendix A) notes that many activities that are unethical are also illegal. However, there are instances in which something is perfectly legal but unethical and other instances in which things might be illegal but otherwise ethical. Thus, when a public relations professional reflects on what course to take in a particular situation, he or she must analyze not only the legal ramifications but also the ethical considerations.[2]

This chapter examines the relationship between the law and public relations and the more prominent role the law plays in public relations practice and vice versa. The discussion introduces the legal concerns of public relations professionals today: First Amendment considerations, insider trading, disclosure law, ethics law, privacy law, copyright law, and the laws concerning censorship of the Internet— issues that have become primary concerns for public relations practitioners in the 21st century.

② The First Amendment

Any discussion of law and public relations should start with the First Amendment, which states: "Congress shall make no law...abridging the freedom of speech or the press." The First Amendment is the cornerstone of free speech in our society: This is what distinguishes democratic nations from many others.

Recent years have seen a blizzard of problems and challenges regarding the First Amendment.

- In 2010, WikiLeaks, an international online organization that billed itself as a "publisher of private, secret and classified media from anonymous news sources, leaks and whistleblowers," shocked the diplomatic world by collaborating with international newspapers to publish secret U.S. State Department diplomatic cables. WikiLeaks' strange founder, an Australian computer programmer/hacker named Julian Assange, defiantly defended the "public's right to know."[3]

- In 2015, after publishing scatological cartoons of the Prophet Muhammad, the satirical French weekly newspaper, Charlie Hebdo, was attacked by Islamist terrorists, who killed 11 staff members and later a French police officer. As offensive as the cartoons were, most democratic nations considered them examples of "freedom of expression." World leaders flocked to Paris to join a crowd of two million, who marched in solidarity with Charlie Hebdo's right to publish such material (**Figure 7-2**).

- That same year, veteran New York Times national security reporter James Risen was subpoenaed by the U.S. Central Intelligence Agency (CIA) to reveal the sources he used to report on a failed secret CIA sabotage operation on Iran's nuclear program. Demanding such disclosures by a reporter may be technically legal, but it flies in the face of journalistic First Amendment concerns. Risen refused to reveal his sources and vowed he'd go to jail first. In the end, U.S. Attorney General Eric Holder backed down and decided not to prosecute

FIGURE 7-2
Je suis Charlie.
In January 2015, 40 world leaders joined two million marchers in Paris to show solidarity with the staff of satirical magazine Charlie Hebdo, 11 of whom were killed by terrorists outraged over the publication's cartoons of the Prophet Mohammed.
Photo: Jean-Bernard Vernier/JBV News/Polaris/ Newscom

the journalist.[4] Nonetheless, a CIA officer believed to be Risen's source was found guilty of leaking classified government information and sentenced to 42 months in prison.[5]

As these cases suggest, interpreting the First Amendment, especially in the Internet age, is no simple matter. One person's definition of obscenity or divulging state secrets or blaspheming may be someone else's definition of art or freedom of expression. Because the First Amendment lies at the heart of the communications business, defending it is a front-line responsibility of the public relations profession.

3 Defamation Law

The laws that govern a person's privacy have significant implications for journalists and other communicators, such as public relations professionals, particularly laws that touch on libel and slander—commonly known as defamation laws—by the media.

Defamation is the umbrella term used to describe libel—a printed falsehood—and slander—an oral falsehood. For defamation to be proved, a plaintiff must convince the court that certain requirements have been met, including the following:

1. The falsehood was communicated through print, broadcast, or other electronic means.

2. The person who is the subject of the falsehood was identified or easily identifiable.

3. The identified person has suffered injury—in the form of monetary losses, reputational loss, or mental suffering.[6]

Generally, the privacy of an ordinary citizen is protected under the law. A citizen in the limelight, however, has a more difficult problem, especially in proving defamation of character through libel or slander.

A Question of Ethics

Whistleblower or Traitor?

The case of Edward Snowden, former CIA employee and government security contractor, who leaked classified information from the National Security Agency (NSA) in 2013 and then fled to Russia to escape spy charges, is one of the most perplexing First Amendment-tinged cases in history **(Figure 7-3)**.

Snowden mysteriously left his national security consulting assignment in Hawaii, flew to Hong Kong and proceeded to work in secret with three journalists to expose thousands of pages of confidential NSA data, including the revelation that the NSA had been surreptitiously making records of nearly every phone call in the United States and monitoring the private activities of ordinary citizens who had done nothing illegal.

The Snowden leaks, released in leading newspapers sent shock waves around the world when it was leaked that the U.S. monitored private calls of some 35 world leaders, including allies like German Chancellor Angela Merkle. The U.S. government immediately branded Snowden a "traitor" and sought his return to face espionage charges. U.S. politicians branded Snowden an "anti-American" and condemned his disclosure actions. Snowden, on-the-run and seeking asylum from U.S. prosecution, was accepted for temporary residence in Russia.

By 2015, attitudes toward the First Amendment fugitive had begun to change.

For one thing, the NSA's call-tracking program was declared unlawful by the courts and disowned by the U.S. Congress that had agreed to it. After a White House-appointed oversight board declared that the program hadn't realized its objective to short-circuit terrorism, President Obama ordered it terminated. Other countries ruled similarly with respect to surveillance activities.

A film about Snowden, his exodus and beliefs, called *Citizenfour,* was critically acclaimed and won an Oscar as the best documentary film of 2015.

With Snowden still a fugitive from U.S. justice, ensconced in an unknown location in Russia, a growing number began to think of the former security consultant as a hero and whistleblower, who sacrificed his own freedom to expose privacy violations by U.S. intelligence agencies. Others continued to

FIGURE 7-3 **Fugitive speaks.**
Edward Snowden appears live from Russia at student-organized world affairs conference in Toronto in 2015.
Photo: MARK BLINCH/REUTERS/Newscom

believe him to be a traitor, whose actions put in jeopardy the very people on whom freedom-loving Americans depend for their security.*

Question

1. Was Edward Snowden a hero or a villain? Why or why not?

*For further information, see "NSA Monitored Phone Calls of 35 World Leaders: Report," *Reuters* (October 24, 2013); Edward J. Snowden, "Edward Snowden: The World Says No to Surveillance," *The New York Times* (June 4, 2015); and Jonathan Turley, "Edward Snowden: Whistleblower or Traitor," *Al Jazeerah* (June 9, 2014).

To prove such a charge, a public figure must show that the media acted with actual malice in their reporting. *Actual malice* in a public figure slander case means that statements have been published with the knowledge that they were false or with reckless disregard for whether the statements were false. In a landmark case in 1964, *The New York Times* v. *Sullivan,* the Supreme Court nullified a libel award of $500,000 to an Alabama police official, holding that no damages could be awarded "in actions brought by public officials against critics of their official conduct" unless there was proof of actual malice. And proving actual malice is a difficult task.

Several historic libel cases have helped pave the case law precedent.

■ In a celebrated case in 1986, Israeli General Ariel Sharon brought a $50 million libel suit against *Time* magazine. The jury criticized *Time* for negligent journalism in reporting Sharon's role in a massacre in a Palestinian refugee camp. However, the jury couldn't conclude *Time* acted with "malice" and didn't render a libel verdict. Sharon got nothing.

■ In 1992, *The Wall Street Journal* and its award-winning reporter Bryan Burrough were served with a $50 million libel suit by Harry L. Freeman, a former communications executive of American Express. The suit stemmed from the way Freeman was characterized in Burrough's book, *Vendetta: American Express and the Smearing of Edmund Safra.*[7]

■ In 1996, Atlanta security guard Richard A. Jewell sued both *NBC News* and the *Atlanta Journal-Constitution* for reporting that he was the lead suspect in the Atlanta Olympic bombing, which led to two deaths. The reports caused a media feeding frenzy, which disrupted Jewell's life and tarnished his name. A decade later, Jewell was cleared of any involvement in the bombing and reached a settlement with his media accusers, averting a libel lawsuit.

The 21st century proliferation of blogs, tweets, Facebook posts, and cable and radio talk shows, where hosts and guests say what they want regardless of factual accuracy or impact on a person's life, has resulted in the definition of "defamation" becoming more complex and more global.

■ In 2008, when he was accused by his former trainer of taking steroids, baseball pitcher Roger Clemens sued for defamation. In 2012, Clemens was hauled into U.S. federal court and was exonerated. When a businessman sued for defamation against actor Sacha Baron Cohen for chasing him down Fifth Avenue in a movie in which Cohen's alter ego, "Borat," pretended to be a documentary producer, a judge tossed out the case on the grounds that the movie, "while vulgar," was an attempt at ironic commentary.[8]

■ In 2011, punk rocker and actress Courtney Love agreed to pay $430,000 to a fashion designer who claimed that the Hole lead singer had defamed her by posting multiple remarks on Twitter that the designer was a "drug-pushing prostitute with a history of assault and battery."[9] Ouch!

■ In 2014, former pro wrestler and Minnesota governor Jesse Ventura, successfully sued author and former Navy SEAL Chris Kyle for defamation. A jury found that Kyle, in his book *American Sniper*, had lied about confronting Ventura in a bar after he made unflattering remarks about the SEALS. The jury found Kyle guilty of "defamation," and Ventura was awarded $1.8 million.[10] Kyle was shot to death by a deranged former soldier in 2015, and the movie of his book became one of history's most successful films **(Figure 7-4)**.

Public relations practitioners must be aware of situations involving libel and slander. Many public relations professionals create, write, and edit internal print and online newsletters. In this context, they must be careful not to defame fellow employees or others in what they write. The same caution should be the rule for public relations professionals who make statements to the media on behalf of their organizations. Care must be the watchword in such public speech.

Insider Trading Law

Every public relations professional should know the laws that govern his or her organization and industry.

With 150 million Americans participating in the securities markets, either directly or through private pension plans, nowhere in public relations practice is an understanding of the law more important than in the area of securities law.

Every public company has an obligation to deal frankly, comprehensively, and immediately with any information that is considered *material*. A material announcement is one that might cause an investor to buy, hold, or sell a stock. The Securities and Exchange Commission (SEC)—through a series of court cases, consent decrees, complaints, and comments over the years—has painted a general portrait of disclosure requirements for practitioners, with which all practitioners in public companies should be familiar. The SEC's mandate stems from the Securities Act of 1933 and the Securities Exchange Act of 1934, which attempted to protect the public from abuses in the issuance and sale of securities.

The SEC's overriding concern is that all investors have an opportunity to learn about material information as promptly as possible. Basically, a company is expected to release news that may affect its stock market price as quickly as possible. Through its general antifraud statute, Rule 10b-5 of the Securities and Exchange Act, the SEC strictly prohibits the dissemination of false or misleading information to investors.

It also prohibits insider trading of securities on the basis of material information not disclosed to the public.

In the first years of the 21st century, one celebrated insider trading case involved ImClone Systems' CEO Sam Waksal, who, along with family members, unloaded ImClone stock after he learned that the Food and Drug Administration was about to reject a key ImClone drug. The stock was subsequently crushed, as was CEO Waksal, his family, his stockbroker, and his good friend media star Martha Stewart all embroiled in an insider trading scandal. Stewart eventually went to jail for events surrounding the insider trading case.[11]

In 2011, billionaire hedge fund manager Raj Rajaratnam was sentenced to 11 years in jail and fined more than $150 million for using insider tips to buy stocks. One of those from whom he allegedly received tips was Rajat Gupta, a former McKinsey and Company CEO, Goldman Sachs director and White House state dinner guest, who was convicted of insider trading charges in 2012. In 2013, the giant hedge fund SAC Capital and its high profile founder Steven A. Cohen paid $1.2 billion to settle a federal insider trading suit and agreed to stop handling other people's money.[12]

Nor did journalists escape the accusation of insider trading convictions. In the late 1990s, a columnist at *The Wall Street Journal* was convicted of illegally using his newspaper column to give favorable opinions about companies in which a couple of his stockbroker friends had already invested heavily. He went to jail.

As to public relations counselors, they, too, must be careful to act only on public information when trading securities. Public relations people are privy to all manner of confidential information. When they violate that confidentiality, they risk not only losing clients but also violating the law. In 2008, for example, the public relations firm Brunswick suspended its Dow Chemical account executive when her husband traded on confidential news that Dow was considering an acquisition. Dow Chemical promptly dropped its relationship with Brunswick.[13] In 2014, an investor relations executive was sentenced to two years in jail for taking positions in stocks mentioned in press release drafts being prepared for his firm's clients and then exiting the positions right after the release was made public.[14]

Disclosure Law

Besides cracking down on insider trading, the SEC has challenged corporations and public relations firms on the accuracy of information they disseminate for clients. Today, in an environment of mergers, takeovers, consolidations, and the incessant rumors that circulate around them, knowledge of disclosure law, a sensitivity to disclosure requirements, and a bias toward disclosing rather than withholding material information are important attributes of public relations officials.

In the new millennium, with securities trading extending beyond the traditional 9:30 A.M.–4 P.M. stock market trading day and with instantaneous online trading a reality for millions of investors, the responsibilities on public relations people for full and fair and immediate disclosure have intensified. The SEC, in turn, has increased its focus on private meetings between companies and analysts, which are closed to the media and therefore to individual investors who rely on the media for financial information.

To combat such selective disclosure, the SEC in 2000 adopted Regulation FD, or "fair disclosure." Basically, Regulation FD requires companies to widely disseminate any material announcement. In recent years, that disclosure has included disseminating corporate announcement via social media, especially Twitter and Facebook.

In the past, companies would share such material news with securities analysts or large investors, who then might act on it before the public found out. Under Regulation FD, even

FYI

Criminal Attorneys—Literally

"Let he who is without sin, throw the first stone." Thus sayeth the Bible. And, of course, it is not nice to disparage those who have fallen on hard times.

But, on the other hand, when a public relations person observes a pompous, sanctimonious, and self-righteous fat-cat lawyer finally getting his comeuppance, well....

Such was the case in 2008, when a number of the world's most high-profile and public relations–savvy trial lawyers, aka plaintiff's attorneys—all known for going after large companies in front-page class action suits, many of which reaped gargantuan settlements (mostly for themselves!)—were sentenced to prison for misdeeds.

- Richard Scruggs, wealthy and flamboyant Mississippi attorney, received the maximum sentence of five years in prison for attempted bribery in suits against insurance companies, after Hurricane Katrina.
- Melvyn Weiss, 72-year-old "dean" of the trial lawyers, got 30 months in the slammer and was ordered to pay $10 million for using kickbacks to gain advantage in class actions **(Figure 7-5)**.
- And William Lerach, Mr. Weiss's partner and perhaps America's highest profile plaintiff's attorney, drew two years in federal prison for his role in helping pay $11 million in kickbacks to people who became plaintiffs in lawsuits targeting, among others, AT&T, Lucent, WorldCom, Microsoft, Prudential Insurance, and Enron.

The sentencing of counselor Lerach, one of the more controversial and press-conscious of the breed, evoked particular glee from corporate executives. Said one unsympathetic CEO, "He's getting what he deserves. I once likened Lerach to a low-life form, somewhat below pond scum. Thank goodness, he's met my highest expectations."

Whatever happened to following the good book?*

FIGURE 7-5 **Bubala.**
Not even high-powered friends like New York Congressman Charley Rangel could prevent crooked plaintiff's attorney Melvyn Weiss from serving hard time due to paying kickbacks to witnesses.
Photo: McMullen Co/Newscom

*For further information, see Andrew R. Sorkin, "Lerach Is Sentenced to 2 Years in Prison," *The New York Times* (February 11, 2008).

if a material announcement slips out to an analyst, the company is obligated to issue a news release within 24 hours "to provide broad, non-exclusionary disclosure information to the public."[15]

In 2002, Regulation FD was bolstered by the passage of the Sarbanes-Oxley Act, sponsored by U.S. Senator Paul Sarbanes and U.S. Representative Michael Oxley. Sarbanes-Oxley came as a result of the large corporate financial scandals involving Enron, WorldCom, Global Crossing, and Arthur Andersen. Among other requirements, Sarbanes-Oxley mandated all publicly traded companies to increase financial disclosure and submit an annual report of the effectiveness of their internal accounting controls to the SEC, with criminal and civil penalties for noncompliance.[16]

After the global financial crisis of 2007-2008, where many of the formerly most solid financial institutions shut down and the world was thrown into financial meltdown, legislators returned to the cause of protecting investors. What emerged in 2010 was the Dodd-Frank Wall Street Reform and Consumer Protection Act, designed to increase transparency of financial reporting and also to create a new consumer protection agency.

Although many corporations, analysts, and investors complained that the combination of Regulation FD, Sarbanes-Oxley and Dodd-Frank would have a costly, even "chilling impact" on financial firms, Congress and the regulators were unwilling to yield, especially in terms of disclosure.[17]

Ethics Law

The laws on ethical misconduct in society have gotten quite a workout over the last two decades.

- In one celebrated case, translated into the 1999 movie *The Insider,* the late public relations counselor John Scanlon faced a grand jury subpoena stemming from his efforts to discredit Jeffrey Wigand, an internal critic of Scanlon's cigarette client Brown & Williamson.[18]

- In the political public relations arena, the activities of lobbyists, in particular, have been closely watched by Congress since the imposition of the Federal Regulation of Lobbying Act of 1946. The late White House Deputy Chief of Staff Michael K. Deaver, a well-known public relations professional, was found guilty of perjury over his lobbying activities, fined $100,000, and sentenced to community service. In 2005, political public relations professional Michael Scanlon, an associate of crooked lobbyist Jack Abramoff, also was sentenced to hard time as a result of conspiracy to bribe public officials.

- In 2012, Governor Nikki R. Haley of South Carolina was cleared of charges that she violated ethics rules when she was a state representative and lobbied on behalf of two businesses she worked for.

In recent years, campaign finance reform to limit—if not eradicate—the acceptance by legislators of favors and money from wealthy interest groups intensified until 2010. In that year, the Supreme Court's decision in the *Citizens United* v. *FEC* case held that the First Amendment prohibited the government from restricting independent political expenditures by corporations and unions. Consequently, the emergence of so-called Super PACs, political action committees that could accept unlimited contributions from individuals, unions, and corporations for the purpose of making independent expenditures, proliferated. So much so, that in the 2016 campaign for President, Republican Jeb Bush's Right to Rise Super PAC collected $100 million a month before the candidate even announced plans to run.[19]

Copyright Law

One body of law that is particularly relevant to public relations professionals is copyright law and the protections it offers writers. Copyright law provides basic, automatic protection for writers, whether a manuscript is registered with the Copyright Office or even published. Under the Copyright Act of 1976, an "original work of authorship" has copyright protection from the moment the work is in "fixed" form. The word *fixed* means that the work is sufficiently permanent to permit it to be perceived, reproduced, or otherwise communicated.

What kinds of works are subject to copyright? According to the law, the following:

- Literary works, including articles
- Songs, including words and music
- Plays and choreographed dance performances
- Art
- Motion pictures and audiovisual works
- Sound recordings
- Architectural works[20]

Copyright law gives the owner of the copyright the exclusive right to reproduce and authorize others to reproduce the work, prepare derivative works based on the copyrighted material, and perform and/or display the work publicly. That's why the late Michael Jackson had to pay $47.5 million for the rights to the Beatles' compositions to the duly sworn representatives and heirs of John, Paul, George, and Ringo.

Copyright law is different from trademark law, which refers to a word, symbol, or slogan, used alone or in combination, that identifies a product or its sponsor—for example, the Nike swoosh.

What courts have stated again and again is that for the purposes of criticism, news reporting, teaching, scholarship, or research, use of copyrighted material is not an infringement but rather constitutes *fair use*. Although precise definitions of fair use—like everything else in the law—is subject to interpretation, such factors as "the effect on the future market" of the copyrighted work in question or the "volume of quotation used" or even whether the "heart" of the material was ripped off are often considered.

That's why the Associated Press (AP), one of the nation's largest news organizations, announced in 2008 that it had had it with bloggers copying its works and would impose strict guidelines on the blogosphere as to how much quoting and copying of AP stories would be tolerated. The AP dictum was aimed squarely at the vague doctrine of *fair use*.[21]

Perhaps the most famous recent example of copyright infringement was the verdict in 2015 that Robin Thicke and Pharrell Williams copied a classic Marvin Gaye song while writing their "Blurred Lines." The jury awarded Gaye's children $7.3 million for the copyright theft[22] **(Figure 7-6)**. Over time, the Supreme Court has strengthened the copyright status of freelance artists and writers—many of whom are independent public relations practitioners—ruling that such professionals retain the right to copyright what they create "as long as they were not in a conventional employment relationship with the organization that commissioned their work." As a result of this ruling, public relations professionals must carefully document the authorization that has been secured for using freelance material. In other words, when engaging a freelance professional, public relations people must know the law.

FIGURE 7-6
Not so happy.
Singer Pharrell Williams
wasn't pleased in 2015
when a jury found
his song with Robin
Thicke, "Blurred Lines,"
guilty of infringing the
copyright of the late
Marvin Gaye.
*Photo: LG/Splash News/
Newscom*

Internet Law

The Internet has changed the rules for the laws affecting free speech. The premise
in American law is that "not all speech is created equal."[23] Rather, there is a hierarchy of speech, under Supreme Court precedents dating back many decades, that
calibrates the degree of First Amendment protection with, among other tests, the
particular medium of expression. For example, speech that would be perfectly acceptable if uttered in a public park could constitutionally be banned when broadcast from a sound truck.

Dealing with the Internet has introduced new ramifications to this legal principal.
Indeed, cyberlaw has brought into question many of the most revered communications
law principles.

Censorship

In 1996, Congress passed the Communications Decency Act (CDA) as an amendment to
a far-reaching telecommunications bill. The CDA introduced criminal penalties, including fines of as much as $250,000 and prison terms up to two years, for making "inde-
cent" speech available to "a person under 18 years of age."

Then, in the summer of 1997, the Supreme Court, in a sweeping endorsement of free speech, declared the CDA unconstitutional. The decision, unanimous in most respects, marked the highest court's first effort to extend the principles of the First Amendment into cyberspace and to confront the nature and the law of this new, powerful medium. In summarizing the Court's finding, Justice John Paul Stevens said the Court considered the "goal of protecting children from indecent material as legitimate and important" but concluded that "the wholly unprecedented breadth of the law threatened to suppress far too much speech among adults and even between parents and children."[24]

In 1998, Congress passed the Children's Online Privacy Protection Act (COPPA), which details what a Web site operator must include in a privacy policy, when and how to seek verifiable consent from a parent or guardian, and what responsibilities an operator has to protect children's privacy and safety online including restrictions on the marketing to those under 13. While children under 13 can legally give out personal information with their parents' permission, many Web sites altogether disallow underage children from using their services due to the amount of COPPA paperwork involved. The Federal Trade Commission enforces COPPA.

In the 21st century, the difficulty in interpreting such rules has become apparent. In 2015, a California court sentenced a so-called "revenge porn" Web site owner guilty for posting intimate, compromising and explicit images of people and then charging the victims to take down the images. This move by a state to challenge First Amendment free speech on the Internet underscored the gray area that Internet censorship has become.[25]

Internet censorship overseas is another ongoing battleground, with countries like China, Iran, Saudi Arabia, and Turkey, among many others, notorious for their Internet filters. The Obama Administration joined other democratic governments in leading a global effort to deploy "shadow" Internet and mobile phone systems to undermine repressive government attempts to censor dissidents.[26]

Intellectual Property

Few cyberlaw cases have drawn more headlines than the 2001 case against Napster, the popular application that allowed users to exchange music files. Because Napster ran the file-swapping through a central server, it was an easy target for legislation.

In the end—for Napster—the protest, led by those heavy-metal defenders of the First Amendment, Metallica, and backed by the large music companies, convinced the Court that the company was infringing on copyright protections of intellectual property. Two years later, the recording industry waged all-out war on those who downloaded intellectual property without paying.

On a broader level, intellectual piracy of everything from video games to music to software has become rampant, with estimates that 90% of virtually every form of intellectual property in China is pirated (including this book!).[27] In 2012, a pitched battle was waged in Congress on the piracy of intellectual property. On one side stood the Hollywood producers of records, books, and movies who fretted that the fruits of their labors were being stolen. On the other side stood Internet firms such as Google, Twitter, Facebook, and Reddit, which saw the Stop Online Piracy Act (SOPA) momentum as a threat to creativity. In the end, the might of the upstart Internet crowd proved too strong, and SOPA was defeated.[28]

The SOPA conflict was a harbinger of battles to come, with media companies on one side and Internet providers on the other. While a number of nations, including the United States, Japan, Canada, South Korea, and Australia, signed the Anti-Counterfeiting Trade Agreement, in July 2012, European legislators rejected the international treaty to crack down on digital piracy. While the United States vowed to put the treaty into effect, even without European Union involvement, the debate into international piracy of intellectual property was destined to continue.[29]

E-Fraud

Fraud is fraud, no matter where it is domiciled. And on the World Wide Web, where anyone who wants to can choose anonymity, strip in a logo, and pretend to be someone he or she is not, fraud runs rampant. (Just check your inbox for "inheritance gift" e-mails from Nigeria!)

The problem is that e-crooks are not only difficult to stop but also difficult to define, at least in legal terms. Often it depends on companies policing the Internet themselves, through clear policies that Internet access and e-mail remain the property of the company and rules on the use of non-work e-mails and Web sites on company time. In recent years, case law has been littered with corporate attempts to prosecute employees suspected of e-fraud. For example:

- Varian Medical Systems of Palo Alto won a $775,000 verdict against two former employees who posted 14,000 messages on 100 message boards accusing the firm of being homophobic and of discriminating against pregnant women.

- A California court ruled against a fired Intel employee who sent e-mails to about 35,000 staffers, criticizing the company.

- St. Paul-based insurer Travelers accused one former vice president of trying to sabotage the company with anonymous blog postings, charging, among other things, that one executive was little more than a "glorified secretary" and another "would stab his own mother in the back to make money." Travelers took the case all the way to federal court.[30]

And then there's "click fraud," which threatens to disrupt the largest search engines. Search engines rank listings by the number of clicks they receive: the more clicks, the higher the ranking. Click fraud occurs when a concerted effort is initiated to register multiple clicks to drive specific listings higher in a search-ranking algorithm. Such fraudulent activity affects marketers, who advertise on a site and pay rates based on usage.[31]

Social Media

The advent of social networking has introduced yet another legal dimension to the Internet. As noted, the SEC has moved in recent years to introduce new disclosure rules that clarify how companies can use Facebook, Twitter, and other social networks to disseminate information provided they meet certain requirements.

One area where social media law is particularly thorny is in terms of employee relations.

In 2010, the National Labor Relations Board accused a company of illegally firing an employee after she criticized her supervisor on her Facebook page. The Board argued that "whether it takes place on Facebook or at the water cooler, it was employees talking jointly about working conditions, in this case about their supervisor, and they have a right to do that."[32]

Or do they?

With organizations now sensitive to the potential use of social media to discuss employment matters, lawyers recommend that employers "review their Internet and social media policies to determine whether they are susceptible to an allegation that the policy would reasonably tend to chill employees in the exercise of their rights to discuss wages, working conditions, and unionization."[33]

Increasingly, universities and potential employers are seeking access to social media to monitor activities. The University of North Carolina at Chapel Hill, for example, adopted a student athlete policy that appointed a coach to be responsible "for having access to and regularly monitoring the content of team members' social networking sites and postings."[34]

These are but a few of the burgeoning legal issues that surround the World Wide Web.

4 Litigation Public Relations

In court cases, plaintiffs and defendants are often scrupulously warned by judges not to influence the ultimate verdict outside the courtroom, especially by seeking positive publicity.

Fat chance.

In the 21st century, with social media, cable news, talk radio and traditional media incessantly jabbering about possible trials, upcoming trials, and current trials, there is little guarantee that any jury—or a judge, for that matter—can be objective about any high-profile legal case.

That's why litigation public relations has become so important.

Litigation public relations can best be defined as managing the media process during the course of any legal dispute so as to affect the outcome or its impact on the client's overall reputation.

Although court proceedings have certain rules and protocols, dealing in the public arena with a matter of litigation has no such strictures. The Sixth Amendment to the Constitution guarantees accused persons "a speedy and public trial, by an impartial jury," but television commentary by knowledgeable—and in many cases, unknowledgeable—"experts" can help influence a potential jury for or against a defendant. Among the most lethal was *Headline News* commentator and former attorney Nancy Grace, who was often wrong but never in doubt. Among other pearls of wisdom, Grace accused members of the Duke lacrosse team of "gang raping" a stripper, and alleged that singer Whitney Houston's death in 2012 might have been the result of foul play. Courts found her wrong on both counts, and her ratings kept right on rising (**Figure 7-7**).

The fact is that communication has become central to the management of modern litigation.[35] Smart lawyers understand that with social media, the Internet, and cable TV, in particular, being so pervasive, they have little choice but to engage in litigation public relations to provide their clients with every advantage.

For example, in 2011, when International Monetary Fund President Dominique Strauss-Kahn was charged with rape by a New York City chambermaid, his surrogates engaged in a blistering publicity attack of the woman's history and character. The case was dropped.

According to one counselor who works exclusively with litigation, there are seven keys to litigation visibility.

1. **Learn the process.** All involved should be aware of the roadmap for the case and the milestones ahead, which may lend themselves to publicity.

2. **Develop a message strategy.** Think about what should be said at each stage of a trial to keep the press and public focused on the key messages of the client.

FIGURE 7-7
Legal loud mouth.
Lawyer-turned-broadcaster Nancy Grace was the dean of on-air personalities who led with their bias about ongoing legal cases, often to the detriment of facts and fairness.

3. **Settle fast.** Settlement is probably the most potent litigation visibility management tool. The faster the settlement, the less litigation visibility there is likely to be. This is often a positive development.

4. **Anticipate high-profile variables.** Often in public cases everybody gets into the act—judges, commentators, jury selection experts, psychologists, and so on. Always anticipate all that could be said, conjectured, and argued about the case. Always try to be prepared for every inevitability.

5. **Keep the focus positive.** Ultimately, it's a positive, productive attitude that leads to effective negotiations with the other side. So the less combative you can be—especially near settlement—the better.

6. **Try settling again.** Again, this ought to be the primary litigation visibility strategy—to end the agony and get it out of the papers.

7. **Fight nicely.** Wars are messy, expensive, and prone to producing casualties. It is much better to be positive. This will give both sides a greater chance of eventually settling.[36]

Last Word

As our society becomes more contentious, fractious, adversarial and litigious, public relations must become more concerned with the law. On the one hand, because management must rely so heavily on legal advice and legal judgments, it is imperative that public relations people understand the laws that govern their organizations and industries. Public relations people must understand that their views may differ from those of an attorney. As a defense lawyer once described his role, "You should do what a client wants, period. That's what you're paid for." By contrast, public relations people are paid to advise their clients what is "the right thing to do." And they should never shrink from that obligation.

On the other hand, public relations advisors must depend on "buy-in" from others in management. Lawyers are among the most influential of these associates. Therefore, knowing the law and forming an alliance with legal counselors must be a frontline objective for public relations professionals.

Beyond the working relationship between public relations people and lawyers, the practice of public relations has, itself, wrestled with legal questions in recent years. The government has gone after firms that "deceptively advertised" online, through such tactics as posting fictitious online reviews of products or restaurants or similarly endorsing clients' wares through blogs and Twitter.[37]

Increasingly, public relations practice is based on legal contracts: between agencies and clients, employers and employees, purchasers and vendors. All contracts—both written and oral—must be binding and enforceable.

In recent years, controversy in the field has erupted over noncompete clauses, in which former employees are prohibited, within certain time parameters, from working for a competitor or pitching a former account. Time and again the courts have ruled in favor of public relations agencies and against former clients in noncompete cases.

Add to this the blurring of the lines between public relations advice on the one hand and legal advice on the other, and it becomes clear that the connection between public relations and the law will intensify dramatically in the 21st century.

Discussion Starters

1. What is the difference between a public relations professional's responsibility and a lawyer's responsibility?
2. What have been recent challenges to the First Amendment?
3. How can someone prove that he or she has been libeled or slandered?
4. What is meant by the term *insider trading*?
5. What is the SEC's overriding concern when considering disclosure?
6. How have Regulation FD and Sarbanes-Oxley changed the disclosure environment?
7. Whom does copyright law protect?
8. What are some of the dominant issues in laws affecting the Internet?
9. What are several general principles with respect to litigation public relations?
10. What general advice should a public relations professional consider in working with lawyers?

Pick of the Literature

Advertising and Public Relations Law, 2nd Edition

Roy L. Moore, Carmen Maye and Erik L. Collins. New York: Routledge, 2011

This book offers an exhaustive examination of the First Amendment as it relates to the advertising and public relations businesses.

It traces the history of the First Amendment and tracks the interpretation of the amendment through the decades. The real merit of this volume is in its discussion of New Media implications on free speech law in terms of both individuals and corporations. Libel, defamation, privacy, and related public relations–oriented statutes are discussed in depth.

Copyright, patents and trademarks, Federal Trade Commission regulations, and others are explained. An excellent legal primer for public relations professionals.

Case Study | Walmart's Legal Crackup

On June 7, 2014 in the wee hours of the morning, a stretch limousine carrying comedian Tracy Morgan and others returning from a gig in Delaware, was rear-ended on the New Jersey Turnpike by a Walmart 18-wheeler tractor trailer.

Morgan, a star of the "Saturday Night Live" and "30 Rock" TV shows, was rushed to the hospital, reportedly unconscious, and in "critical but stable condition." Nonetheless, he was thankful; His friend and fellow comedy writer James "Jimmy Mack" McNair was killed in the crash.

Driving Without Sleep

In the days following the accident, New Jersey police alleged that the Walmart employee driver, who was charged with vehicular homicide and assault by auto, hadn't slept for more than 24 hours at the time of the accident. Under New Jersey law, driving without having slept for 24 hours is considered reckless, with deaths caused in such circumstances charged as vehicular homicide.

According to the police report, the driver failed to see traffic slowing and slammed into Morgan's limo, causing a six-car pileup. Upon receiving the police report, Walmart issued a statement affirming the belief that its driver "was operating within the federal hours of service regulations," which limit work shift to 14 hours with a maximum of 11 of those behind the wheel.

A week earlier, Teamsters Union President James P. Hoffa wrote a letter to the U.S. House of Representatives complaining about the pressures companies put on truck drivers. Wrote Hoffa, *"Drivers feel pressure from their employers to drive more than 60-70 hours a week with insufficient rest."*

In the Turnpike crash, a preliminary report by the National Transportation Safety Board said that Roper was traveling 20 mph over the speed limit and that he was almost at his drive time limit.

Lamentable Legal Leap

In the days that followed the horrible crash, the news from Tracy Morgan's hospital room was somber.

After rumors circulated that the comedian would have to have a leg amputated, Morgan's fiancé, issued a statement dispelling the rumor and reporting that the comic had suffered a broken femur, broken ribs, and a broken nose.

The FX Network, which had planned a new sitcom starring Morgan, announced that it would put the project on hold until the comedian recovered. In a statement, FX said, "The only thing we are concerned with is the health and recovery of Tracy Morgan and the victims of this tragic accident. We will support Tracy and his family in every way possible throughout his recovery. At the point when Tracy has recovered and decides that he is ready to go back to work, his show will be waiting for him. Right now our thoughts and prayers remain with Tracy, the other victims of the accident, and their families."

Similar sentiments were posted online by Morgan's fans and sympathizers. Cards and letter poured into the hospital of Morgan's convalescence. Everyone seemed to be in the comedian's corner—except for one glaring exception.

When Morgan filed suit against Walmart in July, the company responded with a most un-public relations like gesture. It blamed Morgan and his mates for the fatal crash.

Specifically, said Walmart's lawyers in a court filing, the comedian's injuries were "caused, in whole or in part, by plaintiffs' failure to properly wear an appropriate available seat belt restraint device" and that Morgan and company had "acted unreasonably and in disregard of (their) own best interests." Walmart's barristers noted that New Jersey has a strict seat belt law that requires all occupants of a passenger vehicle to wear restraints, and that New Jersey is one of only a few states that allow the "seat belt defense." Were Morgan to be found in a New Jersey court to be negligent for not wearing a seat belt, it could materially impact any settlement that Walmart would be made to pay.

If that wasn't enough, the chain's lawyers also noted the possibility that the injuries "may have been caused by third parties over whom Walmart had no control."

The response from pundits and private citizens around the nation to Walmart's brazen attempt to blame Morgan for the accident caused by its driver was immediate and severe. And no one was more stupefied than the slowly recovering Tracy Morgan, himself.

FIGURE 7-8 **No laughing matter.**
Actor and comedian Tracy Morgan uses a walker as he recovers from a 2014 crash on the New Jersey Turnpike, caused by a Walmart truck, which killed a friend and fellow-comic.
Photo: SPN

"*I can't believe Walmart is blaming me for an accident that they caused,*" said the comedian in a statement, "*My friends and I were doing nothing wrong,*"

Backing Down and Out.

It took Walmart precisely one day to see that the statement its lawyers had filed might have made sense in a court of law but not in the court of public opinion.

Walmart's follow-up statement said, in part:

Walmart is committed to working to resolve all of the remaining issues as a result of the accident. . . . . While we were required to respond to the lawsuit, we have also taken steps to encourage settlement discussions. Our thoughts continue to go out to everyone involved, and we remain committed to doing what's right.

And in the end, the company did just that, settling with McNair's estate for $10 million and with the rest of the limo's occupants, including Morgan, for undisclosed sums.

Almost one year to the day of the accident, Tracy Morgan, hobbling, tentative and still grieving, was interviewed on the NBC Today Show, his first TV appearance since the crash that changed his life forever* **(Figure 7-8)**.

Questions

1. How would you assess Walmart's response to the Tracy Morgan crash?

2. Had you have been Walmart's public relations director, what would you have advised the company do different in response to the crash?

3. What do you think of Walmart's response to its own legal claim that the accident might have been partly Morgan's fault?

*For further information, see Topher Gauk-Rogers and Kevin Conlon, "Tracy Morgan: I Can't Believe Walmart Is Blaming Me," *CNN* (September 20, 2014); Andrea Mandel, Soraya N. McDonald, "911 Audio from Tracy Morgan Crash Released," *Washington Post* (June 11, 2014); Gail Sullivan, "Trucker in Tracy Morgan Crash Hadn't Slept for 24 Hours," *Washington Post* (June 10, 2014); and "Morgan, Walmart Reach Accident Settlement," *USA Today* (May 28, 2015).

From the Top

An Interview with Robert Shapiro

Robert Shapiro (right) and a former client.
Photo: KEN LUBAS/KRT/Newscom

Celebrity attorney Robert Shapiro, co-founder of LegalZoom, has represented many of Hollywood's most famous and notorious defendants, from his tenure as a member of football great and accused murderer O. J. Simpson's "dream team" to his defense of legendary record producer and convicted murderer Phil Spector. After his successful defense of O. J. Simpson in 1995, Shapiro offered the following insights into how a modern-day lawyer views public relations.

How do you view a lawyer's public relations responsibilities?

When we are retained for those high-profile cases, we are instantly thrust into the role of a public relations person—a role for which the majority of us have no education, experience, or training. The lawyer's role as spokesperson may be [as] equally important to the outcome of a case as the skills of an advocate in the courtroom.

How important is the media to a trial?

The importance and power of the media cannot be overemphasized. The first impression the public gets is usually the one that is most important. The wire services depend on immediate updates. Therefore, all calls should be returned as quickly as possible.

"No comment" is the least appropriate and least productive response. Coming at the end of a lengthy story, it adds absolutely nothing and leaves the public with a negative impression.

How important are relationships with the media in a trial setting?

Initial relationships with legitimate members of the press are very important. Many times a lawyer will feel it is an intrusion to be constantly beset by seemingly meaningless questions that take up a tremendous amount of time. But the initial headlines of the arrest often make the sacred presumption of innocence a myth. In reality, we have the presumption of guilt. This is why dealing with the media is so important.

How carefully should lawyers construct answers to reporters' questions?

Just as you would do in trial, anticipate the questions a reporter will pose. Think out your answers carefully....Use great care in choosing your words. Keep your statements simple and concise. Pick and choose the questions you want to answer. You do not have to be concerned with whether the answer precisely addresses the question, since only the answer will be aired.

What about dealing with the tabloids?

My experience is that cooperating with tabloid reporters only gives them a legitimate source of information which can be misquoted or taken out of context and does little good

for your client. My personal approach is not to cooperate with tabloid reporters.

What about dealing with television?

The television media, either consciously or unconsciously, create an atmosphere of chaos. Immediately upon arriving at the courthouse, you are surrounded by television crews. We have all seen people coming to court and trying to rush through the press with their heads down or covering them with newspapers or coats. Nothing looks worse. I always instruct my clients upon arrival at the courthouse to get out in a normal manner, to walk next to me in a slow and deliberate way, to have a look of confidence and acknowledge with a nod those who are familiar and supportive.*

*Excerpted from Robert Shapiro, "Secrets of a Celebrity Lawyer," *Columbia Journalism Review* (September/October 1994): 25–29. Copyright © 1994 Columbia Journalism Review. Reprinted by permission.

Public Relations Bookshelf

Beke, Thomas. *Litigation Communication.* New York, NY: Springer Cham Heidelberg, 2014. Written with a British perspective, the book explores historical and contemporary examples of the meshing of legal and public relations communications considerations.

Bybee, Keith. *Bench Press: The Collision of Courts, Politics and the Media.* Stanford, CA: Stanford University Press, 2007.

Coffey, Kendall. *Spinning the Law.* Amherst, NY: Prometheus Books, 2010. A famous attorney takes a spin at spinning, offering a media primer for barristers.

Goldsmith, Jack and Tim Wu. *Who Controls the Internet? Illusions of a Borderless World.* New York: Oxford University Press, 2008. Two legal scholars examine the reality of the laws that attempt to govern the Internet.

Haggerty, James F. *In the Court of Public Opinion: Winning Strategies for Litigation Communications.* 2nd ed. Chicago, IL: American Bar Association, 2009. Sensible explanation of why a 21st century attorney's job extends beyond the court room to the court of public opinion.

Levick, Richard and Larry Smith. *Stop the Presses: The Crisis and Litigation PR Desk Reference.* 2nd ed. Ann Arbor, MI: Watershed Press, 2008. Two agency veterans focus on litigation public relations in crisis situations. Good book.

Moore, Roy L. and Michael D. Murray. *Media, Law and Ethics.* 3rd ed. New York: Taylor and Francis Group, 2008. An updated compendium of the laws that govern the media.

Parkinson, Michael G. and L. Marie Parkinson. *Public Relations Law.* New York: Routledge, 2008. Candid appraisal of the legal rights and responsibilities of public relations professionals.

Sinclair, Adriana. *International Relations Theory and International Law.* Cambridge, UK: Cambridge University Press, 2010. Good discussion of the legal boundaries of operating in international markets.

Zittrain, Jonathan. *The Future of the Internet and How to Stop It.* Harrisonburg, VA: R.R. Donnelly, 2008. Especially pertinent is the chapter on "cybersecurity."

Endnotes

1. Richard Brownell, "Want to Generate Bad PR and Social Dislikes? Here's General Mills' Strategy," *PR News Online* (April 17, 2014).
2. Gerhart L. Klein, *Public Relations Law: The Basics* (Mt. Laurel, NJ: Anne Klein & Associates, 1990): 1–2.
3. John Burns and Ravi Somaiya, "Wikileaks Founder on the Run, Trailed by Notoriety," *The New York Times* (December 23, 2010).
4. Matt Apuzzo, "Times Reporter Will Not Be Called to Testify in Leak Case," *The New York Times* (January 12, 2015).
5. Matt Zapotosky, "Former CIA Officer Jeffrey Sterling Convicted in Leak Case," *The Washington Post* (January 26, 2015).
6. Dennis L. Wilcox and Glen T. Cameron, *Public Relations Strategies and Tactics.* 8th ed. (Boston: Allyn & Bacon, 2002): 265.
7. Thomas K. Grose, "$50 Million Lawsuit Against WSJ and Burroughs May Make Some Authors-to-Be Think Twice," *TFJR Report* (April 1992): 3.
8. "Judge Tosses Out NY Businessman's 'Borat' Lawsuit," *Associated Press* (April 2, 2008).
9. Jennifer Preston, "Courtney Love Settles Twitter Defamation Case," *The New York Times* (March 4, 2011).
10. Monica Davey, "$1.8 Million for Ventura in Defamation Case," *The New York Times* (July 29, 2014).
11. Constance L. Hays, "Aide Was Reportedly Ordered to Warn Stewart on Stock Sales," *The New York Times* (August 6, 2002): C1–2.
12. Sam Gustin, "'Guilty' Verdict in Biggest U.S. Insider Trading Case," *Time* (February 6, 2014).
13. Andrew Clark, "Brunswick Executive Suspended After Husband Is Charged over Insider Trading," *The Guardian* (December 23, 1908).
14. Stephen R. Brown, "Inside Trader Michael Lucarelli Admits Struggles with Impotence, Cocaine at Sentencing," *New York Daily News* (January 21, 2015).
15. "Managing Tidal Wave of Corporate Disclosure," *Business Wire Newsletter* (April 2002): 2.
16. Joe Nocera, "For All Its Costs, Sarbanes-Oxley Is Working," *The New York Times* (December 3, 2005): C1.
17. Joe Nocera, "Did Dodd-Frank Work?" *The New York Times* (July 21, 2014).
18. Alix M. Freedman and Suein L. Hwang, "Brown & Williamson Faces Inquiry," *The Wall Street Journal* (February 6, 1996): A1.
19. Alex Isenstadt, "Jeb Bush's $100 M May," *Politico* (May 18, 2015).

20. "Copyright Compliance: What Every Media Relations Professional Needs to Know," *Burrelles/Luce* (2008).

21. Saul Hansell, "The Associated Press to Set Guidelines for Using Its Articles in Blogs," *The New York Times* (June 16, 2008).

22. Jacob Kastrenakes, "Jury Finds Robin Thicke and Pharrell Copied a Marvin Gaye Song for Blurred Lines," *The Verge* (March 10, 2015).

23. Linda Greenhouse, "What Level of Protection for Internet Speech?" *The New York Times* (March 24, 1997): D5.

24. Linda Greenhouse, "Decency Act Fails," *The New York Times* (June 27, 1997): 1.

25. Afigo Fadahunsi, "The Communications Decency Act May Disappoint," *Law 360* (March 9, 2015).

26. James Glanz and John Markoff, "U.S. Underwriters Detour Around Censors," *The New York Times* (June 12, 2011).

27. Kristi Heim, "Inside China's Teeming World of Fake Goods," *Seattle Times* (February 12, 2006).

28. Jonathan Weisman, "After an Online Firestorm, Congress Shelves Anti-Piracy Bills," *The New York Times* (January 20, 2012).

29. Eric Pfanner, "Europeans Reject Treaty to Combat International Piracy," *The New York Times* (July 5, 2012).

30. David Hanners, "Travelers in a Spat over Catty E-Chat," *St. Paul Pioneer Press* (March 13, 2008).

31. Kevin Lee, "Click Fraud: What It Is, How to Fight It," *ClickZ Experts* (February 18, 2005).

32. Steven Greenhouse, "Company Accused of Firing over Facebook Post," *The New York Times* (November 8, 2010).

33. Ibid.

34. Mary Pilon, "Maryland Bill Addresses College Athletes' Social Media Policy," *The New York Times* (February 3, 2012).

35. Greg Hazley, "PR, Legal Need to Play on Same Team," *O'Dwyer's PR Services Report* (December 2005): 1.

36. James E. Lukaszewski, "Managing Litigation Visibility: How to Avoid Lousy Trial Publicity," *Public Relations Quarterly* (Spring 1995): 18–24.

37. "Reverberations: The FTC Means Business and What PR Firms Should Do," *Firm Voice, Council of Public Relations Firms* (September 8, 2010.)

Chapter 8

Research

Chapter Objectives

1. To discuss the importance of research as the essential first step in every public relations assignment.
2. To explore research principles, types, and methods.
3. To discuss the various research tools and evaluative techniques available to public relations professionals.
4. To underscore the importance of Web monitoring and tools available for Internet research.

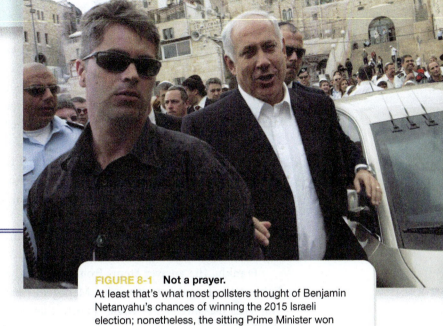

FIGURE 8-1   **Not a prayer.**
At least that's what most pollsters thought of Benjamin Netanyahu's chances of winning the 2015 Israeli election; nonetheless, the sitting Prime Minister won handily, despite the negative prognosticators.
Photo: RONEN ZVULUN/REUTERS/Newscom

It's been a bad few years for public opinion polls.

The problem is that the election polls that have served over decades to indicate potential winners and losers of upcoming elections just don't seem to work anymore. Since 2014, alone, the polls were wrong about several key elections, including:

- The 2014 midterm elections in the United States that swept the Republicans to power with strong majorities in both houses, contrary to what pollsters had predicted,

- The 2015 strong showing by Israeli Prime Minister Benjamin Netanyahu, who most polls predicted would lose (**Figure 8-1**),

- The 2015 landslide victory of British Prime Minister David Cameron and his Conservative Party, despite predictions of gloom by most pollsters.

So what's going on here?

Lots of things. For one, the growth of cell phones has positively wrecked the polling business. With 43% of the U.S. public using only cell phones and another 17% using cell phones most of the time, the traditional polling tactics of interviewing respondents on land lines no longer is particularly relevant. For another, the pervasiveness of answering machines and call-screening has made it more difficult for researchers to get through to citizens. Where once, pollsters experienced an 80% response rate from those called, today the rate hovers below 10%.[1]

All of this means that the probabilities with which pollsters used to predict elections have declined markedly. The lesson: Just because it's "research" doesn't mean it necessarily should be believed.

Such are the peculiarities of research, where the old adage, "Figures lie, and liars figure," must still be considered in evaluating empirical data.

Despite its interpretative issues, research is the natural starting point for any public relations assignment—from plotting a political campaign to promoting a product to designing a program to confronting a crisis. The first step in solving any public relations challenge is to conduct research.

At the same time, it should be recognized that research, particularly in an art form as intuitive as public relations, is no panacea. Research is but a foundation upon which a sensible programmatic initiative must be based. Research must always be complemented by analysis and judgment.

Nonetheless, in public relations it is obligatory to begin with research.

Why?

Frankly, the answer stems from the fact that few managers understand what public relations is and how it works. Managers—particularly those guided by quantitative, empirical measurement—want "proof" that what we advise is based on logic and clear thinking.

In other words, most clients are less interested in what their public relations advisors *think* than in what they *know*. The only real way to know your advice is on the right track is by ensuring that it is grounded in hard data whenever possible. So before recommending a course of action, public relations professionals must analyze audiences, assess alternatives, and generally do their homework.

In other words, do research.

1 Essential First Step

Every public relations program or solution should begin with research. Most don't, which is a shame.

The various approaches to public relations problem solving, discussed in Chapter 1, all start with research.

Instinct, intuition, and gut feelings all remain important in the conduct of public relations work, but management today demands more—measurement, analysis, and evaluation at every stage of the public relations process. In an era of scarce resources, management wants facts and statistics from public relations professionals to show that their efforts contribute not only to overall organizational effectiveness but also to the bottom-line. For example:

- **Outputs**—Did we get the coverage we wanted?
- **Outtakes**—Did our target audience see and/or believe our messages?
- **Outcomes**—Did audience behavior or relationships change and did sales increase?[2]

Questions such as these must be answered through research.

In a day when organizational resources are precious and companies don't want to spend money unless it enhances results, public relations programs must contribute to meeting business objectives. That means that research must be applied to help segment market targets, analyze audience preferences and dislikes, and determine which messages might be most effective with various audiences. Research then becomes essential in helping realize management's goals.

Research should be applied in public relations work both at the initial stage, prior to planning a campaign, and at the final stage to evaluate a program's effectiveness. Early research helps to determine the current situation, prevalent attitudes, and difficulties that the program faces. Later research examines the program's success, along with what else still needs to be done. Research at both points in the process is critical.

What Is Research?

Research is the systematic collection and interpretation of information to increase understanding. Most people associate public relations with conveying information; although that association is accurate, research must be the obligatory first step in any project. A firm must acquire enough accurate, relevant data about its publics, products, and programs to answer these questions:

- How can we identify and define our constituent groups?
- How does this knowledge relate to the design of our messages?
- How does it relate to the design of our programs?
- How does it relate to the media we use to convey our messages?
- How does it relate to the schedule we adopt in using our media?
- How does it relate to the ultimate implementation tactics of our program?

It is difficult to delve into the minds of others, whose backgrounds and points of view may be quite different from our own, with the purpose of understanding why they think as they do. Research skills are partly intuitive, partly an outgrowth of individual temperament, and partly a function of acquired knowledge. There is nothing mystifying about them. Although we tend to think of research in terms of impersonal test scores, interviews, or questionnaires, these methods are only a small part of the process. The real challenge lies in using research—knowing when to do what, with whom, and for what purpose.

2 Public Relations Research Principles

For years, public relations professionals have debated the standards of measuring public relations' effectiveness. Both the PRSA and the Institute for Public Relations have focused on guiding principles in setting standards for public relations research. Among them:

- Establish clear program objectives and desired outcomes tied directly to business goals.
- Differentiate between measuring public relations "outputs," generally short-term and surface (e.g., amount of press coverage received or exposure of a particular message), and measuring public relations "outcomes," usually more far-reaching and carrying greater impact (e.g., changing awareness, attitudes, and even behavior).
- Measure media content as a first step in the public relations evaluation process. Such a measure is limited in that it can't discern whether a target audience actually saw a message or responded to it.

FYI

Figures—and Faces—Lie

If you don't believe the old maxim that "figures lie and liars figure," consider the following: In often repeated research, randomly selected participants are shown the two faces in **Figure 8-2** and asked, "Which woman is lovelier?" Invariably, the answer is split 50–50.

However, when each woman is named; one "Jennifer" and the other "Gertrude," respondents overwhelmingly—more than 80%—vote for Jennifer as the more beautiful woman.

Why? "Jennifer" is more hip, more happening, more, uh, "phat." (Sorry, all you Gertrudes out there!)

The point is that people can't help but introduce their own biases, including even in presumably "objective" research experiments. This factor always should be taken into account in evaluating public relations research.

FIGURE 8-2 **Jennifer/Gertrude.**
Photo: Courtesy Fraser P. Seitel

 Understand that no one technique can be expected to evaluate public relations effectiveness. Rather, this requires a combination of techniques, from media analysis to cyberspace analysis, from focus groups to polls and surveys.

 Be wary of attempts to compare public relations effectiveness with advertising effectiveness. One particularly important consideration is that while advertising placement and messages can be controlled, their equivalent on the public relations side cannot be.

 The most trustworthy measurement of public relations effectiveness is that which stems from an organization with clearly identified key messages, target audiences, and desired channels of communication. The converse of this is that the more confused an organization is about its targets, the less reliable its public relations measurement will be.

Public relations evaluation cannot be accomplished in isolation. It must be linked to overall business goals, strategies, and tactics.

Public Relations Research Types

In general, research is conducted to do three things: (1) describe a process, situation, or phenomenon; (2) explain why something is happening, what its causes are, and what effect it will have; and (3) predict what probably will happen if we do or don't take action. Primary, or original, research in public relations is either theoretical or applied. Applied research solves practical problems; theoretical research aids understanding of a public relations process.

Most public relations analysis, however, takes the more informal form called secondary research. This relies on existing material—books, articles, Internet databases, and the like—to form the research backing for public relations recommendations and programs.

Applied Research

In public relations work, applied research can be either strategic or evaluative. Both applications are designed to answer specific practical questions.

- **Strategic research** is used primarily in program development to determine program objectives, develop message strategies, or establish benchmarks. It often examines the tools and techniques of public relations. For example, a firm that wants to know how employees rate its candor in internal communications would first conduct strategic research to find out where it stands.

- **Evaluative research,** sometimes called summative research, is conducted primarily to determine whether a public relations program has accomplished its goals and objectives. For example, if changes are made in the internal communications program to increase candor, evaluative research can determine whether the goals have been met. A variant of evaluation can be applied during a program to monitor progress and indicate where modifications might make sense.

Theoretical Research

Theoretical research is more abstract and conceptual than applied research. It helps build theories in public relations work about why people communicate, how public opinion is formed, and how a public is created.

Knowledge of theoretical research is important as a framework for persuasion and as a base for understanding why people do what they do.

Some knowledge of theoretical research in public relations and mass communications is essential for enabling practitioners to understand the limitations of communication as a persuasive tool. Attitude and behavior change has been the traditional goal in public relations programs, yet theoretical research indicates that such a goal may be difficult or impossible to achieve through persuasive efforts. According to such research, other factors are always getting in the way.

Researchers have found that communication is most persuasive when it comes from multiple sources of high credibility. Credibility itself is a multidimensional concept that includes trustworthiness, expertise, and power. Others have found that a message generally is more effective when it is simple, because it is easier to understand, localize, and make personally relevant. According to still other research, the persuasiveness of a message can be increased when it arouses or is accompanied by a high level of personal involvement in the issue at hand.

The point here is that knowledge of theoretical research can help practitioners not only understand the basis of applied research findings but also temper management's expectations of attitude and behavioral change resulting from public relations programs.

Secondary Research

Secondary research is research on the cheap. Basically, secondary research allows you to examine or read about and learn from someone else's primary research, such as in a library.

Also called "desk research," secondary research uses data that have been collected for other purposes than your own. Database monitoring is particularly important for public relations researchers. Such online resources as Claritas, which supplies marketing analysis and demographic tools; SurveyMonkey.com, which provides the resources to create tailored online surveys **(Figure 8-3)**; and the omnipresent Google search engine are popular outlets to aid public relations researchers.

Because public relations budgets are limited, it always makes sense first to consider secondary sources in launching a research effort.

3 Public Relations Research Methods

Observation is the foundation of modern social science. Scientists, social psychologists, and anthropologists make observations, develop theories, and, hopefully, increase understanding of human behavior. Public relations research, too, is founded on observation. Indeed, examining human behavior was pivotal to the early public relations work of Edward Bernays, a disciple of his uncle, Sigmund Freud. Three primary forms of public relations research dominate the field.

- *Surveys* are designed to reveal attitudes and opinions—what people think about certain subjects.
- *Communications audits* often reveal disparities between real and perceived communications between management and target audiences. Management may make certain assumptions about its methods, media, materials, and messages, whereas its targets may confirm or refute those assumptions.
- *Unobtrusive measures*—such as fact-finding, content analysis, and readability studies—enable the study of a subject or object without involving the researcher or the research as an intruder.

Each method of public relations research offers specific benefits and should be understood and used by the modern practitioner.

Surveys

Survey research is one of the most frequently used research methods in public relations. Surveys can be applied to broad societal issues, such as determining public opinion about a political candidate, or to more focused issues, such as satisfaction of hospital patients or hotel guests or reporting relationships of public relations people **(Figure 8-4)**. Most survey research is now done online.

Surveys come in two types.

1. *Descriptive surveys* offer a snapshot of a current situation or condition. They are the research equivalent of a balance sheet, capturing reality at a specific point in time. A typical public opinion poll is a prime example.
2. *Explanatory surveys* are concerned with cause and effect. Their purpose is to help explain why a current situation or condition exists and to offer explanations for opinions and attitudes. Frequently, such explanatory or analytical surveys are designed to answer the question "why?" Why are our philanthropic dollars not being appreciated in the community? Why don't employees believe management's messages? Why is our credibility being questioned?

Exit this survey >>

Volunteer Input Requested

1. Survey Regarding Financial Issues

1. Should we be permitted to incur an annual operating deficit?

Yes

No, Never

No, Except in an urgent situation

Other (please specify)

2. Should members be kept informed of projected operating deficits and other material financial issues and the steps being taken to address those issues?

Yes

No

Other (please specify)

3. Should we take steps to reduce or eliminate the projected operating deficit for the current year?

Yes, the deficit should be completely eliminated this year and each following year

Yes, the deficit should be reduced as much as possible this year and fully eliminated starting next year

No

Other (please specify)

4. Would you support an increase in annual membership dues?

No

Yes, up to $25

Yes, up to $50

Yes, up to $75

Yes, up to $100

Yes, more than $100

Other (please specify)

5. Should we take steps to reduce or eliminate the projected operating deficit for the current year?

Yes, the deficit should be completely eliminated this year and each following year

Yes, the deficit should be reduced as much as possible this year and fully eliminated starting next year

No

Other (please specify)

6. Should Board members be required to make a minimum annual contribution?

No,

Yes, $1,000

Yes, $2,000

Yes, $3,500

Yes, $5,000

Yes, more than $5000

Other (please specify)

FIGURE 8-3

Survey monkey. Services, such as SurveyMonkey.com, allow you to design your own online survey, such as the hypothetical one shown here.

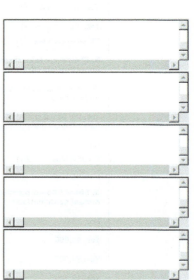

PR News/IABC Joint Survey: Getting a Taste of the C-Suite

Please take a few minutes to fill out the following survey by April 25th. Coverage of the study's results will appear in the May 4th issue of PR News as well as the May 2005 edition of IABC's CW Bulletin. We're hopeful that the results will enable senior PR pros to devise strategies that will help them reach the corporate summit—and stay there.

1. I report directly to the CEO — Please Choose ▼

2. I am a member of the top management team — Please Choose ▼

3. I regularly attend meetings of the top management team (whether or not I am a member) — Please Choose ▼

4. How many employees are there in your corporate affairs/PR department? — Please Choose ▼

5. What country are you in? — Please Select ▼

	Strongly Agree	Agree	Neither Agree nor Disagree	Disagree	Strongly Disagree
6. My CEO:					
a . . . understands the importance of communication, not just when there is an issue or crisis	○	○	○	○	○
b. . . . sees PR as an investment in the future not just a cost	○	○	○	○	○
c. . . . asks my opinion about PR implications of future directions of the business	○	○	○	○	○
d. . . . usually accepts my recommendations	○	○	○	○	○
e. . . . would say I understand the business	○	○	○	○	○
7. My CEO values corporate affairs / PR advice at least as much as that from:					
a. . . . Advertising	○	○	○	○	○
b. . . . Sales	○	○	○	○	○
c. . . . Marketing	○	○	○	○	○
d. . . . Legal	○	○	○	○	○
e. . . . Human Resources	○	○	○	○	○
8. My CEO makes an effort (e.g. willingly puts in time) to maintain good relations with the following stakeholders:					
a. . . . employees	○	○	○	○	○
b. . . . stockholders	○	○	○	○	○
c. . . . analysts	○	○	○	○	○
d. . . . customers/clients	○	○	○	○	○
e. . . . business or alliance partners	○	○	○	○	○
f. . . . media	○	○	○	○	○

9.
a. What do you mostly discuss at your meetings with the CEO? (e.g. high-level strategy, business reputation, communication tactics, your career path, media relations, CEO presentations, analyst relationships, publications?)

b. Has the CEO redefined your role or mandate at any stage (e.g. upgraded it, expanded it, downgraded it, etc.)? Please explain what and why.

10.
a. To what extent does your CEO expect PR results to be measured? Does he/she take PR less seriously because measurement is not easy to do? To what extent is your CEO skeptical of anything without numbers attached?

b. What demands does the CEO have of the PR function that are not currently being met?

c. What three things would you like to see improved in regard to the CEO and PR/coms function or your relationship with him/her?

Surveys generally consist of four elements: (1) sample, (2) questionnaire, (3) interview, and (4) analysis of results. (Direct-mail surveys, of course, eliminate the interview step.) Because survey research is so critical in public relations, let's examine each survey element in some detail.

Sample

The sample, or selected target group, must be representative of the total public whose views are sought. Once a survey population has been determined, a researcher must select the appropriate sample or group of respondents from which to collect information. Sampling, as noted earlier with political polls, is tricky. A researcher must be aware of the hidden pitfalls in choosing a representative sample, not the least of which is the perishable nature of most data. Survey findings are rapidly outdated because of population mobility and changes in the political and socioeconomic environment. Consequently, sampling should be completed quickly.

Two cross-sectional approaches are used in obtaining a sample: random sampling and nonrandom sampling. The former is more scientific, the latter more informal.

Random Sampling In random sampling, two properties are essential—equality and independence. *Equality* means that no element has any greater or lesser chance of being selected. *Independence* means that selecting any one element in no way influences the selection of any other element. Random sampling is based on a mathematical criterion that allows generalizations from the sample to be made to the total population. There are four types of random or probability samples.

1. **Simple random sampling** gives all members of the population an equal chance of being selected. First, all members of the population are identified, and then as many subjects as are needed are randomly selected—usually with the help of a computer. Election polling uses a random approach; although millions of Americans vote, only a few thousand are ever polled on their election preferences. The Nielsen national television sample, for example, consists of only 10,000 homes, encompassing 25,000 people, despite the fact there are 115 million TV households in the United States.[3] Despite the relatively small sample size, TV networks live and die on the basis of Nielsen data.

   How large should a random sample be? The answer depends on a number of factors, one of which is the size of the population. In addition, the more similar the population elements are in regard to the characteristics being studied, the smaller the sample required. In most random samples, the following population-to-sample ratios apply, with a 5% margin of error:

Population	Sample
1000	278
2000	322
3000	341
5000	355
10,000	370
50,000	381
100,000	383
500,000	383
Infinity	384

Random sampling owes its accuracy to the laws of probability, which are best explained by the example of a barrel filled with 10,000 marbles—5000 green ones and 5000 red ones. If a blindfolded person selects a certain number of marbles from the barrel—say, 400—the laws of probability suggest that the most frequently drawn combination will be 200 red and 200 green. These laws further suggest that with certain margins of error, a very few marbles can represent the whole barrel, which can correspond to any size—for example, that of a city, state, or nation.

2. **Systematic random sampling** is closely related to simple random sampling, but it uses a random starting point in the sample list. From then on, the researcher selects every nth person in the list.

3. **Stratified random sampling** is a procedure used to survey different segments or strata of the population. For example, if an organization wants to determine the relationship between years of service and attitudes toward the company, it may stratify the sample to ensure that the breakdown of respondents accurately reflects the makeup of the population.

4. **Cluster sampling** involves first breaking the population down into small heterogeneous subsets, or clusters, and then selecting the potential sample from the individual clusters or groups. A cluster may often be defined as a geographic area, such as an election district.

Nonrandom Sampling   Nonrandom samples come in three types: convenience, quota, and volunteer.

1. **Convenience samples**, also known as accidental, chunk, or opportunity samples, are relatively unstructured, rather unsystematic, and designed to elicit ideas and points of view. Journalists use convenience samples when they conduct person-on-the-street interviews. The most common type of convenience sample in public relations research is the focus group.

2. **Quota samples** permit a researcher to choose subjects on the basis of certain characteristics. For example, the attitudes of a certain number of women, men, blacks, whites, rich, or poor may be needed. Quotas are imposed in proportion to each group's percentage of the population.

3. **Volunteer samples** use willing participants who agree voluntarily to respond to concepts and hypotheses for research purposes.

Questionnaire

Before creating a questionnaire, whether to be mailed or e-mailed, a researcher must consider his or her objective in doing the study. What you seek to find out should influence the specific publics you ask, the questions you raise, and the research method you choose. After determining what you're after, consider the particular questionnaire design. Specifically, researchers should observe the following in designing their questionnaire:

1. **Keep it short.** Make a concerted attempt to limit questions. It's terrific if the questionnaire can be answered in five minutes.

2. **Use structured rather than open-ended questions.** People would rather check a box or circle a number than write an essay.

3. **Measure intensity of feelings.** Let respondents check "very satisfied," "satisfied," "dissatisfied," or "very dissatisfied" rather than "yes" or "no." One popular approach is the semantic differential technique shown in **Figure 8-5**.

4. **Don't use fancy words or words that have more than one meaning.** If you must use big words, make the context clear.

5. **Don't ask loaded questions.** "Is management doing all it can to communicate with you?" is a terrible question. The answer is always no.

6. **Don't ask double-barreled questions.** "Would you like management meetings once a month, or are bimonthly meetings enough?" is another terrible question.

7. **Pretest.** Send your questionnaire to a few colleagues and listen to their suggestions.

8. **Attach a letter explaining how important answers are, and let recipients know that they will remain anonymous.** Respondents will feel better if they think the study is significant and their identities are protected. Also, specify how and where the data will be used.

9. **When mailing, hand-stamp the envelopes, preferably with unique commemorative stamps.** Metering an envelope indicates assembly-line research, and researchers have found that the more expensive the postage, the higher the response rate. People like to feel special.

10. **Follow up your first mailing.** Send a reminder postcard three days after the original questionnaire. Then wait a few weeks and send a second questionnaire, just in case recipients have lost the first.

11. **Send out more questionnaires than you think necessary.** The major weakness of most mail surveys is the immeasurable error introduced by non-responders. You're shooting for a 50% response rate; anything less tends to be suspect.

12. **Enclose a reward.** (One reason to mail and not e-mail.) There's nothing like a token gift of money to make a recipient feel guilty for not returning a questionnaire.

Online questionnaires boast several advantages, among them, being potentially interactive, able to be linked to a Web site and more conducive to asking more questions.

Interviews

Interviews can provide a more personal, firsthand feel for public opinion. Interview panels can range from focus groups of randomly selected average people to Delphi panels of so-called opinion leaders. Interviews can be conducted in a number of ways, including face-to-face, telephone, mail, and through the Internet.

Focus Groups This approach is used with increasing frequency in public relations today. A traditional focus group consists of a 90 to 120-minute discussion among 8 to 10 individuals who have been selected based upon having predetermined common characteristics, such as buying behavior, age, income, family composition, and so on.[4]

Telephone Interviews In contrast to personal interviews, telephone interviews—particularly in a cell phone society—suffer from a high refusal rate. Many people just don't want to be bothered.

FIGURE 8-5
**Measuring
intensity, rewarding
respondents.**
One common device
to measure intensity
of feelings is the
semantic differential
technique, which
gives respondents a
scale of choices from
the worst to the best.
Respondents will
comply more gladly
if a "crisp new bill" is
included—and even
more gladly to two
"crisp new bills."
*Courtesy of Bauman
Research & Consulting
LLC*

Bauman
Research & Consulting, LLC

Dear Susan,

A few months ago you contacted XYZ company about your health condition. We'd like some feedback on how we did – and how you're doing.

Please take 5 minutes to tell us about your experiences and help us do better.

This survey is being conducted for XYZ company by an independent research firm, Bauman Research & Consulting. Your responses are completely confidential and will not be used for any marketing or selling purposes.

As a token of our appreciation for your participation, we have enclosed $5.

If you have any questions about this survey, please contact Sandra Bauman at sandra@baumanresearch.com or 201-444-6894.

Q1.   In general, how would you describe your own health?

EXCELLENT	VERY GOOD	GOOD	FAIR	POOR
$\square_1$	$\square_2$	$\square_3$	$\square_4$	$\square_5$

Q2.   What is your current general level of activity?

Not at all   Extremely
Active   Active

$\longleftarrow$

1   2   3   4   5   6   7   8   9   10

Q3.   Which joint is causing you pain? [Choose one.]

HIP	KNEE	SHOULDER	ELBOW	OTHER
$\square_1$	$\square_2$	$\square_3$	$\square_4$	$\square_5$

Q4.   How effective was XYZ company at communicating information in each of these areas?

	EXTREMELY EFFECTIVE	VERY EFFECTIVE	SOMEWHAT EFFECTIVE	NOT TOO EFFECTIVE	NOT AT ALL EFFECTIVE
a. Information about possible prescription treatment options for your joint pain	$\square_1$	$\square_2$	$\square_3$	$\square_4$	$\square_5$
b. Information about possible physical therapy options for your joint pain	$\square_1$	$\square_2$	$\square_3$	$\square_4$	$\square_5$
c. Information about possible surgical options for your joint pain	$\square_1$	$\square_2$	$\square_3$	$\square_4$	$\square_5$

→ CONTINUED

 44 Abbington Terrace, Glen Rock, NJ 07452 • Phone: 201.444.6894 • Fax: 201.701.0271 • www.baumanresearch.com

E-mail Interviews   This is the least expensive approach, but it often suffers from a low response rate. Frequently, people who return e-mail or even snail mail questionnaires are those with strong biases either in favor of or (more commonly) in opposition to the subject at hand.

Drop-Off Interviews   This approach combines face-to-face and mail interview techniques. An interviewer personally drops off a questionnaire at a household, usually after conducting a face-to-face interview. Because the interviewer has already established some rapport with the interviewee, the rate of return with this technique is considerably higher than it is for straight mail interviews.

Intercept Interviews   This approach is popular in consumer surveys, where researchers "intercept" respondents on the street, in shopping malls, or in retail outlets. Trained interviewers typically deliver a short (5 to 20-minute) questionnaire concerning attitudes, perceptions, preferences, and behavior.

Delphi Panels   The Delphi technique is a qualitative research tool that uses opinion leaders—local influential persons as well as national experts—often to help tailor the design of a general public research survey. Designed by the Rand Corporation in the 1950s, the Delphi technique is a consensus-building approach that relies on repeated waves of questionnaires sent to the same select panel of experts.

Internet Interviews   Web-based surveying is becoming more widely used. In its ubiquitous availability, the Web offers significant advantages over more traditional survey techniques. However, Internet interviews also introduce problems, among them that significant numbers of people either don't have access to or choose not to use the Internet. Several studies have found Internet surveys have significantly lower response rates than comparable mailed surveys.[5]

Analyzing Results

After selecting the sample, drawing up the questionnaire, and interviewing the respondents, the researcher must analyze the findings. Often a great deal of analysis is required to produce meaningful recommendations.

The objective of every sample is to come up with results that are valid and reliable. A margin of error explains how far off the prediction may be. A sample may be large enough to represent fairly the larger universe; yet, depending on the margin of sampling error, the results of the research may not be statistically significant. That is, the differences or distinctions detected by the survey may not be sizable enough to offset the margin of error. Thus, the margin of error must always be determined.

Popular political polls, even notwithstanding the problems caused by cell phones, are fraught with problems. They cannot predict outcomes scientifically. At best, they provide a snapshot, freezing attitudes at a certain point in time—like a balance sheet for a corporation. Obviously, people's attitudes change with the passage of time, and pollsters, despite what they claim, can't categorically predict the outcome of an election. The most notorious example of polls gone awry—even worse than the more recent problems—was the political poll sponsored by *Literary Digest* in 1936, which used a telephone polling technique to predict that Alf Landon would be the nation's next president. Landon thereupon suffered one of the worst drubbings in American electoral history at the hands of Franklin Roosevelt. It was probably of little solace to the *Literary Digest* that most of its telephone respondents, many of whom were Republicans wealthy enough to afford phones, did vote for Landon.

The point is that in analyzing results, problems of validity, reliability, and levels of statistical significance associated with margins of error must be considered before concrete recommendations are volunteered.

Communications Audits

Communications audits are an increasingly important method of research in public relations work. Such audits are used frequently by corporations, schools, hospitals, and other organizations to determine whether a communications group and the products it produces are realizing objectives and also how the institution is perceived by its core constituents. Communications audits help public relations professionals understand more clearly the relationships between management actions and objectives on the one hand and communications methods to promote those objectives on the other.

Communications audits are typically used to analyze the standing of a company with its employees or community neighbors; to assess the readership of routine communication vehicles, such as annual reports and news releases; or to examine an organization's performance as a corporate citizen. Communications audits often provide benchmarks against which future public relations programs can be applied and measured. The data uncovered are frequently used by management to make informed decisions about future communications needs and goals.

A communications audit is not an end in itself. Rather it must be part of a process of measurement and performance improvement.[6] In that context, an extensive audit should be conducted every couple of years to keep an organization's communications fresh and relevant and consistent with 21st century methods and techniques.

Unobtrusive Methods

Of the various unobtrusive methods of data collection available to public relations researchers, probably the most widely used is simple fact-finding. Facts are the bricks and mortar of public relations work; no action can be taken unless the facts are known, and the fact-finding process is continuous.

Another unobtrusive method is simple content analysis, the primary purpose of which is to describe a message or set of messages. For example, an organization with news releases that are used frequently by local newspapers can't be certain, without research, whether the image conveyed by its releases is what the organization seeks. By analyzing the news coverage, the firm can get a much clearer idea of the effectiveness of its communications.

Copy testing, in which public targets are exposed to public relations campaign messages to be used in brochures, memos, online, and so on, in advance of their publication, is another viable method that ensures campaign messages are understandable and effective.

Finally, case study research that analyzes how other organizations handled similar challenges is a constructive, unobtrusive research method.

Clearly, there is nothing particularly mysterious or difficult about unobtrusive methods of research. Such methods are relatively simple to apply—and also inexpensive—yet they are essential for arriving at appropriate refinements for an ongoing public relations program.

A Question of Ethics

Study: Diet Soda Sparks Weight Loss—Whaaaa?

Could diet soda really be better than water for weight loss?

Yes!

Or at least that's what a 2014 study, sponsored by the American Beverage Association, concluded.

The study, published in the journal Obesity included 300 overweight participants, all enrolled in a weight loss and exercise program. One random group was told to avoid all diet drinks and drink mostly water. The other group was told to consume a combination of zero-calorie drinks and water.

At the end of three months, the participants in the diet-drink group had lost about 13 pounds on average; four pounds more than the average of nine pounds lost by those in the water group.

So.....voila! Diet soda is better for weight loss than water. Or is it?

Academic researchers responded to the findings with all thumbs down. Said one Purdue University critic, "This paper is fatally flawed, and leaves us with little science to build on."

Indeed, a Purdue University study found that in the long term, diet soda drinkers may be "at increased risk of excessive weight gain, metabolic syndrome, type 2 diabetes, and cardiovascular disease." As the author of that report told CNN, *"Doing these short-term studies that look at weight can't really tell us anything about whether or not these products are contributing to these increased risks. And it's really hard to look at the (long-term) data and come up with any argument that they're helping."*

Another factor "weighing" on the weight loss study was the admission that the sponsor American Beverage Association's two largest members were none other than Coke and Pepsi* **(Figure 8-6)**.

Questions

1. The American Beverage Association sponsor of the study concluded that "diet soda spurs weight loss." Do you agree? Why or why not?

2. Were you the public relations director of the American Beverage Association, what would be your advice relative to sponsoring this study?

FIGURE 8-6
Research allies.
Long-term rivals Coke and Pepsi put down the gloves to band together for an American Beverage Association study that suggested diet soda was better than water for losing weight.
Photo: Rodney Turner KRT/Newscom

*For further information, see Allison Aubrey, "Could Diet Soda Really Be Better than Water for Weight Loss?" *NPR* (May 28, 2014); and James Best, "Research Claims Diet Soda Is Better than Water for Losing Weight – but Guess Who Paid for the Study," *Takepart.com* (May 29, 2014).

Evaluation

No matter what type of public relations research is used, results of the research and the research project itself should always be analyzed for meaning and action. Evaluation is designed to determine what happened and why by measuring results against established objectives.

The key word in organizations today is *accountability,* which means taking responsibility for achieving the performance promised. With resources limited and competition fierce, managers at every level demand accountability for every activity on which they spend money. That's what evaluation is all about. Public relations professionals are obligated today to assess what they've done to determine whether the expense was worth it.

Outcome evaluation measures whether targets actually *received* the messages directed to them, *paid attention* to them, *understood* the messages, *retained* those messages, and even *acted* on them.

In many respects, a measurement of public relations outcomes is the most important barometer in assessing success or failure of a program.

Measuring Public Relations Outcomes

What kinds of tools are used to measure public relations outcomes? Here are four of the most common.

Awareness and Comprehension Measurement   This measurement probes whether targets received the messages directed at them, paid attention to them, and understood them. Measuring awareness and comprehension levels requires "benchmarking," or determining preliminary knowledge about a target's understanding so that the furthering of that knowledge can be tracked.

Recall and Retention Measurement   This is a commonly used technique in advertising in which sponsors want to know if their commercials have lasting impact. Such measurement analysis may be equally important in public relations. It is one thing for a target to have seen and understood a message but quite another for someone to remember what was said.

Attitude and Preference Measurement   Even more important than how much someone retained from a message is a measure of how the message moved an individual's attitudes, opinions, and preferences. This involves the areas of opinion research and attitude research. The former is easier because it can be realized simply by asking a few preference questions. The latter, however, is derived from more complex variables, such as predispositions, feelings, and motivational tendencies regarding the issue in question.

Behavior Measurements   This is the ultimate test of effectiveness. Did the message get people to vote for our candidate, buy our product, or agree with our ideas?

Measuring behavior in public relations is difficult, especially in "proving" that a certain program "caused" the desired outcome to occur. In other words, how do we know that it was our input in particular that caused people to contribute more to our charity, or legislators to vote for our issue, or an editor to report favorably on our organization?[7]

Regardless of the evaluative technique, by evaluating after the fact, researchers can learn how to improve future efforts. In the fiercely competitive, resource-dear 21st century, the practice of public relations will increasingly be called on to justify its activities and evaluate the results of its programs with formal research.

4 Online Research

Research techniques in evaluating the effectiveness of programs and products and messages on the Web are constantly being perfected.

What can today's Web analytics measure in terms of consumer-generated media (CGR, as it's known in the trade)? Lots of things. Among them:

- Unique visitors
- Returning visitors
- Costs per click through
- Total time spent on a site
- Downloads
- Costs per contact
- Links from other sites
- Google page rank
- Content popularity
- Sales

Search Engine Optimization

The most ubiquitous term in public relations relative to evaluating Web sites or Web pages is Search Engine Optimization or SEO. This is the process of improving the visibility of a Web site or a Web page in a search engine's—primarily Google's—algorithmic search results. The higher ranked a site appears in the search results list, the more visitors it will receive from the search engine's users. SEO may target different kinds of search, including image search, local search, video search, academic search, industry-specific search, etc. Public relations professionals focus on SEO.

Beyond SEO, the two most frequent research terms relative to Web sites are *hits* and *eyeballs*. The former refers to the number of times a Web site is visited by an individual. The latter refers to the orbital lobes affixed to that hit. Obviously, these are but the most rudimentary of measurement tools in that they don't assess the visitors' interest in the product or service or information conveyed, the duration of their stay at the site, or whether they were driven to act on the information—that is, buy the product, subscribe to the service, or vote for the candidate. Indeed, the first 5,000 hits to a new Web site may mean nothing more than the firm's employees checking out the latest communications tool.

One of the most popular measurement vehicles to assess Web sites is Google Analytics, a free service that generates detailed statistics about site visitors. Google Analytics can track visitors from all referrers, including search engines, display advertising, pay-per-click networks, e-mail marketing, and PDF documents.

Social Media Metrics

Research is also a viable way to measure the benefit of an organization's social media output. Social media's ROI—return on investment—can be measured through a number of common sense metrics.

- **Blogger outreach.** Measuring success in reaching bloggers consists of determining how many bloggers wrote about your campaign, how many comments the posts received, how many social shares the posts received, etc.

- **Twitter analytics.** Measuring Twitter value consists of determining how often people used your hashtag, new followers generated by the campaign, cost vs. click-throughs of sponsored tweets, etc.

- **Facebook analytics.** Facebook offers built-in tools and demographic options to help measure success. These include the ability to count how many times people "liked" the particular message, determine if the targeted demographic was reached (using Facebook Insights), and evaluating cost and click-through rates of Facebook ads.

- **YouTube and other video sites** Use of online video can be measured through assessing number of views received, assessing "likes" and "favorites" received, counting new subscribers to the channel, etc.

A complement to these metrics is using and measuring mobile marketing to increase public relations campaign reach. Mobile, too, can be measured through using such devices as QR Codes, mobile app downloads, etc.[8]

Web Research Considerations

The value of Web-oriented research is indisputable. In preparing for such Internet evaluation—just as in preparing for any public relations research—an organization should take several factors into consideration:

1. **Establish objectives.** Again, implicit in any meaningful measurement is the setting of objectives. Why are we on the Web? What is our site designed to do? What are we attempting to communicate?

2. **Determine criteria.** Define success with tangible data—for example, percentage of people likely to purchase from the site and positive interactive publication mentions that the site will receive.

3. **Determine benchmarks.** Project the hits the site will receive. Base this on competitive data to see how this site stacks up against the competition or other forms of communication.

4. **Select the right measurement tool.** Numerous software analytical packages exist to track site traffic and provide other measurements of Internet public relations success, among them:

   - Web traffic: Clicktrax, Web trends, WebSide Story
   - Awareness/preference: SurveyMonkey, Zoomerang
   - Marketplace/Blog engagement: Type pad, Technorati
   - Messages: Dashboards, Vizu
   - Social media: Klout

5. **Compare results to objectives.** Success of online marketing and communications cannot be concluded in a vacuum. Numbers of visitors, hits, and eyeballs must be correlated with original objectives.

6. **Draw actionable conclusions.** Research indicates you've received 100,000 visitors to the site. So what? Interpret the significance of the numbers and do something with the data to make progress.[9]

Finally, in terms of researching the Web, there is the aspect of monitoring what is being said about the organization. With the proliferation of rogue sites, anti-business blogs, and chain letter e-mail campaigns, monitoring the Web has become a frontline public relations responsibility. Web 2.0 has been called the "great equalizer," which means that all individuals can have their say—mean, nasty, belligerent—and organizations must constantly keep track of what is being said about them by consumer-generated media.

Last Word

Research is a means of both defining problems and evaluating solutions. Even though intuitive judgment remains a coveted and important public relations asset, management must see measurable results.

Nonetheless, informed managements recognize that public relations may never reach a point at which its results can be fully quantified. Management confidence is still a prerequisite for active and unencumbered programs. Indeed, the best measurement of public relations value is a strong and unequivocal endorsement from management that it supports the public relations effort. However, such confidence can only be enhanced as practitioners become more adept in using research.

Whether it's as basic as researching through the "thud factor," that is, dumping a pile of publicity on a client's desk to assessing the AVE (advertising value equivalent of publicity)—to the most sophisticated SEO optimization techniques to measure outputs and evaluate outcomes—research must be part of any 21st century public relations enterprise.[10]

Frankly, practitioners don't have a choice. With efficiency driving today's bottom-line and with communications about organizations percolating at a 24/7 clip around the world through a variety of media, organizations must always know where they stand. It is the job of public relations to keep track of, record, and research changing attitudes and opinions about the organizations for which they work.

According to Stuart Z. Goldstein, well-respected communications director of the Depository Trust & Clearing Corporation, strategic public relations research is best achieved through two obligatory databases that form the core of strategy development:

1. An integrated relational database that allows a practitioner to leverage internal information across all public relations disciplines.

2. A diagnostic database that tracks and helps analyze opinion data on a wide range of issues across key segments of an organization's primary constituencies.[11]

The need for greater analytical backup for public relations activities will make it increasingly incumbent on public relations people to reinforce the value of what they do and what they stand for through constantly measuring their contribution to their organization's goals.

Discussion Starters

1. Why is research important in public relations work?
2. What are the differences between primary and secondary research?
3. What are the four elements of a survey?
4. What is the difference between random and stratified sampling?
5. What are the keys to designing an effective questionnaire?
6. What kinds of tools are used to measure public relations outcomes?
7. Why is evaluation important in public relations research?
8. What is Search Engine Optimization?
9. What kinds of questions are pertinent in evaluating a Web site?
10. What are the characteristics that can be measured in Web-based research?

Pick of the Literature

Primer of Public Relations Research, 2nd Edition

Don W. Stacks, New York: The Guilford Press, 2011

Don Stacks has, for decades, been the quintessential public relations researcher. He literally "wrote the book" on public relations research. And this is it.

Stacks reviews the importance of research and why most public relations practitioners fear it. The essence of modern-day public relations research, says the author, is

delivering evidence that the organization's bottom-line has been enhanced by public relations activities. Amen.

The book reviews all matter of public relations research, including an important section on the ethics of research, as well as case studies of qualitative and quantitative research and research reporting methods. An essential text.

Case Study   Researching a Position for Alan Louis General

The administrator at Alan Louis General Hospital confronted a problem that he hoped research could help solve. Alan Louis General, although a good hospital, was smaller and less well-known than most other hospitals in Corpus Christi, Texas. In its area alone, it competed with 10 other medical facilities. Alan Louis needed a "position" that it could call unique to attract patients to fill its beds.

For a long time, the Alan Louis administrator, Sven Rapcorn, had believed in the principle that truth will win out. Build a better mousetrap, and the world will beat a path to your door. Erect a better hospital and your beds will always be 98% filled. Unfortunately, Rapcorn learned, the real world seldom recognizes truth at first blush.

In the real world, more often than not, perception will triumph. Because people act on perceptions, those perceptions become reality. He decided to conduct a communications audit to help form a differentiable "position" for Alan Louis General.

Interview Process

As a first step, Rapcorn talked to his own doctors and trustees to gather data about their perceptions not only of Alan Louis General but also of other hospitals in the community. He did this to get a clear and informed picture of where competing hospitals ranked in the minds of knowledgeable people.

For example, the University Health Center had something for everybody—exotic care, specialized care, and basic bread-and-butter care. CC General was a huge, well-respected hospital whose reputation was so good that only a major tragedy could shake its standing in the community. Mercy Hospital was known for its trauma center. And so on.

As for Alan Louis itself, doctors and trustees said that it was a great place to work, that excellent care was provided, and that the nursing staff was particularly friendly and good. The one problem, everyone agreed, was that "nobody knows about us."

Attribute Testing

The second step in Rapcorn's research project was to test attributes important in health care. He did this to learn what factors community members felt were most important in assessing hospital care.

Respondents were asked to rank eight factors in order of importance and to tell Rapcorn and his staff how each of the surveyed hospitals rated on those factors. The research instrument used a semantic differential scale of 1 to 10, with 1 the worst and 10 the best possible score. Questionnaires were sent to two groups: 1000 area residents and 500 former Alan Louis patients.

Results Tabulation

The third step in the research was to tabulate the results in order to determine community priorities.

Among area residents who responded, the eight attributes were ranked accordingly:

1. Surgical care—9.23
2. Medical equipment—9.20
3. Cardiac care—9.16
4. Emergency services—8.96
5. Range of medical services—8.63
6. Friendly nurses—8.62
7. Moderate costs—8.59
8. Location—7.94

After the attributes were ranked, the hospitals in the survey were ranked for each attribute. On advanced surgical care, the most important feature to area residents, Laredo General ranked first, with University Health Center a close second. Alan Louis was far down on the list. The same was true of virtually every other attribute. Indeed, on nursing care, an area in which its staff thought Alan Louis excelled, the hospital came in last in the minds of area residents. Rapcorn was not surprised. The largest hospitals in town scored well on most attributes; Alan Louis trailed the pack.

However, the ranking of hospital scores according to former Alan Louis patients revealed an entirely different story. On surgical care, for example, although Laredo General still ranked first, Alan Louis came in a close second. Its scores improved similarly on all other attributes. In fact, in nursing care, where Alan Louis came in last on the survey of area residents, among former patients its score was higher than that of any other hospital. It also ranked first in terms of convenient location and second in terms of costs, range of services, and emergency care.

Conclusions and Recommendations

The fourth step in Rapcorn's research project was to draw some conclusions to determine what the data had revealed.

He reached three conclusions:

1. CC General was still number one in terms of area hospitals.
2. Alan Louis ranked at or near the top on most attributes, according to those who actually experienced care there.
3. Former Alan Louis patients rated the hospital significantly better than did the general public.

In other words, thought Rapcorn, most of those who try Alan Louis like it. The great need was to convince more people to try the hospital.

Rapcorn was confident that the data he had gathered from the research project were all he needed to come up with a winning idea.

He then set out to propose his recommendations.

Questions

1. What kind of communications program would you launch to accomplish Rapcorn's objectives?
2. What would be the cornerstone—the theme—of your communications program?
3. What would be the specific elements of your program?
4. In launching the program, what specific steps would you follow—both inside and outside the hospital—to build support?
5. How could you use the Internet to conduct more research about area hospitals and residents' perceptions of the care at these hospitals? How could you use the Internet to research the effectiveness of the communications program you implement?

From the Top

An Interview with Sandra Bauman

Dr. Sandra L. Bauman is founder and principal of Bauman Research & Consulting, LLC. During her two decades in research, Dr. Bauman has designed and managed hundreds of studies for corporate and non-profit clients in the areas of corporate image and brand positioning, employee communications and commitment, strategic marketing, publicity and public affairs, and customer satisfaction and loyalty. She is expert in quantitative methodologies, adept at qualitative research and is an experienced focus group moderator and facilitator for brainstorming, ideation, and strategic planning sessions with executives.

How important is research in public relations?

Research is a means of discovery and exploration, which becomes an important tool in strategic public relations planning. There are different ways research can help in public relations: it can be used to formulate strategy, better define your target or competitors, test reactions to messages and understand the current "environment" impacting your issue or client.

What is the state of research among most public relations professionals?

I think there is a deep appreciation for research in the public relations community. Some large agencies have entire departments that support their research needs. Others use outside research companies or consultants for support. Just peruse the program of any PR conference, articles in PR journals or on the Web sites of PRSA or the Institute for Public Relations and you'll see how much research is a part of the profession.

Is it possible to measure public relations success?

The short answer is yes, of course, but it can be challenging because of the complexity of environment in which PR is operating (often with factors that you can't control for, measure or even identify). First you need to set your objectives and what will determine success. Both need to be measurable. Then, there are generally three types of evaluation: outputs, outtakes, and outcomes. *Outputs* are the easiest to measure and they occur in the short-term—how much press coverage was achieved, how many whitepapers were downloaded, number of tweets, blog posts, etc. *Outtakes* are more challenging and are longer-term—they involve the "reach" of the program. In order to determine who you reached and how they are affected (perceptions, attitudes, messages, awareness), you need to benchmark the "before" and measure the "after" to determine change. Finally, there are *Outcomes*, which are the hardest to measure and really at the heart of the ROI debate: did your program work—by increasing sales, gaining market share, etc.

How do you respond to those who say public relations is based purely on intuition?

No profession can be based purely on intuition. Sometimes research confirms assumptions, hypotheses or conventional wisdom. That's an important role for research—now that intuition has further "proof." But it also can debunk some assumptions or help us discover new areas or relationships that we hadn't considered before.

What kinds of research are valuable for public relations professionals?

There are three types of research that are most valuable for PR professionals.

Secondary research, or desk research, involves collecting and synthesizing all available existing research and intelligence that relates to your topic. This is a critical first step—even if done more informally—before undertaking any primary research.

Qualitative research methods (e.g., focus groups, in-depth interviews, ethnographies) are used for discovery and exploration, to get at the "whys" of human decision making, perceptions and behaviors. Individuals are recruited to participate based on predetermined criteria; they are not a representative sample. Therefore results are directional, not statistical.

Quantitative research (e.g., surveys) is used when you need numeric measures to "quantify" things—behaviors, attitudes, awareness, usage, opinions, etc. Quality surveys use larger samples and statistical techniques that allow us to generalize from the findings to population at large. Quantitative research can look "easy" but often is complex. You need to use a rigorous methodology in order to get attention from national media outlets that have strict "vetting" standards.

How important is reading the daily newspaper as part of public relations "research"?

The answer is obvious. That's basically informal "desk" research. Keep an eye out for how news outlets use research in their stories and you will hone your skills at being an excellent "consumer" of research. Not only will you likely inform the work you do, but you'll probably get ideas for original research to use for your clients.

What are the most important Internet research tools?

The Internet has opened up another medium for conducting research, giving us the ability to expand our geographies, find hard-to-reach populations and reduce costs. We can now do focus groups online, for example, using webcams and collaborative software. There are a number of "do-it-yourself" survey options online, many of which have free versions.

Public Relations Bookshelf

Botan, Carl H. and Vincent Hazleton. *Public Relations Theory II.* Mahwah, NJ: Lawrence Erlbaum Associates, 2009. Strong focus on academic public relations research and theory.

Juggenheimer, Donald W., Larry D. Kelley, Jerry Hudson, and Samuel D. Bradley. *Advertising and Public Relations Research.* 2nd ed. New York, NY: Routledge, 2014. Solid comprehensive analysis of the theories and tactics of public relations research.

Kennedy, Dan. *No B.S.: Marketing to the Affluent.* Irvine, CA: Entrepreneur Media, 2008. Interesting research on the affluent in America, what makes them tick, what intrigues them, and what they buy.

Paine, Katie. *Measuring Public Relationships: The Data-Driven Communicator's Guide to Success.* Berlin, NH: K.D. Paine & Partners, 2007. One of the foremost researchers in public relations expounds on what it takes.

Pavlik, John V. *Public Relations: What Research Tells Us.* Newbury Park, CA: Sage Publications, 1987. Old, but the classic in the field.

Robbins, Donijo. *Understanding Research Methods.* Boca Raton, FL: CRC Press, 2009. Good research primer written for the public policy and nonprofit manager.

Sriramesh, Krishnamurthy and Dejan Vercic (Eds.). *The Global Public Relations Handbook.* New York: Routledge, 2009. Good study of international public relations with strong research base.

Thomas, Alan and Giles Mohan. *Research Skills for Policy and Development.* Thousand Oaks, CA: Sage Publications, Inc., 2007. Discussion of the research questions and approaches appropriate for policy investigation.

Van Ruler, Betteke, Ana T. Vercic, and Dejan Vercic. *Public Relations Metrics Research and Evaluation.* New York: Routledge, 2008. Extensive review of public relations research from the 1980s to the present.

Watson, Tom and Paul Noble. *Evaluating Public Relations.* 3rd ed. London, England: Kogan Page Ltd., 2014. A respected treatise on public relations measurement and research, complete with online environment commentary and case studies.

www.odwyerpr.com. *Jack O'Dwyer's Newsletter* offers online logos, agency statements, and complete listings of 550 PR firms. The best choice on the Web for accessing any part of the Web site, including news from the newsletter and other publications, hyperlinks to articles on PR, job listings, and more than 1000 PR services in 58 categories.

Endnotes

1. Cliff Zukin, "What's the Matter with Polling?" *The New York Times* (June 21, 2015).
2. Katie Delahaye Paine, "Measuring Social Media, Can You Track the Wild West?" *Address to Ragan Communications Conference* (September 2007).
3. Gary Holmes, "Nielsen Media Research Reports Television's Popularity Is Still Growing," *Nielsen Media Research* (September 21, 2006).
4. Tom Greenbaum, "The Gold Standard: Why the Focus Group Deserves to Be the Most Respected of All Qualitative Research Tools," *Quirk's Marketing Research Review* (June 2003).
5. David J. Solomon, "Conducting Web-Based Surveys," *Practical Assessment, Research and Evaluation* (August 23, 2001).
6. "Guidelines and Standards for Measuring and Evaluating PR Effectiveness," The Institute for Public Relations Commission on PR Measurement and Evaluation (2003).
7. Paine, "Measuring Social Media, Can You Track the Wild West?".
8. Danny Brown, "A Guide to Measuring Social Media ROI," *Ragan PR Daily* (May 28, 2014)
9. Frank Walton, "Expect More from PR Research," *PR Café, CommPro.biz* (September 13, 2011).
10. Clare Dowdy, "How to Measure the Value of Public Relations," *Financial Times* (June 20, 2006).
11. Fraser P. Seitel, "Strategic PR Research and Analysis," *odwypr.com* (January 26, 2004).

Chapter 9

Media

FIGURE 9-1   **Most powerful man in media?**
Not exactly but...comedian Marc Maron made national
news when he interviewed President Barack Obama in
the summer of 2015 for his podcast.
Photo: AW3/Arnold Wells/Newscom

Chapter Objectives

1. To discuss the bedrock importance of media relations as the most fundamental skill in public relations work.
2. To explore media communication in all its forms—print, electronic, Internet and social.
3. To discuss the value of publicity as more powerful and credible than advertising.
4. To examine the proper way of dealing with journalists vis-à-vis organizational publicity.

With the nation grieving over the senseless murder of eight African Americans in a Charleston, South Carolina, church in the summer of 2015, President Obama chose a bizarre media channel to bare his soul on the issue of race relations in America.

The President and his entourage pulled up to the Los Angeles home of comedian Marc Maron to tape a podcast **(Figure 9-1)**. Yup, a podcast! During the interview, the President made big news when he used the taboo "N word" to express his frustration.[1]

That the most powerful man in the world would use a podcast to make major news captured vividly how much the media have changed in the 21st century.

In the old days—before social media—several powerful newspapers and three national television networks essentially controlled the news. Public relations people attempted to secure publicity in these leadership media to communicate about their clients.

But today the media are fragmented, omnipresent, busy 24 hours a day/seven days a week. From Twitter feeds to Facebook inclusions to YouTube videos, to breaking news announcements on blogs with names like TMZ.com and Politico and Deadspin and the Drudge Report, to well, podcasts—today's media are constantly evolving, presenting a "moving target" for public relations professionals.

While elements of the traditional media are still vital in shaping the news agenda for the nation and the world, public relations people must begin with the recognition that the media in the 21st century have changed dramatically.

1 Paid vs. Owned vs. Earned

In the days before social media, public relations was aimed, essentially, at one thing: convincing a third party—usually a journalist—to report favorably on your client.

Journalists, who had no affiliation with you or your organization, were looked at as more objective, indifferent, non partisan, and neutral observers. And so, when they reported positively on what you or your organization stood for, this was perceived as an unbiased affirmation of what you or your organization espoused.

In public relations parlance, by winning this unbiased affirmation from a journalist, you had achieved *"third party endorsement"* —the ultimate goal of public relations, worth far more in terms of credibility and value than creating your own, biased advertising. Stated simply, the view of your client or employer expressed by an objective, outside reporter was worth far more than your own view of yourself.

Today, however, thanks primarily to the replacement of traditional media with tablets and mobile devices and the proliferation of social media, public relations has changed. Today, there are multiple media with which public relations people deal.

Basically, they break down into three groups.

1. Paid Media

Paid media is exactly that, media you pay for. The primary format of paid media is advertising. Formerly the province of advertising and marketing departments, public relations advertising has emerged as a combination of advertising and editorial. Ads on such topics as organizational strengths, issues, social responsibility, and philanthropy are more prevalent today than ever before.

The plusses of this format, of any advertising, are that you can control the content, the size, the placement, as well as what the advertising boys call "reach" and "frequency" —how many eyeballs you might "reach" through advertising and the number of times, i.e. the frequency, you'd like the ad to run. You are able to "guarantee" all of these benefits because you *pay* for them. One full page ad in *The New York Times* or *Wall Street Journal* can cost just a bit less than $200,000. So paid media costs plenty.

The big minus of paid media is that, it is far less credible to pat yourself on the back than it is to have some objective source do it for you. Moreover, in today's hyper-cluttered media world—with endless blogs and Web sites and YouTube channels and cable channels and talk radio and print and broadcast, not to mention all the various tablet and mobile and handheld devices that present them to you—it's a lot harder to ensure that anyone will even see your ad, much less pay attention to and act on it.

2. Owned Media

Owned media are the "new media" channels we, ourselves, own and operate. They can be Web sites, mobile sites, blogs, Twitter accounts, YouTube channels, Facebook pages, and anything else that social media comes up with. This is the brave new world of public relations, offering great opportunity for social media-savvy public relations professionals.

The benefits of owned media are that, once again, you can control content. But unlike with advertising, the cost of running a Twitter account or a Facebook page is far less than paying for frequent ads designed to reach many people. The cost efficiency of owned media, as well as its versatility in allowing you to reach niche audiences, is an enticing communications prospect.

The big downside of owned media is that, just like advertising, there is the potential—since you, in fact, *own* it—of not being trusted. Since it's your own Twitter feed or Facebook page or Instagram account, we don't expect you to be objective; or, at the very least, we're suspicious. The key challenge, then, for a public relations person using owned media is to build audience trust. For example, if your organization's tweets can stimulate others to support your cause or embrace your campaign, you have converted your owned media to *earned* media: thus achieving coveted credibility.

3. Earned Media

Earned media represents the legacy public relations value of "third party endorsement."

Earned media is "earned," in that objective reporters are persuaded to write favorably about your organization. Earned media translates into positive publicity and is the result of traditional news releases and story pitches and press conferences and other devices based on building amicable relationships with reporters, editors, bloggers, and other neutral reporters.

Earned media is the most credible format for public relations writers. However, it is not without risks. A negative story about your organization can trigger crisis: fading support, declining stock price, mounting public opposition, and the like. In addition, because there are no guarantees that even the most strategic public relations efforts will result in positive publicity, earned media is elusive.

Stated simply, while you can guarantee a positive ad with paid media or a glowing Facebook account with owned media, you can *"guarantee"* nothing with earned media. But. . . . when earned media works, the resulting publicity is eminently more powerful and valuable than any other format.

That's why the essence of traditional public relations practice—winning "third party endorsement" from objective reporters—is still the bottom-line value of positive public relations.[2] And that will be our focus in this chapter.

Objectivity in the Media

Freedom of the press is a hallmark of American democracy. It is a right guaranteed by the First Amendment to the U.S. Constitution. Written in 1789, the 45 words contained in the First Amendment protect the freedom of speech, press, religion, and assembly.

Over the years, in pursuing that freedom, the media have regularly challenged authority with pointed, nasty, even hostile questions. Their proper role in a democracy, as embodied in the First Amendment, is to independently ferret out the truth. Often this means "breaking eggs" in the process. Whether it means hounding a public figure, invading the privacy of a private figure, or just plain being obnoxious, that is what journalists have become known to do.

What this means to public relations professionals is that dealing with the media—particularly in light of Internet journalism, where 70% accuracy is considered "acceptable"—has never been more challenging.

This is the business of the public relations professional, who serves as the client's first line of defense and explanation with respect to the media. It is the public relations practitioner who meets the reporter head on. In the 21st century, media relations is not a job for the squeamish.

Whether the mass media have lost relative influence to the Internet and its various vehicles, securing positive publicity through the media still lies at the heart of public relations practice.

Why attract publicity?

The answer, as we will see, is that publicity is regarded as more *credible* than advertising. To attract positive publicity requires establishing a good working relationship with the media. This is easier said than done. In the 21st century, faced with intense competition from on-air and online journalists, reporters are by and large more aggressive.

They are also decidedly less "objective."

The presumed goal of a journalist is objectivity—fairness with the intention of remaining neutral in reporting a story. But total objectivity is impossible. All of us have biases and preconceived notions about many things. Likewise, in reporting, pure objectivity is unattainable; it would require complete neutrality and near-total detachment in reporting a story. Reporting, then, despite what some journalists might suggest, is subjective. Nevertheless, scholars of journalism believe that reporters and editors should strive for maximum objectivity **(Figure 9-2)**.

THE JOURNALIST'S Creed

I believe IN THE PROFESSION OF JOURNALISM.

I BELIEVE THAT THE PUBLIC JOURNAL IS A PUBLIC TRUST; THAT ALL CONNECTED WITH IT ARE, TO THE FULL MEASURE OF THEIR RESPONSIBILITY, TRUSTEES FOR THE PUBLIC; THAT ACCEPTANCE OF A LESSER SERVICE THAN THE PUBLIC SERVICE IS BETRAYAL OF THIS TRUST.

I BELIEVE THAT CLEAR THINKING AND CLEAR STATEMENT, ACCURACY, AND FAIRNESS ARE FUNDAMENTAL TO GOOD JOURNALISM.

I BELIEVE THAT A JOURNALIST SHOULD WRITE ONLY WHAT HE HOLDS IN HIS HEART TO BE TRUE.

I BELIEVE THAT SUPPRESSION OF THE NEWS, FOR ANY CONSIDERATION OTHER THAN THE WELFARE OF SOCIETY, IS INDEFENSIBLE.

I BELIEVE THAT NO ONE SHOULD WRITE AS A JOURNALIST WHAT HE WOULD NOT SAY AS A GENTLEMAN; THAT BRIBERY BY ONE'S OWN POCKETBOOK IS AS MUCH TO BE AVOIDED AS BRIBERY BY THE POCKETBOOK OF ANOTHER; THAT INDIVIDUAL RESPONSIBILITY MAY NOT BE ESCAPED BY PLEADING ANOTHER'S INSTRUCTIONS OR ANOTHER'S DIVIDENDS.

I BELIEVE THAT ADVERTISING, NEWS AND EDITORIAL COLUMNS SHOULD ALIKE SERVE THE BEST INTERESTS OF READERS; THAT A SINGLE STANDARD OF HELPFUL TRUTH AND CLEANNESS SHOULD PREVAIL FOR ALL; THAT THE SUPREME TEST OF GOOD JOURNALISM IS THE MEASURE OF ITS PUBLIC SERVICE.

I BELIEVE THAT THE JOURNALISM WHICH SUCCEEDS BEST—AND BEST DESERVES SUCCESS—FEARS GOD AND HONORS MAN; IS STOUTLY INDEPENDENT, UNMOVED BY PRIDE OF OPINION OR GREED OF POWER, CONSTRUCTIVE, TOLERANT BUT NEVER CARELESS, SELF-CONTROLLED, PATIENT, ALWAYS RESPECTFUL OF ITS READERS BUT ALWAYS UNAFRAID, IS QUICKLY INDIGNANT AT INJUSTICE; IS UNSWAYED BY THE APPEAL OF PRIVILEGE OR THE CLAMOR OF THE MOB; SEEKS TO GIVE EVERY MAN A CHANCE, AND, AS FAR AS LAW AND HONEST WAGE AND RECOGNITION OF HUMAN BROTHERHOOD CAN MAKE IT SO, AN EQUAL CHANCE; IS PROFOUNDLY PATRIOTIC WHILE SINCERELY PROMOTING INTERNATIONAL GOOD WILL AND CEMENTING WORLD-COMRADESHIP; IS A JOURNALISM OF HUMANITY, OF AND FOR TODAY'S WORLD.

Walter Williams

DEAN SCHOOL OF JOURNALISM, UNIVERSITY OF MISSOURI, 1908-1935

FIGURE 9-2
Code of objectivity. "The Journalist's Creed" was written after World War I by Dr. Walter Williams, dean of the School of Journalism at the University of Missouri. *Courtesy of Burrelles/Luce*

By virtue of their role, the media view officials, particularly business and government spokespersons, with a degree of skepticism. Reporters shouldn't be expected to accept on faith the party line. By the same token, once a business or government official effectively substantiates the official view and demonstrates its merit, the media should be willing to report this accurately without editorial distortion.

Stated another way, the relationship between the media and the establishment—that is, public relations people—should be one of *friendly adversaries* rather than of bitter enemies. Unfortunately, this is not always the case.

That is not to say that the vast majority of journalists don't try to be fair. They do. Despite the preconceived biases that all of us have, most reporters want to get the facts from all sides. An increasing number of journalists acknowledge and respect the public relations practitioner's role in the process. (Some don't, but there are rotten apples in any profession!) If reporters are dealt with fairly, most will reciprocate in kind.

However, some executives fail to understand the essential difference between the media and their own organizations. That is:

1. The reporter wants the "story," whether bad or good.

2. Organizations, on the other hand, want things to be presented in the best light.

Because of this difference, some executives consider journalists to be the enemy, dead set on revealing all the bad news they can about their organization. These people fear and distrust the media. As a consequence, the practice of public relations—intermediary between the executive and the journalist—gets knocked as a profession of "stonewallers" intent on keeping journalists out.[3] That is an unfair and, hopefully in most cases, undeserved generalization.

A Question of Ethics

Anchors Away

For decades, the individuals who reported the nightly news on the three major television networks—ABC, NBC, and CBS—were eminently respected.

CBS anchor Walter Cronkite, who anchored the nightly news for 19 years, was often cited as "*the most trusted man in America,*" even though the truth was he was little more than a news *reader*, reciting the lines written for him by others.

By the second decade of the 21st century, NBC's Brian Williams had emerged as the heir to the Cronkite throne **(Figure 9-3)**. While the advent of social media and mobile devices had lessened the importance of the nightly news, nonetheless Williams' nightly news cast regularly drew nine million viewers. Williams was respected not only for the ease and authority with which he delivered the news, but also for his knowledge of pop culture and his approachability.

While Brian Williams' 10-year rise to the top of the ratings was relatively swift, his fall in February 2015 was instantaneous.

It all started eight years earlier when Williams reported being shot at in a Chinook helicopter during the first days of the Iraq War. He further reported being rescued by heroic American soldiers, who saved his life. Ten years later in 2013, Williams recounted the incident on the David Letterman Show. And in January 2015, he retold the story on the NBC Nightly News, reporting,

"*The story actually started with a terrible moment a dozen years back during the invasion of Iraq when the helicopter we were travelling in was forced down after being hit by an RPG. Our travelling NBC News team was rescued, surrounded, and kept alive by an armored mechanized platoon from the U.S. Army 3rd Infantry.*"

And that's when the real firing started for Brian Williams. Immediately after the broadcast, the military publication *Stars and Stripes* interviewed soldiers who were present for the incident and denied that Williams was ever in the helicopter that took fire. They said Williams' helicopter arrived an hour after the fire fight, and his recollection and reporting was all wrong. And as it turned out, they were right; Williams, for whatever reason, had made the whole thing up.

After the blockbuster *Stars and Stripes* story, Williams took to the airwaves and apologized. But the damage was done. Additional instances began to be reported, where Williams may have also stretched the truth, including his reporting of seeing a dead body float by his hotel window while covering Hurricane Katrina in New Orleans. NBC suspended the anchor for six months and launched an investigation to determine his fate. In June 2013, the network announced that Williams had been found guilty of "a number of inaccurate statements," would be

FIGURE 9-3 **Shot down.**
NBC anchor man Brian Williams' reporting at the start of the Iraq War in 2003 came back to bite him 12 years later, when he was suspended and demoted for a lie.
Photo: Patrick Andrade/Polaris/Newscom

replaced on the Nightly News by Lester Holt, and would be transferred to the network's MSNBC cable news division.

It was a swift and dramatic fall from grace for America's #1 anchor, victimized by a lapse in ethics.*

Questions

1. How serious an ethical lapse do you consider Brian Williams' misstatements?

2. How would you assess NBC'S handling of the Brian Williams' situation?

3. Had you been NBC's public relations director, what would you have recommended the network do with Williams?

*For further information, see Bryan Burrough, "The Inside Story for the Soul of NBC News," *Vanity Fair* (May 2015); Lauren Carroll, "Timeline of Brian Williams' Statements on Iraqi Helicopter Attack," *Tampa Bay Times* (February 5, 2015); and Rory Carroll, "NBC Suspends Brian Williams Six Months over Iraqi Helicopter Story," *The Guardian* (February 11, 2015).

② Print Media Hangs In

Recent years have not been kind to the print medium, particularly newspapers.

Newspapers

As the recession deepened, once-powerful newspapers—hit by rising costs and declining readership, not to mention challenge from mobile devices, iPads, and comparable tablets—struggled to survive. After a century of daily publishing, the *Rocky Mountain News* in Denver closed. Another mainstay, the *Philadelphia Inquirer*, declared bankruptcy. In 2009, in Seattle, the daily *Post-Intelligencer* became exclusively a Web-based newspaper. In 2012, the historic New Orleans *Times-Picayune*, which reported relentlessly on Hurricane Katrina, fired 200 people and moved to a three-days-per-week publication schedule[4]. Layoffs continued through 2015, including at print leaders like *USA Today* and *The New York Times*, which in 2014 dismissed Jill Abramson, the first woman in its history to be executive editor.[5] Indeed, in 2013, according to the American Society of News Editors, there was a loss of 1300 full-time newspaper journalists.[6]

Despite such sour newspaper news, by the summer of 2015, print circulation, especially measured by time spent on news consumption, was stabilizing. Indeed, research from the Poynter Institute suggested that 92% of the time spent on news consumption is still on legacy, i.e. traditional media, platforms.[7] In terms of newspaper readership, circulation figures have shown some improvement, at least in the most widely read U.S. periodicals, including *USA Today*, *The Wall Street Journal*, and *The New York Times* (**Table 9-1**).

TABLE 9-1 **Top 100 U.S. Newspapers**

This list provided by Burrelles/Luce and compiled by the Audit Bureau of Circulations shows newspaper circulation through September 30, 2013. *Courtesy of Burrelles/Luce*

U.S. Daily Newspapers

Rank	Newspaper	Daily	Sunday	Rank	Newspaper	Daily	Sunday
1	USA Today	2,876,586 ▲	N/A	43	The Baltimore Sun	155,352 ▼	275,782 ▼
2	The Wall Street Journal	2,273,767 ▼	N/A	44	Pittsburgh Post-Gazette	153,078 ▼	279,765 ▼
3	The New York Times	1,897,890 ▲	2,391,986 ▲	45	Orlando Sentinel	152,923 ▼	259,791 ▼
4	Los Angeles Times	671,797 ▲	963,751 ▲	46	Sun-Sentinel (Ft. Lauderdale, FL)	151,413 ▼	206,175 ▼
5	New York Post	576,711 ▲	525,794 ▲	47	The Record (Hackensack, NJ)	148,087 ▼	182,466 ▲
6	San Jose Mercury News	546,282 –	700,437 –	48	The Indianapolis Star	147,342 ▼	279,915 ▼
7	Daily News (New York, NY)	467,110 ▼	587,063 ▼	49	Arkansas Democrat-Gazette (Little Rock, AR)	146,292 ▼	213,881 ▼
8	Chicago Tribune	453,567 ▲	807,189 ▲	50	The Buff News	142,509 ▼	212,757 ▼
9	Newsday (Long Island, NY)	437,457 ▲	496,498 ▲	51	The Columbus (OH) Dispatch	131,276 ▼	246,944 ▼
10	The Washington Post	431,521 ▼	800,643 ▼	52	Austin American-Statesman	130,457 ▲	192,839 ▲
11	Chicago Sun-Times	419,364 ▼	381,471 ▼	53	San Antonio Express-News	130,019 ▼	343,853 ▼
12	The Dallas Morning News	411,929 ▲	703,915 ▲	54	The Miami Herald	129,907 ▼	191,323 ▼
13	The Denver Post	403,039 ▼	618,571 ▼	55	Charlotte Observer	128,344 ▼	182,111 ▼
14	Daily News (Los Angeles, CA)	389,626 ▲	510,873 ▲	56	Omaha World-Herald	125,470 ▼	157,375 ▼
15	The Orange County (CA) Register	362,242 ▲	356,785 ▼	57	The Courier-Journal (Louisville, KY)	124,828 ▼	225,047 ▲
16	Houston Chronicle	356,347 ▼	961,387 ▼	58	The Virginian-Pilot (Hampton Roads, VA)	124,381 ▼	153,787 ▼
17	The Philadelphia Inquirer	310,002 ▲	465,835 ▼	59	The Hartford Courant	124,074 ▼	184,445 ▼
18	Star Tribune (Minneapolis-St. Paul, MN)	300,495 ▼	582,956 ▲	60	The Press-Enterprise (Riverside, CA)	124,051 ▼	146,129 ▼
19	Tampa Bay Times (St. Petersburg)	299,985 ▼	355,853 ▼	61	La Opinión	118,483 ▲	36,616 ▼
20	The Star-Ledger (Newark, NJ)	285,249 ▼	369,723 ▼	62	The Cincinnati Enquirer	117,754 ▼	235,515 ▼
21	Honolulu Star-Advertiser	265,099 ▼	202,487 ▼	63	News & Observer (Raleigh, NC)	115,017 ▼	168,289 ▼
22	The Boston Globe	253,373 ▲	384,931 ▲	64	The Oklahoman (Oklahoma City, OK)	112,225 ▼	160,910 ▼
23	The Atlanta Journal-Constitution	249,390 ▲	667,155 ▲	65	The Detroit News	108,377 ▼	N/A
24	The Arizona Republic (Phoenix, AZ)	245,133 ▼	474,375 ▼	66	The Providence Journal	106,605 ▼	105,810 ▼
25	The Seattle Times	241,320 ▲	363,078 ▲	67	Deseret News (Salt Lake City, UT)	106,424 ▲	183,251 ▲
26	Las Vegas Review-Journal	233,326 ▼	180,949 ▼	68	Baton Rouge Advocate	103,990 –	122,453 –
27	The Oregonian (Portland, OR)	225,868 ▼	284,806 ▼	69	Richmond Times-Dispatch	99,373 ▼	146,063 ▼
28	The San Diego Union-Tribune	222,541 ▼	381,303 ▼	70	Democrat and Chronicle (Rochester, NY)	96,957 ▼	151,905 ▲
29	The Plain Dealer (Cleveland, OH)	213,870 ▼	427,662 ▼	71	The Fresno Bee	96,287 ▼	146,326 ▼
30	San Francisco Chronicle	212,179 ▼	431,203 ▲	72	The Blade (Toledo, OH)	95,939 ▲	127,393 ▲
31	Pittsburgh Tribune-Review	199,182 ▼	222,252 ▲	73	Dayton Daily News	95,282 ▲	163,023 ▲
32	Pioneer Press (St. Paul, MN)	197,727 ▼	282,716 ▼	74	The Tennessean (Nashville, TN)	94,263 ▼	218,491 ▼
33	Detroit Free Press	196,955 ▼	801,663 ▲	75	Tulsa World	91,810 ▼	126,347 ▼
34	Milwaukee-Wisconsin Journal Sentinel	194,321 ▼	318,711 ▼	76	Daily Herald (Arlington Heights, IL)	91,745 ▼	100,313 ▼
35	The Sacramento Bee	190,204 ▼	308,166 ▲	77	Asbury Park Press	89,888 ▼	133,030 ▼
36	The Tampa Tribune	181,589 ▼	255,704 ▼	78	The Des Moines Register	89,684 ▼	187,004 ▼
37	Star-Telegram (Fort Worth, TX)	172,233 ▼	291,614 ▲	79	The Commercial Appeal (Memphis, TN)	89,654 ▼	124,128 ▼
38	Kansas City Star	169,936 ▼	254,111 ▼	80	Boston Herald	88,052 ▼	71,918 ▼
39	El Nuevo Dia (San Juan, PR)	168,274 –	199,945 –	81	The Palm Beach Post	87,699 ▼	110,569 ▼
40	St. Louis Post-Dispatch	161,343 ▼	461,259 ▲	82	Northwest Indiana Times	86,549 ▲	91,102 ▼
41	The Salt Lake Tribune	161,108 ▲	192,090 ▲				
42	Investor's Business Daily (Los Angeles, CA)	156,119 ▼	N/A				

TABLE 9-1 Continued

Rank	Newspaper	Daily	Sunday	Rank	Newspaper	Daily	Sunday
83	Albuquerque Journal	82,416 ▼	102,148 ▼	92	Telegram and Gazette (Worcester, MA)	73,968 ▼	77,544 ▼
84	The Florida Times-Union (Jacksonville, FL)	82,340 ▼	128,376 ▼	93	Lexington (KY) Herald Leader	73,276 ▼	96,733 ▼
85	Wisconsin State Journal (Madison, WI)	81,103 ▼	107,288 ▼	94	El Paso Times	72,517 –	135,013 –
86	Greater Philadelphia Newspaper Group	80,095 ▼	107,294 ▼	95	Knoxville News Sentinel	72,350 ▼	100,175 ▼
87	Arizona Daily Star (Tucson, AZ)	77,547 ▼	123,162 ▼	96	The Morning Call (Allentown, PA)	70,866 ▼	114,723 ▼
88	The Post and Courier (Charleston, SC)	77,433 ▼	86,259 ▼	97	Rockford Register Times (Rockford, IL)	69,253 –	68,720 –
89	The News Journal (New Castle County, DE)	76,185 ▼	107,276 ▼	98	New Haven Register (New Haven, CT)	68,148 –	78,336 –
90	The Akron Beacon Journal	75,622 ▼	107,545 ▼	99	The News Tribune (Tacoma, WA)	67,135 ▼	117,278 ▲
91	Intelligencer Journal/ Lancaster (PA) New Era	74,625 ▼	N/A	100	Times Free Press (Chattanooga, TN)	66,473 ▼	85,707 ▲

Source: Alliance for Audited Media (formerly Audit Bureau of Circulations) Snapshot Report for six-month period ending 09/30/13
▲ an increase in circulation for the period 03/31/13–09/30/13
▼ a decrease in circulation for the period 03/31/13–09/30/13
– did not appear on list of Top U.S. Daily Newspapers 03/31/13

Another significant factor in the continued relevance of the legacy print press is the growth of online newspapers and the reinvention of the newspaper newsroom. Virtually every leading newspaper has placed new emphasis on its online version, with USA Today publisher Gannett launching the *"Newsroom of the Future"* to standardize and digitize job roles across the company. While *USA Today* and *The Wall Street Journal* lead print circulation tables, the king of online newspapers is *The New York Times* **(Table 9-2)**. Another sign of the new Internet dominance of news delivery was the purchase of the venerable *Washington Post* by Amazon.com founder Jeff Bezos in 2013. As one traditional print reporter put it, *"I believe we are getting away from the days of a reporter heading out of the office with notebook in hand. Those situations are still there, but not so common. We are a creature of the Internet now, whether we like it or not."*[8]

Despite the growth of the Internet and electronic media, print still stands as an important medium among public relations professionals.

Why?

The answer probably lies in the fact that many departments at newspapers and magazines use news releases and other publicity vehicles compared to the limited opportunities for such original use on network and cable TV, which frequently schedule stories that have first attracted print coverage. In addition, online databases, blogs, and other Web-based media regularly use organization-originated material destined for print usage, so the Internet—while originating an increasing amount of original copy—still often serves as a residual target for print publicity.

Thomas Jefferson once famously said, *"Were it left to me to decide whether we should have a government without newspapers or newspapers without a government, I should not hesitate a moment to prefer the latter."*

Magazines

Like their newspaper brethren, U.S. magazines have also moved inexorably toward digital.

TABLE 9-2 **Top 50 U.S. Online Newspapers**

This list provided by Burrelles/Luce indicates the popularity of online sites of the leading U.S. newspapers, most especially *The New York Times* and *The Wall Street Journal*. *Courtesy of Burrelles/Luce*

U.S. Daily Newspapers Online

Popularity	Web site	Address	Popularity	Web site	Address
1 *	The New York Times	nytimes.com	26 *	Newsday (Long Island, NY)	newsday.com
2 *	The Wall Street Journal	online.wsj.com			
3 *	USA Today	usatoday.com	27 ▲	Deseret News (Salt Lake City, UT)	deseretnews.com
4 *	The Washington Post	washingtonpost.com			
5 *	Los Angeles Times	latimes.com	28 ▼	The Seattle Post-Intelligencer	seattlepi.com
6 ▲	Houston Chronicle	chron.com			
7 *	San Francisco Chronicle	sfgate.com	29 ▲	Orlando Sentinel	orlandosentinel.com
8 ▼	New York Post	nypost.com	30 ▼	The Examiner (Washington, D.C.)	washingtonexaminer.com
9 *	Chicago Tribune	chicagotribune.com			
10 ▲	The Star-Ledger (Newark, NJ)	nj.com	31 ▲	The Sacramento Bee	sacbee.com
			32 ▲	Salt Lake Tribune	sltrib.com
11 ▲	Washington Times	washingtontimes.com	33 ▼	Chicago Sun-Times	suntimes.com
12 ▼	Christian Science Monitor	csmonitor.com	34 ▼	Milwaukee-Wisconsin Journal Sentinel	jsonline.com
13 ▼	The Philadelphia Inquirer	philly.com	35 ▼	The Tampa Bay Times	tampabay.com
14 ▲	The Atlanta Journal-Constitution	ajc.com	36 ▲	Kansas City Star	kansascity.com
15 ▲	The Denver Post	denverpost.com	37 ▼	Boston Herald	bostonherald.com
16 ▼	The Seattle Times	nwsource.com	38 ▼	Orange County Register	ocregister.com
17 ▼	The Arizona Republic	azcentral.com	39 ▼	The Detroit News	detnews.com
18 ▲	San Jose Mercury News	mercurynews.com	40 ▲	The Indianapolis Star	indystar.com
19 ▲	Star Tribune (Minneapolis-St. Paul, MN)	startribune.com	41 ▼	The Oklahoman Online	newsok.com
			42 ▼	The Palm Beach Post	palmbeachpost.com
20 ▲	Sun-Sentinel (Ft. Lauderdale, FL)	sun-sentinel.com	43 ▼	Times Union (Albany, NY)	timesunion.com
			44 ▼	San Antonio Express-News	mysanantonio.com
21 ▲	The Dallas Morning News	dallasnews.com	45 *	News & Observer (Raleigh, NC)	newsobserver.com
22 ▼	Detroit Free Press	freep.com	46 ▲	Las Vegas Sun	lasvegassun.com
23 ▲	The Baltimore Sun	baltimoresun.com	47 ▼	The Hartford Courant	courant.com
24 ▼	St. Louis Post Dispatch	stltoday.com	48 –	New York Observer	observer.com
25 ▼	The Miami Herald	miamiherald.com	49 –	The Tennessean	tennessean.com
			50 ▼	Honolulu Star-Advertiser	staradvertiser.com

Source: Alexa Top Sites by News Category (filtered by Newspaper) accessed 02/26/14
▲ an increase for 02/26/14 compared with 06/18/13
▼ a decrease for the 02/26/14 compared with 06/18/13
* stayed the same for 02/26/14 compared with 06/18/13
– did not appear on list of Alexa Top Sites by News Category 06/18/13

In 2015, as a sign of the times, the Association of Magazine Media rebranded its flagship American Magazine Conference as the American Magazine Media 360 Conference reflecting a new mission of evolving magazine publishers to multiplatform media companies.[9] Accordingly, venerable Time, Inc., the nation's largest magazine publisher, hired an expert in digital advertising to run its magazine operation.

On the plus side, the magazine industry reported in 2015 a 10% growth in its gross audience, with 91% of U.S. adults reading print magazine. The number of print magazines has held steady at around 7000 for nearly a decade, with 180 print magazines existing for more than 50 years.[10] News magazines, as opposed to other categories, seem to be holding their own in the second decade of the 21st century. While general magazine sales were down 14% in 2014, the equivalent drop in news magazines was only 1%. Some few magazines—among them, *The Atlantic, New York Magazine*, and *Rolling Stone*—showed surprising increases in circulation.[11] On the other hand, magazine hiring was not as robust as dismissals of editors and reporters. And *Rolling Stone*, one of the biggest magazine success stories, became a cause célèbre in 2015 when it ran a cover story about a bogus gang rape at a University of Virginia fraternity house; the university sued the magazine over its discredited report.

Magazines remain available for every taste and peculiarity, with titles from *Bacon Busters* for hog hunters, *Bark* for dog lifestyle fans, and *Crappie* for enthusiasts of a particular freshwater fish to *sheep*! for those fond of, well, sheep. Perhaps understandably, as the nation ages, the most widely read consumer magazines are those published by the American Association of Retired Persons, followed closely (also understandably) by a magazine for video gamers **(Table 9-3)**.

For the public relations professional, then, with so many print outlets—newspapers, magazines, and online publications—the area of public relations publicity remains broad and deep.

TABLE 9-3   Top 25 U.S. Consumer Magazines

This list provided by Burrelles/Luce and compiled by the Audit Bureau of Circulations shows magazine circulation, dominated by senior citizens, gamers, women, and ESPN and Netflix viewers. *Courtesy of Burrelles/Luce*

U.S. Consumer Magazines

Rank	Magazine	Total Paid & Verified Circulation
1	AARP The Magazine	21,931,184 ▼
2	AARP Bulletin	21,701,445 ▼
3	Game Informer	7,829,179 ▼
4	Better Homes and Gardens	7,624,505 ▲
5	Reader's Digest	5,241,484 ▼
6	Good Housekeeping	4,396,795 ▲
7	Family Circle	4,014,881 ▼
8	National Geographic	4,001,937 ▼
9	People	3,542,185 ▼
10	Woman's Day	3,394,754 ▲
11	Time	3,301,056 ▲
12	Ladies' Home Journal	3,229,809 ▼
13	Taste of Home	3,207,340 ▼
14	Sports Illustrated	3,065,507 ▼
15	Cosmopolitan	3,017,987 ▼
16	Prevention	2,884,542 ▼
17	Southern Living	2,824,751 ▼
18	O, The Oprah Magazine	2,417,589 ▼
19	Glamour	2,300,854 ▼
20	Parenting	2,245,062 ▲
21	American Legion Magazine	2,232,287 ▼
22	Redbook	2,229,809 ▲
23	FamilyFun Magazine	2,130,223 –
24	ESPN The Magazine	2,128,345 –
25	Smithsonian	2,121,281 –

Source: Alliance for Audited Media (formerly Audit Bureau of Circulations) figures for six-month period ending 06/30/13
▲ an increase in circulation for the period 12/31/12–06/30/13
▼ a decrease in circulation for the period 12/31/12–06/30/13
– did not appear on list of U.S. Consumer Magazines 12/31/12

Electronic Media Leads

Television remains the main place Americans turn to for news about current events (55%), leading the Internet at 21%, newspapers at 9%, and radio at 6%.[12] And among television news viewers, conservative Fox News Channel beats out CNN as America's most trusted broadcast news source, leaving the liberal MSNBC trailing in the dust. Ironically, although Fox frequently takes issue with the "mainstream media," according to such polls, it has *become* the "mainstream media."[13]

What makes the electronic media's news dominance so disconcerting—some would say scary—is that the average 30-minute television newscast would fill, in terms of words, only one-half of one page of the average daily newspaper! That means that if you're getting most of your news from television, you're *missing* most of the news.

While most cable TV news channels continue to see revenues increase, the other side of the picture is that viewership is decreasing. By almost every measure, fewer people are tuning to cable TV in general and, instead, switching to on-demand and streaming viewing services.[14] With challenges from upstarts like Netflix, Hulu, Amazon, and other on-demand viewing services, the number of daily cable watchers has begun to drop steadily.

Despite these new challenges, cable TV has had a dramatic impact on the nation's news consumption habits.

- The impact of 24/7 cable news meant that Americans were barraged with a continuous loop of Kardashians, Kanyes, and assorted other perpetual pop culture esoterica. While network evening news broadcast showed an uptick into 2015, attempting to retain at least some vestige of "impartial" journalism, cable news made no such attempt. Fox News, with lead hosts Bill O'Reilly and Sean Hannity, was unabashedly conservative, while MSNBC, with anchors Al Sharpton and Rachel Maddow, was unashamedly liberal. In such an environment, it was difficult to discern the true and newsworthy from the inconsequential and biased.

- Specialized cable networks, offering everything from sports and food and fashion to weather and history, beam nonstop across the land. In the financial area, for example, CNBC, Fox Business Channel, Bloomberg Television, PBS Nightly Business Report, and other similar efforts have become enormously popular barometers of the nation's stock market appetite. The most outrageous—some would say "dangerous" —cable phenomenon was the popularity, particularly with younger viewers, of "fake news," served up by the likes of Jon Stewart and Stephen Colbert and their successors on Comedy Central and John Oliver on HBO. These comedians specialized in *"truthiness,"* a brand of *"news"* characterized by strong opinions touching on selective facts. The "danger" was that some viewers took these subjective pronouncements as gospel. Stewart's *The Daily Show* was watched by two million viewers daily, 40% of them in the 18-29 demographic, and Colbert's *The Colbert Report* was watched by nearly as many, 43% in the 18-29 demographic.[15] Indeed, when Colbert announced in 2014 he would leave *The Colbert Report* after nine years to replace David Letterman on CBS and Stewart announced a year later that he would leave The Daily Show after 17 years, it was big news[16] **(Figure 9-4)**.

- Meanwhile, 244 million Americans listen to traditional "terrestrial radio" and 25 million listen to satellite radio every year. Talk radio has become an enormous political and social force, particularly conservative talk radio which dominates the airwaves. Each week, mostly conservative talk show hosts lead call-in discussions of the issues of the day. The undisputed dean of this ilk, Rush Limbaugh—*El Rushbo*—reaches a gargantuan 15 million listeners (known

FIGURE 9-4
Red, white and truthy.
The deans of "fake news," Stephen Colbert and Jon Stewart took their act to the nation's capital for the "Rally to Restore Sanity and/or Fear" in 2010.
Photo: JIM Tripplaar Kristoffer/SIPA/Newscom

as "ditto heads" because they *always* agree with the host!). Limbaugh, who makes $40 million a year, was the leading talk radio talker for nearly a decade.[17]

Despite the evolving strength of the Internet as a communications medium, the electronic media undoubtedly will remain a force in the new millennium. Given the extent to which the electronic media dominate society, public relations people must become more resourceful in understanding how to deal with television and radio.

Online Media Competes But....

The new digital revolutionaries—from the *Huffington Post* and the *Drudge Report* to Buzzfeed and TMZ.com to the Daily Mail Online and Yahoo news—have made significant inroads into the news/opinion nexus but have by no means taken over. These upstarts have had to alter their news-gathering emphasis to compete with television; indeed, streaming video occupies 78% of U.S. Internet bandwidth.[18] So the reports of the imminent demise of the "old media" are very much exaggerated.

That is not to discount the impact of the net. To some, the Internet has ushered in a new age of journalistic reporting: immediate, freewheeling, unbridled. Indeed, when the young people of the Middle East erupted into the ill fated-Arab Spring at the end of 2010, it was Twitter and Facebook that broadcast the news from Tunisia to Libya to Egypt to Syria. To others, however, the Internet is responsible for the collapse of journalistic standards and the ascendancy of rumor mongering. And, as noted, one clear online growth area is the digital presence of daily newspapers. So the irony is that while the Internet may be mortally wounding the daily newspaper as we know it, it is also allowing some papers to increase their readership online.

As to the indigenous news-oriented inhabitants of the Web, "new-age news sources" abound, from the right wing Drudge Report and NewsMax to the left wing Huffington Post and Salon, offering agreeable fodder for believers and increased targets for public relations practitioners. *The Huffington Post*, founded in 2005 by the conservative-turned-liberal gadfly Arianna Huffington, was purchased in 2011 by AOL for a whopping $315 million. (That's some gadfly!) *The Huffington Post*, with 28 million unique Web site visitors per month, has been ranked as the most popular political news Web site, with the conservative Drudge Report second with half the amount of estimated unique monthly users, compared to its liberal rival.[19]

Finally, there are the blogs—all 227 million of them and counting.

Blogs come in all shapes, sizes, and pedigrees. Many are of passing interest, many more are worthless, and several—a precious few, really—have become important sources of news and commentary. Measuring agency Technorati ranks blogs by their links to Web sites. The higher the number of links, the greater the ranking by Technorati. Leading blogs **(Table 9-4)** are all over the lot, from news sites to political sites, from tech sites to gossip sites.

TABLE 9-4 **Most Popular Blogs**

This list, provided by Burelles/Luce and composed by Technorati, shows the most popular English-language blogs through February 26, 2014. *Courtesy of Burelles/Luce*

English-Language Blogs

Rank	Blog	Blog Address	Technorati Authority Figures on 02/26/14
1	The Huffington Post	huffingtonpost.com	956 ▲
2	BuzzFeed	buzzfeed.com	913 ▲
3	The Verge	theverge.com	898 ▲
4	Mashable	mashable.com	889 ▲
5	Business Insider	businessinsider.com	887 ▲
6	Gawker	gawker.com	867 ▲
7	Deadspin	deadspin.com	859 ▲
8	TechCrunch	techcrunch.com	856 ▲
9	Gizmodo	gizmodo.com	850 ▲
10	Ars Technica	arstechnica.com	848 ▲
11	TMZ	tmz.com	844 ▲
12	Mediaite	mediaite.com	842 ▲
13	Bleacher Report	bleacherreport.com	842 ▲
14	SB Nation	sbnation.com	837 ▲
15	The Blaze	theblaze.com	835 ▲
16	Deadline	deadline.com	828 ▲
17	Jezebel	jezebel.com	825 ▲
18	ZeroHedge	zerohedge.com	824 ▲
19	GigoOM	gigaom.com	823 ▲
20	CNN Political Ticker	politicalticker.blogs.cnn.com	821 ▲
21	Think Progress	thinkprogress.org	818 –
22	Hot Air	hotair.com	805 ▲
23	Laughing Squid	laughingsquid.com	805 ▲
24	Bits	bits.blogs.nytimes.com	799 –
25	Venture Beat	venturebeat.com	796 –

Source: Technorati Authority for the Top 100 Blogs on 02/26/14
▲ an increase in authority for 02/26/14 compared with 06/17/13
▼ a decrease in authority for 02/26/14 compared with 06/17/13
* no change in authority for 02/26/14 compared with 06/17/13
– did not appear on list of Top English-Language Blogs 06/17/13

The majority of bloggers are women, and half of bloggers are aged 18–34. About one in three bloggers are moms, and more than half are parents with children under 18 years old. Seventy percent of bloggers have gone to college.[20]

The point is that Internet reporters and bloggers from every political bias and ulterior motive remain busy 24 hours a day, seven days a week, churning out continuous stories—some true, others not—about companies, government agencies, nonprofits, and prominent individuals.

The challenge for public relations professionals in dealing with print, electronic, or online commentators is to foster a closer relationship between their organizations and those who present the news. The key, once again, is fairness, with each side accepting—and respecting—the other's role and responsibility.

Dealing with the Media

It falls on public relations professionals to orchestrate the relationship between their organizations and the media, whether print, electronic, or Internet-based. To be sure, the media can't ordinarily be manipulated (and they *hate* it if you try!). They can, however, be engaged in an honest and interactive way to convey the organization's point-of-view in a manner that may merit being reported. First, an organization must establish a formal media relations policy.

Organizations profit by maintaining positive relations with the media, and the media relations policy should so state. Typical is the National Football League's media relations policy, which begins with the following sentence: *"Reasonable cooperation with the news media is essential to the continuing popularity of our game and its players and coaches."* The league policy goes on to specify that "players must be available to the media following every game" and . . . "it is not permissible for any player or any group of players to boycott the media."[21]

Next, an organization must establish a philosophy for dealing with the media, keeping in mind the following dozen principles:

1. **A reporter is a reporter.** A reporter is never "off duty." Anything you say to a journalist is fair game to be reported. Remember that, and never let down your guard, no matter how friendly you are.

2. **You are the organization.** In the old days, reporters disdained talking to public relations representatives, who they derisively labeled "flacks" (as in "catching flak," or bad news). Public relations people, therefore, were rarely quoted and remained anonymous. Today the opposite is true. The public relations person represents the policy of an organization. He or she is quoted by name and interviewed on camera, so every word out of the public relations professional's mouth must be carefully weighed in advance.

3. **There is no standard-issue reporter.** The sad fact is that many business managers want nothing to do with the press. They believe them to be villains. But that isn't necessarily true. As noted, most are simply trying to do their jobs, like anyone else, so each should be treated as an individual, until, cynics might say, "proven guilty."

4. **Treat journalists professionally.** As long as they understand that your job is different than theirs and treat you with deference, you should do likewise. A journalist's job is to get a story, whether good or bad. A public relations person's job is to present the organization in the best light. That difference understood, the relationship should be a professional one. Some journalists complain

that "PR people are paid to twist reality into pretzels and convince you that they are fine croissants."[22] So seek to earn reporter trust.

5. **Don't sweat the skepticism.** Journalists aren't paid to ask nice questions. They are paid to be skeptical. "Bad news" is *news*, while "good news" isn't usually *news*. Some interviewees resent this. Smart interviewees realize it comes with the territory.

6. **Don't try to "buy" a journalist.** Never try to threaten or coerce a journalist with advertising. The line between news and advertising should be a clear one. No self-respecting journalist will tolerate someone trying to "bribe" him or her for a positive story.

7. **Become a trusted source.** Journalists can't be "bought," but they can be persuaded by your becoming a source of information for them. A reporter's job is to report on what's going on. By definition, a public relations person knows more about the company and the industry than does a reporter. So become a source and a positive relationship will follow.

8. **Talk when not "selling."** Becoming a source means sharing information with journalists, even when it has nothing to do with your company. Reporters need leads and story ideas. If you supply them, once again a positive relationship will follow.

9. **Don't expect "news" agreement.** A reporter's view of "news" and an organization's view of "news" will differ. If so, the journalist wins. (It's the reporter's paper/Web site/TV station, after all!) Don't complain if a story doesn't make it into publication. Sometimes there is no logical reason, so never promise an executive that a story will "definitely make the paper."

10. **Don't cop a 'tude.** Don't have an attitude with reporters. They need the information that you possess. If you're coy or standoffish or reluctant to share, they will pay you back. Although reporters vary in look and type, they all share one trait: They remember.

11. **Never lie.** This is the cardinal rule. Stated bluntly, "Never lie to a reporter or that reporter will never trust you again."[23]

12. **Read the paper.** The number one criticism of public relations people by journalists is that they often don't have any idea what the journalist writes, comments, or blogs about. This is infuriating, especially when a journalist is approached on a story pitch. Lesson: Read the paper or the blog!

Although some may deny it, reporters are human beings, so there is no guarantee that even if these principles are followed, all reporters will be fair or objective. Most of the time, however, following these dozen rules of the road will lead to a better relationship between the journalist and the public relations professional.

3 Attracting Publicity

Publicity, through news releases—mostly via e-mail—and other methods, is eminently more powerful and valuable than advertising. Why? Publicity is "earned"; advertising is bought. There's a big credibility difference.

Publicity is most often gained by dealing directly with the media, either by initiating the communication or by reacting to inquiries. Although most people—especially CEOs!—confuse the two, *publicity* differs dramatically from *advertising*.

First and most important, advertising costs money—lots of it. A color, full-page, one-time, nonrecurring ad in the global edition of *The Wall Street Journal,* for example, costs upwards of $372,000, with black and white, $280,000—for one ad! A full page in *The New York Times* is just slightly lower.[24]

On the other hand, the benefits of paid advertising include the following communications areas that can be "guaranteed":

- **Content:** What is said and how it is portrayed and illustrated
- **Size:** How large a space is devoted to the organization
- **Location:** Where in the paper the ad will appear
- **Reach:** The audience exposed to the ad—that is, the number of papers in which the ad appears
- **Frequency:** How many times the ad is run

Frequency is extremely important. Today, with 500 cable and broadcast television channels, thousands of newspapers and magazines, and millions more Internet sites, people often skip over or surf by the ads or commercials. The only way to get through is to repeat the ad over and over again. In that manner, the largest advertisers—McDonald's, Microsoft, Coca-Cola, and so on—blast their way into public consciousness.

Publicity, on the other hand, offers no such guarantees or controls. Typically, publicity is subject to review by news editors who may decide to use all of a story, some of it, or none of it. Many news releases, in fact, never see the light of print.

When the story will run, who will see it, and how often it will be used are all subject to the whims of a news editor. However, even though attracting publicity is by no means a sure thing, it does offer two overriding benefits that enhance its appeal far beyond that of advertising:

- First, although not free, publicity costs only the time and effort expended by public relations personnel and management in conceiving, creating, and attempting to place the publicity effort in the media. Therefore, relatively speaking, its cost is minimal compared to advertising; the rough rule of thumb is 10% of equivalent advertising expenditures.

- Second and more important, publicity, which appears in news rather than in advertising columns, carries the implicit *third-party* endorsement of the news source that reports it. In other words, publicity is perceived not as the sponsoring organization's self-serving view but as the view of the objective, unbiased, neutral, impartial news source. For years, as noted, when surveys asked people to name their most trusted American, respondents invariably answered not the president or first lady but rather Walter Cronkite, the late former news anchor at CBS. NBC's Tom Brokaw and the late Tim Russert became equally trusted over the years. (Today, of course, it's more likely to be fake newsmen like Trevor Noah or Larry Wilmore!)

So even in a cynical society, news reporters and news organizations still enjoy credibility. When an organization's publicity is reported by such a source, it instantly becomes more credible, believable, and, therefore, valuable *news*.

That, in essence, is why publicity is more powerful than advertising.

Value of Publicity

For any organization, then, publicity makes great sense in the following areas:

- **Announcing a new product or service.** Because publicity can be regarded as news, it should be used before advertising commences. A new product or service is news only once. Once advertising appears, the product is no longer news. Therefore, one inflexible rule—that most organizations, unfortunately, don't follow—is that publicity should always precede advertising (**Figure 9-6**).

FYI

Confessions of a Media Maven

Dealing with the media for fun and profit, even for an experienced public relations hand, is a constant learning experience. It is also risky business. Consider the real-life case of an up-and-coming, daring, but wet-behind-the-ears public relations trainee.

In the 1980s, many of the nation's largest banks were a bit jittery about negative publicity on their loans to lesser developed countries. One of the most vociferous bank bashers was Patrick J. Buchanan, a syndicated columnist who later became President Reagan's communications director and still later ran for president **(Figure 9-5)**.

After one particularly venomous syndicated attack on the banks, the young and impetuous bank public affairs director wrote directly to Buchanan's editor asking whether he couldn't "muzzle at least for a little while" his wild-eyed columnist. The letter's language, in retrospect, was a tad harsh.

Some weeks later, in a six-column article that ran throughout the nation, Buchanan wrote in part:

Another sign that the banks are awaking to the reality of the nightmare is a screed that lately arrived at this writer's syndicate from one Fraser P. Seitel, director of public affairs of the Chase Manhattan Bank.

Terming this writer's comments "wrong," "stupid," "inflammatory," and "the nonsensical ravings of a lunatic," Seitel nevertheless suggested that the syndicate "tone down" future writings, "at least 'til the frenetic financial markets get over the current hysteria."*

Buchanan went on to describe the fallacy in bankers' arguments and ended by suggesting that banks begin immediately to cut unnecessary frills—such as "directors of public affairs!"

Moral: Never get into a shouting match with somebody who buys ink by the barrel.

Secondary moral: Just because you write a textbook doesn't mean you know everything!*

FIGURE 9-5 **Thumbs down media relations.**
Syndicated columnist, TV commentator, and presidential contender Patrick Buchanan didn't suffer a fool gladly when challenged by one bright-eyed media relations novice.
Photo: CHUCK KENNEDY/KRT/Newscom

*For further information, see Patrick J. Buchanan, "The Banks Must Face Up to Losses on Third World Loans," *New York Post* (July 12, 1984): 35.

■ **Reenergizing an old product.** When a product has been around for a while, it's difficult to make people pay attention to advertising. Therefore, publicity techniques—staged events, sponsorships, and so on—may pay off to rejuvenate a mature product.

■ **Explaining a complicated product.** Often, there isn't enough room in an advertisement to explain a complex product or service. Insurance companies, banks, and mutual funds, which offer products that demand thoughtful explanation, may find advertising space too limiting. Publicity, on the other hand, allows enough room to tell the story.

■ **Little or no budget.** To make an impact, advertising requires frequency—the constant repetition of ads so that readers eventually see them and acknowledge the product. But when an organization or individual can't afford the significant sums that advertising demands, seeking publicity is the desired course. In the case of Samuel Adams Lager Beer, for example, the company lacked an advertising budget to promote its unique brew, so it used public relations techniques to spread the word about this different-tasting beer. Over time, primarily through publicity about its victories at beer-tasting competitions, Samuel Adams grew in popularity. It took Sam Adams' founder Jim Koch 12 years to be able to afford its first TV commercial.[25] Today, its advertising budget is in the hundreds of millions, but the company's faith in publicity endures.

FIGURE 9-6 **Earning publicity.**
Making "news" by using celebrities like New York Giants' quarterback Eli Manning is a proven publicity generator.

■ **Enhancing the organization's reputation.** Advertising is, at its base, self-serving. When a company gives to charity or does a good deed in the community, taking out an ad is the wrong way to communicate its efforts. It is much better for the recipient organization to commend its benefactor in the daily news columns.

■ **Crisis response.** In a crisis, publicity techniques are the fastest and most credible means of response. Indeed, in the 21st century, it has become a cliché for celebrities to "apologize" for transgressions by seeking out a high-profile TV interviewer for instant publicity.

These are just a few of the advantages of publicity over advertising. A smart organization, therefore, will always consider publicity a vital component in its overall marketing plan.

4 Pitching Publicity

The activity of trying to place positive publicity in a periodical, on a news site, or in the electronic media—of converting publicity to news—is called *pitching*. Traditionally, public relations people "pitched" journalists through mail. Today, as more editors become more conversant in digital and social media, pitch methods are evolving. Specifically, media outlets are looking for more than text—for example, photos and videos. However, even in the second decade of the 21st century, it's important to recognize that 80% of reporters still want pitches through e-mail; only 2% prefer social media.[26]

The following hints may help achieve placement of a news release:

1. **Be time sensitive.** The Internet means every news organization wants your news now. News events should be scheduled, whenever possible, to accommodate news deadlines.

2. **Generally write first, then call.** Reporters are barraged with deadlines. They are busiest close to deadline time, which is late afternoon for morning newspapers and early afternoon for local television news. Thus, it's preferable to e-mail news releases first, rather than try to explain them over the telephone. Follow-up calls to reporters to "make sure you got our release" also should be avoided. If reporters are unclear on a certain point, they'll call to check.

3. **Direct the release to a specific person or editor.** Newspapers are divided into departments, and bloggers have specialties: business, sports, style, entertainment, and so on. Assignment editors are generally in charge of television news. The release directed to a specific person, editor, or blogger has a greater chance of being read.

4. **Determine how the reporter wants to be contacted.** Call or write, e-mail or tweet? Treat the reporter as the client. How he or she prefers to get the news should guide how you deliver it.

5. **Don't badger.** Journalists are generally fiercely independent about the copy they use. Even a major advertiser will usually fail to get a piece of puffery published. Badgering an editor about a certain story is bad form, as is complaining excessively about the treatment given a certain story.

6. **Use exclusives, but be careful.** News desks receive hundreds of e-mails daily; most, for better or worse, are considered spam. That's the reality. But reporters get credited for getting "scoops" and citing "trends." So public relations people might promise exclusive stories to particular publications. The

exclusive promises one publication or other news source a scoop over its competitors. Best policy is to spread your exclusives to different recipients, so that no journalist is alienated.

7. **Do your own calling.** Reporters and editors generally don't have assistants. So having a secretary place a call to a journalist can alienate a good news contact. Public relations professionals should make their own calls. Above all, be pleasant and courteous.

8. **Don't send clips of other stories about your client.** Often, rather than interesting a journalist in your story, this will just suggest that others have been there already and make the story potential less attractive.

9. **Develop a relationship.** Relationships are the name of the game. The better you know a reporter, the more understanding and accommodating to your organization he or she will be.

10. **Never lie.** This is *the* cardinal rule.

Dealing with the media is among the most essential technical skills of the public relations professional. Anyone who practices public relations must know how to deal with the press. Period.

Online Publicity

With online outlets increasing in numbers and use, it is important to consider how to secure online publicity. While those who predicted that the Internet would change public relations thinking forever are wrong, it's still a "relationship business"—seeking Internet outlets for publicity is an important complement to publicity in more traditional media.

For one thing, journalists are increasingly moving toward social media, at least as a communications mechanism. According to recent studies, 75% of reporters use Facebook as a tool to assist in reporting; 69% use Twitter; 69% use mobile technology to search for stories; and 95% agree that social media has increased in journalistic import.[27]

Therefore, knowledge of social media, Web hosting and Web casting, and blogs and chat rooms and discussion groups and investor "threads" and search engine optimization are critical for modern public relations people. At the top of this list of Internet public relations tools is knowledge of online publicity.

- Paid wires, such as PR Newswire, Business Wire (purchased in 2006 by investor Warren Buffet's Berkshire Hathaway), MarketWire, and Internet Wire, disseminate full-text news releases to media, investors, and online databases. These are wires that guarantee use of your material (you pay them!). Newsrooms regularly check the paid wires for information of interest.

- All these paid wires offer services to enhance Web use, including search engine optimization and social media "tags" to encourage online sharing and a *long tail*, that is, a longer life for the release on the Internet.

- Staging events is another way to draw reporters and other publics online. Popular events include movie sneak previews, concerts broadcast online, candidate debates, roundtable forums, Web site grand openings, conventions, and trade shows.

- As the Internet has become a more commonplace communications vehicle, the bar for Web events has been raised. A new Web site is no longer cause for attention. Nor is an online news conference. So a Web event today, to attract publicity, must be really "big."[28]

As a relationship business, building online contacts is similar to building traditional media contacts. By building relationships with bloggers and other online influencers, public relations professionals can transform bloggers into brand advocates and reach specific demographic groups, a key to success in today's fragmented media environment.[29]

Sponsored Content

A more recent wrinkle in creating online publicity is the whole area of so-called "sponsored content," also labeled "sponsored journalism," "branded content" or "native advertising."

This is the latest blurring of the lines between earned publicity and paid advertising.

Essentially, sponsored content is "news-oriented" content created by a sponsor, in partnership with a legitimate media source. In other words, your organization creates and pays for the content and then it appears online under the banner of *The New York Times* or *The Wall Street Journal* or Buzzfeed or Mashable or hundreds of other online publishers.

Some traditional journalists consider sponsored content the very worst example of "faux news"; others accept it as an unfortunate fact-of-life in a changing media environment constantly searching for new revenue sources.[30]

Sponsored content is a descendant of advertorials, which are ads in the form of news stories and have been around for decades. Some publishers—including Forbes, Washington Post, Gawker and Buzzfeed—have created profit-center departments to work with content providers to develop more enticing, news-oriented copy. While some publications have gotten criticized for sponsored content—the most celebrated case was *The Atlantic* magazine accused of running controversial Church of Scientology propaganda in 2013—sponsored content is a form of online quasi-publicity that is here to stay.[31]

Like it or not, sponsored content in the 21st century is a reality and should be considered as an option for at least "quasi-publicity" in a media relations plan.

Handling Media Interviews

A primary task of public relations people—perhaps the most essential task in the eyes of those for whom public relations people work—is to coordinate interviews for their executives with the media. Most executives are neither familiar with nor comfortable in such interview situations. For one thing, reporters ask a lot of searching questions, some of which may seem impertinent. Executives aren't used to being put on the spot. Instinctively, they may resent it, and thus the counseling of executives for interviews has become an important and strategic task of the in-house practitioner as well as a lucrative profession for media consultants.

The first question before engaging in a media interview is: What purpose will this serve the organization? If the answer is "none," then don't do it! Before any interview, organizational goals and objectives must be considered, homework on the interviewer and outlet must be done, and statistics and figures and anecdotes to spice into the interview must be compiled.[32]

In conducting interviews with the media, the cardinal rule to remember is that such interviews are not "intellectual conversations." Neither the interviewee nor the interviewer seek a lasting friendship. Rather, the interviewer wants only a good story, and the interviewee wants only to convey his or her key messages. Period.

FIGURE 9-7   **Oshkosh, Wisconsin, you're on the air.**
A media interview ought to be perceived as a "friendly chat" between acquaintances, rather
than an inquisition.
Photo: Courtesy of Fraser P. Seitel

Accordingly, the following 11 dos and don'ts are important in media interviews:

1. **Prepare.** An interviewee must be thoroughly briefed—either verbally or in writing—before the interview. Know the interviewer's point-of-view, interests, and likely questions. Preparation is key.

2. **Know your main points.** In other words, know what you will say *before* you begin the interview. The most important thing to remember in any interview is that an interview isn't a conversation. Nor is it the place for original thought. Walk into the interview knowing the three or four points that must make it on the air or in print. Hammer away at those points, so the interviewer uses them.

3. **Relax.** Remember that the interviewer is a person, too, and is just trying to do a good job. Building rapport will help the interview. Even though a media interview isn't a "conversation," it should seem like one **(Figure 9-7)**.

4. **Speak in personal terms.** People distrust large organizations. References to "the company" and "we believe" may sound ominous. So personalize your messages. Speak as an individual, as a member of the public, rather than as a mouthpiece for an impersonal bureaucracy.

5. **Welcome the naive question.** If the question sounds simple, it should be answered anyway. It may be helpful to those who don't possess much knowledge of the organization or industry.

6. **Answer questions briefly and directly.** Don't ramble. Be brief, concise, and to the point—especially on television. And don't get into subject areas about which you know; that's dangerous.

7. **Don't bluff.** If a reporter asks a question that you can't answer, admit it. If there are others in the organization more knowledgeable about a particular issue, the interviewee or the practitioner should point that out and get the answer from them. But play it straight. Bluffing will be obvious to the reporter and any readers/listeners/viewers.

8. **State facts and back up generalities.** Facts and examples always bolster an interview. An interviewee should come armed with specific data that support general statements. Again, the practitioner should furnish all the specifics.

9. **There is no such thing as "off the record."** A person who doesn't want to see something in print shouldn't say it. It's that simple. Reporters may get confused as to what was "off the record" during the interview. Although most journalists will honor an off-the-record statement, some may not. Occasionally, reporters will agree not to attribute a statement to the interviewee but to use it as background. Mostly, though, interviewees should be willing to have whatever they say in the interview appear in print.

Outside the Lines

Two-Minute Media Relations Drill

How well would you do if you were asked to go toe-to-toe with a reporter? Take this yes-or-no quiz and find out. Answers follow:

Questions

1. When addressing a reporter, should you use his or her first name?

2. Should you ever challenge a reporter in a verbal duel?

3. Are reporters correct in thinking that they can ask embarrassing questions of anyone in public office?

4. Should you answer a hypothetical question?

5. Should you ever say "No comment?"

6. When a reporter calls on the phone, should you assume that the conversation is being taped?

7. Do audiences remember most of the content of a television interview 30 minutes after it is broadcast?

8. Should you ever admit you had professional training to handle the media?

9. If you don't know the correct answer to a reporter's question, should you try to answer it anyway?

Bonus Question

What did Henry Kissinger say at the start of his press briefings as U.S. Secretary of State?

Answers

1. **Yes.** In most cases, using first names is the best strategy. It makes the discussion much more conversational and less formal than using Mr. or Ms.

2. "Never say never," but the answer most often is **No**. You can and should challenge a faulty premise. But your goal is to gain goodwill, which is difficult in an acrimonious debate.

3. **Yes.** Journalists don't work for you or your organization. They can ask what they want. Anyone in the public eye must be prepared to respond to such questions.

4. **No.** Avoid hypothetical questions. Rarely can you win by dealing with them.

5. Again never say, "never" but ordinarily, **No**. It is tantamount to taking the Fifth Amendment against self-incrimination. You appear to be hiding something.

6. **Yes.** Many state laws no longer require the "beep" that signals a taped call. Always assume that everything you say is being recorded and will be used.

7. **No.** Studies have found that audiences remember less and less as time wears on. Indeed, on television, it's often more important to "look good."

8. **Yes.** By all means. You should point out that good communication with the public is a hallmark of your organization and that you're proud it has such a high priority.

9. **No.** Don't be afraid to say, "I don't know." Offer to find the answer and get back to the interviewer. Don't dig yourself into a hole you can't get out of.

Bonus Answer

"Does anyone have any questions . . . for my answers?"

10. **Avoid "no comment."** "No comment" sounds evasive and suggests to people you're hiding something or worse. If you can't answer a question for confidential or proprietary reasons, explain why. "No comment" too often sounds "guilty."

11. **Tell the truth.** It sounds like a broken record, but telling the truth is the key criterion. Journalists are generally perceptive; they can detect a fraud. So don't be evasive, don't cover up, and, most of all, don't lie. Be positive but be truthful. Occasionally, an interviewee must decline to answer specific questions but should candidly explain why. This approach always wins in the long run. Once you lose your credibility, you've lost everything.[33]

Last Word

Even in this day of paid and owned media, winning third-party endorsement from journalists with earned media is an essential requisite of most public relations work.

As is true of any other specialty, in public relations work the key to productive media relations is professionalism. Because management relies principally on public relations professionals for expertise in handling the media effectively, practitioners must not only know their own organization and management but also be conversant in and respectful of the role and practice of journalists. That means knowing their deadlines, understanding their pressures, and returning their calls.

Indeed, public relations professionals must understand what a reporter goes through each day—intractable deadlines, spotty information, frequently uncooperative sources, and increasingly in a world marked by terrorism, mortal danger.

All that has been discussed in this chapter must be practiced: transmitting only newsworthy information to journalists; knowing how to reach reporters most expeditiously; understanding that journalists have become more pressured, by the Internet and cable, to produce material that is "immediate" and "entertaining" and therefore potentially controversial; and recognizing that a reporter has a job to do and should be treated with respect.

At the same time, all public relations practitioners should understand that their role in the news-gathering process has become more respected by journalists. As a former business/finance editor of *The New York Times* once said:

> *PR has gotten more professional. PR people can be a critical element for us. It makes a difference how efficiently they handle things, how complete the information is that they have at hand. We value that and understand all the work that goes into it.*[34]

Indeed, the best public relations–journalist relationship today—the only successful one over the long term—must still be based on mutual understanding, trust, and respect.

Discussion Starters

1. What is the difference among paid, owned, and earned media?
2. What is the current state of the newspaper industry?
3. What is the importance of objectivity to a reporter?
4. What are some of the key principles in dealing with the press?
5. What is the difference between advertising and publicity?
6. What is the value of publicity?
7. What are some of the keys in pitching publicity?
8. What are the several dos and don'ts of interviews?
9. What are several methods of online publicity?
10. What's the most important thing to remember in any interview?

Pick of the Literature

On Deadline Managing Media Relations, 5th Edition
Carole M. Howard and Wilma K. Mathews, Long Grove, IL:
Waveland Press, 2013

Outstanding dos and don'ts from two outstanding public relations professionals, both of whom who've been there, as chief spokespersons for Reader's Digest and AT&T, respectively.

The authors' years of experience in dealing with the media allows them to take a reader through the entire process of media relations, beginning with setting up an organization to deal with the press, explaining what "news" is and reviewing the various situations—both pro and con—that may eventuate.

This latest edition adds chapters on dealing with social media and in particular, using the techniques and avenues of social media to achieve media relations goals. Fine book in every respect.

Case Study   They're Heeere!

Suppose you gave a party and *60 Minutes* showed up at the door. Would you let them in? Would you evict them? Would you commit hara-kiri?

Those were the choices that confronted the Chase Bank at the American Bankers Association convention, when *60 Minutes* came to Honolulu to "get the bankers."

The banking industry was taking its lumps. Profits were lagging. Loans to foreign governments weren't being repaid. Financings to bankrupt corporations were being questioned. And it was getting difficult for poor people to open bank accounts.

Understandably, few bankers at the Honolulu convention cared to share their thoughts on camera with *60 Minutes*. Some headed for cover when the cameras approached. Others barred the unwanted visitors from their receptions. In at least one case, a *60 Minutes* cameraman was physically removed from the hall. By the convention's third day, the *60 Minutes* team was decrying its treatment at the hands of the bankers as the "most vicious" it had ever been accorded.

By the third night, correspondent Morley Safer **(Figure 9-8)** and his *60 Minutes* crew were steaming and itching for a confrontation.

That's when *60 Minutes* showed up at our party.

For 10 years, with your intrepid author as its public affairs director, Chase had sponsored a private convention reception for the media. It combined an informal cocktail party, where journalists and bankers could chat and munch hors d'oeuvres, with a more formal, 30-minute press conference with the bank's president. The press conference was on the record, no-holds-barred, and frequently generated news coverage by the wire services, newspapers, and magazines that regularly sent representatives. No television cameras were permitted.

But when we arrived at Honolulu's scenic Pacific Club, there to greet us—unannounced and uninvited—were Morley and the men from *60 Minutes*, ready to do battle.

The ball was in our court. We faced five questions that demanded immediate answers.

■ **First, should we let them in?** What they wanted, said Safer, was to interview our president about "critical banking issues." He said they had been "hassled" all week and were "entitled" to attend our media reception. But we hadn't invited them. And they hadn't had the courtesy to let us know they were coming. It was true that they were members of the working press. It was also true that our reception was intended to generate news. So we had a dilemma.

■ **Second, should we let them film the press conference?** Chase's annual convention press conference had never before been filmed. Television cameras are bulky, noisy, and intrusive. They threatened to sabotage the normally convivial atmosphere of our party. Equally disconcerting would be the glaring camera lights that would have to be set up. The *60 Minutes* crew countered that their coverage was worthless without film. Theirs, after all, was a medium of pictures, and without pictures, there could be no story. As appetizing as this proposition sounded to us, we were worried that if we refused their cameras, what they might film instead would be us blocking the door at an otherwise open news conference. So we had another problem.

■ **Third, should we let them film the cocktail party?** Like labor leader Samuel Gompers, television people are interested in only one thing: "More!" In the case of our reception, we weren't eager to have CBS film the cocktails and hors d'oeuvres part of our party. We were certain the journalists on hand would agree with us. After all, who wants to see themselves getting sloshed on national television when they're supposed to be working?

■ **Fourth, should we let them film a separate interview with our president?** Because few top people at the convention were willing to speak to CBS, *60 Minutes* was eager to question our president in as extensive and uninterrupted a format as possible. Safer wanted a separate

FIGURE 9-8   **Smiling assassins.** For nearly a half century, the correspondents of CBS *60 Minutes* news magazine program have struck fear into the hearts of those politicians and business leaders they've interviewed. At far left, the dreaded—but lovable— Morley Safer.
Photo: TONY ESPARZA/MCT/Newscom

interview before the formal press conference started. So we also had to deal with the question of whether to expose our president to a lengthy, one-on-one, side-room interview with the most powerful—and potentially negative—television news program in the land.

■ **Fifth, should we change our format?** The annual media reception/press conference had always been an informal affair. Our executives joked with the journalists, shared self-deprecating asides, and generally relaxed. Thus, in light of the possible presence of *60 Minutes*, we wondered if we should alter this laid-back approach and adopt a more on-guard stance.

We had 10 minutes to make our decisions. We also had splitting headaches.

Questions

1. Would you let *60 Minutes* in?
2. Would you let them film the press conference?
3. Would you let them film the cocktail party?
4. Would you let them film a separate interview with the president?
5. Would you change the format of the party?
6. How does the American Bankers Association (ABA) deal with the media today? Visit its online press room (www.aba .com/press+room/default.html). What resources can members of the press access on this site? How does ABA make it easy for reporters to make contact?

From the Top

An Interview with Al Neuharth

The late **Al Neuharth** was born a poor country boy in South Dakota in 1924. He became a self-made multimillionaire who built the nation's largest newspaper company, Gannett Co. Inc., and started the nation's most widely read newspaper, *USA Today*. After he retired from Gannett in 1989, he became chairperson of one of the nation's largest private charitable foundations, *The Freedom Forum*, which he founded in 1991 as the successor to the Gannett Foundation, established in 1935 by Frank E. Gannett. This interview was conducted in 2007, on the occasion of *USA Today's* 25th anniversary, and eight years before Mr. Neuharth's death.

How did you know *USA Today* would work?
We didn't. It was a gamble. But we did an awful lot of research. We hired the pollster Lou Harris, who extensively analyzed whether a national newspaper could make it. One of Lou's conclusions was that "The TV generation won't fight its way through dull, gray newspapers." So we shortened stories, added color, and made an exciting product.

What do you read each day?
I read *The New York Times* and *The Wall Street Journal* every day. I travel a great deal. One of the benefits I received in retiring from Gannett is that the company agreed to provide me with the *Times, Journal, USA Today*, and a local newspaper, wherever I am.

Do you think that newspapers are dying?
No way. Critics who predict the death of newspapers are nuts. Circulation falloffs are not nearly as excessive as critics suggest. People said newspapers were dying when television first appeared. Whenever a new medium enters the picture, critics predict the demise of newspapers. The challenge for publishers is to blend newspapers with the most popular features of the Net.

Do you think newspapers can compete with the Internet?
I have great confidence that executives at *USA Today*, the *Journal*, and the *Times* will find the key to successfully marrying the Internet and print. We did it at *USA Today* with the challenge of television. Look at the *Times*, under Arthur Sulzberger, its publisher, who is doing a great job. He took a risk by adding color and other things. People criticized him for changing the look of the "great gray lady." Arthur told me, "I know it's risky. But it's more risky if we didn't do it." That's the kind of attitude that will return people—even young people—to print.

What has been the role of cable television on journalism?
Cable news is largely opinion. But the good thing is that what cable forced editors and reporters to do was focus on what the public was following.

How do you feel about reporters appearing on TV and giving their opinions?
It's absolutely appropriate. For too long, publishers forbade their editors from appearing on television, because it would "compromise the integrity" of the publication. Nonsense. What it does is increase the audience for the paper.

How does this impact the "quality" of journalism?
Who defines "quality"? Readers ought to have a voice in what we're giving them. An editor's job is to diversify and debate but not to dictate. When I was CEO of Gannett, we changed the makeup of the board of directors, because we realized that a bunch of middle-aged white males couldn't possibly make appropriate decisions for a diversified audience.

How do you feel about public relations?
The job of a public relations person is to pedal propaganda. The good ones don't lie. They make it clear when they are providing facts and when they are providing something else. Our job in the media business is to make damn sure PR people aren't lying.

What's the future of the news business?
The future is bright. In the United States, there's a great appetite for "hard news," particularly at night. That's why the "evening news" has survived. In the morning, the desire is more for "entertainment." Outside the United States, there are few news vacuums left in the world thanks to the net and the satellite. In places like China, Africa, India, and the like, people want more news. I see this everywhere I travel, and I travel a lot. Well, we're in the news business. So I'm optimistic.

Public Relations Bookshelf

Ansell, Jeff and Jeffrey Leeson. *When the Headline Is You: An Insider's Guide to Handling the Media*. San Francisco, CA: Jossey-Bass, 2010. Brutally honest take on what to do when confronted by the media, from the perspective of two experienced reporters.

Carney, William W. *In the News: The Process of Media Relations in Canada*. Alberta, Ontario: University of Alberta Press, 2008. The view of the media north of the border.

D'Vari, Marisa. *Building Buzz: How to Reach and Impress Your Target Audience*. Franklin Lakes, NJ: Career Press, 2006. A primer, from soup to nuts, on securing publicity, including news release and interview tips, media training, and branding advice.

Gianconitieri, Donna. *Master Media Relations: The Complete Guide to Getting Better Press Coverage*. Bloomington, IN: iUniverse, 2008. Former news reporter's take on dealing with the media.

Hayes, Richard and Daniel Grossman. *A Scientist's Guide to Talking with the Media*. Cambridge, MA: Union of Concerned Scientists, 2006. Worthwhile perspective for those who must deal with technical language and experts.

Henderson, David. *Making News: A Straight Shooting Guide to Media Relations*. Lincoln, NE: iUniverse, 2006. Mr. Henderson's second work is aimed at gaining credibility and achieving media coverage.

Holstein, William. *Manage the Media: Don't Let the Media Manage You*. Cambridge, MA: Harvard University Press, 2008. Among other things, the author says that CEOs should hire a communications "consigliore" to advise them on offensive media relations. The worst thing, he cautions, is falling into the "airline syndrome," responding to media only when the organization is faced with a plane crash or similar catastrophic occurrence.

Johnston, Jane. *Media Relations*. Crow's Nest, Australia: Allen & Unwin, 2007. A primer from Down Under, not altogether different from dealing with the media in the United States.

Lewis, Benjamin. *Perfecting the Pitch: Creating Publicity Through Media Rapport*. No. Potomac, MD: Larstan Publishing, 2008. A solid primer on how even a sole practitioner can solicit coverage by the media.

Macfarquhar, Neil. *The Media Relations Department of Hisbollah Wishes You a Happy Birthday*. New York: Public Affairs, 2009. Reporter's memoir of how times have changed in the Middle East, where many today are publicity-conscious first.

O'Dwyer, Jack (Ed.). *O'Dwyer's Directory of PR Firms*. New York: J. R. O'Dwyer, Inc., 2015, This directory lists thousands of public relations firms. In addition to providing information on executives, accounts, types of agencies, and branch office locations, the guide provides a geographical index to firms and cross-indexes more than 8000 clients.

Persinos, John. *Confessions of an Ink-Stained Wretch*. No. Potomac, MD: Larstan Publishing, 2006. This former journalist/editor/press secretary explains how marketing can mesh with media to attract publicity.

Phillips, Brad. *The Media Training Bible*. Washington, DC: SpeakGood Press, 2013. Fine primer on the do's and don'ts of interview protocol.

Walker, Tiran J. *Media Training: A to Z*. New York: Media Training Worldwide, 2008. Media trainer Walker knows his stuff. Good advice.

Endnotes

1. Michael D. Shear, "Making a Point, Obama Invokes a Painful Slur," *The New York Times* (June 22, 2015).
2. Fraser P. Seitel, "The Media of Public Relations: Paid v. Owned v. Earned," odwyerpr.com (March 17, 2014).
3. Satham Sanghera, "How Corporate PR Has Turned into the Art of Stonewalling," *Financial Times* (February 10, 2006).
4. "Times-Picayune Editor on Commitment, Accountability amid Cutbacks," *PBS News Hour* (June 13, 2012).
5. Ken Auletta, "Why Jill Abramson Was Fired," *The New Yorker* (May 14, 2014).
6. Gil Rudawsky, "5 Ways to Adjust for Declining Reporter Employment," *Ragan PR Daily* (August 7, 2014).
7. Rick Edmonds, "New Research Finds 92 Percent of Time Spent on News Consumption Is Still on Legacy Platforms," *Poynter Institute* (May 16, 2013).
8. "State of the Media 2015 Report," *Cision*, http://www.cision.com/us/resources/white-papers/state-of-the-media-2015/.
9. Bill Mickey, "MPA's AMMC Looks to Redefine the Magazine Industry," *Folio* (February 5, 2015).
10. "2015 Magazine Media Factbook Released Accompanied by 22 'Tweetable Truths' About the Industry," *PR Newswire* (May 21, 2015).
11. Katerina E. Matsa and Elisa Shearer, "News Magazines: Fact Sheet," *Pew Research Center State of the News Media 2015* (April 29, 2015).
12. Lydia Saad, "TV Is Americans' Main Source of News," *Gallup* (July 8, 2013).
13. Hunter Schwarz, "Fox News Is the Most Trusted National News Channel. And It's Not That Close," *Washington Post* (March 9, 2015).
14. Jesse Holcomb, "Cable News: Fact Sheet," *Pew Research Center State of the News Media 2015*, op. cit.
15. Glynnis Macnicol, "More People Watch Jon Stewart Than Any Show on Fox News Other Than Bill O'Reilly," *Business Insider* (June 7, 2011).
16. Tom McCarthy and Amanda Holpuch, "Jon Stewart Made Fake News Meaningful Without Sacrificing Comedic Bite," *The Guardian* (February 11, 2015).
17. Rodney Ho, "Rush Limbaugh Tops Talkers Heavy Hundred for Ninth Year in Row," *Ajc.com* (March 26, 2015).
18. Michael Wolff, "Old Media, New Again," *The New York Times* (June 29, 2015).
19. Jeremy W. Peters and Verne G. Kopytoff, "Betting on News, AOL Is Buying the Huffington Post," *The New York Times* (February 7, 2011).
20. "Buzz in the Blogosphere: Millions More Bloggers and Blog Readers," *Nielsen Wire* (March 8, 2012).
21. Mike Florio, "Like It or Not, NFL's Media Relations Policy Is Clear," *Pro Football Talk* (November 20, 2014).
22. Bruce Buschel, "The Problem with Public Relations," *The New York Times* (February 22, 2011).
23. Lee Berton, "Avoiding Media Land Mines," *Public Relations Strategist* (Summer 1997): 16.
24. "General Advertising Rate Card 2015," *The Wall Street Journal* (January 2, 2015).
25. "Jim Koch on the Secret to Effective (and Cheap) Marketing," *Inc.* (April 1, 2007).
26. Michael Sebastian, "7 Things PR Pros Should Know About Shifting Media Landscape," *Ragan PR Daily* (January 26, 2012).
27. "Journalists' Use of Facebook, Twitter, Blogs and Company Websites to Assist in Reporting Surges from 2009/2010 Study," *Society for New Communications Research and Middleberg Communications* (May 6, 2011).
28. Steve O'Keefe, *Complete Guide to Internet Publicity* (New York: John Wiley & Sons, 2002).
29. William Comcowich, "The Importance of Bloggers to PR (And How to Woo Them)," *Ragan PR Daily* (April 15, 2015).
30. Janice Cuban, "Sponsored Content Is Here to Stay," *Ragan PR Daily* (December 10, 2013).
31. Taylor Berman, "The Atlantic Is Now Publishing Bizarre, Blatant Scientology Propaganda as 'Sponsored Content,' " *Gawker* (January 14, 2013).
32. Kaylen McNamara, "Interview Savvy: How Spokespeople Can Avoid Media Blunders," *Ragan PR Daily* (September 28, 2010).
33. Fraser P. Seitel, "Preparing the CEO for a Print Interview," odwyerpr.com (July 11, 2001).
34. "Getting into the Times: How Andrews Views PR," *Across the Board* (August 1989): 21.

Chapter 10

Social Media

Chapter Objectives

1. To explore the general parameters of public relations and the Internet.

2. To discuss the digital vehicles with which public relations professionals should be proficient, including Web sites, email and the rest.

3. To discuss the four primary social media vehicles of Facebook, Twitter, LinkedIn, and YouTube and how public relations professionals use them.

4. To examine the pros and cons of dealing with bloggers and the new journalists who populate the Internet.

In the 21st century, the most lethal career-killer for public relations professionals or anyone else is a simple 140-character instantaneous messaging social medium, with the benign name of Twitter **(Figure 10-1)**. Just ask former public relations executive Justine Sacco.

The unfortunate Ms. Sacco was on the front and rear end of a Twitter catastrophe that cost her job in 2013 as senior director of corporate communications at media owner IAC and served as an object lesson to all other gainfully-employed Twitter users. Before boarding a plane for an overseas vacation, the public relations executive tweeted, "Going to Africa. Hope I don't get AIDS. Just kidding. I'm white!"

While she was airborne, Ms. Sacco's tweet unleashed a venomous social media backlash.

Between the time Sacco tweeted and when she landed in South Africa 12 hours later, the hashtag, #HasJustineLandedYet, trended world-wide, and even Donald Trump tweeted that she should be "fired!" Which was exactly what happened to her when her plane touched down. Her former employer IAC issued a statement, "The offensive comment does not reflect the views and values of IAC. We take this issue very seriously, and we have parted ways with the employee in question."[1]

The lesson: Social media giveth, and social media taketh away.

By the second decade of the 21st century, social media's dominance as a communication medium—for good and evil—couldn't be disputed.

After his election in 2009, President Barack Obama created the first official White House blog and appointed the nation's first White House Director of New Media.[2]

That same year, when a downed plane attempted an emergency landing in New York City's Hudson River, the first reports of the floating airliner came from a nearby ferry passenger, who posted this message on Twitter: "There's a plane in the Hudson. I'm on the ferry going to pick up the people. Crazy." Within 30 minutes, the word had spread far and wide, and the original "tweeter" was interviewed live on MSNBC and CNN and would subsequently become a media star.

A year later, the nation marveled as the social media giant, Facebook, went public and was valued at $104 billion after one hectic trading day. By the time the dust had settled, Facebook's hoodie-wearing, 28-year-old founder, Mark Zuckerberg, was worth a cool $19 billion.[3]

In 2015, the White House, in a bow to the universality of social media "selfies," dropped its 40-year ban of taking photos during public tours.[4]

Such was the power of social media as a persuasive vehicle in the 21st century.

As companies tighten their spending in the face of worldwide financial challenges, inexpensive social media is clearly the new marketing and public relations frontier. As with any other phenomenon, social media offers enormous opportunities and also large pitfalls to be avoided.

While it is irrefutable that the Internet and social media have changed communication forever with newfound immediacy and pervasiveness, it isn't the case that the Internet has replaced human relationships as the essence of societal communications. Nor have the new techniques replaced human relationships as the essence of the practice of public relations.

The Internet and social media comprise important tools in the public relations arsenal. But it is important to remember they are but "tools" nonetheless. In this chapter, we will explore how public relations professionals might harness these new technologies to more effectively communicate their messages.

☐ 1 Brief History of the Net

What is the Internet? We all use it, but few of us know from whence it derived. The Internet, technically, is a cooperatively run, globally distributed collection of computer networks that exchange information via a common set of rules. The Internet began as the ARPANET during the Cold War in 1969, developed by the Department of Defense and consultants who were interested in creating a communications network that could survive a nuclear attack. It survived—even though there was, thankfully, no nuclear attack!—as a convenient way to communicate.

The World Wide Web, the most exciting and revolutionary part of the Internet, was developed in 1989 by physicist Tim Berners-Lee to enlarge the Internet for multiple uses. The Web is a collection of millions of computers on the Internet that contain information in a single format: HTML, or Hypertext Markup Language. By combining multimedia—sound, graphics, video, animation, and more—the Web has become the most powerful tool in cyberspace.

Without question, the Internet and the World Wide Web have transformed the way we work, the way we buy things, the way we entertain ourselves, the way business is conducted, and, most important to public relations professionals, the way we communicate with each other. The Internet phenomenon, pure and simple, has been a revolution.

By 2015, the number of worldwide Internet users had risen seven fold, from 738 million in 2000 to 3.2 billion. Almost seven billion individuals were mobile-cellular subscribers. Mobile-broadband penetration levels are highest in Europe (64%) and the Americas (59%), followed by the Commonwealth of Independent States (CIS) (49%), the Arab States (25%), Asia-Pacific (23%), and Africa (19%). Of all the regions of the world, Africa stands out with a 40% growth rate in mobile-broadband subscriptions; the rest of the world averages 20% growth.[5]

The point is that the so-called digital divide between haves and have-nots is closing as the world becomes more dependent on the Net and social media. In particular, the rise of mobile has increased Internet use among minorities. In the United States, African Americans still trail whites by 7% in overall Internet use and 12% in home broadband use, but blacks and whites are on more equal footing when it comes to other types of access, especially on mobile platforms. Younger African Americans are much more likely to use social media, particularly Twitter; 96% of those 18 to 29 use a social media networking service. The numbers for Hispanics are just slightly less, although English-speaking Latinos are as likely as whites to own a mobile phone.[6]

The Internet explosion has taken new forms: tablets, mobile apps, blogs, podcasts, wikis, RSS feeds, social networks from Facebook to YouTube, from LinkedIn to Snapchat, and social commerce like Uber and Air BNB.

The pace of Internet change is so rapid and the addition of new social media communications vehicles so voluminous, in fact, that this summary of Web-based communications tools and tactics may be obsolete by the time you finish reading! Nonetheless, press on.

Public Relations and the Net

The Internet has transformed the way that people communicate and make contact with each other. And the practice of public relations has responded accordingly.

Public relations departments now have interactive specialists and groups responsible for communicating via social media and the Internet. Likewise, public relations agencies boast online departments that help clients access the Internet. A number of public relations firms specialize in Internet-related communications.

Journalists, meanwhile—still the primary customers for many in public relations—have also embraced the Internet as their primary source for research and reporting. Most reporters today are online and prefer e-mail as their primary source of public relations correspondence.[7] Nonetheless, personal contact with a journalist (i.e., building a relationship) is still the best way to ensure that your message will be heard.

Use of the Internet by public relations practitioners inevitably will grow as the century proceeds, for four reasons in particular.

- **The demand to be educated rather than sold.** Today's consumers are smarter, better educated, and more media savvy. They know when they are being hustled by self-promoters and con artists. Communications programs therefore must be grounded in education-based information rather than blatant self-promotion. The Internet is perhaps the world's greatest potential repository of such information.

■ **The quest for conversation.** The Internet has enabled anyone to become a publisher, broadcasting views and opinions far and wide. In so doing, the Internet has empowered users by leveling the playing field between them and the organizations trying to reach them. The net result is that Internet dialogue is just that—a conversation—between supplier and consumer. And the more conversational the organization, the more likely it will be to persuade prospects to buy its products, support its issues, and believe its ideas.

■ **The need for real-time performance.** The wired world is moving quickly. Everything happens instantaneously and in real-time. When insurgents in Egypt blow up government leaders, the bombing is beamed immediately via social media around the world. Public relations professionals can use this ability to their advantage to structure their information to respond instantly to emerging issues and market changes.

■ **The need for customization.** There used to be three primary television networks. Today there are hundreds of television channels. Today's consumers expect more focused, targeted, one-on-one communications relationships. Increasingly, organizations must broadcast their thoughts to ever-narrower population segments. The Internet offers such narrowcasting to reporters, shareholders, analysts, opinion leaders, consumers, and myriad other publics.

For individual public relations practitioners, then, familiarity with the Internet and social media and mastery of its effective use have become frontline requisites of the practice. Consequently, it is important that practitioners are familiar with the primary areas of cyberspace communications.

2 Web Sites

Today, virtually everybody, from the largest corporation to the smallest nonprofit, has a Web site **(Figure 10-2)**. Perhaps the most familiar, broadly used, and oldest social media tool, Web sites provide organizations, individuals, and governmental agencies the ability to offer information to the public in an organized, consolidated manner.

Most of the time today, it is the Web site that serves as an organization's "first face" to the public. Web sites serve multiple functions, are commonly interactive, and afford viewers the ability to browse for information and in many cases, conduct business, create profiles, manage their accounts, and a plethora of other convenient options. Web sites permit an organization to speak in its own voice—unfettered and unadulterated by the media or other intermediaries.

Web site development is very much the province of public relations professionals. Public relations professionals need to be cognizant of the methods in which audiences prefer to receive information on Web sites. They need to make Web sites as navigable as possible, providing the necessary tools to facilitate ease of delivery of content. "Static," non-user friendly Web sites are more of a detriment than a tool. Web sites also must be "media friendly"; journalists should be able to navigate the Web site with ease. This means having a clearly identifiable "Media" icon and organized subsections, including a page for news and video clips, reports, and publications.

A Web site gives an individual or institution the flexibility and freedom of getting news out without having it filtered by an intermediary. There are literally millions of Web sites, all of them open for visitors.

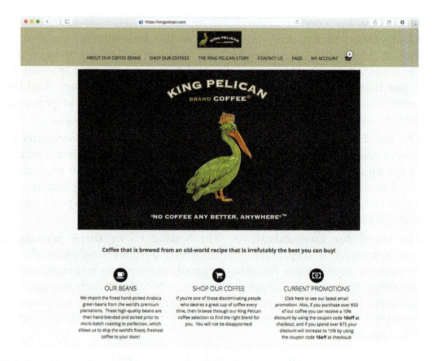

Developing a Winning Web Site

In many ways, the organization's Web site is its most important interface with the public. Today, journalists and others turn to the Web site first for an introduction to the organization.

The aim of any Web site is to provide information that visitors are looking for. The more you achieve that objective, the more "sticky" your site becomes. Stickiness is often measured by the amount of time visitors spend at a site and how many pages they view. For example, if visitors spend 10 minutes at the Web site and view five or more pages, you've achieved stickiness.[8]

How should you create a winning Web site? By first asking and answering several strategic questions.

1. **What is our goal?** To extend the business? Sell more products? Make more money? Win support for our position? Turn around public opinion? Introduce our company? Answer these fundamental questions first.

2. **What content will we include?** The reason some Web sites are tedious and boring as they are is because little forethought has gone into determining the content of a site. Cramming news releases onto a Web site won't advance an organization's standing.

3. **How often will we edit?** Often the answer to this question is not often enough. Stale news and the lack of updating are common. Sites must regularly be updated.

4. **How will we enhance design?** The style of the site is most important. If an organization's homepage isn't attractive, it won't get many hits. Good design makes complicated things understandable, and this is essential in a Web site.

5. **How interactive will it be?** Traditional communication is unidirectional, one way. The great attraction of the Web, on the other hand, is that it can be bidirectional.

6. **How will we track use?** As in any other communications project, the use of a Web site must be measured. Measuring site performance should be a multi-faceted exercise that includes such analysis as volume during specific times of day, kind of access, specific locations on the site to which visitors are clicking first, and the sequencing through the site that visitors are following.

7. **Who will be responsible?** Managing a Web site must be someone's full-time job. Companies may subordinate the responsibility to someone; it is much better to treat the Web site as a first line of communication to the public, which requires full-time attention.

Web site developers are most concerned about SEO—search engine optimization—the tweaking of keywords, copy, and design so that a site comes up toward the top of Internet search results, primarily on Google. SEO has become an art form in itself, with Internet-oriented agencies promoting themselves as SEO specialists. The key is to identify, promote, and repeat searchable keywords and phrases that will propel a site up the search list.

E-mail

E-mail may seem passé to a self-respecting millennial but more than 90% of adult Internet users regularly use e-mail, which remains the most pervasive form of communication in the business world.

The number of worldwide e-mail accounts is expected to grow by one billion, reaching five billion accounts by the end of 2018. By that same year, the total number of worldwide e-mail users, including both business and consumer users, will reach nearly three billion. So while other technologies, such as social networking, instant messaging (IM), mobile IM, and others are also taking hold, e-mail remains the most ubiquitous form of business communication.[9]

Since e-mail is quick and almost effortless, a manager can deliver praise or concern without leaving the office. Thus, e-mail has, by and large, improved organizational communications. That is not to say that face-to-face communication isn't always best. It is. But the ease and effectiveness of e-mail makes it a viable alternative.

Internal E-mail Newsletters

E-mail has also supplanted the traditional employee print newsletter.

Online internal newsletters are both more immediate and more interactive than print counterparts. Employees can "feed back" to what they've read or heard instantaneously. The organization, in turn, can apprise itself quickly of relevant employee attitudes and opinions. Such online vehicles also lend an element of timeliness that print magazines and newspapers simply couldn't do **(Figure 10-3)**.

Internal e-mail newsletters differ from their print brethren in several important areas:

1. **No more than one page.** Employees won't read lengthy newsletters on the computer, newsletters must be succinct.

2. **Job-relevant information.** Employees want to know what's going on at the organization and how they fit in; e-mail newsletters must be strong on relevance, short on fluff.

3. **Link content.** Copy should be peppered with links to other material, such as the organization's Web site.

4. **Regular dissemination.** It is also important to send email newsletters at regular intervals so that recipients expect them.

FIGURE 10-3
E-mail newsletter.
NCH Healthcare
System CEO Allen
Weiss kept staff and
the Florida community
aware of recent
developments through
a weekly e-mail
newsletter.
*Photo: Courtesy of NCH
Healthcare System*

Straight Talk NCH

A weekly update from management on the issues that matter most

Healthcare
System

July 2, 2015

Dear Friends and Colleagues,

The 4th of July is a time to recognize the heroes who have helped make our nation the ideal of the world. Here in our own community, I'd like to use the 4th to recognize three such healthcare heroes—or, more correctly, *heroines*—who help make NCH a model of concerned caring for patients.

1. Ellen Spencer. While making rounds to deliver bonus checks to Pulmonary Rehab, **CFO Mike Stephens** asked staff their plans for using the recent employee bonus. Ellen Spencer, respiratory therapist, said she planned to buy a puppy for one of the patients. The patient has been in Pulmonary Rehab for some time and had recently lost her own dog due to illness. During her time in rehab, the patient fell in love with Ellen's puppy, a miniature red dachshund. Ellen reached out to her local breeder, who just happened to have a new litter of puppies. Through friendship with the breeder, Ellen was able to negotiate a favorable deal on a new pup, typically costing upwards of $1,200. Ellen presented the new puppy to her patient, who, understandably, was thrilled and grateful. To this day, the patient doesn't know Ellen spent her own money to purchase this new puppy. What a hero!

2. Gabriela Mora, Environmental Service Supervisor, assists cancer survivors in our support group at North Naples Hospital. Gabriela noticed a woman, stressed and short of breath, wandering the campus looking for the meeting room for a cancer survivors support group. Gabriela escorted the woman to the designated meeting room, which wasn't yet set up for the meeting. So Gabriela set up the chairs and chatted comfortably with the patient for 20 minutes, until other folks arrived. In this simple yet meaningful way, Gabriela proved herself a true healthcare hero.

3. Theresa Hansen, Human Resources specialist, joined the NCH family in 2013 as the Workers Compensation and LOA Specialist. In her role, she works with employees going through rough times due to a work-related injury or, more often, a serious personal or family member's health issue. Often, the employee is out on extended leave of absence. As anyone who has found themselves in such an unfortunate position knows, Theresa is a compassionate and caring person, always attentive to an individual's personal and often sad story. Recently, Theresa learned that an employee was in the hospital recovering from surgery. Theresa wanted to brighten this individual's day so she purchased fresh flowers and delivered them herself, spending time talking to the employee patient. Nobody asked Theresa to drop in on the patient or buy the flowers or deliver them personally. She did it because she *cares*, and that's why she's a hero.

We are fortunate at NCH to have a great many Ellens and Gabrielas and Theresas, who care deeply about our patients and prove it in their compassionate service every day. We are proud of all our NCH heroes. Happy 4th of July.

Respectfully,

Allen

Allen S. Weiss, M.D., President and CEO

P.S. DO YOU HAVE A COLLEAGUE OR FRIEND WHO WOULD BE INTERESTED IN THESE UPDATES? Please enter their email address below, and we will add them to our complimentary mailing list. No cost or obligation. And of course they may unsubscribe at any point they find the content uninteresting. Just enter their email address, and we shall send them a "Welcome" note, indicating you have recommended them to receive the newsletter (again, this is free and without obligation of any sort).
Present Reader's Email Address:

Name:

Please add my colleague or friend to your distribution: His/her name and email address is:

Instant Messaging/Texting

Instant messaging—or "IM"—is an online, nonlinear, real-time form of communication that allows two or more users to exchange information quickly via text and to send pictures any place in the world. A related vehicle is text messaging or texting, the common term for sending short—160 characters or fewer—messages from cell phones, using the Short Message Service (SMS).

Increasingly, as texting becomes "old school," IM continues to see strong growth, particularly fueled by mobile technology. IM is generally free, or inexpensive, immediate, easy to use and pervasive on a wide range of different platforms and devices. Worldwide IM user accounts are expected to grow from over 3.2 billion in 2015 to over 3.8 billion by year-end 2019, representing an average annual growth rate of about 4%.[10]

In today's world of the smart phone, more and more people are sending messages through Web-based applications like WeChat, WhatsApp, and Snapchat. These apps allow consumers to send messages from their mobile devices to other mobile devices without paying for wireless service.[11] One area where text and instant messaging has been applied is at colleges to warn students of emergencies on campus.

Blogs

By the second decade of the 21st century, bloggers had come of age. In 2010, the Associated Press (AP), the world's foremost network of editors and reporters, announced that henceforth, bloggers would be recognized as bona fide news sources.[12] The AP, like so many others in the news business, recognized that bloggers, who span the gamut from political to social, from entertainment to sports, deserve recognition.

A blog, technically, is an online diary, a personal chronological log of thoughts published on a Web page, sometimes referred to as Web blog. Once used only by fringe media, blogs have now been embraced by professional communicators as well as mainstream print and broadcast media. Blogs are used to encourage as well as enhance dialogue among publics on subjects from politics to current events, from ethical issues to hobbies and sports. Blog sharing allows individuals to locate, share, and subscribe to blogs of interest.[13]

The blogosphere is immense. There were more than 227 million blogs in operation by April 2015, with 14 million new blogs launched in 2014. The vast majority of blogs—81%—are the written from home and, accordingly, are the product of hobbyists. On the other hand, blogging is increasing among corporations, too. In 2014, one in three Fortune 500 companies maintained active blogs; with 58 of the 72 industries included having blogs. So blogging has become an accepted public relations activity among companies.[14]

One viable outlet for organization blogging is the so-called "CEO blog," published under the byline of the individual who runs the organization. CEO blogs have gotten mixed reviews. On the one hand, CEOs at companies such as Zappos, Marriott International, Dallas Mavericks, and Pitney Bowes have received credit for blogging consistently in good and bad times. On the other hand, in many cases, "blogs read like tired, warmed-over press releases . . . with companies yakking away about their companies and products, seemingly oblivious to whether their audience is listening or not."[15]

One reason for the proliferation of blogs is that audience preferences are shifting—many can see through a company's traditional "ad speak" and have begun to turn elsewhere for information and opinion. This phenomenon is important for public relations professionals in that it reflects the need for respected, third-party "endorsers" of products and services.

FYI

King Blogs; Subjects Cheer

July 11, 2014, will forever live in Cleveland, Ohio, sports history. That was the day that the prodigal son announced his return.

Four years earlier, Lebron James, the undisputed King of the National Basketball Association, departed his home state's NBA team, the Cleveland Cavaliers, to join the star-filled Miami Heat, leaving anger and bitterness and an open letter on the Cavaliers' home page from team owner Dan Gilbert, which called James "narcissistic"…"heartless"…and "callous."

And then on a magical day in 2014, all was forgiven, when King James announced, via a blog post on the Sports Illustrated Web site as told to writer Lee Jenkins, what was a masterpiece in blogsmanship. It said in part:

"Before anyone ever cared where I would play basketball, I was a kid from Northeast Ohio. It's where I walked. It's where I ran. It's where I cried. It's where I bled. It holds a special place in my heart".

And for good measure, Lebron even posted that he held no ill will towards the hot-headed owner who once trashed him. "Everybody makes mistakes. I've made mistakes as well. Who am I to hold a grudge."

It's good to be the King.

FIGURE 10-4

The king and his court. When NBA king Lebron James decided to return to his native Cleveland to play again for the Cavaliers, he announced via blog.
Photo: TYRONE SIU/ REUTERS/Newscom

The most popular blogs on the Internet are now "required reading" for journalists. Among them are Politico.com, a running rundown of the latest political news and gossip; The Drudge Report, a conservative-slanted news review; TMZ.com, a leading post for celebrity news and the latest salacious showbiz gossip; and Huffingtonpost.com, a liberal-leaning news site, begun by liberal commentator Arianna Huffington. There are blogs for every taste, with industry blogs becoming especially important, not only in the information technology sphere, where there are numerous well-followed blogs that pace industry discussion, but also in industries from education to finance to fashion to public relations.

The vast majority of blogs on the Internet attract little following and are hardly worth the attention of public relations practitioners. And just as they do with reporters, public relations people must target bloggers they wish to reach, create relationships with them before pitching them on a particular story, personalize the appeal toward the blog targeted and have something unique to sell.[16]

The real point with blogging, as noted by one veteran blogger, was that rather than focusing on the tool itself, organizations need to zero in on "the principles behind social media that make it work, like participating in a larger community and not controlling the conversation."[17]

③ Social Networks

The theoretical concept of social networking stemmed from an article in a telecommunications journal by David Isenberg, a former employee of AT&T Labs Research. He described the Internet as a "stupid network"—that relied on "dumb transport in the middle, and intelligent user-controlled endpoints" and where information was provided "by the needs of the data, not the design assumptions of the network."[18] Isenberg proposed his own "stupid network" with the outmoded "intelligent network," which relied on a technological hierarchy dictated by others.

Thus was born the "dumb transport" of social networking sites, originally such as MySpace and later Facebook, that allowed communities of participants with common interests, opinions, and activities, to interact with others to manage messaging, e-mail, video, file sharing, blogging, discussion groups, and all other manner of Internet discussion.

The growth of social networks—from the emergence of Netscape in the 1990s to the inception of MySpace in 2004 to the phenomena of Facebook and Twitter shortly thereafter to YouTube and Instagram and Pinterest, et al., as nexus for people around the world with varied similar interests—introduces expanding opportunities for public relations practice.

Indeed, in the second decade of the 21st century, every company, politician, nonprofit organization, university, hospital, not to mention one billion citizens of the world communicate via social media.

The short history of social networking has been characterized by upstarts capturing tech lightning for brief stretches—see MySpace, Second Life, Bebo, Friendster, Orkut, Spotify, Quora, etc.—only to sputter and fade. Thus far in the development of social networking, several sites have stood the test of time— among them, Facebook, Twitter, YouTube, and LinkedIn. Public relations professionals must be conversant with and proficient in using each.

Facebook

The biggest social networking service—and arguably, the most successful in terms of earnings and stock market following—is Facebook. With 936 million daily users and 1.44 billion monthly active users, including one-third of the American public, Facebook is in a social media class of its own.[19]

Founded in 2004 by Harvard sophomore Mark Zuckerberg, who was once as poor as you are, the cultural phenomenon began as a glorified, well, "Facebook," a name-and-photo directory that colleges distribute to incoming first-year students. Members answer as many questions about themselves as they feel comfortable sharing, from name and relationship status to favorite music and photos. They then search for "friends," past and present, and link up.

In public relations terms, Facebook is ideal for sharing news, photos, and videos for groups that support various causes or interests or for sending messages or for playing games. Facebook also is prone to exposing personal information and makes money by letting advertisers place ads on the pages of targeted members, for example, divorced, 40+-year-old females from Connecticut. Facebook went public in 2012, making its iconic founder and his colleagues instant billionaires. Zuckerberg himself was the subject of a not-so-flattering blockbuster movie, The Social Network, in 2010. Facebook has thoroughly eclipsed its nearest competitor and former rival, MySpace, which has become a pop music–focused site for teenagers and preteenagers. The average Facebook user spends 21 minutes on the site per visit.

For public relations professionals, Facebook serves multiple community-building purposes, among them the following:

- **Attract attention.** Organizations may use their Facebook page to clarify who they are and what they stand for.

- **Two-way communication.** The real sine qua non of Facebook, the medium can be used to get together virally with followers, fans, customers, and friends to help build third-party credibility.

- **Conversation monitor.** Facebook allows one to see who is talking about us, what they are saying, and upon what basis they are making their arguments. This monitoring function, in particular, is a must for any organization.

- **Interactive activities.** Many organizations sponsor opinion polls, games, contests, and other interactive platforms on their Facebook page.

- **Internal communication.** Facebook can build morale, create employee groups, and create a sense of community among the staff.

- **Halo effect.** Facebook is also excellent for promoting charitable activities or encouraging fundraising campaigns or calling a group to action to lobby for a cause.

- **Network with the media.** Facebook may be used best when one has an existing relationship with a journalist. If so, Facebook can be an excellent medium for brainstorming story angles or in showcasing one's expertise and experience as a potential interview source.

- **Crisis management.** Increasingly, organizations use Facebook to issue statements and post updates in times of crisis. Journalists have become accustomed to checking Facebook pages to monitor crisis management approaches.

- **Link. Link. Link.** Finally, Facebook facilitates linking Web sites, videos, content pages, hosted material, and any other sites that may be relevant to communicating an organization's view.

One emerging blemish in the Facebook complexion is the realization that only 4% of Americans, aged 15 to 25, consider Facebook brand pages as "a credible source of information." This may indicate that to these young consumers, promoting a brand on Facebook is no more credible than a paid ad.[20] Such is the inherent difficulty in public relations initiatives in owned media. Nonetheless, of all the social networks, Facebook continues to offer the most promise and remains, therefore, a potentially potent marketing and public relations mechanism and a powerful tool for building brand affinity.

Twitter

By the second decade of the 21st century, premier micro-blogging service Twitter had also graduated to a "keeper," with 270 million active users, including one-fifth of all U.S. Internet users; some 500 million tweets are sent out every day in 33 languages.[21] However, where Facebook had learned how to "monetize"—"make money" to those of us not on Wall Street—its product, Twitter had not. Twitter's expansion included its purchase of Vine video-sharing service in 2012. Nonetheless, by the summer of 2015, the company had shaken up its management, searching for new answers to profitability.

Twitter is the micro-blogging service that allows you to "tweet"—type short messages (140 characters maximum) to alert friends and followers "what you're doing now." Like a multi-person text message service, Twitter allows you to send and receive messages to and from tens or hundreds or even thousands of cell phones.

Twitter is frequently used to follow celebrities and athletes, and, indeed, the Ashton Kutchers and Lindsay Lohans and Nicki Minajes and Shaquille O'Neals of the world pay public relations people either to tweet for them or, at least, advise them what to write. Corporations also pay celebrities to tweet about their products. The queen of this brave new world is Kim Kardashian (surprise!), with more than 30 million Twitter followers, who reportedly receives anywhere from $10 to $20,000 per Twitter endorsement.[22] Not bad for 140 characters!

Twitter has also earned a place as a breaking news source. In 2012, Twitter broke the news about singer Whitney Houston's death 27 minutes before mainstream media reported the story. Twitter became the go-to breaking news source, when terrorists struck the Boston Marathon in 2013 and a San Bernardino state function in 2015.

In terms of public relations, Twitter can prove a powerful tool used thusly:

- **Finding your Tweeple.** Following conversations about your issues, product, candidate, etc. on Twitter can be enormously valuable in determining what people think is important and in building a supporter base. The Twitter search function can be used to tap into conversations on particular subjects.

- **Finding the Tweetfluentials.** Closely related is identifying tweeters who might be influential in speaking about your brand.

- **As a news source.** As noted, Twitter increasingly has been used to break news. Twitter, like Facebook, can be used to pitch stories. More regularly, Twitter serves as a kind of circulatory system of the news cycle, yielding a constant stream of commentary and information for public relations people to observe.

- **Providing valuable content.** Twitterites value insider tips and insights and information not available elsewhere. Also, live-tweeting from events, using a hashtag that has been set up for the event, is another viable public relations initiative. Tweet is an excellent place to build buzz around companies and products.

- **Recycling valuable content.** Retweeting what other people have said about your company or your client is another excellent way to spread the word.

- **Building a community.** That means tweeting daily to show followers you're serious and engaged.

- **Crisis management.** Also like Facebook, Twitter can be used to issue statements and post updates in times of crisis.[23]

Twitter has imitators, the most popular of which is Tumblr, known for its functionality and ease of use, which has more than three million users and is reportedly growing at the rate of 15,000 new users each day. Twitter also has its critics, who suggest that it is little more than a passing fad for "people with nothing to say . . . writing for people with nothing to do." However, the consensus seems to be that Twitter, like Facebook, is another social networking vehicle that is here to stay.

LinkedIn

LinkedIn is Facebook for the professional set.

The guiding concept behind LinkedIn is establishing a "who you know" network of current and former business colleagues. Begun in 2003, LinkedIn membership has grown to 364 million in more than 200 countries. Unlike Facebook, whose Initial Public Offering (IPO) in 2012 was marred by mishap, LinkedIn's public debut in 2011 saw its stock pop 90% over the IPO price. LinkedIn's revenue comes from three fairly even sources—advertising, premium subscriptions, and corporate recruiting.[24] And the stock has done well ever since.

LinkedIn is popular with public relations professionals connected to like-minded professionals to discover new business or employment opportunities and to develop a network of contacts. LinkedIn is particularly helpful in finding a new job because you're not limited to asking immediate colleagues for referrals. LinkedIn allows you to ask colleagues of colleagues, which greatly expands one's network. Another popular LinkedIn feature called "Answers" encourages business-oriented questions of people who might know—from résumé writing tips to business software advice.

In terms of public relations, LinkedIn services include the following:

- **Notes.** Notify others of events, job openings, and vendor recommendations.
- **Groups.** LinkedIn accesses more than 150,000 groups, including business forums, alumni groups, fan clubs, conferences, etc.
- **Answer Forum.** Provides advice proffered by professionals, advised to treat the discussion as you would a business lunch.
- **Polls.** LinkedIn enables the creation of polls.
- **Card Munch.** Mobile app that scans business cards and converts them into contacts.
- **Job Openings.** LinkedIn has become a viable source for employment searches, as a complement to or replacement for paid search agencies.

YouTube

YouTube, hatched in 2005 as a video-sharing Web site by three former PayPal employees, is already the stuff of media legend, what with its cute cats, dramatic chipmunks and ubiquitous Katy Perry/Bruno Mars/Pitbull videos. It is also the source of fantastic wealth for its founders, who sold the enterprise in 2006 to Google for $1.65 billion.

Although YouTube began as the outlet for "15 minutes of fame" for millions of individuals around the world, organizations have increased their use of the channel, primarily for marketing and crisis management purposes. One benefit is that marketers can target specific user groups for such topics as medical issues, self-help subjects, even public relations guidance. YouTube users have notoriously short attention spans, so marketing messages must be kept simple and short, and savvy marketers—from Ford to GoPro to Nike—have found that the more videos made available, the more YouTube traffic is generated for a particular organization's offerings.[25]

Another primary public relations use of YouTube has been as a quick response to crisis. The most famous example was Domino's use of the channel when two moronic employees posted a disgusting video, impugning the company's pizza, in 2006. Domino's CEO responded quickly—on YouTube—promising swift action against the now-former employees and reassuring the public about the goodness of the product. In more recent years, organizations from Netflix to Lufthansa to the U.S. General Services Administration (GSA) have all taken to YouTube to issue mea culpas for some wrong or

FIGURE 10-5
Is that you (tube)?
When a GSA $1 million Las Vegas party went viral on YouTube in 2012, the official responsible—captured in a hot tub photo—and his agency were called on the carpet by Congress.
Photo: JASON REED/ Reuters/Newscom

another. In the case of the latter, after GSA employees were seen on a 2012 YouTube video rapping about taxpayer naiveté at a lavish, $1 million, all-expenses-paid junket in Las Vegas. GSA officials quickly responded, again via YouTube, to try to quell the uproar. In 2015, Jeff Neely, the GSA official responsible for the outrageous party—famously photographed in a Las Vegas hot tub—was fined and sentenced to three months in the slammer[26] **(Figure 10-5)**. So YouTube, like all social media, taketh and giveth away.

Networking Sites to Consider

High-tech enthusiasts and Silicon Valley venture capitalists constantly search for "the next big thing" in terms of social networks. Among those in contention as we write (meaning they'll be obsolete by next Thursday!).

Pinterest   Pinterest is a social network that allows its users to share what's important to them, as long as this includes a picture somewhere on the Web page. Like many other social media services before it, Pinterest, for a time, was the hottest new social media technology for public relations professionals after the wives of both 2012 presidential candidates, Ann Romney and Michelle Obama, created accounts. Pinterest is a visual tool that allows users to create collections ("boards") of visuals ("pins") and share them with others. The Pinterest platform allows public relations professionals to speak in a language everyone understands—pictures.

The pictures are displayed or "pinned" on a virtual bulletin board in Pinterest. Pinterest users can have "pinboards" that are a collection of "pins" that revolve around a common theme. Users can share their tastes and interests with others and discover like-minded people.

In terms of public relations, Pinterest advocates cite the following uses:

- **Visual stories.** Tell the story of the organization or candidate or issue or product visually, to enhance customer interest.

A Question of Ethics

Ain't No Sunshine for Wikipedia Alteration

Few Web sites have experienced more enormous acceptance than Wikipedia, the free-access, crowd-sourced Internet encyclopedia, whose articles and inclusions can be edited by anyone, as long as they follow Wikipedia policies.

Founded in 2001 by Jimmy Wales and Larry Sanger, the site includes 35 million articles in 288 different languages and 69,000 active editors, whose job it is to police the inclusions—particularly from incursion by advocates for those about whom they're writing, often public relations professionals. While Wikipedia management professes the "pristine" nature of Wikipedia commentaries, the reality is that many, if not most, of the site's articles are written by biased supporters or critics.

But in 2015, when one such biased editor, the public relations firm Sunshine Sachs, acknowledged that its employees had violated the Wikipedia rules, it was major news.

Specifically, Sunshine Sachs operatives surreptitiously deleted a reference to client Naomi Campbell about the super model's less-than-auspicious record album, "Babywoman," a universally panned R&B flop, about which Ms. Campbell, herself, acknowledged, "At least I tried" (Figure 10-6). Accordingly, her Wikipedia entry dubbed the album "a critical and commercial failure." At least it did before it was mysteriously removed by an "editor."

To its credit, Sunshine Sachs admitted its violation and promised to observe the Wikipedia regulations going forward. As to Wikipedia, the head of the Wikipedia Foundation vowed to enforce its regulations more rigorously, tut-tutting that paid advocacy editing by public relations firms "violates the core principles that have made Wikipedia so valuable for so many people." *

FIGURE 10-6 **Warble a Wikipedia tune.**
As a model, Naomi Campbell was super; as a singer, though, not so much, which is why her public relations firm tried to alter her Wikipedia bio in 2015.
Photo: AO1/Andres Otero/WENN/Newscom

Questions

1. What is your view on Sunshine Sachs' surreptitious editing of its client's Wikipedia page?

2. Do you think Wikipedia's regulations to prohibit "advocates" from editing its copy are realistic?

3. How might you modify the Wikipedia rules?

*For further information, see Michael Cieply, "P.R. Firm Alters the Wikipedia Page of Its Star Clients," *The New York Times* (June 22, 2015).

■ **Industry stories/organizational retrospectives.** Pin interesting developments in the industry and invite the community to a social media board and to Media Pinterest happenings.

■ **Videos.** Tie sponsored YouTube videos to the Pinterest site.

■ **Employee participation.** Ask employees to become involved by creating their own Pinterest boards.

■ **Sharing product launches/consumer stories/events, etc.** Articles, stories, and blog posts can all be shared through Pinterest.[27]

Infographics   Another social media visual platform that has sparked the interest of public relations professional is that of Infographics, which, as noted, are visual representations of information, data, or knowledge intended to present complex information quickly and clearly. As opposed to Pinterest, Infographics are more detailed and demand writing talent to convey information succinctly.

In creating Infographics, one must cut straight to the point, simplify complex information and impress the reader—in an instant. Infographics must be relevant, interesting and, because there are pictures involved, visually arresting. An effective Infographic elicits an instant reaction and compels readers to seek more information.

Infographics might apply to any public relations subject, but the following in particular:

- Survey results that may be cumbersome in a lengthy text format
- Statistical data that can lose the fleeting interest of a reader
- Comparison research that will have a more a dramatic effect with visuals
- Messages targeted to multilingual audiences (images are a universal language)

Increasingly, newspapers and other print publications, sensitive to readers' preference for pictures, have turned to infographics to help describe news events.

Instagram   Instagram, begun in 2010, is a photo-sharing application that can be downloaded for iPhones, iPads, and Android devices. You can upload a photo from your phone or take one while using the program and then apply a filter to it to make it look weathered, faded, vintage, or enhanced in some way.

In terms of public relations, Instagram is a venue to help bolster brands. Starbucks is perhaps the most recognized brand that uses Instagram as a social channel with more than 500,000 followers; posts tend to be product-heavy but also reveal an opportunity to show a bit of personality by featuring baristas and some behind-the-scenes action as well. Another user, Vans clothing, posts photos of people using the products in their natural environment: skateboarding events, surfing, and BMX events.[28]

One area where Instagram's success is irrefutable was in making its founders rich. In 2012, Mark Zuckerberg's Facebook bought the company and its 13 employees for a cool $1 billion!

Snapchat   In a related sense, the fastest-growing social networking app—at least at this writing—is Snapchat, started as a Stanford University class project in 2011 and has today an estimated 200 million users.[29]

Snapchat is another video messaging app where users can take photos and videos, i.e. "snaps," and add text and then send to a list of recipients, who view them for a set time period before they are deleted from the recipient's device. Snapchat's addition of what it called, "Stories," a collection of "Snaps" that can be viewed for 24 hours, enables the app to be used as a marketing tool for public relations professionals.

Reddit   Reddit, founded at the University of Virginia in 2005, is a social networking news site where members, known as "Redditers," vote content up or down in terms of its "importance" in a variety of categories, called "sub-Reddits." Thus, Reddit becomes an online bulletin board for trending news and information.

Public relations professionals may submit stories to Reddit, which holds enormous potential of generating online interest, inasmuch as 169 million monthly visitors use the site. One viable use of Reditt is the site's AMA—Ask Me Anything feature—which is a sort of online media briefing where a host briefly describes his or her specialty and then fields questions from users. In 2013, one such "host" was the President of the United States, Barack Obama,[30] etc.

A number of other social sites, as we speak, have shown promise for public relations practitioners. Among them:

Tumblr Another micro-blogging platform, owned by Yahoo! (who paid the founders a cool $1.1 billion!), where users trend toward videos, images and GIFs more than text, companies like Coca-Cola, Whole Foods, Sesame Street, and others have used Tumblr to highlight their content in a more dynamic way. Organizational users may prefer this service over more cumbersome blogs and more restrictive 140-character Twitter feeds.

Periscope Owned by Twitter, this app launched in 2015 instantly broadcasts events for worldwide viewers to see and comment on. Companies are experimenting with Periscope as another channel through which to announce product or service launches. The U.S. Department of the Interior was an early user with its "Find Your Park" campaign.

Meerkat An independent competitor to Periscope, which also depends on streaming content broadcast through Twitter, to broadcast live events, like the South by Southwest festival, which boosted its popularity in 2015. Meerkat broadcasts, however, as opposed to those on Periscope, disappear immediately.

Social apps like these are appearing every day, each full of promise and hope. Public relations professionals must be aware of the latest social media applications that may prove helpful to their practice. But they should always assess them with a critical eye, focused on the sustained value that such services may or may not bring.

Social Media Measurement

Public relations agencies have embraced social media as the next great frontier of public relations. One of the largest, Edelman Public Relations, headed by social media advocate and the industry's leading social media voice Richard Edelman (see From the Top in this chapter), has a division of Digital Integration, which actively markets the Internet and social media to clients.

The Public Relations Industry

The public relations industry is also developing standards to track outcomes of social media use. Social media analytics target several priority areas to track, among them:

- Content sourcing and methods, so that evaluations can be standardized.
- Reach and impressions, similar to advertising analysis, which is more difficult to come by in terms of social media.
- Engagement, which might include business outcomes such as sales or less engaging outcomes such as blog posts, video comments, retweets, etc.
- Influence and relevance, which must be rated by more subjective human research rather than computer algorithms.

- Opinion and advocacy, also a more qualitative measure, analyzing feedback.
- Impact and value, including measuring financial results as well as nonfinancial factors such as "reputation impact."[31]

Again, social media measurement is just in its infancy. But just like any other public relations activity, some analytical analysis is obligatory to capture a true picture of value and contribution.

4 Online Communication Vehicles

Like a discussion of social networks, a discussion of online communications vehicles available on the Internet is, by definition, obsolete as soon as it hits the page. Nonetheless, public relations practitioners should be knowledgeable of the full range of Web-based communications vehicles, most certainly including the following:

- Intranets are a pervasive internal communications phenomenon. Generally defined, an intranet is an internal vehicle that integrates communication with workflow, process management, infrastructure, and all other aspects of completing a job. Intranets allow communicators, management, and employees to exchange information quickly and effectively, much more quickly and effectively than any similar vehicle.
- Extranets, on the other hand, allow a company to use the Internet to communicate information to finely segmented external groups, such as the media, investors, vendors, key customers, left-handed female reality TV stars, security-cleared video archiving soccer players, blonde East Side yoga-going supermodels, whatever. In segmenting the information in such a focused fashion—and protecting its dissemination through a complex series of firewalls—the targeted audience is assured that the data will remain confidential.

    Wikis, which derive from the Hawaiian word for "quick," are collaborative Web sites that combine the work of many authors. Similar to a blog in structure and logic, a wiki differs from a blog in that it allows anyone to edit, delete, or modify content that has been placed on the Web site, including the work of previous authors. The most prominent online wiki example is Wikipedia, from which its name derives.

- Podcasting, which gained its name and fame after Apple's iPod burst onto the scene in 2001, refers to the act of making audio programs available for download. Listeners already have an enormous selection of podcasts from which to choose; the pod revolution is limited only by the supply of and demand for content.
- RSS, which literally stands for really simple syndication, is an easy way to distribute content on the Internet, similar to a newsgroup. RSS feeds are widely used by the blog community, for example, to share headlines or full text. Major news organizations, including Reuters, CNN, PR Newswire, and the BBC, use RSS feeds to allow other sites to incorporate their "syndicated" news services.

    QR codes and LBS, or quick response codes and location-based services, have become an essential component of the overall communication marketing experience as cell phones have overwhelmed society. QR codes, most often embedded in magazines, can be scanned by smartphones to demonstrate product uses or take advantage of special offers. Most such uses are designed to drive consumers online and visit a Web site. LBS often targets consumers within close proximity to retailers selling the items identified. Both QR codes and LBS may hold potential application for public relations use.[32]

These are but a sample of the online communications vehicles available to public relations professionals. The important thing for public relations people is to stay aware of the changing nature of Internet communications vehicles. The Internet menu changes at lightning speed, and it's the responsibility of the communications professional to change right along with it.

The Online Dark Side

Monitoring the Internet is another frontline public relations responsibility. The World Wide Web is riddled with unhappy consumers spilling their guts, disgruntled stockholders badmouthing management in chat rooms, and rogue Web sites condemning this or that organization.

The Internet is free, wide open, international, and anonymous—the perfect place to start a movement and ruin an organization's reputation. And so it is imperative that public relations people monitor the Internet in consideration of the following.

- **Blogs** are hotbeds for discontented shareholders, unscrupulous stock manipulators, and disgruntled consumers. Any local or service provider message board that solicits public input about an organization is ripe for messaging contrary to the official position. Finance boards on Yahoo! and others, for example, are the source of continuing commentary about public companies from anonymous commentators, all using mysterious pseudonyms.

- **Rogue Web sites** must also be monitored by the organizations they attack. Rogue Web sites seek to confront an organization by presenting negative, often-unfounded information. One device that companies use to throttle rogue sites is to buy up all the names that might be chosen by adversaries, most including words like. Rogue Web sites must also be monitored by the organizations they attack. Rogue Web sites seek to confront an organization by presenting negative, often-unfounded information. One device that companies use to throttle rogue sites is to buy up all the names that might be chosen by adversaries, most including words like "sucks," "stinks," "bites," etc.

- **Urban legends** are yet another requisite for online monitoring. There is a growing body of corporate horror stories from bogus Internet rumors that have taken on legendary proportions. Most are spread by e-mail at lightning speed across the country and the world. For example:

  - Upscale retailer Neiman Marcus was accused by an anonymous e-mailer of charging a $200 fee for its special cookie recipe. Outrageous, cried the thousands who received the e-mail. It's also completely untrue. Neiman Marcus doesn't have a cookie recipe.

  - Mrs. Fields also outraged the populace when an e-mail dispatch reported that she had sent a batch of her famous cookies to O. J. Simpson after he won his infamous 1990s murder trial. This is also totally false.

> **Subject:** Tommy Hilfiger
>
> **MESSAGE:**
>
> I'm sure many of you watched the recent taping of the *Oprah Winfrey Show* where her guest was Tommy Hilfiger. On the show she asked him if the statements about race he was accused of saying were true. Statements like if he'd known African-Americans, Hispanics and Asians would buy his clothes he would not have made them so nice. He wished these people would *not* buy his clothes, as they are made for upper class white people. His answer to Oprah was a simple "yes". Where after she immediately asked him to leave her show.

FIGURE 10-7 Stuff of legends.
Urban legends like this e-mail, discussing a bogus appearance by Tommy Hilfiger on *The Oprah Winfrey Show*, have become increasingly frequent as more people, some with questionable motives, access the Internet.

■ In perhaps the most pervasive and pernicious urban legend of all, retailer Tommy Hilfiger was, according to the official-sounding e-mail, evicted from *The Oprah Winfrey Show* by the lady herself when the clothes manufacturer admitted his garments weren't made for "African Americans, Hispanics, and Asians" **(Figure 10-7)**. The reality was that Tommy Hilfiger never met Oprah Winfrey, was never on her show, and certainly didn't design his clothing solely for white people. In the end, the false Internet legend proved so virulent that Oprah invited Hilfiger on her show to "clear the air" once and for all.

What should a proper public relations response be to such online efforts to derail the organization? Typical responses range from doing nothing to throwing money at an aggrieved party to engaging the aggrieved party to releasing the lawyers. The smartest organizations adopt "inoculation strategies" that establish clear communication channels on the Web, through which customers and employees can relay concerns to management, sometimes privately, before frustrations mount. Such preemptive public relations make solid business sense.

The real lesson: Public relations professionals must constantly monitor and beware of the Web.

Last Word

The Internet, as a popular communications medium, has been around barely for two plus decades; social media even less. In that short time, these new applications have evolved into indispensable communications tools for organizations and favored weapons for angry customers, disaffected employees, and consumer activists bent on attacking those same organizations. As a consequence, mastering and monitoring the Internet and social media have become a front-burner priority for public relations professionals.

As the number of the world's citizens using the Internet expands exponentially, it is urgent that public relations professionals understand the new technology and its capabilities and increase their competence in employing and monitoring it. Those who can blend the traditional skills of writing and media and communications knowledge with the online skills of the Internet—particularly the generation that has grown up with social media as its preferred communication default mechanism—will find a rewarding calling in the practice of public relations in the 21st century.[33]

Discussion Starters

1. What is the status of the Internet and World Wide Web in public relations today?
2. How has social media affected journalism? Commerce? Internal communications?
3. How has e-mail changed the way people and organizations communicate?
4. How has social media changed the way journalists look at e-mail?
5. How have blogs influenced public relations practice?
6. What is the significance of Facebook relative to public relations practice?
7. What is the significance of Twitter relative to public relations practice?
8. How have companies used YouTube in crisis?
9. How should organizations protect themselves from online attack?
10. What is the difference between an intranet and an extranet?

Pick of the Literature

Social Media and Public Relations

Deidre Breakenridge, Upper Saddle River, NJ: Pearson Education, 2012

There is no more knowledgeable public relations counselor on uses of social media and the Internet than Deidre Breakenridge. The New Jersey consultant has written a number of books on public relations uses of the new media. This is the best.

Early in the book, author Breakenridge confronts public relations practitioners with the exhortation that "Social media requires you to shift your mindset to unite communications and collaborative technology." She then goes on to introduce and explain eight new practices that social media introduces to public relations professionals: (1) policy maker, (2) internal collaborator, (3) technology tester, (4) communications organizer, (5) pre-crisis doctor, (6) relationship analyzer, (7) reputation task force member, and (8) metrics master.

She examines each of these elements in creative detail, diagramming their relationship to the overall business entity and their navigation in terms of social media. This is original thinking at its finest.

Case Study   Don't Mess with the Queen of Social Media

In the 21st century, record sales are depressed. Yet her albums sell by the millions. She has 60 million followers on Twitter and another 100 million friends and subscribers among Facebook, YouTube and Instagram.

She is pop singer Taylor Swift, and in the second decade of the 21st century, she is the undisputed queen of social media.

How she has mastered the social medium should serve as a primer for any individual or organization eager to understand and penetrate the world's most potent communications force. Here's how she's done it.

Building Relationships

Public relations begins with building relationships, and here Taylor Swift is a master. The singer may be a millionaire many times over, but she never loses sight of her "Swifties."

Answering the appeals of the Swift fan base appears to be the singer's number one interest. She builds a relationship with her audience by responding to random appeals on Twitter and Instagram. For example:

■ A girl named Hannah wrote to the singer that she was being bullied, so Swift decided to send a heartfelt message encouraging her to "keep walking in the sunlight." The Instagram comment Swift posted on the girl's fan account went viral.

■ Another fan told the singer of her heartbreak over a lost boy friend, and Swift told her to, "Hang in there." Again, the Instagram went viral.

■ Swift used Instagram to wish another fan a happy 16th birthday, congratulated another on her engagement, and another on earning her driver's license. She even commended the "sense of humor" of another teenage follower.

Such interactions occasionally open Swift to attack from the some of the more cynical denizens of the Internet, but the more Swift embraces the hate, the more popular she gets. With strategic social media messages like these to individual fans, Swift has developed a reputation for caring that transcends that of any other superstar. Indeed, one Swiftie even devotes a Tumblr account to follow Swift's likes and comments on Instagram.

Keeping It Real

In the 21st century, everyone from corporate CEOs to entertainers to the President of the United States to the Queen of England communicate via social media. But how many of them have ghost writers, i.e. public relations assistants who draft the missives for them? Answer: Nearly all of them. Except for…Taylor Swift!

While most celebrities, like Britney Spears whose manager tweets from her client's account to the 39 million Britney followers, have social media experts writing for them round-the-clock, Swift, by all accounts, engages with fans in a raw and natural way, personalizing her social media communications.

When a Swift fan tweeted her how she went "bonkers" over a particular song at a concert, the singer retweeted that the girl had "made her day!!!!" When another fan tweeted about a local dance party with all Swift songs, the singer tweeted back, "Wish I was there!!!!"

The Swift social media "touch," including the multiple!!!! exclamation marks, adds to the singer's authenticity as a social media presence and, by extension, as a "real" person. Indeed, in her interviews and personal appearances—including the time she threw a private concert for a six-year-old Leukemia patient and her two-hour lunch with a 17-year-old girl battling cancer—Swift comes across as confident, enthusiastic, and the "real deal."

Promoting Creatively

The fact that everybody uses social media means that just like any other medium, to really score with the new technology, one must use it creatively. Here again, Taylor Swift excels.

In 2014, when the singer was about ready to drop her new album, "1989," she enticed a larger audience by dropping clues on Instagram. In the video, an unseen person presses the 18th floor button of an elevator, followed by a screen shot of her phone, showing the time, 5 P.M. Another screen shot mysteriously showed Yahoo!'s search engine.

This creative gamification strategy gave her audience an additional reason to care about what the singer was leading up to. The outgrowth: Swift would debut the album with a live stream on Yahoo at 5 P.M. on August 18.

Not only did the singer leave the social media clues to entice interest in the new album, but she also proceeded to comment, favor, and retweet individual fan posts about the campaign.

And beyond the social media games, Taylor Swift also is canny enough to avail herself of social media's most fetching commodity—the cat. So when the singer walks her cats or goes shopping with them, she makes a point of posting the photo for her adoring fans. Predictably, those fans have awarded Swift's cats, Meredith and Olivia, with numerous social profiles **(Figure 10-8)**.

Such are the initiatives that separate celebrities who merely understand and use social media from those who are true social media prodigies.

Standing for Something

Taylor Swift also distinguishes herself from other social media users by demonstrating, through social media postings, that she stands for something.

This gutsiness was amply demonstrated in the summer of 2015 when Apple announced that it didn't plan to pay artists royalties during a free, three-month trial of its new streaming music service.

Immediately after the Apple announcement, Swift posted an online announcement of her own, saying she would withhold her latest album from the service because Apple wasn't planning to pay artists and labels directly for the use of their music. In part, the singer posted on her Tumblr page:

To Apple, Love Taylor

"We don't ask you for free iPhones. Please don't ask us to provide you with our music for no compensation."

She closed by expressing hope that the company might change its policy and "change the minds of those in the music industry who will be deeply and gravely affected by this."

And within hours, that's exactly what the most powerful tech company in the world decided to do. Said Apple's senior vice president, "When I woke up this morning and I saw Taylor's note that she had written, it really solidified that we needed to make a change." And so Apple did, gently brought to its knees by the Queen of Social Media **(Figure 10-8)***.

Questions

1. What distinguishes Taylor Swift's social media strategy from that of other celebrities?

2. How does Taylor Swift benefit from her social media strategy?

3. What other public relations options did Taylor Swift have with respect to the Apple streaming music decision?

For further information, see Brandon Bailey, "Apple Changes Tune on Royalties After Swift Complains," *Associated Press* (June 22, 2015); Rebecca Borison, "Taylor Swift Is Incredibly Good at Being a Celebrity," *Business Insider* (September 10, 2014); Ben Sisario, "With a Tap of Taylor's Swift's Fingers, Apple Retreated," *The New York Times* (June 22, 2015); and Joshua Swanson, "The Taylor Swift Guide to Social Media Marketing," *Digiday* (January 7, 2015).

From the Top

An Interview with Richard Edelman

Richard Edelman is president and CEO of Edelman, the world's largest public relations firm with 3500 employees in 66 offices worldwide. Mr. Edelman is also the public relations executive most associated with the Internet and new technology. Under his leadership, Edelman has distinguished itself not only in traditional public relations areas but as a pioneer in the new media. A graduate of Harvard College and the Harvard Business School, Mr. Edelman is one of the only public relations executives to write his own blog.

How has the Internet changed the public relations business?

The Web has changed the PR business by giving us access to budgets that we never saw before...by allowing us to make each of our clients its own media company...by broadening our array of addressable media to include bloggers...to force us to have relationships with a whole new set of influencers who may not be at top magazines but are frequently posting content.

How proficient in terms of the Net should a public relations professional be today?

The PR person who does not read important blogs (e.g., in DC you should read Drudge Report, Politico) is missing the game. You also must be posting comments to blogs that matter. You need to be reading the mainstream media's blogs (e.g., Andrew Ross Sorkin's blog at NY Times—Deal Book).

What are the primary online communications methods that you recommend to your clients?

Primary online methods are listening to the conversation by reading or viewing video blogs, making comments as appropriate, making relationships with key bloggers. For example, I had lunch the old-fashioned way with Laurel Touby of Mediabistro, who was Tweeting during our lunch about our conversation.

Why do you blog?

I blog because I enjoy writing, because I like to walk the talk about social media, because too few executives in PR agencies are willing to take a stand on issues.

Do you recommend that other CEOs blog internally?

I do recommend that other CEOs blog. I would rather have them make their blog posts accessible to the general public. But internal only is a good first step.

Do you recommend that clients get involved in online forums that are critical of them?

I believe that companies must participate in the horizontal axis of communications. You need to correct misinformation and to be part of the conversation. At least point people to alternative interpretations of the data on the company site or another site.

Who do you consider the leadership companies in terms of online communications?

Best companies are Walmart, GE, and GM. They offer access to mid-level staffers. Note, for example, the blog for Walmart which has buyers posting from around the world as they find new garments or electronics; also the GE research blog on future innovations.

What lies on the horizon for public relations use of the Web?

PR will have to improve the quality of its content. All of it must be ready for prime time—not as much selling mode as it will have to be conversational and factual. Also, it must include more visual content as words are no longer sufficient. We will be the means by which business can open up to conversation.

Public Relations Bookshelf

Barger, Christopher. *Social Media Strategist*. New York: McGraw-Hill, 2012. Sophisticated look at using social media strategically to accomplish public relations goals.

Bragman, Howard. *Where's My Fifteen Minutes?* New York: Penguin, 2008. Ricki Lake's public relations counselor offers behind-the-scenes secrets to optimize publicity, including using the Internet.

Breakenridge, Deirdre. *PR 2.0: New Media, New Tools, New Audiences*. Upper Saddle River, NJ: Pearson Education, 2008. This is a terrific explanation, in layperson's language, of everything one needs to know about practicing public relations on the Internet.

Evans, Liana. *Social Media Marketing*. Indianapolis, IN: Que Publishing, 2010. Solid explanation of dealing with Facebook and Twitter.

Falls, Jason and Erik Deckers. *No Bull*&** Social Media*. Upper Saddle River, NJ: Pearson Education, 2012. My very own publisher, proving that it, too, can publish a book with a curse word in the title.

Gehrt, Jennifer and Colleen Moffitt. *Strategic Public Relations*. Bloomington, IN: Xlibris Corporation, 2009. General strategies including Internet discussion.

Green, Andy. *Creativity in Public Relations*. 3rd ed. London, England: Kogan Page, 2008. This updated version includes creativity via the Internet.

Handley, Ann and Charles C. Chapman. *Content Rules*. Hoboken, NJ: John Wiley & Sons, 2012. Focus on perfecting blogs, podcasts, webinars, and other Internet fare.

Kabani, Shana H. *Social Media Marketing*. Dallas, TX: BenBella Books, 2010. Straightforward presentation on online marketing.

Kelleher, Thomas. *Public Relations Online*. Thousand Oaks, CA: Sage Publications, 2007. This book offers a good explanation of relationship-based interactive public relations.

Kerpen, Dave. *Likeable Social Media*. New York: McGraw-Hill, 2011. Tongue-in-cheek approach to explaining the pros and cons of avenues of social media.

King, Janice M. *Copywriting That Sells High-Tech*. Sammamish, WA: WriteSpark Press, 2006. This book is for public relations writers who deal primarily with high-tech companies and products.

Lawson, Russell. *The PR Buzz Factor*. London, England: Kogan Page, 2006. One way to create "buzz" is through a creative online presence and Website, says this counselor.

Lynn, Jaqueline. (Ed.). *Start Your Own Public Relations Business*. New York: Entrepreneur Media, 2009. This provides a route—largely Internet-related—through which a practitioner might start his or her own public relations organization.

Martin, Gail Z. *30 Days to Social Media Success*. Pompton Plains, NJ: The Career Press, 2010. A book dedicated to getting you to rethink, restart, and reenergize your social marketing—in 30 days.

Phillips, David and Philip Young. *Online Public Relations*. Philadelphia, PA: Kogan Page, 2011. Fine soup-to-nuts tour, including definitions and strategies, of using the Internet and social media.

Safko, Lon. *The Social Media Bible*. 3rd ed. Hoboken, NJ: John Wiley & Sons, 2012. Bible? Well, it is pretty comprehensive in discussing everything from podcasts and video sharing to social networking and micro blogging.

Scott, David M. *The New Rules of Marketing and PR*. 3rd ed. Hoboken, NJ: John Wiley & Sons, 2011. Marketing-oriented text emphasizes raising online visibility to enhance sales volume.

Singh, Shiv. *Social Media Marketing for Dummies*. Hoboken, NJ: Wiley Publishing, 2010. Social media primer.

Solis, Brian and Deirdre Breakenridge. *How Social Media Is Reinventing the Aging Business of PR*. Upper Saddle River, NJ: Pearson Education, 2009. Not sure if public relations is exactly "aging" (although your author clearly is!). But social media has, clearly, arrived, and this book is a good introduction to it.

Sponder, Marshall. *Social Media Analytics*. New York: McGraw-Hill, 2012. Searching for the Return on Investment with social media.

Swann, Patricia. *Cases in Public Relations Management: The Rise of Social Media and Activism*. 2nd ed. New York, NY: Routledge, 2014. Good review of contemporary public relations cases involving social media.

Sweeney, Susan, Andy MacLellan, and Ed Dorey. *3G Marketing on the Internet*. Gulf Breeze, FL: Maximum Press, 2006. It's third-generation time for the Internet, and this book provides business strategies for using the Internet today.

Van Den Hurk, Ann M. *Social Media Crisis Communications*. Indianapolis, IN: Pearson Education, Inc., 2013. Interesting social media take on crisis from a self-described "hybrid public relations counselor, bridging the gap between traditional PR and social media."

Endnotes

1. Roxane Gay, "Justine Sacco's Aftermath: The Cost of Twitter Outrage," *Salon* (December 23, 2013).
2. Eric Benderoff, "Macon Phillips: Obama's New-Media Messenger," *Chicago Tribune* (March 9, 2009).
3. Evelyn M. Rusli and Peter Eavis, "Facebook Raises $16 Billion in IPO," *The New York Times* (May 17, 2012).
4. Nicholas Fandos and Gardiner Harris, "To Delight of Tourists, White House Ends 40-Year-Old Ban on Photos," *The New York Times* (July 2, 2015).
5. Brahima Sanou, "2014 ICT Facts and Figures," April 2014, http://www.itu.int/en/ITU-D/Statistics/Documents/facts/ICTFactsFigures2014-e.pdf.
6. Aaron Smith, "African Americans and Technology Use," *Pew Research Center* (January 6, 2014).
7. "Journalists' Use of Facebook, Twitter, Blogs and Company Websites to Assist in Reporting Surges from 2009/2010 Study," *Society for New Communications Research and Middleberg Communications* (May 6, 2011).
8. "Corporate Websites Still Coming Up Short," *The Holmes Report* (February 18, 2002): 1–2.
9. Sara Radicati (Ed.), "E Mail Statistics Report: 2014-2018," *The Radicati Group, Inc.* (April 2014), http://www.radicati.com/wp/wp-content/uploads/2014/01/Email-Statistics-Report-2014-2018-Executive-Summary.pdf.
10. Sara Radicati (Ed.), "Instant Messaging Market, 2014-2019," op. cit.
11. Catherine Clifford, "Top 10 Apps for Instant Messaging," *Entrepreneur* (December 11, 2013).
12. Lauren Fisher, "AP Begins Crediting Bloggers as News Sources," *TNW Social Media* (September 7, 2010).
13. Fraser P. Seitel, "Blog-Communications Weapon," *O'Dwyer's PR Services Report* (November 2005): 39.
14. Susan Gunelius, "The State of Blogging in 2014," *ACI Information Group* (December 27, 2014), http://aci.info/2014/12/27/the-state-of-blogging-in-2014/.
15. Chris Kent, "Why Your CEO's Blog Is Fading into Oblivion," *The Ragan Report* (December 2008): 9.
16. Lisa Barone, "5 Dos & Don'ts for Getting Blog Coverage," *Ragan PR Daily* (June 30, 2010).
17. Beth S. Bulik, "Does Your Company Need a Chief Blogger?" *Advertising Age* (April 14, 2008): 24.
18. Isenberg David, "The Rise of the Stupid Network," *Computer Telephony* (August 1997): 16–26.
19. Craig Smith, "By the Numbers: 200+ Amazing Facebook Statistics," *DMR* (June 29, 2015), http://expandedramblings.com/index.php/by-the-numbers-17-amazing-facebook-stats/.
20. Joeri Van den Bergh, "Youngsters Think Facebook Pages of Brands Are Not Credible," *InSites Consulting* (February 5, 2013), http://www.slideshare.net/joerivandenbergh/the-truth-and-nothing-but-the-truth-by-generation-y-around-the-world-16358470.
21. "10 Remarkable Twitter Statistics for 2015," *Social Caffeine*, http://lorirtaylor.com/twitter-statistics-2015/.
22. Jennifer Weiner, "The Cost of Buying Someone's Soul. Or Tweets," *The New York Times* (April 24, 2015).
23. Shonali Burke, "How to Use Twitter for Public Relations," *Social Media Today* (June 21, 2013).
24. Irina Slutsky, "Why LinkedIn Is the Social Network that Will Never Die," *Advertising Age* (December 6, 2010).
25. Christa Toole, "Ten Tips for Those Who Still Aren't Using YouTube," *Advertising Age* (October 19, 2010).
26. Jason Miller, "Judge Sentences Former GSA Official Jeff Neely to 3 Months in Jail," *Federal News Radio* (July 1, 2015), http://federalnewsradio.com/management/2015/07/judge-sentences-former-gsa-official-neely-3-months-jail/.
27. Gin Dietrich, "16 Ways to Use Pinterest for PR," *Ragan PR Daily* (May 10, 2012).
28. Kevin Allen, "A Complete Guide to Instagram," *Ragan PR Daily* (May 21, 2012).
29. Will Oremus, "Is Snapchat Really Confusing or Am I Just Getting Old?" *Slate* (January 29, 2015).
30. Caroline Farhat, "3 Ways to Use Reddit for PR," *Ragan PR Daily* (June 7, 2013).
31. Angela Jeffrey, "PR Industry Developing Social Media Measurement Standards," *Ragan PR Daily* (July 24, 2012).
32. JoAnn De Luna, "QR Codes," www.dmnews.com (May 2012).
33. Fraser P. Seitel, "Know Your Social Media," *O'Dwyer's PR Report* (November 2006): 34.

Chapter 11

Employee Relations

Chapter Objectives

1. To discuss an often-overlooked but core critical constituency for organizational management, the internal public.
2. To explore the philosophy of dealing with employees in an era of layoffs and meager job growth.
3. To discuss the various tactics—print, online, and broadcast—of communicating with the internal public.
4. To examine the ways that social media have complicated and made more challenging the function of communicating with employees.

FIGURE 11-1 **Back on the street.**
Groupon co-founder didn't mince words to the staff in 2013 when he was unceremoniously booted as CEO by the Groupon board.
Photo: BRENDAN MCDERMID/REUTERS/Newscom

The pervasiveness of social media has brought a new honesty—brutal honesty—to the realm of employee relations.

The people who know the most about your organization are the individuals who work for that organization. Therefore, it's a wise management that talks truth and stays transparent when communicating with the employees.

For example, in 2013 when his board of directors decided to replace Andrew Mason, co-founder of the daily deals site Groupon, as CEO, Mr. Mason rejected suggestions that he provide the time-honored alibi of fired CEOs everywhere, i.e. "I want to spend more time with my family" (Figure 11-1). Rather, he decided to tell the truth, tweeting the staff:

People of Groupon,

After four and a half intense and wonderful years as C.E.O. of Groupon, I've decided that I'd like to spend more time with my family. Just kidding—I was fired today. . . .

I'm O.K. with having failed at this part of the journey. If Groupon was Battletoads, it would be like I made it all the way to the Terra Tubes without dying on my first-ever play through. I am so lucky to have had the opportunity to take the company this far with all of you. I'll now take some time to decompress.

F.Y.I. I'm looking for a good fat camp to lose my Groupon 40, if anyone has a suggestion, and then maybe I'll figure out how to channel this experience into something productive.[1]

Mr. Mason's bluntness notwithstanding, in the second decade of the 21st century, relations between employees and the people they worked for remained brittle. As world economies from Greece to Latin America to China continued to suffer fits and starts and more people either got fired or worried that unemployment might lie around the corner, relations with employees—to keep them loyal and believing—emerged as a front burner public relations responsibility.

In the United States, rising pressure to reduce income inequality was fueled by the fact that CEO pay vs. average worker pay had ballooned in 50 years from 20 to 300 times.[2] Layoffs, once the exception, had become a crushing periodic reality, as companies prospered from computer-fueled productivity growth at the expense of human labor.

While states like California, where unemployment had continued to grow, showed new found strength in 2014, adding 498,000 jobs, the state's unemployment rate remained at 20% with the highest poverty rate in the nation.[3] While cheaper oil prices drove energy costs lower for most Americans, the U.S. oil industry lost 51,000 jobs in a year.[4] Meanwhile, consolidation and efficiency efforts in other industries also meant worker job losses. Wall Street's six largest banks were responsible for cutting more than 80,000 jobs over five years.[5] And in the summer 2015, Microsoft, a company doing well, announced a round of 7800 layoffs, following another layoff a year earlier that sacked 18,000 people.[6]

Even as many workers around the world continued to toil in this climate of uncertainty, according to an Edelman study, companies with "highly engaged employees" outperformed the total stock market and enjoyed total shareholder returns 19% higher than the average; those with low engagement levels saw total shareholder returns 44% lower than average.[7]

So what's an organization to do, especially to reassure these younger participants in the workforce?

According to the Edelman study, rethinking employee engagement to drive better results isn't easy. Management, Edelman says, must be willing to answer several questions in attempting to lift employee morale, commitment, and engagement.

1. Is your leadership rolling out a new strategy or initiative that will require more engagement than ever from your employees?

2. Do you need to activate or reengage your employees as advocates or ambassadors?

3. How well is the urgency for change understood and acted on within your organization?

4. Should leadership communication be a critical component of delivering on your company's strategy or organizational performance goals?

5. Are you searching for novel ways to renew or reinvent the employee experience? Are leaders looking for better ways of engaging their teams?

6. Does your employee engagement research provide sufficient insights for leaders to build trust, cultivate two-way dialogue, and engage employees on critical priorities?

7. Do your current drivers of employee engagement support the business you need to become?

8. If employee engagement remains at its current level or decreases within your company, is there a downside risk?[8]

In the midst of such turmoil between employees and management, an organization's communications to and with employees must be candid, clear, and credible That's why organizing effective, believable, and persuasive internal communications—particularly in the midst of economic uncertainty and organizational change—is such a challenging and critical public relations responsibility in the 21st century.

1 A Critical Function

In the 21st century, employee relations matters—a lot.

One significant measure, the 2015 Edelman Trust Barometer, revealed an alarming evaporation of trust across all institutions, reaching the lows of the Great Recession in 2009. Trust in government, business, media, and NGOs in the general population was below 50% in two-thirds of countries, including the United States, UK, Germany, and Japan. Among the most significant declines in trust was that of the CEO as a credible spokesperson, which showed a third consecutive year of trust declines.[9]

The reasons for this loss in credibility are varied and underscore the importance of employee communication.

- First, the pace of downsizings and layoffs that dominated business and industry in the United States and worldwide after the overleveraging in the first decade of the 21st century, may have subsided, but it hasn't ceased altogether. Such vulnerability and uncertainty has taken its toll on employee loyalty. Although employees once implicitly trusted their organizations and superiors, today they are more hardened to the realities of a job market dominated by technological change that reduces human labor. Today, when companies lay off workers, they are often rewarded by the stock market for becoming more productive and efficient. This phenomenon has caused employees to understand that in today's business climate, every employee is expendable and there is no such thing as "lifetime employment." Consequently, companies must work harder at honestly communicating with their workers.

- Second, as noted, the wide gulf between the pay of senior officers and common workers is another reason organizations must be sensitive to employee communications. Income inequality between top management and common workers has exploded in recent years to become a cause célèbre particularly in the United States.

- Third, the move toward globalization has hastened the integration of business and markets around the world. Customers on far-away continents are today but a mouse-click away. Alliances, affiliations, and mergers among far-flung companies have proliferated. Organizations have become much more cognizant of the importance of communicating the opportunities and benefits that will enhance support and loyalty among worldwide staffs.

- Finally, as the Edelman research suggested, companies that communicate effectively with their workers financially outperform those that don't. The Edelman data suggested that nearly two-thirds of respondents refused to buy products and services from a company they did not trust. Conversely, 80% chose to buy products from companies they trusted, with 68% recommending those companies to a friend.[10]

Employee communications, then, has become a key way to nurture and sustain trust and loyalty among workers.

This was not always the case. For years, employee communications was considered less important than the more glamorous and presumably more "critical" functions of media, government, and investor relations.

Today, with fewer employees expected to do more work, staff members are calling for empowerment—for more of a voice in decision making. Just about every researcher who keeps tabs on employee opinion finds evidence of a "trust gap" that exists between management and workers. To narrow that gap demands that more effective employee communication play a pivotal role.

2 The Employee Public

Just as there is no such thing as the "general public," there is also no single "employee public."

The employee public is made up of numerous subgroups: senior managers, first-line supervisors, staff and line employees, union laborers, per diem employees, contract workers, and others. Each group has different interests and concerns. A smart organization will try to differentiate messages and communications to reach these segments.

Indeed, in a general sense, today's staff is younger, increasingly female, more diverse, ambitious, and career oriented, less complacent, and less loyal to the company than in the past. Today's more hard-nosed employee demands candor in communications. Internal communications, like external messages, must be targeted to reach specific subgroups of the employee public.

Grounding in effective employee communications requires management to ask three hard questions about the way it conveys knowledge to the staff.

- Is management able to communicate effectively with employees?
- Is communication trusted, and does it relay appropriate information to employees?
- Has management communicated its commitment to its employees and to fostering a rewarding work environment?

In many instances, the biggest problem is that employees don't know where they stand in the eyes of management. This is particularly true in a period of high unemployment. The more workers understand how they fit into the big picture, the more secure and loyal they will become.

The bottom-line: If the people inside who work for you don't believe your story, then the people outside will never buy in. Therefore, organizing effective, believable and persuasive internal communications is a core critical public relations responsibility in the 21st century.

Communicating "Trust"

How does a public relations professional counsel his management to communicate the coveted commodity of "trust?"

According to the coauthors of the *100 Best Companies to Work For in America*, who later became editors of the Fortune magazine exercise of the same name, six criteria, in particular, have stood the test of time:

1. **Willingness to express dissent.** Employees want to be able to "feed back" to management their opinions and even dissent. They want access to management.

They want critical letters to appear in internal publications. They want management to pay attention.

2. **Visibility and proximity of upper management.** Enlightened companies try to level rank distinctions, eliminating such status reminders as executive cafeterias and executive gymnasiums. They act against hierarchical separation. Smart CEOs practice MBWA—"management by walking around."

3. **Priority of internal to external communication.** The worst thing to happen to any organization is for employees to learn critical information about the company on a renegade blog or the 10 o'clock news. Smart organizations always release pertinent information to employees first and consider internal communication primary.

4. **Attention to clarity.** How many employees regularly read benefits booklets? Although the answer should be "many" because of the importance of benefit programs to the entire staff, most employees never do so. Good companies deliver such messages with an emphasis on clarity as opposed to legalities—to be readable for a general audience rather than for human resources specialists.

5. **Friendly tone.** The best companies "give a sense of family" in all that they communicate. One high-tech company makes everyone wear a name tag with his or her first name in big block letters. When management creates a culture more "fiend" than "friend," employees—especially in a day of Twitter and Facebook—occasionally rebel with a vengeance.

6. **Sense of humor.** People are worried principally about keeping their jobs. Corporate life for many is grim, where people can't wait to get to the end of the day. So employees seem to enjoy themselves more at companies such as Southwest Airlines, where legendary founder Herb Kelleher used to say, "If you create an environment where people truly participate, you don't need control"[11] **(Figure 11-2)**.

FIGURE 11-2
Alien company.
Southwest Airlines is one company that prides itself on its sense of humor. Here the company, in conjunction with Sue Bohle Public Relations and Infogames Entertainment, decked out these passengers in out-of-this-world masks on the way to the E3 Entertainment Trade Show.
Photo: Courtesy of the Bohle Company

A Question of Ethics

How Not to "Cosi" Up to Employees

CEOs in the 21st century dread facing their shareholders after a bad quarter. So no one could blame Cosi CEO Stephen Edwards if he wasn't looking forward to the restaurant chain's 2013 quaterly conference call with investors, after the company lost $2 million in the quarter.

What they might have blamed the CEO for was laying the reason for the quarterly shortfall squarely at the feet of one group in particular, Cosi employees. Stated CEO Edwards to the assembled analysts and portfolio managers:

> People love our sandwiches; they love our salads. We hear it time and time again. It's never a complaint. A complaint is because someone was rude to me, my sandwich or my salad was incomplete in the ingredients that it was supposed to have…or I got the wrong order or it took me 20 minutes to get my order when there was nobody else in the store.

To remedy the problem, CEO Edwards promised to focus on *"Class A hospitality and service experience."*

The CEO clearly had his work cut out for him in encouraging the workers to pick up the pace. According to Glassdoor, a Web site where employees and former employees anonymously review companies and their management, Cosi received a 2.6-star rating, vs. a 2.9 rating and a 3.1 rating at competitors Burger King and McDonald's, respectively. Many of the Cosi employee reviews criticized the company for not offering training and chastised management for treating employees with little respect.

In light of the CEO's comments about his workforce, maybe they had a point **(Figure 11-3)**.

Questions

1. How would you assess the Cosi CEO's comments to investors?

2. Had you been the Cosi public relations director, how would you have suggested the CEO frame his remarks?

FIGURE 11-3
All is not Cosi.
Employees at the nation's 150 Cosi restaurants weren't feeling the love when the CEO blamed them for the chain's losses in 2013.
Photo: RICHARD B. LEVINE/Newscom

*For further information, see Ashley Lutz, "Cosi's CEO Blames the Chain's Troubles on His Employees," *Yahoo! Finance* (August 20, 2013); and Matt Wilson, "Cosi CEO Blames Staff for Losses," *Ragan PR Daily* (August 22, 2013).

What internal communications comes down to—just like external communications—is one word, *credibility*. The task for management is to convince employees that it not only desires to communicate with them but also wishes to do so in a truthful, frank and direct manner. That is the overriding challenge that confronts today's internal communicator.

Credibility Holds Key

The employee public is a savvy one. Employees can't be conned because they live with the organization every day. They generally know what's going on and whether management is being honest with them. That's why management must be truthful.

Employees want managers to level with them. They want facts, not wishful thinking. The days when management could say "Trust us, this is for your own good" are over. Employees like hearing the truth, especially in person. Indeed, survey after survey suggests that face-to-face communication—preferably between a supervisor and subordinate—is the hands-down most effective method of employee communications.

Employees also want to know, candidly, how they're doing. Research indicates that trust in organizations would increase if management (1) communicated earlier and more frequently, (2) demonstrated trust in employees by sharing bad news as well as good, and (3) involved employees in the process by asking for their ideas and opinions. Effective employee communication means that an organization's leaders have taken the time to clearly and succinctly articulate the vision of the business and show how employees can contribute to it in their daily jobs.

Today, smart companies realize that well-informed employees are the organization's best goodwill ambassadors. Managements have become more candid in their communications with the staff. Gone are the days when all the news coming from management is all good. In today's environment, being candid means treating people with dignity, addressing their concerns, and giving them the opportunity to understand and share in the realities of the marketplace. When that credibility isn't forthcoming, social media often finds out, and that's when the trouble starts.

3 S-H-O-C the Troops

Enhancing credibility, being candid, and winning trust must be the primary employee communications objectives in the new century. Earning employee trust may result in more committed and productive employees. But scraping away the scar tissue of distrust that exists in many organizations requires a strategic approach.

The question is: How does management build trust when employee morale is so brittle?

Part of the answer lies in an approach to management communication built around the acronym S-H-O-C. That is, management should consider a four-step communications approach—built on communications that are **strategic, honest, open,** and **consistent**—to begin to rebuild employee trust.

- **First, all communications must be strategic.** What strategic communication essentially boils down to is this: Most employees want you to answer only two basic questions for them:
    1. Where is this organization going?
    2. What is my role in helping us get there?

That's it. Once you level with the staff as to the organization's direction and goals and their role in the process, even the most ardent bellyachers will grudgingly acknowledge your attempt to "keep them in the loop."

- **Second, all communications must be honest.** The sad fact is that while most executives may pay lip service to candor and honesty, in the end, too many turn out like the managements at Bear Stearns, Washington Mutual, Lehman Brothers, Countrywide Financial, and all the other 21st century companies caught dissembling, obfuscating, pulling their punches, and eventually fading into oblivion.

  They seem to fear, as Jack Nicholson raged in *A Few Good Men*, that the staff "can't handle the truth."

  Such trepidation is foolish. For one thing, the staff already may discount anything management tells them. For another, you can't hope to build credibility through prevaricating or sugarcoating.

- **Third, all communications must be open.** This is another way of saying that there must be feedback. The best communications are two-way communications. That means that no matter how large the organization, employee views must be solicited, listened to, and most important, acted on.

  That latter aspect is most important. Often, managers stage elaborate forums and feedback sessions, listen to employee gripes and suggestions, and yet do nothing. The key must be *action*.

- **Fourth, all communications must be consistent.** Once you've begun to communicate, you must keep it up. Maintain a regular, on-time, and predictable program of internal newsletters, employee forums, leadership meetings, and reward celebrations.

  On-again, off-again communications or programs that start with bold promises only to peter out question management's commitment to keeping the staff informed.

  This obviously is wrong. Communications, if they are to work, must be steadily, sometimes painfully, consistent.[12]

Internal Tool Kit

Once internal communications objectives are set, a variety of tactics may be adopted to reach the staff. The initial tool again is research. Before any communications program can be implemented, communicators must have a good sense of staff attitudes toward management, the organization and the communications climate.

Internal Communications Audits

Both a strategy and a tactic, the internal communications audit is the most beneficial form of research on which to lay the groundwork for effective employee communications. Ideally, this starts with old-fashioned, personal, in-depth interviews with both top management and communicators. It is important to find out from top management what it "wants" from the communications team. It is also important to find out what communicators "think" management wants. Often the discontinuities are startling. The four critical audit questions to probe are:

1. How do internal communications support the mission of the organization?
2. Do internal communications have management's support?

FYI

Disney's Credibility Correction

In today's social media environment, companies are more compelled than ever to do the right thing. If they don't, more often than not, they get caught—even the good companies.

Few corporations are more admired than entertainment colossus The Walt Disney Company **(Figure 11-4)**. But admiration turned to shock in the summer of 2015, when it was revealed that months earlier, 250 Walt Disney World data systems employees were replaced by lower-paid immigrants on temporary visas, who were brought in by an outsourcing firm based in India. If that wasn't bad enough, many of the out-of-work Disney employees were required, before they left, to train their replacements to do the jobs they had lost.

"I just couldn't believe they could fly people in to sit at our desks and take over our jobs exactly," said one former worker, quoted in *The New York Times.*

The criticism of Disney on social media and in the press was as categorical as it was withering. The conclusion: Disney and others were using a loophole in the U.S. temporary visa law to recruit highly-trained immigrants to do the work of Americans for less money.

What united the critics was the hypocrisy of a company like Disney, which portrayed itself as wholesome and honest, stooping to such questionable hiring practices. And Disney was listening.

When the *Times* subsequently reported that 35 technology employees at Disney/ABC Television would be replaced by immigrants brought in by an outsourcing company, it took Disney just a few days to—quietly—inform the 35 employees that plans had changed and they would all be keeping their jobs.*

FIGURE 11-4   Minnie crisis.
All was not sweetness and smiles in the Magic Kingdom in the summer of 2015, when The Walt Disney Company was forced to rescind a decision to replace workers with lower-paid immigrants on temporary visas.
Photo: Courtesy Raina Seitel

*For further information, see Julia Preston, "In Turnabout, Disney Cancels Tech Worker Layoffs," *The New York Times* (June 16, 2015); and Julia Preston, Disney Has No Comment on Recent Reversal of Layoffs," *The New York Times* (June 23, 2015).

3. Do internal communications justify the expense?

4. How responsive to employee needs and concerns are internal communications?

The ultimate aim of a communications audit should be to evaluate how effectively your channels are performing against your strategic communication objectives.[13]

Online Communications

Internal online communications vehicles—from instant messaging to mobile and video, from tailored organizational intranets to employee and CEO blogs to social media—have largely replaced print media as go-to internal communications vehicles. Such online communications reach employees at their desks or on their mobile device and are more likely to be read, listened to and acted on. Indeed, employees without computer access are increasingly losing their "voice" and ability to be heard, especially the ability to submit ideas for improvement or to access a company intranet remotely.

Online communications also have the capability of reaching virtual employees at their desks in their homes, on their smart phone and tablets, in their cars, or wherever they remotely may be.

As print publications become steadily fewer, tailored online newsletters have begun to replace them. In many cases, organizations are using print vehicles to push readers to new intranet portals.[14]

Among growing online, internal communications vehicles are the following:

- *Blogs* provide an easy way for employees to post opinions and views of the company on the Internet.

- *Podcasts*, in which audio or video monologue, interview or on-location content is broadcast online to employees. At Hewlett-Packard, for example, division presidents are podcasting discussions of new products and organizational developments with rank-and-file employees. The HP podcasts have proven immensely popular.[15]

- *Video* has grown as an online internal communications device. More and more companies are adopting a YouTube-like approach to video, introducing video libraries that let employees search for videos, comment on them, tag them, embed them, and upload their own as a means of sharing information and knowledge.

- *Mobile*, too, has grown as an employee communications vehicle, with the most forward-thinking companies recognizing that employees use their personal devices for work-related communication. Indeed, BYOD (Bring Your Own Device) is a grass-roots movement that smart companies will seize on to improve internal communications.[16]

In addition to these online tactics, social media, primarily through social software adaptation of networks like Facebook and Twitter, are growing and have caused companies to adopt specific social media policies and strategies, which we will discuss in a moment.

The Intranet

Today, in many organizations, the intranet has overtaken print communications. Intranet investments remain strong as companies continue to convert sites to portal technology and add streaming video capability. At IBM, for example, where just about everyone is computer savvy, the company eliminated every other internal communications medium but the corporate intranet to reach IBM's 300,000 employees. Today, the intranet—known internally as W3—is has become the voice of the company.[17]

At British American Tobacco, 25,000 intranet users can create their own Facebook-like profiles and networks by linking with other members. Members of the company's *Connect* network can link up with others in the 40-country company through a variety of social media derivatives.[18]

Unfortunately, having an intranet site doesn't mean employees will necessarily go there for information. Sites high in visual appeal but low in usefulness will likely be ignored. To prevent that, intranet creators should keep in mind several important considerations, learned early on in the intranet experience:

1. **Consider the culture.** If the organization is generally collaborative and collegial, it will have no trouble getting people to contribute information and materials to the intranet. But, if the organization is not one that ordinarily shares, a larger central staff may be necessary to ensure that the intranet works.

2. **Set clear objectives and then let it evolve.** Just as in setting up a corporate Web site, intranets must be designed with clear goals in mind: to streamline business processes, to communicate management messages, and so on.

3. **Treat it as a journalistic enterprise.** Company news gets read by company workers. Employees must know what's going on in the company and complain bitterly if they are not given advance notice of important developments.

4. **Market, market, market.** The intranet needs to be "sold" within the company. Publicize new features or changes in content. Weekly e-mails can be used to highlight noteworthy additions and updates.

5. **Senior management must commit.** Just like anything else in an organization, if the top executive is neither interested nor supportive, the idea will fail. Therefore, the perceived value of an organization's intranet will increase dramatically if management actively supports and uses it.

Finally, just like any other important internal communications vehicle, the intranet must be managed, maintained and updated by a communications professional who has sole responsibility for keeping the intranet current and vital as a trusted source of corporate communication.[19]

Print Publications

While the advent of online internal communications has been hard on print publications, print as a useful internal communications medium is making a modest comeback. Clearly, print is more expensive than online, but in cases where employees don't have online access—hospitals, for example—print still plays a vital role in reaching and motivating the staff.

Print defenders argue that print still must play a role, particularly in helping create a "climate" that bears the stamp of management **(Figure 11-5)**. For example, after BP suffered the disastrous spill in the Gulf of Mexico in 2010, the company used its internal publication, "Planet BP," to update employees on the efforts to clean up the gulf and help damaged communities.[20]

Writing and editing employee publications are traditional entry-level public relations responsibilities. In many firms, the mandate is to integrate print and online publications, with each vehicle realizing a different communication objective **(Figure 11-6)**.

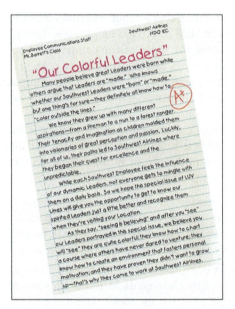

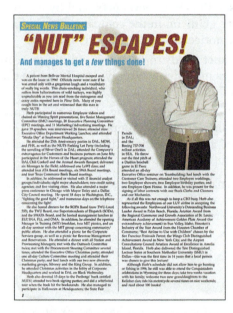

FIGURE 11-5
Prince of print.
Southwest Airlines is a one-of-a-kind company, thanks principally to its founder and former CEO Herb Kelleher. For five decades, Kelleher helped build a climate of creativity, productivity, and fun at Southwest by sponsoring some of the most far-out internal print publications ever seen on this planet (and perhaps any other!).
Reprinted courtesy of Southwest Airlines

One organization devoted originally to internal communications, the International Association of Business Communicators (IABC), founded in 1970, has come to rival the older PRSA. With more than 12,000 members throughout the United States and in 80 countries, the IABC helps set journalistic standards for internal communicators of both print and online publications.

Bulletin Boards

Bulletin boards—not necessarily *electronic* ones but the decidedly low-tech kind—may be among the most ancient of employee communications vehicles, but they have made a comeback in recent years.

FIGURE 11-6
Edgy photo.
Publicity photos for internal and external uses don't have to be mundane. So when the CN Tower in Toronto, declared one of the modern Seven Wonders of the World by the American Society of Civil Engineers, created a publicity photo, it captured the world's highest full circle hands-free walk, 168 stories above the ground.
Photo: Courtesy CN Tower

For years, bulletin boards were considered second-string information channels, generally relegated to the display of federally required information and policy data for such activities as fire drills and emergency procedures. Most employees rarely consulted them. But the bulletin board has experienced a renaissance and is now being used to improve productivity, cut waste, and reduce accidents on the job. Best of all, employees are taking notice.

How come?

For one thing, yesterday's bulletin board has become today's news center. It has been repackaged into a more lively visual and graphically arresting medium. Using enlarged news pictures and texts, motivational messages, and other company announcements—all illustrated with flair—the bulletin board has become an important source of employee communications.

Town Hall Meetings/Suggestion Boxes

Two other traditional staples of employee communication are the suggestion box and the town hall meeting.

In the old days, suggestion boxes were mounted on each floor, and employees, often anonymously, deposited their thoughts on how to improve the company and its processes and products. Often rewards were awarded for the most productive or profitable suggestions.

Today, the only necessity in implementing a successful suggestion box program is to ensure that there is "feedback"—that is, that management takes action to deal with valid suggestions and then communicates what it did to respond.

Town hall meetings are large gatherings of employees with top management, where no subject is off limits and management–staff dialogue is the goal. Town hall meetings can be invaluable in exposing top management to employees and answering what's on the minds of the staff.

Town hall meetings must encourage unfettered two-way communication. While it would be nice if employee groups were spontaneous and confident in asking questions, often this is not the case. That's why town hall organizers should "prime the pump," to encourage staffers to get things rolling with relevant questions.[21] Most important, when managers tell town hall meeting goers they will "look into" something or "get action" on something, they need to do it. If not, they impair their own credibility.

Internal Video

As noted, video is an increasingly important internal communications medium to cut through the communications and reach people in a way that moves them.

As important as YouTube and broadcast and cable television are as communication media in society today, video has had an up-and-down history as an internal communications medium. On the plus side, internal television, including streaming video, can be demonstrably effective. A 10-minute Web video of an executive announcing a new corporate policy imparts hundreds of times more information than a podcast of that same message, which in turn contains hundreds of times more information than a printed text of the same message.

On the downside, internal video is a medium that must be approached with caution. Unless video is of broadcast quality, few will tolerate it—especially an audience of employees weaned on television. So there are always risks in producing an internal video.

The keys to any internal video production are first to examine internal needs; next to plan thoughtfully before using the medium; and finally to keep it short and keep it exciting. How? One proven technique is to feature real people telling meaningful stories about corporate change. In this way, video creates the opportunity to renew a sense of shared experience and community that other internal vehicles may not provide.[22] One caveat: Broadcast quality is a tough standard to meet. If an organization can't afford high-quality video, it shouldn't get involved.

Face-to-Face Communications

What is hands-down, the most compelling and valuable internal communications vehicle?

Face-to-face communications.

Supervisors, in fact, are the preferred source for the vast majority of employees, making them the top choice by far. The reason is obvious. You report to your supervisor, who awards your raise, promotes you, and is your primary source of corporate information.

Some departments formalize the meeting process by mixing management and staff in a variety of formats, from gripe sessions to marketing or planning meetings. Many organizations embrace the concept of skip-level meetings in which top-level managers meet periodically with employees at levels several notches below them in the organizational hierarchy. As with any other form of communication, the value of meetings lies in their substance, their regularity, and the candor managers bring to face-to-face sessions.[23]

4 Internal Social Media

The popularity of social media among employees has caused problems for employers. About half of U.S. employers block their employees from using social media sites at work.

Typical was the experience of Procter & Gamble, which blocked 129,000 employees from accessing video-streaming site Netflix and music site Pandora. Why? Employees were watching so many movies and downloading so many songs, it was "hobbling the company's digital backbone to the point of slowing down Internet service."[24]

An increasing number of companies have social media policies. The best are based in common sense.

- Best Buy's policy is underpinned by an approach that dictates: "Be smart. Be respectful. Be human." Because Best Buy's 170,000 employees are mostly young people, the company allows employees to use social media, including sponsoring a "Watercooler" online forum that allows employees to voice concerns, uncensored by management. Employees also participate in great numbers in the company's "Twelpforce" Twitter account, which is also open to customers.[25]

- FedEx "moderates," that is, reviews, all comments posted to its internal blog. Blog comments are screened for relevance to the topic and compliance with the company's "Rules of Engagement." E-mail addresses are mandatory for posted comments.

- Wells Fargo, too, moderates all comments on its internal community blogs, ensuring that submissions subscribe to guidelines relative to such things as personal attacks, offensive language, confidential information, or spam designed to sell products.

- Walmart reminds any of its 2.2 million associates around the world that if they want to use any of the company's Twitter sites—among them, "walmartmeeting," "samsclubrobert," and "walmartgames"—they must identify themselves on a "landing page" where identities are captured.

Just like any other communications vehicle, for social media to be effective within an organization environment, it (1) must have a business purpose, (2) be entertaining as well as informative, and (3) be composed of riveting content.

The Grapevine

In far too many organizations, it's neither print nor social media that dominates communication but rather the company grapevine. The rumor mill can be treacherous. As one employee publication described the grapevine:

> Once they pick up steam, rumors can be devastating. Because employees tend to distort future events to conform to a rumor, an organization must work to correct rumors as soon as possible.

Identifying the source of a rumor is often difficult, if not impossible, and it's usually not worth the time. However, dispelling the rumor quickly and frankly is another story. Often a bad-news rumor—about layoffs, closings, and so on—can be dealt with most effectively through forthright communication. Generally, an organization makes a difficult decision after a thorough review of many alternatives. The final decision is often a compromise, reflecting the needs of the firm and its various publics, including, importantly, the workforce.

In presenting a final decision to employees, management often overlooks the value of explaining how it reached its decision.

A company grapevine can be as much a communications vehicle as internal publications or employee meetings. It may even be more valuable because it is believed, and everyone seems to tap into it.

Last Word

The best defense against damaging social media discussion and grapevine rumors is a strong and candid internal communication system. Employee communication, for years the most neglected communications opportunity in corporate America, is today much more appreciated for its strategic importance. Organizations that build massive marketing plans to sell products have begun today to apply that same knowledge and energy to communicating with their own employees.

A continuing employee relations challenge for public relations communicators is to work hand in hand with human resources officials. In the 1950s, personnel departments began to change their name to "human resources" to more accurately reflect the personal focus of their responsibilities. Over the past half century, human resources functions have concentrated on such areas as organization, staffing, benefits, and recruitment rather than communications.

The responsibility for communicating to employees has largely fallen on the public relations function, which must coordinate its initiatives with human resources priorities to create a culture of professionalism, accountability, and candor.

In the 21st century, organizations have no choice but to build rapport with and morale among employees. The shattering of morale and distrust of top management prevalent in the early years of the century will take time to repair. Building back internal credibility is a long-term process that depends on several factors—among them, listening to employees, developing information exchanges to educate employees about changing technologies, empowering them with new skills and knowledge through strategic business information they require, and adapting to the new culture of job "mobility" that is replacing job "stability."

Most of all in this new century, effective employee communications requires openness and honesty on the part of senior management. Public relations professionals must seize this initiative to foster the open climate that employees want and the two-way communications that organizations need.

Discussion Starters

1. What societal factors have caused internal communications to become more important today than in the past?
2. What is the general mood of the employee public today?
3. What are the key elements to effective employee relations?
4. What are some important employee communications strategies today?
5. What are the key questions of an employee communications audit?
6. What is the status of internal print communications?
7. What are the key considerations in communicating through an intranet?
8. How should an organization respond to and use social media with employees?
9. What are the primary considerations in adopting internal social media?
10. What is the best way to combat the grapevine?

Pick of the Literature

Strategic Internal Communication: How to Build Employee Engagement and Performance

David Cowan, Philadelphia, PA: Kogan Page Ltd., 2014

This book provides a fresh, questioning analysis of all the accepted assumptions about and approaches to internal communications that have served through the years.

The author approaches the task of communicating with the staff from the viewpoint of both communications and human resources and offers a hybrid approach to communications, linking internal communications to employee engagement and what he calls "cultural integration."

As his contribution to the field, the author offers a "dialogue box" to examine the "dialogue" an organization must adopt to better communicate with its internal publics. He spends much time detailing the "zones" that comprise the dialogue box, which are intelligence, emotion, interpretation, narrative, and dialogue. Such a unique approach is worth a hard look.

Case Study   Sony Shoots the Messenger

In the old days of employee relations—before there was an Internet or a computer or a typewriter or even an America—there were Greek and Roman rulers who never like to receive bad news. Whenever they did, they lashed out at the (blameless) poor souls who delivered the unfriendly tidings. In some cases—if the messenger delivered news of a lost battle or fallen city—the envoy would be dealt with in the harshest manner; merely for delivering bad news.

Today, of course, the bearers of bad news are often public relations professionals, whose essential mandate, as we have learned, is to tell management the truth. Modern managers, by and large, appreciate this candor from their public relations associates.

But occasionally, as in the case of Sony Pictures Entertainment in the winter of 2014, a disgruntled manager harkens back to 46 A.D. and shoots the poor public relations messenger.

Boy King Strikes Back

Sony's problems began in November 2014, after the company released the trailer for an infantile satirical comedy about North Korea, *The Interview*, starring Seth Rogen and James Franco **(Figure 11-7)**. Among other bits of hilarity, the movie included the killing of North Korea's boy ruler Kim Jong-un.

From all reports, North Korea's supreme leader evidently didn't see the humor in the Sony movie. And shortly thereafter, cybercriminals hacked into Sony's computer system and leaked a treasure trove of 32,000 internal e-mails, revealing all sorts of confidential and embarrassing correspondence. The anonymous criminals promised to stop leaking documents if Sony canceled release of the offensive, anti-Kim Jong-un movie.

Within weeks, the U.S. government concluded that North Korea was behind the Sony cyber attack, which it labeled, "a

serious national security matter." For its part, Sony got cold feet and canceled *The Interview's* theatrical release, compelling Rogen and fellow Hollywood actors to condemn Sony for its cowardice.

Eventually, after the release of a tidal wave of damaging documents, Sony changed its mind and initiated a low-scale release of the movie, which landed with a thud and was quickly resigned to the Hollywood scrap heap; at an estimated cost to Sony of $75 million.

The Damage Is Done

In the face of a steady flow of leaked revelations—including top employees' salaries, nasty Hollywood e-mails, and illicit movie downloads—Sony hired hardball attorney David Boies to warn publishers that they would be held responsible if they dared release any of the purloined material.

Good luck.

Boies' entreaties were laughed at, as the nation's gossip network, fueled by Wikileaks, Gawker, TMZ.com, and a host of other willing enablers, proceeded to fill the airwaves with a month's worth of stinging and embarrassing stories, including:

- Facebook founder Marc Zuckerberg wrote desperately to Sony executives to try to get them to stop the movie, *"The Social Network,"* which he found "hurtful."

- Sony Co-Chairman Amy Pascal ran up a tab of $66,500 for car services, air travel, meals, etc. on a two-day movie premiere in Washington, D.C.

- In an e-mail to Pascal, another Sony executive called comedian Kevin Hart *"a whore,"* for demanding money to write a tweet promoting his new Sony movie, for which he received a $3 million paycheck.

FIGURE 11-7
The provocateurs.
James Franco and
Seth Rogen, stars of
The Interview.
Photo: SPNNewscom

■ Before a fund-raising dinner for Barack Obama, Pascal e-mailed producer Scott Rudin, with both playfully pondering if she should ask the President how he liked the movies *Django Unchained*, *12 Years a Slave,* and other black-themed films.

Co-Chairman Pascal was criticized for the Hart and Obama e-mails, interpreted by many as "racist," and she was also taken to task for a set of e-mails, surrounding her decision to fire Sony's director of communications.

"Off With His Head, Darling"

Among the leaked e-mails were several between the Sony co-chair and her husband, former New York Times reporter Bernard Weinraub **(Figure 11-8)**.

Subject of this marital correspondence was the publication by the *Hollywood Reporter* newspaper of a roundtable interview with the heads of the major film studios. For some reason, the only studio chief who wasn't invited was Pascal.

That didn't sit well with concerned hubby Weinraub, who tersely e-mailed his wife, *"I would fire your P.R. guy immediately...or at least tell him you're not going to deal with him anymore."*

Pascal forwarded her spouse's note to Sony's head of human resources, George Rose. *"He's right,"* the independent-minded human resource chief wrote back. Six days later, Sony Pictures' head of corporate communications, Charles Sipkins, was out of a job. He made a base salary of $600,000-a-year, according to leaked documents.

According to other leaked e-mails from Sipkins to Pascal, *Hollywood Reporter* apologized to Sony for not inviting its chief, explaining that the roundtable lineup shifted after some people initially passed and then reconsidered.

The explanation wasn't enough to save the public relations man's job.

FIGURE 11-8 **The e-mail executioners.**
Amy Pascal and husband, former *New York Times* reporter Bernard Weinraub.
Photo: FRED PROUSER/REUTERS/Newscom

After the "shoot the messenger" e-mails were made public, co-chair Pascal scrambled to explain that the missed roundtable wasn't the cause of the dismissal of her communications chief. *"That's ridiculous,"* Pascal said. *"That has nothing to do with it. Charlie's very talented at what he did."*

But in public relations, as in life, "what goes around comes around." And shortly after she lowered the boom on her public relations director, Amy Pascal, herself, was fired as Sony's co-chairman, basically for what she revealed in her e-mails.

Another messenger had bitten the dust.*

Questions

1. How would you assess Sony's handling of the hacking scandal?

2. Had you been Amy Pascal's public relations advisor, how would you have suggested she handle the fallout from the e-mails, adjudged as "racist?"

3. Had Pascal asked you to counsel her on what to do in light of her husband's e-mail about the roundtable, what would you have suggested?

*For further information, see Jake Coyle, "Amy Pascal, Ex Sony Chief, Acknowledges She Was Fired," *Associated Press* (February 12, 2015); Sean Fitz-Gerald, "Everything That's Happened in the Sony Leak Scandal," *Vulture* (December 22, 2014); Chris Palmeri and Lucas Shaw, "Fire Your PR Guy' E-Mail Sends Sony Exec Out the Door," *Bloomberg Business Week* (December 12, 2014); and Aly Weisman, "Leaked: Sony Exec Calls Out Kevin Hart for Requesting Money to Promote His Movies on Social Media," *Business Insider* (December 11, 2014).

From the Top

An Interview with Jay Rayburn

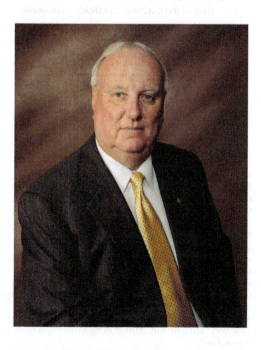

Jay Rayburn, APR, CPRC, Ph.D., Fellow PRSA is Division Director for Public Relations and Advertising in the School of Communication at Florida State University and one of the nation's most eminent professors of public relations. He is a former president of the Florida Public Relations Association and the founding chairman of FPRA's Counselors' Network. He is also a past chair of the Universal Accreditation Board. For more than a decade he was on the professional development faculty of the PRSA, where he conducted seminars in building and evaluating employee communication programs.

What's the general state of employee relations today?

Overall, the relationship between organizations and their employees seems to be relatively good, and for the most part, improving. Of course there are still the constant differences between management and unions. Just pick up *The Wall Street Journal* and you'll find an example of the stress between these two groups. But even here, management and labor seem to be coming to terms quicker and in a more pleasant circumstance.

One thing we are seeing more and more are lists of "best places to work" being published by business publications, chambers of commerce and other business-related entities. Just reading what employees say about these organizations indicates there are a lot of employees who are very happy with their work situations.

What do employees want to know from management?

As they always have, employees want to know what's happening in their business. They want to know the negatives as well as the positives, and how each of these affects them and their future. They want to know what management expects of them, and how they can improve and contribute to the overall wellbeing of the organization.

For the most part, management has been pretty good at telling employees the "what," but especially in the current business climate, employees also want to know the "why." A good explanation of the why behind the decision goes a long way, especially when the news is bad.

How has social media affected employee communications?

The jury is still out on social media as a tool of employee communication although more and more organizations are starting to incorporate social media as part of the overall employee communication program. Obviously, social media are more important to the individuals currently entering the workforce than they are for the baby boomers or even generation X. For the millennials, texting is their primary means of communications. Organizations with the more effective communication programs are the ones who have figured out how to incorporate and control social media in the overall employee communication plan.

What can management do to improve the climate of trust within an organization?

The best way to improve trust within an organization is to use the same model effective organizations use during a crisis: tell the truth, tell it all, and tell it quickly (or at least as quickly as you can). Equally important, management must follow up on what it says it will do. Unkept promises are a guaranteed way to ensure employees will never again believe anything you say. If management learns about a problem from a communication audit, for example, and can fix the problem immediately, tell the employees what will be done and do it. If the problem can't be fixed immediately, tell them what can be done and by when, and work toward fixing the issue. If the problem can't be fixed, tell the employees but find something that can be done to at least ameliorate the situation. And don't forget the "why" behind the "what."

What communications advice would you give any CEO?

Same advice as above: tell the truth, tell it all, and tell it quickly. And don't be afraid to say "I don't know." Be visible. Employees like to put a face with a name. Find ways to interact sincerely with employees. Keep an open door—great ideas often come from unusual places. Hewlett-Packard proved almost half a century ago that management by wandering around leads to productive employees and a successful organization.

What can students do to prepare for public relations employment?

- First, read. Read everything you can find about the practice of public relations—tactics, strategy, research, case studies, EVERYTHING.

- Second, write. If you can't write, you can't make it in this business. Good public relations writers write something almost every day. And don't be afraid to ask for help. Even the best editor needs a good editor.

- Third, do an internship, or two, or three. Once you have learned the skills in courses or workshops, apply them, even if you are just volunteering.

- Fourth, know your business. It is one thing to be a well-prepared practitioner, but the really successful practitioner has a thorough understanding of the business (and that includes the not-for-profits, government, and any other organization that uses the public relations function). When you get that first job, become a student of the business as quickly as possible.

- And fifth, find out what keeps your boss awake at night, and fix it. And don't bring management problems, bring solutions.

Public Relations Bookshelf

Barton, Paul. *Maximizing Internal Communication*. Lake Placid, NY: Aviva Publishing, 2014. The book begins with the perspective that employees are the organization's most important audience and provides sound methods to inspire them.

Duncan, Wendy. *Lead Employees to Success*. Parker, CO: Books to Believe In, 2010. An explanation of what constitutes an internal "leader."

Falcone, Paul. *101 Tough Conversations to Have with Employees*. New York: Amacom, 2009. The rules of engagement in dealing with employees.

Fitzpatrick, Liam and Klavs Valskov. *Internal Communications: A Manual for Practitioners*. Philadelphia, PA: Kogan Page Ltd., 2014. The premise of this manual is that an organization's ultimate success must start on the inside with an informed and enthusiastic cadre of employees. Amen, Brother.

Guffey, Mary E. and Dana Loewy. *Essentials of Business Communications*. 9th ed. Mason, OH: South-Western, 2013. Comprehensive text on business communication.

Leat, Mike. *Exploring Employee Relations*. 2nd ed. Burlington, MA: Butterworth-Heinemann, 2007. Used in colleges, this text is an excellent introduction to the art of dealing with employees.

LeMenager, Jack. *Inside the Organization: Perspectives on Employee Communications*. Winchester, MA: Fells Publishing, 2011. The book's overriding theme: Treat employees as "human beings," especially in terms of trusting them and letting them know what's going on around the organization at which they spend most of their daily lives.

Quirke, Bill. *Making the Connections*. 2nd ed. Hampshire, England: Gower Publishing Limited, 2008. Outstanding analysis of how businesses can use internal communications to enhance everything from productivity to differentiation.

Ragan PR Daily. Chicago: Ragan Communications. Daily online report and weekly newsletter, written in an irreverent tone, that captures the best and worst in internal communications.

Ruck, Kevin (Ed.). *Exploring Internal Communication*. 3rd ed. Burlington, VT: Grover Publishing, 2015. Several internal communications experts offer contributions, ranging from language and tone to using social media.

Runion, Meryl. *Perfect Phrases for Managers and Supervisors*. 2nd ed. New York: McGraw-Hill, 2010. Among them: "synergize, dynamize, personalize."

Vengel, Alan. *20 Minutes to a Top Performer*. New York: McGraw-Hill, 2010. A primer on how to motivate, develop, and engage employees.

Xenitelis, Marcia. *Repositioning Employee Communications*. Camberwell, Australia: Communication at Work, 2009. The internal view from Down Under.

Endnotes

1. David Streitfeld, "Hello, I Must Be Going," *The New York Times* (March 2, 2013).
2. Alyssa Davis and Lawrence Mishel, "CEO Pay Continues to Rise as Typical Workers Are Paid Less," *Economic Policy Institute* (June 12, 2014).
3. Robert C. Lapsley, "Another View: California Is Losing Middle Class Jobs," *The Sacramento Bee* (April 4, 2015).
4. "Oil Fallout: U.S. Companies Kill over 51,000 Jobs," *CNN Money* (April 8, 2015).
5. Portia Crowe, "The Big Banks on Wall Street Have Fired 80,000 People in the Past 5 Years," *Business Insider* (April 20, 2015).
6. Nick Wingfield, "Microsoft to Cut Up to 7800 Jobs, Mostly in Its Phone Units," *The New York Times* (July 8, 2015).
7. "Edelman Change and Employee Engagement," *Edelman Company* (May 22, 2012): 2.
8. Ibid.
9. "Trust in Institutions Drops to Level of Great Recession," *2015 Edelman Trust Barometer* (January 19, 2015).
10. "Edelman Change and Employee Engagement," op. cit.
11. Milton Moskowitz and Robert Levering, "Beyond Perks: Lessons from Tracking the '100 Best,'" *Fortune* (January 20, 2011).
12. Fraser P. Seitel, "Rebuilding Employee Trust Through S-H-O-C," *odwyerpr.com* (July 11, 2005).
13. Luke Dodd, "Three Channel Audit Killers," *Melcrum SCM* (May/June, 2013).
14. Kevin J. Allen, "Overhaul Your Intranet from A to Z," *ragan.com* (October 24, 2007).
15. Steve Crescenzo, "How to Make Social Media Successful at Your Company," *ragan.com* (February 28, 2008).
16. Shel Holtz, "The 11 Viral Internal Communications Trends You'd Be Crazy to Ignore," *Holtz Communication+Technology* (October 30, 2013), http://holtz.com/blog/visual-communication/the-11-vital-internal-communications-trends-youd-be-crazy-to-ignore/4223/.
17. Steven Rosenbaum, "IBM: Communication and Curation Go Hand in Hand," *Forbes.com* (April 10, 2012).
18. Jamie Pietrus, "Employee Networking: The Next Generation," *ragan.com* (October 2, 2008).
19. Helen Robinson, "How to Build a Successful Intranet for Your Company," *Northern Lights Public Relations & Marketing PR Blog* (March 12, 2013), http://www.northernlightspr.com/how-to-build-a-successful-intranet-for-your-company/.
20. Michael Sebastian, "BP Internal Pub Extols the Virtues of the Oil Disaster," *Ragan PR Daily* (June 23, 2010).
21. Ryan Williams, "4 Ways to Engage Employees in Your Town Hall," *Ragan PR Daily* (April 16, 2013).
22. Ron Shewchuk, "For Your Approval," *Ron Shewchuk Blog* (February 15, 2015), http://ronshewchuk.blogs.com/.
23. Robert J. Holland, "Seven Ways to Use Face-to-Face Communication," *ragan.com* (August 7, 2008).
24. Matt Wilson, "P&G Blocks Employee Access to Pandora, Netflix," *Ragan PR Daily* (April 6, 2012).
25. Matt Wilson, "Best Buy Engages Young Staff Through Online Dialogue," *Ragan PR Daily* (December 15, 2011).

Chapter **12**

Government Relations

Chapter Objectives

1. To discuss the prevalence of government at all levels of daily life and the impact that public relations plays in communicating the platforms and programs of legislators.

2. To discuss the use of public relations by the president and in government departments, agencies, and at the state and local levels.

3. To review the unique role of the Press Secretary to the President of the United States; perhaps the top public relations job in the world.

4. To examine the role, responsibilities, and tactics of those who "lobby" the government to influence legislation.

FIGURE 12-1 **Public relations brain trust.**
President Barack Obama depended on a cadre of public relations experts to guide his communications strategy, including from left, Press Secretary Josh Earnest; Chief of Staff Denis McDonough; Senior Advisor Dan Pfeiffer; Deputy National Security Advisor for Strategic Communications Ben Rhodes; Counselor to the President John Podesta; and Director of Communications Jennifer Palmieri.
Photo: Official White House Photo by Pete Souza

In America, as we will learn shortly, federal law prohibits the President or political appointees to use publicity, i.e. public relations, to promote their policies. Nonetheless, there is no more powerful force in U.S. government than the practice of public relations—of persuading through effective communication.

The greatest example of government public relations was the 44th President of the United States, Barack Obama.

In his two terms as President, Barack Obama embraced the public relations power of social media as no chief executive before him. Relying heavily on a cadre of strategic communications advisors, Obama rewrote the rules for public engagement through public relations tactics

(Figure 12-1). Among other public relations innovations, Obama:

■ Announced his original choice for Vice President in 2008 by text messaging his supporters at 3 A.M. to declare, *"Barack has chose Senator Joe Biden to be our VP nominee."*

■ Recruited a team of social media experts to social mediatise his 2015 State of the Union Address, producing a series of videos, digital op-eds, Facebook and Twitter posts, and six-second animated GIFS.[1]

■ Began tweeting from his own POTUS account in 2015, amassing one million followers in five hours, which shattered a Guinness World Record.[2]

- Appeared on podcasts, Reddit chats and even on *"Between Two Ferns"* on the Web site Funny or Die, for a sit down with comedian Zach Galifianakis.[3]

- Appointed the White House's first Chief Digital Officer, a Silicon Valley veteran of Google and Twitter, to spread the Obama message across digital platforms in 2015.[4]

Obama's unprecedented efforts to spread his Administration's messages across a growing number of digital platforms caused traditional media representatives to cry, "foul." One Associated Press reporter phrased the suspicions about Obama's online communications predilection in no uncertain terms:

It is limiting press access in ways that past administrations wouldn't have dared, and the president is answering to the public in more controlled settings than his predecessors. It's raising new questions about what's lost when the White House tries to make an end run around the media, functioning, in effect, as its own news agency.[5]

Despite the groans of the representatives of the traditional print and broadcast media, President Obama's tilt toward communicating via social media and online platforms was understandable.

By 2012, 98% of Congress was using at least one social media platform, with 72% using the big three platforms of Twitter, YouTube, and Facebook. For the 20116 campaign, all presidential candidates had digital media directors and were active social media users. One, the irrepressibly bombastic Donald Trump, announced his announcement as a Republican nominee via Periscope, which helped him trend worldwide on Twitter and other platforms during his speech.[6]

The practice of public relations, whether social media–based or not, is a huge factor in politics and government around the world. By 2016, the faith in governments across the globe—what with financial meltdowns, bank bailouts, Greek challenges to the fate of the European Union, censorship and economic downturns in China, nuclear disasters in Japan, and terrorist threats across the Middle East—hovered at low levels. According to the Edelman Trust Barometer, government was essentially distrusted in 19 of the 27 markets surveyed.[7]

In light of the universal mistrust of government agencies and officials, the importance of honest and open communication can't be understated.

☐1 Don't Call It "Public Relations"

It is ironic that the practice of "public relations"—so defined—has been barred from the federal government since 1913. Congress at the time was worried that those who inhabited the corridors of power might be tempted to use the privileges granted and the attention paid to them by the American people for the advancement of their own agendas or, heaven forbid, the promotion of themselves.

So in 1913, Congress enacted the Gillette Amendment, which almost barred the practice of public relations in government. The amendment stemmed from efforts by President Theodore Roosevelt to win public support for his programs through the use of a network of publicity experts. The law was a specific response to a Civil Service Commission help wanted advertisement for a "publicity man" for the Bureau of Public Roads. Congress, worried about the potential of this unlimited presidential persuasive power, passed an amendment stating: "Appropriated funds may not be used to pay a publicity expert unless specifically appropriated for that purpose."

Several years later, still leery of the president's power to influence legislation through communication, Congress passed the gag law, which prohibited "using any part of an appropriation for services, messages, or publications designed to influence any member of Congress in his attitude toward legislation or appropriations." Even today, no government worker may be employed in the "practice of public relations." Public affairs, yes. But public relations, no. As a result, the government is flooded with "public affairs experts," "information officers," "press secretaries," and "communications specialists."

One wonders, in light of this background, how the legislators of that day would think of their 21st century publicity-seeking successors.

Every day, the Washington, D.C., seat of the federal government is a public relations free-for-all, with 435 congressmen and congresswomen, 100 senators, 15 cabinet secretaries, and thousands of federal employees supporting them, all jockeying to make the morning newspapers and evening talk shows. Where business leaders frequently are *unavailable to the press*," politicians are more often *unavoidable to the press*." Typical of the latter ilk, Democrat Sen. Charles Schumer of New York is legendary for holding press conferences every Sunday—some (most?) of dubious value—simply because Sunday is a notoriously slow news day. Schumer's push for personal publicity knew no bounds. On the state and local levels, where the situation is just slightly less blatant, politicians similarly jockey for attention in the media.

Legislators in the 21st century, it seems, have come a far distance from the days of President Dwight D. Eisenhower, a former general, who once famously remarked, "If the Army is good, the story will be good, and the public relations will be good. If the Army is bad, the story will be bad, and the public relations will be bad."[8]

Today, by contrast—good, bad, or indifferent; story or no story—politicians crave publicity; apparently, according to most Americans, in lieu of seeking meaningful policy change. Indeed, by the start of 2015, with the American government hopelessly mired in dysfunction, upwards of 80% of Americans "disapproved" of Congress and an abysmal 16% "approved."[9]

In many ways, the importance of constant government communications became more profound after the terrorist attacks on America on September 11, 2001.

The war on terrorism depended on candid, frank, and informative communications with the American people and the world. Said President Bush's first press secretary, Ari Fleischer, "The American people are appreciative of the forthrightness of the government. I think the government has an obligation to be forthright" **(Figure 12-2).**[10]

"Why do they hate us?" the president asked rhetorically about the Muslim attackers and their sympathizers in his historic speech before Congress the week after the terrorist attacks.[11] To combat such hate and to reassure the American people about the goodness of the war effort, the government's public relations initiatives took center stage, particularly in the initial stages of the conflict. Ironically, it was Bush—not a particularly adept communicator—who put in place lasting public relations measures. Among those initiatives:

■ The White House created a permanent Office of Global Communications to coordinate the administration's foreign policy message and supervise America's image abroad.

FIGURE 12-2
Hail to the public relations chief.
As a wartime president, George W. Bush, here with first-term Press Secretary Ari Fleischer, met the media challenge immediately after 9/11 with strength and confidence.
Photo: Courtesy of the White House Photo Office

■ The position of Undersecretary for Public Diplomacy and Public Affairs was created in the State Department to work to convince the Muslim world, in particular, of the true values and ethics of America. President Obama's Undersecretary for Public Diplomacy and Public Affairs Richard Stengel, former editor of *Time,* dealt with a world more integrated by social media, where countries spend, *"billions of dollars to get their information out, to get their message out, they can narrow the information space."*[12]

It is indisputable that the practice of public relations is broadly represented throughout government—not only at the presidential level but in each government branch, in all government agencies, on the state and local levels, and also in lobbying the government to maintain or change legislation. All of these functions are part of the multiple levels of public relations communication in and around government.

2 Government Public Relations

The growth of public relations work both with and in the government has exploded in recent years. Although it is difficult to say exactly how many public relations professionals are employed at the federal level, it's safe to assume that thousands of public relations–related jobs exist in the federal government and countless others in government at the state and local levels. Thus, the field of government relations is a fertile one for public relations graduates.

Over the past 50 years, more than 20 new federal regulatory agencies have sprung up—including the Office of Homeland Security, the Environmental Protection Agency, the Consumer Product Safety Commission, the Department of Energy, the Department of Education, and the Drug Enforcement Administration. Moreover, according to the Government Accounting Office (GAO), more than 120 government agencies and programs now regulate business. As society is shaken by new problems, the government response is to create a new bureaucracy. Such was the case when the near-total collapse of the financial system in 2007–2008 gave rise to the Dodd-Frank Bill and another new agency, the Consumer Financial Protection Bureau.

The nation's defense establishment offers some 27,000 jobs for recruiting, advertising, and public relations—although, again, none are labeled "public relations" in Department of Defense (DOD) military and civilian positions. Indeed, with military service now purely voluntary and an increasingly difficult war on terrorism nearly a decade old, the nation's defense machine must rely on its public information, education, and recruiting efforts to maintain a sufficient military force. One 2009 audit found that the DOD budget to win "hearts and minds" increased by 63% in one year alone to $4.7 billion.[13]

Government Practitioners

Most practitioners in government communicate the activities of the various agencies, commissions, and bureaus to the public. As consumer activist and perpetual presidential candidate Ralph Nader once said, "In this nation, where the ultimate power is said to rest with the people, it is clear that a free and prompt flow of information from government to the people is essential."

It wasn't always as essential to form informational links between government officials and the public. In 1888, when there were 39 states in the Union and 330 members in the House of Representatives, the entire official Washington press corps consisted of 127 reporters. Today, as cutbacks have occurred in the ranks of mainstream media reporters, there has been a surge in niche media representatives, among the more than 2000 full-time journalists covering the capital. In addition the contingent of foreign reporters covering Washington has grown to nearly 10 times the size it was a generation ago, with 1500 foreign journalists based in the nation's capital.[14]

The closest thing to an audit of government public relations functions came in 1986 when Senator William Proxmire, a notorious gadfly, asked the GAO to tell him "how much federal executive agencies spend on public relations."

At the time, the GAO reported that the 13 cabinet departments and 18 independent agencies spent about $337 million for public affairs activities during fiscal 1985, with almost 5600 full-time employees assigned to public affairs duties. In addition, about $100 million was spent for congressional affairs activities, with almost 2000 full-time employees assigned.

Now fast-forward to 2005, where a similar GAO report revealed that the Bush administration paid $1.6 billion—that's $1.6 *billion*—on advertising and public relations contracts over a two-and-a-half-year period, with $88 million spent in 2004 alone. The DOD spent $1.1 billion of that for recruitment campaigns and public relations efforts. A total of 54 public relations firms were contracted as part of this effort.[15]

Now, fast fast forward to 2012, where an independent study found that the U.S. government spent more than $16 billion on advertising, marketing, and public relations contractors. That expense was beyond the millions of dollars a year that agencies already spend on their full-time press, communications and media operations, and it has gone to pay for projects as varied as sports sponsorships, recruitment efforts for the military services, veterans benefits, welfare aid, and programs that help multibillion-dollar multinational corporations pitch their products to overseas customers.[16]

The bottom line: There may well be no "public relations" allowed in government, but it sure costs plenty!

Two Prominent Departments

Even before the war on terrorism, the most potent public relations voices in the federal government, exclusive of the president, were, first, the U.S. Department of State, and second, the U.S. Department of Defense. After the terrorist attacks of September 11, 2001, the communications importance of both increased, but their relative positions were reversed.

The State Department The State Department, like other government agencies, has an extensive public affairs staff, responsible for press briefings; maintaining secretary of state homepage content; operating foreign press centers in Washington, New York, and Los Angeles; as well as managing public diplomacy operations abroad.

In 1999, the State Department inherited and absorbed the United States Information Agency (USIA), from 1953 the most far-reaching of the federal government's public relations arms, devoted to "public diplomacy," whose job was to explain and support American foreign policy and promote U.S. national interests through a wide range of overseas information programs and educational and cultural activities.

The director of the USIA had reported directly to the president and received policy guidance from the secretary of state. Under the 1999 integration plan, an undersecretary for public diplomacy and public affairs within the State Department was chosen to head the operation. The annual appropriation for this public relations activity has exceeded $1 billion since the late 1980s.

In the 21st century, with America's motives for the war on terrorism challenged around the world, the former USIA's mission—"to support the national interest by conveying an understanding abroad of what the United States stands for"—has been modified to include new challenges:

- Build the intellectual and institutional foundations of democracy in societies around the globe.
- Support the war on drugs in producer and consumer countries.
- Develop worldwide information programs to address environmental challenges.
- Bring the truth to any society that fails to exercise free and open communication.

In its nearly half a century, the USIA was a high-level public relations operation and not without controversy. Under the direction of such well-known media personalities as Edward R. Murrow, Carl Rowan, Frank Shakespeare, and Charles Z. Wick, the agency prospered.

One element of this program was the Voice of America (VOA), the nation's official international radio and TV broadcasting platform. VOA broadcasts in some 40 languages around the world, from Albanian to Somali to Urdu. In 2015, VOA was led by former ABC correspondent David Ensor.

The communication initiatives of the successor to USIA to spread the "gospel of America" are far-reaching. Among them are the following:

1. **Radio.** VOA, which first went on the air in 1942, broadcasts more than 1000 hours of programming weekly in its 40 languages, including English, to an international audience of more than 100 million listeners. In 2006, the U.S. Congress appropriated $166 million for VOA. In addition to VOA, the USIA in 1985 began Radio Marti, in honor of José Marti, father of Cuban independence. Radio Marti's purpose was to broadcast 24 hours a day to Cuba in Spanish and "tell the truth to the Cuban people" about ruler Fidel Castro and communism. By March 2015,

the Office of Cuba Broadcasting, which oversaw Radio and TV Marti, reported that 20% of Cubans tuned in "to objective news coverage Cubans cannot receive anywhere else."[17] **By** the summer of 2015, with the thaw in U.S.-Cuba relations, **the** ultimate fate of Radio Marti was very much up in the air.

VOA keeps current with the world's changing dynamics. In 2002, a new Arabic service, called the Middle East Radio Network or Radio Sawa, was instituted, with an initial budget of $22 million. In 2010, VOA added radio broadcasts in Sudan to coincide with growing U.S. interests in Southern Sudan. In 2014, VOA dropped its service in Greece.

2. **Film and television.** VOA annually produces and acquires an extensive number of films and videocassettes for distribution in 125 countries. VOA produces more than 30 hours of television per week in 24 languages, from Albanian to Urdu. TV Marti in Cuba, for example, telecasts four-and-a-half hours daily.

3. **Internet.** VOA uses a distributed network, including more than 14,000 servers in 65 countries, to deliver Internet content. News is also available via e-mail subscription service in English and an increasing number of broadcast languages. Electronic journals were created to communicate with audiences overseas on economic issues, political security and values, democracy and human rights, terrorism, the environment, and transnational information flow.[18]

4. **Education.** The agency is also active overseas in sponsoring educational programs through 111 bi-national centers where English is taught and in 11 language centers. Classes draw about 350,000 students annually.

The Defense Department The importance of the Department of Defense (DOD) communications has been intensified in wartime. The DOD's public affairs network is massive—3727 communicators in the Army, 1250 in the Navy, 1200 in the Air Force, 450 in the Marines, and 200 at headquarters. The DOD public affairs department is headed by an assistant secretary of defense for public affairs, one of six direct reports to the deputy secretary of defense **(Figure 12-3)**.

With the DOD consisting of more than three million active duty forces, reserves, and civilian employees, information is the strategic center of gravity. Communications must be organized, secure, and rapid to fulfill the department's mission.

Although each service has its own public affairs organization and mission, DOD's American Forces Information Service (AFIS) promotes cooperation among the various branches. AFIS is responsible for maintaining the Armed Forces Radio and Television Service, *Stars and Stripes* newspaper, communications training at the Defense Information School, and a variety of other functions.

Public relations efforts of the DOD in the 21st century have run the gamut from drawing universal praise to generating opprobrium. When the United States invaded Iraq in 2003, the department was lauded for "embedding" reporters with the troops in the field in order for Americans to get firsthand information about the battle.

Other Government Agencies Beyond the State and Defense departments, other government departments also have stepped up their public relations efforts. The Department of Health and Human Services has a public affairs staff of 700 people. The Agriculture, State, and Treasury departments each have communications staffs in excess of 400 people, and each spends more than $20 million per year in public relations–related activities. Even the U.S. Central Intelligence Agency has an active public affairs office. As a sign of the times, one element of CIA public affairs is an "Entertainment Industry Liaison" to assist the motion picture industry and other entertainment representatives, so that they portray an accurate picture of America's spying apparatus.

Office of the Secretary of Defense

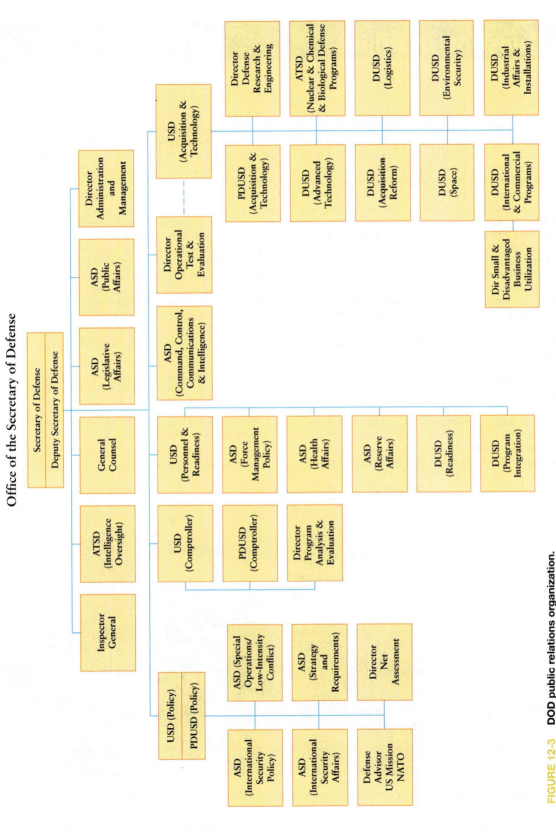

FIGURE 12-3 **DOD public relations organization.**

The Assistant Secretary of Defense for Public Affairs was one of six who reported to the Defense Secretary's chief deputy.

Photo: Courtesy of Department of Defense

A Question of Ethics

Schock-ing the Downton Abbey Congressman

In the early days of 2015, everything was going swimmingly for Rep. Aaron Schock of Illinois.

The 34-year-old Republican had just won reelection with 75% of his district's vote, had been chosen by Speaker of the House John Boehner to lead the Congressional delegation to the funeral of Nelson Mandela, and was reportedly meeting with party leaders to discuss a run for Illinois governor. After being sworn in again in January, the young congressman was riding high.

And then *The Washington Post* paid a visit to his new office in the Rayburn Office Building.

As the *Post* reported, Schock's new digs stood out in the otherwise drab confines of a drab building.

"Bright red walls. A gold-colored wall sconce with black candles. A Federal-style bull's-eye mirror with an eagle perched on top. And this is just the Illinois Republican's outer office" (Figure 12-4).

The *Post* then quoted a friendly receptionist, who offered, "It's actually based off of the red room in 'Downton Abbey,'" comparing the uniquely appointed office to the luxurious set piece at the heart of a popular Public Broadcasting British-period drama. And that was only the beginning. Another woman, who identified herself as Schock's interior decorator, showed the reporter the congressman's private office, revealing another dramatic red room *"with a drippy crystal chandelier, a table propped up by two eagles, a bust of Abraham Lincoln and massive arrangements of pheasant feathers."*

It was then, according to the reporter, that the congressman's communications director came rushing out to try to restore order. Argued the harassed public relations associate, *"You've got a member [of Congress] willing to talk to you about other things. Why sour it by rushing to write some gossipy piece?"*

Alas, that's precisely what the Post did, alluding to the congressman's bizarre office, as well as his six-pack ab photo on the cover of *Men's Health* magazine, his Instagram feed featuring him surfing, hiking across glaciers, tangoing on the streets of Buenos Aires, and smiling next to pop star Ariana Grande.

A month after the *Post* article appeared and placed Rep. Schock and his creative office squarely on the agenda of every Washington tourist and late night comedian, a sadder-but-wiser congressman announced his resignation. His Downton Abbey red dining room office was repainted beige.*

Questions

1. Had you had been Rep. Schock's communications advisor, what would you have counseled relative to his interior decorating plans?

2. How would you have handled the Post reporter once he found out about the office?

3. What is the public relations lesson in this tale for other members of Congress?

FIGURE 12-4 **Media magnet.**
Media visitors flocked to see the red Downton Abbey office of Illinois Rep. Aaron Schock, right up until he announced his resignation from Congress.
Photo: Nancy Stone/TNS/ Newscom

*For further information, see Ben Terris, "He's Got a 'Downton Abbey' –Inspired Office But Rep. Aaron Schock Won't Talk About It," *The Washington Post* (February 2, 2015).

The President

Despite early congressional efforts to limit the persuasive power of the nation's chief executive, the president today wields unprecedented public relations clout. The president travels with his own media entourage, controls the "bully pulpit," and with it, a large part of the nation's agenda. Almost anything the president does or says makes news.

The political blogs, cable and broadcast networks, daily newspapers and national magazines and talk radio follow his—or her—every move. His press secretary provides the White House press corps (a group of national reporters assigned to cover the president) with a constant flow of announcements supplemented by live televised daily press briefings. Unlike many organizational news releases that seldom make it into print, many White House releases achieve national exposure.

Prior to President Obama, Ronald Reagan and Bill Clinton were perhaps the most masterful, modern presidential communicators. Reagan gained experience in the movies and on television, and even his most ardent critics agreed that he possessed a compelling stage presence. As America's president, he was truly the "Great Communicator." Reagan and his communications advisors followed seven principles in helping to "manage the news":

1. Plan ahead.
2. Stay on the offensive.
3. Control the flow of information.
4. Limit reporters' access to the president.
5. Talk about the issues you want to talk about.
6. Speak in one voice.
7. Repeat the same message many times.

George H. W. Bush was not as masterful as his predecessor in communicating with the American public. Indeed, Bush met his communications match in 1992 when Bill Clinton beat him soundly in the presidential race.

The press had a love–hate relationship with President Clinton. On the one hand, Clinton's easygoing, "just folks" demeanor, combined with an unquestioned intelligence and grasp of the issues, was praised by the media. On the other hand, the president's legendary "slickness," accentuated by his false statements and downright lying to the American people during the Monica Lewinsky affair, caused many journalists to treat him warily.

President Clinton's accessibility to the media—except during the saga with the White House intern—and his common sense approach to dealing with media were greatly responsible for his popularity, despite the series of embarrassing scandals afflicting his administration during both terms of his presidency.

George W. Bush, like his father, wasn't particularly comfortable with the press and public speaking. After the terrorist attacks of September 11, 2001, Bush delivered a historic speech before Congress, addressed workers at the World Trade Center site through a bullhorn, and conducted frequent press conferences in Washington and at his ranch in Crawford, Texas. The terrorist challenge of Bush's first term had awakened his communications instincts. In his second term, however, particularly due to his premature announcement of "Mission Accomplished" in Iraq and disastrous handling of Hurricane Katrina in New Orleans, Bush's relationship with the media soured significantly.

In his first months in office in 2009, President Barack Obama proved himself an adept communicator with a natural, easygoing, and believable style. Faced with

FIGURE 12-5

Historic speech.
President Obama's use
of the "bully pulpit,"
including an historic
speech in Charleston,
SC, honoring
those killed by a
crazed young white
supremacist.
Photo: RICHARD ELLIS/
EPA/Newscom

mounting economic crises, Obama immediately became the most telegenic president in U.S. history, with daily televised press conferences and announcements characterizing his early presidential tenure. As the rigors of the presidency wore on and the nation's economy staggered along, Obama drew criticism, for "over-communicating" particularly on television, where some accused it of being, "All Obama All the Time."[19] As Obama's second term wore down, he regained his communications mojo, with several policy breakthroughs and memorable speeches, including an historic one in 2015 at a black church in Charleston, South Carolina, where he led parishioners in the hymn *"Amazing Grace,"* to honor those killed in a mass shooting by a white supremacist **(Figure 12-5).**

③ White House Press Secretary

The press secretary to the President of the United States is the most visible public relations position in the world.

Some have called the job of presidential press secretary the second-most-difficult position in any administration. The press secretary is the chief public relations spokesperson for the administration. Like practitioners in private industry, the press secretary must communicate the policies and practices of the management (the president) to the public. Often it is an impossible job.

In 1974, Jerald ter Horst, President Ford's press secretary, quit after disagreeing with Ford's pardon of former President Richard Nixon. Said ter Horst, "A spokesman should feel in his heart and mind that the chief's decision is the right one so that he can speak with a persuasiveness that stems from conviction."[20] That's one view of the role of the press secretary.

A contrasting view was expressed by ter Horst's replacement in the job, former NBC reporter Ron Nessen, who said, "A press secretary does not always have to agree with the president. His first loyalty is to the public, and he should not knowingly lie or mislead the press."[21] A third view of the proper role of the press secretary was offered by a former public relations professional and Nixon speechwriter who became a *New York Times* political columnist, William Safire:

> *A good press secretary speaks up for the press to the president and speaks out for the president to the press. He makes his home in the pitted no-man's land of an adversary relationship and is primarily an advocate, interpreter, and amplifier. He must be more the president's man than the press's. But he can be his own man as well.*[22]

Over the years, the position of press secretary to the president has taken on increased responsibility and has attained a higher public profile. Jimmy Carter's press secretary, the late Jody Powell, for example, was among Carter's closest confidants and frequently advised the president on policy matters. He went on to found his own Washington public relations agency. James Brady, the next press secretary, who was permanently paralyzed in 1981 by a bullet aimed at President Reagan, later joined his wife, Sarah, to lobby hard for what would become known as the Brady Bill, establishing new procedures for licensing handguns.

Over time, the position of press secretary has been awarded more to career political public relations people than to career journalists. Larry Speakes, who followed Brady, was a former Hill and Knowlton executive and was universally hailed by the media for his professionalism. During Reagan's second term, Speakes apparently was purposely kept in the dark by Reagan's military advisors planning an invasion of the island of Grenada. The upset press secretary later apologized to reporters for misleading them on the Grenada invasion.

The next press secretary was a low-key, trusted, and respected lifetime government public relations professional, Marlin Fitzwater. His successor was another career political public relations professional, Dee Dee Myers, who was respected by the media and brought a refreshing perspective to her role as President Clinton's press secretary. She went on to become a cable talk show host and magazine editor.

The trend toward retaining experienced communications people continued through the administrations of Presidents Clinton and George W. Bush. For his first choice as White House Press Secretary, President Barack Obama chose Robert Gibbs, a career political public relations strategist who gained the new president's trust over four years as a wise and trusted advisor **(Figure 12-6)**. Gibbs, in the tradition of the best press secretaries, was an alter ego to Obama. Because of his closeness, Gibbs could speak with impunity and absolute confidence in the name of the president. Gibbs described his unique role thusly:

> *"The Press Secretary occupies a unique position in the physical structure of the White House. Your office is equidistant from the Oval Office and the Briefing Room. So your role is one of spokesperson to and advocate for the President, but you are also the representative of the press inside the White House, in order for them to get the facts, information, and access they need."*[23]

When Gibbs left the administration to help run Obama's reelection campaign, he was replaced by Jay Carney, a former *Time* magazine journalist. Unlike Gibbs, Carney, a taciturn and serious sort, had no particular relationship with President Obama, and it showed in his. painfully deliberative manner, always giving the impression of "walking on eggshells" each time he responded to a reporter's question.

When Carney resigned in 2014 to take a top job at Amazon.com, he was replaced by his deputy, Josh Earnest, a career political public relations professional, whose mastery of the subject matter, confidence in answering prickly questions and sense of humor was a welcome change from the lugubrious Carney and reestablished the importance of the job of Press Secretary. (See From the Top in this chapter.)

Over the years, the number of reporters hounding the presidential press secretary—dubbed by some "the imperial press corps"—has grown from fewer than 300 reporters during President Kennedy's term to around 3000. During the Obama administration, the position of director of new media was created. With the White House having 1.7 million followers on Twitter, 500,000 fans on Facebook, and 70,000 e-mail subscribers, the traditional power of the press corps following the president began to erode, as Obama frequently chose social media to "go direct" to the people. While traditional editors and reporters complained about "White House secrecy," future presidents were likely to take a page from the Obama book and increasingly adopt social media as a medium through which to reach the American people.[24]

Dealing with the media on an international stage is no easy task, and the role of press secretary is never simple nor totally satisfactory. As former Bill Clinton Press Secretary Mike McCurry, who began the practice of televising the daily White House press secretary press briefing, put it, "Having a single person standing at a podium and answering questions and trying to explain a complicated world is not a very efficient way to drive home the idea that government can make a difference."[25] **Perhaps** President Lyndon Johnson, the first chief executive to be labeled an "imperial president" by the Washington press corps, said it best when asked by a television reporter what force or influence he thought had done the most to shape the nature of Washington policy. "You bastards," Johnson snapped.[26]

4 Lobbying the Government

The business community, foundations, and philanthropic organizations have a common problem: dealing with government, particularly the mammoth federal bureaucracy. Because government has become so pervasive in organizational and personal life, the

FYI

Are Ya' Havin' a Laugh?

Reporters, those in power often forget, are people, too. (At least most of them are!)

And public relations people who handle the media for a living should treat them with humanity and even, at times, a sense of humor. Thus it was refreshing in the winter of 2014 to see President Obama's Press Secretary Josh Earnest issue his *"Top 10 Things That Happened in the White House Briefing Room This Year That Hopefully Won't Happen Next Year,"* at the White House Correspondents' Association holiday reception **(Figure 12-7)**.

Here they are with explanation.

Number 10   *Creating a fake Twitter account for the next Secretary of Defense.* (Someone had mysteriously created such an account for the incoming DOD Secretary Ashton Carter.)

Number 9   *The Press Secretary awkwardly hugging the President of the United States on live television.* (Which is what the outgoing Jay Carney did with Obama.)

Number 8   *Veritable White House institutions—like Ann Compton, Peter Maer and Roger Runningen—announcing their retirement.* (All retiring respected reporters.)

Number 7   *Explaining why our Ebola czar is not a doctor.* (He wasn't.)

Number 6   *A scruffy beard appearing without warning on the face of the White House Press Secretary.* (Inexplicably, Carney sported one for a month.)

Number 5   *Fainting White House interns.* (On her first day, an intern fainted at Earnest's press briefing.)

Number 4   *The White House spokesman forgetting to do the Week Ahead at the end of Friday's briefing—oh, wait, that happens every week.* (It did.)

Number 3   *White House reporters jockeying for an invite to the White House holiday party to take a picture with the President and First Lady—oh, wait, that happens every year.* (It does.)

Number 2   The President donning a tan suit and calling a news conference to say that the United States doesn't have a strategy. (Which the President did when asked about the U.S. response to the terrorist Islamic State.)

FIGURE 12-7   **Jocular Josh and friend.**
White House Press Secretary Josh Earnest with President Obama.
Photo: Official White House Photo by Pete Souza

Number 1   *And the #1 Thing That happened in the White House Briefing Room This Year That Hopefully Won't Happen Next Year: Seeing the White House Press Secretary being replaced by a smart-aleck deputy.* (Deputy Earnest replaced Carney.)

Needless to say, the crowd, composed of gruff, grizzled and grousing reporters, loved it.

*For further information, see Mike Allen, "Josh Earnest's Top 10 List," *Politico* (December 3, 2014).

number of corporations and trade associations with government relations units has grown steadily in recent years.

The occupation of lobbyist has shown steady growth. The number of registered lobbyists in Washington, many of them situated along legendary K Street, totals 12,281 responsible for spending at an annual level of more than $3 billion—more than $8 million a day—to influence legislators and legislation.[27] Who spends the most to lobby the federal government? At the top of the lobbying chart was General Electric, which spent $134 million since 2009, followed by communications giants like AT&T, Verizon, and Comcast and defense contractors like Northrop Gunman, Boeing, and Lockheed Martin.[28] Trade associations, led by the U.S. Chamber of Commerce, the American Medical Association, American Hospital Association, Pharmaceutical Manufacturers of America, and the American Association of Retired Persons, also spend millions annually to influence legislation. Many trade associations and lobbying firms are populated by former congressmen, eager to cash in on their D.C. contacts. Typical was former Connecticut Sen. Chris Dodd, who despite vowing he would never lobby after leaving the Senate in 2011, pocketed a cool $3.3 million as chief lobbyist for the Motion Picture Association of America.

Beyond federal government lobbying, state government and local lobbying is only slightly less active. In 2009, local, state, and territorial governments spent more than $83.5 million of taxpayer money lobbying federal lawmakers and public officials. And who leads the parade in local lobbying? None other than the U.S. territory of Puerto Rico, which spends well over $1 million a year in lobbying expenses and has received generous tax credits to build its economy. But what Congress giveth as a result of lobbying, it can also taketh away. And when Congress phased out one crucial tax credit in 2005, the island was plunged into a long recession, culminating in. the summer of 2015, when Puerto Rico sadly announced it was unable to repay its creditors.[29]

To the uninitiated, Washington (or almost any state capital) can seem an incomprehensible maze. Consequently, organizations with an interest in government relations usually employ a professional representative, who may or may not be a registered lobbyist with responsibility to influence legislation. Lobbyists are required to comply with the federal Lobbying Act of 1946, which imposed certain reporting requirements on individuals or organizations that spend a significant amount of time or money attempting to influence members of Congress on legislation.

In 1995, the Lobbying Disclosure Act took effect, reforming the earlier law. The new act broadened the activities that constitute lobbying and mandated government registration of lobbyists. Under the new law, a lobbyist is an individual who is paid by a third party to make more than one "lobbying contact," defined as an oral or written communication to a vast range of specific individuals in the executive and legislative branches of the federal government.

Lobbyists, at times, have been labeled everything from influence peddlers to fixers to downright crooks. In 2005, with the admissions of convicted super-lobbyist Jack Abramoff—and his equally convicted public relations consigliere, Michael Scanlon—about luring members of Congress on golf outings and in the process ripping off Native American tribe clients for millions of dollars, the practice of lobbying reached a new low. President Obama made a point of going after lobbyists in his campaigns and State of the Union messages. But his Democrat colleagues, typical of Washington's tradition of not wanting to bite the hand that feeds it, failed to pass legislation that would have required greater disclosure of donors to outside lobbying groups.[30]

Despite the slings and arrows and Congressional reluctance to do anything about the influence of lobbyists, the fact is that today's lobbyist is likely to be a person who is well informed in his or her field and who furnishes Congress with facts and information necessary to make an intelligent decision on a particular issue. This task—the lobbyist's primary function—is rooted in nothing less than the First Amendment right of all citizens to petition government.

What Do Lobbyists Do?

For sure, lobbying has become big business.

But what exactly do lobbyists do?

The essence of a lobbyist's job is to inform and persuade. The specific activities performed by individual lobbyists vary with the nature of the industry or group represented. Most take part in these activities:

1. **Fact-finding.** The government is an incredible storehouse of facts, statistics, economic data, opinions, and decisions that generally are available for the asking.

2. **Interpretation of government actions.** A key function of the lobbyist is to interpret for management the significance of government events and the potential implications of pending legislation. Often a lobbyist predicts what can be expected to happen legislatively and recommends actions to deal with the expected outcome.

3. **Interpretation of company actions.** Through almost daily contact with congressional members and staff assistants, a lobbyist conveys how a specific group feels about legislation. The lobbyist must be completely versed in the business of the client and the attitude of the organization toward governmental actions.

4. **Advocacy of a position.** Beyond the presentation of facts, a lobbyist advocates positions on behalf of clients, both pro and con. Hitting a congressional representative early with a stand on pending legislation can often mean getting a fair hearing for the client's position.

5. **Publicity springboard.** More news comes out of Washington than from any other city in the world. It is the base for thousands of social media, press, television, radio, and magazine correspondents. This multiplicity of media makes it the ideal springboard for launching organizational publicity. The same holds true, to a lesser degree, in state capitals.

6. **Support of company sales.** The government is one of the nation's largest purchasers of products. Lobbyists often serve as conduits through which sales are made. A lobbyist who is friendly with government personnel can serve as a valuable link for leads to company business.[31]

Emergence of Social Media Lobbying   As it has in every other area of society and public relations work, the Internet has influenced the practice of lobbying as well. In terms of political campaigning and grassroots lobbying, as noted, the two-term presidency of Barack Obama cemented the role of the Web in political campaigning. Obama became the first "digital presidential candidate." He raised millions in campaign contributions via the Internet. He announced his vice presidential running mate via instant messaging. He created a blog, "Fight the Smears," to extinguish scurrilous rumors. He had more than 1.5 million "friends" on MySpace and Facebook He set the record of five hours for fastest to one million Twitter followers (which was broken by Caitlyn Jenner, who got there in four hours in 2015).[32]

The Obama presidency was the greatest indication that social media and the Internet had changed politics and lobbying forever. One Democratic Web site, in particular, MoveOn.org, financed by the billionaire George Soros, was credited as "one of the most influential . . . organizations in U.S. politics." Founded in 1998 by Clinton sympathizers opposed to impeachment and eager for the Congress to "move on," the site has become a rallying point for liberal issues. A host of conservative sites, including The Drudge Report, News Max, and Real Clear Politics, fuel the fervor on the other side of the aisle.[33]

Political Action Committees

The rise of political action committees (PACs), as sources of funding to promote political lobbying, has been among the most controversial political developments in recent years—second only to the rise of the "super" political action committee (super PAC).

A political action committee is the name commonly given to a private group, regardless of size, organized to elect political candidates. In the mid-1970s, there were about 600 PACs. By 2009, there were more than 4600 PACs, which are formed by companies, unions, or other groups to raise and spend money to help presidential and congressional candidates. The largest PACs were Emily's List, the Service Employees International Union, American Federation of Teachers, American Medical Association, National Rifle Association, Teamsters Union, and the like—all donating millions of dollars to get candidates elected.[34]

Each PAC can give a maximum of $5000 to a federal candidate in a primary election and another $5000 for the general election. Political campaign fund-raising, through PACs, has become a year-long process. Every day, political PACs reach out along these lines:

Rapid Response

Rosemary—The Clintons have both e-mailed you.

The Obamas have both e-mailed you.

It's because the South and the Senate WILL be decided by what happens before the FINAL quarterly deadline in 12 hours. **We need YOU to step up NOW.**

Six races are virtually tied, and the GOP needs just three to take control. **It's our FINAL chance to go on the ATTACK and win.**

President Clinton just warned, this deadline "is the most important we've ever faced…**If you don't want Republicans to run this country, you can't wait for someone else to pick up the slack."**

We're begging now: Please donate before midnight, and we'll triple match your gift. It will go IMMEDIATELY to battleground states. This is our FINAL CHANCE.

If you've saved your payment information with ActBlue Express, your donation will go through immediately:

Pitch in $3 IMMEDIATELY>>

Pitch in $8 IMMEDIATELY>>

Pitch in $17 IMMEDIATELY>>

Pitch in $25 IMMEDIATELY>>

Pitch in $35 IMMEDIATELY>>

Or donate another amount.

Tonight marks our BIGGEST deadline yet, and our LAST chance to fully fund our voter mobilization program. That's why President Clinton is calling you to action in this moment.

Let's do this!

DSCC Rapid Response

Source: Democratic Senatorial Campaign Committee, 430 S. Capitol St. SE, Washington, DC, 2003.

The increased influence of such groups on candidates is one reason why Senators John McCain and Russ Feingold led the Congress in 2002 to pass new strictures on campaign financing and particularly advertising for or against a candidate just prior to an election. But then in 2010, in the landmark case *Citizens United* v. *Federal Election Commission*, the U.S. Supreme Court held that the First Amendment to the U.S. Constitution prohibited the government from restricting independent political expenditures by corporations and unions.

Citizens United opened the flood gates for the introduction of super PACs, groups able to accept unlimited political donations from wealthy donors to use in favor of or against a particular candidate. In 2012, the super PACs supporting Mitt Romney spent $142 million, the vast majority on attack ads.[35] In the 2016 campaign, candidates on either side of the aisle were fueled by Super PACs, driven by people like billionaire brothers David and Charles Koch and Las Vegas casino owner Sheldon Adelson on the Republican side and computer software entrepreneur Tim Gill and hedge fund owners Tom Steyer and Soros on the Democrat side.

While a few praised super PACs as representing free speech, many others argued that the tremendous amount of money being spent on negative advertising unfairly influences elections and steers "political favors" to mega-donors. With the approval ratings of politicians at an all-time low, largely because of their never-ending quest for money, it was likely, sad to say, that money and politics would continue to be inextricably linked for the foreseeable future.

Dealing with Local Government

In 1980, Ronald Reagan rode to power on a platform of New Federalism, calling for a shift of political debate and public policy decisions from national to state and local levels. Presidents Clinton and Bush picked up the same initiative when they assumed power. But by the time the second decade of the 21st century rolled around, after financial system collapse, auto industry implosion, terrorism overseas and domestically and persistent problems in job growth and wage expansion, sentiment shifted back to a more fortified national government role and increased regulation. Indeed, this battle between federal vs. local government power largely framed the narrative of the 2016 presidential election.

Although the federal government's role in wielding power and employing public relations professionals is significant, state and local governments also are extremely important. Indeed, one viable route for entry-level public relations practitioners is through the local offices of city, county, regional, and state government officials.

Local agencies deal directly—much more so than their counterparts in Washington—with individuals. State, county, and local officials must make themselves available for local media interviews, community forums and debates, and even door-to-door campaigning. In recent years, local and state officials have found that direct contact with constituents—often through call-in radio programs—is invaluable not only in projecting an image but also in keeping in touch with the voters.

The public information function at state and local levels—to keep constituents apprised of legislative and regulatory changes, various government procedures, and notices—is a front-line public relations responsibility on the local level.

Last Word

The pervasive growth of government at all levels of society may not be welcome news for many people. But with the nation and the world confronting unprecedented economic challenges in the second decade of the 21st century, an increased government role is inevitable.

Government's growth has stimulated the need for increased public relations support and counsel. On the one hand, the importance of communicating directly with individual voters has become paramount for politicians. On the other hand, individuals disgusted with the system where "money talks" need communication mechanisms to fight back. Such was the case in 2011 when far-sighted Starbucks CEO Howard Schultz launched an effort to convince his fellow CEOs to forego giving political donations to any candidate until Washington "delivers a fiscally, disciplined long term debt and deficit plan to the American people."[36] Valiant idea, but good luck!

The fact is we're stuck with this massive federal government bureaucracy, organized through individual agencies that seek to communicate with the public. The best news is that this means a vast repository of public relations jobs. Indeed, the most powerful government position in the Free World—that of President of the United States—has come to rely on public relations counsel to help maintain a positive public opinion of the office and the incumbent's handling of it.

On state and local levels, public relations expertise also has become a valued commodity. Local officials, too, attempt to describe their programs in the most effective manner. In profit-making and nonprofit organizations alike, the need to communicate with various layers of government also is imperative.

Like it or not, the growth of government in our society appears unstoppable, particularly now that the United States is faced with continued economic challenges and engaged in a long-term war on terror. One direct outgrowth is that need for public relations support in government relations will clearly continue to grow in the 21st century.

Discussion Starters

1. Why is the public relations function regarded as something of a stepchild in government?
2. What is the current status of the Voice of America, and what are its responsibilities?
3. What is meant by the term *embedded reporter*?
4. Why was Ronald Reagan called the Great Communicator?
5. Contrast the performances of Scott McClellan and Tony Snow as White House press secretaries.
6. What are the objectives of government relations officers?
7. What are the primary functions of lobbyists?
8. What impact has the Internet had on lobbying?
9. What are the pros and cons of PACs?
10. What is the significance of the *Citizens United* Supreme Court case?

Pick of the Literature

All the Presidents' Spokesmen

Woody Klein, Westport, CT: Praeger Publishers, 2008

A former *Washington Post* reporter reviews the ups and downs of press secretaries through the ages. With forewords by former press secretaries Marlin Fitzwater and Dee Dee Myers, Klein discusses the special responsibilities that press secretaries share. The book begins with Franklin Roosevelt and his press secretary, Stephen Early. It then tracks through history through the presidency of George W. Bush, describing in some detail every press secretary to occupy the White House briefing room podium.

Klein focuses on seminal events, from Pearl Harbor and Vietnam to Richard Nixon's pardon and Hurricane Katrina. He extensively examines "spin" and how beauty—or more specifically, "truth"—lies in the eye of the administration and the spokesperson representing it.

Case Study   Bridgegate

In the second decade of the 21st century, few politicians were quite as imposing as New Jersey's two-term Republican Gov. Chris Christie.

Christie was larger than life—literally. And residents of the Garden State, a notorious Democrat stronghold, loved him until one day in 2013 when Christie's bridge came tumbling down—again, literally.

Bully's Pulpit

A lifelong resident of New Jersey, Christie rose to power in the state as a brash, no-nonsense U.S. Attorney, who specialized in exposing New Jersey's rampant, legendary political corruption. Christie's no-nonsense approach in prosecuting political criminals and others paved the way for his gubernatorial victory in 2009 over Jon Corzine, a former senator who, himself, would later face corruption charges in mismanaging a commodities futures firm.

As governor, Christie earned a reputation of governing with an iron hand, rigorously controlling his loyal staff, talking tough and letting the chips fall where they may. The governor seemed to relish run-ins with Democrat opponents, union representatives and even common citizens with the audacity to challenge his wisdom. In one YouTube-celebrated town hall appearance, Christie called a Rutgers law student an *"idiot"* for interrupting him. While some (mostly Democrats) bridled at Christie's bullying nature, others (mostly Republicans) loved their in-your-face governor.

By 2013, with Christie running for reelection as New Jersey governor, Republicans around the nation contemplated the large governor's ultimate run for the White House. Christie was elected chairman of the Republican Governor Association, did a good job of raising money, and readied himself for the 2016 President campaign.

"Time for Some Traffic Problems"

With the Christie bandwagon rolling on, a strange thing happened in the midst of the Christie reelection campaign, one day in early September of 2013.

Traffic on the nation's busiest bridge, the George Washington that connected New Jersey to New York, came to a screeching halt. And nobody could quite explain why. For some inexplicable reason, traffic patterns on the bridge were being altered and lanes closed, causing havoc among the thousands of commuters who daily traversed the bridge. One 91-year-old woman died, when EMS crews were delayed in reaching her car.

The traffic delays at the bridge were particularly maddening for the mayor of Fort Lee where the bridge was anchored. Mayor Mark Sokolich, a Democrat who refused to endorse Christie for reelection, frantically appealed to Christie associates at the Port Authority, the agency controlling the bridge, that the lane closures were preventing kids from getting to school. *"Help please, it's maddening,"* he texted. By the fourth day of the closures, Sokolich informed Christie aides he suspected the lanes were closed as a *"punitive measure."*

The next day, the bridge lanes were reopened and the Port Authority announced belatedly that it had closed the lanes as part of a *"traffic study."* But unconvinced Democrats in the state senate

launched an investigation, and *The New York Times* and Jersey media began reporting on the suspicious circumstances.

Christie, characteristically, dismissed growing accusations of political retaliation. Said the pugnacious governor, *"I worked the cones. Unbeknownst to anyone, I was working the cones."* Christie said he had asked his staff about the closures, and no one in his administration was involved.

Wrong.

By late December, subpoenaed e-mails revealed that Christie's longtime deputy chief of staff, Bridget Anne Kelly, had written to her contact at the Port Authority, *"Time for some traffic problems in Fort Lee.";* apparently in retaliation for Mayor Sokolich's refusal to support Christie.

Bridgegate had now become a cause célèbre in the halls of Congress and in the national news.

FIGURE 12-8   Joining the race.
Despite suspicions about his role in the national scandal of Bridgegate, Gov. Chris Christie still thought he could win the Republican nomination for president in 2016.
Photo: Wenzelberg/NYPost/SplashNews/Newscom

Duped by the Little People

By early January 2014, the nation's most ferocious governor suddenly became sheepish.

After canceling several public appearances, Christie issued a subdued statement that he *"had been misled"* and knew nothing about the bridge problems. A day later, he faced reporters at the Trenton State House, announced that he had fired Kelly *"because she lied to me"* and asserted how hurt he was that his staff had let him down. Said Christie to skeptical reporters who challenged him about failing to shake the truth out of his subordinates, *"I am who I am, but I am not a bully."*

Over the next several months—as investigations and lawsuits and critical press coverage mounted—Gov. Christie essentially washed his hands of the bridge scandal. While acknowledging how *"embarrassed and humiliated"* he was, he made no subsequent attempt to reach out to those involved to determine what happened or to those personally impacted by the outrageous delays, nor did he choose to answer any questions about Bridgegate. Rather, he chose to hire his own personally selected law firm to do an "independent" study of what happened, at government expense. Not surprisingly, the law firm came back, $8 million taxpayers' dollars later, and declared the governor not guilty of anything.

In effect, the governor moved on.

By the fall of 2015, with former Christie aides admitting in federal court they had, indeed, engaged in a politically-motivated plot to cause the traffic jam, the involvement of Gov. Christie in the whole sordid affair was still not completely known. Former Deputy Chief of Staff Kelly and others under indictment were scheduled to go on trial later in 2016.

Meanwhile, Christie continued to insist on his innocence and declared himself a candidate for the Republican presidential nomination. Two years earlier, Chris Christie might have been considered the front runner, but after Bridgegate, he didn't have a prayer **(Figure 12-8).***

Questions

1. How would you assess Chris Christie's handling of Bridgegate?

2. Had you been his public relations advisor, what would you have advised he do upon first reports of the traffic scandal?

3. Were you in charge of Christie's campaign for the Republican nomination for president, what public relations strategy would you adopt, in light of Bridgegate?

*For further information, see Steven Malanga, "A Tale of Two Scandals," *City Journal* (August 5, 2014); Tom Moran, "Christie's Bridgegate Spin Withers Under Scrutiny," *NJ.com* (July 12, 2015); and Steve Strunsky and Ted Sherman, "Bridgegate Fallout: Chris Christie Apologizes in Wake of Bridge Scandal, Fires Top Aide," *NJ.com* (January 9, 2014).

From the Top

An Interview with Josh Earnest

Photo: Official White House Photo by Pete Souza

Josh Earnest was named Assistant to the President and White House Press Secretary by President Barack Obama in May 2014, the third to occupy the position in the Obama Administration Mr. Earnest has two decades of experience in political communications, nearly half of that time in the service of Mr. Obama. After serving in communications posts in mayoral and gubernatorial campaigns, in Congress and for the Democratic National Committee, Mr. Earnest moved to Iowa, eventually joining Sen. Obama's presidential campaign in 2007 as Obama's Iowa Communications Director and then as Deputy Communications Director during the 2008 general election. Mr. Earnest started at the White House on President Obama's first full day in office as Deputy Press Secretary under Robert Gibbs and later as Principal Deputy White House Press Secretary and Chief of Staff to Jay Carney, before becoming White House Press Secretary.

What do you consider your primary mission as press secretary?

At its most fundamental, my job is to help the American public and therefore, the press, to process what the President is doing and why he is doing it. We must present the basic facts and help people understand the President's priorities and the values that underlie them.

How much access do you have to the President?

The short answer is as much as I need and whenever I want it. When I took the job, the President told me that I could feel free to walk into his office whenever I felt it was necessary. Obviously this is a great privilege which I take seriously and use judiciously.

What's been your greatest challenge?
Well, there are a lot of challenges in this job. One of the most significant is to deal with a news media going through dramatic changes brought about by the constant flow of news over the Internet. The day-to-day responsibilities of a White House reporter are no longer what they once were in terms of filing daily stories. Every reporter today is a wire service reporter, expected to file to the Net all the time. This poses a unique set of new challenges for the reporters, themselves, and for those of us whose job it is to provide them information.

We are under more pressure not only quickly to marshal details and facts but also to help reporters understand the perspective in which decisions are made. There is often a big difference between really important things and the latest developments which might not be that important. Sometimes the newest thing isn't the most essential. In this environment of continuous reporting, it's a challenge for reporters to ensure that this important perspective is made clear.

How does President Obama feel about the press?
I believe the President believes that the judgment of a professional, independent press is integral to our democracy. Further, he believes it is our responsibility not only to respect this independent press corps, but we must also help reporters do their jobs more professionally by providing the facts and context they require. He also believes that leaders in this democracy must be held accountable for their actions; and the press has an important role in ensuring this.

One illustration of this is the daily White House press briefing. You could argue that in this day where reporters constantly file stories that this daily press briefing is an antiquated concept; that it doesn't reflect the reality of today's journalistic environment.

But the President feels duty bound that we invest senior management time every morning and continue this daily reporting—on camera and on-the-record—of what he is doing and why. This, I would say, is a daily display of the President's accountability to the American people.

How would you characterize the White House press corps?
They understand how important their role and responsibility is—to keep the citizens informed and to hold the people in power accountable to the public. As I've noted, there is a real challenge to apply this principle in today's dynamic media environment.

Is the press "fair" in its coverage of the President?
By and large, the press is fair in its coverage. But I would also say that it's o.k. if sometimes, they're a little unfair. We don't expect the media's standard to be to make the President look good. But we do expect accuracy—or fairness—in reporting what the President is doing and why he is doing it. That's a standard that a majority in the press would agree is reasonable. And most, I would say, adhere to that standard most of the time.

What should be the proper relationship between the Press Secretary and the press?
It's understandable that there's an inherent 'friction' built into the relationship. If that friction were to disappear, then one side or the other isn't doing its part. It's the responsibility of the media to push for more access, more insight and greater accountability. My role, in response, is at times to serve as a force among my colleagues for greater transparency and at other times, to push back when we feel greater access isn't needed.

Just as there's a built-in friction between the Press Secretary and the press, there also ought to be mutual respect. That's what reporters should expect of a person in my position, and that's what we, in turn, expect of them.

Public Relations Bookshelf

Bacevitch, Andrew J. *The Limits of Power*. New York: Henry Holt and Company, 2008. A university international relations professor analyzes what's behind America's international relations problems.

Beck, Glenn. *An Inconvenient Book: Real Solutions to the World's Biggest Problems*. New York: Simon & Schuster, 2007. The conservative commentator takes'em all on—from poverty and marriage to liberalism and radical Islam.

Chemerinsky, Erwin. *Enhancing Government: Federalism for the 21st Century*. Stanford, CA: Stanford University Press, 2008. A political science professor explores the evolution of government in U.S. society.

Clarke, Torie. *Lipstick on a Pig*. New York: Free Press, 2006. The former Department of Defense communication director and originator of the effort to "embed" reporters in warzones offers a worthwhile memoir of her time running perhaps the largest government public relations operation.

Dunn, Geoffrey. *The Lies of Sarah Palin*. New York: St. Martin's Press, 2011. A less-than-friendly portrait of the woman who might have been second-in-command.

Lee, Mordecai, Grant Neeley, and Kendra Stewart. *The Practice of Government Public Relations*. Boca Raton, FL: CRC Press, 2012. Dissection of various government relations functions by guest chapter writers.

Levin, Linda L. *The Making of FDR*. Amherst, NY: Prometheus Books, 2008. The story of Stephen T. Early, FDR's and America's first modern-day press secretary.

McClellan, Scott. *What Happened*. New York: Perseus Books Group, 2009. Hatchet job from a disappointed and disappointing George W. Bush spokesman.

Morris, Dick and Eileen McGann. *Fleeced*. New York: HarperCollins, 2008. A reborn, former Bill Clinton advisor rants about what's wrong with liberals.

Murray, Ian. *Stealing You Blind*. Washington, DC: Regenery Publishing, 2011. Red meat for conservatives, where the "rich" are composed primarily of Democrats.

Nessen, Ron. *Making the News*. Middletown, CT: Wesleyan University Press, 2011. Memoir from a press secretary to President Richard Nixon.

Perino, Dana. *And the Good News Is.....* New York, NY: Hachette Book Group, 2015. Reminiscences of another former George W. Bush White House Press Secretary-turned Fox News host; quite a bit cheerier than the McClellan book.

Phillips, Kevin. *Bad Money*. New York: Penguin Group. 2008. A sobering look at American foreign policy from a former White House strategist.

Smith, Kevin R. (Ed.). *State and Local Government 2007–2008 Edition*. Washington, DC: CQ Press, 2008. Practitioners discuss various aspects of government on the state and municipal levels.

Smith, Sally B. *For Love of Politics*. New York: Random House, 2007. The unadulterated story of America's favorite political couple, Bill and Hillary Clinton.

Woodward, Bob. *The War Within: A Secret White House History 2006–2008*. New York: Simon & Schuster, 2008. The *Washington Post* reporter convinced Bush administration people to speak with him about this inside story. They learned to regret it.

Woodward, Bob. *Obama's Wars*. New York: Simon & Schuster, 2010. The same reporter also convinced the Obama administration people to speak with him. They, too, learned to regret it.

Endnotes

1. Michael D. Shear, "Obama's Social Media Team Tries to Widen Audience for State of Union Address," *The New York Times* (January 19, 2015).

2. Amit Chowdhry, "President Obama Joins Twitter, Hits One Million Followers in 5 Hours," *Forbes.com* (May 19, 2015).

3. Chris Cillizza, "Barack Obama, The World's Most Famous Social Media Editor," *The Washington Post* (March 11, 2014).

4. David Jackson, "Obama Appoints New Senior Advisor, Chief Digital Officer," *USA Today* (March 14, 2015).

5. Nancy Benac, "Obama Limiting Press Access in Ways that Past Administrations Wouldn't Have Dared," *Associated Press* (April 1, 2013).

6. Alex Swoyer, "Donald Trump Trumps Fellow GOP Candidates on Social Media," *Breitbart.com* (June 17, 2015).

7. "2015 Edelman Trust Barometer," Edelman Public Relations, 2015, http://www.edelman.com/2015-edelman-trust-barometer/.

8. David Murray, "PR Is Not the Problem—or the Solution," *Ragan Report* (November 24, 2003): 1.

9. Andrew Dugan, "U.S. Congress Starts Off Year with 16% Job Approval," *Gallup* (January 6, 2015), http://www.gallup.com/poll/180962/congress-starts-off-year-job-approval.aspx.

10. Fraser P. Seitel, *The Practice of Public Relations*, 9th ed. (Upper Saddle River, NJ: Prentice-Hall, 2004): 341.

11. Karen De Young, "Bush to Create Formal Office to Shape U.S. Image Abroad," *Washington Post* (July 30, 2002): A1.

12. Remarks by Richard Stengel, "Undersecretary for Diplomacy and Public Affairs, University of Southern California Center on Public Diplomacy" (October 15, 2014).

13. "Pentagon Spending Billions on PR to Sway World Opinion," *Associated Press* (February 5, 2009).

14. "The New Washington Press Corps," *Journalism.org* (July 16, 2009).

15. "GAO: Bush Administration Paid $200M for PR," *Jack O'Dwyer's Newsletter* (February 22, 2006): 2.

16. Phillip Swarts and John Solomon, "Feds Spent $16B on Outside PR, Ads," *Washington Times* (November 25, 2012).

17. "20% of Cubans Report Listening to Radio Marti," Broadcasting Board of Governors, http://www.bbg.gov/blog/2015/04/09/20-of-cubans-report-listening-to-radio-marti/, April 9, 2015.

18. "About VOA," Voice of America, Office of Public Affairs, 330 Independence Avenue, S.W., Washington, DC. 20237, http://www.voanews.com/.

19. Roger Simon, "It's All Obama All the Time," *Politico.com* (April 16, 2009).

20. Robert U. Brown, "Role of Press Secretary," *Editor & Publisher* (October 19, 1974): 40.

21. William Hill, "Nessen Lists Ways He Has Improved Press Relations," *Editor & Publisher* (April 10, 1975): 40.

22. William Safire, "One of Our Own," *The New York Times* (September 19, 1974): 43.

23. Fraser P. Seitel, *The Practice of Public Relations*, 12th ed. (Upper Saddle River, NJ: Pearson Education, Inc., 2014).

24. Michael Tarm, "Journalists Say Obama's Press Restrictions 'Significantly Worse' Than Past Administrations," *Associated Press* (September 18, 2014).

25. Remarks by Mike McCurry, "A View from the Podium," *New York* (May 5, 1999).

26. Michael J. Bennett, "The 'Imperial' Press Corps," *Public Relations Journal* (June 1982): 13.

27. Lee Fang, "Where Have All the Lobbyists Gone?" *The Nation* (February 19, 2014).

28. "Top 10 Companies Lobbying Washington," *CNN Money* (October 1, 2014).

29. Michael A. Fletcher and Steven Mufson, "How Washington Helped Create Puerto Rico's Staggering Debt Crisis," *The Washington Post* (July 17, 2015).

30. Dan Eggen, "The Influence Industry: Obama's Ban on Lobbyist Bundlers Has Unclear Prospects," *Washington Post* (February 1, 2012).

31. Fraser P. Seitel, "Lobbying Do's and Don'ts," *O'Dwyer's PR Services Report* (December 2005): 31.

32. Jethro Nededog, "Caitlyn Jenner Breaks Barack Obama Record for Fastest to One Million Twitter Followers," *Business Insider* (June 1, 2015).

33. Robert S. McCain, "MoveOn.org: Don't Believe the Hype," *Ripon Forum* (Fall 2004): 16.

34. Alan Fram, "Number of Political Action Committees Hits Record," *Associated Press* (March 14, 2009).

35. Alex Altman, "How Super PACs Are Taking Over," *Time* (March 25, 2015).

36. Charles Riley, "Starbucks CEO to DC: You've Been Cut Off," *CNN Money* (August 16, 2011).

Chapter 13

Community Relations

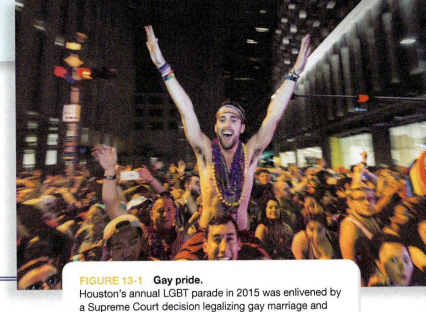

FIGURE 13-1 Gay pride.
Houston's annual LGBT parade in 2015 was enlivened by a Supreme Court decision legalizing gay marriage and also by a contingent of marchers from Exxon-Mobil.
Photo: F. Carter Smith/Polaris/Newscom

Chapter Objectives

1. To discuss the importance of dealing with "communities," both geographic and ethnic.

2. To review the tradition of corporate social responsibility that has uniquely characterized U.S. institutions.

3. To discuss the multicultural publics that populate society, including Hispanics, blacks, Asians, and groups beyond nationalities, such as seniors and gays.

4. To examine the role of public relations in orchestrating the activities of nonprofit organizations.

Business has come a long way since railroad magnate William Henry Vanderbilt told a reporter in 1883, *"The public be damned."* Today, organizations large and small realize they have an obligation to their communities and that to earn trust and support, they must practice positive community relations.

Traditionally, community relations included not only supporting the local area but also the "communities" of the larger society, most especially including minorities and those less fortunate. And in the second half of the 21st century, dealing with all those diverse communities—from African Americans to Hispanics, straights to gays, senior citizens to millennials and everybody in between—is no easy matter.

Consider the following:

- In the holiday season of 2013, Hallmark, the greeting card company, found itself besieged when it chose to adorn one of its Keepsake ornaments with an altered version of the lyrics to "Deck the Halls;" removing the word, "gay." "Don we now our gay apparel" became "don we now our fun apparel." When Hallmark was challenged on the curious switch, it responded that because the word, "gay," today has multiple meanings, they opted to substitute the word, "fun."[1]

- Two years later in 2015, a day after the Supreme Court affirmed same sex marriage, something truly unusual happened. In Houston, TX, more than 125 Exxon Mobil employees, all sporting rainbow-hued Exxon T-shirts, marched in the annual LGBT (Lesbian Gay Bi-sexual Transgender) parade. As The New York Times put it, *"That Exxon, long excoriated by gay rights advocates, would allow itself to be identified with a public expression of support for gay rights is perhaps even more surprising than the Supreme Court's historic ruling"*[2] **(Figure 13-1).**

■ That same year, the beloved Washington Redskins found their 81-year-old name in serious jeopardy, when a federal judge ruled to uphold the cancellation of the Redskins trademark because the name could be perceived as disparaging to Native Americans.[3]

Such was the state of controversy and change that surrounded the various communities with which organizations dealt. Nor were nonprofit charitable organizations —another essential aspect of community relations—free of controversy.

■ In 2012, Susan G. Komen for the Cure, a laudatory charity devoted to fighting breast cancer, was excoriated when it announced it would no longer fund Planned Parenthood, the nation's largest abortion provider.

■ In 2015 with Hillary Clinton running for President, the Bill, Hillary and Chelsea Clinton Foundation, with $199 million in contributions, was the subject of numerous exposes of its suspect, deep-pocketed foreign contributors and suspicious failures to disclose required information.

■ Even the nation's institutions of higher learning were called on the carpet for everything from steadily escalating tuition fees to increasing incidences of on-campus sexual violence.

As the importance of community relations in the 21st century had increased, so, too, had the challenge in steering a positive community relations course through the shoals of controversy.

1 Multicultural Diversity

Today's society is increasingly multicultural. America has always been a melting pot, attracting freedom-seeking immigrants from countries throughout the world. Never has this been more true than today, as America's face continues to change. In 2012, America reportedly hit a demographic milestone, with census figures showing for the first time more than half the children born in the United States were minorities. However, on analysis, that report may have been premature; more recent indications are that non-Hispanic whites account for 50.4% of the population less than one-year-old.[4]

While growth rates among minorities seemed to have slowed down in the second decade of the 21st century, their march to majority status in the United States appeared inexorable. Consider the following:

■ The country's minority population increased from 32.9% of U.S. residents in 2004 to 37.9% in 2014, according to the Census Bureau. Four states—Hawaii, California, New Mexico, and Texas—along with Washington, D.C., are now majority-minority. Nevada reported a 48.5% minority population.[5]

- According to the U.S. Census Bureau, 54 million Hispanics live in the United States, approximately 17% of the U.S. population. Mexicans ranked as the largest group at 64%, followed by Puerto Ricans at 9%. By 2060, Hispanics are expected to reach nearly 129 million, constituting 31% of the U.S. population.[6]

- The population of African Americans including those of more than one race was estimated at 45 million, making up 15% of the total U.S. population. Those who identified only as African American made up 13.2% of the U.S. population—over 41.7 million people.[7]

- The population of Asian Americans was a little over 23 million, representing 5.6% of the U.S. population. The largest ethnic group in the census was Chinese (3.79 million), Filipino (3.41 million), Indian (3.18 million), Vietnamese (1.73 million), Korean (1.7 million), and Japanese (1.3 million).

- The fastest growing population in the United States is those who identify themselves as "multi-racial." According to the U.S. Census Bureau, about 9 million Americans chose two or more racial categories when asked about their race. Between 2000 and 2010, the number of white and black biracial Americans more than doubled, while the population of adults with a white and Asian background increased by 87%. And during that decade, the nation elected President Barack Obama, the son of a black father from Kenya and a white mother from Kansas. The share of multiracial babies has risen from 1% in 1970 to 10% in 2013. And with interracial marriages also on the rise, demographers expect this rapid growth to continue, if not quicken, in the decades to come.[8]

- Millennials, meanwhile, who number 83.1 million, have now surpassed Baby Boomers at 75.4 million and are the most diverse generation in history.[9]

Such is the multicultural diversity enjoyed today by America and the world. The implications for organizations are profound. For example, half of the 320 million U.S. population are women, but 71% of women high school graduates enroll in college, compared to 61% of males, with women more likely to graduate than men.[10]

As the arbiters of communications in their organizations, public relations people must be sensitive to society's new multicultural realities.

☐2 CSR—Corporate Social Responsibility

In the old days—pre-1990s—corporations prided themselves on their "social responsibility." Their premise was that with the great opportunities they were afforded, companies needed to "give back" to society through participation in and contributions to not-for-profit organizations committed to confront society's most pressing problems—from poverty to education to cultural and health enrichment **(Figure 13-2)**.

Then came the go-go 1990s and the "bubble years" of the early 2000s, when Internet stocks zoomed to dizzying heights, and corporate social responsibility took a backseat to making money—as much money as possible. When the stock market bubble burst at the end of the first decade of the 21st century and economic doldrums morphed into worldwide recession and then near-systemic Armageddon, companies further cut back on charitable support and charities struggled to support their constituents.

The good news is that as the economy has at least gradually come back in the first five years of the century's second decade, charitable giving, including that of companies, has come back. For 2014, charitable giving rose for the fifth consecutive year to a total of $358 billion, according to the Giving USA Foundation.[11] A large

FIGURE 13-2 **Mighty community relations.** Catan Communications created the Mighty Milk Nutritional Drink campaign, devising the "Be Mighty, Get Active" essay contest to raise awareness among children to learn about living a healthier lifestyle. Winners got to meet the one and only former pro basketball giant Shaquille O'Neal.
Photo: Courtesy of O'Dwyer Company

part of that increase was due to individual givers, led by billionaires like Microsoft founder Bill Gates and his wife, Melinda, and corporate stock guru Warren Buffet. Buffet and Gates, infact, began the *"Giving Pledge"* of billionaires pledging to give at least half their fortune to philanthropic causes. By 2015, the Giving Pledge had 137 members from 14 nations.[12]

The concept of "corporate social responsibility"—of "giving back" to one's community and the larger society through voluntarism and financial support—is very much an American phenomenon, slow to catch on around the world. That's why membership in the Gates-Buffet group form overseas billionaires was particularly heartening.

In light of the increasing diversity of U.S. society, both profit and nonprofit organizations are also becoming more diverse and learning to deal and communicate with those who differ in work background, education, age, gender, race, ethnic origin, physical abilities, religious beliefs, sexual orientation, and other perceived differences.

In 2013 alone, the top 10 companies aggregately contributed approximately $1.5 billion to charity. Companies were paced by companies like Novartis, Wal-Mart, General Electric, Coca-Cola, Exxon-Mobil, Caterpillar, and the nation's largest banks **(Table 13-1)**.

Corporate giving in the second decade of the 21st century also has shown three decided trends:

- **Corporate giving is becoming more focused.** Companies are choosing to make larger gifts to fewer causes. Instead of spreading their gifts widely across

TABLE 13-1 **Largest Corporate Foundations by Total Giving**
The list below includes the 10 largest corporate foundations ranked by total giving. All figures are based on the most current audited financial data in the Foundation Center's database as of fiscal year ending December 31, 2013.

Rank	Name/(State)	Total Giving
1.	Novartis Patient Assistance Foundation, Inc. (NJ)	$452,981,816
2.	Wells Fargo Foundation (CA)	186,775,875
3.	The Wal-Mart Foundation, Inc. (AR)	182,859,236
4.	The Bank of America Charitable Foundation, Inc. (NC)	175,299,789
5.	GE Foundation (CT)	124,512,065
6.	The JPMorgan Chase Foundation (NY)	115,516,001
7.	The Coca-Cola Foundation, Inc. (GA)	98,175,501
8.	Citi Foundation (NY)	78,372,150
9.	ExxonMobil Foundation (TX)	72,747,966
10.	Caterpillar Foundation (IL)	55,998,836

multiple program areas, corporations are choosing one or two societal issues to focus on, according to one study of nearly 200 companies. Which issues were most of these companies choosing to target? Basic health and social service programs topped the list, followed by education and community and economic development.[13]

■ **Matching gifts are a high priority.** Companies with a workplace giving campaign rose to 59% in 2012, and those with a "dollars for doers" program encouraging volunteerism rose to 63%. Matching gifts are a great way for employees to maximize the value of their personal giving.

■ **International giving is on the rise.** This is partly driven by overseas profits, which are difficult to bring home without incurring big tax liabilities. But overseas giving also rose as a result of company-sponsored volunteerism, where employees are given time off to take part in local causes around the world. Indeed, employers are increasingly willing to let workers engage in causes that are important to them anywhere in the world. Companies are embracing the "giving back" mindset and establishing the strategies and programs to back it up.[14]

Increasingly, corporate leaders—long absent from the public dialogue on community issues—have begun again to take an active stance in confronting societal challenges, such as protecting the environment. General Electric CEO Jeffrey Immelt, for example, led his company's effort to reduce its greenhouse gas emission by 1% over time, really a 40% reduction when factoring in GE's presumed growth. Ford Motor Company executives also have worked to shift the company's energy use to renewable sources, which account for 3% of Ford's energy use.[15] Tiger Management founder and legendary Wall Street investor and hedge fund legend Julian Robertson has also devoted significant foundation money to curbing greenhouse gasses.

Again, corporate contributions like these depend on profits, a reality that those who rail against big business and capitalism should keep in mind. Another element of CSR "giving back to the community" is voluntarism. A new generation of millennials entering the business world has increased focus on their own and their firm's contribution to society.

FIGURE 13-3
From this…
*Photo: Courtesy of
Alex's Lemonade Stand
Foundation*

Most companies today understand that in the 21st century an organization must be a *citizen* of the community in every respect and accept its role as an agent for social change in the community **(Figure 13-3/13-4)**.

Community Relations Expectations

For an organization to coexist peacefully in its community, three skills in particular are required: (1) determining what the community knows and thinks about the organization, (2) informing the community of the organization's point of view, and (3) negotiating or mediating between the organization and the community and its constituents should there be a significant discrepancy.

Basically, every organization wants to foster positive reactions in its community. This becomes increasingly difficult in the face of protests from and disagreements with community activists. Community relations, therefore—to analyze the community, help understand its makeup and expectations, and communicate the organization's story in an understandable and uninterrupted way—are critical.

What the Community Expects

Communities expect from resident organizations such tangible commodities as employment, wages, and tax revenues. But communities have come to expect intangible contributions, too:

- **Appearance.** The community hopes that the firm will contribute positively to the quality of life in the area. It expects facilities to be attractive, with care

FIGURE 13-4
...to this.
Volvo for Life Days celebrated the memory of Alexandra Scott, a young Philadelphia cancer patient who earned a *Volvo for Life* award by selling lemonade to raise money for pediatric cancer. A year after Alex died, the car company sponsored Alex's Lemonade Stands throughout the country, such as this one in Minneapolis, to raise funds for pediatric cancer research.
Photo: Courtesy of Alex's Lemonade Stand Foundation

spent on the grounds and structures. Increasingly, community neighbors object to plants that belch smoke and pollute water and air.

- **Participation.** As a citizen of the community, an organization is expected to participate responsibly in community affairs, such as civic functions, park and recreational activities, education, welfare, and support of religious institutions.

- **Stability.** A business that fluctuates sharply in volume of business, number of employees, and taxes paid can adversely affect the community through its impact on municipal services, school loads, public facilities, and tax revenues. Communities prefer stable organizations that will grow with the area.

- **Pride.** Any organization that can help put the community on the map simply by being there is usually a valuable addition. Communities want firms that are proud to be residents. For instance, to most Americans, Battle Creek, Michigan, means cereal; Armonk, New York, means IBM; and Hershey, Pennsylvania, *still* means chocolate. Organizations that help build the town generally become revered symbols of pride.

What the Organization Expects

Organizations, in turn, expect to be provided with adequate municipal services, fair taxation, good living conditions for employees, a good labor supply, and a reasonable degree of support for the business and its products. When some of these requirements are missing, organizations may move to communities where such benefits are more readily available.

In light of the more portable and productive Internet-oriented business environment of today, the one benefit increasingly more important to businesses is the state's tax rate. The states that offer the most business-friendly taxes are Wyoming, South Dakota, Nevada, Alaska, and Texas, and those that offer the worst are New Jersey, New York, California, Minnesota and Vermont.[16] States like Texas have made a concerted push to attract business by improving infrastructure, cost of living and business policies relative to taxation, innovation, and technology made Texas the most "business friendly state in the nation."[17]

Community Relations Objectives

Research into community relations indicates that winning community support for an organization is no easy matter. Studies indicate difficulty in achieving rapport with community neighbors, who expect support from the company but object to any dominance on its part in community affairs.

Organizations profit by a written community relations policy that clearly defines the philosophy of management as it views its obligation to the community.

Typical community relations objectives may include the following:

1. To tell the community about the operations of the firm: its products, number of employees, size of the payroll, tax payments, employee benefits, growth, and support of community projects.

2. To correct misunderstandings, reply to criticism, and remove any disaffection that may exist among community neighbors.

3. To gain the favorable opinion of the community, particularly during strikes and periods of labor unrest, by stating the company's position on the issues involved.

4. To inform employees and their families about company activities and developments so that they can tell their friends and neighbors about the company and favorably influence opinions of the organization.

5. To inform people in local government about the firm's contributions to community welfare and to obtain support for legislation that will favorably affect the business climate of the community.

6. To find out what residents think about the organization, why they like or dislike its policies and practices, and how much they know of its policy, operations, and problems.

7. To establish a personal relationship between management and community leaders by inviting leaders to visit the plant and offices, meet management, and see employees at work.

8. To operate a profitable business to provide jobs and to pay competitive wages that increase the community's purchasing power and strengthen its economy.

9. To cooperate with other local businesses in advancing economic and social welfare through joint community relations programs.

Finally, there are the community relations activities available on the Internet. The heart of the Net is "community;" the Net holds immense potential to further human relations and progress—across common communities and for the larger society. Nowhere was this more on display than in the summer of 2014, when thousands of Americans participated in the Internet-driven ALS Ice Bucket Challenge to fight amyotrophic lateral sclerosis (see Case Study in this chapter).

A Question of Ethics

How *NOT* to Win Friends & Influence Communities

Minorities today may quickly becoming majorities, but you wouldn't know it the way that some public organizations and individuals deal with them. Take fashion designer Dolce & Gabbana.

In the spring of 2015, with LGBT individuals on the cusp of an historic same sex marriage decision and gay men and women becoming more powerful in all sectors of society, the firm's founders, Stefano Gabbana and Domenico Dolce, inserted themselves directly into a no-win position regarding in vitro fertilization and nontraditional families,

In an interview with an Italian magazine, Mr. Dolce said, *"I am not convinced by those I call children of chemicals, synthetic children. Rented uterus, semen chosen from a catalog."* Mr. Gabbana added, *"The family is not a fad. In it there is a supernatural sense of belonging."*

Woops! Social media went wild.

Almost immediately, the comments caught the attention of the singer and songwriter Elton John, who took to Instagram to urge a boycott of the high-end label, a perennial favorite of celebrities and socialites. Sir Elton, who had two sons through I.V.F. with his husband, David Furnish, wrote, "How dare you refer to my beautiful children as 'synthetic.' Shame on you for wagging your judgmental little fingers at I.V.F. Your archaic thinking is out of step with the times, just like your fashions. I shall never wear Dolce and Gabbana ever again" **(Figure 13-5)**.

The hashtag. #BoycottDolceGabbana quickly became a rallying cry on social media. Among others, the actress Courtney Love, the singer Ricky Martin, and the former tennis star Martina Navratilova condemned the fashion label on Twitter. Celebrities and civilians alike threatened to burn their Dolce & Gabbana apparel. Users posted pictures of their children conceived through artificial insemination.

FIGURE 13-5   **Happy family.**
Elton John, David Furnish, and their two sons, Zachary and Elijah.
Photo: Matthew Impey/REX/Newscom

Mr. Gabbana reacted immediately, by calling Mr. John a "Fascist" on Instagram. But in little time, when the controversy became too intense, Messrs. Dolce and Gabbana quickly backtracked to try to stem the backlash.

A sadder but wiser Mr. Gabbana said: *"We firmly believe in democracy and the fundamental principle of freedom of expression that upholds it. We talked about our way of seeing reality, but it was never our intention to judge other people's choices."**

Questions

1. Do you believe Dolce and Gabbana should have mentioned their views on I.V.F.? Why or why not?
2. What might the impact be on the Dolce & Gabbana brand as a result?
3. Were you the firm's public relations director, what plan of action would you initiate to regain brand traction and credibility?

* For further information, see Sandy Cohen, "Stars Join Elton John's Calls for Dolce and Gabbana Boycott," *Associated Press* (March 17, 2015); and Sydney Ember, "Remarks on Family by Dolce and Gabbana Bring Swell of Criticism," *The New York Times* (March 16, 2015).

③ Serving Diverse Communities

What were once referred to as minorities are rapidly becoming the majority. Today, 41 million Americans, 16% or one out of every six U.S. adults, are foreign born. Mexicans accounted for the largest immigrant population by far, with 11.6 million legal and illegal immigrants living in the United States.[18]

Women, African Americans, Hispanics, Asians, LGBT, seniors, persons with disabilities, and a variety of other groups have become not only important members of the labor force but also important sources of discretionary income.

Public relations professionals must be sensitive to the demands of all for equal pay, promotional opportunities, equal rights in the workplace, and so on. Communicating effectively in light of the multicultural diversity of society has become an important public relations challenge.

Women

In the 21st century, women became the majority of college enrollees and graduates and of near-equal strength in the U.S. workforce.

According to the Bureau of Labor Statistics, labor participation among women was 57% in 2013, down from its peak of 60% in 1999, but still high by historical standards. In addition, a large share of women work full-time and year-round. At the same time, women's earnings have increased as a proportion of men's earnings. In 1979, women's earnings were 62% of men's; in 2013, women's earnings were 82% of men's.[19]

In 2013, women accounted for 51% of all workers employed in management, professional, and related occupations, somewhat more than their 47% share of total employment. In terms of specific occupations, women represent 20% of software developers, 33% of lawyers and physicians, 62% of accountants and 81% of elementary and middle school teachers.

Women today head large corporations from General Motors to Hewlett Packard to Pepsi Cola. There are more than 100 women in Congress between the House and the Senate, representing about 20% of each body, and five female state governors.[20] Women have held the highest positions in the American government from Attorney General to Secretary of State to Secretary of Homeland Security, and, soon enough, President of the United States.

The point is that in the 21st century, women have made great strides in leveling the playing field between their roles and compensation schedules and those of their male counterparts. The days of "mommy tracks" and "mommy wars," glass ceilings and pink-collar ghettos are rapidly falling by the wayside.

So, too, in public relations, women have steadily climbed into middle- and upper-management positions, both at corporations and public relations agencies. Indeed, with the Public Relations Student Society of American now reporting 90% women, the field is among the strongest for opportunities for women.[21] One blemish, however, remains in the area of equal pay. According to a Public Relations Society of America (PRSA) study, women made 78 cents on the dollar compared to men. While an improvement over prior decades, researchers concluded that "gender discrimination as related to pay" still exists in public relations.[22]

Hispanics

There is little question that companies need to reach Hispanics. Currently 54 million strong, Hispanics are the fastest growing minority in the nation. From 2000 to 2010, more than half of the nation's population growth was due to Hispanics. The Census Bureau predicts that by 2050, they will comprise one-third of the population, nearly 100 million people.

The U.S. Hispanic population already ranks as the fifth largest in the world, behind Mexico, Spain, Colombia, and Argentina. In the United States, 77% of Hispanics reside mainly in six states—California, Texas, Florida, Arizona, New Jersey, and Illinois. Each has more than a million Hispanic residents and collectively, 31% of their population is Hispanic. As a group, those states house 30 million Hispanics, according to the 2010 Census.[23]

New York City has the largest Latin population with 2.2 million residents. Los Angeles rates second with 1.8 million and then Houston with 908,000. Mexicans, numbering 34 million, are by far the biggest national group within the United States, accounting for 64% nationwide and constituting the majority of Hispanics in 40 of the 50 states.

In terms of the importance of the Latin community to marketers and organizations of all types, Hispanic buying power is estimated at around $1.5 trillion, and Hispanic households earning more than $50,000 are projected to grow at a faster rate than the total number of households.[24]

Hispanics also comprise 12 million voters—a number expected to double by 2030. Accordingly, Hispanics comprise a potent political and economic force. For public relations counselors in business, government and other fields then, it's imperative to understand the Hispanic market. For example:

- Most U.S. Hispanics don't think of themselves as "Hispanic," but more in terms of their country of origin, as in "Latino," or a person of Latin American origin. So messages that resonate with Mexicans may not be appreciated by those of Puerto Rican or Dominican or Salvadoran descent.

- With just over half of Hispanics in America bilingual, it's important to "se habla Espanol," or to speak Spanish, which shows respect for a person's heritage.

- Latinos are also socially trendy, as studies indicate Hispanics take more of a social approach to shopping on and offline than non-Hispanics. So they are heavy users of social media.

- Hispanics appreciate organizations that work with them and their own organizations within their community. CSR and community relations programs, in partnership with Hispanic Chambers of Commerce or other community organizations, help identify organizations and brands as caring and concerned about Hispanics.[25]

Finally, Hispanics are voracious media consumers, relying heavily on television and radio to stay informed. Thirty years ago, there were 67 Spanish-language radio stations in the United States; today that number has increased to 500. Two large Spanish-programming TV networks, Univision, the largest Spanish-language media company in the United States, and Telemundo, dominate the airwaves, with Univision drawing 83% of the country's adult, prime-time, Spanish-language viewing audience. That's why in 2015, when Republican presidential candidate Donald Trump bad-mouthed Mexicans, Univision immediately dropped its relationship to broadcast Trump's Miss USA Pageant **(Figure 13-6)**. English-language players, such as CNN, Fusion, and Latin Post also offer daily programs in Spanish.[26]

African Americans

Growth of the black population in the United States, stalled for many years, has increased to 45 million by a surge in black immigrants, largely from Africa and the Caribbean, with a record 3.8 million foreign-born blacks now in the United States.[27] What this means is that, just as in dealing with the "Hispanic population," the black population is equally diverse in terms of customs, language and culture. Most of the nation's U.S.-born blacks trace their heritage to African ancestors who were brought here as slaves, thus the term, African American.

New York has the largest black population, followed by Florida, Texas, Georgia, and California. For the bulk of the past century, most blacks lived in the south. New York City, with three million black people, leads the nation, followed by Atlanta, Chicago, Washington, D.C., Philadelphia, Miami, Houston, and Los Angeles, each with more than one million blacks.[28]

The socioeconomic status of blacks has improved in recent years primarily due to large increases in women's incomes. While black median family income has improved, black men have recently experienced a decline in income. Black disposable income has increased markedly in recent years, now nearly $1 billion yearly. Black buying power is expected to continue its trajectory—from $316 billion in 1990 to $600 billion in 2000, to $947 billion in 2010, to $1038 billion in 2012 and a projected $1307 billion in 2017.[29]

FIGURE 13-6 **Take my dinero, por favor.** Republican presidential candidate Donald Trump got in aqua caliente in 2015, when he labeled Mexican immigrants, "drug dealers, rapists and crooks."
Photo: Matthew Healey/ UPI/Newscom

One important reason for this economic growth has been the impact of foreign-born blacks, who have fared better than U.S.-born blacks in terms of college graduation rates and household income.[30]

Despite their continuing evolution in the white-dominated workplace, the nation's 45 million blacks can still be reached effectively through special media:

- Black Entertainment Television is a popular network that has done well.
- Local African American radio stations have prospered.
- Pioneering Internet sites, such as TheRoot.com, BlackFamilies.com, Blackvoices.com, NetNoir.com, and the Black World Today (www.tbwt.com), have created a culture of acceptance and desirability for Web access among African Americans.
- Publications such as *Black Enterprise* and *Essence* are national vehicles. *Ebony,* the largest African American–oriented publication in the world and publishing since 1945, has a circulation of 1.6 million.[31]

One area of frustration in improving the livelihood of African Americans is the practice of public relations. (See From the Top in this chapter.) The field has failed to attract sufficient numbers of African American practitioners to its ranks. In recent years, the PRSA has increased outreach efforts to attract and retain African Americans. However, attracting African Americans to the field remains a great challenge to public relations leaders in the new century.

Asians

The U.S. Asian population totals approximately 23 million and grew faster than any other major race group since 2000. The distinction of being the fastest-growing racial/ethnic group in the United States has alternated between Asians and Hispanics in recent decades. Since 2010, though, Asians have had the edge, increasing by 43%. Census Bureau data estimate that the U.S. Hispanic population increased by 2.1% from December 20, 2013, while Asian population had a slightly higher growth rate of 2.9%.[32] California has the largest Asian population (6.1 million), and Hawaii is the only state in which Asians are a majority at 56% of the population.

Not only are Asians the fastest-growing racial group in the United States, they are also the highest-income and best-educated. Asians in the United States, according to studies, are distinguished by their emphasis on traditional family mores, such as having a successful marriage and being a good parent. Asians also place greater importance on career and material success, values reflected in child-rearing styles. Where once Asian Americans were low-skilled, low-wage laborers, today they are the most likely of any major racial or ethnic group in America to live in mixed neighborhoods and to marry across racial lines.[33]

Muslims

Without question, the most misunderstood and put-upon American public in this post-9/11 world are Muslims. Since the attacks on America in 2001, life has become more difficult for many of the estimated 2.6 million Muslims living in the United States. While only 1% of Americans are Muslim, research indicates that most people believe the Muslim population is 15 times greater than it really is.[34] The largest U.S. Muslim populations are found in Detroit, Washington, D.C., Cedar Rapids, IA, Philadelphia, and New York City.

Despite the fact that Muslim Americans report they unfairly bear the brunt of the negative publicity caused by Islamic terrorist attacks overseas and even occasionally in the United States, the U.S. Muslim population is expected to swell to more than 6 million by 2030, due to immigration.[35]

In terms of U.S. media, Arabic television stations, such as Al Jazeera or PTV, the state-run Pakistan Television, are accessible and employ American journalists. In 2004, Bridges TV, an English-language network with programming aimed at American Muslims, made its debut. The primary purpose of Bridges TV, said its founder, was to "build bridges of understanding between American Muslims and mainstream America."[36] In 2012, the channel ceased operations.

LGBT, Seniors, Etc.

In the 21st century, a diverse assortment of special communities has gravitated into the mainstream of American commerce. One such group is the LGBT market. To some, homosexuality may remain a target of opprobrium, but in the 21st century, the LGBT market, estimated at 9 million Americans, comprises a target of opportunity estimated at $830 billion in buying power. As a consequence of this buying power and the increasing acceptance of gays in society, the vast majority of American companies market to this community.[37] Accordingly, mainstream media now cater to the LGBT market, and a vibrant gay media market—from magazines *The Advocate* and *Out* to Internet portal GayWired.com to premium gay cable TV network Here—has emerged.[38]

Senior citizens also have become an important community for public relations professionals and the organizations they represent. The baby boomer generation has begun to steam into their Social Security years. Together, the over-50 crowd controls more than 50% of America's discretionary income. The American Association of Retired Persons, founded in 1958 for women and men over 50, has a membership of more than 35 million, about half of whom, despite the group's name, still work for a living.

Beyond gays and seniors, other racial and ethnic minorities abound in the United States, where freedom of religion and democratic ideals reign. Depending on one's position in public relations, knowledge of specific minorities may be relevant.

4 Nonprofit Public Relations

Among the most important champions of multiculturalism in any community are not-for-profit or just plain *nonprofit* organizations. Nonprofit organizations serve the social, educational, religious, and cultural needs of the community around them. So important is the role of public relations in nonprofit organizations that this sector is a primary source of employment for public relations graduates.

The nonprofit sector is characterized by a panoply of institutions: hospitals, schools, trade associations, labor unions, chambers of commerce, social welfare agencies, religious institutions, cultural organizations, and the like. Unlike corporations, nonprofits also seek to broaden volunteer participation in their efforts, often through the use of controversial communications tactics to raise public awareness through *media advocacy*. Media advocacy, simply defined, is public relations without resources. Protests, marches, demonstrations, media photo opportunities, stealth Internet campaigns, and the like are all fair game in media advocacy.

Master of Many Trades

Also unlike corporations, nonprofits generally don't have much money for key activities—especially in times of economic downturn. That's why public relations professionals in nonprofits must be masters of many functions; key among them are positioning the organization, developing a marketing or promotional plan, orchestrating media relations, and supporting fundraising.

Positioning the Organization   With thousands of competitors vying for support dollars, a nonprofit must stand out from the rest. This positioning initiative, to differentiate itself, depends largely on the public relations function.

No organization, particularly a resource-challenged nonprofit, can afford to be all things to all people. The best nonprofits, like the best corporations, stand for something. And they are unafraid to "break a few eggs" in order to achieve a clear and differentiable identity **(Figure 13-7)**.

Developing a Marketing/Promotional Plan   Often in nonprofits, the public relations director serves as the marketing director, advertising director, and promotion director. The job, simply, is marketing the organization to raise its profile, respect, and levels of support. This requires planning in terms of audiences, messages, and vehicles to deliver those messages to those audiences. Crucial in framing these messages is to recognize the *cause-related* quotient—that is, what the organization stands for—around which the marketing campaign is based.

Media Relations   Because most nonprofits lack sufficient resources for advertising or formal marketing, the use of "free" media is a critical public relations function. As the late National Public Radio broadcaster Daniel Schorr once put it, "If you don't exist in the media, for all practical purposes you don't exist." Nonprofits desperately need media advocates who champion their cause and mission.

Supporting Fundraising   Nonprofits depend on donors for support. Fundraising, therefore, is a key nonprofit challenge that must engage the attention of the organization's key executives. Public relations professionals must be intimately involved in fundraising communications and appeals so that messages can be targeted and consistent with the organization's general position.

FIGURE 13-7   Grin and bear it.
A "polar bear" sliced into the world's largest "Baked Alaska" during an "Earth Day" demonstration against drilling in the Arctic National Wildlife Region.
Photo: Courtesy of O'Dwyer Company

A successful fundraising campaign should include the following basic steps:

1. **Identify campaign plans and objectives.** Broad financial targets should be set. A goal should be announced. Specific sectors of the community from which funds might be extracted should be targeted in advance.

2. **Organize fact-finding.** Relevant trends that might affect giving should be noted. Relations with various elements of the community should be defined. The national and local economies should be considered, as should current attitudes toward charitable contributions.

3. **Recruit leaders.** The best fundraising campaigns are those with strong leadership. A hallmark of local United Way campaigns, for example, is the recruitment of strong business leaders to spearhead contribution efforts.

4. **Plan and implement strong communications activities.** The best fundraising campaigns are also the most visible. Publicity and promotion must be stressed. Special events should be organized, particularly featuring national and local celebrities to support the drive.

5. **Periodically review and evaluate.** Review the fundraising program as it progresses. Make midcourse corrections when activities succeed or fail beyond expectations. Evaluate program achievements against program targets. Revise strategies constantly as the goal becomes nearer.[39]

Because many public relations graduates enter the nonprofit realm, knowledge of fundraising strategies and techniques is especially important. Beginning practitioners, once hired in the public relations office of a college, hospital, religious group, charitable organization, or other nonprofit organization, are soon confronted with questions about how public relations can help raise money for the organization.

FYI

13 Rules for Radicals

Want to know how to organize a winning protest in a community or on campus with no money?

No problem.

Here are the time-honored suggestions of labor leader and notorious business disruptor Saul Alinsky, from his 1971 classic *Rules for Radicals* (see Pick of the Literature in this chapter). They are just as relevant now as they were nearly four decades ago. *(Just don't tell anybody where you learned 'em!)*

1. Power is not only what you have but what the enemy thinks you have.

2. Never go outside the experience of your people.

3. Whenever possible, go outside the experience of the enemy.

4. Make the enemy live up to its own book of rules.

5. Ridicule is a person's most potent weapon.

6. A good tactic is one that your people enjoy.

7. A tactic that drags on too long becomes a drag.

8. Keep the pressure on.

9. The threat is usually more terrifying than the thing itself.

10. The major premise for tactics is the development of operations that will maintain a constant pressure on the opposition.

11. If you push a negative hard and deep enough, it will break through to its counter side.

12. The price of a successful attack is a constructive alternative.

13. Pick the target, freeze it, personalize it, and polarize it.

Last Word

The increasing cultural diversity of society in the 21st century has spawned a wave of "political correctness (PC)," particularly in the United States. Predictably, many—famously including comedians Jerry Seinfeld and Bill Maher, who accused PC students and liberals of killing comedy—have questioned whether sensitivity to women, people of color, the physically challenged, gays, seniors, and other groups has gone too far.[40] One thing, however, is certain. The makeup of society—of consumers, employees, political constituents, and so on—has been altered inexorably. The number of discrete communities with which organizations must be concerned will continue to increase.

Intelligent organizations in our society must be responsive to the needs and desires of their communities. Positive community relations must begin with a clear understanding of community concerns, an open door for community leaders, an open and honest flow of information from the organization, and an ongoing sense of continuous involvement and interaction with community publics.

The public relations profession, responsible as it is for managing the communications of an organization, must take the lead in dealing with diversity. The society's Public Relations Student Society of America has chapters at 13 historically black colleges, and 27 schools have been accredited by the Hispanic Association of Colleges and Universities. Still, 87% of PRSA membership has remained Caucasian, with only a 6% increase in minority membership since 2005. So there is a ways to go for the profession.

Community relations itself is only as effective as the support it receives from top management. Once that support is clear, it becomes the responsibility of the public relations professional to ensure that the relationship between the organization and all of its multicultural communities is one of mutual trust, understanding, and support.

Discussion Starters

1. How is the atmosphere for community relations different today than it was even at the turn of the century?
2. What is meant by the term *multicultural diversity*?
3. In general terms, what does a community expect from a resident organization?
4. What are typical community relations objectives for an organization?
5. What was the philosophy of corporate responsibility espoused by economist Milton Friedman?
6. What is meant by the term *media advocacy*?
7. Why do companies need to reach the Hispanic community?
8. What are the primary responsibilities of a nonprofit public relations professional?
9. What is meant by the term *corporate social responsibility*?
10. What are the basic steps of a fundraising campaign?

Pick of the Literature

Rules for Radicals: A Practical Primer for Realistic Radicals
Saul D. Alinsky, New York: Vintage Books, 1989

Sure it's ancient, but so am I, and besides ... Alinsky's *Rules for Radicals*, originally published in 1971, is still the classic handbook for those bent on organizing communities, rattling the status quo, and effecting social and political change as well as for those who wish to learn from a legendary master.

Alinsky, a veteran community activist who fought on behalf of the poor from New York to California, provides strategies for building coalitions and for using communication, conflict, and confrontation advantageously.

In "Of Means and Ends," Alinsky lists his 13 tactics of engagement (see Outside the Lines in this chapter) and 11 rules of ethics that define the uses of radical power.

Alinsky supports his principles with numerous examples, the most colorful of which occurred when he wanted to draw attention to a particular cause in Rochester, New York. Alinsky and his group attended a Rochester Symphony Orchestra performance—after a meal of nothing but beans. The results were predictable—and very funny.

Alinsky died in 1972, but his lessons endure in this offbeat guide to seizing power. Whether your goal is to fluster the establishment or defend it, *Rules for Radicals* is the organizer's bible.

Case Study   Up Your Bucket for a Wonderful Cause

It isn't easy earning publicity for a nonprofit organization, despite its inherent worthiness.

That's why it was so remarkable in the summer of 2014 when an initiative to promote giving to amyotrophic lateral sclerosis or ALS, the disease that killed baseball legend Lou Gehrig, became an instant, overnight success—one of the most extraordinary public relations campaigns for any organization in history.

Cold Shower for Cold Cash

The campaign got its impetus from 27-year-old Boston philanthropist Corey Griffin, who spread the world about a "challenge" in support of his friend, Pete Frates, a former Boston College baseball player, who contracted ALS and couldn't walk or speak. Griffin called it, the "ALS Ice Bucket Challenge," designed to promote awareness of and raise contributions for ALS, by dumping an ice bucket over a willing volunteer's head in return for contributing to ALS.

Mr. Griffin began the campaign in July, when he posted a video on Facebook, Instagram and other social media of Mr. Frates dumping a bucket of ice on his head. He then challenged three friends similarly to take the challenge.

The campaign went viral, and then it was discovered by television. *Today Show* host Matt Lauer took the challenge, said that he would donate money to the Hospice of Palm Beach County and then challenged Brian Williams, Martha Stewart, and Howard Stern.

Soon, *Tonight Show* host Jimmy Fallon followed, and so did virtually every celebrity and non-celebrity with a cell phone camera.

Bucket Becomes Tidal Wave

The ALS Ice Bucket Challenge became the talk of the nation and the world and the undisputed hit of the summer of 2014. From Oprah Winfrey to Bill Gates to Taylor Swift to international basketball star Yao Ming **(Figure 13-8)**, everybody participated. Within weeks, Internet video featuring sports stars, politicians, celebrities, and just plain folks—each video wackier than the next—erupted in a tidal wave of support for ALS **(Figures 13-9)**.

People shared more than 1.2 million videos on Facebook over two months and mentioned the phenomenon more than 2.2 million times on Twitter. Donations to the ALS Association spiked as

FIGURE 13-8 From big current celebrities to ....
Photo: JONES JIN/FEATURECHINA/ Newscom

FIGURE 13-9 .... **little future celebrities.**
Photo: Courtesy Raina Seitel

never before, with the association receiving $13 million for the month of August, alone; compared to $1.7 million for the same period a year earlier.

The campaign spread, nonprofit experts said, because of its "authenticity" and "voluntarism" to help a good cause. On the other hand, critics also began to emerge—from philanthropy purists condemning the self-serving, frivolous nature of the challenge to animal advocates decrying the use of animals in ALS research to the Catholic Church, which objected to the use of embryonic stems cells by ALS. Some criticized the campaign for so-called "slacktivism," where people will click and post online for social causes with little actual impact on the cause. Said one critic,

"There are a lot of things wrong with the Ice Bucket Challenge, but the most annoying is that it's basically narcissism masked as altruism."

For its part, the beneficiary of the national largesse, the ALS Association, stayed above the fray. Said the ALS spokeswoman, *"One of the big takeaways is the power of individuals who are so tightly connected to a cause can really make a difference. I'm pretty sure that if any company or any nonprofit had all of the public relations dollars in the world to come up with a campaign, we never would've seen this kind of success."*

Bitter Sweet Conclusion

In the end, the Ice Bucket Challenge spread around the world and recorded contribution numbers never before enjoyed by any similar event.

By the fall of 2014, more than $100 million in donations had been raised from some 3 million donors. That compared to $2.8 million that the ALS Association had raised in the same period the year before. The ALS Association reported that it would spend the windfall raised primarily on research. Said ALS Association President Barbara Newhouse, *"We have a sense of urgency, but we also we recognize that we have to be good stewards of the donor dollars as we move this forward as quickly as researchers can research."*

The Ice Bucket Challenge effectively raised the bar for other organizations. How, for example, would the much larger American Cancer Society or American Heart Association compete with the Ice Bucket Challenge? Indeed, the importance of user-generated social media content for marketing purposes in the nonprofit world became topic #1 for philanthropic institutions.

One sad note in the campaign was that its originator, young Mr. Griffin, tragically died on August 16, 2014, in an early morning diving accident off the coast of Nantucket; just hours after his Ice Bucket Challenge reported reaching the $100 million donation mark.

Corey Griffin's legacy would be one of the most successful nonprofit campaigns in the history of philanthropy.*

Questions

1. What lessons can a nonprofit public relations manager learn from the Ice Bucket Challenge?

2. Were you the public relations advisor to ALS, how would you answer the critics of the Ice Bucket Challenge?

3. How should ALS build on the recognition and donations it received from the Ice Bucket Challenge?

* For further information, see Kevin Allen, "How the ALS Ice Bucket Challenge Could Change PR for Nonprofits," *Rayan PR Daily* (August 26, 2014); Sarah Gray, "Co-founder of ALS 'Ice Bucket Challenge' Drowns at Age 27," *Salon* (August 20, 2014); Emily Steel, "Ice Bucket Challenge Has Raised Millions for ALS Association," *The New york Times* (August 18, 2014); Mary E. Williams, "The Ice Bucket Challenge's Stem Cell Controversy," *Salon* (August 20, 2014); and Justin Worland, "Here's What's Happening with the Ice Bucket Challenge Money," *Time* (November 4, 2014).

From the Top

An Interview with Mike Paul

Mike Paul, the "Reputation Doctor," is a veteran of strategic public relations, corporate communications, and reputation management. He is president and senior counselor of MGP and Associates PR (MGP). MGP was founded by Paul in 1994 and is a leading boutique public relations and reputation management firm based in New York, providing senior counseling services to top corporate, government, nonprofit, sports, and entertainment clients. In 2012, Trust Across America named Mr. Paul one of the "Top 100 Thought Leaders in Trustworthy Behavior."

How important is an organization's or individual's reputation?

Reputations of all types are so important, I made it our firm's tag line: "Because Your Reputation Is Everything!"™ A reputation is the greatest asset we have, for both a public company and an individual. It must be built, maintained, and repaired to thrive for a lifetime. Sadly, many corporations, organizations, and individuals talk the talk of the importance of reputation, but don't walk the walk.

How can reputation be managed?

The big "bricks" of managing an excellent reputation include truth, humility, transparency, accountability, consistency. Honesty and humility are the most important tools in a reputation management tool belt. Like any disease, a reputation in crisis is a disease that can be cured or can grow out of control and cause severe damage in other areas. Admitting mistakes, lies, and deceit is the first step in reputation management.

What is the state of community relations among organizations today?

Community relations among U.S. organizations are becoming much better, but there is still much work to be done and further commitment and accountability from senior management is necessary to achieve excellence. For example, many community organizations are not teaming up with similar organizations in their arena to achieve community goals. Many are islands among themselves and believe partnering with other community organizations is not part of their mission. One goal of any community relations campaign should be to mirror the population in which you serve.

What is the state of social responsibility among corporations?

Corporate social responsibility has become a key communications and business tool for most corporations today. However, corporations must realize social responsibility has both a community responsibility and a business obligation. For example, a successful social responsibility campaign—local, national, or global—cannot be just a pet project of a CEO or senior management. It must include social and community responsibility interests important to many key audiences, including employees, investors, customers, and the communities in which the corporation operates.

How important is it for an organization to focus on dealing with minorities?

Minorities have become the majority in many communities across the United States and around the world. As a result, minority is not an accurate word to use any more for communities or people of color. People, employees, or executives of color are now the appropriate terms to use because of the huge demographic shift in the world. As a result, corporate America and other organizations have begun to truly embrace diversity, but there is much more work to be done. However, the executive ranks are still void of many people of color, and sadly, racism is still alive in many corporations, organizations, and communities in the United States and around the world.

What is the state of African Americans in the public relations business?

Two words: in crisis. There are still few African Americans in public relations overall and even fewer executives of color in leadership positions. Most work for community organizations and in government. There has still not been an African

American CEO within any of the top 10 global PR firms and very few top global corporate communications executives. Until the CEOs of PR firms and corporate America embrace the problem with the same intensity from both the bottom and the top levels, diversity in PR will continue to be in crisis. Accountability and transparency are both necessary to develop lasting change.

What advice would you give young minority members interested in a public relations career?
First, for young people of color, there are not many executives of color in our business. As a result, seeking a career in our business is a tougher road. The numbers don't

lie. Second, seek employment at a top global PR firm to best learn the business and work in as many different divisions as possible. The training programs at these firms are superior to others, and the type of clients you will work with are top notch and best for building skills and an excellent resume. Third, seek out an excellent mentor, and the mentor does not have to be an executive of color. For example, I have the best mentor in our business, Harold Burson of Burson-Marsteller. He gave me excellent advice years ago when I was at B-M, and he still gives me excellent advice today. Many young professionals of color make the mistake of only seeking executives of color. This is a big mistake.

Public Relations Bookshelf

Beal, Brent D. *Corporate Social Responsibility: Definition, Core Issues and Recent Developments*. Los Angeles, CA: Sage Publications, Inc., 2014. University management professor offers a well-researched and comprehensive review of CSR, what it is and how it works.

Benn, Suzanne and Dianne Bolton. *Key Concepts in Corporate Social Responsibility*. Thousand Oaks, CA: Sage Publications, 2011. Strong discussion on sustainability and environmental programs.

Coombs, W. Timothy and Sherry J. Holladay. *Managing Corporate Responsibility: A Communication Approach*. Malden, MA: Wiley-Blackwell, 2012. Excellent examples of companies practicing effective CSR, from Home Depot to Nike.

Crane, Andrew, Dirk Matten, and Laura J. Spence. *Corporate Social Responsibility: Readings and Cases in a Global Context*. 2nd ed. New York, NY: Routledge, 2014. Scholarly analysis of CSR.

Derickson, Rossella and Krista Henley. *Awakening Social Responsibility*. Silicon Valley, CA: Derickson and Henley, 2007. This text calls for individuals to lead their companies down the path of sustainable development, business ethics, philanthropy, and giving.

Harrison, Bruce E. *Corporate Greening 2.0: Create and Communicate Your Company's Climate Change and Sustainability Strategies*. Exeter, NH: Publishing Works, 2008. The most knowledgeable person in public

relations about climate change analyzes the positions on the environment of 40 companies and business groups.

McElhaney, Kellie A. *Just Good Business*. San Francisco, CA: Berret-Koehler Publishers, 2008. Step-by-step approach in implementing CSR.

Tench, Ralph and Liz Yeomans. *Exploring Public Relations*. Essex, England: Pearson Education, 2006. A general public relations text, written by British authors, with a strong section on community and society, as well as corporate social responsibility.

Visser, Wayne, Dirk Matten, Manfred Pohl, and Nick Tolhurst. *The A to Z of Corporate Social Responsibility*. Chichester, England: John Wiley & Sons, 2007. Literally soup to nuts in organizing for corporate social responsibility.

Werther, William B., Jr. and David Chandler. *Strategic Corporate Responsibility*. 2nd ed. Thousand Oaks, CA: Sage Publications, 2011. Good primer on the various elements of corporate social responsibility.

Zandvliet, Luc and Mary B. Anderson. *Getting It Right: Making Corporate-Community Relations Work*. Sheffield, England: Greenleaf Publishing Ltd., 2009. Exhaustive analysis of international community relations programs.

Endnotes

1. Kevin Allen, "Hallmark Changes Christmas Carol's Lyrics to Remove the Word 'Gay,'" *Ragan PR Daily* (October 31, 2013).
2. James B. Stewart, "Exxon Lumbers Along to Catch Up to Gay Rights," *The New York Times* (July 1, 2015).
3. Nick Gass, "Judge Rules Against Redskins Trademark," *Politico* (July 8, 2015).
4. D'Vera Cohen, "Are Minority Births the Majority Yet?" *Pew Research Center "FactTank"* (June 4, 2014).
5. Josh Sanbum, "U.S. Steps Closer to a Future Where Minorities Are the Majority," *Time* (June 25, 2015).
6. "Hispanics or Latino Populations," *U.S. Centers for Disease Control and Prevention* (May 5, 2015).
7. "Black or African American Populations," *U.S. Centers for Disease Control and Prevention* (June 8, 2015).
8. "Multiracial in America," *Pew Research Center "Social and Demographic Trends"* (June 11, 2015).
9. D'Vera Cohen, op. cit.
10. Allie Bidwell, "Women More Likely to Graduate College But Still Earn Less Than Men," *US News & World Report* (October 31, 2014).
11. Diane Cardwell, "Charitable Giving Rises Past Prerecession Mark," *The New York Times* (June 16, 2015).
12. "10 More Billionaires Join Buffet-Gates Giving Pledge," *CNN Money* (June 3, 2015).
13. Llona Bray, "Corporate Giving Gets More Issue-Focused," *Nolo.com* (November 11, 2011).
14. Dan Kadlec, "Charitable Giving: How Companies Are Doing More with Less," *Time* (June 5, 2012).
15. "CEO Forum: Environmental Impact," *NYSE Magazine* (January/February 2006): 13.
16. David Allen, "How Business-Friendly Is Your State?" *Tax Foundation "The Daily Signal"* (November 14, 2014).
17. Scott Cohn, "Texas Is America's Top State for Business 2012," *CNBC.com* (July 10, 2012).
18. Karen Zeigler and Steven A. Camarota, "U.S. Immigrant Population Record 41.3 Million in 2013," *Center for Immigration Studies* (September 2014).
19. "BLS Reports," *US Bureau of Labor Statistics*, Report 1052 (December 2014).
20. Jena McGregor, "More than 100 Women in Congress for the First Time, but Not Much Growth," *The Washington Post* (November 5, 2014).
21. Tom Martin, "A Few Good Men," *PR Week* (July 21, 2008).

22. Bey-Ling Sha, "PR Gender Gap Research Under Fire," *CommPRO .biz* (May 20, 2011).

23. Jeffrey S. Passel, "How Many Hispanics in the U.S.?" *Pew Hispanic Center* (March 15, 2011).

24. Doris Nhan, "Buying Power of Hispanics Worth $1 Trillion, Report Says," *National Journal* (May 8, 2011).

25. Joel Staley, "8 Things PR Pros Should Know About the U.S. Hispanic Audience," *Ragan PR Daily* (April 15, 2013).

26. Katerina E. Matsa, "Hispanic Media: Fact Sheet," *Pew Research Center* (April 29, 2015).

27. Fredrick Kunkle, "Black Immigration Is Remaking Black Population, Report Says," *The Washington Post* (April 9, 2015).

28. "Ten Major Cities with the Largest Black Populations," *MadameNoir.com* (September 24, 2011).

29. Jeffrey M. Humphreys, "Black Buying Power Continues to Rise," *ReachingBlackConsumers.com* (2012).

30. Monica Anderson, "6 Key Findings About Black Immigration to the U.S.," *Pew Research Center "FactTank"* (April 9, 2015).

31. Richard Prince, "Ebony and Jet Increase Circulations," *TheRoot.com* (August 14, 2011).

32. Anna Brown, "U.S. Hispanic and Asian Populations Growing but for Different Reasons," *Pew Research Center "FactTank"* (June 26, 2014).

33. "The Rise of Asian Americans," *Pew Research Center "Social and Demographic Trends"* (April 4, 2013).

34. Carol Kuruvilla, "Americans Think the Country's Muslim Population Is Much Bigger than It Really Is" *Huffington Post* (November 2, 2014).

35. Julia Hahn, "Immigration to Swell U.S. Muslim Population to 6.2 Million," *Breitbart.com* (July 16, 2015).

36. Robert Spencer, "U.S. Muslim Cable TV Channel Aims to Build Bridges," *Jihad Watch* (November 28, 2004).

37. Blanca Villagrana, "Understanding the Multi-Billion LGBT Market," *Florida State University Center for Hispanic Marketing Communication* (April 20, 2015).

38. Claudia Eller, "Building an Empire of Gay Media," *Los Angeles Times* (June 29, 2008): C2.

39. Nicole Lewis, "Multiple Missions and a Thousand Ideas," *Chronicle of Philanthropy* (December 8, 2005): 37.

40. Lydia O'Connor, "Bill Maher Calls College Student 'A Little Sh*t' for Criticizing Jerry Seinfeld," *Huffington Post* (June 20, 2015).

Chapter 14

International Consumer Relations

Chapter Objectives

1. To examine the important public of "consumers," both in the United States and around the world.
2. To explain the nuances of consumer relations; dealing persuasively with customers and prospects to build an agreeable consumer experience.
3. To discuss the growth of the "consumer movement" in America and around the world.
4. To discuss the differences in media and management between international organizations and those in the United States.

It used to be in a public relations text like this, you could talk about "consumer relations" in the context of the United States.

No longer.

In the second half of the first decade of the 21st century, this is one big integrated world, connected by social media and the Net, with companies operating around the globe. And companies—even the largest and most powerful—must be sensitive to the customs and culture and feelings of their host countries.

Consider the greatest consumer company of them all, Apple of Cupertino, California, and its relations in one of its most important and growing markets, China (**Figure 14-1**). In the second quarter of 2015 alone, Apple made $13 billion in China, with iPhone sales rising 87%.[1] But two years earlier, Apple's future in its most important emerging market was clouded by a public relations crisis that demanded quick action to salvage the local franchise. Complicating the Apple response was the fact that such a crisis could never happen in the United States but only in a country like China, where the state controlled the media.

Specifically, China's powerful national broadcaster, China Central Television and The People's Daily—the official mouthpiece of the Chinese Communist Party—accused Apple of skirting warranty periods, adopting customer-service policies that discriminated against Chinese customers and formulating an inadequate and arrogant response to the reports. The

291

government-controlled media claimed that Apple refused to provide customers with new iPhones if they brought in damaged or defective phones, unlike in other countries. They also said Apple didn't give consumers a new one-year warranty after their Phone was fixed.

After two weeks of constant media pounding, Apple CEO Tim Cook took the rare step of writing a personal letter—written in Chinese and posted to Apple's Chinese Web site—apologizing for the customer service policies and promising to revamp them.

Wrote Mr. Cook, *"We are aware that a lack of communications . . . led to the perception that Apple is arrogant and doesn't care or attach enough importance to consumer feedback. We express our sincere apologies for any concerns or misunderstandings this gave consumers."*[2]

China's state-run media similarly went after Germany's Volkswagen, America's Yum Brands, and similar multinationals, letting one and all understand that consumer relations in China needed to be scrupulously tailored and carefully conducted.

Thanks largely to e-commerce, the world has continued to evolve into a society of consumers, with increased consumption propelling economies in good times and declining consumption perplexing economies in bad times. Global companies, then, must be sensitive to local surroundings, where *"thinking global and acting local"* is more than a business cliché.

Dealing with consumers around the world—often in conjunction with product and marketing professionals—is another front-line responsibility of public relations. At the core of international consumer relations lies an attitude of delivering dependable products in a manner that is service-oriented and ethical. As in all areas of public relations, the aim is to offer products and brands that are stellar not only in quality but also in reputation.

① Worldwide Consumer Class

The world is awash with consumers.

By one calculation, there are now more than 1.7 billion members of "the consumer class"—nearly half of them in the developing world. A lifestyle and culture that became common in Europe, North America, Japan, and a few other pockets of the world in the 20th century has gone global in the 21st. Worldwide, private consumption expenditures—the amount spent on goods and services at the household level—topped $20 trillion in 2000, a four-fold increase over 1960 (in 1995 dollars).[3]

What is the "consumer class?" It's the group of people characterized by diets of highly processed food, the desire for bigger houses and more and bigger cars, higher levels of debt, and lifestyles devoted to the accumulation of nonessential goods. Rising consumption has helped meet basic needs and create jobs around the world. Consumer spending also lies at the heart of a nation's gross domestic product. And, therefore, its economic well-being. Today, nearly half of global consumers reside in developing countries, where the wealthiest 20% of the world accounts for more than three-quarters of world consumption.

FIGURE 14-2
Open the gates.
Countries like Spain, with attractions like Madrid's Royal Palace, or Palacio Real if you prefer, took advantage of the world's burgeoning tourist trade and problems in nearby nations like Greece, to entice global consumers.
Photo: Courtesy of S. Drewes

The global market for consumption keeps increasing. Driving this charge to consumer is tourist spending around the world. Revenue from international tourism reached a mind-boggling record of $1.5 trillion in 2014.[4] Even as the world suffers currency fluctuations, persistent economic weakness in Europe and external forces, such as terrorism, civil strife in the Middle East, the Crimean crisis in the Ukraine and globally pervasive economic inequality between the have's and have not's, tourism, and with it, consumption, flourish. When tourists fear the impact of a debt crisis in Greece, they merely move to Italy or Spain, where economic uncertainty is not quite as great **(Figure 14-2)**.

The spread of consumerism has placed fresh pressures on multinational companies to act ethically, in the best interests of their global customers. Globalization and the spread of social media and the Internet mandate that such companies walk a fine line between behaving "responsibly" and promoting their products. Often it is public relations techniques and societal sensitivities that help distinguish a company and its products from the competition. For example:

■ The Walt Disney company, addressing the concerns of parents over child nutrition, decided to curtail the use of its name and popular characters such as Buzz Lightyear and Lightning McQueen with food items that didn't meet acceptable nutritional standards. The new guidelines affected Disney licensing agreements with a variety of snacks and foods that were too rich in sugar, calories, and fat.[5]

■ The Mattel Company battled ferociously to protect the reputation of its toys. A lead paint scandal emanating from China, where many of the company's toys were made, caused Mattel to revamp safety measures at Chinese manufacturing plants and caused the firm's CEO to film an online video apology to parents.[6]

- Burger King, the world's second largest hamburger chain, announced it would begin buying eggs and pork only from suppliers that did not confine their animals in cages and crates. The decision was hailed by animal rights activists as a "historic advance."[7]

- Meanwhile, the world's largest burger chain, McDonald's, and KFC found themselves fighting for their international reputations, when local Chinese suppliers were exposed as processing expired meat.[8]

Such were the socially responsible public relations initiatives and complications that companies faced in confronting worldwide consumer relations in the 21st century.

In an era overwrought with advertising "noise"—tens of thousands of blaring messages beamed in the direction of a single consumer—public relations solutions can help cut through the clutter and distinguish one company from the next, enhancing the sale of a firm's products. This chapter examines how public relations helps attract, win, and keep consumers, often dealing in a worldwide perspective.

2 Consumer Relations Objectives

Building sales is the primary consumer relations objective. A satisfied customer may return; an unhappy customer may not. Here are some typical goals:

- **Keeping old customers.** Most sales are made to established customers. Consumer relations efforts should be made to keep these customers happy.

- **Attracting new customers.** Every business must work constantly to develop new customers. In many industries, the prices and quality of competing products are similar. In choosing among brands, customers may base decisions on how they have been treated.

- **Marketing new items or services.** Customer relations techniques can influence the sale of new products. When GE's research revealed that consumers wanted personalized service and more information on new products, it established the GE Answer Center, a national toll-free, 24-hour service that informs consumers about new GE products and services. Building such company and product loyalty lies at the heart of a solid consumer relations effort.

- **Expediting complaint handling.** Few companies are free of complaints. Customers protest when appliances don't work, errors are made in billing, or deliveries aren't made on time. Many large firms have established response procedures, often outsourcing call centers to places like Lakeland, Florida; Johnson City, Tennessee; or Bangalore, India.

- **Reducing costs.** For three decades, the Sym's clothing company used to advertise that "An educated customer is our best customer." Indeed, to most companies, an educated consumer is, indeed, the best consumer.

Consumer-Generated Media

For decades, publicity to consumers about products and services revolved around the mass media. While the traditional media are still important avenues through which to promote organizational offerings, the new lead voice in town is social media. It has given consumers a voice, a publishing platform, and a forum where their collective voices on products and services can be heard, shared, and researched.

Consumer-generated media (CGM) encompasses the millions of consumer-generated comments, opinions, and personal experiences posted in publicly available online sources on a wide range of issues, topics, products, and brands. CGM is also referred to as "online consumer word-of-mouth," originated from a variety of sources:

- social/review sites
- blogs
- message boards and forums
- public discussions (Usenet newsgroups)
- discussions and forums on large e-mail portals (Yahoo!, AOL, MSN)
- online opinion/review sites and services
- online feedback/complaint sites

As the use of social media increases, so, too, does the amount of CGM about particular companies. In addition to social sites like Facebook and Twitter, review sites like Angie's List, TripAdvisor, and Yelp, all are used by consumers to learn about products and services. The challenge, then, for marketers is to align CGM with one's consumer objectives. Such techniques as engaging in dialogue with consumers via social media, encouraging consumers to talk about brand experiences, while analyzing what people are saying and acting on their comments, all make sense in optimizing consumer-generated content.[9]

The point is that consumers seem to place trust in their fellow consumers. For any marketer trying to be heard or to break through the clutter, understanding and managing CGM may be critical.

Handling Consumer Complaints

Research indicates that only a handful of dissatisfied customers—4%—will ever complain. But that means that there are many others with the same complaint who never say anything. And the vast majority of dissatisfied customers won't repurchase from the offending company.

In the old days, a frequent response to complaint letters was to dust off the so-called *bedbug letter*—a term that stemmed from occasional letters to the railroads complaining about bedbugs in the sleeper cars. To save time, railroad consumer relations personnel simply dispatched a prewritten bedbug letter in response. Today, with the volume of mail, e-mail, and faxes at a mountainous level, 21st century versions of the bedbug letter still appear from time to time. Really good companies, however, understand the benefit of applying the "personal touch" to rectify consumer problems **(Figure 14-3)**.

Today, the risk of consumer complaints going viral is always present. Airlines seem to suffer more than others, with Twitter becoming the go-to source for instantaneous complaints about everything from cancellations to lost luggage. Retail chains are also frequent targets for consumer approbation. In 2014, for example, Urban Outfitters— no stranger to controversy—was excoriated on social media for a $129 "vintage Kent State" sweatshirt, appearing to be blood-spattered, evoking a 1970 campus shooting, where students were killed. After an immediate outcry about the bad taste marketing, the retailer removed the shirt from its offerings.[10] On the other hand, retailers like Target have demonstrated how responding to consumer criticism can be used as an impetus for positive innovation. (See *A Question of Ethics* in this chapter.)

FIGURE 14-3
Personal touch.
There's a reason Four
Seasons hotel chain
is always ranked at
the top of customer
service lists; it takes
pains to deal properly
with clients.
*Photo: Courtesy Fraser
Seitel*

Dear Mr. Seitel,

I'm writing to apologize for the e-mail sent to you on April 13, 2012, which incorrectly identified you as "Mr. Mamela."

The error occurred during the programming of the salutation and resulted in the e-mail being addressed to a Four Seasons employee (the recipient for purposes of testing), instead of you, the intended recipient. This technical oversight is not representative of the standard we have set for ourselves in creating customized experiences and communications for our guests. We have put measures in place to ensure that it does not happen again.

At Four Seasons, we take guest privacy very seriously. Please rest assured that your personal data has not been compromised in any way and your Four Seasons guest profile remains secure.

I apologize for any inconvenience or concern this may have caused you.

Sincerely,
Susan Helstab
Executive Vice President, Marketing
Four Seasons Hotels and Resorts

To respond quickly to complaints, companies established ombudsperson offices. The term *ombudsman* originally described a government official—in Sweden and New Zealand, for example—appointed to investigate complaints about abuses committed by public officials. Today, more often than not, the ombudsperson function is outsourced to a central (often overseas) location that customers can call to seek redress of grievances.

Typically, call center personnel monitor the difficulties customers are having with products. Often they can anticipate product or performance deficiencies. Corporate complaint handlers are in business to inspire customer confidence and to influence an organization's behavior toward improved service.

The companies that express such understanding and courtesy will be the ones that keep the business.

③ The Consumer Movement

Although consumerism is considered to be a late 20th century concept, legislation to protect consumers first emerged in the United States in 1872, when Congress enacted the Criminal Fraud Statute to protect consumers against corporate abuses. In 1887, Congress established the Interstate Commerce Commission to curb freewheeling railroad tycoons.

However, the first real consumer movement came right after the turn of the century when journalistic muckrakers encouraged legislation to protect the consumer. Upton Sinclair's novel *The Jungle* revealed scandalous conditions in the meatpacking industry and helped usher in federal meat inspection standards as Congress passed the Food and Drug Act and the Trade Commission Act. In the second wave of the movement, from 1927 to 1938, consumers were safeguarded from the abuses of manufacturers,

A Question of Ethics

Targeting Plus-Sized Critics

Every organization has critics—especially with social media. But it's the rare company that engages with its critics respectfully, even leading to product innovation.

Behold, Target Corporation, the American discount retailer second only to Walmart.

In 2014, Target was roundly chastised on social media for its new Altuzarra line, which went only up to size 16. One retail blogger called for a boycott, claiming, *"Year after year, season after season, you put out these gorgeous designer collections and you almost never include a plus range. Every time each of these collections is about to be released, it feels like a slap in the face."* The media quickly followed by taking the company to task for "ignoring plus sizes."

A year later, Target had learned from its run-in with the critics.

Not only did the retailer announce its new Ava & Viv plus-sized collection, but it chose several of the critical bloggers to serve as models for the new line. **(Figure 14-4)** After visiting Target's Minneapolis headquarters, one former critic-turned model blogged, *"I was able to see firsthand how hard the team is working and how much they truly care about their plus size customer. They hear the feedback of the community and are really putting in effort to making the changes necessary to get it right."*

By recruiting its critics to help with its new line, Target proved more adept than most retailers in turning the proverbial lemons to lemonade. As another former critic blogged about the new line, *"It's really wonderful as a consumer to know a brand is listening."**

Questions

1. Did Target make a mistake in limiting the Altuzarra line only to size 16?

2. How would you assess its response to its critics? What other options did it have?

FIGURE 14-4   Shaping up.
Responding to its critics, Target introduced a plus-size collection, which drew praise as well as sales.
Photo: Handout/MCT/Newscom

*For further information, see Mary E. Williams, "Target Uses Its Plus-Sized Critics to Launch a New Line," *Salon* (January 15, 2015).

advertisers, and retailers of well-known brands of commercial products. During this time, Congress passed the Food, Drug, and Cosmetic Act.

Later, the movement was boosted by the activities of a lone consumer crusader, Ralph Nader, who brought the world's most powerful auto company, General Motors, to its knees. Nader's thin 1965 book, *Unsafe at Any Speed,* pointed out how the GM Corvair was literally a "death trap." After trying to stop Nader at every turn—including assigning private detectives to trail his every move—GM relented and stopped production of the Corvair. Consumerism had won its most significant battle.

By the early 1960s, the movement had become stronger and more unified. President John F. Kennedy, in fact, proposed that consumers have their own bill of rights, containing four basic principles:

1. **The right to safety:** to be protected against the marketing of goods hazardous to health or life.

2. **The right to be informed:** to be protected against fraudulent, deceitful, or grossly misleading information, advertising, labeling, or other practices and to be given the facts needed to make an informed choice.

3. **The right to choose:** to be assured access, whenever possible, to a variety of products and services at competitive prices.

4. **The right to be heard:** to be assured that consumer interests will receive full and sympathetic consideration in the formulation of government policy.

Subsequent U.S. presidents have continued to emphasize consumer rights and protection. Labeling, packaging, product safety, and a variety of other issues continue to concern government overseers of consumer interests. Indeed, the federal consumer-protection bureaucracy extends through multiple agencies, which protect everything from trade and product performance to stock holder rights and financial disclosure. The most recent such agency was the Consumer Financial Protection Bureau, created in the wake of Wall Street scandals in 2011 "to promote fairness and transparency for mortgages, credit cards and other consumer financial products and services."

Just as the practice of philanthropy has begun to migrate from the United States to an international phenomenon, so, too, is the practice of consumer activism reaching overseas. For example, in the United States, antismoking laws and policies have been widely adopted. Indeed, in 2015, CVS Health Corporation resigned from the U.S. Chamber of Commerce after revelations that the chamber and its foreign affiliates were undertaking a global lobbying campaign against antismoking laws.[11] The Chamber was reacting to the dramatic increase in antismoking activism in countries from China to Great Britain.

④ Operating Around the Globe

The actions of individuals and organizations in one part of the world are felt instantly and irrevocably by people around the globe. As a consequence, multinational corporations, in particular, must be sensitive to how their actions might affect people of different cultures in different geographies.

Companies, in fact, have become the most prominent standard bearers of their countries. American companies, with seven of the 10 most powerful brands in the world (plus Samsung, Toyota, and Mercedes-Benz) and 14 of the top 20 are the most prominent of the prominent **(Figure 14-5)**.

Consider the challenges multinational companies face.

■ In 2012, both McDonald's and Coca-Cola, two core sponsors of the London Summer Olympics, drew criticism from local politicians and nongovernmental organizations for offering products that promote obesity. That same year, McDonald's, Burger King, and KFC were subject to a new law in Chile, barring them from offering toys with children's meals. Like the Brits, Chilean officials worried about their increasingly chubby children.[12]

Rank	Previous Rank	Brand	Country	Sector
1	1	Apple	United States	Technology
2	2	Google	United States	Technology
3	3	Coca-Cola	United States	Beverages
4	4	IBM	United States	Business Services
5	5	Microsoft	United States	Technology
6	6	GE	United States	Diversified
7	8	Samsung	Korea	Technology
8	10	Toyota	Japan	Automotive
9	7	McDonalds	United States	Restaurants
10	11	Mercedes-Benz	Germany	Automotive
11	12	BMW	Germany	Automotive
12	9	Intel	United States	Technology
13	14	Disney	United States	Media
14	13	Cisco	United States	Technology
15	19	Amazon	United States	Retail
16	18	Oracle	United States	Technology
17	15	HP	United States	Technology
18	16	Gillette	United States	FMCG
19	17	Louis Vuitton	France	Luxury
20	20	Honda	Japan	Automotive

FIGURE 14-5
Global brand leaders.
Each year, Interbrands determines the top 100 most valuable brands ranked on financial performance, the role the brand plays in influencing customer choice and the strength of the brand to command a premium price and earnings.
Photo: Courtesy of Interbrand

- Also in 2012, the mighty Apple company found itself embroiled in a scandal involving working conditions at the Chinese plants manufacturing its iPads and iPhones. One iPad factory in Foxconn, near the booming southern city of Shenzhen, experienced a spate of 13 suicides or attempted suicides. Amid increased criticism, Apple called in assessors from the same organization that was set up to stamp out sweatshops in China's clothing industry a decade earlier.[13]

- In 2015, the European Union's (EU) Executive Commission, the anti-competitive watchdog which earlier had gone after companies like Microsoft and Google, launched an anti-trust case against six major U.S. movie studios, including Disney and Warner Brothers, contending the companies didn't make their services available equally throughout the EU.[14]

All foreign companies operating internationally must constantly reinforce the notion that they are responsible and concerned residents of local communities. Most resort to the public relations philosophy of leading with proper action and then communicating it. KFC, for example, has 158 franchises in Indonesia, most of which are locally owned and operated. McDonald's has a poster in the window of the Jakarta McDonald's that reads:

> *In the name of Allah, the merciful and the gracious, McDonald's Indonesia is owned by an indigenous Muslim Indonesian.*

Smart multinationals also support local causes and incorporate international audiences and celebrities in their philanthropic efforts. Stated another way, the most well-known companies and best brands in the world observe the mantra of *"thinking global, acting local"* to win lasting friendship and support in other countries.

Consumer Internet Activists

In the 21st century, with the Internet as stimulus, organic consumer movements—directed at individual companies, industries, or even multinational agencies such as the World Trade Organization—have spread like wildfire around the globe. As one harassed executive put it, "In the old days, if you had an unlisted number, it was hard to find you. Now you do a Google search and find out the most intimate details."[15]

Such was the case in 2011 when the Occupy Wall Street movement rallied its troops with ongoing social media contact about rallies and protests, not to mention marches to the Manhattan homes of several Wall Street big shots, including JP Morgan CEO Jamie Dimon, News Corp. CEO Rupert Murdoch, and several hedge fund billionaires, all addresses compliments of Internet search. The Net also served as a unifying catalyst in the drive to raise the minimum wage for fast-food workers that swept through the United States in 2015, resulting in a more than doubling of hourly wages for workers from New York to California.

Likewise, although private testing organizations that evaluate products and inform consumers about potential dangers have proliferated, the most significant activity to keep companies honest has occurred on the Internet.

Perhaps the best-known testing group, Consumers Union, was formed in 1936 to test products across a wide spectrum of industries. It publishes the results in a monthly magazine, *Consumer Reports*, which reaches about 3.5 million readers. Often an evaluation in *Consumer Reports*, either pro or con, greatly affects how customers view particular products. Another consumer watchdog, the Consumer Federation of America was formed in 1968 to unify lobbying efforts for pro-consumer legislation. Today the federation consists of 200 national, state, and local consumer groups, labor unions, electric cooperatives, and other organizations with consumer interests.

A great deal of digital consumer activism deals with helping consumers make better decisions and more quickly resolve problems. Recommendations for travel, lodging, and eating through such Net firms as TripAdvisor, Yelp, Angie's List, eBay, Craigslist, Airbnb, and others have helped educate millions of consumers.

Perhaps, the most striking recent example of Internet activism has stemmed not from consumers but from political activists, particularly in the Middle East from Tunisia to Libya to Egypt to Syria, who raged against established dictatorships and in some cases, brought them down.

Although companies often find activists' criticism annoying, the emergence of the consumer watchdog movement has generally been a positive development for

FYI

Think Multilingual—or Else

Steve Rivkin is America's foremost "nameologist," having written extensively on what organizations and products must consider before they choose a name **(Figure 14-6)**. When it comes to organizations dealing overseas, the nameologist warns, you'd better think multilingual—or else.

Or else what? Or else this:

- A food company named its giant burrito a *Burrada*. Big mistake. The colloquial meaning of that word in Spanish is "big mistake."

- Estée Lauder was set to export its Country Mist makeup when German managers pointed out that *mist* is German slang for, uh, well, to put it gently, "manure." (The name became Country Moist in Germany.)

- Colgate introduced a toothpaste in France called Cue, the name of a notorious French porno magazine.

- The name Coca-Cola in China was first rendered as *ke-kou-ke-la*. Unfortunately, Coke did not discover until after thousands of signs had been printed that the phrase means "bite the wax tadpole." Coke then researched 40,000 Chinese characters and found a close phonetic equivalent, *ko-kou-ko-le*, which loosely translates as "happiness in the mouth." Much better.

FIGURE 14-6 **Namemeister extraordinaire.**
Steve Rivkin.
Photo: Courtesy of Rivkin & Associates.

- A leading brand of car de-icer in Finland will never make it to America. The brand's name: *Super Piss*.

- Ditto for Japan's leading brand of coffee creamer. Its name: *Creap*.

---

consumers. What started with one man's campaign against unsafe autos a half century ago has today morphed into a global movement that forces organizations to consider, even more than usual, the downside of the products and services they offer. Smart companies have come to take seriously the pronouncements of consumer activists.

Business Gets the Message

Obviously, few organizations can afford to shirk their responsibilities to consumers. Consumer relations divisions have sprung up, either as separate entities or as part of public relations departments.

In many companies, consumer relations began strictly as a way to handle complaints, an area to which all unanswerable queries were sent. Such units have frequently provided an alert to management. More recently, companies have broadened the consumer relations function to encompass such activities as developing guidelines to evaluate services and products for management, developing consumer programs that meet consumer needs and increase sales, developing field-training programs, evaluating

FYI

Straighten Out Your English—or Else

On the other hand, it might be equally beneficial for our friends in foreign lands to make sure of their own English.

Consider these actual signs posted in various establishments around the world.

- In a Copenhagen airline ticket office: "We take your bags and send them in all directions."

- In a Norwegian cocktail lounge: "Ladies are requested not to have children in the bar."

- At a Budapest zoo: "Please do not feed the animals. If you have any suitable food, give it to the guard on duty."

- In a doctor's office in Italy: "Specialist in women and other diseases."

- In a Paris hotel elevator: "Please leave your values at the front desk."

- From the brochure of a Tokyo car rental firm: "When passenger of foot heave in sight, tootle the horn. Trumpet him melodiously at first, but if he still obstacles your passage then tootle him with vigor."

- In an advertisement by a Hong Kong dentist: "Teeth extracted by the latest Methodists."

- In an Acapulco hotel: "The manager has personally passed all the water served here."

- In a Bucharest hotel lobby: "The lift is being fixed for the next day. During that time we regret that you will be unbearable."

service approaches, and evaluating company effectiveness in demonstrating concern for customers.

The investment in consumer service apparently pays off. Marketers of consumer products say that most customer criticism can be mollified with a prompt, personalized reply. Throw in a couple of free samples and consumers feel even better. In any case, consumers are impressed when a company takes the time to drop them a line for whatever reason.

On the other hand, failing to answer a question, satisfy a complaint, or solve a problem can result in a blitz of bad word-of-mouth advertising.

In adopting a more activist consumerist philosophy, firms have found that consumer relations need not take a defensive posture. Consumer relations professionals must themselves be activists to make certain that consumers understand the benefits and realities of using their products.

The consumer philosophy of JetBlue Airways, embodied in the company's "Customer Bill of Rights," is typical of the more enlightened attitude of most companies today.[16]

JetBlue issued its Customer Bill of Rights in 2007, a week after a disastrous Valentine's Day ice storm stranded thousands of customers and saddled the formerly beloved airline with oppressive national opprobrium. Said embattled CEO David Neeleman (who was replaced shortly thereafter), *"We had a weakness in our system. We were completely overwhelmed. I don't blame our customers for being upset with this. This was a big wakeup call for JetBlue"* (**Figure 14-7**).

No question that in the second decade of the 21st century, business understood that with heightened competition, scarcer resources, and more immediate and public ways to complain, the consumer most certainly was "king."

FIGURE 14-7
JetBlue mea culpa.
JetBlue published this apology in full-page newspaper ads and included the signed letter from its CEO on the JetBlue Web site, after a Valentine's Day ice storm grounded its fleet.
Photo: Courtesy of JetBlue

Last Word

Without consumers, there would be no multinational companies. Increased worldwide concerns about climate change, packaging and pollution, rising outrage about trans fats and second hand smoke, and numerous other causes indicate that the push for product safety and quality will likely increase in the years ahead.

Indeed, the smartest companies are those that tie their products and services to larger societal causes, thus establishing a link in the minds of consumers that represents "loftier" goals than merely making money.

That is not to say there is anything wrong with making money. Companies depend on their profits to exist. Without profitability, corporations can't pay people, provide products, or contribute to bettering society.

Safeguarding the relationship with consumers of products and services is fundamental to continuing to earn profits. That's why the efforts of public relations professionals, assigned to maintaining, sustaining, and enhancing a company's standing with its customers, is a core communications challenge in the 21st century.

Discussion Starters

1. Why is dealing with consumers so important for public relations?
2. What are typical consumer relations objectives?
3. What is the office of the ombudsperson?
4. What is consumer-generated marketing?
5. What key federal agencies are involved in consumerism?
6. What is the purpose of the Consumer Financial Protection Bureau?
7. What is a consumer bill of rights?
8. What is the impact of the Internet on a company's consumer relations?
9. Who is Ralph Nader, and what is his significance to consumerism?
10. What constitutes a quality international consumer-oriented company?

Pick of the Literature

Business as Usual

Brian Solis, Hoboken, NJ: John Wiley & Sons, Inc., 2012

A Silicon Valley-based, new media expert dissects the new ways that business reaches consumers.

His premise is that new communication networks—through social media, the mobile Web, gamification, and other Web-based technology—have created an ever-expanding "egosystem," such that each individual believes he or she deserves 24-hour customer service.

The author attempts to decipher the significance of all this socializing and egotism and draw lessons for business so that organizations might understand how to respond to this new breed of consumer.

Case Study   Hiding "Under the Dome"

China is a nation with 1.3 billion people, the vast majority of them consumers, a great many of them entrepreneurs, and a growing number of them investors in the stock market. Any visitor to the bustling cities of Beijing or Shanghai or Tianjin or Guangzhou can testify to the passion of the Chinese people for commerce and making money.

But as consumer-friendly and market-oriented as China may be, there is another, less attractive side of the Chinese economy; a government that at times represses dissent and restricts dialogue. It is this foreboding characteristic—the uncertainty of dealing with China's government—that concerns the expanding number of free market companies that do business in China as well as all of those around the world who invest in China securities.

Nowhere was this concern and uncertainty more on vivid display than in the spring of 2015, when a simple documentary film about the environment became an overnight sensation among China's citizens and the bane of the Chinese government.

The Government Giveth......

In March of 2015, a self-financed, 104-miunte documentary film about China's air pollution, *"Under the Dome,"* created by Chai Jing, a former China Central Television journalist, was released.

Chai Jing reportedly made the documentary when her as yet unborn daughter developed a tumor in the womb, which had to be removed soon after her birth. Ms. Chai blamed the tumor on China's stifling air pollution. Her film adopted its straightforward style—weaving graphs, statistics, vivid photographs, interviews, and personal emotion—from former U.S. Vice President Al Gore's award-winning *"An Inconvenient Truth."* Indeed, just as Gore had narrated his film, Ms. Chai, a slight woman in jeans and a white blouse, narrated *Under the Dome* from a dimly lit stage **(Figure 14-8)**.

The film was an immediate blockbuster, tugging at the emotional heartstrings of the Chinese people, especially on social media. It drew more than 110 million views within 24 hours and

150 million views on video portals like Youku and Tencent within the first days of its release.

Under the Dome's impact in the country was immediate, stirring up conversations about environmental protection on social media and doubling the sale of air purifiers in the days after the documentary's release. Foreign media throughout the world hailed the film as a breakthrough, not only for its impact on the citizenry but also for the reaction it stimulated in the Chinese government.

Despite the fact the film openly criticized the state-owned energy companies, steel producers, and coal factories and showed the inability of the Ministry of Environmental Protection to act against the big polluters, the government of China gave the documentary a "vote of confidence."

China's government-controlled People's Daily Web site and other outlets posted the film, along with an interview with Ms. Chai. The newly-appointed minister of environmental protection, Chen Jining, praised the video as China's *"Silent Spring"* moment, referring to the landmark 1962 U.S. book by environmentalist Rachel Carson. The minister declared, *"Chai Jing deserves our respect for drawing the public's attention to the environment from a unique public health perspective."*

The government's positive response to such a critical film was unprecedented. As it turned out, it was also short-lived.

......And the Government Taketh Away

Two days after praising *Under the Dome* and receiving worldwide publicity for its judgment, the Chinese government changed its mind.

In a chilling announcement that was leaked to the media, the Shanghai Propaganda Department issued these instructions: *"Media and web sites of all types and levels...must absolutely discontinue coverage of the documentary 'Under the Dome'*

and its creator." An employee of *China Business News* was suspended for leaking the order.

Complicating matters, at the same time it was lowering the boom on Ms. Chai, it was publicly declaring its new commitment to cleaning up the environment. Premier Li Keqiang told the National People's Congress, *"Environmental pollution is a blight on people's quality of life and a trouble that weighs on their hearts. We must fight it with all our might."*

A day after Li's declaration, the government ratcheted up its earlier order: *"Video websites are to delete 'Under the Dome.' Take care to control related commentary."* And a day after that, President Xi Jinping emphatically declared, *"We are going to punish, with an iron hand, any violators who destroy ecology or the environment, with no exceptions."*

Even while it tried to suppress Ms. Chai's film and control debate, the Chinese government reinforced its environmental concern. In short order, Chinese officials said they would cut coal consumption by 160 million tons over the next five years, while the vice mayor of Beijing said the capital would shut down 300 factories and take 200,000 heavily polluting vehicles off the roads by the end of 2015.

So even though *Under the Dome* might have been stopped dead in its tracks, the film's message was heard and being responded to not only by the Chinese government but more important, by the Chinese people.*

Questions

1. Why do you think the Chinese government immediately endorsed Chai Jing's film?

2. Why do you think the government reneged on its endorsement?

3. How would you assess the success or failure, in a public relations sense, of *Under the Dome?*

FIGURE 14-8
Powerful activist.
Although slight of stature, former journalist Chai Jing's riveting anti-pollution documentary film, *Under the Dome*, created a firestorm of controversy with the Chinese government in 2015.
Photo: Dai Tianfang Xinhua News Agency/Newscom

*For further information, see Daniel K. Gardner, "Why 'Under the Dome' Found a Ready Audience in China," *The New York Times* (March 18, 2015); and Didi Tang, "Environmental Issues Top Major Legislative Meeting in China," *Associated Press* (March 7, 2015).

From the Top

An Interview with Kathy Bloomgarden

Dr. Kathy Bloomgarden is CEO of Ruder Finn, one of the world's leading independent public relations agencies, serving more than 250 corporations and nonprofit organizations. With more than 25 years of experience in communications for multinational companies, Dr. Bloomgarden has developed particular skills in global communications consulting. She is a member of the Council on Foreign Relations and the Atlantic Council and author of *Trust: The Secret Weapon of Effective Business Leaders*.

What is the key to doing public relations work in international markets?

It is absolutely critical to distinguish between global PR—using channels and thought leadership that have the flexibility to be relevant to people worldwide—and execution of PR in local markets around the world—tailoring approaches to specific audiences. While some campaigns can be broad enough to have a universal impact, it is often necessary to adjust strategies for each country or region. For example, since countries have varying levels of Internet usage, the channels used to reach target audiences must be adjusted by market.

In particular, it is crucial to understand that different markets often have vastly different needs and cultural nuances. Today, the simplicity of disseminating messages instantly and globally through the Internet can easily camouflage the importance of language and culture needed to engage local audiences.

What is the largest difference between public relations work in the United States and overseas?

Some international markets, like those in Western Europe, are actually quite similar to the United States, especially with respect to the position of journalists, the ways people consume media, and levels of government involvement. For example, in both the United States and France, Germany, Italy, Spain, and the UK, consumers are likely to access media through their phones. However, the approach to PR content and messaging to the media in the United States is often more technical and in-depth than in other markets, like the UK, where journalists tend to prefer succinct messaging and colloquial language.

On the other hand, PR in emerging markets is distinct from the United States and can vary drastically between countries. For example, while Internet penetration is still spotty in India, China has the largest population of Internet users in the world. This allows PR campaigns to reach large audiences through these channels. Cultural differences also affect PR messaging and approach. In the West, for instance, differing opinions are usually valued, while in China, a higher premium is placed on consensuses. Taking this cultural dissimilarity into account can help PR practitioners ensure that they target the right influencers.

What is the most advanced international location for public relations?

If you think of PR in terms of traditional media relations, London is among the most advanced international locations because its media culture is probably the most established in the region and absolutely ingrained in popular culture. Germany is similar in rank and is important due to its economic role in Europe and geographic position at the heart of the continent. There is a high concentration of international journalists based in these locations—some international publications, such as *Al Hayat* and *Al-Arab*, have their global headquarters in London despite the fact that their distributions are concentrated in the Middle East.

Beijing is also very developed in certain PR specialty areas, such as Corporate Social Responsibility, the environment, mobile technology, and luxury.

What is the most common mistake that American firms make in international public relations?

Many American agencies use a one-size-fits-all approach, failing to take into account the scale and diversity of their target audiences, and, with budget constraints in mind, stick to regional planning without adequate local budgets for adaptation and execution. The "Europe-in-a-box" approach, for example, in which agencies run a continent-wide campaign from one location with a limited budget, almost never works. Pitching media in France and Spain from an office in London is not the same as securing coverage in Illinois and Ohio from a desk in New York!

What is the state of public relations in Europe?

It's very difficult to generalize when it comes to Europe. The continent has some very mature and developed PR markets such as the UK, Germany, and France, which are on a par with the United States, and the Nordic countries, which are similar, but have a more limited media environment. However, other countries, such as Poland and the Czech Republic, have a less developed PR industry, but are moving quickly and showing signs of progress.

What is the state of public relations in Latin America?

With increased focus on Brazil and other emerging economies in Latin America, there is a growing demand for public relations services in this region. This market is particularly dynamic due to the demographic differences and similarities across the region. For example, PR can benefit from the fact that, with the notable exception of Brazil, the vast majority of people in this region speak Spanish, but must also consider that drastic income and wealth disparity impacts how audiences can be reached. Age demographics, such as the fact that half of Mexico's population is under the age of 27, also influence the content and channels that are effective in particular areas.

What is the state of public relations in Asia generally?

Public relations in Asia varies tremendously by market, primarily due to differences in economic development and the extent of government involvement in the media. In countries that have a robust economy and low government control, like the Philippines, the practice of PR is more similar to developed markets like the United States and Western Europe. On the other hand, in countries where the government has more influence over the media, like Singapore, China, and Indonesia, public relations operates differently, as local contexts must be taken into account.

In particular, differing demographics play a large role in PR across the region. India, for example, is a relatively young market age-wise and the population speaks more than 22 languages.

What is the state of public relations in China?

China is a very dynamic and fast-growing market for public relations. We've seen the market dramatically evolve, from 15 years ago, when the government led all media, and 10 years ago, when business and commercial publications began to take over, to today, when social plays a critical role in influencing young audiences. Third party influencers are also a growing factor, as NGOs increase their presence.

Public relations in China has flourished, developing at an annual growth of around 30% over the past 10 years, according to the China International Public Relations Association.

With the boom of the PR industry there are also a lot of issues to deal with today in China. For instance, PR needs to be more clearly defined for the public if we don't want it to be known as buying ads or paying media. The PR industry needs to tackle these ethics issues and educate clients and the public about what behaving responsibly means for the industry.

Public Relations Bookshelf

Bloom, Robert H. and Dave Conti. *The Inside Advantage: The Strategy That Unlocks the Hidden Growth in Your Business.* New York: McGraw-Hill, 2007. The premise here is that in order to grow your consumer base, a firm must tap its "inner strength" by looking internally for that which differentiates you.

Burley, Ron. *Unscrewed.* Berkeley, CA: Ten Speed Press, 2006. A consumer's guide to getting what you pay for.

Carland, Maria P. and Candace Faber. *Careers in International Affairs.* 8th ed. Washington, DC: Georgetown University Press, 2008. Fine primer on what it takes to serve in international relations and how to secure employment.

Cone, Steve. *Powerlines: Words That Sell Brands, Grip Fans & Sometimes Change History.* New York: Bloomberg Press, 2008. These are the lines that moved marketing, according to the author, from "Only You Can Prevent Forest Fires" to "Virginia Is for Lovers."

Eisenberg, Bryan and Jeffrey Eisenberg. *Waiting for Your Cat to Bark?* Nashville, TN: Thomas Nelson Publishers, 2006. The Eisenberg brothers are best-selling authors who have made their living examining the communication gap between marketers and the buying public, and what marketers can do to redress the problem. They begin by declaring "mass marketing" deader than Saddam Hussein.

Epstein, Charlotte. *The Power of Words in International Relations.* Boston, MA: Massachusetts Institute of Technology, 2008. This is a fascinating analysis of how the whaling industry evolved from an attitude of widespread acceptance to one of worldwide opprobrium.

Jackson, Robert and George Sorenson. *Introduction to International Relations: Theories and Approaches.* New York: Oxford University Press, 2007. An excellent introductory text to international relations.

Johnson, Lisa and Cheri Hanson. *Mind Your X's & Y's: Satisfying the 10 Cravings of a New Generation of Consumers.* New York: Free Press, 2006. There are 62 million Americans aged 27–41 and 74 million aged just below. This book tells how to reach these Gen X and Yers, who grew up on the Internet.

Martin, Dick. *Rebuilding Brand America.* New York: Amacom, 2007. Dick Martin is a longtime public relations professional and a smart fellah. His prescription to build back the American brand makes great good sense.

McPhail, Thomas L. *Global Communication: Theories, Stakeholders and Trends.* 2nd ed. Malden, MA: Blackwell Publishing, 2006. In addition to tracking the elements that impact global communication, the author also provides a primer on the latest global theories of communication, from electronic colonialism theory to world-system theory.

Ries, Laura and Al Ries. *The Fall of Advertising and the Rise of PR.* New York: Harper Business, 2002. Legendary positioning guru and his talented daughter declare that their former business has had it. Long live public relations!

Schiffman, Stephan. *E-Mail Selling Techniques: That Really Work.* Avon, MA: Adams Media, 2007. This book is all about creating targeted e-mails to reach potential customers and earn coveted face time with them.

Spizman, Robyn and Rick Frishman. *Where's Your WOW? 16 Ways to Make Your Competitors Wish They Were You.* New York: McGraw-Hill,

2008. All about growing creatively by seeking and winning new business.

Stevens, Howard and Theodore Kinni. *Achieving Sales Excellence: The 7 Customer Rules for Becoming the New Sales Professional.* Avon, MA: Platinum Press, 2007. The result of 14 years of research into how people can become better salesmen. (And all of us in public relations are—"salespeople.")

Wilkinson, Paul. *International Relations.* New York: Oxford University Press, 2007. Learned treatise on government entities and the challenges they face.

Endnotes

1. Daisuke Wakabayashi, "Apple's Market Cap Loses $60 Billion After iPhone Sales Disappoint," *The Wall Street Journal* (July 22, 2015).
2. Paul Mozer, "Tim Cook Apologizes for China Customer Service," *The Wall Street Journal* (April 1, 2013).
3. "The State of Consumption Today," *Worldwatch Institute* (July 21, 2015), http://www.worldwatch.org/node/810.
4. "Exports from International Tourism Rise to US $1.5 Trillion in 2014," *World Tourism Organization* (April 15, 2015).
5. Landon Thomas, Jr., "Disney Says It Will Link Marketing to Nutrition," *The New York Times* (October 17, 2006).
6. Nicholas Casey and Nicholas Zamiska, "Mattel Does Damage Control After New Recall," *The Wall Street Journal* (August 15, 2007): B1.
7. Andrew Martin, "Burger King Shifts Policy on Animals," *The New York Times* (March 28, 2007): C1.
8. Amit Jaim, "China Food Scandal Rocks McDonald's and KFC," *PR Week* (July 22, 2014).
9. Robert Kwortnik, "3 Ways to Manage Consumer Generated Media," *eCornell Blog* (February 11, 2013).
10. Beki Winchel, "Urban Outfitters Offends with Red-Stained 'Vintage' Kent State Sweatshirt," *Ragan PR Daily* (September 17, 2014).
11. Danny Hakim, "CVS Health Quits U.S. Chamber Over Stance on Smoking," *The New York Times* (July 7, 2015).
12. Luis A. Henoa, "No McDonald's Happy Meal Toy? Chile Bans Toys in Children's Meals," *Christian Science Monitor* (August 2, 2012).
13. Matt Warmen, "iPhone Workers Beg Apple for Better Working Conditions," *The Telegraph* (February 23, 2012).
14. Raf Casert, "EU Opens Antitrust Case Against 6 Major U.S. Studios," *Associated Press* (July 23, 2015).
15. Noam Cohen, "Doorstep Protest: Very Real, Very Virtual," *The New York Times* (November 26, 2007): C3.
16. *JetBlue Airways Customer Bill of Rights*, JetBlue Airways, Forest Hills, NY.

Chapter **15**

Public Relations
Writing

Chapter Objectives

1. To discuss the reasons that the public relations professional must be the best writer in the organization.
2. To explore the fundamentals of writing, from drafting to style to ensuring worthwhile content.
3. To discuss, in detail, the rationale for and elements of the news release, the most practical and ubiquitous of public relations writing vehicles.
4. To examine the requisites of writing for the ear that differ from writing for the eye.

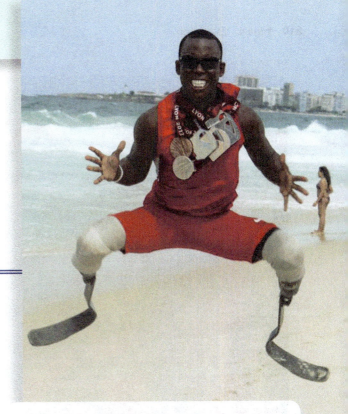

FIGURE 15-1   Publicity leaper.
Paralympic star Blake Leeper sashayed through a publicity blitz that took him from the Espy Award's red carpet with football legend Brett Favre **(Figure 15-2)** to an appearance with TV host Arsenio Hall **(Figure 15-3)** to the competition to win a spot on a Wheaties box **(Figure 15-4)**.
Photo: Courtesy of Steven Barber

The vast majority of public relations writing is designed to attract positive publicity about a product, organization, issue, or person.

The public relations writer has a vast arsenal of writing weapons at his or her disposal; from basic news releases and pitch letters to features and op eds, from social media Facebook and Twitter copy to sophisticated testimony, presentations, and formal speeches.

Achieving results from public relations writing requires, in addition to possessing a newsworthy subject and preparing sound copy, perseverance. Stated another way, converting publicity to "news" depends on aggressiveness, salesmanship, and commitment.

Consider the example of U.S. Paralympic athlete Blake Leeper and his whirlwind manager/public relations front man, Steven Barber. Leeper, who was born with both legs missing below the knee, has worn prosthetics since nine months of age. Using those prosthetic limbs and benefiting from a perpetually-positive attitude, Leeper excelled in baseball and basketball in school and made his international debut in the 2009 Paralympic Games in Rio de Janeiro.

As Mr. Leeper progressed athletically, Mr. Barber waged a non-stop campaign of news releases and pitch letters and publicity photos that traced the Paralympian's development. The result: Chockablock appearances on national television, at the 2015 NBA All-Star Celebrity Game, at the 2015 ESPN Espy Awards, and even as a candidate for a Wheaties box![1] **(Figure-15 1/4)** Leeper was also the subject of a dramatic Nike Internet documentary.[2] The Leeper/Barber combination proved a public relations writing publicity bonanza.

FIGURE 15-2 **Publicity leaper.**
Photo: Courtesy of Steven Barber

FIGURE 15-3 **Publicity leaper.**
Photo: Courtesy of Steven Barber

FIGURE 15-4 **Publicity leaper.**
Photo: Courtesy of Steven Barber

Even in the age of social media and the Internet, writing remains the key to public relations: Public relations practitioners are professional communicators. And communications means writing.

All of us know how to write and speak. But public relations professionals should write and speak *better* than their colleagues. Communication—that is, effective writing and speaking—is the essence of the practice of public relations.

There is no substitute for clear and precise language in informing, motivating, and persuading. The ability to write and speak with clarity is a valuable and coveted skill in any organization. Stated another way, the pen (or keyboard, if you will) is, indeed, mightier than the sword.

The ability to write easily, coherently, and quickly distinguishes the public relations professional from others in an organization. It's not that the skills of counseling and marketing and judgment aren't just as important; some experts argue that these skills are often *more* important than knowing how to write. Perhaps. But not knowing how to write—how to express ideas on paper—may reduce the opportunities to ascend the public relations success ladder.

Stated bluntly, beginning public relations professionals are expected to have mastery over the written word. So this chapter will explore the fundamentals of writing: (1) discussing public relations writing in general and the staple of that writing, news releases, in particular; (2) reviewing writing for reading; and (3) briefly discussing writing for listening.

☐ Writing for the Eye and the Ear

The sad fact is that public relations people, by and large, are horrible writers. This is the unfortunate conclusion of public relations teachers, supervisors, and executive recruiters assigned to find jobs for public relations applicants.[3] That is unacceptable in a field in which the fundamental skill must be the ability to write.

What does it take to be a public relations writer?

For one thing, it takes a good knowledge of the basics. Although practitioners probably write for a wider range of purposes and use a greater number of communications methods than do other writers, the principles remain the same whether writing for the Internet, an annual report or a case history, an employee newsletter, or a public speech.

Writing for a reader differs dramatically from writing for a listener. A reader has certain luxuries a listener does not have. For example, a reader can scan material, study printed words, dart ahead, and then review certain passages for better understanding. A reader can check up on a writer; if the facts are wrong, for instance, a reader can find out pretty easily. With the emergence of online reading, the requirements and scrutiny have increased. Online readers are fickle and impatient. Unless your copy corrals them, they move on. To be effective then, especially in the second decade of the 21st century, writing for the eye must be able to withstand the most rigorous standards.

The stakes are even higher with writing for listening. A listener gets only one opportunity to hear and comprehend a message. If the message is missed the first time, there's usually no second chance. This situation poses a special challenge for the writer—to grab the listener quickly. A listener who tunes out early in a speech or a broadcast is difficult to draw back into the listening fold.

Public relations practitioners—and public relations students—should understand the differences between writing for the eye and the ear. Although it's unlikely that any beginning public relations professional would start by writing speeches, it's important to understand what constitutes a speech and how it's prepared and then be ready for the assignment when opportunity strikes. Because writing lies at the heart of the public relations equation, the more beginners know about writing, the better they will do.

Again, your *primary* skill as a public relations professional is "writing."

Any practitioner who doesn't know the basics of writing and doesn't know how to write—even in the age of social media—is vulnerable and expendable.

2 Fundamentals of Writing

Few people are born writers. Like any other discipline, writing takes patience and hard work. The more you write, the better you should become, provided you have mastered the basics. Writing fundamentals do not change significantly from one form to another.

What are the basics? Here is a foolproof, four-part formula for writers, from the novice to the novelist:

1. **The idea must precede the expression.** Think before writing. Few people can observe an event, immediately grasp its meaning, and sit down to compose several pages of sharp, incisive prose. Writing requires ideas, and ideas require thought.

   Sometimes ideas come quickly. Other times, they don't come at all. But each new writing situation doesn't require a new idea. The trick in coming up with clever ideas lies more in *borrowing* old ones than in creating new ones. What's that, you say? Is your dear old author encouraging "theft"? You bet! The old cliché "Don't reinvent the wheel" is absolutely true when it comes to good writing. So never underestimate the importance of maintaining good files.

2. **Don't be afraid of the draft.** After deciding on an idea and establishing the purpose of a communication, the writer should prepare a rough draft. Drafting is a necessary and foolproof method for avoiding a mediocre, half-baked product. Writing, no matter how good, can usually be improved with a second look. The draft helps you organize ideas and plot their development before you commit them to a written test. Sadly, few public relations writers go through the drafting process. (That's why public relations people, by and large, are horrible writers!) Writing clarity is often enhanced if you know where you will stop before you start.

3. **Simplify, clarify.** In writing, the simpler, the better. Today, with more and more consumers reading from computer screens, simplicity is imperative. The more people who understand what you're trying to say, the better your chances for stimulating action. Shop talk, jargon, and "in" words should be avoided. Standard English is all that's required to get an idea across. In

FYI

The Greatest Public Relations Writer of All Time

You're too young to remember Sir Winston Churchill. (Even I'm too young to remember him!)

But the former Prime Minister of Great Britain, who led the Brits to victory in World War II, was history's greatest public relations writer, an inspiration to any poor schnook who ever pecked at a keyboard. Churchill, also one of history's greatest speakers, began as a back bencher in Parliament, who lacked confidence because of a stutter.

But Churchill worked hard at his writing and, through it, developed into one of history's most charismatic figures, with memorable passages that will live forever **(Figure 15-5)**.

How did he do it? Here's the writing formula Churchill followed.*

1. **He got straight to the point.**
   Churchill delivered bad news, in particular, in a no-nonsense, straightforward way, for example, "The news from France is very bad."
   So get to your point.

2. **He wrote the truth.**
   Jack Nicholson famously intoned in the movie *A Few Good Men* that "You can't handle the truth."
   Well, Churchill could and did, all the time.
   "The whole fury and might of the enemy must very soon be turned on us," he told the British people about the Nazis. It was true, and they needed to hear it.

3. **He painted pictures.**
   Writing teachers in the 21st century talk about "telling stories" and "painting pictures." Churchill did this beautifully a full century earlier.
   When he talked of the evil Hitler, Churchill told his countrymen and women, "If we can stand up to him, all Europe may be freed and the life of the world may move forward into broad, sunlit uplands."
   "But if we fail, then the whole world, including the United States, including all that we have known and cared for, will sink into the abyss of a new dark age made more sinister and perhaps more protracted, by the lights of perverted science."
   Nuff said.

4. **He used simple words.**
   "Let us therefore brace ourselves to our duties, and so bear ourselves, that if the British Empire and its Commonwealth last for a thousand years, men will still say, 'This was their finest hour.'"
   Simple, straightforward, perhaps the most famous written passage in military history.

5. **He worked his verbs.**
   In writing, verbs are always the key. Churchill understood that and wouldn't be caught using an "is" or "am"

FIGURE 15-5 Stone cold writer.
Toronto statue of Sir Winston Churchill, history's greatest public relations writer.
Photo: Pierre Roussel/Agence Quebec Presse—Pierre Ro/Newscom

or "achieve." Rather, the Churchill verb lexicon stressed words of action:

- Grieve
- Fall
- Rise
- Defend
- Fight

Not a dead, corporate verb among em.

*Based on Clare Lynch, "5 Writing Tips from Winston Churchill," *Ragan's PR Daily* (May 15, 2012).

practically every case, what makes sense is the simple rather than the complex, the familiar rather than the unconventional, and the concrete rather than the abstract. Clarity is another essential in writing.

4. **Finally, writing must be aimed at a particular audience.** The writer must have the target group in mind and tailor the message to reach that audience. To win the minds and hearts of a specific audience, one must be willing to sacrifice the understanding of certain others. Writers, like companies, can't expect to be all things to all people.

Flesch Readability Formula

Through a variety of writings, the late Rudolf Flesch staged a one-man battle against pomposity and murkiness in writing. According to Flesch, anyone can become a writer. He suggested that people who write the way they talk will be able to write better. In other words, if people were less inclined to obfuscate their writing with 25-cent words and more inclined to substitute simple words, then not only would communicators communicate better but receivers would also receive more clearly.

There are countless examples of how Flesch's simple dictum works.

■ Few would remember William Shakespeare if he had written sentences such as "Should I act upon the urgings that I feel or remain passive and thus cease to exist?" Shakespeare's writing has stood the test of centuries because of sentences such as "To be or not to be?"

■ A scientist, prone to scientific jargon, might be tempted to write, "The biota exhibited a 100% mortality response." But how much easier and infinitely more understandable to write, "All the fish died."

■ One of President Franklin D. Roosevelt's speechwriters once wrote, "We are endeavoring to construct a more inclusive society." FDR changed it to "We're going to make a country in which no one is left out."

■ Even the most famous book of all, the Bible, opens with a simple sentence that could have been written by a 12-year-old: "In the beginning, God created the heaven and the earth." Simple but brilliant!

Flesch gave seven suggestions for making writing more readable.

1. Use contractions such as *it's* and *doesn't*.

2. Leave out the word *that* whenever possible.

3. Use pronouns such as *I, we, they,* and *you.*

4. When referring back to a noun, repeat the noun or use a pronoun. Don't create eloquent substitutions.

5. Use brief, clear sentences.

6. Cover only one item per paragraph.

7. Use language the reader understands.

Inverted Pyramid Simplicity

Journalistic writing style is the Flesch approach in action.

Reporters learn that words are precious and are not to be wasted. In their stories every word counts. If readers lose interest early, they're not likely to be around at the

FYI

Churchill's Worst Nightmare

Worried about fitting in a corporate environment? Concerned that the suits speak and write a different language than do you—more convoluted, hyperextended, and obtuse?

Relax. You can rely on this version of "Jargon Master Matrix," developed by a former bank communicator, a chart consisting of three columns of jargon words that can be mixed and matched for any occasion.

Just select any three words from the three columns, such as *value-based process model* or *overarching support centralization*, and you will fit right in. (Just don't tell Sir Winston!)

overarching	visionary	objectives
strategic	support	alternatives
special	customer-oriented	expectations
specific	stretch	excellence
core	planning	assessment
long-term	marketing	update
quality	service	model
technology-based	process	product
formal	fundamental	centralization
exceptional	sales	incentive
value-based	budget	initiatives
executive	operating	feedback
immediate	discretionary	infrastructure
interactive	tracking	proposition

end of the story. That's where the inverted pyramid comes in. Newspaper story form is the opposite of that for a novel or short story. The climax of a novel comes at the end; but the climax of a newspaper story comes at the beginning.

Generally, the first tier, or lead, of the story is the first one or two paragraphs, which include the most important facts. From there, paragraphs are written in descending order of importance, with progressively less important facts presented as the article continues—thus, the term *inverted pyramid*.

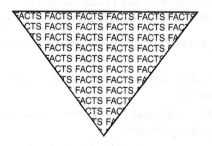

The lead is the most critical element, usually answering the questions concerning who, what, why, when, where, and occasionally how. For example, the following lead effectively answers most of the initial questions a reader might have about the subject of the news story.

> *The Walt Disney Company today announced today it had signed actress Felicity Jones to star in Rogue One, the first of a series of Star Wars adventures, to be released in 2017.*

That sentence tells it all; it answers the critical questions and highlights the pertinent facts. It gets to the point quickly without a lot of extra words. In just about 30 words, it captures and communicates the essence of what the reader needs to know. Factual. Straightforward. Simplicity at its clearest.

This is the style of straightforward writing that forms the basis for the most fundamental, practical, ubiquitous, and easiest of all public relations tools: the news release.

③ The News Release

A valuable but much-maligned device, the news release is the granddaddy of public relations writing vehicles. The first recorded news release was issued by Ivy Lee in October of 1906, as a "Statement from the Road," offering an explanation from client Pennsylvania Railroad about that month's crash that killed 50 people. The release was published verbatim by *The New York Times*. (That may have been the last release the *Times* ever published verbatim!)

Most public relations professionals swear by news releases. Some editors and reporters swear *at* them. Some, in fact, have predicted that with social media and Internet communicating, the "end of news releases" is nigh. Nah. Releases, done correctly, are the easiest, most straightforward, most understandable, and ubiquitous communication vehicles. Indeed, PR Newswire, a paid wire service used by public relations people, distributes hundreds of news releases—virtually all by e-mail—every day to more than 5000 Web sites and online databases.

A news release may be written as the document of record to state an organization's official position—for example, in a court case or in announcing a price or rate increase. More frequently, however, releases have one overriding purpose: to influence a publication to write favorably about the material discussed. Each day, in fact, professionals e-mail releases to editors in the hope of stimulating favorable stories about their organizations.

Most news releases are not used verbatim, although there are rare exceptions **(Figures 15-6 and 15-7)**. Rather, they may stimulate editors to consider covering a story. In other words, the release becomes the point of departure for a newspaper, magazine, radio, or television story. Professor Linda Morton of the University of Oklahoma's Herbert School of Journalism suggested five newsworthy topics for news releases:

- *Impact:* a major announcement that affects an organization, its community, or even society.
- *Oddity:* an unusual occurrence or milestone, such as the one-millionth customer being signed on.
- *Conflict:* a significant dispute or controversy, such as a labor disagreement or rejection of a popular proposal.
- *Known principal:* the greater the title of the individual making the announcement—president versus vice president—the greater the chance of the release being used.
- *Proximity:* how localized the release is or how timely it is, relative to the news of the day.[4]

FIGURE 15-6   **Ready for prime time news release. So...** This release concerns a captivating topic and is well-written and newsworthy. *Courtesy Rivkin & Associates*

NEWS RELEASE

CONSUMERS PREFER "HOSPITALS" OVER "MEDICAL CENTERS," ACCORDING TO NEW SURVEY

June 21, 2011 – Do consumers prefer a "Hospital" over a "Medical Center," or vice versa? According to a new survey of 1027 American adults, the clear answer is: "Hospital."

On four separate measures, consumers showed strong preferences for a "Hospital" over a "Medical Center." Survey highlights:

	HOSPITAL	MEDICAL CENTER
Which would have a wider range of services?	61%	31%
Which would provide better care?	32	52
Which would be on the cutting edge of medicine?	53	37
Which would have physicians who are experts?	46	34

These consumer perceptions come from a survey conducted this month by Rivkin & Associates LLC and Bauman Research & Consulting LLC, both based in Glen Rock, NJ.

"The conventional wisdom for years has been that the word 'Hospital' was tired and old-fashioned," said Steve Rivkin, founder of Rivkin & Associates, a marketing and communications consultancy. "As a result, hundreds of hospitals have dropped the word and renamed themselves Medical Centers."

"Our data indicates this conventional wisdom is wrong," said Sandra Bauman, PhD, founder of Bauman Research & Consulting. "This national study shows that consumers favor a 'hospital' across the board on the four attributes we measured."

Survey results were consistent across respondents' gender, age, income, race, region, household income, size of household, and educational levels, according to Dr. Bauman.

"We've encountered many internal reasons for using the term 'medical center,'" said Rivkin. "As hospitals expanded, added facilities and services, and partnered with physicians, they came to see themselves as 'centers' of healthcare for their communities. And for some, the term 'medical center' also has an academic pedigree, conveying prestige to physicians and other practitioners."

Beyond these characteristics, *human interest* stories, which touch on an emotional experience, are regularly considered newsworthy.

With this as a backdrop, it is not surprising that research indicates that in terms of the popular press, most news releases never see the light of print. Early studies, in fact, even before the exponential growth of releases, indicated that less than 10% of all news releases were published.[5] Nonetheless, each day's *The Wall Street Journal, The New York Times, USA Today*, CNN, Fox News, MSNBC, CNBC, Associated Press wire, Yahoo News, Google News, and other daily media around the nation devices and world—all streaming on mobile devices—are filled with stories generated from news releases issued by public relations professionals.

So the fact is that the news release—despite the harsh reviews of some—remains the single most important public relations vehicle.

News Release News Value

The key challenge for public relations writers is to ensure that their news releases reflect news. What is *news*? That's an age-old question in journalism. Traditionally, journalists said, when "dog bites man, it's not news, but when man bites dog, that's news." The best way to learn what constitutes news value is to scrutinize the daily press, online and broadcast news reports and see what they call news. In a general sense, news releases ought to include the following elements:

- Have a well-defined reason for sending the release.
- Focus on one central subject in each release.

FIGURE 15-7
....prime time.
Sometimes (not always), news releases serve their purpose perfectly.
Courtesy Rivkin & Associates

L-2 THE RECORD   LOCAL

HEALTH CARE NEWS

 Submit news items to **northjersey.com/calendar**

Most favor hospitals over medical centers, poll shows

By BARBARA WILLIAMS
STAFF WRITER

Americans believe they will receive better services in a "hospital" than in a "medical center," according to a phone survey conducted by two local consulting firms.

More than 1,000 people were asked four questions about whether they believed they would have better outcomes in a hospital or medical center during the survey conducted by Rivkin & Associates LLC and Bauman Research & Consulting LLC, both based in Glen Rock.

When asked "which would have a wider range of services," 61 percent said a hospital and 31 percent chose a medical center. Six percent said there would be no difference, and 2 percent didn't know or refused to answer.

Fifty-two percent said a hospital provides "patients with better quality medical care" while 32 per-

> **"The conventional wisdom for years has been that the word 'hospital' was tired and old-fashioned."**
> STEVE RIVKIN,
> RIVKIN & ASSOCIATES

cent said a medical center. Twelve percent thought the care would be the same; 4 percent weren't sure.

Asked "which would be on the cutting edge of medicine, using the most up-to-date technologies and procedures," 53 percent chose a hospital while 37 percent picked a medical center. Just 8 percent thought there would be no difference.

Forty-six percent said they thought a hospital would have "physicians who are experts in their fields" compared with 34 per-

cent who thought a medical center would have more expertise, and 19 percent who thought there would be no difference.

"The conventional wisdom for years has been that the word 'hospital' was tired and old-fashioned," Steve Rivkin, founder of Rivkin & Associates, said in a statement. "As a result, hundreds of hospitals have dropped the word and renamed themselves medical centers."

But "our data indicates this conventional wisdom is wrong," Sandra Bauman, founder of Bauman Research, said in a statement. "This national study shows that consumers favor a "hospital" across the board on the four attributes we measured."

The survey was conducted in June using random-digit dialing to 1,027 people nationwide who were at least 18 years old.

E-mail: williamsb@northjersey.com

- Make certain the subject is newsworthy in the context of the organization, industry, and community.
- Include facts about the product, service, or issue being discussed.
- Provide the facts "factually"—with no puff, no bluff, no hyperbole.
- Rid the release of unnecessary jargon.
- Include appropriate quotes from principals but avoid inflated superlatives that do little more than boost management egos.
- Include product specifications, shipping dates, availability, price, and all pertinent information for telling the story.

FYI

Write the Release

Writing in news release style is easy. It is less a matter of formal writing than it is of selecting, organizing, and arranging facts in descending sequence.

Here are 10 facts:

Fact 1: Supreme Court Chief Justice John Roberts will speak in Madison, Wisconsin, tomorrow.

Fact 2: He will be keynote speaker at the annual convention of the American Bar Association.

Fact 3: He will speak at 8 p.m. at the Kohl Center.

Fact 4: His speech will be a major one.

Fact 5: His topic will be capital punishment.

Fact 6: He will also address university law classes while in Madison.

Fact 7: He will meet with the university's chancellor while in Madison.

Fact 8: He became the 17th Chief Justice, replacing the late William Rehnquist in 2005.

Fact 9: He is a former practicing attorney.

Fact 10: He has, in the past, steadfastly avoided addressing the subject of capital punishment.

Organize these facts into an American Bar Association news release for tomorrow morning's Wisconsin State Journal newspaper. One right answer appears soon in this chapter. Just don't peek.

- Include a brief description of the company (also called a "boilerplate") at the end of the release—what it is, and what it does.
- Write clearly, concisely, forcefully.

News Release Content

When a release is newsworthy and of potential interest to an editor, it must be written clearly and concisely in proper newspaper style. It must get to the facts early and answer the six key questions. From there it must follow the inverted pyramid structure to its conclusion. For example, consider the following lead for the John Roberts news release posed in this chapter's "Outside the Lines."

MADISON, WISCONSIN—Supreme Court Chief Justice John Roberts will deliver a major address on capital punishment at 8 p.m. tomorrow in the Kohl Center before the annual convention of the American Bar Association.

This lead answers all the pertinent questions:

1. **Who?** Chief Justice John Roberts
2. **What?** A major address on capital punishment
3. **Where?** Kohl Field House
4. **When?** Tomorrow at 8 p.m.
5. **Why?** American Bar Association is holding a convention

In this case, *how* is less important. Whether or not the reader chooses to delve further into the release, the gist of the story has been successfully communicated in the lead.

To be newsworthy, news releases must be objective. All comments and editorial remarks must be attributed to organization officials. The news release can't be used as the private soapbox of the release writer. Rather, it must appear as a fair and accurate representation of the news that the organization wishes to be conveyed.

And news releases—even in the form of tweets or Facebook postings—must also be written in a certain professional style, or there can be real trouble (see *A Question of Ethics* in this chapter).

News Release Essentials

Beyond the necessity of being newsworthy, news releases must include several time-honored essentials that will help get them considered for inclusion in print.

- **Rationale.** There must be a well-defined reason for sending the release. Releases should answer the two critical questions: *What's new?* and *So what?* Stated another way, the subject matter of the release must be relevant to the readers or viewers of the target media. Lack of relevance should be enough to scuttle the release.

- **Focus.** Each release should speak about only one central subject. Lack of focus—that is, discussing many different things—is a guaranteed non-starter for a journalist.

- **No puffery.** Releases, to paraphrase Fox News commentator Bill O'Reilly, should be "puffery-free zones." Even mediocre reporters can sniff out hyperbole and puffiness, which may make them suspicious of the entire product. At all costs, avoid the buzzwords and taboo terms listed in the next *FYI* box.

- **Nourishing quotes.** Include quotes, but make them count. "We think this is the best product of its type" doesn't add much. But "This product will add 20% to our annual revenue growth" advances the story by providing important projections that will help put the announcement in corporate context.

- **Company description.** Many reporters may not be familiar with a particular organization and what it does. Therefore, a succinct organizational description, commonly called *boilerplate*, is eminently appropriate to conclude a release. The best boilerplate should contain market position, scope of business activity, geographic coverage, aspiration, size, and even company personality.

- **Spelling, grammar, punctuation.** Ask journalists to describe the *quality* of the public relations releases they receive, and they'll invariably roll their eyes. If the most rudimentary writing principles of spelling, grammar, and punctuation aren't observed, how important can the release be? And how important can the reporter recipient be if the public relations writer doesn't even take the time to proofread?

- **Clarity, conciseness, commitment.** The best releases from the best organizations are straightforward, understated, and confident. Just like any other communications vehicle, a public relations news release can reveal much about the company that produces it.

A Question of Ethics

No "Pardon" for Anti-Obama Facebook Poster

Never forget that any time you put keyboard to word, you are taking your life into your hands. And that goes especially for combustible social media.

Just consider the fate of one, Elizabeth Lauten, communications director for Republican Rep. Stephen Fincher of Tennessee. Ms. Lauten objected to the casual dress and perceived lack of decorum of First Daughters Sasha and Malia Obama at the annual White House Thanksgiving turkey pardoning ceremony in 2014. Ms. Lauten took her objections out in the following Facebook post:

Dear Sasha and Malia,

I get you're both in those awful teen years, but you're a part of the First Family, try showing a little class. At least respect the part you play. Then again your mother and father don't respect their positions very much, or the nation for that matter, so I'm guessing you're coming up a little short in the "good role model" department. Nevertheless, stretch yourself. Rise to the occasion. Act like being in the White House matters to you. Dress like you deserve respect, not a spot at a bar. And certainly don't make faces during televised public events.

Almost immediately, Ms. Lauten was vilified for picking on the teenagers. Typical was this tweet:

A chagrined Lauten reacted immediately to the criticism, tweeting *"I wanted to take a moment and apologize for a post I made on Facebook earlier today judging Sasha and Malia Obama at the annual White House turkey pardoning ceremony....After many hours of prayer, talking to my parents, and re-reading my words online I can see more clearly just how hurtful my words were."*

Alas, the apology proved too little, too late. The next day Ms. Lauten resigned her position with the congressman.*

Question

1. What would your advice have been to Ms. Lauten in considering her Facebook post on the turkey pardoning ceremony.

Elizabeth Lauten in happier times

*For further information, see Jessica Durando, "GOP Aide Resigns After Comments on Obama Girls," *USA Today* (December 1, 2014).

FYI

21st Century News Release 10 Taboo Terms

Back in the old days of 1978, the late comedian George Carlin found himself in deep turbulence for uttering seven "dirty words" that the Supreme Court found to be "patently offensive" to radio listeners. (Because this is a "family textbook," we will leave the seven words to your imagination or your next visit to the *Howard Stern Show* on satellite radio.)

In the second decade of the 21st century, there is nothing more patently offensive to a reporter than a news release that contains the following 10 most overused buzzwords and phrases.

1. **Synergy.** An overused word that suggests that everything fits together in one, neat little organization. Again, show us how you work together; don't tell us you're "synergistic."

2. **Value-added.** Shouldn't all your suggestions/solutions/innovations add value? If they don't, why introduce them?

3. **Outside-the-box.** This might have meant something once, but not so much today, since everybody uses it. Save yourself the trouble and avoid.

4. **Leading.** Every company thinks it's a leader and most use the term liberally in their releases. If you can prove how you are a "leader," fine. But most can't so don't.

5. **Innovative.** Another term that must be used with caution. Prove that you truly are innovative; then, you can say it.

6. **Disruptive.** This is geek speak, a popular 21st century term that generally refers to technologies or companies that disrupt the common wisdom with some new, radical thinking. It has become a common news release term, and is unworthy of the description in the vast majority of cases.

7. **World class.** What makes your university or association or technology world class? Under what criteria? Against whom are you measuring?

8. **Game changer.** At some point, this made sense, but its ad nauseam use in stories from business to baseball to politics has rendered the phrase clichéd.

9. **Paradigm shift.** Here, too, overuse has caused this phrase—which technically means a seismic change in an existing concept—to lose its meaning and sound pretentious.

10. **End of the day.** Is there any term more annoying? Answer: Nope!

You have to prove, justify, or quantify how specifically your organization is "leading, world class, innovative, disruptive, etc." If you can't prove it, don't use it. (Especially at the end of the day!) *

For further information, see Fraser P. Seitel, *Public Relations Promotional Writing* (San Diego, CA: Bridgepoint Education, Inc., 2015).

Internet Releases

The vast majority of journalists today prefer to receive news releases via e-mail.

In terms of news release writing for the Internet, brevity and succinctness are paramount. Reading from a computer screen is more difficult and tedious than extracting from paper. Therefore, Internet news release writing must conform to the following requisites:

- **One reporter per "To" line.** Nobody—least of all, reporters—likes to be lumped in with everybody else. That's why journalists despise press conferences. They want to be considered "special." So don't group journalists together on the "To" line of an e-mail release.

- **Limit subject line headers.** Most reporters are cursed with a daily e-mail inbox that runneth over. Therefore, enticing them with a provocative subject line is a necessity if you want your release to be considered. You should limit subject headers to four to six words, no more.

- **Hammer home the headline.** E-mail release headlines are as important as print headlines to attract immediate interest and subsequent coverage. E-mail headlines should be written in boldface upper- and lowercase and, as in all e-mail writing, should be limited in length—to 10 words or less.

- **Limit length.** E-mail news releases should be shorter than print versions; PR Newswire reports that the average print release is 500 words.

- **Observe 5W format.** E-mail news releases should observe traditional news release style, leading with the 5W format, to answer the key questions of who, what, why, when, where, and even how.

- **No attachments.** Never. Never. Never. Journalists wish neither to face the risk of a virus nor take the time to download. So don't attach anything. Rather . . .

- **Remember readability.** E-mail releases must balance information with readability. That means short paragraphs, varied paragraph length, bullets, numbers, and lists—devices that make the release more eye-friendly and scannable.[6]

Art of the Pitch

The most fundamental way to reach a journalist, beyond the news release, is through a pitch letter.

When in "publicity mode," public relations people are *"pitch people."* They "pitch" stories and interviews, press conferences and product demonstrations to reporters, hopeful to receive positive coverage that will promote their organization's efforts. Such pitching is regularly initiated through correspondence in the form of e-mail pitch letters.

Pitching generally refers to the act of a public relations professional attempting to interest a journalist in covering what the organizational communicator is selling. Public relations writers pitch stories all day, every day; indeed reporters are inundated by e-mails inviting them to write about this product or interview that executive or cover this cause.

Public relations pitching is an art; tip your hand too much in a promotional direction or fail to show the relevance or newsworthiness of that which you are pitching—and your pitch will be rejected. And even if your pitch is newsworthy, with competition from hundreds or even thousands of others pitching their products and services to the same journalists, the odds are stacked against you.

That's why crafting a successful pitch requires the following fundamentals.

- **First, do your homework.** Every public relations writing assignment begins with research; that's particularly important with respect to pitching. You must know who you are pitching. Read what they write in the paper or report on the air or record in their blog. The more familiar you are with the target of your pitching, the more likely your pitch will resonate. So go to school on the reporter you're after.

- **Second, personalize.** Most public relations pitches are randomly distributed, with no particular target in mind; the goal being to throw everything against the wall and see what sticks. It never works. Since one positive mention in an objective, indifferent, third-party media source is worth a lot more than a paid ad or your own Facebook posting, the best pitches are those that are directed, personally, to one particular reporter and tailored to his or her interests.

- **Third, be polite and honest.** Many reporters, as noted, are skeptical of public relations people as "spin meisters." So once you've reached a specific reporter, be up front and explain who you are and what the client campaign is all about. Be honest, and don't "spin."

- **Fourth, localize.** Reporters report locally, so they prefer local news. If you're pitching from out-of-town, you've got a built-in problem. But if you're local and pitching a local product or service, you're ahead of the game. Similarly, pitching a local angle to a "timely" topic that is currently in the news also is a potential winner.

- **Fifth, use celebrities.** Does anybody really care if Kim Kardashian or Ryan Seacrest or Drake is involved with your product? Sadly, yes. Celebrities, like it or not, sell. So if you can tie a celebrity to your pitch, do so.

- **Sixth, be creative.** Reporters receive scores of pitches every day from public relations writers. So your pitch must stand out from the rest. Simply saying the product or service you're pitching is "unique" won't convince anyone. You must demonstrate that this time, it's different. Creativity can pay off **(Figures 15-8 and 15-9).**

Subject: **The 30 Year Sweatshirt**

Dear Fraser,

I apologise in advance for getting in touch out of the blue. I am a 24 year old designer and my brand, Tom Cridland, has just launched The 30 Year Sweatshirt.

The 30 Year Sweatshirt is a groundbreaking sustainable fashion project, designed to lead a trend towards protecting our natural resources by making truly durable clothing, in the form of a premium crewneck sweatshirt backed up with a 30 Year Guarantee.

Do have a look at our brief video if you have a moment:

https://www.kickstarter.com/projects/tomcridland/the-30-year-sweatshirt

Would you be interested in covering our story?

Key details:

- *The 30 Year Sweatshirt is Guaranteed for 30 Years but built to last a lifetime.*

- *The 30 Year Sweatshirt is ethically made using organic loopback cotton, reflecting our commitment to quality, respect for the environment and responsible production ethos.*

- *The Tom Cridland brand already has a star studded following. Leonardo DiCaprio, Ben Stiller, Stephen Fry, Rod Stewart, Hugh Grant, Brandon Flowers, Robbie Williams, Nile Rodgers, Frankie Valli, Nigel Olsson, and Daniel Craig all own Tom Cridland clothing.*

Thank you very much in advance for your time,

Tom Cridland

Let's talk fabric in detail:

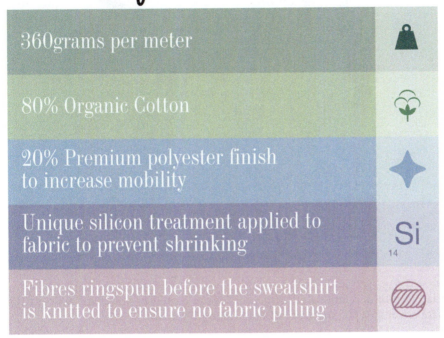

360grams per meter

80% Organic Cotton

20% Premium polyester finish to increase mobility

Unique silicon treatment applied to fabric to prevent shrinking

Si
14

Fibres ringspun before the sweatshirt is knitted to ensure no fabric pilling

The 30 Year Sweatshirt's fabric is

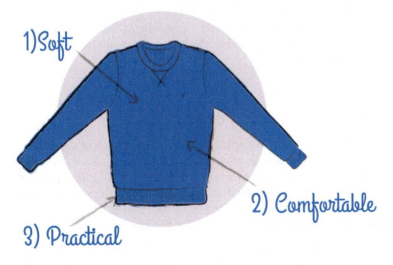

1) Soft

2) Comfortable

3) Practical

Built to withstand a lifetime of wear and tear.

FIGURE 15-8   **Creative pitch.**
Sweatshirt designer Tom Cridland was honest, respectful, and creative in pitching his guaranteed 30-year sweatshirt in 2015.
Photo: Courtesy Tom Cridland

FIGURE 15-9
Creative pitch.
Photo: Courtesy Tom Cridland

A myriad of public relations writing vehicles are regularly "pitched" to journalists to stimulate coverage. The most prominent among them are:

1. Round up stories—which collect or "round up" industry or societal trends, including examples.
2. Case histories—which cite specific solutions for organizational problems, that hold more generalizeable industry application.
3. Op-eds—opinion editorials, typically confronting timely and newsworthy issues, that are submitted on an unsolicited basis to daily and online publications.

④ Writing for Listening

Writing for the ear requires a special skill. After all, unlike something in print to which you can return over and over, you generally get only one crack at listening to a speech or hearing a radio or TV commentary **(Figure 15-10)**. So the impact of the oral presentation has to be delivered immediately. That's a significant challenge for a writer.

The key to writing for listening is to write as if you are speaking. The following half dozen rules are helpful in writing for the ear.

1. **Use short words:** Big words sound impressive. But multi-syllabic words are rarely as good as their simpler counterparts when writing for the ear. As Churchill said, *"Short words are the best and old words when short are the best of all."*
2. **Use short sentences:** Likewise, short sentences are more impactful than longer ones. The speech excerpts we remember—*"We have nothing to fear but fear itself." . . . . "Ask not what your country can do for you; ask what you can do for your country."* —are generally shorter rather than longer.

FIGURE 15-10
You're on!
Writing for listening—
whether for TV broadcast,
speech or presentation
requires different
fundamentals than writing
for the eye.
Photo: Courtesy Raina Seitel

3. **Use 10-cent words:** Rather than 50-cent words. There are more than 500,000 words in the dictionary (You remember the "dictionary!"), yet TV newscasts impose a 7000-word ceiling. The reason is that while people know thousands of words, they are prone to use the same limited pool of words in conversation. When writing for an oral presentation, then, you should use words that everyone understands.

4. **Forget jargon:** Every industry—from basketball to ballet to ballistic missiles—has its own jargon, i.e. words and phrases indigenous to those in the industry. As a general rule, jargon should be avoided; it may sound pretentious or worse, be misunderstood or confusing to listeners. Always better, not to mention more economical, is to substitute those 10-cent words.

5. **Use contractions:** Barring the most formal speeches, oral delivery requires the use of contractions. "Do not" and "I will" work best for the eye. "Don't" and "I'll" work best for the ear. In a moment, we'll review, in detail, elements of Oral Style for a speech. But as a general rule of thumb, in writing for the ear, it's the informal over the formal, the conversational over the stuffy, the simple over the complex.

6. **Speak it aloud:** When you're finished drafting a speech or presentation, read it aloud. Indeed, the best way for a speech writer to learn how to write a speech is by practicing or giving speeches him or herself. That's the best way to observe what works and what doesn't, what's difficult to say and what isn't, what flows naturally and what doesn't.

In brief, be brief. That's what writing for the ear is all about. And nowhere is that more true or more important than in drafting the principle document for the ear, the speech. The most important spoken word vehicle—the acid test for PR writers—is the speech.

The Speech

The most important written vehicle—the acid test for public relations writers—is the speech. In the practice of public relations, access is power; that is, the closer you are to the CEO and the more comfortable he or she is with your production, the more power you will possess within the organization.

President Lyndon Johnson once said, *"Access is power."* For a public relations writer, there is no greater "access" than that provided by drafting the CEO's speech. For a CEO, a speech is unlike any other communications product. He or she must stand before an audience, internal or external, that may or not be friendly or familiar with the CEO, expecting to be informed, entertained, and persuaded. To meet this challenge, CEOs call on public relations "ghosts" to draft their speeches and presentations.

In drafting a speech, the speech writer must approach the assignment cognizant of five simple characteristics.

- **It is designed to be heard, not read.** The mistake of writing for the eye instead of the ear is the most common trap of bad speeches. Speeches needn't be literary gems, but they ought to sound good.

- **It uses concrete language.** The ear dislikes generalities. It responds to clear images. Ideas must be expressed sharply for the audience to get the point.

- **It demands a positive response.** Every word, every passage, every phrase should evoke a response from the audience.

- **It must have clear-cut objectives.** The speech and the speaker must have a point of view—a thesis that is clear and unmistakeable. If there's no point, then it's not worth the speaker's or the audience's time to be there.

- **It must be tailored to a specific audience.** An audience needs to feel that it is hearing something special. The most frequent complaint about organizational speeches is that they all seem interchangeable—they lack uniqueness and are instantly forgettable. A good speech is unique and stands out from the rest.

With these principles as an underpinning, the speech or presentation may be adapted in any number of ways. There's no one size that fits all speeches However, every speech must contain four sections:

1. **Introduction**—This is the critical part of the speech where the speaker introduces himself to the audience and tries to win their immediate trust. *"You never get a second chance to make a first impression,"* goes the old saw. And in a speech, it's brutally true.

2. **Thesis**—This is the most critical element of the speech, and alas, is often overlooked. The thesis, a sentence or two written directly after the introduction, is the heart or central idea that will be corroborated throughout the talk.

3. **Body**—This is the bulk of the speech that reinforces the thesis with three or four main points, all "proven" with examples, anecdotes, facts, statistics, and illustrations.

4. **Conclusion**—This is the final chance the speaker has of encouraging the audience's support and action. It must be dynamic, dramatic and brief, or to paraphrase the poet Stephen Spender, *"leave the vivid air signed with your honor."*[7]

Writing a speech means filling 10-12 blank pages. Rarely will an audience sit through more than 20 minutes, two minutes/page. This is as bone-chilling a prospect as public relations writers can face. However, speech writing, itself, is among the most creative writing exercises available to public relations professionals. Once mastered, it can be a source of immense writing pleasure, not to mention, spending cash.

Importance of Editing

Editing is the all-important final touch for the public relations writer. You must edit your work. One error can sink a perfectly worthwhile release.

In a news release, a careful self-edit can save the deadliest prose. An editor must be judicious. Each word, phrase, sentence, and paragraph should be weighed carefully. Good editing will "punch up" dull passages and make them sparkle. The key again: verbs. For instance, "The satellite flies across the sky" is dead, but "The satellite roars across the sky" is alive.

In the same context, good editing will get rid of passive verbs. Invariably, this will produce shorter sentences. For example, "George Washington chopped down the cherry tree" is shorter and better than "The cherry tree was chopped down by George Washington."

A good editor must also be gutsy enough to use bold strokes—to chop, slice, and cut through verbiage, bad grammar, misspellings, incorrect punctuation, poorly constructed sentences, misused words, mixed metaphors, non sequiturs, clichés, redundancies, circumlocutions, and jargon. Redundant sentences such as "She is the widow of the late Marco Picardo." and "The present incumbent is running for reelection." are intolerable to a good editor.

Editing should also concentrate on organizing copy. One release paragraph should flow naturally into the next. Transitions in writing are most important. Sometimes it takes only a single word to unite two adjoining paragraphs.

Writing, like fine wine, should flow smoothly and stand up under the toughest scrutiny. Careful editing is a necessary and important final step.

FYI

Twitterspeak

The Internet and social media, particularly Twitter, have a writing style all their own. In chat rooms, a correctly spelled word may be a sign of the inarticulate. Consider, for example, this conversation:

Wuzup?

n2m

well g/g c ya

The translation by anyone who spends 8 to 10 hours a day texting or tweeting: Not too much is up with the respondent, and so the writer has got to go and will see his friend later.

Indeed, in terms of e-mail vocabulary, the following shortened vernacular can be adjudged as "chat ready":

■ please	pls
■ feel free	flfre
■ by the way	btw
■ be right back	brb
■ best friend forever	bff
■ in my humble opinion	IMHO
■ laughing out loud	lol
■ rolling on the floor laughing	rotfl
■ you are	u r
■ information	info
■ document	doc
■ conversation	convo
■ later	latr

Last Word

Writing is the essence of public relations practice. The public relations professional, if not the best writer in his or her organization, must at least be one of the best.

That means mastering the traditional fundamentals of sound writing and staying aware of changing, 21st century techniques in writing. Specifically, "in an era where buttoned-up corporate culture is giving way to hoodie-clad executives and job titles like 'chief happiness officer,'" public relations people must be sensitive to stylistic writing changes brought about by blogs, tweets, to say nothing of haiku.[8]

It's up to the public relations professional to decide which of these new wrinkles is either lasting or worth considering. Indeed, writing remains the communications skill that sets public relations professionals apart from others.

Or should.

The most frequent complaint of employers is that "public relations people can't write." That's why any public relations student who "can write" is often ahead of the competition.

Some writers are born. But most are not.

Writing can be learned by understanding the fundamentals of what makes interesting writing; by practicing different written forms; and by working constantly to improve, edit, and refine the written product. When an executive needs something written well, one organizational resource should pop immediately into his or her mind: public relations.

Discussion Starters

1. What is the foremost technical skill of public relations professionals?
2. What are several of the writing fundamentals one must consider?
3. What is the essence of the Flesch method of writing?
4. What is the purpose of a news release?
5. What is the inverted pyramid, and why does it work?
6. What is the essential written communications vehicle used by public relations professionals?
7. What are style considerations of news releases?
8. What is an SMR and what distinguishes it?
9. What are the keys in writing releases for the Internet?
10. Why shouldn't public relations writers include attachments on e-mail releases?

Pick of the Literature

Public Relations Writing, 10th Edition

Doug Newsom and Jim Haynes, Boston, MA: Wadsworth Cengage Learning, 2014

This updated work is as much the bible on public relations writing as any other text. Two distinguished public relations professors provide a soup-to-nuts compilation of the philosophy, strategy and tactics of public relations writing.

The book begins with an exhaustive discussion of how people become persuaded, moves into the preparation that a public relations writer must take before approaching the keyboard and then launches into the publics and principles of public relations writing.

The final part of the book is devoted to specific writing vehicles and situations, from writing for legacy media and government to writing for advertising, social media, and newsletters. As comprehensive an analysis of public relations writing as you'll find.

Case Study   The Raina, Inc. News Release

Background: The Raina carborundum plant in Blackrock, Iowa, has been under pressure in recent months to remedy its pollution problem. Raina's plant is the largest in Blackrock, and even though the company has spent $5.3 million on improving its pollution-control equipment, black smoke still spews from the plant's smokestacks, and waste products are still allowed to filter into neighboring streams. Lately, the pressure on Raina has been intense.

- On April 7, J. K. Krafchik, a private citizen, called to complain about the "noxious smoke" fouling the environment.
- On April 8, Janet Greenberg of the Blackrock Garden Club called to protest the "smoke problem" that was destroying the zinnias and other flowers in the area.
- On April 9, Clarence "Smoky" Salmon, president of the Blackrock Rod and Gun Club, called to report that 700 people had signed a petition against the Raina plant's pollution of Zeus Creek.
- On April 10, WERS Radio editorialized that "the time has come to force area plants to act on solving pollution problems."
- On April 11, the Blackrock City Council announced plans to enact an air and water pollution ordinance for the city. The council invited as its first witness before the public hearing Leslie Sludge, manager of the Raina carborundum plant.

News Release Data

1. Leslie Sludge, manager of Raina's carborundum plant in Blackrock, appeared at the Blackrock City Council hearing on April 11.
2. Sludge said Raina had already spent $5.3 million on a program to clean up pollution at its Blackrock plant.
3. Raina received 500 complaint calls in the past three months protesting its pollution conditions.
4. Sludge said Raina was "concerned about environmental problems, but profits are still what keeps our company running."
5. Sludge announced that the company had decided to commit another $2 million for pollution-abatement facilities over the next three months.
6. Raina is the oldest plant in Blackrock and was built in 1900.
7. Raina's Blackrock plant employs 10,000 people, the largest single employer in Blackrock.
8. Raina originally planned to delay its pollution-abatement program but speeded it up because of public pressure in recent months.
9. Sludge said that the new pollution-abatement program would begin in October and that the company projected "real progress in terms of clean water and clean air" as early as two years from today.
10. Five years ago, Raina received a Presidential Award from the Environmental Protection Agency for its "concern for pollution abatement."
11. An internal Raina study indicated that Blackrock was the "most pollutant laden" of all Raina's plants nationwide.

12. Sludge formerly served as manager of Raina's Fetid Reservoir plant in Fetid Reservoir, New Hampshire. In two years as manager of Fetid Reservoir, Sludge was able to convert it from one of the most pollutant-laden plants in the system to the cleanest, as judged by the Environmental Protection Agency.
13. Sludge has been manager of Blackrock for two months.
14. Raina's new program will cost the company $2 million.
15. Raina will hire 100 extra workers especially for the pollution-abatement program.
16. Sludge, 35, is married to the former Polly Yurathane of Wheeling, West Virginia.
17. Sludge is author of the book *Fly Fishing Made Easy*.
18. The bulk of the money budgeted for the new pollution-abatement program will be spent on two globe refractors, which purify waste destined to be deposited in surrounding waterways, and four hyperventilation systems, which remove noxious particles dispersed into the air from smokestacks.
19. Sludge said, "Raina, Inc. has decided to move ahead with this program at this time because of its long-standing responsibility for keeping the Blackrock environment clean and in response to growing community concern over achieving the objective."
20. Former Blackrock plant manager Fowler Aire was fired by the company in July for his "flagrant disregard for the environment."
21. Aire also was found to be diverting Raina funds from company projects to his own pockets. In all, Aire took close to $10,000, for which the company was not reimbursed. At least part of the money was to be used for pollution control.
22. Aire, whose whereabouts are presently not known, is the brother of J. Derry Aire, Raina's vice president for finance.
23. Raina's Blackrock plant has also recently installed ramps and other special apparatus to assist employees with disabilities. Presently, 100 workers with disabilities are employed in the Raina Blackrock plant.
24. Raina's Blackrock plant started as a converted garage, manufacturing plate glass. Only 13 people worked in the plant at that time.
25. Today the Blackrock plant employs 10,000 people, covers 14 acres of land, and is the largest supplier of plate glass and commercial panes in the country.
26. The Blackrock plant was slated to be the subject of a critical report from the Private Environmental Stabilization Taskforce (PEST), a private environmental group. PEST's report, "The Foulers," was to discuss "the 10 largest manufacturing polluters in the nation."
27. Raina management has been aware of the PEST report for several months.

Questions

1. If you were assigned to draft a news release to accompany Sludge to the Blackrock City Council meeting on April 11, which items would you use in your lead (i.e., who, what, why, where, when, how)?

2. Which items would you avoid using in the news release?

3. If a reporter from the *Blackrock Bugle* called and wanted to know what happened to former Blackrock manager Fowler Aire, what would you tell the reporter?

4. How could Raina, Inc. use the Internet to research public opinion of the pollution problem? How could the company use the Internet to communicate its position in advance of the Blackrock City Council meeting?

From the Top

An Interview with Hoa Loranger

Hoa Loranger is a User Experience Specialist at Nielsen Norman Group. She consults with many large, well-known companies in various industries such as entertainment, finance, technology, e-commerce, and government. She is a frequent speaker, conducts usability research worldwide, and has published reports on a variety of Web usability topics. Ms. Loranger is co author of the book *Prioritizing Web Usability (2006)*.

Ms. Loranger holds a Masters degree in Human Factors and Applied Experimental Psychology from California State University, Northridge, and a BA in Psychology from University of California, Irvine.

holds a masters degree in Human Factors and Applied Experimental Psychology from California State University, Northridge, and a BA in Psychology from University of California, Irvine

What is the state of online writing?
Web site interaction design is getting better, but Web content is lagging behind. Organizations underestimate the role of effective writing in creating a successful Web site. In our studies, we often see people purposefully navigate to the correct areas of a site and be frustrated by verbose content. Companies are dumping information on Web sites without much thought of how usable it is. Employing shortcuts such as plastering content intended for printed material on the Web leads to disastrous outcomes. The traditional narrative writing style commonly used in printed media repels online readers. Unlike print, the Web is a user-directed medium, where people adopt information–seeking strategies to save time. People rely on visual cues to direct their attention to areas of interest and ignore everything else. People on the Web are impatient and expect to get answers quickly. Good Web sites design their content for the way people actually behave on the Web. Bad Web sites design their content the way they want people to behave.

What are the most common errors that online writers make?
Writers often overwrite and choose hype over simplicity. Using sophisticated verbiage makes people work hard to find the information they need. Writers assume that their readers understand internal terminology or jargon. The terminology your organization or industry uses is not usually part of your user's vernacular. Simple language might not seem glamorous, but it is preferred by customers.

What are the most essential elements of online writing?
Keep it short and sweet. Long rambling text frustrates audiences. People on the Web scan, and do not read text word for word. Nothing is more daunting on the Web than being confronted by a large wall of text. In general, the word count for Web content should be about half of that used in conventional writing. Conventional writing calls for complete sentences. Not so much online. If the same information can be conveyed effectively in fewer words, do it.

Start with key terms. Our eye-tracking studies show that people are extremely frugal with their gazes. Web pages are often packed with competing stimulus. Audiences develop selective attention to combat information overload; they notice little and ignore a lot. Headings that start with key terms get more attention than those that don't. For example, the link "Press Releases" is much more effective than "Click here to read press releases." Why? People focus on the first few words of headings while ignoring the rest. Saying "Click here" does not convey anything useful. So it's not good to save your information-carrying keywords for the end of the phrase.

Layer the content. Rather than overwhelm site visitors with extensive content, layer the information on different pages. Start with the key points first and then make it easy for people to drill down. Layering your content satisfies the needs of both casual browsers and serious researchers without sacrificing scannability and completeness. This approach facilitates people's nonlinear information-seeking behavior on the Web.

How important to online writing is the inverted pyramid style?
Start with the summary of key points, then reveal supporting facts is a technique adopted by many successful journalists. This structure gives readers the gist quickly and then lets them burrow into the details of they choose to read on. A long rambling introduction is a sure way to bore readers. People will more likely be captivated if the first part of an article is interesting and focused.

How important are bullets, fragments, white space, and brevity?
Formatting text for readability is essential in attracting and keeping people's attention. Proper Web-formatting techniques break up content into small chunks. Short paragraphs surrounded by white space or a bulleted list appear more approachable than a sold wall of text.

How does a public relations writer distinguish his news releases from those of others online?
Have concise and descriptive titles. Titles that have descriptive keywords are important in garnering interest as well as for search engine optimization. Headlines and titles are often devoid of context, so sarcasm and word play can easily be misunderstood. The Web is truly a worldwide medium, and idioms don't translate easily across borders. Remember, your audience is coming to your site for direct content, not for cleverness.

Follow well-established Web-formatting techniques on all news releases. Repurposing a press release from print for the Web is lazy and should be avoided.

Public Relations Bookshelf

Altman, Rick. *Why Most PowerPoint Presentations Suck*. 3rd ed. Pleasanton, CA: Harvest Books, 2012. This book, from a computer expert, is worth the time for anyone who complements presentations with PowerPoint. And that's everyone!

Aronson, Merry, Don Spetner, and Carol Ames. *The Public Relations Writer's Handbook*. 2nd ed. San Francisco, CA: Jossey-Boss, 2007. Simple, step-by-step approach to creating a wide range of writing, from basic news releases and pitch letters to writing for digital media.

Bartlett, David. *Making Your Point*. New York: St. Martin's Press, 2008. This comprehensive book covers every area of how to communicate more effectively in today's society.

Bivins, Thomas. *Public Relations Writing*. 8th ed. Lincolnwood, IL: NTC/Contemporary Publishing Group. 2013. A popular text, updated to include all aspects of public relations writing, including writing for digital media.

Dean, Fletcher. *10 Steps to Writing a Vital Speech*. Phoenix, AZ: Vital Speeches of the Day, 2011. An experienced corporate speech writer shares his wisdom on preparing for, researching and writing a memorable speech.

Foster, John. *Effective Writing Skills for Public Relations*. 4th ed. Philadelphia, PA: Kogan Page, 2008. Another solid writing text from a former journalist and public relations professional.

Kennedy, Mickie. *Beginner's Guide to Writing Powerful Press Releases*. Baltimore, MD: ereleases.com, 2014. The proprietor of a news release service offers a most knowledgeable perspective on getting the most out of news releases.

Pacelli, Lonnie. *The Truth about Getting Your Point Across...and Nothing but the Truth*. Saddle River, NJ: Prentice Hall, 2006. This is a guide to communicating in all settings—at meetings, presentations, interviews, and more.

Scott, David M. *The New Rules of Marketing and PR*. Hoboken, NJ: John Wiley & Sons, 2007. This book primarily discusses the Internet and how such vehicles as news releases and blogs should be used.

Smith, Ronald D. *Becoming a Public Relations Writer*. 4th ed. New York: Routledge, 2012. Important section on "ethical writing"; good primer.

Strunk, William and Elwyn B. White. *Elements of Style*. New York: Allyn & Bacon, 1999. A classic that *must* be in any public relations writer's library.

Weissman, Jerry. *Presenting to Win: The Art of Telling Your Story*. Upper Saddle River, NJ: Prentice-Hall, Inc., 2006. An experienced speech trainer shares his secrets.

Wilcox, Dennis L. and Bryan H. Reber. *Public Relations Writing and Media Techniques*. 7th ed. Boston, MA: Allyn & Bacon, 2012. Comprehensive review of writing skills and media relations principals.

Zitron, Ed. *This Is How You Pitch: How to Kick Ass in Your First Years of PR*. Muskegon, MI: Sunflower Press, 2013. A take-no-prisoners report from the battlefield experience of a transplanted Brit, complete with an introduction by the author of the literary work *"Dead Pig Collector."* Approach with care.

Endnotes

1. Elizabeth Lancaster, "Paralympic Star Makes History on NBA Stage," *CBS News* (February 16, 2015).
2. "Inner Strength: For Blake Leeper, the Only True Disability in Life Is a Bad Attitude," *Nike News "Inner Strength Series"* (June 16, 2015), http://news.nike.com/news/inner-strength-for-blake-leeper-the-only-true-disability-in-life-is-a-bad-attitude.
3. Fraser P. Seitel, "PR Pros Are Horrible Writers," *odwyerpr.com* (March 5, 2001).
4. "How to Get Editors to Use Press Releases," *Jack O'Dwyer's Newsletter* (May 26, 1993): 3.
5. Linda P. Morton, "Producing Publishable Press Releases," *Public Relations Quarterly* (Winter 1992–1993): 9–11.
6. Fraser P. Seitel, "E-mail News Releases," *odwyerpr.com* (February 23, 2004).
7. Stephen Spender, "The Truly Great," *Collected Poems 1928-1953*. (London, England: Ed Victor Ltd., 1955).
8. Kevin Roose and Peter Lattman, "New-Form Press Release, in Blog, Tweet and Haiku," *The New York Times* (September 8, 2011).

Chapter 16

Integrated Marketing
Communications

Chapter Objectives

1. To discuss the synthesis of advertising, marketing, and public relations to yield an integrated marketing approach in promoting products, services, and brands.

2. To discuss, in detail, the two marketing differentiators of public relations—publicity and third-party endorsement.

3. To explore how international brands build a differentiable identity across geographies.

4. To examine the various tactics and techniques that distinguish integrated marketing, from the traditional—public relations advertising, trade shows, cause-related marketing, etc.—to the 21st-century innovations—social media marketing, brand integration, buzz marketing, etc.

In the old days—before social media, TMZ, or even the computer, for that matter—there was the "Avon lady," who went door-to-door, marketing her line of cosmetics by introducing it to community neighbors.

In these days of 24/7 communication and "communities" composed of social media friends and followers, products and services market themselves a whole lot differently. To wit:

- In 2012, *U.S. News & World Report* magazine offered the hospitals it ranked in its *"Top 100 Hospitals"* a complete merchandising package to promote the distinction, including sample news releases, promotional badges for use in electronic media, print media, and broadcast media, reprints, Best Hospitals 2012–2013 lapel pins, and advertising on USNews.com.

- That same year, New York Life Insurance signed a deal with 10 Major League Baseball teams to provide a promotional plug every time a player slid safely into home plate. As soon as the umpire called the runner safe, a New York Life logo appeared on the TV screen, and the announcer was contracted to say, "Safe at home. Safe and secure, New York Life."[1]

- In 2015, the real hero of the action movie "Jurassic World" movie wasn't an action hero, but rather a 68-year-old man in sunglasses, who casually runs away from attacking pteranodons, clutching margaritas in both hands. The man? None other than Mr. Margaritaville himself, singer Jimmy Buffet, whose Margaritaville saloon chain appeared prominently in the film.[2]

- And then there's the world of sponsored tweets, where boldfaced names from Snoop Dogg to Wendy Williams to Padma Lakshmi get paid by companies to tweet about their products. The queen of the tweeters is everybody's favorite boldface, Kim Kardashian, with 34 million Twitter followers, who reportedly received $10–$20,000 for her 140-character endorsements of everything from eos lip balm to Reebok Easy Tone training kicks to Carl's Jr. hamburgers[3] (**Figure 16-1**).

What's going on here?

Welcome to the global market society where, according to one expert, "everything is up for sale. . . . where market values govern every sphere of life."[4] Perhaps that's an overstatement. But it is true that the various discrete disciplines that have always added up to "marketing" are, today, integrated more than ever before.

Integrated marketing is the intersection of public relations and publicity, advertising, sales promotion, and marketing to promote organizations, products, and services. Creating marketing-oriented tweets and Facebook messages, Instagram photos, YouTube videos, Internet publicity, using celebrities as spokespersons, inserting product placements in movies, sponsoring concerts, creating street theater, and a host of other publicity-seeking techniques are all examples of *integrated marketing communications*.

All are important to sell products and ideas.

While traditional advertising and marketing can build brand awareness, public relations establishes credibility and tells the brand story more comprehensively. Database marketing touches consumers one-on-one. Sales promotion motivates them to action.

The integration of these marketing techniques helps build a cohesive presence for a brand.

Some have suggested that advertising is dying and that public relations is taking over. That may be a bit overzealous.[5] Advertising isn't quite dead yet. In 2014, the top 200 advertisers in the United States spent a record $137.8 billion—with a "b"—on advertising. Procter & Gamble led the way, spending $4.6 billion, with an increasing share devoted to online advertising. AT&T was next at $3.3 billion, followed by General Motors and Comcast, both of which spent $3 billion on advertising.[6] So neither advertising nor marketing is anywhere near "dead." But it is true that public relations and publicity integrated with these other disciplines are very much the rule in many organizations today.

Therefore, the need for integration . . . for *communications cross-training*—to learn the different skills of marketing, advertising, sales promotion, and public relations—becomes a requirement for all communicators.

1 Public Relations vs. Marketing/Advertising

What is the difference between marketing, advertising, and public relations?

Marketing, literally defined, is the selling of a service or product through pricing, distribution, and promotion. Marketing ranges from concepts such as free samples in the hands of consumers to buzz campaigns.

Advertising, literally defined, is a subset of marketing that involves paying to place your message in more traditional media formats, from newspapers and magazines to radio and television to the Internet and outdoors.

Public relations, liberally defined, is the marketing of an organization and the use of unbiased, objective, third-party endorsement to relay information about that organization's products and practices.[7]

With so many media outlets bombarding consumers daily, most organizations realize that public relations can play an expanded role in marketing.

In the past, marketers treated public relations as an ancillary part of the marketing mix—almost an afterthought. They were concerned primarily with making sure that their products met the needs and desires of customers and were priced competitively, distributed widely, and promoted heavily through advertising and merchandising. Gradually, however, these traditional notions among marketers began to change.

The increased number of advertisements in newspapers and on the airwaves caused clutter and placed a significant burden on advertisers who were trying to make the public aware of their products. In the 1980s, the trend toward shorter television advertising spots contributed to three times as many products being advertised on television as there were in the 1970s. In the 1990s, the spread of cable television added yet another multi-channeled outlet for product advertising. In the 2000s, the proliferation of cable TV and Internet advertising intensified the noise and clutter.

In the 2010s, the social media revolution ushered in an era where organizations increasingly used owned media to market their products, services, and ideas via Facebook, Twitter, Instagram, YouTube, Reddit, and myriad other vehicles.

Against this backdrop, the potential of public relations as an added ingredient in the marketing mix has become an imperative. Indeed, marketing guru Philip Kotler was among the first to suggest two decades ago that to the traditional four Ps of marketing—product, price, place, and promotion—a fifth P, *public relations*, should be added.[8]

In the second decade of the 21st century, Kotler's suggestion has increasingly become reality.

2 Product Publicity

Product publicity is the most traditional method of integrating public relations and marketing. In light of how difficult it now is to raise advertising awareness above the noise of so many competitive messages, marketers turn to product publicity as an important adjunct to advertising. Although the public is generally unaware of it, a great deal of what it knows and believes about a wide variety of products comes through press coverage.

In certain circumstances, product publicity can be the most effective element in the marketing mix. For example:

- **Introducing a new product.** Product publicity can start introductory sales at a much higher level of demand by creating more buzz around the "news" of a new product. This is why Apple, for example, will typically "announce" its breakthrough products through press conferences, as opposed to advertising.

- **Eliminating distribution problems with retail outlets.** Often the way to get shelf space is to have consumers demand the product. Product publicity can be extremely effective in creating consumer demand.

- **Small budgets and strong competition.** Advertising is expensive. Product publicity is cheap. Often publicity is the best way to tell the story. That's why Samuel Adams Boston Lager beer became a household name—and a huge franchise—almost solely through early publicity opportunities.

- **Explaining a complicated product.** The use and benefits of many products—particularly financial services—are difficult to explain to mass audiences in a brief ad. Product publicity, through extended news columns, can be invaluable.

- **Tying the product to a unique representative.** Try as it might, the advertising industry can't escape the staying power of unique mascots who become tied inextricably to products. Consider the following:

  - GEICO's gecko has earned its place as the insurance company's mascot and spokesman across many media platforms.

  - The Jolly Green Giant has "ho ho ho'ed" so long at General Mills that he now has his own Green Giant Food Company and Web site.

  - Burger King's "King" is back with a vengeance in the new century, cavorting on football fields and in other venues for a whole new generation.

  - The real "king," however, is McDonald's standard bearer, Ronald McDonald, who first appeared in 1963 and has since starred on national television, at Academy Awards ceremonies, and around the world. No other iconic figure in history has become more synonymous with any company (**Figure 16-2**).

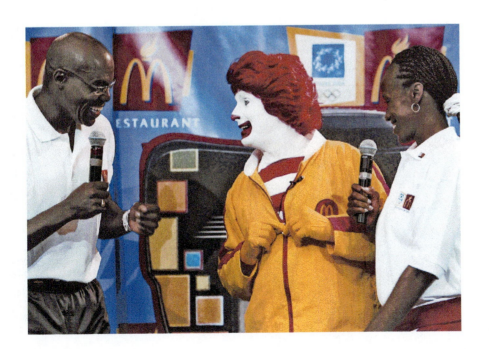

FIGURE 16-2
The king.
Maybe not of burgers but certainly of corporate icons. Ronald McDonald, here with former Olympic gold medalists Carl Lewis and Jackie-Joyner Kersee to celebrate "Go Active Day" in Athens, Greece.
Photo: Courtesy of O'Dwyerpr.com

Third-Party Endorsement

Perhaps more than anything else, the value of third-party endorsement is the primary reason smart organizations value product publicity. Third-party endorsement, as noted, refers to the tacit support given a product by an "objective" third-party observer—a blog, newspaper, magazine, tweet, or broadcast—which mentions the product as "news."

Advertising often is perceived as self-serving. People know that the advertiser not only created the message but also paid for it. Publicity, on the other hand, generally carries no such stigma. Editors, after all, are considered objective, impartial, indifferent, unbiased, neutral. Therefore, publicity appears to be news and is more trustworthy than advertising that is paid for by a clearly nonobjective sponsor.

Traditional journalists, sensitive to the proliferating raft of product placements in the media, have become sensitive to mentioning product names in print. Some, in fact, have a policy of deleting brand or company identifications in news columns. Bloggers, newer to the media world, often have no such reluctance. Indeed, although not widely discussed, companies may well pay bloggers for a product posting or to put up a link or graphic. Organizations will seek out quality blogs in their industry and pay bloggers to link to the product Web site. The more blog readers who click through to the site, the higher an organization's Google page rank.[9]

In recent years, one integrated marketing practice that has drawn journalistic scorn is that of companies using well-known spokespersons to promote products without identifying that they are being paid for the endorsement. Journalists argue that such presentations are patently unethical paid endorsements designed to appear objective.[10] Broadcast networks have become particularly sensitive when celebrities don't disclose financial relationships with products they mention. CNN changed its policy on paid spokespersons after suffering an embarrassing incident with actress Kathleen Turner, who promoted drug company products without disclosing her financial relationship with the company. Fox News suffered a similar embarrassment when future presidential candidate Dr. Ben Carson endorsed a medical supplement that was paying him.[11] Nonprofits seem to suffer decidedly less anguish when they use celebrities to promote their activities (**Figure 16-3**).

FIGURE 16-3

It's my third party, and I'll sign if I want to.

Actress and former Girl Scout Elizabeth Banks supplies third-party endorsement to Nestle, signing a poster and talking about Nestle Crunch Girl Scout Candy Bars.

Photo: Courtesy of O'Dwyerpr.com

A Question of Ethics

End of a Subway Super Spokesman

For decades, companies have used celebrities to sell products. Why? It works. People—for whatever ungodly reason—find comfort in using a product or service that is used by a well-known personality.

In 2000, the Subway sandwich company went one better. It hired an unknown college student, who became obese from eating junk food and then found his salvation—and lost 200 pounds—by going on a Subway sandwich diet and exercising. That college student, Jared Fogle, became Subway's spokesman for the next 15 years. By 2015, Jared the Subway Guy had become one of the nation's most well-known product representatives. He had also become wealthy, with a reported net worth of $15 million (**Figure 16-4**).

And then in July 2015, Jared Fogle's connection with Subway—and for all intents, his life as he had known it—came crashing down.

Subway suspended its relationship with Fogle after federal and state authorities raided his Indiana home as part of a child pornography investigation. The raid came after an employee of Fogle's charitable foundation was arrested on child pornography charges. More than 400 videos of child pornography were found in the employee's possession.

Within weeks, the FBI had subpoenaed an affidavit reportedly containing alleged texts between Fogle and a former female Subway franchisee in 2008, in which the former spokesman reportedly said he paid for sex with a 16-year-old girl. The woman, who initially met Fogle at a Subway function, hired a lawyer to determine whether the communication violated her franchiser-franchisee contract with Subway. She also claimed she shared the texts and her concerns about Fogle with Subway management at the time, but Subway did nothing. Subway responded that it had no record of the woman's complaint.

Suspending its relationship with its long-term spokesman ended Subways most lucrative endorsement deal in its history. According to the company's chief marketing officer, Fogle was likely responsible for one-third to one-half of Subway's growth over 15 years.

Only to have the relationship end disastrously for the spokesman, who was sentenced to 15 years in federal prison, and embarrassingly for the company.*

FIGURE 16-4   **No more super hero.**
Subway Guy Jared Fogle lost his job and more when he became embroiled in a child pornography investigation in 2015.
Photo: Birdie Thompson/AdMedia/Newscom

Questions

1. How do you feel about the way Subway handled the Jared Fogle controversy?

2. Should Subway hire a new spokesman? Why or why not?

3. What is the larger lesson here about hiring spokespeople?

* For further information, see Sydney Ember, "Jared Fogle and Subway Suspend Ties After Raid at His Home," *The New York Times* (July 7, 2015); Tom Murphy and Rick Callahan, "Raid Spotlights Subway Pitchman's Ties to Ex-Foundation Head," *Associated Press* (July 8, 2015); and Hayley Peterson, "The FBI Has Subpoenaed Lewd Text Messages Between Subway's Jared Fogle and a Former Subway Franchisee," *Business Insider* (July 31, 2015).

Native Advertising

The latest element in the product publicity arsenal would have been antithetical to both professional journalists and public relations practitioners in an earlier day.

Native advertising—also known as branded content or sponsored journalism or sponsored content—is just that: content authored by and paid for by public relations professionals, placed in news site news columns, shoulder-to-shoulder with real news, to appear to look like the real thing.

In the past, no self-respecting newspaper or magazine would even consider such a blatant attack on the firewall between advertising and news. Indeed, some journalists worry that the blurring of the traditional lines between advertising and product publicity will also erode a consumer's ability to differentiate between the two.[12] Despite such concerns, native advertising is thriving for one simple reason: Publications need revenue, and native advertising is one way to achieve it. The broadcast equivalent of print native advertising is a new symbiotic relationship between advertisers and TV feature programs, in which organizations from amusement parks to restaurants to car companies pay broadcasters to report on their products.

Indeed, the most venerable names in the media—from *The Washington Post* to the *Financial Times* to *The New York Times* have joined the less venerable *Politico, Business Insider,* and *BuzzFeed* as repositories for sponsored content. In fact, native advertising was on target to reach $8 billion by the end of 2015 and grow to $21 billion in 2018.[13]

So like it or not, the sponsored content of digital advertising is here to stay and should be considered as part of the product publicity arsenal. The real question is, how should a public relations professional approach this new hybrid vehicle? Here are a few suggestions:

- **Realize this isn't really "news."** Consider sponsored content, the advertising supplements, and vanity magazine articles of the Internet Age.

  Understand that readers know that these articles are "biased" in favor of the sponsoring agency—often to pitch a product or service or underscore a community relations or philanthropic commitment or talk up an industry for a trade association group. (Many are bylined by vice presidents of public affairs or similar corporate officers.)

  So hyperbole and boastful claims and adjectives that could be questioned should be avoided. Articles should be written straight, heavy on facts, and short on superlatives. Let the facts of the program about which you are writing speak for themselves.

- **Place the content in context.** Assume—even if it's not true in many cases—that readers understand that native advertising isn't especially objective, public relations writers must take pains to place the subject matter in broader context— to underscore the "significance" of the content being discussed.

  For example, CTIA—the Cellular Telecommunications Industry Association— was a regular *Washington Post* native advertising contributor, which used its submissions to place the industry's role into broad context so that readers might understand the importance of the content, sponsored or not.

- **Emphasize consumerism.** Much sponsored content—no surprise—concerns products and services for sale. After all, why else would an organization pay a public relations person to ghost editorial copy for a news site? In native advertising, the best way to "pitch" products and services is by reinforcing their "value" to society. Such creative, consumer-oriented sponsored content can be a valuable complement to a broader public relations media campaign.

- **Discuss philanthropy.** Even when people used to read newspapers and magazines, editors were loathe to say nice things about all the good works for which those reviled capitalist giants might be responsible. So philanthropy—how organizations "give back" to society—is an excellent topic for native advertising.

- **Avoid the hard sell.** Finally, hard sell should be avoided at all costs. One of the most blatant examples of over-the-top selling was The Atlantic's disastrous experience with native advertising from the Church of Scientology in 2013.

This post, which lauded Scientology leader David Miscavige for creating a *"new breed of church, ideal in location, design, quality of religious service and social betterment programs,"* lasted about a nanosecond before outraged critics caused a chagrined *Atlantic* to replace the Scientologist's self-congratulatory content with a circumspect note: "*We have temporarily suspended this advertising campaign pending a review of our policies that govern sponsor content and subsequent comment threads.*"[14]

The lesson for journalists and public relations professionals availing themselves of native advertising: Cuidado.

3 Building a Brand

Once upon a time, a brand was an identifying mark burned onto livestock with a branding iron. Today, a brand is the way to identify a particular type of something. Indeed, the watchwords in business today are brands and branding—creating a differentiable identity or position for a company or product.

In more traditional times, it took years for brands such as Pepsi, Coke, McDonald's, Hertz, FedEx, and Walmart to establish themselves. Today, with the advent of social media and the Web, thriving technology companies from Apple and Google to Amazon and to Uber have become household words in a historical nanosecond.

The act of branding is something communicators can control. A branding program is all about managing perceptions by using the many tools of integrated marketing communication and observing the following principles.

- **Be early.** We remember the "first" in a category because of the *law of primacy*, which posits that people are more likely to remember you if you were the first in their minds in a particular category.

- **Be memorable.** Equally important is to fight through the clutter by creating a memorable brand. With hundreds of participants in categories from bottled

FIGURE 16-5
Street cred.
Friendly Ice Cream
Corporation took to
the streets with free
samples in an effort
to reinforce brand
recognition.
*Photo: Courtesy
of O'Dwyerpr.com*

water to bathing suits, a brand needs to stand out by distinguishing itself in some way—through uniqueness or advertising slogan or social responsibility or whatever. Creating brand awareness requires boldness.

- **Be aggressive.** A successful brand also requires a constant drumbeat of publicity to keep the company's name before the public. Potential customers need to become familiar with the brand. Potential investors need to become confident that the brand is an active one. So take it to the customers aggressively (**Figure 16-5**). The new competitive economy leaves little room for demure integrated marketing communications.

- **Use heritage.** Baby boomers are old. Gen Xers are getting older. And *heritage* is very much in vogue. This means citing the traditions and history of a product or organization as part of building the brand. As consumers live longer, an increasing number of citizens long for "the good old days."

- **Create a personality.** The best organizations are those that create "personalities" for themselves. Who is number one in car safety? Volvo. What company stands for overnight delivery? FedEx. What's the East Coast university that boasts the best and the brightest? Harvard. Or at least that's what most people think. The organization's personality should be reflected in all communications materials the organization produces.

As more and more companies each year attempt to bust through the advertising and marketing clutter by increasing marketing efforts in such areas as social media, banner ads, proprietary Web sites, free classified advertising, e-zines and e-mail marketing, the challenge to create a differentiable brand becomes that much more difficult.

FYI

World's Top 10 Sports Team Brands

In the second decade of the 21st century, few worldwide brands are more valuable than professional sports teams—especially those in soccer, football, baseball, and basketball.

Professional sports team brands are booming as communication takes the most prominent teams—through television broadcasts, jersey sales, and social media presence—around the world. In 2014, the National Football League entered into multi-year TV deals that delivered nearly $7 billion in annual revenue. The National Basketball Association was close behind with its $2.66 billion-a-year deal with ESPN and TNT networks, which was three times the previous rate. Soccer's English Premier League signed a $2.7 billion-a-year contract with Sky TV. And the Los Angeles Dodgers' signed a 25-year, $8.35 billion contract for regional broadcasts on Time Warner Cable.

As to the number one sports brand in the world, the honor went to soccer's—or if you prefer, futbol's—Read Madrid, with a brand valued at $3.6 billion. Real Madrid's rise to the #1 spot upended the former #1 New York Yankees, who lost the face of the franchise in 2014, when Derek Jeter retired after 20 years **(Figure 16-6)**. The dethroned Yankees could take comfort in the knowledge, as detailed in the following Forbes list of "Most Valuable Sports Teams," that the brand was still worth a not-too-shabby $3.2 billion.

FIGURE 16-6   Jeter in training.
After Derek Jeter retired in 2014 as the shortstop of the New York Yankees, the brand slipped to second in the world, valued at a paltry $3.2 billion.
Photo by Raina Seitel, courtesy of Fraser Seitel

1. Real Madrid — $3.6 billion
2. Dallas Cowboys — $3.2 billion
3. New York Yankees — $3.2 billion
4. Barcelona — $3.16 billion
5. Manchester United — $3.1 billion
6. Los Angeles Lakers — $2.6 billion
7. New England Patriots — $2.6 billion
8. New York Knicks — $2.5 billion
9. Los Angeles Dodgers — $2.4 billion
10. Washington Redskins — $2.4 billion*

*For further information, see Kurt Badenhausen, "The World's 50 Most Valuable Sports Team 2015," *Forbes* (July 15, 2015).

4 Traditional Integrated Marketing

Among the more traditional public relations activities used to market products are public relations advertising, article reprints, trade show participation, use of spokespersons, cause-related marketing, and in-kind promotions.

Public Relations Advertising

Traditionally, organizations used advertising to sell products. In 1936, a company named Warner & Swasey initiated an ad campaign that stressed the power of America as a nation and the importance of American business in the nation's future. In the 1980s, Mobil Oil—predecessor of ExxonMobil—doubled down on the technique, advertising its views and issues on op-ed pages across the nation. This technique to advertise non-products became known variously as institutional advertising, image advertising, public service advertising, issues advertising, and ultimately public relations advertising.

Public relations advertising is still widely used today to communicate everything from corporate mergers, personnel changes, and important announcements to organizational views on issues of the day. Such paid advertising is often used to complement public relations campaigns or even as a last resort if other "free" publicity channels aren't accessible.

Article Reprints

Once an organization has received product publicity in a newspaper or magazine, whether in print or online, it should market the publicity further to achieve maximum sales punch. Marketing can be done through article reprints aimed at that part of a target audience—wholesalers, retailers, or consumers—that might not have seen the original article. Reprints, included on a Web site and direct mailed, also help reinforce the reactions of those who read the original article.

Trade Show Participation

Trade show participation enables an organization to display its products before important target audiences. The decision to participate should be considered with the following factors in mind:

1. **Analyze the show carefully.** Make sure the audience is one that can't be reached effectively through other promotional materials, such as article reprints or local publicity. Also, be sure the audience is essential to the sale of the product.

2. **Select a common theme.** Integrate public relations, publicity, advertising, and sales promotion. Unify all organizational elements for the trade show to avoid any hint of interdepartmental rivalries.

3. **Emphasize what's new.** Talk about the new model that's being displayed. Discuss the additional features, new uses, or recent performance data of the products displayed. Trade show exhibitions should reveal innovation, breakthrough, and newness.

4. **Consider local promotional efforts.** While in town during a trade show, an organization can enhance both the recognition of its product and the traffic at its booth by doing local promotions.

5. **Evaluate the worth.** Always evaluate whether the whole exercise was worth it. This involves counting, qualifying, and following up on leads generated as well as looking at other intangibles to see if marketing objectives were met.[15]

Spokespersons

In our celebrity-dominated culture, the use of spokespersons to promote products has increased. As noted, spokespersons shouldn't disguise the fact that they are advocates for a particular product.

Spokespersons must be articulate, fast on their feet, and thoroughly knowledgeable about the subject. When these criteria are met, the use of spokespersons as an integrated marketing tool can be most effective.

FIGURE 16-7
The greatest.
Michael Jordan, dubbed by many as the "greatest basketball player of all time", was still making $100 million through endorsement deals, like that for Hanes underwear, more than a decade after retiring from the NBA.
Photo: Feature Photo Service/Newscom

In recent years, the use of spokespersons to promote products has become so crazed that in 2003, Coca-Cola signed high school basketball phenom LeBron James to a six-year, $12 million contract to promote Sprite. James hadn't even stepped foot onto an NBA court. At the time Coke signed him, the Ohio high schooler already had signed a shoe deal with Nike for a cool $100 million. Of course, a decade later those earlier signings proved prescient, as King James endorsement income with Coke, Nike, Upper Deck, Samsung, Audemars Piguet, Dunkin Donuts, and others totaled a cool $42 million annually.[16]

As successful a spokesman as LeBron was, he still ranked a distant second to history's most successful athlete endorser; none other than James' predecessor as the "king of professional basketball," Michael Jordan. M.J., although having retired more than a decade ago, made a whopping $100 million in 2014, largely as a result of his Nike Air Jordan brand and his ubiquitous Hanes underwear commercials (**Figure 16-7**).

Cause-Related Marketing

Public relations sponsorships tied to philanthropy are another effective integrated marketing device. Again, in an economy where advertising is omnipresent and differentiation is at a premium, companies turn to sponsorship of the arts, education, music, festivals, anniversaries, sports, and charitable causes for promotional and public relations purposes.

Cause-related marketing will continue to grow in the 21st century, as aging baby boomers and milennials, alike, express concern about issues that affect their lives, such as protecting the environment and aiding the less fortunate. This, coupled with the need of corporations to reassure the citizenry they are "not evil," should drive the creation of events and decision-making by corporate sponsors.

In-Kind Promotions

When a service, product, or other consideration in exchange for publicity exposure is offered, it is called an *in-kind promotion*. Examples of in-kind promotions include the following:

1. Providing services or products as prizes offered by a newspaper or charity in exchange for being listed as a cosponsor in promotional materials.
2. Providing services or products to a local business in exchange for having fliers inserted in shopping bags or as statement stuffers.
3. Providing services or products to doctors' offices, auto repair shops, or other businesses in exchange for having brochures prominently displayed.
4. Providing posters of the product or service at well-trafficked locations.

The point of in-kind promotions is to leverage the name and use of products and services, so that more potential buyers are exposed to the organization.

21st-Century Integrated Marketing

Like any other public relations technique, integrated marketing, too, must keep pace with the ever-changing world of promotional innovations to help sell products and services. Among them are television brand integration, infomercials, word-of-mouth marketing, television, movie, and social media product placement and more.

Social Media Marketing

The fastest growing category of advertising in the 21st century is digital, and the emerging mechanism to deliver online is mobile, through smart phones and tablets. And the most rapidly emerging integrated marketing technique is using social media to create "buzz" for a product.

Traditional marketers from Coca-Cola to Kraft Foods to Procter & Gamble have all shifted significant marketing dollars to online marketing and social media. As proof:

- 23% of Fortune 500 companies have a corporate blog, a number that has remained fairly steady over recent years.
- 62% of Fortune 500 companies have an active corporate Twitter account, and just about every Fortune 500 company has a Twitter presence. Companies with the highest number of Twitter followers include Google, Whole Foods, Starbucks, Southwest Airlines, *The Washington Post*, Verizon Wireless, Coca-Cola, and McDonalds.
- 58% of Fortune 500 companies have a corporate Facebook page, with insurance, specialty retail (apparel, home, appliances, furniture) and food production, services, and drug store categories leading the way.[17]

Social media enables companies to create direct relationships with their customers, who use these same tools in their daily lives. In terms of integrated marketing, social media is becoming the fastest and most cost efficient way to build relationships with individual consumers worldwide.

Brand Integration

Another burgeoning phenomenon in television, movies, and music is to integrate products into the fabric of what is being presented on the screen or in the song. When one of ABC's *Desperate Housewives* found herself hard up for cash, she donned an evening gown and extolled the virtues of a Buick Lacrosse at a car show. In Sony's smash hit, *The Lego Movie*, protagonist Lord Business speaks glowingly about Apple's iPod Shuffle. Singer Chris Brown's *"Forever"* included a reference to *"double your pleasure,"* a passing reference to Wrigley's Double Mint gum, for which Brown would make a commercial.[18]

Clearly, such product emphases were not just coincidence.

As technology and clutter blunt the effectiveness and reach of traditional 30-second commercials, more advertisers are paying to integrate their products directly into the action of a show or film or even a song. In 2012, in fact, an entire episode of the hit NBC sitcom *30 Rock* was devoted to a look back in time to what the announcer called *"The Kraft Product Placement Comedy Hour,"* sponsored by Kraft Singles. The bit made sense because not only was Kraft an early NBC sponsor, but the corporation also entered into a "branded integration" contract that combined real-life commercials with fake on-the-air ones.[19]

The process of brand integration on television probably owed its jump start to CBS's *Survivor*, which financed itself largely through product tie-ins with advertisers whose products were mentioned in the course of the show. This was a far cry from serendipitous—that is, unpaid—earlier TV product mentions, such as Junior Mints and Pez on *Seinfeld*.[20]

In pop music, Lady Gaga enlisted sponsorships from a variety of companies, from Miracle Whip to Polaroid to Virgin Mobile to the Plenty of Fish dating site for her 2009 *Telephone* song with Beyonce. And Courvoisier came up with a brand integration deal with rapper Busta Rhymes, after his song *"Pass the Courvoisier"* lifted product sales.[21]

Product Placements

Once removed from brand integration are product placements, the decades-old practice of inserting name-brand cans of soda, clothes, accessories, cars, whatever, into the scenes and dialogue of novels, TV programs, movies, video games, and even cartoons. These have proliferated at a rapid—and to some, alarming—rate.

- Advertisers from Dunkin' Donuts to Intel to Honda have all signed up with the publishers of game consoles to embed their messages in video games.[22]

- Comedy Central introduced its adult cartoon show, *Shorties Watchin' Shorties*, which prominently featured Domino's Pizza, Red Bull energy drink, and Vans sneakers.[23]

- General Motors (GM), seeking new ways to market cars in its comeback, even made its Camaro and Traverse brands central parts in the NBC series, *My Own Worst Enemy*. Unfortunately for GM, the show was canceled after only four episodes.[24]

In recent years, with more video available via digital streaming, TV marketers, at least, have begun to look elsewhere for placement opportunities. For example,

Coca-Cola pulled its signature red cups from the judges' table on *American Idol*, and Hyundai removed its kiwi-green Tucson vehicle from AMC's *The Walking Dead*.

While product placements aren't nearing extinction, the wide variety of other techniques to showcase products have caused communication channels to go the extra mile for the products they endorse; for example using tweets or Facebook pages to promote the placement to followers.[25]

Infomercials

Infomercials were greeted with universal catcalls in the 1980s when they were introduced as program-length commercials, shamelessly hawking products.

Nonetheless, infomercials remain strong for one reason: They work. Collectively, the U.S. market for infomercial products stood at $170 billion in 2009 and is expected to exceed $250 billion by 2016. That's a lot of money for baldness cures, fitness equipment, potato peelers, and sauna belts.[26]

Celebrities from Alex Trebek to Brooke Shields, from Suzanne Somers to Donald Trump are staples among the growing parade of shameless infomercial hawkers. The all-time infomercial champ, though, is former boxer George Foreman, whose immortal infomercial about his Lean Mean Fat-Reducing Grilling Machine reportedly earned him in excess of $137 million!

Buzz Marketing

Also known as word-of-mouth, *buzz marketing* is another alternative to traditional advertising that enlists "influencers" or "trend setters" to spread the word about a particular product. Today, with social media so ubiquitous, paying such influencers to facilitate the "buzz" has become yet another source of celebrity income.

The practice began with teenagers, who appeared to be popular. It evolved to marketers reaching out for "evangelists" who are already diehard fans of a particular product and persuading them to "spread the gospel." Its proponents hail word-of-mouth as the most honest and ethical of advertising media. "People don't want to hurt their friends and family and colleagues with bad information," is the way one believer put it.[27]

Today, buzz marketing is more often done with the help of celebrities on social media, particularly to reach the most robust buying sector in the economy, young people. As marketers have struggled to connect with young audiences, they turn to people like Ricky Dillon (Who??), a video and social media star with millions of followers on Twitter and Instagram and a YouTube channel with 2.5 million subscribers. So Coca-Cola, for one, paid young Mr. Dillon to post two cans of Coke on Instagram, one marked *"Ricky,"* the other marked *"Dillon."* The reaction? *"Awesome,"* tweeted one fan, and another urged him to sell the cans on Ebay.[28]

The flip side to paying for creating buzz is that celebrities—particularly those who appeal to young followers—may be accused of "selling out." So while such endorsements might assist the credibility of sponsoring companies, it may have just the reverse effect on the celebrity doing the endorsing. Nonetheless, media companies like Viacom and Tumblr have developed marketing platforms that connect influencers with brands in search of buzz.

You Name It

What other 21st-century integrated marketing venues exist? How fertile is your imagination? Consider the following:

■ **Sports teams.** It used to be that stadiums were named for the highest bidder. Today, the team itself takes on the name of the sponsor who pays for it. Venues such as the St. Louis Cardinals' Busch Stadium and the Washington Redskins' FedEx Field have given way to teams such as the New York Red Bulls, the Major League Soccer franchise named after the sports energy drink, which paid more than $100 million for the integrated marketing privilege. But when the New York Giants tried to sell stadium naming rights to a German insurance company linked to the Nazis, the franchise was forced to reverse field and shelve the $25-million-a-year bonanza.[29] The venue is now called MetLife Stadium, a much safer choice.

■ **Online game shows.** What national advertiser hasn't sponsored a game show? But what JetBlue did in 2012 was way different. JetBlue designed its own online game show to be the centerpiece of a $2 million campaign to build awareness of its JetBlue vacation package travel service. The show was to take place on the JetBlue Web site for one week, complete with its own slick host and fabulous prizes for contestant volunteers.[30]

■ **Whaaaa?** No space is too odd to integrate marketing messages. US Airways sells ads on airsickness bags. Hockey teams sell ads on Zamboni ice machines. School districts sell ads on the outside of school buses. Folgers Coffee buys ads on the top of manhole covers. Hands down, the most bizarre 21st-century integrated marketing technique was the use of a person's body—literally from head to toe—for marketing purposes. In 2008, a father looking for money to buy a new car sold rights to a permanent tattoo on his neck to Web-hosting company Globat. And if that wasn't enough, the same company purchased a temporary tattoo ad on the pregnant belly of a St. Louis woman—to promote its product (not the woman's baby).

Ridiculous? Perhaps. But if we're writing about it here—it worked!

Last Word

The key marketing question in the 21st century is, *How do we generate buzz?* How do we distinguish ourselves and get our voice heard in the midst of hundreds of thousands of competing voices?

To marketing expert Al Ries, who cut his teeth in the advertising industry, the answer was obvious. "In the past, it may have been true that a beefy advertising budget was the key ingredient in the brand-building process. . . . Today brands are born, not made. A new brand must be capable of generating favorable publicity in the media or it won't have a chance in the marketplace."[31]

In other words, said Ries, it is public relations and its attendant communications forms—not advertising alone—that differentiate an organization, product, or issue.

Perhaps more precisely stated, what is needed now is an integrated approach to communications, combining the best of marketing, advertising, sales promotion, and public relations with all forms of media from online to print to broadcast to face-to-face.

The clear marketing need for organizations and those who serve them is to build lasting client relationships. A successful communications professional must be knowledgeable about all aspects of the communications mix. Integrated marketing communications, then, becomes paramount in preparing public relations professionals for the challenges of the second decade of the 21st century.

Discussion Starters

1. What is meant by *integrated marketing communications*?
2. Describe the differences among advertising, marketing, and public relations.
3. What is meant by *third-party endorsement*?
4. In what situations is product publicity most effective?
5. Describe the pros and cons of using a well-known individual as a spokesperson.
6. What is *native advertising*?
7. How can integrated marketing help build a brand?
8. What are the purposes of public relations advertising?
9. What is the significance of Warner & Swasey and Mobil Oil in terms of public relations advertising?
10. What are several 21st-century techniques of integrated marketing communications?

Pick of the Literature

Integrated Marketing Communication, 2nd Edition

Robyn Blakeman. London, UK: Rowman & Littlefield, 2015

This is an excellent introduction to how using a variety of marketing methods and techniques can aid a strategic campaign.

The author begins with an all-encompassing definition of integrated marketing and then explores the components of branding and positioning, media advertising, social media, and mobile marketing and also, public relations.

The public relations discussion looks at how the function might be used strategically to support integrated marketing and then walks readers through the documents that public relations writers produce to support marketing campaigns. A number of instructive case studies complement each section of this comprehensive work.

Case Study — Arrogant Alex Learns Humility—Finally

Alex Rodriguez, inarguably, was one of the most gifted baseball players of all time. Born in New York City, his family moved to the Dominican Republic and then to Miami, where young Alex became so famous as a ball player that he was drafted first in the nation by the Seattle Mariners in 1993.

Within a matter of a few years, he became one of the most heralded, in-demand and highest paid players in Major League history—until it all came crumbling down in 2014.

Stellar Performer

From the beginning, ARod, as he was known, was destined for baseball greatness.

In his first six years in the big leagues, toiling for the mediocre Mariners, Rodriguez not only led the American League in batting, but registered the highest right-handed batting average since the legendary Joe DiMaggio in 1939. He went on to post the highest totals ever for a shortstop in runs, hits, doubles, extra base hits, and slugging and established Seattle club records for average, runs, hits, doubles and total bases, in a 1996 season that statistical analysts considered the best year ever for a shortstop.

But Seattle turned out to be just a warm up for what would follow.

Beginning in 2001, first with the Texas Rangers and then with the New York Yankees, Alex Rodriguez blazed an exceptional trail of achievement and made more money than any player in the history of baseball. In 2001, ARod signed a deal with the Rangers that paid him $252 million for 10 years, the highest baseball deal ever up to that time. He went on to become the league's Most Valuable Player (MVP) in 2003. Then, with Texas now wishing to unload his lucrative contract, the Yankees were more than happy to pick it and him up in 2004.

With New York, ARod grew to an even bigger star on a bigger stage; becoming only the third player in history, along with two Hall of Famers, to rack up seven consecutive seasons of 35 home runs, 100 runs scored and 100 runs batted in.

Off the field, the endorsements rolled in, with Rodriguez serving as spokesman for Nike, Rawlings, Wheaties, Pepsi, and even the "Got Milk" campaign, all for significant payouts.

Nothing, it seemed, could knock this extraordinary player and star marketer off his pedestal.

Arrogant Actor

In 2007, his third year with the Yankees and in the last year of his contract, even as his baseball feats accelerated, Rodriguez seemed to become a different person—less likeable, more attitude, more arrogant.

Never shy to talk to the press about his exploits, he joked on the *David Letterman Show* about his new, leaner look. He acknowledged to a reporter as to how he and team captain Derek Jeter—one of the most beloved Yankees of all time—weren't particularly close friends. When he was awarded his third league MVP award, he claimed he would like to remain a Yankee for the rest of his career. But his agent, the inimical Scott Boras, announced that his client wouldn't renew his Yankee contract, because he was unsure of the team's future direction. Both Rodriguez and Boras were roundly criticized for their blatant brinksmanship, in a transparent ploy to hold the Yankees up for more money. Sure enough, ARod ultimately signed the highest contract in baseball history for 10 years and $275 million, loaded with incentives if he reached future record-breaking milestones.

Trouble soon followed. In spring training, when ARod's name appeared on a list of players suspected of taking performance-enhancing drugs, he first declined comment; but since there were then no penalties for steroid use, he later admitted—in a press conference attended by his teammates—he had, indeed, taken the performance-enhancing drugs **(Figure 16-8)**. Things only

FIGURE 16-8   Fallen hero.
A somber team of New York Yankees showed solidarity with Alex Rodriguez in the spring of 2009, as he reluctantly acknowledged at a press conference, his use of performance-enhancing drugs.
Photo: Brian Cassella/Rapport Press/Newscom

deteriorated when the team returned to New York. ARod became a recurring target for the New York City tabloids, which charted his every misstep as he caroused the New York City nightlife scene. He reportedly demanded special treatment from the team and grew distant from the same teammates who had supported him, especially the beloved captain Derek Jeter.

In 2013, after continuing to thrive on the field but suffer in the Court of Public Opinion, ARod was sidelined by hip surgery and became a central figure in another scandal involving now-banned, performance-enhancing drugs. While headlines warned that charges were coming, ARod continued to deny any involvement. He tweeted that his personal doctor had cleared him to return to the field. The Yankees disagreed, and a public battle between team and star commenced on the back pages of the tabloids.

In 2014, the roof fell in. Major League Baseball, claiming enough proof that Rodriguez was guilty, suspended him for the entire season for violating the league's Performance Enhancing Drug Policy. The Yankees declined to come to their fallen star's aid and said little.

Rather than serving his suspension peacefully, Rodriguez lit up the tabloids with sinister charges against both the league and the team including:

- He hired a high-profile, big-mouthed lawyer who accused the league of staging a *"crusade"* and a *"witch hunt"* and a *"shameful endeavor"* to destroy his client.

- The lawyer then accused the Yankees of medical malfeasance, of trumping up the player's injuries so as not to have to pay him.

- Rodriguez stormed out of a baseball hearing, claiming he was being railroaded, and then told a radio interviewer, *"My position hasn't changed. I didn't do it. I shouldn't serve one inning."*

Repentant Sinner

By the time the 2015 baseball season rolled around, most people in and outside of baseball had given up on the bizarre and off base antics of Alex Rodriguez. Even the Yankees, contractually obligated to allow him to play again, didn't expect much from their disgraced former star.

And then, Alex Rodriguez got public relations religion.

- First, he acknowledged, finally, what everyone had suspected all along, that he had been guilty of taking steroids and lying about his steroid use. He apologized and hoped he might be forgiven over time.

- Second, his production on the field, expected to suffer as a result of the layoff, actually improved. He was once again a team leader in hitting. And when the Yankees announced that he would no longer play the field but rather serve as the "designated hitter," Rodriguez accepted the limited duty without complaint.

- Third and most important, ARod became a model public citizen. While his hits won games and set records, his words were always in praise of his teammates and in gratitude to the Yankee fans, who had accepted him back into the fold. He even refused to be drawn into the controversy that erupted when the Yankees announced that, in light of his prior steroid use, they wouldn't honor the portion of his contract that called for incentives as he reached milestones.

Typical of the new Alex was his reaction the night he passed the immortal Willie Mays for fourth place on the all time list. Said the chastened pinstriped diplomat, *"I can tell you this (I wish I could) thank every fan personally for not only the way they've treated me all tonight, but for the way they've treated me all season."**

*For further information, see Mike Axisa, "Just How Much Has A-Rod Made During His Career?" *River Ave Blues* (February 16, 2010); Erik Matuszewski, Eben Novy, and Williams M. Levinson, "Rodriguez Loses Far More than $25 Million Salary in MLB Ban," Bloomberg Businessweek (January 13, 2014); Fraser P. Seitel, "Winning Back Public Trust," Odwyerpr.com (June 1, 2015); and Steve Serby, "Alex Rodriguez on His Miracle Comeback, the World Series and Being Clean," The New York Post (August 1, 2015).

Questions

1. What would you have advised Alex Rodriguez upon his being charged with steroid use?

2. How would you assess his public relations approach upon being suspended from baseball?

3. What were the public relations elements that helped return Rodriguez to favor when he returned from his suspension in 2015?

4. What are the larger public relations lessons of the Rodriguez case?

From the Top

An Interview with Tadd Schwartz

Tadd Schwartz is the founder and president of Schwartz Media Strategies, a public relations, marketing, and digital media firm based in Miami, Florida. Schwartz Media Strategies has national practices in real estate; financial and legal services; hospitality and lifestyle; destination marketing; consumer affairs; and cultural arts. Offering services ranging from media relations, crisis management, and targeted marketing, to Hispanic communications and social media, the firm helps clients reach their core audiences with the goal of generating new business and building increased brand value.

How helpful can public relations be for a marketer?

Public relations amplifies the value of a marketing campaign, lending an element of third-party credibility to advertising, direct marketing, collateral material development, and even events. Prospective clients or customers who have read about your business or product in the news are much more likely to accept your marketing proposition when it comes time to reach out to them directly.

How can public relations help build a brand?

Every brand has a story, and public relations is a vehicle for broadcasting that story, whether it's through traditional media or social media. Publicity gives your brand a sense of depth and substance that can't be bought. It has to be earned.

Is public relations more important than advertising in selling products?

Depends who you ask, but no matter your school of thought, a well-balanced communications campaign is one that combines several mediums—PR, marketing, social media, and advertising in many cases. Public relations provides the credibility that comes when someone else is talking about your business or product. The challenge is that you don't control the message, which is why a strategic media relations counselor is so valuable when it comes to managing the message. Advertising allows you to convey your points in a predictable manner, but it lacks the journalistic integrity that comes with earned editorial coverage.

How important is social media in public relations work?

It's everything. In today's 24/7 world where information can be shared with the click of a mouse, or the tap of an app, a savvy PR campaign doesn't solely focus on traditional media or social media. It emphasizes and gives equal weight to all media, period. And in many cases, journalists are relying on social media for news tips and expert source identification. Media, whether it's social engagement or publicity and marketing driven, is all encompassing and really includes any forum in which you are communicating publicly.

What social media devices are most important?

It depends on the client, and we tailor our campaigns accordingly. A hotel or consumer product launch will rely heavily on photo and video-centric social media platforms such as Pinterest or Instagram; a real estate client with a clearly-identified target customer base is a good fit for Facebook; a business-to-business company may be a better fit for LinkedIn. There's no catch-all strategy for any one client. A successful campaign will align the social media tactics with the client's underlying business goals. The one common denominator is that all social media platforms have the potential to drive brand awareness if implemented strategically.

How important is knowledge of mobile devices for public relations professionals?

PR professionals must use social media every day to communicate with their followers, to raise awareness, and start meaningful conversations. Twitter, Facebook, YouTube, and others, have quickly become important tools in a PR person's communications toolkit.

Food for thought: Every year, fewer people read print or use computers, and are communicating and consuming their news via mobile devices. According to Microsoft Tag, by 2014, mobile Internet should take over desktop Internet usage! One half of all local searches are performed on mobile devices, and 91% of mobile Internet access is to socialize. This gives PR professionals many other avenues to connect and inform the public.

Public Relations Bookshelf

Belch, George and Michael Belch. *Advertising and Promotion: An Integrated Marketing and Communications Perspective*. New York: McGraw-Hill, 2008. A view of integrated marketing from the advertising side of the house.

Berger, Jonah. *Why Things Catch On*. New York, NY: Simon & Schuster, 2013. Interesting read on the power of viral marketing, through analysis of cases from NASA to Disney to Kit Kat Bars.

Gospe, Mike. *Marketing Campaign Development*. Silicon Valley, CA: Happy About, 2008. How a guerilla marketer might use integrated marketing.

Hanlon, Patrick. *Primal Branding*. New York: Free Press, 2006. The author says there is a "primal code" that makes a product successful, all based on creating a "belief system" for your brand.

Kabani, Shama H. *The Zen of Social Media Marketing*. Dallas, TX: Ben Bella Books, 2013. A non-stress introduction to social media marketing, if you've got the "Zen."

Nazarudin, Heidi and Ponn Sabra. *Blog Social Media Rules*. Venice, CA: Pink Press, 2015. Focus here is on helping bloggers—preferably women!—learn how to use social media buzz to create an audience.

Percy, Larry. *Strategic Integrated Marketing Communications*. Oxford, England: Butterworth-Heinemann, 2008. Chapter and verse discussion of the roots and implementation of integrated marketing communications.

Rein, Irving and Philip Kotler. *High Visibility*. New York: McGraw-Hill, 2006. What do Oprah Winfrey, Donald Trump, and Bill Gates have in common? High visibility, which the authors claim is necessary to succeed today.

Rostica, Christopher, with Bill Yenne. *The Authentic Brand: How Today's Top Entrepreneurs Connect with Customers*. Paramus, NJ: Noble Press, 2007. Case studies from the viewpoint of CEOs, whose companies stood apart from the competition.

Scott, David M. *The New Rules of Marketing & PR*. 4th ed. Hoboken, NJ: John Wiley & Sons, 2013. Creative approach to reaching consumers directly, primarily via owned media. Perhaps not as open-and-shut a case as the author suggests, but worth considering.

Schaefer, Mark W. *Return on Influence*. New York: McGraw-Hill, 2012. Excellent explanation and discussion about Klout scores and how they're derived and used.

Shiffman, Denise. *The Age of Engage: Reinventing Marketing for Today's Connective, Collaborative and Hyperinteractive Culture*. Ladera Ranch, CA: Hunt Street Press, 2008. This book charts a way to market on the Web and has a very long title.

Shimp, Terence A. *Advertising, Promotion and Other Aspects of Integrated Marketing Communications*. Mason, OH: South-Western Cengage Learning, 2008. Good discussion here of introducing new brands.

Endnotes

1. Thomas L. Friedman, "This Column Is Not Sponsored by Anyone," *The New York Times* (May 12, 2012).
2. Logan Rhoades, "The Hero of 'Jurassic World' Is Not Chris Pratt, but the Man Double-Fisting Margaritas," *BuzzFeed* (June 15, 2015).
3. Jennifer Weiner, "The Cost of Buying Someone's Soul. Or Tweets," *The New York Times* (April 24, 2015).
4. Friedman, op cit.
5. Al Ries and Laura Ries, *The Fall of Advertising and the Rise of PR* (New York: Harper Business, 2002): 251.
6. Lara O'Reilly, "These Are the 10 Companies that Spend the Most on Advertising," *Business Insider* (July 6, 2015).
7. "Getting Word Out Involves 3 Strategies," *Poughkeepsie Journal* (October 16, 2005).
8. Tom Harris, "Kotler's Total Marketing Embraces MPR," *MPR Update* (December 1992): 4.
9. Andrea Whitmer, "The Truth About Sponsored Blog Posts," *Nuts and Bolts Media* (February 22, 2013).
10. James Bandler, "How Companies Pay TV Experts for On-Air Product Mentions," *The Wall Street Journal* (April 19, 2005): A1.
11. Oliver Willis, "Did Ben Carson Violate Fox News' Policy on Product Endorsements?" *Media Matters* (January 12, 2015).
12. Bob Garfield, "Even Blurrier Lines," *On the Media blog* (September 5, 2014).

13. Mark Hoelzel, "Spending on Native Advertising Is Soaring as Marketers and Digital Media Publishers Realize the Benefits," *Business Insider* (May 20, 2015).

14. Julie Moos, "The Atlantic Publishes Then Pulls Sponsored Content from Church of Scientology," *Poynter Media Wire* (January 15, 2013).

15. Kathy Burnham, "Trade Shows: Make Them Worth the Investment," *Tactics* (September 1999): 11.

16. Kurt Badenhausen, "LeBron James' Endorsements Breakdown: By the Numbers," *Forbes* (January 22, 2014).

17. Shelly Kramer, "How Fortune 500 Companies Use Social Media," *V3B Marketing* (May 28, 2012), http://www.v3b.com/2012/05/how-fortune-500-companies-use-social-media/#ixzz3hrDL8QIQ.

18. Scott Timberg, "Pop Music's Biggest Sellout: How Many Brands Paid for Product Placement in Your Favorite Songs," *Salon* (May 28, 2015).

19. Stuart Elliott, "'30 Rock' Satire of Kraft Sponsorship Is Sponsored by Kraft," *The New York Times* (April 27, 2012).

20. Lorne Manly, "On Television, Brands Go from Props to Stars," *The New York Times* (October 2, 2005): B1.

21. Timberg, op. cit.

22. Matt Richtel, "A New Reality in Video Games: Advertisement," *The New York Times* (April 11, 2005).

23. Stuart Elliott, "Product Placement Moves to Cartoons," *The New York Times* (October 21, 2004).

24. Brian Stelter, "Low Ratings End Show and a Product Placement," *The New York Times* (November 14, 2008).

25. Brian Steinberg, "TV's Old Product Placement Era Could Be Nearing Its End," *Variety* (February 4, 2015).

26. Joe Nathanson, "The Lucrative Secret Behind Infomercials," *The Week* (December 15, 2013).

27. Julie Bosman, "Advertising Is Obsolete: Everyone Says So," *The New York Times* (January 23, 2006): C7.

28. Sydney Ember, "Cool Influencers with Big Followings Get Picky About Their Endorsements," *The New York Times* (August 2, 2015).

29. Clyde Haberman, "Sell the Naming Rights and You May Sell Much More," *The New York Times* (September 16, 2008).

30. Stuart Elliott, "Live and Online, a Game Show Developed for the Internet Age," *The New York Times* (June 4, 2012).

31. Al Ries and Laura Ries, op. cit.

Chapter 17

Crisis
Management

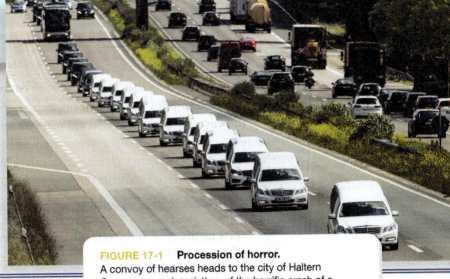

FIGURE 17-1 **Procession of horror.**
A convoy of hearses heads to the city of Haltern
Germany, carrying victims of the horrific crash of a
Germanwings plane, brought down by a mentally-ill
co-pilot in 2015.
Photo: ROLF VENNENBERND/EPA/Newscom

Chapter Objectives

1. To discuss the importance in counseling on the actions and managing the communication of an organization in crisis.

2. To explore the role of public relations in managing issues and risks and communicating in a crisis.

3. To discuss, in detail, the aspects of crisis planning, message mapping, and implementing crisis communication.

4. To examine how media relations differs in time of crisis than in normal everyday operations.

"A lie," Mark Twain once said, "can travel halfway around the world while the truth is still putting on its shoes."

In the age of social media and the Internet, so can a crisis.

No individual or organization—no matter how public, how large, or how newsworthy—is immune from crisis. Public relations professionals must be ready to confront crisis at any moment—whether said crisis has been festering for years or occurs in an instant.

Two examples from the spring and summer of 2015 are typical of the atypical evolution of crises.

■ In March, a Germanwings international passenger flight from Barcelona to Dusseldorf mysteriously crashed in the French Alps, shortly after signing off with air traffic control. All 144 passengers and

six crew members, from some 18 countries, were killed.

Immediately upon receiving the devastating news, Lufthansa, Germany's largest air carrier and the owner of Germanwings, labeled the crash an "accident," also expressing "shock and sadness" for the victims and their families. Lufthansa also reported that the airbus, itself, had no prior mechanical difficulties.

It took only a day later, upon analysis of the plane's cockpit voice recorder, to learn the awful truth. The plane's co-pilot, a 27-year-old man with hidden mental problems, had locked the pilot out of the cabin and purposely crashed the plane.

The co-pilot's apartment was searched and a letter found in a waste bin indicating that he had been declared "unfit to work" by a doctor.

Germanwings reported that it hadn't received any sick note from the man and concluded that the co-pilot had hidden his mental illness from his employer.[1]

In the ensuing days, as the world grieved for the poor people killed in the crash, Lufthansa—which had built a reputation over years as one of the world's safest airlines—faced a withering crisis surrounding its training regimen, medical record-keeping, and air safety protocols (**Figure 17-1**).

■ Four months later, a crisis of a very different variety showed the sad state to which 21st century media had descended; the dangers even to private citizens of a media gone wild and the need for professional public relations counsel in the new media reality.

In July, Gawker.com, the sleaziest of a spate of sleazy gossip blogs, "outed" a media industry financial executive, whose only claim to fame was that he was the brother of a former Obama Administration high-ranking executive. Gawker's *"news"* was that the man (who it named, but we won't) had contacted a male prostitute, who then breathlessly notified Gawker to gain personal publicity. The man, with a wife and small children, was understandably mortified.

Within days, even Gawker's founder and chief editor Nick Denton, a veteran of Britain's take-no-prisoners tabloids, acknowledged that needlessly embarrassing a private person in this manner was not only inexcusable but also just plain wrong.[2] Denton took the blame for the malicious post and took it down. In response, several Gawker "reporters" announced that they were quitting, because Denton had defied the blog's charter of "putting truths on the Internet" and letting the chips fall where they may. In other words, these misguided gossip mongers took the right action for the wrong reason.

In any event, the existence of Gawker and its fellow-gossip sites, like TMZ and Radar Online and Perez Hilton, was a bitter reminder that in the second decade of the 21st century, thanks largely to the digital speed and pervasiveness and perniciousness of viral communications, organizations, and individuals—from the highest profile to the most private—are always one step away from crisis.

1 Crisis Pervades Society

Crisis has become so pervasive, so crippling, that insurance companies, such as AIG and Chubb, now offer crisis management insurance to pay for corporations turning to crisis management agencies for help in defending damaged brands from such issues as food contaminations, environmental disasters, executive scandals, or even government bailouts (which AIG, by the way, received as a result of the U.S. financial meltdown!).[3]

Indeed, in recent years, the practice of public relations has become most well known for assisting those who find themselves in such crises and, as a consequence, has benefitted handsomely.

Crisis, which public relations counselor James Lukaszewski once described as "unplanned visibility," can strike anyone at any time.[4] Indeed, in the new century, among the most well-regarded and highest-paid professionals in public relations are those who have achieved this status through their efforts in attempting to "manage" crises.

In a world of instantaneous Internet communications, round-the-clock social media, cable news commentary, talk radio, tabloid news journalism, and exploding communications challenges, the number and depth of crises affecting business, government, labor, nonprofits, and even private individuals have expanded exponentially.

No sector of society is immune from crisis.

- In *government,* scandals—from the tax finagling of New York Congressmen Charley Rangel and Michael Grimm to the cracking-smoking charges against mayors in Washington, DC and Toronto, Canada to the impeachment of former Illinois Governor Rod Blagojevich to the sexual shenanigans of various politicians—have recurrently dominated the news.

- In *business*, the outrageous ineptitude of the financial industry leading to the subprime lending crisis of 2008 and the subsequent financial meltdown, complemented by the outrageous pay packages awarded failed CEOs, caused sweeping changes in government regulation of business during the Obama administration; including the 2015 SEC mandate that companies must publish how much more money the CEO makes compared to the average worker.[5]

- In *education,* Duke University was rocked in 2006 by what proved to be bogus accusations of rape and racism among the college's lacrosse players. And Penn State University's legendary football program was scandalized in 2006 by the imprisonment of a popular assistant coach, who committed sexual crimes against children.

- In the area of *religion,* the Catholic Church, under Pope Francis, finally began to recover from the shame of the pedophile priest scandals at the beginning of the decade.

- In the world of *charitable institutions,* in January 2009 universities and foundations across the nation discovered their investment portfolios savaged by the actions of one rogue investor, Bernard Madoff, a former chair of the NASDAQ Stock Exchange.[6] Madoff's actions caused a crisis of biblical proportions for charities, which suffered the brunt of the $60 billion he had reportedly bilked investors. In 2015, a crisis of a different nature confronted Planned Parenthood, when an anti-abortion group filmed unsuspecting representatives, talking about getting money for aborted fetal parts.[7]

- In *journalism,* a story in *Rolling Stone* magazine in 2015 about a campus rape, which turned out to be created out of whole cloth, caused great crisis for the University of Virginia in general and one fraternity in particular. The crisis shifted to *Rolling Stone* when the fraternity wound up suing *the magazine for* the journalistic miscarriage.[8]

- Nor was scandal absent in the *public relations* industry. Some of the industry's most respected agencies were guilty of ethical violations, including Burson-Marsteller's surreptitious attempt in 2011 to poison the waters for Google, in behalf of client.[9] Earlier scandals involving Ketchum Public Relations in a pay-for-play broadcaster scheme and Fleishman-Hillard in padding bills brought crisis to the crisis counselors themselves. Indeed, the subject of which client to support or decline occasionally presents a crisis itself to public relations firms (see *A Question of Ethics,* this chapter).

The list of such issues—and of the crises they often evoke—is unending. In the second decade of the 21st century, society is flooded with front-burner issues that affect individuals and organizations. From war to peace, poverty to abortion, discrimination to downsizing, environmentalism to energy conservation, the domain of "issues management" has become increasingly important for public relations professionals.

2 Issues Management

In guarding against crisis, public relations professionals must constantly be aware of the primary issues that impact their organizations. The term *issues management* was coined in 1976 by the late public relations counselor W. Howard Chase, who defined it this way:

> *Issues management is the capacity to understand, mobilize, coordinate, and direct all strategic and policy planning functions, and all public affairs/public relations skills, toward achievement of one objective: meaningful participation in creation of public policy that affects personal and institutional destiny.*[10]

In specific terms, issues management encompasses the following elements:

- **Anticipate emerging issues.** Normally, the issues management process is about precrisis planning. It deals with an issue that will hit the organization a year later, thus distinguishing the practice from the normal crisis planning aspects of public relations.

- **Identify issues selectively.** An organization can influence only a few issues at a time. Therefore, a good issues management process will select several—perhaps 5 to 10—specific priority issues with which to deal.

- **Deal with opportunities and vulnerabilities.** Most issues, anticipated well in advance, offer both opportunities and vulnerabilities for organizations. For example, in assessing higher oil prices, an insurance company might anticipate that fewer people will be driving and therefore there will be fewer accident claims. This would mark an opportunity. On the other hand, higher gas prices might mean that more people are strapped to pay their premiums. This would be a vulnerability that a sharp company should anticipate well in advance.

- **Plan from the outside in.** The external environment—not internal strategies—dictates the selection of priority issues. This is especially true in a day where social media and the Internet set the conversation. This approach differs from the normal strategic planning approach, which, to a large degree, is driven by internal strengths and objectives. Issues management is driven by external factors.

- **Bottom-line orientation.** Although many people tend to look at issues management as anticipating crises, its real purpose should be to defend the organization in light of external factors as well as to enhance the firm's business by seizing imminent opportunities.

3 Risk Communication/Message Maps

Risk communication is an outgrowth of issues management. Risk communication began as a process of taking scientific data related to health and environmental hazards and presenting them to a lay audience in a manner that is both understandable and meaningful.

Models of risk communication have been developed based on the position that *perception is reality*—a concept that has been part of public relations for years. Indeed,

A Question of Ethics

Lion Killer, Qu'est-ce que c'est?

In the United States, few criminals are more vilified than those who do mean things to animals. In fact, sometimes the backlash against animal cruelty is more ferocious than that when human beings hurt one another.

And if you don't believe that, you weren't paying attention in the summer of 2015, when citizens across the nation responded with great vengeance and furious anger when they learned that a poor, defenseless lion was shot and killed by a Minnesota dentist on safari in Africa.

Dr. Walter Palmer, an experienced big game hunter, reportedly paid $50,000 to Zimbabwe guides to secure the necessary licenses to track down and kill a lion. But the lion that the dentist's guides lured out of a national park turned out to be a well-known, 13-year-old, jet-black maned specimen, known to one and all as "Cecil" **(Figure 17-2)**.

Immediately, public opinion turned against Dr. Palmer, who went into hiding and tried to hire a public relations firm. That's when things got even dicier.

First, J. Austin & Associates, a Minnesota firm, issued a statement on Dr. Palmer's behalf which included an apology: *"I deeply regret that my pursuit of an activity I love and practice responsibly and legally resulted in the taking of this lion."* But a couple of days later, the Austin firm tweeted that it had apparently had a change of heart, *"Yesterday another PR firm asked to help distribute Dr. Palmer's statement. Having completed that task, we've ended our work on this issue."*

Then, a sign was posted on the besieged dentist's office door, referring all related queries to Minneapolis agency Spong PR. But Spong tweeted that the dentist was not its client: *"To confirm, Spong does not represent Walter Palmer. Please direct all media inquiries to Jon Austin at jon@jaustin-group.com."*

Dr. Palmer, it seemed, was that rare commodity who couldn't seem to find a public relations firm that would take his money. As public relations professor and blogger Jeff Morosoff noted, *"An important maxim in the PR profession is that you have to believe in—or at least be comfortable supporting—your client."*

And while in the past, public relations firms were apparently "comfortable" representing everyone from gun manufacturers to gambling casinos, from ball players charged with felonies like sexual assault and even murder to foreign dictators, like Libya's Mohammer Khadafy and Syria's Bashar Al-Assad, who killed people, a dentist who mistakenly ended the life of a man-eating lion was evidently too hot to handle.*

Questions

1. Where would you draw the line in representing a public relations client?

2. Do you think Dr. Palmer should have been entitled to public relations representation?

3. Would you have represented him? Why or why not?

FIGURE 17-2   **Rest in peace.** Cecil, the lion, was lured out of a Zimbabwe reserve to be killed by an American hunter, who immediately became public enemy #1.
Photo: Brent Stapelkamp/Polaris/Newscom

*For further information, see Arthur Chu, "Big Game Hunters Are Easy Targets for Our Anger," *Huffington Post* (August 3, 2015); Jeff Morosoff, "Hot Potato Hunter," *Public Relations Nation* (August 2, 2015); and Katie Rogers, "American Hunter Killed Cecil, Beloved Lion Who Was Lured Out of His Sanctuary," *The New York Times* (July 28, 2015).

the disciplines of risk communication and public relations have much in common. Risk communication is based on behavioral scientific research, which shows how behavior changes when a person processes messages during high-stress situations. When stressed, the ability to hear, understand, and remember diminishes. Research indicates that in times of high stress, people can miss up to 80% of message content. Of the 20% they do hear, most messages are negative. In crisis, you must adjust for these effects to communicate effectively.

To confront this reality, risk communicators have developed a message-mapping process, based on seven steps.

1. Identify stakeholders.
2. Determine specific concerns for each stakeholder group.
3. Analyze specific concerns to fit underlying general concerns.
4. Conduct structured brainstorming with input from message-mapping teams.
5. Assemble supporting facts and proof for each key message.
6. Ask outside experts to systematically test messages.
7. Plan delivery of resulting messages and supporting materials.[11]

Message maps generally adhere to the following standard requirements:

- Three key messages
- Seven to 12 words per message
- Three supporting facts for each key message

Like any other area of public relations, risk communication depends basically on an organization's actions. In the long run, deeds, not words, are what count in communicating risk.

Signs of a Crisis

The most significant test for any individual or organization comes when it is hit by a major accident or disaster—that is, a *crisis*.

What is a crisis? According to the *Harvard Business Review*, "A crisis is a situation that has reached a critical phase for which dramatic and extraordinary intervention is necessary to avoid or repair major damage."[12] Others define a crisis more simply, as "anything the CEO says it is!"

A corporate "problem" is generally a more short-term issue that affects one element or department of the organization and can be limited. A "crisis," on the other hand, is a longer-term issue that impacts the entire organization, affects many parts of that organization, and runs the risk of damaging the organization's reputation.

How an individual or organization handles itself in the midst of a crisis may influence how it is perceived for years to come. Poor handling of events with the magnitude of past crises such as Exxon's *Valdez* oil spill, President George W. Bush's handling of Hurricane Katrina, President Obama's handling of the BP oil spill, the Catholic Church's pedophile priest crisis, Wall Street's banking crisis or the National Football League's concussion and domestic violence scandals can cripple a reputation. and cause it enormous monetary loss. When front-running presidential candidate Donald Trump lost his cool in the very first Republican debate in the summer of 2015, his popularity (momentarily) subsided. On the other hand, thinking logically and responding thoughtfully and quickly in a crisis, such as how Johnson

& Johnson reacted to its Tylenol tablet poisoning episodes, can cement a positive reputation and establish enormous goodwill for an organization (see Case Study, Chapter 4).

It is essential, therefore, that such emergencies be managed intelligently and forthrightly with the news media, employees, and the community at large.

As any organization unfortunate enough to experience a crisis recognizes, when the crisis strikes, seven instant warning signs invariably appear:

1. **Surprise.** When a crisis breaks out, it's usually unexpected. Sometimes it's a natural disaster—a tornado or hurricane, for example. Sometimes, it's a human-made disaster—robbery, embezzlement, or large loss. Frequently, a public relations professional first learns of such an event when the media calls and demands to know what immediate action will be taken.

2. **Insufficient information.** Many things happen at once. Rumors fly. Blogs and social media come alive with wild stories. Wire services want to know why the company's stock is falling. It's difficult to get a grip on everything that's happening.

3. **Escalating events.** The crisis expands. The stock exchange wants to know what's going on. Will the organization issue a statement? Are the rumors true? While rumors run rampant, truthful information is difficult to obtain. You want to respond in an orderly manner, but events are unfolding too quickly.

4. **Loss of control.** The unfortunate natural outgrowth of escalating events is that too many things are happening simultaneously. Erroneous stories hit the Internet, the wires, and the airwaves.

5. **Increased outside scrutiny.** Bloggers, the media, stockbrokers, talk-show hosts, and the public in general feed on rumors. "Helpful" politicians and observers of all stripes comment to cable television on what's going on. Talk radio is abuzz with innuendo. The media want responses. Investors demand answers. Customers must know what's going on.

6. **Siege mentality.** The organization understandably feels surrounded. Lawyers counsel, "Anything we say will be held against us." The easiest thing to do is to say nothing. So, "No comment" is urged by the attorneys. But does that make sense?

7. **Panic.** With the walls caving in and with leaks too numerous to plug, a sense of panic pervades. In such an environment, it is difficult to convince management to take immediate action and to communicate what's going on.[13]

Planning for Crisis

The first rule of crises is that they never appear on your schedule. But that doesn't mean you shouldn't plan as much as you can for the inevitable.

Thus, heightened preparedness is always in order, with five planning issues paramount.

■ **First, for each potentially impacted audience, define the risk.** "The poison in the pill will make you sick." "The plant shutdown will keep you out of work." "The recall will cost the stockholders $100 million." The risk must be understood—or at least contemplated—before framing crisis communications.

■ **Second, for each risk defined, describe the actions that mitigate the risk.** "Don't take the pill." "We are recalling the product." "We are studying the possibility of closing the plant." If you do a credible job in defining the risk, the public will more closely believe in your solutions. When bird flu pandemic threatened the world, the parent of Kentucky Fried Chicken readied a consumer education and advertising program to reassure consumers that eating cooked chicken is perfectly safe.[14]

■ **Third, identify the cause of the risk.** If the public believes you know what went wrong, it is more likely to accept that you will quickly remedy the problem. That's why people get back on airplanes after crashes.

■ **Fourth, demonstrate responsible management action.** Most essential to the planning phase is to move toward fixing the problem—in other words, take proper action. Cosmetics are never the solution. Much more important is acting to correct the issue that got you in the soup in the first place.

■ **Fifth, create a consistent message.** Agree on an official spokesperson who can disseminate one voice for the organization. Most of all, be honest, and never, ever cover up or lie. That just exacerbates the crisis.

Letting people know that the organization has a plan and is implementing it helps convince them that you are in control. Defining the issues means both having a clear sense internally of what the focus of action should be and communicating that action into the marketplace to reach key constituents.

Communicating in a Crisis

The key communications principle in dealing with a crisis is not to clam up when disaster strikes. A lawyer, correctly, is focused on defense in a court of law and advises clients to say nothing.

Public relations advice, on the other hand, is concerned about a different court—the court of public opinion—and therefore takes a different tack.

A lawyer advises a client what he or she *must* say—to comply with the law. A public relations counselor advises a client what he or she *should* say—to do the right thing.

Keep in mind that every crisis is different. And just like anything else in public relations, there is no one answer to solve every crisis. However, in a general sense, there are a series of do's and don'ts that should be observed in a crisis. Let's start with the....

Crisis Don'ts

We start with the "Don'ts" because in a crisis, often what you "don't" do is equally important as what you "do" do. For instance:

1. **Don't keep all channels of communication open.** Public relations practitioners must have, as their general operating premise, a bias to "disclose" and not "withhold" information.

    In normal times, it makes sense to expose many corporate officers to the media, so that positive relationships with the press can be developed at various levels in the organization. However, when crisis strikes, these channels must be closed down. The organization must speak with a unified voice in crisis, so as not to either confuse the issues or exacerbate the organization's dilemma.

    The only way to prevent errant remarks being uttered or verbal misguided missiles being launched inadvertently, is to appoint one—and only one—designated spokesperson. He or she, then, becomes the only authorized organizational spokesperson for the media.

2. **Don't always make the CEO the spokesman.** The media, of course, prefer to speak "to the top person" and the public relations spokesman.

    Tough. Sometimes, the worst thing you can do is send the CEO out to face the media firing squad. That's what BP did in 2010 when it flooded the Gulf of Mexico with oil. BP immediately dispatched its clueless CEO Anthony "Tony" Hayward to Louisiana, where, in rapid succession, Hayward incorrectly predicted a speedy conclusion to the crisis, painted an unrealistically upbeat picture, whined incessantly and when the going got tough, flew to England to go sailing. The media ate it up, and BP suffered.[15]

    Moral: Don't always send the CEO to the crisis.

3. **Don't always take the lawyers' advice.** This may sound like heresy, but it makes great sense.

    As noted, a lawyer's job is to protect the organization from challenge in a Court of Law. Lawyers, correctly, must counsel their clients on the dangers of making public statements that can be used against them. So most of the time, the advice is, "Say nothing."

    But in a crisis, when the fate of the organization may be at stake, CEOs can't remain silent. A public relations professional's job is to help guide the CEO and the organization through the thicket of crisis with clear and thoughtful communication.

4. **Don't lean toward withholding information.** In a crisis, management is overwhelmed by lawyers and liability. The tendency is to say as little as possible and "hope" that the trauma will subside. It rarely does—particularly for a visible company, non profit or individual.

    Therefore, as difficult as it is for management to swallow, it makes much more sense for an organization to attempt to "control" the damage, by constantly issuing briefings and updates that "advance" the story. "The media beast," the old saying goes, *"needs to be fed."* That's especially true today when social media ensure that no crisis will be ignored.

5. **Don't answer every question.** On the other hand, just because the media ask doesn't mean you have to answer.

    In any crisis, there are questions that you simply cannot or should not answer. That is not to say you should ever intentionally cover up, mislead, or lie. But your allegiance, your bias, must be toward your employer, i.e. the one who signs your paycheck. Hypothetical questions, proprietary questions, speculative questions, and the like should be politely turned away.

6. **Don't ever, ever lie.** This is the cardinal rule of proper public relations.

    All you have in public relations, as in life, is your credibility, your reputation. Once you and your organization lose that, you lose everything. If you lie to a reporter once, you won't get a second chance. They will forever be suspect, and you will be hurt in the long run.

    The greatest, saddest example was President Bill Clinton, who, arguably, was a most competent and charismatic chief executive officer. But in the midst of the single worst crisis of his administrations, he lied, continually and habitually, over a period of months, even to those who supported him unequivocally. Like most public figures or organizations, in the end he was found out.

    As a consequence, the legacy of an otherwise solid Presidency will forever be shrouded by his refusal to tell the truth.

Crisis Do's

Now what about the "Do's?"

1. **Do be flexible.** Certainly, it is important to "be prepared" for crisis. Crisis manuals, role simulations, emergency preparedness checklists, and the like are valuable tools.

   But anyone who has lived through a crisis understands that sometimes, you can't even *find* the crisis manual, much less follow it! Therefore, you have to be ready to move quickly. In the Tylenol crisis, the CEO of Johnson & Johnson said at the time that his company *"had to remain flexible, responding to changing facts and rumors almost on a minute-to-minute basis."*

   Today, with the Net, social media, cable TV, radio, and all the other 21st-century communications media continuously reporting on rapidly changing developments, a smart company must keep its crisis options open and not be tied to a rigid formulaic response plan.

2. **Do answer early.** In crisis, the most critical stage is what crisis managers call *"the golden hour."* Literally translated, this means the first several hours—or days if you're lucky—set the tone for the rest of the ordeal.

   This is when the media—both traditional and online—are framing their stories and, in effect, setting the "agenda" for crisis coverage. Therefore, it is incumbent on the organization enmeshed in the problem to come out early with a statement or, at the very least, establish contact.

   When an airplane crashes, for example, airline public relations professionals make themselves available immediately at headquarters to try to handle the media onslaught. Meanwhile, personnel are simultaneously dispatched to rush to the crash site.

   When organizations fumble early on in a crisis, the results can be catastrophic. In 2015, when FIFA, the organization that runs world soccer, was enmeshed in an international bribery scandal, its autocratic President Sepp Blatter refused to relinquish his post and was reelected FIFA head. A week after his reelection, the U.S. government indicted several FIFA officials, and Blatter was forced to announce that he would step down as FIFA president (**Figure 17-3**). For its indecision, FIFA suffered even more.

3. **Do speak with one voice.** The media prefer lots of spokespeople. They want access. And as a general communications premise, candor and openness should be the rule. But.................in a crisis, multiple communications channels must be shut down. The institution must speak with one voice.

   It is important in crisis to communicate a sense of confidence and control and coordination. There are few things more embarrassing—or damaging—to corporate credibility than one spokesperson having to "correct" on the evening news, the comments of a previous spokesperson quoted in the morning news.

   Therefore, it must be understood by everyone from the CEO on down, that the company will speak through only one spokesperson. More often than not, that spokesperson will be the public relations professional.

4. **Do be prepared to move without all the facts.** Sure, the lawyers get antsy if you speak up quickly. And certainly, there is always a risk of saying too much, too soon. But there is often a greater risk of remaining silent.

FIGURE 17-3
Crisis buddies.
FIFA President Sepp
Blatter made nice to
Russian President
Vladimir Putin during
the preliminary draw
for the FIFA 2018
World Cup. A month
later Blatter was forced
to announce he would
step down as crisis-
weary FIFA's chief
executive.
*Photo: Photoagency
Interpress/ZUMA Press/
Newscom*

If you sit still too long, you could still be "sitting" there as social media and cable news spew out uncorrected negative assertions about you and the next day's papers brand you "guilty as charged."

Certainly, you should never say anything that you don't know to be true. But saying something—even if it's *"We're efforting the answer to that question"*—is better than saying nothing.

5. **Do squawk if you're wronged.** Auto pioneer Henry Ford used to say, *"Never complain, never explain."* But that's often bad advice in a crisis.

In a crisis, you must fire back if the organization is accused unfairly, or if information reported is flat out wrong. The fact is that in today's Net-accelerated news environment where speed is most important, reporters don't necessarily write the truth. The write what people tell them is the truth. And sometimes, what they tell them simply ain't true. So it's your job, as public relations keeper of the truth, to set the record straight.

Putting news sources on notice early that you don't plan to accept untruths or false accusations or inaccuracies just because they report them—will pay benefits later on as you navigate through the crisis.

6. **Seek out your allies.** Invariably in crisis, organizations clam up. They surround the wagons. They descend off the radar screen. The operative communications posture is often one of *"withholding"* rather than *disclosing.* Companies refer to this as doling out information on a "need to know basis." Government refers to this as "for your eyes only."

This is often bad advice in crisis.

FYI

When "No Comment" and "Comment" Are Equally Catastrophic

Normally, public relations crisis counselors advise avoiding "no comment" at all costs. White House press secretaries, working for administrations generally disdainful of the media's prying eyes, constantly have to parry reporters' questions with the dreaded phrase.

No presidential press secretary in history had a tougher job in this respect than President Bill Clinton's Press Secretary Mike McCurry, who had to invoke a Kabuki-dancing strategy when his boss got mixed up with a White House intern in 1998 and went public to adamantly deny the liaison (**Figure 17-4**).

McCurry, who years later intimated that he had his doubts about his boss's honesty, refused, personally, to deny the allegations—because he wasn't privy to the facts; in the process, he kept his own reputation pure. How? When McCurry was asked if President Clinton had sexual relations with the 22-year-old intern, Monica Lewinsky, McCurry's standard answer was, *"The President said he did not."* In other words: *"No comment."*

On the other hand, sometimes a comment is even worse than "no comment." This turned out to be the case in early 2006, when 12 miners were caught in a West Virginia mine explosion. After 41 hours underground, the miners, according to a statement by the mine's owner, were "found alive." The media communicated the news, and the nation rejoiced.

A day later, the earlier report was found to be mistaken—wishful thinking based on misunderstood communications. The CEO of the mine company apologized immediately and profusely, but the damage perpetrated by the false report had been done.

Most public relations professionals consider the cardinal rule for communications during a crisis to be *Tell it all and tell it fast!*

As a general rule, when information gets out quickly, rumors are stopped and nerves are calmed. There is nothing complicated about the goals of crisis management. They are (1) terminate the crisis quickly, (2) limit the damage, and (3) restore credibility. And always. . . . be careful what you say.

FIGURE 17-4
"I did not have sex with that woman."
On second thought..........
"No comment."
Photo: CHUCK KENNEDY/ KRT/Newscom

In times of crisis, corporations need all the good will and support they can muster. They need their employees, customers, retirees, suppliers and all the other constituent publics that believe in them.

The cornerstone of the practice of public relations is "third-party endorsement"—getting someone else to talk about how good you are. Accordingly in crisis, the more that can be shared with key publics—the more third-party support can be generated.

The public relations aim in any crisis—the objective of both "Don'ts" and "Do's" is to get the crisis over as quickly as possible.

4 Handling the Beast

No element in a crisis is more critical for a public relations professional than handling the media. Normally, treating the press as friendly adversaries makes great sense. But when crisis strikes, media attention quickly turns to "feeding frenzy." So dealing with the media in crisis demands certain "battlefield rules," among them:

- **Set up media headquarters.** In a crisis, the media will seek out the organizational soft spots where the firm is most vulnerable to being penetrated. To try to prevent this, organizations in crisis must immediately establish a media headquarters through which all authorized communication must flow.

- **Establish media rules.** In a crisis, the media are sneaky. Their goal is to unearth any salient or salacious element that will advance the story line of the crisis. It is imperative, therefore, that the organization in the crucible set firm rules—which parts of the operation are off limits, which executives won't be available, and so on—for the media to follow.

- **Media live for the "box score."** Crisis specifics make news— number fired, injured, dead, property damage estimates, etc. —the grislier, the better. Stated another way, crisis is about numbers. And an organization in crisis must be ready to provide enough numbers to keep the media at bay.

- **Don't speculate.** If you don't know the numbers or the reasons or the extent of the damage, don't pretend you do. Speculation is suicidal in crisis.

- **Feed the beast.** The media in crisis are insatiable. Blogs, cable news, and wire services all must be fed 24/7. In the 21st century, with faux journalists blogging and tweeting round the clock, the media never sleep. "Nature abhors a vacuum," goes the old saying.

  So a smart organization in crisis will strive to keep the media occupied— even distracted—with new information that advances the story.

- **Speed triumphs.** In crisis, the media mantra is speed first, accuracy second. That's why the Net and social media are so dangerous in crisis. This sad but true fact holds major implications for public relations people, who must monitor what is being wrongly reported so that it can be nipped quickly before others run with the same misinformation.

As to what is said to the media, the following 10 general principles apply:

1. Speak first and often.
2. Don't speculate.

3. Go off the record at your own peril.

4. Stay with the facts.

5. Be open and concerned, not defensive.

6. Make your point and repeat it.

7. Don't wage war with the media; when you do, you lose.

8. Establish yourself as the most authoritative source.

9. Stay calm and be truthful and cooperative.

10. Never lie.[16]

Social Media Crisis Management

While traditional media still dictate the vast majority of communications during crisis, social media's role is steadily increasing. In 2013, when two terrorist wannabe brothers exploded two pressure cooker bombs at the Boston Marathon, journalists used Twitter to get the news out quickly around the world (**Figure 17-5**).

The less positive news is that even during the Boston Marathon crisis, researchers found that only 20% of nearly eight million tweets conveyed factual information; and disturbingly, 29% were "rumors and fake content."[17] So the rule of thumb for a public relations professional still is to communicate well with mainstream media and monitor social media 24/7.

One social media strategy increasingly popular for corporations is the development of a so-called dark Web site, a pre-developed site that doesn't become "live" until crisis strikes. A dark Web site is equipped with documents perceived to be necessary

FIGURE 17-5
Instant crisis communication.
Twitter became the go-to communication vehicle for journalists, the moment a pressure bomb detonated at the 2013 Boston Marathon.
Photo: Michael Leary/ Polaris/Newscom

in a crisis. When the crisis hits, the dark Web site is activated, and other documents, graphics, videos, etc., are added, as needed. Once again, the point of a dark Web site—just as any other communication vehicle—is to serve as a source of information for the outside world, so that the organization becomes the go-to contact for explanations and updates about the crisis.[18]

Last Word

In 2012, angry MSNBC anchor Rachel Maddow labeled crisis communication specialists "disgusting," "mercenary," "open sewer," and "the most morally repellant, indefensible thing out of American corporate culture." Ow! What made Ms. Maddow so mad—Ow!—was her view that crisis communications was primarily an underhanded exercise in pouring perfume on a skunk.[19]

Professional crisis managers, of course, would beg to differ. The fact is that in the second decade of the 21st century, although prevention remains the best insurance for any organization, crisis management has become one of the most revered skills in the practice of public relations. Organizations of every variety are faced, sooner or later, with a crisis. The issues that confront society—from income inequality and the environment to health care and nutrition to corporate accountability and minority rights—will not soon abate.

Social media and the Internet, with blogs and tweets and Facebook friends banging about at all times, have added a new dimension of complexity to communicating in crisis. Nonetheless, research indicates that in time of crisis, consumers still turn to traditional media. Half of those polled turn to network television in times of crisis, followed by 42% radio; 37% newspapers; 33% cable networks; and 25% the Internet.[20]

All of this suggests that experienced and knowledgeable crisis managers who can skillfully navigate and effectively communicate, turning crisis into opportunity, will be valuable resources for organizations into the 21st century.

In the final analysis, communicating in a crisis depends on a rigorous analysis of the risks versus the benefits of going public. Communicating effectively also depends on the judgment and experience of the public relations professional. Every call is a close one, and there is no guarantee that the organization will benefit, no matter what course is chosen. One thing is clear: Helping to navigate the organization through the shoals of a crisis is the ultimate test of a public relations professional. And crisis managers are very much in demand.

In the years ahead, as the world continues to present new and more complex challenges, crisis management promises to be a *growth* area in the *growth* profession that is the practice of public relations.

Discussion Starters

1. What is meant by the term *issues management*?
2. How can an organization influence the development of an issue in society?
3. What is meant by "message mapping?"
4. What is meant by the term *risk communications*?
5. What are the usual stages that an organization experiences in a crisis?
6. What are the principles in planning for crisis?
7. What are important rules in dealing with the media in crisis?
8. What is the cardinal rule for communicating in a crisis?
9. What are the keys to successful crisis communication?
10. What is a dark Web site?

Pick of the Literature

Crisis Management in the New Strategy Landscape, 2nd Edition
William "Rick" Crandall, John A. Parnell, and John E. Spillan, Thousand Oaks, CA: Sage Publications, 2013

This book presents a solid framework in crisis management, from planning to execution.

The emphasis here is on strategy, including the context of crisis and the elements that must be considered in preparing for a crisis and extricating the organization. Case studies are liberally mentioned, including weather-related disasters, Royal Caribbean hijacking, Perrier water contamination, BP Gulf of Mexico spill, and others.

The back part of the book deals with implementation, in terms of the action that crisis managers must take in dealing with customers, media, social media, etc. through each stage of an emerging crisis. Finally, the extensive discussion on ethics in a crisis is a welcome addition to a comprehensive text.

Case Study | The Rise and Fall and Rise of Queen Martha

One of the most famous and significant cases in 21st century public relations history is the crisis that threatened the reputation and empire of domestic queen Martha Stewart.

In the winter of 2001, few Americans could dispute that Martha Stewart was "Queen of the Kitchen." Few Americans enjoyed more robust acclaim in terms of public opinion.

The tough-willed, hot-tempered, blunt-speaking perfectionist had morphed from a modest upbringing to become the undisputed, multimillionaire-closing-in-on-billionaire, domestic doyenne—the homemaker's homemaker, arbiter of all things tasteful in the home, *numero uno* in all matters of domesticity.

Her parents, Martha and Edward Kostyra, were Polish Americans, her mother a school teacher and her father a pharmaceutical salesman, who raised their five children in Nutley, New Jersey. Her mother taught young Martha cooking and baking and sewing, and her father taught her how to garden. That was just the start the serious-minded model student needed. After a brief fling in the stock brokerage business and a failed marriage, Stewart began to build an empire that would become the stuff of legends.

- She coauthored a book called *Entertaining*, which became an instant bestseller.
- She followed that with lucrative publishing ventures, producing videotapes, dinner-music CDs, television specials, and dozens of books on matters of domesticity—from hors d'oeuvres to pies, from weddings to Christmas, from gardening to restoring old houses.
- She appeared regularly on NBC's *Today Show*, becoming a household name.
- She became a board member of the New York Stock Exchange.
- She delivered lectures for $10,000 a pop and charged eager attendees $900 a head to attend seminars at her farm.

- She signed an advertising/consulting contract with department chain Kmart for $5 million.
- She presided over a long-running syndicated television show, *Martha Stewart Living*.
- She parlayed the program into the creation of multimillion-dollar company Martha Stewart Living Omnimedia (MSO), with branches in publishing, merchandising, and Internet/direct commerce, selling products in eight discrete categories.

Without exaggeration, Stewart was Queen of the Kitchen, until one day when it all came tumbling down.

Selling in the Nick of Time
In December 2001, Stewart sold nearly 4,000 shares of biotech company ImClone Systems stock under mysterious circumstances. The company was run by Stewart's pal Samuel Waksal, who had presided over a rapid stock price ascension, due principally to the company's promising cancer-fighting drug, Erbitux, which had been submitted for approval to the Food and Drug Administration (FDA).

With everything looking good for the company, it was surprising on December 27 that Stewart decided suddenly to unload all her shares at a $60 price. The next day, the case got even more curious: On December 28, the FDA rejected ImClone's application for Erbitux. The stock cratered. But Stewart, having presciently decided to sell the day before, avoided a $51,000 loss.

Serendipity perhaps?

The government didn't think so.

Charges of Insider Trading
Stewart may have been smart, but according to the U.S. attorney for the Southern District of New York, she was not smart enough to know about the FDA's timing in rejecting Erbitux. Rather,

argued the government, Stewart had learned about the FDA's intention from her stockbroker. The stockbroker had received an urgent call from Waksal, then relayed the information to Stewart, who immediately decided to sell.

If true, Stewart had acted on classic insider information, a federal crime, which gives privileged investors an unfair advantage over all other shareholders. Indeed, prosecutors argued that this was precisely what had happened and that Stewart and her stockbroker were both guilty of illegally acting on insider information. Accordingly, in June 2003, the U.S. Attorney formally indicted both of them.

Stewart's attorneys argued that this was not the case at all. Stewart, they said, had always had a "plan" to sell her stock when it reached the $60 level.

After Waksal was sentenced to seven years in prison and family members he had tipped off were fined, attention turned to Stewart. The question was: Would she come forward and acknowledge "mistakes," or would she hold firm and deny any impropriety?

Silence of the Diva

The answer, painfully revealed over the next excruciating two years, was that Stewart became the "silent diva." She said little to elaborate on the case, preferring instead to allow her attorneys to speak for her. In one celebrated appearance on the *CBS Morning Show,* Stewart defiantly cut cabbage while an exasperated host tried to get her to react to the charges against her.

Soon thereafter, Stewart's guest appearances on television became fewer and fewer. She stopped lecturing. Her ubiquitous Kmart ads ceased to appear. She resigned as chair and CEO of MSO. Indeed, the woman who had seemed to be everywhere was now virtually out of sight.

In her place, a battery of lawyers negotiated with the Feds and argued with the judge to have her charges reduced. U.S. District Judge Miriam Cedarbaum, taking a page from the domestic doyenne herself, adamantly refused to throw out the charges.

Those who expected the typically feisty Stewart to come out fighting were sadly disappointed. In June 2003, Stewart unveiled a personal Website on which she proclaimed her innocence and insisted she would fight to clear her name. But beyond those Website notations, she remained tight-lipped. Meanwhile, in the vacuum of Stewart's silence, the Internet, cable television, and the public press were flooded with "experts" surmising on just what poor Martha Stewart had done to herself.

An Excruciating Trial

Stewart's trial began January 27, 2004, two full years after the alleged insider trading violation.

The trial was excruciating for Martha. For two months, she was forced to endure a phalanx of cameras greeting her in the morning for her arrival at the lower Manhattan courthouse and waiting for her each evening when the day's session was over **(Figure 17-6)**. She said nothing, again relying on attorneys to explain to the media exactly what went on that day in court. As her lawyers spoke each night, a stone-faced Stewart would stare straight ahead. Meanwhile, the share price of her company's stock plummeted, and her reputation wasn't far behind.

On March 5, 2004, with the world waiting breathlessly for the verdict, Stewart was found guilty on all four counts of obstructing justice and lying to federal investigators. Her broker was also found guilty, and both faced prison time.

About an hour after the verdict was read, Stewart—radiant as ever with a fur around her neck, a black overcoat, and a tasteful,

brown leather bag at her side—strode poker-faced down the stairs of the courthouse, accompanied by her lawyers. She did not respond to questions shouted at her by reporters. Instead, the following statement was posted on her Website:

Dear Friends,

I am obviously distressed by the jury's verdict but I take comfort in knowing that I have done nothing wrong and that I have the enduring support of my family and friends.

Her lawyers vowed to appeal.

Four months later, after losing her job, her company, close to $500,000 in stock market wealth, and her reputation, Martha Stewart lost her freedom. She was sentenced to five months in prison and two years' probation.

Still, Stewart was defiant, telling a television interviewer that "many, many good people have gone to prison" and comparing herself to Nelson Mandela, South Africa's persecuted anti-apartheid hero. And outside the courthouse, after her sentencing, an unrepentant Stewart vowed, "I'll be back."

Winter at Camp Cupcake

Stewart's attorneys, taking the lead from their defiant client, appealed her conviction and vowed to spare her hard time. But suddenly, in mid-September 2004, Stewart had a change of heart.

Shocking her supporters, the domestic doyenne announced that she would not wait for the verdict on her appeal and rather wished to begin serving her five-month prison sentence early "to put this nightmare behind me, both personally and professionally."

And so on October 8, 2004, Stewart, 63 and a multimillionaire, slipped into the women's federal prison in Alderson, West Virginia, to join petty thieves and embezzlers and drug offenders, all performing day labor at rates between 12 and 40 cents an hour.

And wonder of wonder, Stewart was an ideal prisoner. Reports from "Camp Cupcake," as it was labeled, were glowing in their praise of Stewart.

- She praised her guards, the warden, and fellow prisoners.
- She wrote passionately about the unfairness of federal sentencing guidelines, which shackled many of those whom she met behind the walls.
- She even participated in prison events—failing to win the "prison bakeoff."

On Thursday, March 3, 2005, when Stewart was sprung from the slammer to return to her 153-acre Westchester Estate, she was met with cameras, microphones, and a hero's welcome.

Comeback Kid

It was a new Martha Stewart who emerged from prison. She was more relaxed, more open, and more available to questioners. She also was very much back in business.

- She signed deals to begin two new television shows— one a daytime lifestyles show, the other a spinoff of Donald Trump's *The Apprentice.*
- She signed a $30 million deal for a Sirius satellite radio program.
- She signed a lucrative book deal to produce a Martha memoir, discussing her time in prison.

FIGURE 17-6   **The diva falls.**
Grim-faced Martha Stewart is flanked by lawyers after she was
sentenced to five months in prison in July 2004.
Photo: BRIAN FLANNERY/ACEPIXS.COM/Newscom

By the winter of 2005, Stewart was back with a vengeance.
She still hadn't acknowledged—even after her conviction and
subsequent jail time—that she had done anything "wrong." But
there would be ample opportunity for an admission, as Martha
momentum—"Martha Mo"—began to build and the "queen" set
out to retake her throne.

On January 6, 2006, the United States Court of Appeals for the
Second Circuit rejected the arguments of Stewart's lawyers and
upheld her conviction.

With time, Martha Stewart was back on television and prominent once again. But the layoff in prison had clearly taken its
toll. While Martha was gone, a number of other homemaking
heroines—led by the younger Rachel Ray—and celebrity chefs
had moved eagerly to supplant her.

By 2015, Martha Stewart had regained her footing as a
media force to be reckoned with. She introduced new television shows, wrote new books and lent her name to retail chains
looking to hitch their wagon to a star. And while it was clear that
the domestic diva would never again want for money, fame, or
power, nonetheless it was also safe to assume that in terms of
public opinion and reputation, Martha Stewart would never fully
get back to where she had been prior to taking her fatal fall.

Questions

1. How would you characterize Martha Stewart's initial public
   relations response to the charges against her?

2. What key public relations principle did Martha Stewart violate?

3. Had you been advising her, what public relations strategy
   and tactics would you have recommended? How "vocal"
   should she have been?

4. How important, from a public relations perspective, was her
   decision to go to jail early?

5. What public relations strategy should Stewart adopt now?

6. Should she acknowledge that she made mistakes?

For further information, see Michael Barbaro, "Court Rejects Appeal by Martha Stewart," *The New York Times* (January 7, 2006): C3; Krysten Crawford,
"Martha: I Cheated No One," *CNN Money* (July 20, 2004); Krysten Crawford, "Martha, Out and About" (March 4, 2005); Gene Healy, "Lessons of Martha
Stewart Case," *Cato Institute* (July 16, 2004); "Martha Stewart Wants to Enter Prison Early," *CBC News* (September 16, 2004); Brooke A. Masters, "Stewart
Begins Prison Term," *Washington Post* (October 9, 2004): EO1; Fraser P. Seitel, "Martha's Final PR Hurdle," www.odwyerpr.com (March 6, 2005); Fraser P.
Seitel, "Martha Finally Gets PR Religion" (August 26, 2005); "Stewart Convicted on All Charges," *CNN Money* (March 5, 2004); "Timeline of Martha Stewart
Scandal," *Associated Press*, Copyright 2005.

From the Top

An Interview with Sandra Macleod

Sandra Macleod is Director of Reputation Dividend
and CEO of Mindful
Reputation based in
London, England, advising
senior leaders and boards
on better managing their
credibility and reputa-
tion. Ms. Macleod set
up the first international
franchises for a media
analysis company before
launching her own firm,
Echo Research, as a full-
service global research
group with offices in Asia, Europe, and the US, which secured
over 89 industry awards for innovation and excellence prior to
being acquired. Ms. Macleod also founded the International
Association of Measurement & Evaluation Companies. She is
on the boards of the Arthur W Page Society and University of
Oxford's Public Affairs Advisory Group. Ms. Macleod has also
been cited among the 100 most influential people in public
relations.

How important is "reputation" for an organization today?
Corporate success is all about that intangible thing called
Reputation—and its output called trust—which drives behaviors essential for organizational success. Reputation
has proven itself to be measurable, manageable and yes,
valuable. By some accounts, reputation is estimated to be

worth some 30% of all shareholder value, and that amount has been increasing year on year. In the latest study by Reputation Dividend, US corporate reputation was found to be worth $3.3 trillion. The same study also found that perceptions of corporate reputation were actively destroying value in 10% of S&P. Reputation is also means to grow shareholder value as stronger reputations increase the confidence the investment community has in the ability of companies to deliver the economic returns they promise. It's been found that on average, a 5% improvement in the strength of a reputation will lead to an increase of 2.0% in market capitalization.

What are the most essential components of "reputation?"
Leading business schools and management consultants agree on the principle levers of reputation as: 1) Quality of Goods & Services, 2) Quality of Management, 3) Financial Performance, 4) Workplace Environment, 5) Innovation, 6) Marketing, 7) Corporate Responsibility, 8) Ethics, and 9) Governance.

How can a communications department help build reputation?
If one considers communications departments as the stewards or curators of reputation, then one of their chief roles is to provide that necessary insight of how the organization is seen internally and externally, and support the leadership team embrace the best that it can. The role here is not one of ownership. Rather it is as the eyes, ears, and conscience of the organization and its chief facilitations officers across all segments, silos, and levels throughout the organization. The first step is knowing where and how the organization sees itself as compared and contrasted to the "outside world" and the wider discussions in media/social media and influencer channels. Evidence —from quantitative to qualitative research and even "big data"— is an essential partner in this process.

How important is the CEO in building positive public opinion so that an organization might suffer less in crisis?
Leadership and quality of management are widely recognized as among the key drivers of reputation. So the CEO's role in setting out the vision, strategy, direction, and tone for the organization externally is essential. Some CEO's have said that it's anywhere between 20 to 50% of their "day job." *If it's not in their job description, I think we have a problem, Houston.*

How important is it for the communications department to report to the CEO?
Not *reporting* to the CEO is less troublesome than not having *access* to the CEO. That is the key If the communications department it to be the strategic "weather vane" and "supporting band," it needs to be in sync with the leader and be able to challenge and provide other perspectives with solid evidence-based counsel when needs be.

What are the skills that public relations people need to help build reputation in the 21st century?
Unless we each understand how our companies make money, how they grow or gain marketshare, and how they compete directly in the marketspace, our story-telling is likely to come off as superficial or shallow. Our narratives must link into those strategic business goals of the organizations that employ us. The Arthur W Page Society found that there are three core skill "sets" that will be essential.

1. The longstanding skills of the CCO as strategic counselor, protector of corporate reputation, critical thinker who clearly communicates and influencer of the few, who in turn influence the many.

2. The heightened need for business acumen, leadership competencies and integration skills.

3. Creating capability to engage individuals at massive scale such as using data to detect understand and engage individuals vs. segments, creating channels and platforms to engage individuals directly, and using engagement to drive the cycle from belief-to-advocacy.

To that, I would add diplomacy, tact and a deep, quiet passion for the craft. There is much at stake.

Public Relations Bookshelf

Anthonissen, Peter. *Crisis Communication*. London, England: Kogan Page, 2008. This book was written by members of the IPREX group of 64 worldwide, independent public relations agencies and offers a novel take on crisis communications in the 21st century; the Internet, they say, has changed everything.

Barton, Laurance. *Crisis Leadership Now*. New York: McGraw-Hill, 2008. This book is written from the perspective of averting corporate disasters, from threats to sabotage to scandal.

Boin, Arjen, Paul t'Hart, Eric Stern, and Bengt Sundelius. *The Politics of Crisis Management*. Cambridge, England: Cambridge University Press, 2006. This is a treatise on major government crises, including 9/11 and the anthrax scare in the United States.

Coombs, Timothy W. *Applied Crisis Communication and Crisis Management*. Thousand Oaks, CA: Sage Publications, 2014. This is chock full of interesting cases, including those of several chocolate makers, from Nestle to Hershey to Cadbury.

Devlin, Eric S. *Crisis Management Planning and Execution*. Boca Raton, FL: Auerbach Publications, 2007. This is a good compilation of case studies, emphasizing the planning aspects that go into crisis management.

Dezenhall, Eric and John Weber. *Damage Control*. New York: Penguin Group, 2011. The authors contend that "everything you learned about crisis communication is wrong." (Not quite.) But they do have a good chapter on Wikileaks.

Fearn-Banks, Kathleen. *Crisis Communications*. 4th ed. New York: Routledge, 2011. Solid primer on full spectrum of crises and how to handle them.

Fink, Steven. *Crisis Communications: The Definitive Guide to Managing the Message*. New York, NY: McGraw-Hill, 2013. Written for managers at every level, this book offers sound advice, based on lessons learned in 21st century crises, from BP's Gulf of Mexico spill to Penn State University's sex scandal.

George, Bill. *Seven Lessons for Leading in Crisis*. San Francisco, CA: Jossey-Bass, 2009. If only it were this easy.

Gilpin, Dawn R. and Priscilla J. Murphy. *Crisis Management in a Complex World*. New York: Oxford University Press, 2008. This book does a good job of tracing the roots and progression of crises, including the long, sad saga of Enron.

Henry, Rene. *Communicating in Crisis*. Seattle, WA: Gollywobbler Productions, 2008. Leaning on his 40 years of experience in industry, sports, education, and government, the author warns, "Lawyers make little money preventing crisis and a lot resolving them."

Jordan-Meier, Jane. *The Four Stages of Highly Effective Crisis Management*. Boca Raton, FL: CRC Press, 2011. Focus here is on managing the media in a digital age.

Levick, Richard and Larry Smith. *Stop the Presses*. 2nd ed. Ann Arbor, MI: Watershed Press, 2008. The authors contend that one important change in 21st century crisis communication is the "sea change in Internet communications that now ties the world's most powerful corporations to the humblest public interest groups in an unholy dance of 'gotcha' and 'gotcha back.'"

Lewis, Gerald. *Organizational Crisis Management*. Boca Raton, FL: Auerbach Publications, 2006. This book focuses on crises involving personnel, premises, and the like, all affecting reputation.

O'Dwyer, Jack (Ed.). *Jack O'Dwyer's Newsletter*. 271 Madison Ave., New York, NY 10016. The industry bible.

Powell, Conrad. *Sandy Hook Slaughter*. New York: First World Publishing, 2012. A quickly-done e-book that details the horrendous shooting of elementary school children in Connecticut and how authorities reacted to the crisis.

Rampton, Sheldon and John Stauber. *The Best War Ever*. New York: Penguin Press, 2006. Two public relations industry critics offer a thorough trashing of the War on Terror, the Bush administration, and the entire public relations industry. (Look out below!)

Smith, Denis and Dominic Elliot. *Key Readings in Crisis Management*. New York: Routledge, 2006. A series of essays on major international crises and how they were handled.

Stein, Matthew. *When Disaster Strikes*. White River Junction, VT: Chelsea Green Publishing Company, 2011. Written from the point of view of what to do when disaster strikes you or your family; not exactly traditional crisis management but, hey, 377 pages ain't easy to fill!

Ulmer, Robert R., Timothy L. Sellnow, and Matthew W. Seeger. *Effective Crisis Communication*. Thousand Oaks, CA: Sage Publications, 2011. This provides a good explanation of steps in crisis management, illustrated by famous cases.

Zdziarski, Eugene L., Norbert W. Dunkel, and Michael J. Rollo. *Campus Crisis Management*. San Francisco, CA: Jossey-Bass, 2007. This provides background on university crises, beginning with the University of Texas tower shootings in 1966 to the present.

Endnotes

1. Melissa Eddy and Nicola Clark, "Before Crash, Germanwings Pilot Searched Web for Ways to Die," *The New York Times* (June 12, 2015).
2. Nick Denton, "Taking a Post Down," *Gawker.com* (July 17, 2015).
3. Erik Holm, "Got a Crisis? Tap AIG (Really)," *The Wall Street Journal* (October 12, 2011).
4. Helio F. Garcia, *Crisis Communications 1* (New York: American Association of Advertising Agencies, 1999): 9.
5. Peter Eavis, "S.E.C. Approves Rule on CEO Pay Ratio," *The New York Times* (August 5, 2015).
6. Vernon Silver and David Glovin, "Madoff Scandal Ensnares Patron Saint for Moralists," *Bloomberg News* (February 13, 2009).
7. Jennifer Steinhauer, "Taking Aim at Planned Parenthood, Conservatives Use Familiar Tactic," *The New York Times* (July 30, 2015).
8. Jonah Goldberg, "Rolling Stone Ignored Basic Journalism with Bogus UVA Rape Story," *Los Angeles Times* (April 6, 2015).
9. Josh Halliday, "Facebook Paid PR Firm to Smear Google," *The Guardian* (May 12, 2011).
10. Howard W. Chase, "Issues Management Conference—A Special Report," *Corporate Public Issues and Their Management 7*, no. 23 (December 1, 1982): 1–2.

11. Richard C. Hyde, "In Crisis Management, Getting the Message Right Is Critical," *The Strategist* (Summer 2007): 32–35.
12. Richard K. Long, "Seven Needless Sins of Crisis (Mis) Management," *PR Tactics* (August 2001): 14.
13. Fraser P. Seitel, "Spotting a Crisis," *odwyerpr.com* (March 20, 2001).
14. Kate MacArthur, "KFC Preps Bird-Glue Fear Plan," *Advertising Age* (November 7, 2005): 1.
15. Fraser P. Seitel and John Doorley, *Rethinking Reputation* (New York, NY: Palgrave MacMillan, 2012).
16. Fraser P. Seitel, "Crisis Management Lessons from the Astor Disaster," *O'Dwyer's PR Report* (December 2006): 30.
17. Colin Schultz, "Marathon Bombing, Twitter Was Full of Lies," *Smithsonian.com* (October 24, 2013).
18. Melissa Agnes, "Dark Websites as a Social Media Crisis Management Strategy," White Paper, www.MelissaAgnes.com, 2012.
19. Shel Holtz, "In Defense of Crisis PR: An Open Letter to Rachel Maddow," *Ragan PR Daily* (August 8, 2012).
20. "Traditional Media Still Win in Crises," *Jack O'Dwyer's Newsletter* (October 9, 2006): 8.

Chapter 18

Launching a Career

FIGURE 18-1   **Wrong key.**
The late Steve Jobs was happy to be with singer Alicia Keyes at the launch of the iTunes online music store but much less so when an enterprising college student asked the Apple founder for assistance on a school project.
Photo: Ray Tang/REX/Newscom

Chapter Objectives

1. To explore the role of public relations in time of economic uncertainty, charting how the field has improved its position even in times of stress.

2. To discuss how a public relations student or novice finds a position in the practice of public relations.

3. To discuss, in detail, the aspects of organizing the search, job letters, résumés, interviewing, and follow-up.

4. To examine how an individual can map his or her course for long-term public relations success.

In the old days, you got a job in public relations by "networking." In the new days, you get a job in public relations by "networking" in social media. At least that's how young David Murray found communications work in 2009.

■ First, he reached out to followers on his Twitter account that he was officially "looking for work." He immediately received several prime leads.

■ Second, he augmented these by entering keywords in Twitter Search, like "Hiring Social Media," "Online Community Manager," and "Blogging Jobs."

■ Third, he pulled RSS feeds of his keyword conversations into Google Reader and checked his incoming mail every morning.

■ Fourth, he followed up on promising leads by introducing himself via Twitter, inquiring about job leads, some of which hadn't been officially posted. Several executives were receptive to his social media entreaties.

And before he knew it, voilà, he had landed a Web-based communications post at a Web site design firm.[1]

As positive as Mr. Murray's experience in reaching out to corporate bigwigs for assistance, there are others who are less fortunate, such as Long Island University senior Chelsea Kate Issacs, who in 2010 had a most unpleasant exchange with a well-known CEO (**Figure 18-1**).

Ms. Issacs e-mailed none other than living (at the time) legend Steve Jobs, founder and CEO of Apple, and asked why the Apple public relations department refused to give her a quotation for a school project on the use of iPads in academic settings.[2]

Wonder of wonders, Mr. Jobs himself, the iconic Apple impresario e-mailed back—bluntly: *"Our goals do not include helping you get a good grade. Sorry."*

Ms. Issacs was shocked by the dismissive tone and e-mailed again, wondering again whether it was Apple's job to be responsive to the public. Mr. Jobs again responded cryptically: *"Nope. We have over 300 million users and we can't respond to their requests unless they involve a problem of some kind. Sorry."*

Ms. Issacs tried again, informing the CEO that she was, in fact, "one of the 300 million Apple users" and asked if she might, simply, receive the quote she sought. To which, the world's greatest innovator responded: *"Please leave us alone."*

Dealing with cranky executives—and sometimes even worse, their protective secretaries!—isn't easy for public relations students. Finding a job in the practice of public relations—especially in times of economic downturn—is probably the most formidable task that an entry-level communicator faces. Once inside an organization, competence rises to the top. So if you're competent, you've got it made. But how do you get "through the door" in the first place? The challenge—the one we'll focus on in this final chapter—is "launching a career."

1 | Public Relations Rebounds

Traditionally, public relations jobs were the first to fall when economic times got rough. Not so much anymore.

Smart organizations today understand the critical importance of communications that are honest, candid, and transparent. Moreover, the advent of social media and the Internet have made the traditional corporate "vow of silence," especially in the face of continuous criticism, a dangerous proposition. CEOs, who by nature are tight-lipped, need only consider the carcasses of once-great companies laid to waste by arrogant leaders, who, in recent years, refused to level with the public about the state of their corporations.

As a consequence, the impact on the public relations industry of the economic downturn that afflicted the United States and the world in the second decade of the 21st century was rather muted. A study of nearly 200 organizations by the University of Southern California indicated that public relations and communications functions of U.S. companies suffered only moderate decreases as the recession wore on. Instead of cutting staffs, as had been done in previous downturns, most companies opted to freeze or reduce staff compensation, rather than cutting headcount.[3]

The understanding and mastery of social media proved a primary reason in the renewed popularity and staying power of public relations positions in economic downturn. As one Toronto marketing CEO, whose firm purchased three public relations agencies, told *The New York Times*: "Marketers want to find firms that can deliver performance, and public relations agencies are excelling in understanding the changing dynamics of the marketplace, as what happens with a campaign in social media and earned media has become as important as its presence in paid media and owned media."[4]

While the practice of public relations isn't immune from cuts in bad times, it is no longer "the first to go." Most important, organizations today understand that especially in bad times, candid communication isn't an option; it's a necessity.

② Getting a Jump

Public relations jobs used to be available for anybody who wanted them. Since nobody understood exactly what public relations was, standards weren't high. (How d'ya think I got a job?) But today, with standards raised, competition fierce and the labor market tight, the search for a public relations position must begin in school.

The reality today is that when a potential employer considers a candidate, he or she is also thinking, as Pulitzer Prize winner Tom Friedman has put it, "Can this person add value every hour, every day—more than a worker in India, a robot, or a computer? Can he or she help my company adapt by not only doing the job today but also reinventing the job for tomorrow?"[5] "Friedman concluded that unless an applicant measures up to these criteria, he or she won't get hired in today's "hyperconnected world."

For public relations students, this translates into using the college years to get a jump on the competition by doing the following:

1. **Improve your communication skills.** Communication is what you do in public relations. So make sure you do it better than others.

2. **Start networking.** Don't wait until you're submitting your résumés before you begin networking. Start doing it now. Make friends and keep them. Attend business gatherings and get around.

3. **Focus . . .** on what you do—and like—best. Which part of public relations do you like the most—corporate, agency, nonprofit, political, what?

4. **Look at companies you like.** Keep a running roster of the public relations firms or companies to which you'd like to apply. Follow them on LinkedIn for news on the company and to learn who is leaving and moving up the ladder.

5. **Intern, intern, intern.** Use college to try employment during the off months. Sure, you may not get paid and may be given tedious assignments that others don't want. But it's worth it—a great way to get your foot in the door, both literally and figuratively.

To paraphrase the old saw, an education is a terrible thing to waste—so get started in the field before you graduate.[6]

③ Organizing the Job Search

Organizing a job search, in good times or bad, requires just that—"organization."

Just as in any assignment, public relations job seekers should follow a predetermined path to get them through the door to meet a person with a potential job offer. Again, it's getting *through* the door that's the problem.

As public relations practice has become more enticing to communications students, lawyers, journalists, and others, positions in the field have become more competitive.

So what's an entry-level, fresh-eyed graduate to do as he or she commences the post-commencement job search?

According to experienced public relations executive and teacher Martin Arnold, the following ought to be considered:

- **First, consider what interests you, and start early.**
  Determine where, if you had your druthers, you would like to work. In sports? Fashion? Government? Big business? With a grassroots nonprofit? Where?

- **Second, get a name.**
  Avoid writing blind to potential employers.

  To avoid the "dead letter response," network with colleagues to see if an associate might suggest a name at a target organization. Failing that, consult directories to discover the names of public relations professionals on staff. Failing that, call the organization directly and secure the name of the public relations director.

- **Third, dispatch a personal letter.**
  Write directly to the contact, requesting an interview. Explain in the note who you are, your rationale for choosing this organization as a target, and why you're interested in speaking with the addressee.

  But don't make the interview contingent on job openings at the company in question. Even if no job is currently available—and most of the time that's the case—you still want to get through the door.

- **Fourth, call.**
  The sad truth is that few job applicants ever do.

  While it's true that some potential employers—the nasty ones—refuse to be "bothered" by job seekers, most potential public relations employers are nicer than that. Some, in fact—the enlightened ones—will even allow you 30 minutes to come in and discuss opportunities.

- **Fifth, prepare an elevator speech.**
  Be prepared with a 30-second talk on who you are, what you are doing, and what you are trying to achieve. Memorize it and use it whenever you can. Most people will help if they know what you want.[7]

Organizing the Résumé

Just like everything else in the second decade of the 21st century, résumés have become big business, with their own set of consultants to help you master the process. As to what to do—and not to do—here are some "dos" from résumé consultant extraordinaire Paulette Barrett:

1. What's your intro? Who are you? What do you want? Why should anyone care?

2. What three impressions do you want to create immediately?

3. What can you say about your achievements that will make someone say, "Tell me more."

4. Be able to cover a time sequence, most recent, backward. Don't leave any gaps.

5. How did you add value in each slot? Solve a problem? Lead colleagues? Sell more?

6. Have an anecdote about each post.

7. List your professional awards, educational achievements, and community service.

8. Aim for a two-page résumé with no less than 12 pt. type.[8]

A Question of Ethics

Hiding the Truth/Padding the Resume

What would you do were you the public relations manager in these two hiring situations, based on real life?

■ After interviewing five candidates for the director of philanthropy job at the global bank, you settle on one front-runner. You invite him in for one final interview, which he passes with flying colors. The man is highly qualified, articulate and passionate about doing good in the community.

You check his references, and all give him glowing reviews. So you offer the man the job and ask him to start a week from today. Two days later, you receive an urgent call from your new hire, asking to see you.

He comes in, looking tired and forlorn. He explains that he has spent "several sleepless nights," because of one fact he withheld during his interviews. Specifically, as a teenager, he had been arrested and convicted for shoplifting. *"I know your security check would have turned this up, and I understand if this changes your mind about my employment,"* he says. You ask him what he stole, and he answers, *"a Peter, Paul & Mary album"* **(Figure 18-2)**.

■ The bank's annual report is the most prestigious document and highest budget item for which the public relations department is responsible.

You interview four well-known design firms, each of which has many years of experience working for large companies, and one small firm that seems singularly creative but has never landed a major corporate assignment.

You interview the CEOs of each firm and find the small firm's leader, a Harvard graduate, according to his resume, to be a young man of great vision and passion. So you decide to "roll the dice" and give the upstart a shot. *"Understand,"* you tell the young CEO, *"I am taking a real chance here, so you've got to come through."* *"Don't worry,"* the young man replies, *"you can count on us."*

The next day you call the other competitors and tell them of your choice. One competitor is particularly upset his firm didn't win. *"You're making a big mistake,"* he says on the phone, *"that guy is lying about Harvard. He attended but never got his degree."*

You call Harvard admissions and find out the bitter competitor is right; the young man never graduated.

Question:

1. What do you do in each case?

FIGURE 18-2
The answer my friend ....
was *what* when a job candidate belatedly admitted to stealing a Peter, Paul, and Mary album as a teenager?
Photo: PF1 WENN Photos/Newscom

As to the "don'ts," here are some of the more egregious from career expert Dawn Rasmussen:

1. **Goofy or inappropriate e-mail address.** Grow up. Don't use your hotlix23@ aol.com account on your résumé. Names like that suggest that you aren't taking your job search seriously, and quite possibly lead to a "delete."

2. **Including an objective statement.** Employers don't care what *you* want; they care what you are going to do for *them*.

3. **Forgetting skill sets.** Knock, knock. Who's there? Keywords. Keywords who? Keywords are key to getting your résumé noticed. Okay, that's a lousy joke, but it's not any worse than a résumé without keyword skill sets included. (The Web site onetonline.org offers the mother lode of keywords. Pass it on.)

4. **Placing awards and top achievements at the end of the document.** Please, insert a "Notable Achievements" section right after the top third of the résumé where you've included your keywords. Remember, the cream rises to the top.

5. **Lumping multiple jobs at one employer into one position.** This is a dealbreaker. Some people have had a wonderful career at one employer, holding multiple positions as they worked their way to the top. However, this does *not* entitle them to lump the entirety of their time at that employer under that one position. It's a *big* no-no.

6. **Stretching your employment dates.** If you started on 11/2007 and left in 2/2008, that does not mean you can put "2007–2008" on your résumé. That's called lying.

7. **Upgrading your job title.** The title listed on the résumé should match what is on file in the personnel office—or you're creating a terrible first impression.

8. **Not keeping up to date.** If the last class you took to boost your on-the-job knowledge was in 1999, then you need to get cracking. Employers are hiring subject matter experts, and your job—until you retire (I know, tall order)—is to constantly think about the professional development classes, workshops, conferences, etc., that will enhance your job knowledge. Most of all remember, there is no such thing as job security anymore—especially in public relations.[9]

Organizing the Job Interview

Once an applicant is fortunate enough to land an interview, he or she must understand that 9 times out of 10, it is their responsibility to control the meeting agenda.

This meeting is your chance—often your *only* chance—to find out the information you need about other firms and other individuals to keep your search progressing.

So walk in with a game plan and the "script" that will keep the interview going.

■ **First, take charge.** To take your best shot, you have to—in a nice and subtle way—take charge of the interview.

So lead. Don't wait to be asked. Raise questions about the organization and the interviewer. Demonstrate your interest in the organization and a job by taking charge of the interview.

■ **Second, lead with your knowledge and strength.** Suggest through your questions and answers that you've done your homework on the organization.

FYI

Online Public Relations Job References

The Internet offers an expanding list of reference sites that access "public relations openings." Among them:

- **Indeed.com**
  The job search engine Indeed.com is an excellent resource for finding public relations job listings fast. Indeed.com is free and enables you to search millions of job listings from thousands of Web sites, job boards, newspapers, blogs, company career pages, and associations to find job listings that match or are similar to your search query. Indeed.com has the look and feel of Google and the other top search engines. It's user-friendly, uncluttered, simple, and easy to navigate. (www.Indeed.com/)

- **International Association of Business Communicators (IABC)**
  The IABC's site lists 240 or so primarily internal communications openings at corporations and nonprofits. With its significant presence in Canada, IABC boasts the added advantage of listing Canadian job openings. (http://jobs.iabc.com/home/index.cfm?site_id=65)

- **Media Bistro**
  This site lists all manner of media jobs, from online and newspaper editors to broadcast journalists. It also includes a healthy sampling of public relations posts. (www.mediabistro.com/joblistings/)

- **Monster**
  Every day, approximately 20–50 "new" public relations positions are listed. Many are of the promotional/marketing cold call variety, but others are at legitimate public relations firms. Monster.com is a good source for "public relations" positions that often don't appear elsewhere. (http://jobsearch.monster.com/Browse.aspx)

- **O'Dwyerpr.com**
  Among its 70 or so availabilities, the inestimable Odwyerpr.com site generally lists higher level openings at firms, nonprofits, and companies. In addition to the high-level posts, O'Dwyer also lists a number of "intern" availabilities. (http://jobs.odwyerpr.com/home/index.cfm?site_id=258)

- **PR News Online**
  PR News offers another excellent online source for corporate, nonprofit, and agency public relations positions. As with other sites, PR News offers a service for job seekers to post résumés for employers to peruse. (www.prnewsonline.com/resources/pr_jobs.html)

- **PRSA Job Center**
  The Public Relations Society of America (PRSA) site lists 1700 job openings, many from agency members from around the nation. In addition, individual PRSA chapters, such as Cleveland and Houston, keep their own local job openings updated on a regular basis. (www.prsa.org/jobcenter/)

- **PR Talent**
  This service, begun by several public relations professionals, says that it "operates much like an entertainment talent agency, except that we identify and represent top full-time and freelance public relations and communications talent." (www.prtalent.com/-jobSearch.aspx)

- **Public Affairs Council**
  The Public Affairs Council in Washington lists primarily lobbying, government relations, and government agency job openings, not only in the nation's capital but throughout the nation. (http://pac.org/jobs)

- **Ragan Communications Career Center**
  Ragan.com's 250 or so offerings span the gamut from internal to external positions, including public relations posts at government agencies, such as the U.S. Coast Guard and the IRS. (www.ragan.com/jobadvice/)

- **The Fry Group**
  The Fry Group is a public relations executive search firm that lists some of its job searches on the Internet, where interested talent may inquire. Other search firms offer similar job quests in progress. (www.frygroup.com/listings.php)

Many of the job opening postings on these sites are redundant from one site to the next. Some are recurring month-to-month adverts designed to troll the waters to see what turns up. Still others are little more than low-level sales come-ons, looking for warm bodies.

Whatever.

All these site are worth a look from prospective public relations job seekers.

Remember, it only takes one.

Show the interviewer that you've gone the extra mile by researching the firm and becoming knowledgeable about it.

- **Third, beware the "gotcha" questions.** Every interviewer asks standard questions. They seem innocuous enough, but cuidado: They're tricky. Here are a few:

  - **Do you have any questions?** This is a great opportunity to turn around the interview. The best way to answer this standard question is to stir up a conversation by asking the interviewer more about how he or she started at the company, and even what he or she loves most about the job.

  - **What is your biggest weakness?** This is dangerous. The standard "weakness" question is usually answered with strength by the majority of job applicants. But careful, hiring managers are tired of hearing every single candidate that walks through the door stating that being a "perfectionist" is their biggest weakness.

  - **Tell me about yourself.** Your answer to this interview question is where your "elevator pitch" can work like a charm. Be prepared for it.

  - **What do you know about our company?** The best strategy you can have in tackling this question is to research the most recent news about the employer and turn this interview question around by starting a conversation about the direction the business is moving in. On the other hand, the biggest mistake an applicant can make in answering this common interview question is to not know anything about the company at all.[10]

- **Fourth, indicate what you'll add to the mix.** Take the opportunity to allude to what that college training has afforded you, particularly in enhancing the expertise and scope of the department you'd love to join.

  For example, all those social media tools that you took for granted in school—Facebook, Twitter, LinkedIn, Tumblr, Pinterest, blogs, and all the rest—may reveal potential new avenues for an interviewer. Your facility with such social media may, therefore, suggest attractive possibilities to the interviewer. Remember, people want to work with people they like.

- **Fifth, get more names.** This is your most important task at the interview.

  Use the interviewer to provide more names—advice, leads, contacts, colleagues at competitors with whom you might speak, etc. Don't walk out the door unless you have been given two or three other people you can call to continue the job search.

- **Sixth, follow up.** Ensure that the interviewer won't mind if you "keep in touch," as situations with you and at the organization change. Once you've made the contact, you don't want to lose it.

The reassuring point to keep always in mind is that as frustrating and maddening and ego-deflating as the job-seeking process sometimes seems to be, all it takes is one "You're hired" to start you on a lifelong career.

4 Ensuring Public Relations Success

For years, practitioners of the practice of public relations have searched for the "holy grail" to advise them on getting ahead.

While many have speculated on achieving senior management success in public relations, a comprehensive study of 97 highest-level public relations leaders isolated the seven factors that can help pave the way to the top of the practice.

Recruiter William C. Heyman (see From the Top in this chapter) and University of Alabama Professor Bruce Berger produced a study that pinpointed what it takes to pursue a successful career in public relations. They discovered seven keys—some expected, others counterintuitive—to a successful public relations career.

1. **Diversity of experience.** While the executives polled averaged 23 years of experience, most indicated that it was "the accumulation of experiences over time" that forged the "tipping point" in their success. Study recipients clearly felt that focusing on one specialty throughout a career was counterproductive.

2. **Performance.** Successful public relations executives must deliver one tangible commodity—results. Survey respondents agreed that the power of performance—solving problems, meeting goals, providing counsel, and producing results—was an absolute requirement for success in public relations.

3. **Communications skills.** Public relations practitioners are, at base, professional communicators. Therefore, highly honed technical communications skills, according to the study—from writing and design to the production of sophisticated communication materials—are imperative for public relations success.

4. **Relationship building.** Common wisdom suggests that in public relations, "it's not what you know but who you know that counts." To a great degree, according to the study, common wisdom is correct.

   Nearly half of the executives, in fact, said the most valuable source of influence they possessed was relationships with senior executives, peers, and subordinates. Indeed, the findings hint that relationships may provide more power to professionals than their titles or formal positions in their organization.

5. **Proactivity and passion.** The executives said that public relations people must be go-getters, self-starters, risk-takers, opportunity-seekers with boundless energy, great curiosity, and passionate in their commitment to the practice.

6. **Teamliness.** Most respondents agreed that achievement depended on three levels—the individual, organizational, and group or work unit, in that order.

7. **Intangibles.** Chemistry. Likeability. Personality. Presence. Cultural fit.

Nearly 90% of the executives polled cited positive personal character traits as the single most desired characteristic among job candidates.

One disturbing aspect of their study, said the researchers, was that nearly half of those interviewed said the most significant limitation on public relations practice and influence was the "inaccurate or incomplete perceptions of the function's role and value," particularly among organizational executives.

One way to upgrade that perception is for those who practice public relations—particularly young practitioners—to take seriously the list of successful attributes revealed in the Heyman-Berger study.[11]

FYI

Don't You Dare...

After all this, anyone guilty of repeating the following 20 faux pas in their cover letters or résumés for employment (culled from the files of career expert Andrew Kucheriavy) deserve what they get:

20. "I have a known track record and excellent experience with accuracy and fixing errors"
19. "Strong Work Ethic, Attention to Detail, Team Player, Attention to Detail"
18. "My experience include filing, billing, printing and coping"
17. "Demonstrated ability in multi-tasting."
16. "My work ethics are impeachable."
15. "I have nervous of steel."
14. "I consistently tanked as top sales producer for new accounts."
13. "I am a perfectionist and rarely if ever forget details."

12. "Dear Sir or Madman,"
11. "I can type without looking at the keyboard."
10. "Instrumental in ruining entire operation for a Midwest chain store."
9. "I am anxious to use my exiting skills"
8. "Speak English and Spinach"
7. "I am a Notary Republic"
6. "I attended college courses for minor public relations"
5. "Following is a grief overview of my skills."
4. "I'm attacking my resume for you to review."
3. "I am experienced in all faucets of accounting."
2. "Hope to hear from you, shorty."

And the most embarrassing one to finish off our list:

1. "Directed $25 million anal shipping and receiving operations." *

*Andrew Kucheriavy, "Top 20 of the Most Hilarious Mistakes on Resumes and Cover Letters," www.resumark.com/blog/author/andrew/, March 19, 2010.

Last Word

Public relations dialogue still revolves around finding that elusive "seat at the management table," that is, convincing management that the public relations function is as imperative as legal or human resources or finance. To be sure, the practice has come a long way since patriarchs such as Edward Bernays and Ivy Lee first practiced the art form in the early 20th century.

Indeed, notwithstanding the tremendous strides the field has made in recent years, the practice is still often challenged by those who don't fully understand or appreciate it. The burden, then, is on the public relations practitioners of the 21st century.

Employers will increasingly seek experienced and competent public relations professionals to help them communicate. How can entry-level professionals accommodate this Catch-22 need for

"experience"? According to experienced counselor and LIM College public relations professor Barry Zusman, at least three specific courses should be considered:

- **Hone writing skills.** Says Professor Zusman, "While the current generation gets it as far as technology and digital media are concerned, we don't yet live in a world ruled by 140 Twitter characters." Well-written content is still king.
- **Seize internships.** These are among the best ways to learn about the field with real-life experience. Although many internships are unpaid, they're still often worth it, since firms hire based on internship experience.

■ **Join a professional communications organization.** And become involved in professional committees. Says Zusman, "Listen and learn everything you can from the organization's members, who have been in the field and can serve as mentors."[12]

To the Zusman Principles, others suggest five additional keys to moving ahead in public relations.

1. **Use technology to your advantage.** You can often teach employers how to use social media for public relations value, so don't be shy.

2. **Pay attention to details.** Treat everything like a "big deal," using every opportunity to demonstrate your worth.

3. **Read, read, read.** The key to good writing, say veterans, is "good reading," so pick up newspapers, magazines, and books, and then *read* them.

4. **Be a student.** Just because you've graduated into the workplace doesn't mean you should stop *learning*. Learn constantly.

5. **Find a mentor.** Often, the old adage is right: It's not what you know but who you know that counts. So find someone or *someones*

who can advise and help you as you proceed through the public relations profession.[13]

In the second decade of the 21st century, the practice of public relations has never been stronger or more valuable to the individuals and organizations that depend on it. The field still has its share of debates—the value of a public relations degree vs. a degree in liberal arts, the role and knowledge of digital media vs. traditional media, the goodness of a public relations education vs. on-the-job training, the relative pay of women vs. men, whether marketing should be subordinated to public relations, etc. Indeed, as the CEO of Ketchum public relations put it, "The fact there's debate over whether marketing and public relations should remain separate is evident of PR's growing importance."[14]

One point, however, is incontestable: The practice of public relations has never been as accepted or respected as it is today. That's why jobs in the field are coveted, and competition is great. But for an individual of dedication and competence, who writes well and communicates clearly and who understands that integrity and reputation are critical for success—the practice of public relations will continue to offer bountiful opportunities for generations to come.

Discussion Starters

1. How is the practice of public relations doing in the midst of economic downturn?
2. What steps can a college student take to get a jump on public relations employment?
3. Is it worth sending a form letter to a potential public relations employer?
4. Why is it important to have a "name" at an organization before applying?
5. What are the elements that make a winning job letter?
6. What are the principles in creating an effective résumé?
7. How can an applicant "control the agenda" of a job interview?
8. Should an interviewee follow-up the interview with further communication?
9. What additional steps should an up-and-coming professional follow to ensure success?
10. How important is writing in a public relations career?

Pick of the Literature

Ready to Launch: The PR Couture Guide to Breaking into Fashion PR

Crosby Noricks, New York: Crosby Noricks, 2013

Sure, this is self-published, but it's good.

A great many public relations students today, infused by Fashion Week and VH1, wish to enter the wild world of fashion public relations. This is a great introduction to that ethereal world.

The book begins by distinguishing among marketing, advertising, and public relations, emphasizing that it is media relations and publicity that largely defines the latter (true, especially in the fashion world).

The book takes the novice through interviewing, pitching, social media networking, and what to expect from a career in fashion public relations. Written by an agency executive knowledgeable in the subject matter, this book provides a true-to-life explanation about what public relations—at least as it relates to fashion—is all about.

From the Top

Ultimate Word to the Wise (Student): An Interview with Bill Heyman

Bill Heyman, founder, president, and CEO of Heyman Associates, has been the dean of public relations recruiters for more than two decades. He manages senior-level searches for blue-chip and emerging companies, leading public relations firms, nonprofit organizations, and government agencies. He is a board member of the Lagrant Foundation, which awards scholarships to minority students planning public relations careers. He is also an inaugural member of the advisory board for the Plank Center for Public Relations Studies in the College of Communication and Information Sciences at the University of Alabama. For additional information about Heyman Associates, visit www.heymanassociates.com.

What is the employment outlook for public relations graduates today?

Public relations has become an essential business tool, not something that could be eliminated. On the whole, companies want to do a better job telling their stories. But, job seekers need to be realistic: The employment market is tied to the performance of capital markets. Those seeking jobs must recognize that salaries and perks will not match those of only a few years ago, when "new economy" companies ruled, and that more will be expected from them for lower initial salaries. It also is likely to take longer for most to earn their stripes—[that is, job seekers can expect to] rise more slowly within an organization, because organizations are smaller and leaner.

Where are the most attractive public relations employment skill areas?

The most employment opportunities today are in media relations, internal communications, issues management, financial public relations, branding and image development, and social responsibility. Each one of these specialties tends to target an audience that was underserved prior to corporations' rebuilding their images. Companies are no longer taking any audience for granted. Transparency is critical.

What are the most attractive industries for public relations employment?

The health care industry consistently looks at communications as an important way to deliver its message. Pharmaceutical and biotechnology companies lead the public relations job market. Almost on a level field is the financial services industry. Also, an increased number of the largest corporations are in the process of remaking their images, especially those whose reputations have been challenged. With communications, they can demonstrate they are broad thinkers, technologically advanced, and contemporary.

What's the best preparation for public relations employment?
Become a strong writer. There is no greater need than having a strong writing ability. Key areas of employment today are in media relations and speechwriting, and both require strong writing skills.

Students must take as many writing classes as possible and intern (for pay or not) in places where they can get real-world experience (local newspapers, public relations agencies, companies, or philanthropic organizations).

And, because they must be increasingly well-rounded in their knowledge, they need to take a wide range of liberal arts classes (especially ethics) and meld that with exploring cultural experiences in the community (opera, theater, museums, etc.) and read, read, read newspapers, magazines, corporate Web sites, and books.

The most successful practitioners will be those that the CEO will want as a seatmate flying across the country or at a dinner table with the organization's most important client.

What is the ideal starting point for public relations beginners?
Often, an agency is the best training ground because of the diverse experiences. The broader the experience, the better it is. Corporate jobs, especially entry-level, tend to be more narrowly focused. Starting at a news organization enables people to learn up close what a reporter goes through and needs every day. Another area where people can consider working in the early stages of their career is a political campaign.

What are the public relations prospects in the nonprofit sector?
Public relations is becoming a valued commodity in the nonprofit sector, especially after 9/11. These jobs tend to have lower salaries, but the experience can be similar to that of a public relations agency and therefore a good training ground.

Also, corporate foundations are doing more to articulate their specific business message and are looking for strong public relations executives.

What are the essential characteristics that public relations employers look for in potential employees?
There are five nontechnical characteristics that are most important: one, integrity; two, self-confidence; three, likeability (including respect for others); four, energy (including noticeable enthusiasm); and five, intellect (including business knowledge and judgment).

Added to that are two technical characteristics: the ability to write and to present well. These seven criteria transcend communications posts and organizations.

What's the best way to find a public relations job?
There is no greater way to find a position than to develop a network from the earliest stages of your career.

- Contacting people, joining professional organizations, and being involved in volunteer work are all critical ways to meet other people.

- Conducting research and learning more about the companies you want to work for is key, as is finding a specific contact within each company.

- Learning about the alumni association at your college or university and who might be working within the field can help you start your career.

- During internships, reach out to anyone you meet.

- Always follow up with people, writing courteous notes asking for help. Two key characteristics in finding a job are to be courteous and tenacious. Always let people know how appreciative you are of any time they spend with you.

Public Relations Bookshelf

Aronson, Merry, Don Spetner, and Carol Ames. *The Public Relations Writer's Handbook.* San Francisco, CA: Jossey-Bass, 2007. This presents a good explanation of how the digital age has altered the requirements in the public relations field.

Breakenridge, Deirdre. *Social Media and Public Relations.* Upper Saddle River, NJ: Pearson Education, 2012. The queen of social media public relations holds forth on a comprehensive explanation of what social media means to the practice of public relations.

Croft, Arthur C. *Managing a Public Relations Firm for Fun and Profit.* Binghamton, NY: Haworth Press, 2006. Once you've entered the field, prospered in it, and now are ready to become your own CEO, read this book to find out how to do it.

Fitzpatrick, Kathy and Carolyn Bronstein. *Ethics in Public Relations.* Thousand Oaks, CA: Sage Publishing, 2006. This offers a fresh approach on why public relations people should be "responsible advocates" for the views they represent.

Freitag, Alan R. and Ashli Q. Stokes. *Global Public Relations.* New York: Routledge, 2009. This presents the cross-border cultural impact of different societies on public relations practice.

Green, Andy. *Creativity in Public Relations.* 3rd ed. London, England: Kogan Page, 2007. The author emphasizes "creative thinking" as the road to inspired public relations.

Hall, Phil. *The New PR.* N. Potomac, MD: Larsten Publishing, 2007. Emphasis here is on how "experiential marketing strategies" will change the face of public relations.

Harris, Thomas L. and Patricia T. Whelan. *The Marketer's Guide to Public Relations in the 21st Century.* Mason, OH: Texere, 2006. The emphasis here is on marketing public relations.

Henderson, David. *Making News.* Lincoln, NE: iUniverse Star, 2006. This is an experienced look at how to effectively practice media relations.

Kelleher, Tom. *Public Relations Online.* Thousand Oaks, CA: Sage Publications, 2007. This is a fine explanation of the new technologies in public relations and how to use them.

Morris, Trevor and Simon Goldworthy. *PR: A Persuasive Industry?* New York: Palgrave MacMillan, 2008. The authors describe public relations as more gray than black and white, in terms of ethics; as "amoral," neither a tool for good nor bad but rather dependent on the specific ethic or motives of its professionals. They deride journalists who deride public relations, because without the field, "there would be little news." Amen.

Stimson, Sarah. *How to Get a Job in PR.* London, England: Sarah Stimson, 2013. British perspective on getting a public relations job, providing good grounding in opportunities in Britain.

Weiner, Mark. *Unleashing the Power of PR.* San Francisco, CA: Jossey-Bass, 2006. A measurement expert reminds practitioners that public relations measurement has become essential.

Yaverbaum, Eric. *Public Relations for Dummies.* 2nd ed. Hoboken, NJ: Wiley Publishing, 2006. A seasoned public relations professional talks about how "word of mouth" can move mountains.

Zappala, Joseph M. and Ann R. Carden. *Public Relations Worktext.* Mahwah, NJ: Lawrence Erlbaum, 2008. This is an excellent writing resource for the public relations professional.

Endnotes

1. David M. Scott, "How David Murray Found a New Job via Twitter," *ragan.com* (February 25, 2009).
2. Adrian Chen, "Steve Jobs in Email Pissing Match with College Journalism Student," *Gawker.com* (September 16, 2010).
3. Lindsey Miller, "Recession Reprieve for Communicators," *ragan.com* (February 27, 2009).
4. Stuart Elliott, "Growing Appreciation for P.R. on Madison Avenue," *The New York Times* (September 8, 2010).
5. Thomas L. Friedman, "The Start-Up of You," *The New York Times* (July 12, 2011).
6. Mickie Kennedy, "5 Things Students Should Do Now to Secure a PR Job Later," *Ragan PR Daily* (July 5, 2011).
7. Fraser P. Seitel, "Finding a PR Job," *odwyerpr.com* (June 13, 2005).
8. Paulette Barrett, "Working with a Resume Consultant: 10 Tips to Help You Through the Process," *thehiringclub blog* (July 22, 2011).
9. Dawn Rasmussen, "12 Dangerous Résumé Mistakes," *Ragan PR Daily* (May 15, 2012).
10. Christine Rochelle, "Standard Interview Questions That Will Make or Break You," *AOL.jobs* (February 26, 2010).
11. Fraser P. Seitel, "The 7 Keys to Success in Public Relations," *odwyerpr.com* (July 15, 2004).
12. *Interview with Barry Zusman* (March 2, 2009).
13. Jessica Levco, "Veteran Communicators Share Advice with Newbies," *ragan.com* (March 16, 2009).
14. Michael Bush, "How Social Media Is Helping Public-Relations Sector, Not Just Survive but Thrive," *Advertising Age* (August 23, 2010).

Appendix A

PRSA Member Code of Ethics 2000

Approved by the PRSA Assembly October, 2000

Letter from the PRSA Board of Directors

It is with enormous professional pleasure and personal pride that we, the Public Relations Society of America Board of Directors, put before you a new Public Relations Member Code of Ethics for our Society. It is the result of two years of concentrated effort led by the Board of Ethics and Professional Standards. Comments of literally hundreds and hundreds of members were considered. There were focus groups at our 1999 national meeting in Anaheim, California. We sought and received intensive advice and counsel from the Ethics Resource Center, our outside consultants on the project. Additional recommendations were received from your Board of Directors, PRSA staff, outside reviewers, as well as District and Section officers. Extensive research involving analysis of numerous codes of conduct, ethics statements, and standards and practices approaches was also carried out.

In fact, this Member Code of Ethics has been developed to serve as a foundation for discussion of an emerging global Code of Ethics and Conduct for the practice of Public Relations.

This approach is dramatically different from that which we have relied upon in the past. You'll find it different in three powerfully important ways:
1. Emphasis on enforcement of the Code has been eliminated. But, the PRSA Board of Directors retains the right to bar from membership or expel from the Society any individual who has been or is sanctioned by a government agency or convicted in a court of law of an action that is in violation of this Code.
2. The new focus is on universal values that inspire ethical behavior and performance.
3. Desired behavior is clearly illustrated by providing language, experience, and examples to help the individual practitioner better achieve important ethical and principled business objectives. This approach should help everyone better understand what the expected standards of conduct truly are.

Perhaps most important of all, the mission of the Board of Ethics and Professional Standards has now been substantially altered to focus primarily on education and training, on collaboration with similar efforts in other major professional societies, and to serve an advisory role to the Board on ethical matters of major importance.

The foundation of our value to our companies, clients, and those we serve is their ability to rely on our ethical and morally acceptable behavior. Please review this new Member Code of Ethics in this context:

- Its Values are designed to inspire and motivate each of us every day to the highest levels of ethical practice.
- Its Code Provisions are designed to help each of us clearly understand the limits and specific performance required to be an ethical practitioner.
- Its Commitment mechanism is designed to ensure that every Society member understands fully the obligations of membership and the expectation of ethical behavior that are an integral part of membership in the PRSA.

This approach is stronger than anything we have ever had because:

- It will have a daily impact on the practice of Public Relations.
- There are far fewer gray areas and issues that require interpretation.
- It will grow stronger and be more successful than what we have had in the past through education, through training, and through analysis of behaviors.

The strength of the Code will grow because of the addition of precedent and the ethical experiences of other major professional organizations around the world.

Our new Code elevates our ethics, our values, and our commitment to the level they belong, at the very top of our daily practice of Public Relations.

PRSA Board of Directors

A Message from the PRSA Board of Ethics and Professional Standards

Our Primary Obligation

The primary obligation of membership in the Public Relations Society of America is the ethical practice of Public Relations.

The PRSA Member Code of Ethics is the way each member of our Society can daily reaffirm a commitment to ethical professional activities and decisions.

- The Code sets forth the principles and standards that guide our decisions and actions.
- The Code solidly connects our values and our ideals to the work each of us does every day.
- The Code is about what we should do, and why we should do it.

The Code is also meant to be a living, growing body of knowledge, precedent, and experience. It should stimulate our thinking and encourage us to seek guidance and clarification when we have questions about principles, practices, and standards of conduct.

Every member's involvement in preserving and enhancing ethical standards is essential to building and maintaining the respect and credibility of our profession. Using our values, principles, standards of conduct, and commitment as a foundation, and continuing to work together on ethical issues, we ensure that the Public Relations Society of America fulfills its obligation to build and maintain the framework for public dialogue that deserves the public's trust and support.

The Members of the 2000 Board of Ethics and Professional Standards

Robert D. Frause, APR, Fellow PRSA
Chairman BEPS
Seattle, Washington

Kathy R. Fitzpatrick, APR
Gainesville, Florida

Linda Welter Cohen, APR
Tucson, Arizona

James R. Frankowiak, APR
Tampa, Florida

James E. Lukaszewski, APR, Fellow PRSA
White Plains, New York

Roger D. Buehrer, APR, Fellow PRSA
Las Vegas, Nevada

Jeffrey P. Julin, APR
Denver, Colorado

David M. Bicofsky, APR, Fellow PRSA
Teaneck, New Jersey

James W. Wyckoff, APR
New York, New York

Preamble

Public Relations Society of America Member Code of Ethics 2000

- Professional Values
- Principles of Conduct
- Commitment and Compliance

This Code applies to PRSA members. The Code is designed to be a useful guide for PRSA members as they carry out their ethical responsibilities. This document is designed to anticipate and accommodate, by precedent, ethical challenges that may arise. The scenarios outlined in the Code provision are actual examples of misconduct. More will be added as experience with the Code occurs.

The Public Relations Society of America (PRSA) is committed to ethical practices. The level of public trust PRSA members seek, as we serve the public good, means we have taken on a special obligation to operate ethically.

The value of member reputation depends upon the ethical conduct of everyone affiliated with the Public Relations Society of America. Each of us sets an example for each other—as well as other professionals—by our pursuit of excellence with powerful standards of performance, professionalism, and ethical conduct.

Emphasis on enforcement of the Code has been eliminated. But, the PRSA Board of Directors retains the right to bar from membership or expel from the Society any individual who has been or is sanctioned by a government agency or convicted in a court of law of an action that is in violation of this Code.

Ethical practice is the most important obligation of a PRSA member. We view the Member Code of Ethics as a model for other professions, organizations, and professionals.

PRSA Member Statement of Professional Values

This statement presents the core values of PRSA members and, more broadly, of the public relations profession. These values provide the foundation for the Member Code of Ethics and set the industry standard for the professional practice of public relations. These values are the fundamental beliefs that guide our behaviors and decision-making process. We believe our professional values are vital to the integrity of the profession as a whole.

Advocacy
- We serve the public interest by acting as responsible advocates for those we represent.
- We provide a voice in the marketplace of ideas, facts, and viewpoints to aid informed public debate.

Honesty
- We adhere to the highest standards of accuracy and truth in advancing the interests of those we represent and in communicating with the public.

Expertise
- We acquire and responsibly use specialized knowledge and experience.
- We advance the profession through continued professional development, research, and education.
- We build mutual understanding, credibility, and relationships among a wide array of institutions and audiences.

Independence
- We provide objective counsel to those we represent.
- We are accountable for our actions.

Loyalty
- We are faithful to those we represent, while honoring our obligation to serve the public interest.

Fairness
- We deal fairly with clients, employers, competitors, peers, vendors, the media, and the general public.
- We respect all opinions and support the right of free expression.

PRSA Code Provisions

Free Flow of Information

Core Principle
Protecting and advancing the free flow of accurate and truthful information is essential to serving the public interest and contributing to informed decision making in a democratic society.

Intent
- To maintain the integrity of relationships with the media, government officials, and the public.
- To aid informed decision making.

Guidelines
A member shall:
- Preserve the integrity of the process of communication.
- Be honest and accurate in all communications.
- Act promptly to correct erroneous communications for which the practitioner is responsible.
- Preserve the free flow of unprejudiced information when giving or receiving gifts by ensuring that gifts are nominal, legal, and infrequent.

Examples of Improper Conduct Under This Provision
- A member representing a ski manufacturer gives a pair of expensive racing skis to a sports magazine columnist, to influence the columnist to write favorable articles about the product.
- A member entertains a government official beyond legal limits and/or in violation of government reporting requirements.

Competition

Core Principle
Promoting healthy and fair competition among professionals preserves an ethical climate while fostering a robust business environment.

Intent
- To promote respect and fair competition among public relations professionals.
- To serve the public interest by providing the widest choice of practitioner options.

Guidelines
A member shall:
- Follow ethical hiring practices designed to respect free and open competition without deliberately undermining a competitor.
- Preserve intellectual property rights in the marketplace.

Examples of Improper Conduct Under This Provision
- A member employed by a "client organization" shares helpful information with a counseling firm that is competing with others for the organization's business.
- A member spreads malicious and unfounded rumors about a competitor in order to alienate the competitor's clients and employees in a ploy to recruit people and business.

Disclosure of Information

Core Principle
Open communication fosters informed decision making in a democratic society.

Intent
- To build trust with the public by revealing all information needed for responsible decision making.

Guidelines
A member shall:
- Be honest and accurate in all communications.
- Act promptly to correct erroneous communications for which the member is responsible.
- Investigate the truthfulness and accuracy of information released on behalf of those represented.
- Reveal the sponsors for causes and interests represented.
- Disclose financial interest (such as stock ownership) in a client's organization.
- Avoid deceptive practices.

Examples of Improper Conduct Under This Provision
- Front groups: A member implements "grass roots" campaigns or letter-writing campaigns to legislators on behalf of undisclosed interest groups.
- Lying by omission: A practitioner for a corporation knowingly fails to release financial information, giving a misleading impression of the corporation's performance.
- A member discovers inaccurate information disseminated via a Web site or media kit and does not correct the information.
- A member deceives the public by employing people to pose as volunteers to speak at public hearings and participate in "grass roots" campaigns.

Safeguarding Confidences

Core Principle
Client trust requires appropriate protection of confidential and private information.

Intent
- To protect the privacy rights of clients, organizations, and individuals by safeguarding confidential information.

Guidelines
A member shall:

- Safeguard the confidences and privacy rights of present, former, and prospective clients and employees.
- Protect privileged, confidential, or insider information gained from a client or organization.
- Immediately advise an appropriate authority if a member discovers that confidential information is being divulged by an employee of a client company or organization.

Examples of Improper Conduct Under This Provision

- A member changes jobs, takes confidential information, and uses that information in the new position to the detriment of the former employer.
- A member intentionally leaks proprietary information to the detriment of some other party.

Conflicts of Interest

Core Principle
Avoiding real, potential, or perceived conflicts of interest builds the trust of clients, employers, and the publics.

Intent

- To earn trust and mutual respect with clients or employers.
- To build trust with the public by avoiding or ending situations that put one's personal or professional interests in conflict with society's interests.

Guidelines
A member shall:

- Act in the best interests of the client or employer, even subordinating the member's personal interests.
- Avoid actions and circumstances that may appear to compromise good business judgment or create a conflict between personal and professional interests.
- Disclose promptly any existing or potential conflict of interest to affected clients or organizations.
- Encourage clients and customers to determine if a conflict exists after notifying all affected parties.

Examples of Improper Conduct Under This Provision

- The member fails to disclose that he or she has a strong financial interest in a client's chief competitor.
- The member represents a "competitor company" or a "conflicting interest" without informing a prospective client.

Enhancing the Profession

Core Principle
Public relations professionals work constantly to strengthen the public's trust in the profession.

Intent
- To build respect and credibility with the public for the profession of public relations.
- To improve, adapt, and expand professional practices.

Guidelines
A member shall:
- Acknowledge that there is an obligation to protect and enhance the profession.
- Keep informed and educated about practices in the profession to ensure ethical conduct.
- Actively pursue personal professional development.
- Decline representation of clients or organizations that urge or require actions contrary to this Code.
- Accurately define what public relations activities can accomplish.
- Counsel subordinates in proper ethical decision making.
- Require that subordinates adhere to the ethical requirements of the Code.
- Report ethical violations, whether committed by PRSA members or not, to the appropriate authority.

Examples of Improper Conduct Under This Provision
- A PRSA member declares publicly that a product the client sells is safe, without disclosing evidence to the contrary.
- A member initially assigns some questionable client work to a non-member practitioner to avoid the ethical obligation of PRSA membership.

Resources

Rules and Guidelines
The following PRSA documents, available in The Blue Book, provide detailed rules and guidelines to help guide your professional behavior:
- PRSA Bylaws
- PRSA Administrative Rules
- Member Code of Ethics

If, after reviewing them, you still have a question or issue, contact PRSA headquarters as noted below.

Questions

The PRSA is here to help. Whether you have a serious concern or simply need clarification, contact Judy Voss at judy.voss@prsa.org.

PRSA Member Code of Ethics Pledge

I pledge:

To conduct myself professionally, with truth, accuracy, fairness, and responsibility to the public; to improve my individual competence and advance the knowledge and proficiency of the profession through continuing research and education; and to adhere to the articles of the Member Code of Ethics 2000 for the practice of public relations as adopted by the governing Assembly of the Public Relations Society of America.

I understand and accept that there is a consequence for misconduct, up to and including membership revocation.

And, I understand that those who have been or are sanctioned by a government agency or convicted in a court of law of an action that is in violation of this Code may be barred from membership or expelled from the Society.

_____

Signature

_____

Date

Public Relations Society of America
33 Irving Place
New York, NY 10003
www.prsa.org

Appendix B

PRIA Code of Ethics

The Public Relations Institute of Australia is a professional body serving the interests of its members. In doing so, the Institute is mindful of the responsibility which public relations professionals owe to the community as well as to their clients and employers. The Institute requires members to adhere to the highest standards of ethical practice and professional competence. All members are duty-bound to act responsibly and to be accountable for their actions.

The following Code of Ethics binds all members of the Public Relations Institute of Australia.

1. Members shall deal fairly and honestly with their employers, clients and prospective clients, with their fellow workers including superiors and subordinates, with public officials, the communications media, the general public and with fellow members of PRIA.

2. Members shall avoid conduct or practices likely to bring discredit upon themselves, the Institute, their employers or clients.

3. Members shall not knowingly disseminate false or misleading information and shall take care to avoid doing so inadvertently.

4. Members shall safeguard the confidences of both present and former employers and clients, including confidential information about employers' or clients' business affairs, technical methods or processes, except upon the order of a court of competent jurisdiction.

5. No member shall represent conflicting interests nor, without the consent of the parties concerned, represent competing interests.

6. Members shall refrain from proposing or agreeing that their consultancy fees or other remuneration be contingent entirely on the achievement of specified results.

7. Members shall inform their employers or clients if circumstances arise in which their judgment or the disinterested character of their services may be questioned by reason of personal relationships or business or financial interests.

8. Members practising as consultants shall seek payment only for services specifically commissioned.

9. Members shall be prepared to identify the source of funding of any public communication they initiate or for which they act as a conduit.

10. Members shall, in advertising and marketing their skills and services and in soliciting professional assignments, avoid false, misleading or exaggerated claims and shall refrain from comment or action that may injure the professional reputation, practice or services of a fellow member.

11. Members shall inform the Board of the Institute and/or the relevant State/Territory Council(s) of the Institute of evidence purporting to show that a member has been guilty of, or could be charged with, conduct constituting a breach of this Code.

12. No member shall intentionally injure the professional reputation or practice of another member.

13. Members shall help to improve the general body of knowledge of the profession by exchanging information and experience with fellow members.

14. Members shall act in accord with the aims of the institute, its regulations and policies.

15. Members shall not misrepresent their status through misuse of title, grading, or the designation FPRIA, MPRIA or APRIA.

Adopted by the Board of the Institute on November 5, 2001, this Code of Ethics supersedes all previous versions.

Index

Page numbers followed by "*f*" refer to figures and "*t*" refer to tables.